THIRD CANADIAN EDITION

essentials of managing human resources

Eileen B. Stewart
Program Head, Human Resource Management Program
British Columbia Institute of Technology

Monica Belcourt
Professor of Administrative Studies
York University

George Bohlander
Professor of Management
Arizona State University

Scott Snell
Professor of Human Resource Studies
Cornell University

THOMSON

NELSON

Australia   Canada   Mexico   Singapore   Spain   United Kingdom   United States

THOMSON

NELSON

Essentials of Managing Human Resources
Third Canadian Edition
by Eileen B. Stewart, Monica Belcourt,
George Bohlander, and Scott Snell

**Associate Vice-President,
Editorial Director:**
Evelyn Veitch

Acquisitions Editor:
Anthony Rezek

Marketing Manager:
Charmaine Sherlock

Senior Developmental Editor:
Karina Hope

Photo Researcher/Permissions Coordinator:
Kristiina Bowering

Production Editor:
Tannys Williams

Copy Editor:
Joan Rawlin

Proofreader:
Wendy Thomas

Indexer:
Belle Wong

Production Coordinator:
Kathrine Pummell

Design Director:
Ken Phipps

Interior Design:
Katherine Strain

Cover Design:
Liz Harasymczuk

Cover Image:
©2002 Stockbyte

Compositor:
Integra

Printer:
CTPS

**Library and Archives Canada
Cataloguing in Publication**

Essentials of managing human resources / Monica Belcourt ... [et al.]. — 3rd Canadian ed.

ISBN 0-17-640723-5

1. Personnel management—Textbooks. I. Bohlander, George W II. Snell, Scott, 1958– III. Belcourt, Monica, 1946–

HF5549.E85 2006   658.3   C2005-905797-1

BRIEF CONTENTS

DETAILED CONTENTS

PART 2: ATTRACTING AND SELECTING PEOPLE FOR THE ORGANIZATION

PART 3: DEVELOPING PEOPLE IN THE ORGANIZATION

PART 4:   EMPLOYEE RELATIONS

PREFACE

The second edition of *Essentials of Managing Human Resources*, published at the beginning of the 21st century, made reference to the major economic and political events in North America that have escalated the need for improved organizational results and the confidence of employees, consumers, and shareholders. Further, we continue to deal with skill shortages and will shortly be dealing with the impact of many provinces abolishing mandatory retirement.

All of these issues have once again magnified the need for organizations to focus on the people in the company: the company's "human resources." This book is written to help you understand the HR "language"—the processes and systems integral to the success of the people in the organizations, and, therefore, the success of the organization. For example, one of the more important systems in an organization is recruiting capable and skilled people.

This textbook builds on concepts you have learned or been introduced to in either a general management or a general organizational behaviour course. It is written primarily for those of you who will become (or are) supervisors and line managers rather than HR professionals. However, since the text covers the major human resources management processes and systems, it will provide a good overview if you are thinking about moving into the HR profession.

Essentials is a shorter and a more relevant book for general business students with simpler language. It is important, however, to remember that the field of HR has its own "jargon" or specialized language. Therefore, one of the goals of this book is to help you learn the terminology so that you can deal with HR issues in a more informed way.

Finally, this book is designed to cover all the materials you will need for a good general understanding of all the HR activities in a company, as well as your role in managing people.

WHAT'S NEW IN THE THIRD EDITION

Building on the successes of the second edition, and incorporating suggestions from users of the text, the following changes have been made:

- Review questions at the end of each chapter
- Critical thinking questions at the end of the At Work with HRM boxes
- A boxed feature entitled "The Manager's Toolkit"
- A section at the end of each chapter titled "Developing Your Skills"
- More service-based references and examples
- New case study material in each chapter
- Additional Web sites within each chapter
- Significant revision of Chapters 1 and 4, including additional content on human resource planning, Internet recruiting, and human resource information systems
- Data and information from the 2001 Census
- Updated references

FEATURES OF THE BOOK

Each chapter contains the following materials:

Objective 1

- **Learning objectives** are listed at the beginning of each chapter, with reference icons indicating the objective within the chapter.
- **HRM Close-Up** chapter opening relates a story about a supervisor's experience in human resources management.
- **Manager's Toolkit** boxes contain tools and resources for handling HR matters, including tips for supervisors.
- **At Work with HRM** boxes feature real-world applications relating to a specific topic with critical thinking questions at the end.
- **HRM and the Law** boxes help explain the legal implications of HR.
- **Around the World with HRM** boxes show HR issues in an international light.
- **Ethics in HRM** boxes highlight sensitive issues supervisors might face.
- **Key terms** appear in boldface and are defined in margin notes. The key terms are also listed at the end of the chapter and in the glossary.
- **Figures with graphs** and **research information** appear throughout the chapters.
- **Illustrations** reinforce points and maintain reader interest.
- A **Summary** at the end of each chapter reinforces the learning objectives.
- A **Need to Know/Need to Understand** box at the end of each chapter helps to identify key topics.
- **Review Questions** and **Critical Thinking Questions** provide basic recall as well as stimulating critical thinking questions for discussion.
- **Developing Your Skills** contain both text-based and Web-based experiential exercises.
- Two **case studies** in each chapter present current HRM issues in real-life settings that allow for critical analysis.
- **Notes and References** are included for further research and information.
- **Web site addresses** are provided throughout the text and are indicated with a symbol in the margin.

SUPPLEMENTARY MATERIALS

A complete package of teaching and learning support materials accompanies this text:

- **Instructor's Resource CD-ROM**—Key instructors ancillaries (Instructor's Manual, Test Bank, ExamView, PowerPoints) are provided on CD-ROM, giving instructors the ultimate tool for customizing lectures and presentations.
- An **Instructor's Manual** designed to increase the effective use of the text. It includes chapter overviews, video guides, detailed lecture outlines, answers to the end-of-chapter material, and case solutions.
- A **Computerized Test Bank** with a balance of true/false, multiple-choice, and essay-type questions. The test bank is cross-referenced with the learning objectives for fast and relevant testing.
- **PowerPoint Slides** created by the author for continuity.

- **Turning Point**—JoinIn™ on TurningPoint®. Now you can author, deliver, show, assess, and grade all in PowerPoint . . . with *no* toggling back and forth between screens! JoinIn™ on TurningPoint® is the only classroom response software tool that gives you true PowerPoint integration. With JoinIn™, you are no longer tied to your computer . . . you can walk about your classroom as you lecture, showing slides and collecting and displaying responses with ease. There is simply no easier or more effective way to turn your lecture hall into a personal, fully interactive experience for your students. If you can use PowerPoint, you can use JoinIn™ on TurningPoint®!

- **Web site (www.stewart3e.nelson.com)**—One of the most comprehensive Web sites available in human resource management that includes test yourself exercises and Web links divided by subject: In the News; Human Resources Associations; Statutes, Regulations, and Government Agencies; Career Development; and General Interest Links, concerning job analysis, recruitment, compensation, and health and safety.

ACKNOWLEDGEMENTS

This third edition could not have happened without the hard work of many people, particularly the users of the first and second editions. We are grateful to the supervisors and HR practitioners who have shared their stories and helped influence the thinking.

We are very appreciative of the excellent research work done by Aaron McIntee. He excelled in finding useful, recent, and informative items as well as interviewing people on a picket line.

Thanks also go to John Beckett, Vancouver Airport Authority, for his writing contribution, and to Deborah Broznitsky, for help in reviewing manuscript at key stages. Many thanks to Deborah Sanborn and Caroline Bonham and to the featured individuals for their work on "HRM Close-Up."

The efforts of the Nelson team were excellent. Thanks to Evelyn Veitch, Anthony Rezek, and Karina Hope for their guidance, wisdom, and patience.

The authors and publisher also wish to thank those people who reviewed this project during its development and provided important insights and suggestions:

Barinder Bhavra, CDI College of Business, Technology, and Healthcare
Julie Bulmash, George Brown College
Sarah Holding, Malaspina University College
Dave Inkster, Red Deer College
Nelson Lacroix, Niagara College
Laurent M. Lapierre, University of Ottawa
Jill Leedham, Mohawk College
Melanie Peacock, Mount Royal College
Deborah Sauer, Capilano College
Bob Van Someren, Red Deer College

Our greatest thanks go to our families, particularly this author's son, Jason Robertson. They have provided help, support, research, and encouragement that were most welcome for the project to succeed. And the previous authors' spouses—Michael

Belcourt, Ronnie Bohlander, and Marybeth Snell—have also provided invaluable guidance and assistance. We are grateful to all of them for their enthusiasm and guidance.

Eileen B. Stewart
British Columbia Institute of Technology

Monica Belcourt
York University

George Bohlander
Arizona State University

Scott Snell
Cornell University

ABOUT THE AUTHORS

EILEEN B. STEWART

Eileen B. Stewart is Program Head, Human Resource Management Programs, and Faculty in the School of Business, at the British Columbia Institute of Technology. She is a senior human resources professional with extensive experience in all areas of human resource management, including labour relations in both the public and private sectors. As an HR executive, she has managed human resource units in several of British Columbia's large public-sector organizations. With a diverse background that includes mining, banking, education, and municipal government, Ms. Stewart has a strong overall business orientation.

After receiving a B.A. in economics and commerce from Simon Fraser University, British Columbia, she joined Teck Mining as its first personnel manager. She then moved to the British Columbia Institute of Technology where she specialized in labour relations. She obtained her senior management experience at BCIT as director of personnel and labour relations; the University of British Columbia, as director of human resources; and the City of Vancouver, as general manager of human resources.

While working full-time, Ms. Stewart completed her M.B.A. at Simon Fraser University. She currently teaches management and HRM courses at BCIT and continues to provide consulting services to private, public, and not-for-profit organizations. She is currently working on a Ph.D. in Human and Organizational Development at the Fielding Graduate University.

Ms. Stewart is active in the HR community through her continued involvement with the BC Human Resources Management Association (BCHRMA), where she chairs the HR Leadership Forum. She also served on the executive of the BCHRMA for a number of years, including serving as President. In addition to her professional involvement, she chairs the Board of Directors of the YWCA of Vancouver and sits on the board of Science World of British Columbia.

MONICA BELCOURT

Monica Belcourt is a full Professor, Human Resources Management, and Director of the Graduate Program in HR at the Atkinson Faculty of Liberal and Professional Studies, York University. She has an extensive and varied background in human resources management. After receiving a B.A. in psychology from the University of Manitoba, Winnipeg, she joined the Public Service Commission as a recruitment and selection specialist. During her tenure with the federal government, she worked in training, HRM research, job analysis, and HR planning.

Dr. Belcourt alternated working in HRM with graduate school, obtaining an M.A. in psychology from York University, an M.Ed. in adult education from the University of Ottawa, and a Ph.D. in management from York University. She also holds the designation of Certified Human Resource Professional (CHRP). Her research is grounded in the experience she gained as Director of Personnel for CP Rail, Director of Employee Development, National Film Board, and as a functional HR specialist for the federal government. Monica has taught HRM at Concordia, UQUAM, McGill, and York, where she founded and managed the largest undergraduate program in HRM in Canada. She created Canada's first degrees in human resources management: B.HRM, B.HRM (honours) and a Masters in HRM (www.atkinson.yorku.ca/mhrm/).

Monica is Director of the International Alliance for HR Research (IAHRR) (www.yorku.ca/hrresall) which is a catalyst for the discovery, dissemination, and application of new knowledge about HRM. Professor Belcourt's research interests focus on strategic HRM. She has published over 100 articles, several of which received best paper awards.

Monica is Series Editor for the ITP Nelson Canada Series in HRM: *Performance Management through Training and Development, Occupational Health and Safety, Human Resources Management Systems, Recruitment and Selection in Canada, Compensation in Canada, Strategic Human Resources Planning, Research, Measurement and Evaluation in HRM*, and *The Canadian Labour Market.*

Active in many professional associations and not-for-profit organizations, Monica was President of the Human Resources Professionals Association of Ontario and served on the national committee for HR certification, and is a past board member of CIBC Insurance and the Toronto French School. She is a frequent commentator on HRM issues for CTV, *Canada AM*, CBC, *The Globe and Mail, The National Post, Report on Business Television, The Canadian HR Reporter,* and other media.

GEORGE BOHLANDER

George Bohlander is Professor of Management at Arizona State University. He teaches undergraduate, graduate, and executive development programs in the field of human resources and labour relations. His areas of expertise include employment law, training and development, work teams, public policy, and labour relations. He is the recipient of six outstanding teaching awards at ASU and has received the Outstanding Undergraduate Teaching Excellence Award given by the College of Business at ASU. In 1996, Dr. Bohlander received the prestigious ASU Parents Association Professorship for his contributions to students and teaching.

Dr. Bolander is an active researcher and author. He has published over 40 articles and monographs covering various topics in the human resources area ranging from labour–management cooperation to team training. His articles appear in such academic and practitioner journals as *Labor Studies Journal, Personnel Administrator, Labor Law Journal, Journal of Collective Negotiations in the Public Sector, Public Personnel Management, National Productivity Review, Personnel,* and *Employee Relations Law Journal.*

Before beginning his teaching career, Dr. Bohlander served as personnel administrator for General Telephone Company of California. His duties included recruitment and selection, training and development, equal employment opportunity, and labour relations. He was very active in resolving employee grievances and in arbitration preparation. Dr. Bohlander continues to be a consultant to both public- and private-sector organizations, and he has worked with such organizations as the U.S. Postal Service, Kaiser Cement, McDonnell Douglas, Arizona Public Service, American Productivity Center, Rural Metro Corporation, and Del Webb. Dr. Bohlander is also an active labour arbitrator. He received his Ph.D. from the University of California at Los Angeles and his M.B.A. from the University of Southern California.

SCOTT SNELL

Scott Snell is Professor of Human Resource Studies at Cornell University. During his career, Dr. Snell has taught courses in human resources management, principles of management, and strategic management to undergraduates, graduates, and executives. He is actively involved in executive education and served as faculty director for Penn State's Strategic

Leadership Program as well as faculty leader for programs in human resources, developing managerial effectiveness, and managing the global enterprise. In addition to his teaching duties, Dr. Snell also served as director of research for Penn State's Institute for the Study of Organizational Effectiveness.

As an industry consultant, Professor Snell has worked with companies such as Arthur Andersen, AT&T, GE, IBM, and Shell Chemical to redesign human resource systems to cope with changes in the competitive environment. His specialization is the realignment of staffing, training, and reward systems to complement technology, quality, and other strategic initiatives. Recently, his work has centred on the development of human capital as a source of competitive advantage.

Dr. Snell's research has been published in the *Academy of Management Journal, Human Resource Management Review, Industrial Relations, Journal of Business Research, Journal of Management, Journal of Managerial Issues, Organizational Dynamics, Organizational Studies, Personnel Administrator, Strategic Management Journal,* and *Working Woman.* He is also co-author of *Management: The Competitive Edge,* with Thomas S. Bateman. In addition, Dr. Snell is on the editorial boards of *Journal of Managerial Issues, Digest of Management Research, Human Resource Management Review,* and *Academy of Management Journal.*

He holds a B.A. in psychology from Miami University, as well as M.B.A. and Ph.D. degrees in business administration from Michigan State University. His professional associations include the Strategic Management Society, Academy of Management, and the Society for Human Resource Management.

PART 1

HRM Challenges and the Legal Context

Chapter 1: The Challenge of HRM

Chapter 2: The Legal Framework of HRM

CHAPTER 1

The Challenge of HRM

HRM
Close-Up

"It's a joy to see people perform well on their own and with confidence. That's when I know our company has done a good job in managing human resources."

Tamsin Plaxton, Co-owner and Director of Sales and Marketing, Tamwood International College

It was on their first date that Tamsin Plaxton and Matthew Collingwood talked about their dreams and discovered a common desire to run a summer camp for kids. But it wasn't for many years that the dream was realized. Plaxton become a successful lawyer and Collingwood established himself in banking. But in the fall of 1992, the two made the leap to become entrepreneurs. Tamwood International College was born and has developed a niche teaching English to both youth and adults at three locations in Canada.

For the younger students arriving from places including Asia, South America, Europe, and Quebec, Tamwood combines English-language immersion with fun activities, such as glacier skiing, snowboarding, horseback riding, and golf at its summer camps in Vancouver, Whistler, and London, Ontario. And in Vancouver and Whistler, Tamwood also runs year-round English-language instruction programs for adults.

As the company has expanded, roles have evolved with Collingwood directing operations, and Plaxton is responsible for sales and marketing. Responsibility for human resources and people management is shared between the owners and the directors in charge of educational programming at Tamwood. Except for full-time management staff at head office and some of the academic staff in the adult year-round facilities, staffing is temporary and contract-based, hired according to the enrolment and needs for the high-season programming. Typical of many smaller firms, Plaxton seeks human resource expertise when she needs it. "We engage a recruiting firm to assist with applicant screening for management positions," explains Plaxton. "We're also seeking HR consulting services to assist us with a new compensation structure because we're getting to the size that we need the outside expertise."

In the early years, Tamwood's HR practices were more casual and informal. "Our communications regarding people management were verbal for the most part," says Plaxton. "Now, we have formal job descriptions, policies in place for vacation and benefits, and last year, we published our first employee manual complete with a dress code!"

Formal human resources practices became a necessary element of running a successful business. So did getting employees engaged in business strategy and planning. Tamwood completed a branding exercise in 2004 to identify the company's strengths and opportunities. Using focus groups, client and employee surveys, and an intense two-day strategic planning session, Plaxton was able to engage most employees in the company and feels that the process helped to bring everyone on board and get them working from the same page. "Each employee our clients have contact with is a touch-point for us. Clients need a consistent impression of Tamwood International College as a high-quality, professional, yet personal organization," she explains. "Having staff knowledgeable about our company vision and how their work impacts our success is critical."

Being an entrepreneur herself, Plaxton tends to recruit employees who are self-starters. Knowing that human resources management is one of the many hats that she wears, Plaxton is up front with all new hires. She explains that she and her partner are "hands-off" owners, inclined to guide and support staff as opposed to direct and oversee them. "I get such a great feeling when I can send our people out to represent our company and have clients tell me that they felt they were dealing with the owner of the company. It's a joy to see people perform well on their own and with confidence. That's when I know our company has done a good job in managing human resources."

INTRODUCTION

The managing of people in an organization continues to be at the top of the business agenda. New phrases, such as "human capital," have crept into business jargon to emphasize the value that the people in the organization have. As Tamsin Plaxton says in the opening vignette, hiring the right people for the business is important to her. But what is human resources management (HRM) and why is it important?

Just for a moment, imagine an organization without people. No employees, no supervisors, no managers, executives, or owners. It's a pretty tough assignment. Without people, organizations would not exist. And while this idea may not be much of a revelation, it brings home the point that organizations are made up of people. Successful organizations are particularly good at bringing together different kinds of people to achieve a common purpose. This is the essence of human resources management. As students, you are the future of any organization—whether you become employees, supervisors, or managers.

WHAT IS HUMAN RESOURCES MANAGEMENT?

Objective 1

Human resources management (HRM)
An integrated set of processes, programs, and systems in an organization that focuses on the effective deployment and development of its employees

Human resources management is more than hiring, paying, and training people. **Human resources management (HRM)** is an integrated set of processes, programs, and systems in an organization that focuses on the effective deployment and development of its employees.

The word "employee" is also intended to cover contract workers, people from other organizations who are working on a project, or any other similar working relationship. This is indicative of the new workplace that is far more fluid and flexible than the workforce of 10 to 20 years ago.

Managers use a lot of words to describe the importance of people to their organizations. The term "human resources" implies that people are as important to the success of any business as other resources are, such as money, materials, machinery, and information.

WHAT ARE THE HRM PROCESSES AND ACTIVITIES?

Objective 2

Before there can be a discussion about why to study HRM, let's look at the various individual systems and processes that fit together. There are some very traditional activities as well as some new and emerging activities. You will also notice that this book is structured on the typical HR activities in an organization.

1. *Organizational, work, and job design*—determining what tasks need to be done, in what order, with what skills, and how individual tasks fit together in work units. For example, in the HRM Close-Up, Plaxton and Collingwood had to decide what tasks fit together for their educational business.
2. *Planning*—ensuring that people in the organization are the right people with the right skills at the right time in the right place. In the HRM Close-Up, Plaxton had to plan when enrollment was high enough to add more staff.

3. *Recruitment and selection*—sourcing, attracting, and hiring the people with the necessary skills and background. Again, Plaxton had to find and hire the people who can best represent the company and do the work as expected.
4. *Training and development*—providing the resources to assist employees in developing the necessary knowledge and skills to do their job today and in the future. Plaxton indicated that having knowledgeable staff is part of the success and that she must ensure they have information about the business.
5. *Performance management*—ensuring that there are appropriate mechanisms in place to provide feedback to employees on a regular basis. For Plaxton and Collingwood to ensure that the business objectives are being met, they will need to have a way of measuring employees' performance or contribution to the firm.
6. *Compensation (pay and benefits)*—developing and administering pay and benefits programs that will attract and retain employees. As an entrepreneurial business, Tamwood found that as the firm grew, a more structured system for compensation was necessary.
7. *Occupational health and safety*—ensuring that the safety and health of employees are maintained. Plaxton and others in the company need to ensure that the physical premises have a safe and healthy work environment.
8. *Employee and labour relations*—ensuring that there are positive and constructive relations between the employees and their supervisors or managers and/or union representatives. Plaxton notes that part of her job is to ensure that staff are actively participating in changes to business practices.

While the above lists the more traditional areas, a number of areas are emerging as the field of HR grows and responds to the concerns of both employees and employers. Some of these are (1) organizational development and learning (an extension of training and development); (2) high-performance work groups or teams (an extension of job design); (3) flexible work arrangements (ways to engage employees and address demographic issues); and (4) HRIS—human resource information (and management) systems. HRIS will be discussed more fully in this chapter's section under "Technology." These processes and activities and their relationship to the organization and the employees are shown in Figure 1.1.

WHY STUDY HUMAN RESOURCES MANAGEMENT?

Objective 3

To work with people in any organization, it is important to understand human behaviour and be knowledgeable about the various systems and practices available to effectively use as well as build a skilled, knowledgeable, and motivated workforce. At the same time, managers must be aware of economic, technological, social, and legal issues that either help or hinder their ability to achieve organizational success. The line manager or supervisor is the key link between the employee and the organization. Therefore, the manager must have a thorough knowledge and understanding of contemporary HRM and how these practices influence the output of any organization. You are the managers and employees of tomorrow: studying HRM will help you understand your roles and responsibilities in helping to manage your company's people—its human resources.

In the process of managing human resources, increasing attention is being given to the individual needs of the employees. Thus, this book will not only emphasize the importance of the contributions that HRM makes to the organization but will also show how, through good people management in an organization, the individual and our overall society are improved. Consider how you feel and behave if your work isn't enjoyable and

FIGURE 1.1   Overall Framework for HR

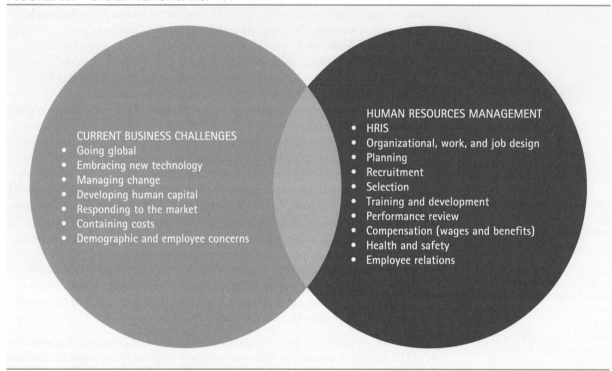

CURRENT BUSINESS CHALLENGES
- Going global
- Embracing new technology
- Managing change
- Developing human capital
- Responding to the market
- Containing costs
- Demographic and employee concerns

HUMAN RESOURCES MANAGEMENT
- HRIS
- Organizational, work, and job design
- Planning
- Recruitment
- Selection
- Training and development
- Performance review
- Compensation (wages and benefits)
- Health and safety
- Employee relations

you don't feel that you understand your role in the organization or that your work doesn't appear to be valued. You might respond in a variety of ways, including being unconcerned about a customer complaint. By acting in this way, you are not contributing to the success of the organization, which includes your own success. If enough people do this, our overall productive capacity as a society will decrease.

In addition, employees and the public at large are demanding that employers demonstrate greater social responsibility in managing their people. Complaints that some jobs are deadening the spirit and injuring the health of employees are not uncommon. Complaints of discrimination against women, visible minorities, the physically and mentally challenged, and the elderly with respect to hiring, training, advancement, and compensation are being levelled against some employers. Issues such as comparable pay for dissimilar work, the high cost of health benefits, daycare for children of employees, and alternative work schedules are ones that many employers must address as our workforce grows more diverse.

THE PARTNERSHIP OF LINE MANAGERS AND HR PROFESSIONALS

Role of the Line Manager

Objective 4

Managing people depends on effective supervisors and line managers. Although HR professionals may have responsibility for coordinating programs and policies pertaining to people-related issues, managers and employees themselves are ultimately responsible for making the organization successful. All line managers, in effect, are people managers—not the HR professional or HR unit. It is through the effective leadership of the line manager or supervisor that the talent or "intellectual capital" of the organization is enhanced. Remember that it is the line manager who directly interacts with the employees and is responsible for the effective contribution of those employees to the organization. For example, when an organization wishes to place an increased emphasis on the growth and development of its people, it is the line manager who is front-and-centre in identifying the gaps in any skill sets. It is only then that the HR practitioner can offer some ways and means of bridging the gap.

It is also important to understand that the supervisor or manager has "line authority"—being directly responsible for the product or service. Unlike line managers who are directly responsible for a product or service, HR professionals are typically "staff"—people who help and support the line manager. HR professionals may have "functional authority"; that is, they have the legitimate authority in HR areas, such as recruitment strategies or developing organizational programs, to recognize employees. In today's organizations, most HR professionals no longer have total functional authority and are expected to provide advice and guidance to the line. However, there might be a situation that could have very serious consequences for the organization. In this case, the HR professional will be expected to provide advice in a strong and influential way ensuring that the line manager understands the impact on the organization prior to taking action.

Since most readers of this book will be line managers, supervisors, and employees rather than HR professionals, this text is oriented toward helping people manage people more effectively, whether they become first-line supervisors or chief executive officers. Students now preparing for careers in organizations will find that the study of HRM provides a background that will be valuable in managerial and supervisory positions. Discussions concerning the role of the HR department can provide a better understanding of the functions performed by this department. A familiarity with HRM will help facilitate closer cooperation between HR professionals, whether they are part of the organization or are a contracted service, and will provide an opportunity to more fully use the expertise of HR professionals. For example, an HR professional can assist the supervisor in developing steps to improve the performance of a particular employee. The consequences for the supervisor of developing a poor approach could result in the employee either not improving the performance or the employee feeling unsupported or criticized by the supervisor's approach. In either situation, the primary objective of improving performance would not be achieved.

Role of the HR Professional

It is important for line managers to understand the role or function HR professionals play, whether these individuals are part of the organization or are external resources retained by the organization. HR practitioners are increasingly becoming more professional and are being trained with common bodies of knowledge and information. Besides knowing how to recruit and pay people appropriately, HR professionals need sound business knowledge, good problem-solving and influence skills, and personal credibility (trust and the ability to build personal relationships). The HR practitioner's primary role in today's organizations is to help equip the line manager with the best people practices so that the organization can be successful. HR professionals can provide service activities, such as recruiting and training. Further, they can be active in policy formulation and implementation in such areas as workplace

In the highly competitive hospitality industry, it is important that hotel managers work closely with HR professionals to hire and retain capable employees.

harassment, healthy work environments, and change management. Lastly, an HR professional can be an employee advocate by listening to employee concerns and ensuring that the organization is aware of and responding to those concerns. HR professionals are expected to fulfill their role by actively involving others in the organization, particularly the supervisors and managers, in the development and design of HR programs.

For example, a company may want the HR professional to develop an overall recruitment approach to attract individuals with key skill sets. This approach would then generate a pool of applicants with the required skills. However, it would be the line manager who would actually select the best person from this pool.

Dave Ulrich,[1] a leading author on human resources practices, states that an HR professional must understand and deliver value to the various stakeholders in any organization—the line managers, the investors, and the employees.

Above all else, HR professionals must be able to integrate business skills, HR skills, and skills in helping employees handle change so that their organization can build and maintain a competitive advantage through its people.

The Ongoing Partnership

As we look at the competitive and social challenges facing human resources management in the next section of this chapter, it is important to reinforce the idea that managing people is not something that occurs in a back room or is done by HR professionals alone. Managing people is every manager's responsibility and obligation, and successful organizations are those that equip their line managers with a thorough understanding of good HRM practices—either through having an HR unit or retaining expertise when needed. The key is to find ways to develop and utilize the talents of employees so that they reach their greatest potential. If an organization has an HR unit, the HR professionals are there to provide guidance and assistance as internal consultants to the line manager or to help design and deliver programs and services to better equip employees, supervisors, and managers to contribute to organizational success. Even without an HR professional, the manager is still responsible for effective human resources management.

In organizations that have an HR unit, HR managers assume a greater role in top-management planning and decision making, a trend that reflects the growing awareness among executives that HRM can make important contributions to the success of an organization. A recent study conducted by Watson Wyatt Worldwide demonstrated that specific human resource practices can add (or subtract) millions of dollars from the bottom line.[2] The authors also indicate that shareholders understand this and will insist that the organizations make effective use of their people. For additional information on the studies conducted by Watson Wyatt in this area, access their Web site at **www.watsonwyatt.com**.

Let's reconsider the comments made by Plaxton in the chapter's opening story. Even though the company is still small, at what point would she consider hiring an HR professional? Frequently when an organization has 75 to 100 employees, the owners or senior management may decide that it would be best to have professional assistance. Figure 1.2 shows what the relationship between HR and other business units might be in a small organization.

This means that if Jack needed to hire a customer service agent, he would work with Sarita in confirming the job requirements, identifying possible recruitment sources, doing the final interviewing, and making the decision on which candidate to hire. Sarita, on the other hand, would assist Jack as required, including the development of appropriate interview questions and conducting reference checks.

In a larger organization, the HR department may have several professionals to work with employees, supervisors, and managers. Frequently, a particular HR person might be assigned to Jack Smith and be the key contact for all HR services.

Watson Wyatt Worldwide
www.watsonwyatt.com

FIGURE 1.2 Relationship of HR to Other Business Units

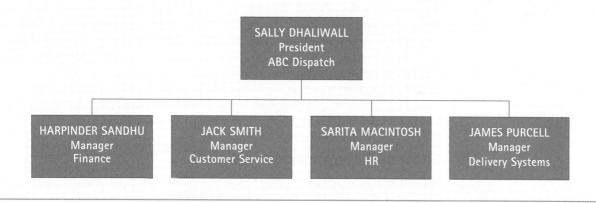

CURRENT BUSINESS CHALLENGES

Objective 5

Conference Board of Canada
www.conferenceboard.ca

Society for Human Resource Management (SHRM)
www.shrm.org

The Human Resource Planning Society
www.hrps.org/

Organizations, such as the Conference Board of Canada (**www.conferenceboard.ca**), the Society for Human Resource Management (**www.shrm.org**), and the Human Resource Planning Society (**www.hrps.org/**), conduct ongoing studies of the most important competitive trends and issues facing firms. By seeking the input of chief executives and HR professionals, these organizations track major trends. There has been a consistent theme of the following issues:

1. Going global
2. Embracing new technology
3. Managing change
4. Developing human capital
5. Responding to the market
6. Containing costs
7. Demographic and employee concerns

Challenge 1: Going Global

In order to grow and prosper, many companies are seeking business opportunities in global markets. Competition—and cooperation—with foreign companies has become an important focal point for business. Indeed, exporting accounts for a large portion of the Canadian economy. Canadian exports were expected to account for about $500 billion a year by 2004.[3] At Work with HRM 1.1 provides insights about a number of Canadian companies who are dependent on the global market for success.

Impact of Globalization

By partnering with firms in other regions of the world and using information technologies to coordinate distant parts of their businesses, companies, such as Bombardier, General Electric, and SNC Lavalin, have shown that their vision for the future is to offer customers "anything, anytime, anywhere" around the world. But **globalization** is not just something of interest to large firms. While estimates vary widely, 70 to 80% of the Canadian economy today is affected by international competition. This means, for a small distributor in Kamloops, British Columbia, or a small manufacturer in Alliston, Ontario, that the competition today is no longer the distributor or manufacturer in the next town or province. Trade agreements that allow a freer flow of goods and services mean that competitors may be located anywhere around the world. For example, Finning International, one of the world's largest dealers in Caterpillar heavy equipment, based in Vancouver, British Columbia, generates about 60%, more than $3 billion, in annual revenue from its world-wide markets. Meanwhile, international companies are looking to Canada to expand, as it has been rated by the *Economist* magazine as the best country in the world to do business.[4] In order to remain competitive, managers of today's organizations, both large and small, must ensure that they manage their human resources in the most productive, efficient, and effective way possible.

Globalization
Trend toward seeking out the most economical place in the world to do business

Effect of Globalization on HRM

When managers start to "go global," they have to balance a complicated set of issues related to different geographies, cultures, laws, and business practices. Human resources issues underlie each of these concerns and include such things as identifying capable

at work **with HRM 1.1** at work with HRM 1.1

EMPLOYEES: THE KEY DRIVERS FOR GLOBAL SUCCESS

Organizations, such as Canadian National Resources Ltd., Syncrude Canada Ltd., Shell Canada Ltd., and the world-wide management consulting firm of McKinsey & Company, acknowledge that their success in the global market is dependent on the skills and capabilities of their employees. Syncrude has undertaken an aggressive approach to encourage people to work in places such as Fort McMurray, Alberta. They offer very high pay and quick advancement, as well as offering work to partners and spouses. Even though much of the work is traditional blue collar (construction, drilling, etc.), today's employees also want to continue with their education and development and thus expect a variety of different educational programs.

Likewise, McKinsey & Company demonstrates its commitment to valuing its employees by a variety of developmental approaches, such as the traditional training and educational offerings as well as individual coaching. Each consultant has an individual development plan which is reviewed on a regular basis with the person's manager but also with the coach. It appears to be working as McKinsey tends to attract top performers who stay with the company.

CRITICAL THINKING QUESTIONS

1. What other businesses in your geographic area have a global marketplace?
2. What type of skills might their employees need to continue being a global player?

Source: Adapted from Claudia Cattaneo, "Oilsands Battleground for Skilled Workers," *Financial Post*, August 19, 2002, FP1; and Christopher A. Bartlett and Sumantra Ghosal, "Building Competitive Advantage through People," *MIT Sloan Management Review*, Winter 2002, 38.

expatriate managers who live and work overseas; designing training programs and development opportunities to enhance the managers' understanding of foreign cultures and work practices; and adjusting compensation plans to ensure that pay schemes are fair and equitable across individuals in different regions with different costs of living.

So, while managing across borders provides new and broader opportunities for organizations, it also represents a quantum leap in the complexity of human resources management. Whether you are working for a large multinational company or a small parts distributor, HRM in other countries has an impact on you. The Around the World with HRM boxes, located in several chapters, will help you understand this complexity. For example, Around the World with HRM 7.1 in Chapter 7 lists the differences in vacation days for several countries.

Challenge 2: Embracing New Technology

Advancements in information technology have enabled organizations to take advantage of the information explosion. With computer networks, unlimited amounts of data can be stored, retrieved, and used in a variety of ways, from simple record keeping to controlling complex equipment. The effect is so dramatic that at a broader level, organizations are changing the way they do business. Use of the Internet to transact business has

CHANGES TO BUSINESS PRACTICES

"Air Traffic Controllers' Strike Disrupts Flights in Europe"

During the height of summer travel in 2002, holidays were disrupted for thousands of people, and this disruption cost the airlines millions of dollars. Why did this happen and what does this have to do with changing business practices?

Prior to the creation of the European Union, each country was responsible for managing its own airspace with a multitude of different air control centres and different monitoring systems. As with many of the other reasons for creating the European Union, a decision was made to create a single, unified plan aimed at reducing congestion and delays by bringing all air traffic controllers under a centralized authority. While this may seem like a logical step from the air traveller's perspective, air traffic controllers are more fearful that there will be job loss and safety risks. Even though the EU has existed for a number of years, it is only now getting around to creating a central authority for air travel.

What do you think?[5]

Job Futures
www.jobfutures.ca

Monster.ca
www.monster.ca

Workopolis
www.workopolis.com

Manpower
www.manpower.ca

Knowledge workers
Workers whose responsibilities extend beyond the physical execution of work to include decision making, problem solving, and troubleshooting

become so pervasive for both large and small companies that *e-commerce* is rapidly becoming the organizational challenge of the new millennium. Even following the "dot-com bust," in which many promising new Internet companies failed rapidly, the Web is transforming the way traditional brick-and-mortar companies do business. Organizations are connected via computer-mediated relationships, and they are giving rise to a new generation of "virtual" workers who work from home, hotels, their cars, or wherever their work takes them. The implications for HRM are at times mind-boggling.

As a consequence, the skills necessary to be successful are different. For example, this text provides you with Web sites for additional information. You can access **www.jobfutures.ca** for information on trends in jobs and occupations, earnings, and work prospects in Canada. Likewise, some of you will get work after you finish school by posting your résumé online through **www.monster.ca**, **www.workopolis.com**, **or www.manpower.ca**, or by having your own home page with your résumé.

From Touch Labour to Knowledge Workers

The economic changes throughout the world have seen a 300% growth in service-based trade compared to goods-producing trade.[6] According to the World Trade Organization (WTO), 64% of the world's trade is now service-based.[7] In keeping with that trend, Canada has moved from being a production-based economy (industrial economy) to a service-based economy. This, along with the introduction of advanced technology, has reduced the number of jobs that require little skill and has increased the number of jobs that require considerable skill. In general, this transformation is referred to as a shift from "touch" or manual labour to **knowledge workers**, in which employee responsibilities expand to include a richer array of activities, such as planning, decision making, and problem solving.[8] In many cases, current employees can be retrained to assume new roles and responsibilities and behave in new ways. However, those employees who are displaced also require retraining. We thus experience the dilemma of having pages and pages of newspaper advertisements for applicants with technical or scientific training while large numbers of job seekers without such training register for work with employment agencies.

A person working in a pharmaceutical laboratory needs not only technical skills but also skills in working with others.

Technology training makes up a growing portion of all formal training provided by employers. Today, fully one-third of all courses are devoted to computer skills training (compared with 25% in 1996). Manpower Inc., the largest employment agency in the world, offers free information technology training through its Manpower Global Learning Center, an online university for its two million employees. The learning centre enables employees to access material at their leisure on a variety of technical subjects. In fact, Manpower is so focused on developing technical skills in potential employees that it has set up the system so that some training and career planning information is available to those who simply send the company a résumé.[9]

Influence of Technology in HRM

Human resources information system (HRIS)
Computerized system that provides current and accurate data for purposes of control and decision making

Information technology has, of course, changed the face of all business processes in Canada and abroad. Perhaps the most central use of technology in HRM is an organization's **human resources information system (HRIS)**. An HRIS provides current and accurate data for purposes of control and decision making; in this sense it moves beyond simply storing and retrieving information to include broader applications, such as producing reports, forecasting HR needs, assisting in strategic planning and career and promotion planning, and evaluating HR policies and practices. These systems are designed as a resource to be used by the line manager and the HR practitioner to make the best decisions for the organization.

The impact of information technology (IT) within HR has been both pervasive and profound. IT allows firms to store and retrieve large amounts of information quickly and inexpensively. It also enables them to rapidly and accurately combine and reconfigure data to create new information and institutionalize organizational knowledge. With IT networks, managers can communicate more easily and selectively with others in remote parts of the world, thereby allowing for even better use of the information at their disposal. In that regard, IT can be a potent weapon for lowering administrative costs, increasing productivity, speeding response times, improving decision making, and enhancing service. It may also be vital for coordinating activities with parties external to the firm. Ultimately, IT can provide a data and communications platform that helps HR link and leverage the firm's human capital to achieve a competitive advantage.

IT influences HRM in three basic ways. The first is its operational impact; that is, automating routine activities, alleviating the administrative burden, reducing costs, and improving productivity internal to the HR function itself. The most frequent uses of IT in HRM include automating payroll processing, maintaining employee records, and administering benefits programs. At Merck and Company, Inc. there is a major initiative under way to create a global HR data warehouse that provides a uniform architecture for HR reporting (such as payroll, benefits enrolment, address changes, and retirement). To ensure consistency across databases in various locations—a condition necessary for analysis and decision making on a global scale—IT and HR managers are working together to develop standardized data definitions and coding structures for all transactions. The goal of this project is to establish one comprehensive repository for employee data while simultaneously making the reporting process more timely and accurate.[10]

The second way IT influences HR is by enhancing services to line managers and employees. At Merck, several HR practices have been redesigned to enable line managers and employees to enter, retrieve, and edit data (by themselves) from remote locations in order to make better decisions. Perhaps the best example is in the area of staffing. Merck's staffing management system supports the hiring process by tracking application information, scanning résumés, and making the information immediately accessible to line managers so they can search for skills systematically. The system allows Merck managers to search online for internal and external talent by posting jobs, reviewing résumés, or running searches of candidates who have been categorized by skill set. Another example of HR technology in use is with the Toronto Police Services where the HR system tracks uniforms and handcuffs for over 5,000 officers.[11]

The third influence of IT on HR is the Internet as it has revolutionized our ability to access information. A growing number of companies, such as Canada Post, Sun Microsystems, Hewlett-Packard (Canada), and the City of Calgary, are using the Internet and company-specific "intranets" to establish home pages that allow employees and others to read current job postings and even apply for the positions online. In a recent study, more than 90% of organizations used Web-based applications to connect with their employees on everything from changes to benefits to enrolling in training courses.[12] Further, the firm that conducted the study has indicated that line managers are using Web resources to get the tools they need to increase the effectiveness of their departments and better realize the business goals of their company.[13] Lastly, IT has a transformational impact by redefining the activities that HR undertakes. A specific example of HR transformation at Merck can be seen in the evolution of education and training. Rather than relying solely on traditional approaches to learning, Merck is developing a "blended" approach to learning. In combination with traditional classroom experiences, Merck is creating Web-based e-learning opportunities as well. For example, in association with Forum Corporation, Merck piloted the use of an online 360-degree diagnostic tool called *Performance Compass* for its Leadership Development Program. The tool helps managers assess their developmental needs and then connects them to a wide array of external training and educational resources. In addition, the City of Calgary is anticipating that its new HR system will reduce the number of people required to manage the various HR services.[14]

Equipped with only a laptop, managers can take advantage of online services designed especially for HRM activities. Thus, technology can influence where and how a manager retrieves and gets information and can be an "instant assistant" for the manager. The above examples clearly show the way in which employee information is gathered and used and changes the relationship between the HR professional and the line manager or supervisor. Instead of being a record-keeping activity, HR can help the line manager understand and make use of technology to improve service and productivity. Manager's Toolkit 1.1 provides helpful current Web site addresses for the supervisor or manager.

Manager's Toolkit **1.1** Manager's Toolkit 1.1

A GUIDE TO INTERNET SITES

Cyberspace offers managers and HR professionals a large and growing set of resources for research, news, recruitment, and networking with people and organizations. Listed below are some Internet sites related to the HR field. Their addresses (URLs) are printed here for reference, but once you get started, it's easier to access the rest by following the links to related sites.

General HR Sites

www.workforceonline.com
This site posts articles regarding the latest trends and topics in human resources. It also provides links to HR specialist consultants.

www.hrreporter.com
An excellent Canadian resource for current news, information on the latest trends and practices, expert advice, experiences and insights from HR practitioners, research and resources.

www.hronline.com
This site is an independent, Canadian information service devoted to human resources.

www.human-resources.org
This site provides up-to-date information on human resources benchmarking, best practices, new tools and technology, and HR re-engineering.

www.hrprosgateway.com
This is an excellent source of up-to-date human resources information, featuring online articles, discussion forums, and links to related sites.

Specialized Sites

www.canoshweb.org
Offers a variety of information regarding safety in the workplace, reports and statistics, and industry trends. This site also provides online access to the Workers' Compensation legislation in Canadian jurisdictions.

www.acjnet.org
The "Access to Justice Network" site provides online access to federal and provincial statutes and regulations.

www.statcan.ca
The Statistics Canada site offers daily news updates, census information, and free tabular data on various aspects of the Canadian economy.

www.chrpcanada.com
This site provides information about membership in HR associations, information resources, links to relevant HR sites, and information about the new HR professional designation, Certified Human Resources Professional (CHRP).

In addition to the above sites, this book's Web site, **www.stewartessentials3e.nelson.com**, provides useful and up-to-date Web site links to accompany this text.

Challenge 3: Managing Change

Technology and globalization are only two of the forces bringing about change in organizations and HRM. Changes in business practices and approaches require professionals to adopt a different perspective. Stéphan Crétier, CEO of Garda World Security Corp., a Montreal-based security firm that competes with non-Canadian security service providers, describes his perspective:

> We're a bunch of dreamers—hard-edged dreamers. You have to have a dream, make it happen, and continue dreaming even if people try to wake you up. Many organizations tend to focus only on services or products within their own country. In order to compete successfully outside the home country, people need to have a much larger view of the world, understand issues in other countries and create a larger vision—a dream.[15]

In addition to technology and globalization, other forces of change include government laws, competitors, economic changes, employee attitudes, and consumer demands.

Types of Responses to Change

Reactive response to change
Change response that occurs after external forces have already affected performance

Proactive response to change
Change response initiated to take advantage of targeted opportunities

Programs focused on total quality, continuous improvement, downsizing, re-engineering, outsourcing, and the like are all examples of ways organizations have found to manage or cope with change in order to be more successful. Some of these responses are **reactive** to external pressures, such as increased competition. Other responses are more **proactive**, being initiated by managers to take advantage of targeted opportunities, particularly in fast-changing industries where followers are not successful. Bob Nardelli, for example, recognized the need for change when he took over as CEO of Home Depot. Even though the company was the leader in the home improvement industry, Nardelli understood the unrealized potential of the company and its capacity for growth. In the first year of his term, Nardelli and Dennis Donovan, executive vice-president of HR, utilized their experience at GE (working under Jack Welch) to initiate an organization-wide transformation of the company. The main thrust of the change-management program was to involve employees in instituting continuous innovation and excellent customer service. These types of change initiatives are not designed to fix problems that have arisen in the organization so much as they are designed to help renew everyone's focus on key success factors.[16]

Managing Change through People

Change initiatives continue to move forward in many organizations. Yet many of these same organizations have no formal change-management program to support the initiatives. This is unfortunate since successful change rarely occurs naturally or easily.

Most employees—regardless of occupation—understand that the way things were done five or ten years ago is very different from how they are done today (or will be done five or ten years from now). Responsibilities change, job assignments change, work processes change. And this change is continuous—a part of the job—rather than temporary. Nevertheless, people often resist change because it requires them to modify or abandon ways of working that have been successful or at least familiar to them.

All managers play an important role in managing change. Home Depot has been a leader in involving employees in its change initiatives.

Challenge 4: Developing Human Capital

The idea that organizations "compete through people" highlights the fact that success increasingly depends on an organization's ability to manage "human capital." **Human capital** is an overall term used to describe the value of knowledge, skills, and capabilities that may not show up on a company's balance sheet but nevertheless have tremendous impact on an organization's performance.

Human capital
The individual's knowledge, skills, and abilities that have economic value to an organization

Human capital is intangible and elusive and cannot be managed the way organizations manage jobs, products, and technologies. One of the reasons for this is that employees, not the organization, own their own human capital. If valued employees leave a company, they take their human capital with them, and any investment the company has made in training and developing those people is lost. Once again, it is important to emphasize that the supervisor/manager is the link between the organization and the employees. Therefore, managers are key in helping the organization maintain and develop its human capital.

To build human capital in organizations, managers must begin to develop ways of ensuring superior knowledge, skills, and experience within their workforce and to find ways to distribute this "capital" throughout the organization. Staffing programs focus on identifying, recruiting, and hiring the best talent available. Training and development programs complement these staffing practices to provide talent enhancement, particularly in areas that cannot be transferred to another company if an employee should leave.[17] In addition, employees need opportunities for development on the job. The most highly valued intelligence tends to be associated with competencies and capabilities that are learned from experience and are not easily taught.[18] Consequently, managers have to do a good job of providing developmental assignments to employees and making certain that job duties and requirements are flexible enough to allow for growth and learning. To successfully develop people, supervisors and managers have to "let go." The supervisor has to understand where the employees are and where they need to go, but then the supervisor needs to get out of the way and still provide support if something goes wrong.[19]

Core competencies
Sets of integrated knowledge and capabilities in an organization that distinguish it from its competitors

Further, more and more organizations are recognizing that sets of knowledge capabilities—**core competencies**—are part of their human capital. These competencies are necessary in order to be different from their competition and provide ongoing value to their customers. For example, listed below are some core competencies and their definitions:

a. *Analytical and problem-solving skills*: ability to identify issues accurately; get to the root cause not just the symptoms of the problem; break a problem into its component parts.
b. *Focus on customer*: ability to make an effort to identify internal and external customers and understand what adds value for them; to create an environment that appreciates delivery of good customer service.
c. *Active listening skills*: ability to read body language and perceive group dynamics.

While many core competencies are similar from one organization to another, such as focus on customer or active listening skills, each organization will develop its own set and define the competency to fit the particular organization. Thus, it is the combination of competencies of all employees in that organization that makes it stand out from its competition.

Once competencies are identified, organizations have to find ways of using the competencies that currently exist. This has to go beyond the investment in employee development. Too often, employees have skills that go unused. As Robert Buckman, CEO of Buckman Laboratories, noted,

> If the greatest database in the company is housed in the individual minds of the associates of the organization, then that is where the power of the organization resides. These individual knowledge bases are continually changing and adapting to the real world in front of them. We have to connect these individual knowledge bases together so that they do whatever they do best in the shortest possible time.[20]

Bruncor, the parent company of NB Tel (New Brunswick's telecommunications company), has created the Living Lab, a think tank that produces, applies, and sells knowledge. Efforts to empower employees and encourage their participation and involvement utilize the human capital available more fully.

Various HR programs and processes have aided in learning and knowledge being shared among employees. For example, Royal Bank has a Learning Institute, which makes use of technology for interactive communication so that employees throughout Canada can be linked together at one time. Likewise, Boeing Satellite Systems has created a "lessons learned architecture" on the Internet where all areas of the company can store the knowledge they have learned. As information and intellectual capital are posted to the company's electronic newsgroups, it can be analyzed and consolidated by editorial teams. Employees can access and use this new codified knowledge directly from the Internet. Executives at Boeing estimate that this form of intellectual capital has reduced the cost of developing a satellite by as much as $25 million.[21]

In another example, Northwood Pulp and Paper has used interactive video to help train sawmill and forestry operations supervisors in its remote locations. By making use of technology, such as the Internet, organizations throughout Canada can increase their human capital.[22] Organizations have continued to express a concern about the skills shortage and the need to upgrade skills and focus additional training on younger workers.[23]

Developmental assignments, particularly those involving teamwork, can also be a valuable way of facilitating knowledge exchange and mutual learning. Effective communications (whether face to face or through information technology) are instrumental in sharing knowledge and making it widely available throughout the organization. As Dave Ulrich noted, "Learning capability is *g* times *g*—a business's ability to *generate* new ideas multiplied by its adeptness at *generalizing* them throughout the company."[24] A recent report by Statistics Canada summed up the critical need to develop human capital:

> . . . increasingly, human resources are seen to be the lifeblood of a growing economy, along with technological advancement. This view has led to calls for greater attention to the management and development of human resources. Education and training are increasingly seen as a central policy prescription for improved prosperity.[25]

For additional online resources that help small organizations develop their human capital, see **www.leadershipmanagement.bc.ca**.

Challenge 5: Responding to the Market

Meeting customer expectations is essential for any organization. In addition to focusing on internal management issues, managers must also meet customer requirements of quality, innovation, variety, and responsiveness. These standards often separate the winners from the losers in today's competitive world. How well does a company understand its customers' needs? How fast can it develop and get a new product to market? How effectively has it responded to special concerns? "Better, faster, cheaper"—these standards require organizations to constantly align their processes with customer needs. Management innovations, such as total quality management, Six Sigma, and process reengineering, provide comprehensive approaches to responding to customers. These have direct implications for HR: the requirement to hire staff that can work in teams, the necessity of having compensation systems that support TQM objectives, and the need to have performance appraisal systems that recognize the importance of customer satisfaction.

Total quality management (TQM)
A set of principles and practices—core ideas include understanding customer needs, doing things right the first time, and striving for continuous improvement

Six Sigma
A process used to translate customer needs into a set of optimal tasks that are performed in concert with one another

ISO 9000
World-wide quality standards program

Total quality management (TQM) is a set of principles and practices whose core ideas include understanding customer needs, doing things right the first time, and striving for continuous improvement. The TQM revolution began in the mid-1980s, pioneered by companies such as Motorola, Xerox, and Ford. Unfortunately, early TQM programs were no panacea for responding to customer needs and improving productivity. In many cases, managers viewed quality as a quick fix and became disillusioned when results did not come easily. More recently, companies, such as Motorola, GE, and Home Depot, have adopted a more systematic approach to quality, called Six Sigma, which includes major changes in management philosophy and HR programs. **Six Sigma** is a statistical method of translating a customer's needs into separate tasks and defining the best way to perform each task in concert with the others. The use of Six Sigma at a Goodyear tire plant in Medicine Hat, Alberta, is described in At Work with HRM 1.2. What makes Six Sigma different from other quality efforts is that it catches mistakes before they happen. In a true Six Sigma environment, variation from standard is reduced to only 3.4 defects per million.[26]

In addition to TQM and Six Sigma, other organizations focus on the importance of quality through ISO 9000 and 14000 certification or benchmarking. **ISO 9000** is a worldwide approach to quality management standards that can cover both product design and product delivery. ISO 14000 focuses on standards for environmental management.

at work **with HRM 1.2** at work with HRM 1.2

SIX SIGMA

Nine months after conducting a pilot class for Six Sigma Black Belts in October 2002, Goodyear Canada was in the midst of a major business transformation. At that point there were 19 Black Belts (full-time project leaders) and 7 Green Belts (part-time project leaders, working in offices, warehouses, and the 8 Canadian tire and rubber products manufacturing plants). Projects currently under way are projected to yield $10 million in waste reduction, capital equipment purchase avoidance, and increased sales through elimination of production bottlenecks.

Goodyear's tire manufacturing facility in Medicine Hat, Alberta, needed to produce more rubber from its Banbury rubber mixer in order to meet its daily quota and lessen its dependence on rubber produced by outside sources. In buying material, the factory was paying freight charges to get the rubber to the factory. By optimizing the Banbury uptime and increasing the Banbury output, the factory could reduce the amount of rubber it needed to purchase. Using the tools of Six Sigma, the factory determined that it could stagger shift rotations so that an operator was always available to keep the Banbury mixer running. They also were able to increase the batch weight sizes of some of the compounds by 4 to 11%. In addition, staging batches at the top of the conveyor and reducing the gate delay realized gains of two to three seconds per batch. Although three seconds does not sound like a great amount, over the course of a week, it adds about 150 minutes of productivity. After six months, the factory increased its Banbury mixer output by more than 5%, generating savings of over $110,000. The Medicine Hat plant estimates that it can save $250,000 to $400,000 annually by implementing the new procedures.

Gary Blake, Goodyear Canada Six Sigma champion, and a Black Belt, says that it is a problem-solving model that applies rigorous statistical thinking to reduce defects, improve cycle time, and increase customer satisfaction. The methodology is being applied not only to traditional manufacturing processes, but also to transactional processes—supply chain, purchasing, invoicing, sales, and marketing.

CRITICAL THINKING QUESTION

Is use of Six Sigma another management fad to get more work out of people? Explain the reasons for your answer.

International Quality Systems Directory

www.iso.org

Benchmarking
Finding the best practices in other organizations that can be brought into a company to enhance performance

Companies go through a certification process to demonstrate that they have achieved certain quality standards. Some of the Canadian companies certified include Dawson Seed Company Ltd. (British Columbia), Iron Ore Company of Canada (Newfoundland), Levitt-Safety Limited (Alberta), City of Windsor (Ontario), and Acadia Polymers (Ontario). A complete list of companies certified throughout the world can be accessed through **www.iso.org**.

Benchmarking looks at the "best practices" in other companies, whether they are competitors or not. By looking at other companies, managers and employees can assess whether something could be used in their organization to improve overall performance. For example, Royal Bank is involved in benchmarking customer service practices with other financial institutions in North America.

Key to all of these techniques is good HR practices. One of the reasons that HR programs are so essential to programs such as Six Sigma is that they help balance two opposing forces. Six Sigma's focus on continuous improvement drives the system toward

International Quality Systems Directory
www.iso.org

Standards Council of Canada
www.scc.ca

Quality Digest
www.qualitydigest.com

Q-Base
www.qbase.com

disequilibrium, while Six Sigma's focus on customers, management systems, and the like provide the restraining forces that keep the system together. HR practices help managers balance these two forces. This means that the manager plays a key role in motivating employees to care about quality and helping the company foster a work environment that will allow employees to succeed in quality initiatives.

Visit the following sites for the most current information about quality initiatives: **www.iso.org**, **www.scc.ca**, **www.qualitydigest.com**, and **www.qbase.com**.

Challenge 6: Containing Costs

Investments in TQM, intellectual capital, technology, globalization, and the like are all very important for organizational competitiveness. Yet, at the same time, there are increasing pressures on companies to lower costs and improve productivity to maximize efficiency. Labour costs are one of the largest expenditures of any organization, particularly in service and knowledge-intensive companies. Organizations have tried a number of approaches to lower costs, particularly labour costs. These include downsizing and outsourcing, each of which has a direct impact on HR policies and practices.

Downsizing

Downsizing
The planned elimination of jobs

Downsizing is the planned elimination of jobs. The pain of downsizing has been widespread throughout Canada. Virtually every major corporation within the country has undergone some cycle of downsizing. About 50% of Canadian employers have engaged in some type of downsizing and have reduced their workforces by an average of 13%.[27] Interestingly, a recent survey indicated that 72% of firms eliminating jobs were also creating new positions. The reasons for this can include both poor planning and a necessary change in the required skill sets.[28]

Unfortunately, the record on the value of downsizing is pretty spotty. While the stock market usually reacts positively to such announcements, only about half the companies that have eliminated jobs have seen an increase in profits. To minimize the impact on recruitment and retention, some firms have developed a "no layoff" approach. A study by Watson Wyatt of 750 companies showed that companies with excellent recruiting and retention policies provide a return to shareholders nearly 8% higher than those that don't. Those with a strong commitment to job security earned an additional 1.4% for shareholders.

Outsourcing and Employee Leasing

Outsourcing
Contracting outside the organization for work that was formerly done by internal employees. The small-business owner saves money, time, and resources by outsourcing tasks such as accounting and payroll.

Outsourcing simply means hiring someone outside the company or bringing in a company to perform tasks that could be done internally. Companies often hire the services of accounting firms, for example, to take care of financial services. Interest in outsourcing has been spurred by executives who want to focus their organization's activities on what they do best. Increasingly, activities such as maintenance, security, catering, and payroll are being outsourced in order to increase the organization's flexibility and to lower overhead costs. Provigo stores in Montreal has achieved both cost efficiencies and flexibility by outsourcing services as unusual as its cosmetics.[29]

There are several HR concerns with regard to outsourcing, not the least of which is that if employees are likely to lose their jobs when the work is outsourced, morale and productivity can drop rapidly. To minimize problems, line and HR professionals have to work together to define and communicate transition plans, minimize the number of unknowns, and help employees identify their employment options.[30]

In some situations a large portion of a company is outsourced in order to create a new business. This occurred in early 2002 when Hydro One Inc. (formerly Ontario Hydro) transferred approximately 20% of its employees to a new company it created that would provide technology, payroll, supply chain, and accounting services.[31] As an alternative to layoffs and outsourcing, some companies are exploring the idea of employee leasing, where employees are let go and then hired by a leasing company that contracts back with the original company. The Bank of Montreal outsourced its human resources processing services (payroll and benefits administration, HR call centres, and employee records) to Exult, a company specializing in outsourcing, in a contract that saw the transfer of 100 BMO employees to Exult.

In addition to downsizing, outsourcing, and employee leasing, organizations are also making more use of contract workers and part-time workers as a way to contain costs. All of these are HRM concerns as managers work to ensure these individuals understand the mission of the organization and are actively engaged and committed to the organization.

Productivity Enhancements

Pure cost-cutting efforts, such as downsizing, outsourcing, and leasing, may prove to be disappointing interventions if managers use them as simple solutions to complex performance problems. Overemphasis on labour costs perhaps misses the broader issue of productivity enhancement.

Since productivity can be defined as the "output gained from a fixed amount of inputs," organizations can increase productivity either by reducing the inputs (the cost approach) or by increasing the amount that employees produce.

$$\text{Productivity} = \frac{\text{Output (goods and services)}}{\text{Inputs (people, capital, materials, energy)}}$$

It is quite possible for managers to cut costs only to find that productivity falls at even a more rapid rate. Conversely, managers may find that increasing investment in employees (raising labour costs) may lead to even greater returns in enhanced productivity. This in turn may lead to increased profits, and better pay, benefits, and working conditions for employees. Except in extremely cash-poor organizations, managers may find that looking for additional ways to boost productivity may be the best way to increase the value of their organizations.

Canada trails other leading industrial economies in manufacturing productivity, defined as output per worker. From 1991 to 2001, manufacturing productivity in Canada rose only 22%, compared to 90% for Sweden, 51% for France and Japan, and 45% for the United States. This gap may continue as Canadian companies invest in machinery and equipment at rates lower than the United States.[32]

Employee productivity is the result of a combination of employee abilities, motivation, and work environment. When productivity improves the change is usually traceable to enhanced skill, motivation, or a work environment conducive to high performance. In general, this can be summarized in the following equation:

Performance = f(motivation, environment, ability)

If any of these three dimensions is low, productivity is likely to suffer. Figure 1.3 shows some of the topics that we cover in this textbook that help managers increase productivity in their organizations.

FIGURE 1.3   **Productivity Enhancements**

Challenge 7: Demographic and Employee Concerns

Objective 6

Statistics Canada
www.statcan.ca

In addition to the competitive challenges facing organizations, managers in general, and HR professionals in particular, need to be concerned about changes in the makeup and expectations of their employees. Some of these issues will be discussed here and others will be discussed in other chapters.

Among the most significant challenges to managers are the demographic changes occurring in Canada. You can find current information about the labour force through Statistics Canada (**www.statcan.ca**). Because they affect the workforce of an employer, these changes—in employee background, age, gender, and education—are important topics for discussion.

Diversity of Backgrounds

Canadian workers will continue to be a diverse group. According to the 2001 census, immigrants represent almost 70% of labour force growth and now constitute one-fifth of the workforce. By 2016, visible minorities will account for one-fifth of the Canadian population.[33] In cities such as Toronto and Vancouver visible minorities represent a significant portion of the population. Toronto is the most ethnically diverse city in North America, with 44% of its citizens born in other countries. The majority of immigrants coming to Canada are from China, India, the Philippines, and Hong Kong. Aboriginals make up 3.3% of the population, and more than half are under 25 years of age.

Age Distribution of Employees

The working-age population in Canada is becoming older—there are more individuals than ever before in the older age brackets (age 45 to 64) and fewer individuals than ever in the younger brackets. During the past 10 years, the 45 to 64 age bracket increased 35.8% to almost 7.3 million. This age bracket accounted for virtually one-quarter of Canada's total population of just over 30 million in 2001, compared with only 20% in 1991. Data show that there are fewer young people entering the working-age population to replace individuals in the age group nearing retirement.[34]

Companies are responding in a number of ways to this demographic shift. For example, major Canadian corporations, such as CIBC, Canadian National Railway Company, and TransCanada PipeLines, Inc., are looking to Aboriginal youth, which is

The Aboriginal Human Resources Development Council of Canada

www.ahrdcc.com

the fastest-growing segment of the Canadian population, to replace some of the older workers.[35] For additional information on the Aboriginal talent pool in your local community, visit **www.ahrdcc.com** (The Aboriginal Human Resources Development Council of Canada). Read Manager's Toolkit 1.2 to read about some of the other HR practices affected by an aging population.

Imbalance in the age distribution of the labour force has significant implications for employers. Companies such as Inco and sectors such as education are finding that large portions of their workforces are nearing retirement. Beyond the sheer number of employees they will have to replace, managers are concerned that the expertise of these employees is likely to be drained too rapidly. As a stopgap measure, employers are making positive efforts to attract older workers, especially those who have taken early retirement. "We're looking to recruit additional senior workers," says Lynn Taylor, director of research at staffing firm Robert Half International. "They have a vast amount of experience that is invaluable and irreplaceable—and our clients are thrilled to tap that expertise." Older workers, for example, have significantly lower accident rates and absenteeism than younger workers. Further, they tend to report higher job satisfaction scores. And while some motor skills and cognitive abilities may start to decline (starting around age 25), most individuals find ways to compensate for this fact so that there is no discernible impact on their performance.[36]

The other problem that accompanies age imbalances in the workforce might be referred to as the "echo boom" effect. Similar to the trends with baby boomers, those who constitute the new population bulge are experiencing greater competition for advancement from others of approximately the same age. This situation challenges the ingenuity of managers to develop career patterns for employees to smooth out gaps in the numbers and kinds of workers.[37]

Manager's Toolkit **1.2** Manager's Toolkit 1.2

OLD, BUT NOT OUT

The number of Canadians 55 and older is about 27% of the workforce, compared to 29% under 35, and 44% between 35 and 55. The average age of retirement is declining, from 65 in the early 70s to about 61 in 2003. By 2010, older workers will have higher education levels, more training, and more transferable skills, all of which will make them more employable. Many older workers want to continue to work after they retire, mostly because they enjoy work. Their ability to learn and adapt to new technologies does not differ from that of younger workers. However, they do want flexible arrangements, such as reduced hours, special assignments, temporary work, job sharing, telecommuting, and consulting work.

As employers face labour shortages in specific sectors such as health care, there will be more attempts to provide innovative HR programs to retain older workers. For example, the average age of retirement for a registered nurse is 57, so in an attempt to retain these experienced nurses, the Province of New Brunswick is introducing a phased-in retirement program. Nurses can reduce their work hours by about 50% and access their pension plans to supplement their incomes.

Sources: Adapted from Jennifer Thomas and Marianne Chilco, "Coming of Age," *Benefits Canada* 25, no. 3, March 2001: 36–38; Nicole Wassink, "Your Workforce Is Ageing . . . Are You Ready?" *The Conference Board of Canada*, May 2001; "Retention Strategies for Older Nurses Could Ease Shortages," *Canadian HR Reporter*, August 1, 2003: 1.

Gender Distribution of the Workforce

According to Statistics Canada 59.7% of labour force participants are women.[38] Employers are under constant pressure to ensure equality for women with respect to employment, advancement opportunities, and compensation. They also need to accommodate working mothers and fathers through parental leaves, part-time employment, flexible work schedules, job sharing, telecommuting, and childcare assistance. Employers are also finding that many working people are now faced with being caregivers to aging parents. Thus, the whole area of "dependent care" is creating issues in organizations that will require creative solutions. In addition, because more women are working, employers are more sensitive to the growing need for policies and procedures to eliminate sexual harassment in the workplace. Some organizations have special orientation programs to acquaint all personnel with the problem and to warn potential offenders of the consequences. Many employers are demanding that managers and supervisors enforce their sexual harassment policy vigorously.

Rising Levels of Education

The educational attainment of the Canadian labour force has steadily risen over the years. Not coincidentally, the most secure and fastest-growing sectors of employment over the past decade have been in those areas requiring higher levels of education. In fact, almost all job creation in Canada has been in professional and managerial positions, which typically require higher educational requirements.[39] While employment for those with university degrees has risen 26%, employment for those with less than a high school diploma has plummeted by 26%.[40] Figure 1.4 shows the average payoff in annual earnings from education. Women, who make up 58% of university graduates and 58% of community college graduates, are actively employed (82%) but tend to have more part-time work than full-time work.[41]

As more and more employees strive to balance the demands of their jobs with the needs of their families, employers are responding by offering greater flexibility such as part-time work and parental leave.

FIGURE 1.4   Average Annual Earnings from Education

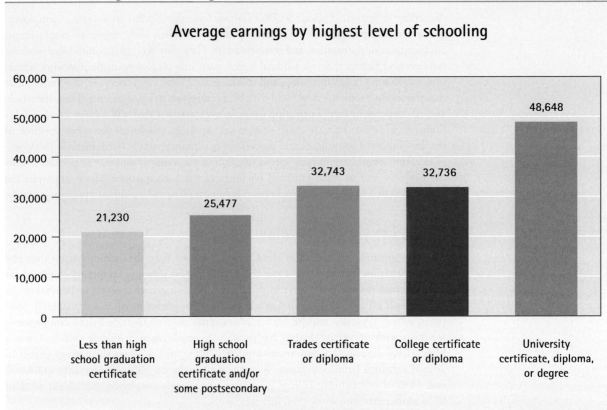

Average earnings by highest level of schooling

Source: Adapted from "Average Earnings of the Population 15 Years and Over by Highest Level of Schooling by Provinces and Territories (2001 Census)," http://www.statcan.ca/english/Pgdb/labor50a.htm. Reprinted with permission of the Minister of Industry Canada.

It is important to observe that while the educational level of the workforce has continued to rise, there is a widening gap between the educated and noneducated, leading to different types of work experiences. At the lower end of the educational spectrum, many employers are coping with individuals who are functionally illiterate—unable to read, write, calculate, or solve problems at a level that enables them to perform even the simplest technical tasks, such as reading an operating manual or reading safety procedures. Almost half of the Canadian adult population lacks the basic literacy skills to meet everyday requirements in today's knowledge-based society.[42] Employees with inadequate literacy skills make it difficult for employers to adopt new technology or new work methods.[43] However, people with computer skills scored higher on the skills assessment than those that had limited or no computer skills.[44]

The Changing Nature of the Job

The era of the full-time permanent job seems to have disappeared. Nearly half of all jobs created during the last two decades were nontraditional—that is, part-time, temporary, or contract work. As job security erodes, so do pension plans and health-care benefits, particularly for part-timers. These individuals hold about 18% of all jobs in Canada. Nearly 50% of all companies now employ part-timers, up from 35% in 1989. The number of Canadians who are self-employed has also risen, from 10% in 1991 to 15% in 2001.[45] With the change in the traditional notion of "job," companies, however, do place high value on team-structured work and on projects. This also leads to new issues in creating effective HR processes.

Cultural Changes

The attitudes, beliefs, values, and customs of people in a society are an integral part of their culture. Naturally, their culture affects their behaviour on the job and the environment within the organization, influencing their reactions to work assignments, leadership styles, and reward systems. Like the external and internal environments of which it is a part, culture is undergoing continual change. HR processes and systems, therefore, must be adjusted to accommodate and integrate these changes.

Employee Rights

Over the past few decades, legislation has radically changed the rules for managing employees by granting them many specific rights. Among these are laws granting the right to equal employment opportunity, union representation if desired, a safe and healthy work environment, minimum working conditions (hours of work, wages, vacations, etc.), and privacy in the workplace.

Ethics

With the various business scandals occurring in North America recently, more attention is being paid to business ethics. While employees are not overly suspicious of all business practices, there is an expectation that organizations behave ethically. Ethics in HRM 1.1 describes a recent study in the United States regarding employees' views of ethics.

Concern for Privacy

HR managers and their staffs, as well as line managers, generally recognize the importance of discretion in handling all types of information about employees. The *Personal Information Protection and Electronic Documents Act* (PIPEDA) is a federal law that deals with the collection, use, and disclosure of personal information (note that Quebec is the only province with similar laws, although Ontario and others have draft legislation in place). This law requires federally regulated organizations holding personal information on customers or employees to obtain their consent before it uses, collects, or discloses this information. Employer responses to the issue of information privacy vary widely. IBM was one of the first companies to show concern for how personal information about employees was handled. It began restricting the release of information as early as 1965 and in 1971 developed a comprehensive privacy policy. The Royal Bank, the Hudson's Bay Company, and Zero Knowledge Systems in Montreal are among other employers that have developed privacy programs.[46]

Changing Attitudes toward Work

Another well-established trend is for employees to define success in terms of personal self-expression and fulfillment of potential on the job. They are frequently less obsessed with the acquisition of wealth and now view life satisfaction as more likely

ethics **in HRM 1.1** ethics in HRM 1.1

LEADERS AND ETHICS

Walker Information, a firm that specializes in measuring employee and customer satisfaction, recently conducted a benchmark survey on ethics. There were some interesting results!

While a majority felt that their organizations were highly ethical, less than half believed that their leaders were people of high integrity. However, more employees feel comfortable in reporting ethical violations although they don't always do so. Many said that they do not report violations because they lack confidence in how such reporting would be handled.

The study concluded that it is critical that leaders model ethical behaviour and that the organizations' HRM practices must also exhibit ethical behaviour. It is important for employees to learn the ethical do's and don'ts.

Source: Extracted from *2001 National Employee Benchmark Study—Ethics,* Walker Information, December 14, 2001.

to result from balancing the challenges and rewards of work with those of their personal lives. Though most people still enjoy work and want to excel at it, they tend to be focused on finding interesting work and may pursue multiple careers rather than being satisfied with just "having a job." People also appear to be seeking ways of living that are less complicated but more meaningful. These new lifestyles cannot help but have an impact on the way employees are motivated and managed. Figure 1.5 outlines the research results by the Canadian Policy Research Network regarding job attributes desired by employees, a survey done in 2000 using a sample population of 2,500 employed Canadians.

Balancing Work and Family

Work and the family are connected in many subtle and not-so-subtle social, economic, and psychological ways. Because of the new forms that the family has taken—for example, the two-wage-earner and the single-parent family—work organizations find it necessary to provide employees with more family-friendly options. "Family friendly" is a broad term that may include unconventional hours, daycare, part-time work, job sharing, pregnancy leave, parental leave, executive transfers, spousal involvement in career planning, assistance with family problems, and telecommuting. Another emerging issue is that of eldercare. Many employees not only balance work and childcare but are also responsible for aging parents. It is projected that within the next five years, employees will be more concerned about caring for aging relatives than for children.[47]

Some progressive companies promote flexibility throughout their organizations. In general, these companies calculate that accommodating individual needs and circumstances is a powerful way to attract and retain top-calibre people. Aetna Life and Casualty, for example, has cut turnover by 50% since it began to offer six-month parental leaves, coupled with an option for part-time work when employees return to the job. Such programs, however, have their costs. In professional firms, such as

FIGURE 1.5   What Employees Want in a Job

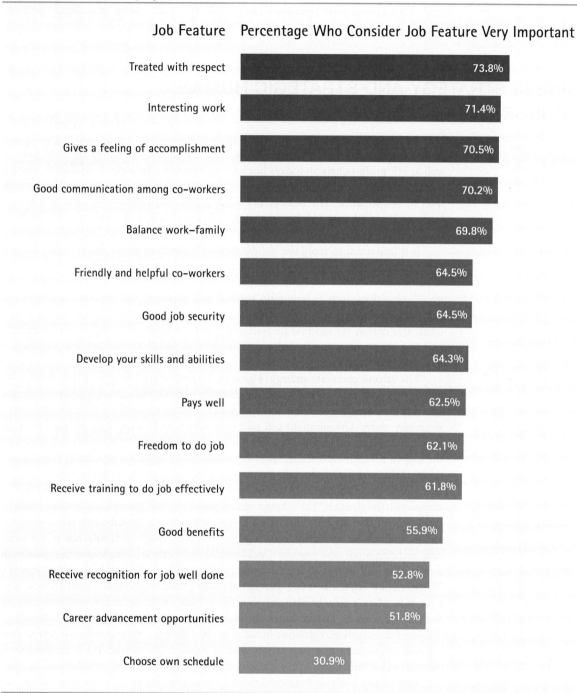

Job Feature   Percentage Who Consider Job Feature Very Important

Job Feature	Percentage
Treated with respect	73.8%
Interesting work	71.4%
Gives a feeling of accomplishment	70.5%
Good communication among co-workers	70.2%
Balance work–family	69.8%
Friendly and helpful co-workers	64.5%
Good job security	64.5%
Develop your skills and abilities	64.3%
Pays well	62.5%
Freedom to do job	62.1%
Receive training to do job effectively	61.8%
Good benefits	55.9%
Receive recognition for job well done	52.8%
Career advancement opportunities	51.8%
Choose own schedule	30.9%

Source: Graham S. Lowe and Grant Schellenberg, "Employee basic value proposition: Strong HR strategies must address work values," *Canadian HR Reporter*, July 15, 2002, Vol. 15, No. 12, p. 18. www.jobquality.ca. Adapted by permission of Carswell, a division of Thomson Canada Limited.

accounting and law, career paths and promotion sequences are programmed in a lock-step manner. Time away from work can slow down—and in some cases derail—an individual's career advancement.

BUSINESS STRATEGY AND STRATEGIC HUMAN RESOURCES MANAGEMENT

Objective **7**

As you can see, there are many challenges and issues facing supervisors and managers, as well as HR professionals, in today's business environment. In order to affectively manage these challenges, organizations develop a business strategy to enable it to achieve a high level of performance. The strategy helps the organization determine what business or businesses it will be in, why it exists, what its key goals are, and what actions it needs to take to realize those goals.

It is important to recognize the distinction between *corporate strategies* and *business strategies.* Corporate strategy deals with questions such as these: Should we be in business? What business should we be in? Corporate strategies are company-wide and focus on overall objectives, such as long-term survival and growth. There are two main types of corporate strategies: The first is a restructuring strategy, to ensure long-term survival, and under this option, we can find turn-around situations (Loewen Group Inc.), divestitures (Air Canada getting rid of its regional airline Jazz), liquidation (Eaton's), and bankruptcy (Confederation Life).

The second corporate strategy is growth. Organizations can grow incrementally (by adding new products or new distribution networks). For example, Procter & Gamble added skin care lotion and hair conditioners for babies and began to distribute to drugstores as well as grocery stores. Organizations can gain new customers by expanding internationally as Finning International Ltd. accomplished when it started selling Caterpillar equipment to the United Kingdom and Chile. Growth can also be achieved through mergers and acquisitions. Telus was created through the merger of BC Tel and Alberta-based Telus.

Unlike corporate strategy, business strategy focuses on one line of business and is concerned with the question "How should we compete?" Michael Porter has developed a classification system that helps us understand five ways in which a business unit can compete.[48] Let us illustrate his model by analyzing how hamburgers are sold. Restaurants can compete by being a low-cost provider (McDonald's); by trying to differentiate its products in a way that will attract a large number of buyers (e.g., Burger King introduces the Whopper); by being a best-cost provider through giving more value for the money (e.g., East Side Mario's sells hamburgers, but on a plate in an attractive environment); by focusing on a niche market based on lower cost to a select group of customers (e. g., offering fish burgers or vegetarian burgers); or by offering a niche product or service customized to the tastes of a very narrow market segment (Bymark restaurant in downtown Toronto sells a hamburger, with a specialty cheese, for $35).

Part of any business strategy is to be competitive. However, to be competitive, an organization needs to think about its people as part of its "competitive advantage." Thus, the people in the organization need to be managed in a manner that enables achievement of the business strategy.

While people have always been central to organizations, today's employees are critical in helping to build a firm's competitive advantage. Competitive advantage is a capacity or quality that an organization has that gives it an edge over its competition. The advantage could be productivity, price, quality, delivery, or service. Therefore, the focus of current HRM thinking and research is identifying and implementing people processes and systems that can make a particular firm stand out above the rest. Thus, an HR strategy is the link and integration of the business objectives with the people processes and systems.[49] It is important to remember that these processes and systems need to be consistent with the thrust of the business strategy. For example, Finning International's HR strategy has goals and actions that support the company's growth strategy, such as an international recruitment strategy along with a sophisticated management development program.[50] And this strategy identifies the role the line manager plays in, for example, management development.

An HR strategy aligned with the business strategy is particularly critical in knowledge-based industries, such as software and information services. Success in these types of companies increasingly depends on "people-embodied know-how," the knowledge, skills, and abilities (KSAs) embedded in an organization's members—commonly called "knowledge workers."[51]

Research has confirmed that the better an organization makes use of the knowledge contained in all the people in the organization, the higher the financial performance of the organization.[52] As a result, the HR areas of recruitment, learning and development, and retention—or "talent management"—become crucial to the attainment of the business goals.[53]

But an organization can sustain its competitive advantage only if the HR systems and processes ensure that the people can bring value to the organization, have appropriate skills, and have skills that are difficult to replace.[54]

For example, companies such as MDS Nordion, DaimlerChrysler Canada, and CIBC are intentionally designed to increase the value that employees add to the bottom line and to customer satisfaction. They actively involve employees in day-to-day decisions, such as determining what solutions can be discovered and applied to diseases of the body, how to more quickly manufacture an automobile, or what specific steps can be taken to reduce customer complaints. Also, companies such as the Four Seasons Hotels invest a great deal to hire and train the best and brightest employees in order to gain advantage over their competitors.

What then is the link between business strategies and strategic HRM? As stated earlier, **strategic human resources management** involves identifying key HR processes and linking those to the overall business strategy.[55] When one company buys another company, often the success of the new business revolves around how well the people side of the merger was handled. For example, in late 2003, Alcan Canada purchased Pechiney, a French aluminum producer, thus creating one of the world's largest aluminum companies. This merger created the need to review all their HR systems and processes to ensure that they supported the new direction of the merged giant.

Organizations of all sizes, public or private, will undertake a set of HR practices that enhance the employees' contribution for organizational success—the success as defined by the business strategy. Thus, all managers play a tremendous role in developing and maintaining effective HR practices and assisting the organization in acquiring a competitive advantage. If a manager believes that employees must be carefully monitored, when the business strategy suggests that employees need to be empowered, then it is highly likely the business will not succeed.[56] When a company (or a line manager) doesn't link the people processes and practices with the business objectives, the company may not be able to achieve the necessary competitive advantage.[57] For example, if a company wished to focus on providing superb customer service, then the company would have an employee selection process that hired people with those skills. Further, it might also have

Strategic human resources management
Identifying key HR processes and linking those to the overall business strategy

a training program that reinforced the expectations regarding customer service. And it would also have a performance appraisal system that rated how well the employee did in customer service.

While "competing through people" may be a key theme for human resources management, the idea remains only a framework for action. On a day-to-day basis, managers frequently focus on specific business challenges and issues and may not always focus as critically on the people issues. You can see from Figure 1.1 that HRM helps blend many aspects of management—business pressures, such as technology and the global market, with the changing nature of the workforce. By balancing what are sometimes competing demands, HRM plays an important role in getting the most from employees for organizational success and providing a work environment that meets the employees' short- and long-term needs.

SUMMARY

1. Define human resources management (HRM).
   - Integrated set of processes, programs, and systems that focus on effective deployment and development of employees.

2. Identify the processes and activities of HRM.
   - Organizational, work, and job design
   - Planning
   - Recruitment and selection
   - Training and development
   - Performance management
   - Compensation—developing and administering pay and benefits programs that will attract and retain employees
   - Occupational health and safety
   - Employee and labour relations

3. Explain the importance of HRM to the line manager.
   - Line manager is key link between employee and organization.
   - Helps you understand roles and responsibilities in managing employees.
   - People have always been central to organizations, but their strategic importance is growing in today's knowledge-based industries.

4. Explain the relationship between the line manager and the HR practitioner.
   - Every manager's job is managing people.
   - Successful organizations equip their line managers with a thorough understanding of HRM.
   - HR professionals help the line manager be a good people manager by providing advice as well as direct services.
   - Combining expertise of HR professionals with the experience of line managers can develop and utilize the talents of employees to their greatest potential.

5. Describe current business challenges that are forcing organizations to put more emphasis on people in organizations.
   - Globalization is creating pressure for managers to effectively manage people.
   - Technology has shifted work and skills from manual labour to knowledge workers.

- Forces of change are making organizations find better ways to help employees learn new skills.
- Managers need to have a style that encourages people to develop.
- Responding to customer needs has led to total quality management (TQM), Six Sigma, re-engineering programs, ISO, and benchmarking.
- Since employee costs are typically the single biggest item in any company's operation, managers are expected to find ways to contain costs while at the same time treating people as an investment.

6. Identify key demographic and employee concerns.
- There is a diverse and aging workforce with an increased participation of females.
- Canadian labour force is more educated.
- There is less full-time work, more part-time work.
- Employees have more rights.
- Employees want a balance between work and family.

7. Describe the link between business strategy and strategic HRM.
- Business strategy involves formulation of company's mission, goals, and action plans.
- Part of any business strategy is to be competitive; to be competitive, an organization needs to think about its people as part of its "competitive advantage."
- Strategic HRM focuses on linking and aligning the HRM processes to the business strategy.
- The HR processes and programs will reflect the particular strategy, such as growth.

Need to Know

- Definition of HRM
- Definition of TQM, re-engineering, and outsourcing
- Definition of strategic human resources management
- Nature of employee expectations and concerns

Need to Understand

- Impact of current business challenges on HRM
- Link of strategic HRM with business planning
- Role of line managers in responding effectively to the expectations and concerns of employees

Key Terms

benchmarking 20	knowledge workers 12
core competencies 18	outsourcing 21
downsizing 21	proactive response to change 16
globalization 10	reactive response to change 16
human capital 17	Six Sigma 19
human resources information system (HRIS) 13	strategic human resources management 31
human resources management (HRM) 4	total quality management (TQM) 19
ISO 9000 19	

REVIEW QUESTIONS

1. What is the definition of human resource management?
2. What are the eight HRM processes and activities?
3. How would you describe the relationship between the line manager and an HR professional?
4. What are the current business challenges facing Canadian organizations?
5. What is the important link between a business strategy and the HR strategy?

CRITICAL THINKING QUESTIONS

1. Your manufacturing company is considering the creation of another plant in South America. What are the major human resource management issues that need to be considered?
2. You are a supervisor in a fast-food restaurant. You have a very diverse customer base. What might be your HR concerns in attracting and retaining employees who can provide excellent customer service?
3. What are three pros and three cons of creating or forcing organizational change? Does it help or hurt organizational performance? Do you like change? Why or why not?
4. The major utility company in your province has just announced that it is outsourcing its customer service functions. What reasons might have led to this decision?
5. What would be the human resource implications if Canada decided to change its immigration policy and significantly reduce the number of immigrants from all parts of the world?
6. List at least three pros and cons of having a more diverse workforce. Is Canada in a better position to compete globally because of our diverse population?

DEVELOPING YOUR SKILLS

1. Working in groups of four to six students, identify what role the line manager would play and the HR professional would play in the following activities. Where would overlaps occur and where would any problems arise?

   a. Job design
   b. Recruitment and selection
   c. Training and development
   d. Performance management
   e. Pay and benefits
   f. Disciplinary matters

2. In groups of three to four students, prepare a list of both positive and negative experiences you've had as an employee. Once the list is generated, identify what HRM practice or activity might have improved the negative experiences, and what HRM practice contributed to the positive experiences.

3. Visit each of the Web sites listed in Manager's Toolkit 1.1. Identify two or three sites that would be useful to you in a supervisory role and give reasons for your choices. Working in groups of four to five students, share your information with each other. Discuss any sites the groups had in common.

4. Visit the following Web sites and determine which site would be more useful to you when looking for work. What if you were a supervisor? Write a one-page summary giving reasons why you chose the site(s).

www.hrdc-drhc.gc.ca/
www.robmagazine.com/
www.monster.ca
www.workplace.ca
www.workinfonet.ca
www.human-resources.org/

Case Study   1

Outsourcing HR at BMO

In 2003, the Bank of Montreal outsourced all the HR processing work to Exult Inc., a human resources outsourcer. Exult will take over BMO's HR systems and administrative functions in a deal worth $75 million over ten years. Exult will handle all payroll, HR call centre management and information systems and support, employee data, staffing, and records management for BMO's 34,000 employees. BMO is Exult's first Canadian client. Rose Patten, executive vice-president of HR for BMO, sees the arrangement as a partnership, not a hand-off. According to Ms. Patten, the outsourcing arrangement will allow BMO to concentrate its HR strategy on four key areas: "talent management, performance alignment and compensation, equity and employment, and learning and development."

Exult chairman and CEO Jim Madden is very pleased with the 100 BMO employees who have accepted offers to manage the HR outsourced functions and to expand the number of Canadian clients. A BMO former manager of Information Management says, "The one thing that is exciting is being able to see outside the box that we are in today, being able to see different businesses." The majority of the 250 employees affected by the outsourcing arrangement have been offered positions with Exult or other BMO departments.

More companies are turning to self-service applications by which clients or employees can do such things as change their home address online as a way to empower customers and employees and cut down on administrative costs. If Exult performs as promised, BMO will save 20% over what it would cost to do the same functions in-house. "It's no surprise that companies are outsourcing functions as a way to save money and focus on core business," says David Rhodes, a principal at management-consulting firm Towers Perrin. He says businesses are "buying expertise and the ability to work very effectively" when they decide to outsource.

Source: George Tischelle and Elisabeth Goodridge, "Prudential Financial Expects Savings by Outsourcing HR," *InformationWeek* (January 28, 2002): 873–81; Virginia Galt, "Take Our Business; Take Our People," *The Globe and Mail*, May 19, 2003: B1.

Questions

1. What are the pros and cons of outsourcing the HR function?
2. What do you think BMO should worry about most?
3. How can Exult make certain that BMO is happy with its service?

Case Study 2

The Airline Industry in Canada

There is probably no industry in Canada as volatile as the airline industry. Over the last several years all carriers have experienced a significant impact to their business due to such external conditions as 9/11, SARS, the tsunami in Asia, and other similar world events.

With such changing conditions, there are challenges to the various Canadian carriers in relation to their employees. And it is not just a matter of how much to compensate them. In some cases it is a situation of determining if there is enough work to keep all the people employed. Or it could be the dilemma of encouraging people to look toward the future and then having to tell them that the company is going into bankruptcy. For Air Canada, it was a matter of helping paint a brighter picture for the future; for Jetsgo, it was informing employees that they would no longer be employed.

Jetsgo was Canada's third largest airline, with a business model offering the cheapest airfares, relying on low costs to operate. On March 11, 2005, it ceased operations, terminating the employment of 1,400 employees and filing for creditor protection. Michael LeBlanc, president, indicated to the public on May 2, 2005, that he would be able to restructure, satisfy creditors, and fly again. The initial bankruptcy filing showed that it carried over 1.6 million passengers in 2004 but lost almost $230 million in that year. It further stated that the prime tool for marketing and selling tickets was over the Internet. In addition, Jetsgo had initiated a lawsuit against WestJet claiming that WestJet was trying to ruin Jetsgo by offering the same cheap airfares as Jetsgo. LeBlanc was unsuccessful in convincing the creditors that he could re-invigorate the ailing airline and on May 14, the bankruptcy took effect allowing the assets to be sold. However, as recently as June 2004, LeBlanc had been announcing the expansion of the airline and the promise to rival the others. So, what happened?

Airline analysts have suggested that the business model was unsustainable—that the company could not continue to offer such cheap fares. Others suggest that LeBlanc, who has had several other failed airline operations, attempted to expand too quickly. Some others have suggested that there were too many operational problems, such as a wild landing in Calgary in January. But whatever the reasons for the failure, it does mean that 1,400 employees no longer have work.

Sources: Adapted from Nicolas Van Praet, "Jetsgo Working With Monitor To Fly Again," *The Gazette*, March 24, 2005, http://www.canada.com/montreal/montrealgazette/news/business/story.html?id=c25381c5-7ffa-4ef0-8f9f-aade3d28c4e8 (retrieved May 24, 2005); "Dear Future Jetsgo Customers," *The National Post*, www.canada.com/search/results.html?searchfor=Jetsgo (retrieved May 24, 2005); "Jetsgo Folds Its Wings," *The Windsor Star*, May 14, 2005,

http://www.canada.com/windsor/windsorstar/news/business/
story.html?id=5c821a5f-6504-4e67-aff6-18f119fcd2d2 (retrieved May 24, 2005);
and Bankruptcy Filing, http://www.canada.com/vancouver/vancouversun/news/
story.html?id=e538ebbe-f520-42bb-9e8d-e1eb1cbb89fd (retrieved May 24, 2005).

Questions

1. Identify the business challenges affecting LeBlanc and Jetsgo.
2. What HRM issues did LeBlanc face once operations ceased?
3. What HRM issues would LeBlanc face if the airline started operations again?

NOTES AND REFERENCES

1. Dave Ulrich and Norman Smallwood, "What's Next for the People Function? A Missing Link for Delivering Value," *Human Resource Resources in the 21st Century* (Hoboken, N.J.: John Wiley & Sons, Inc., 2003): 251–25.
2. The Human Capital Edge: 21 People Management Practices Your Company Must Implement (or Avoid) to Maximize Shareholder Value (February 2002).
3. Bruce Little, "We're Less Dependent but More Entangled," *The Globe and Mail*, May 15, 2000, A-2.
4. Gordon Pitts, "Finning CEO Paves the Way for British, Chilean Expansion," *The Globe and Mail*, July 29, 2002, B7; Simon Tuck, "Canada Will Be No. 1 Spot for Business, Study Says," *The Globe and Mail*, July 17, 2003, B3.
5. "Air Traffic Controllers Strike over Plan to Consolidate European Skies," Canadian Press, June 19, 2002, http://www.canada.com/search/site/story.asp?id=DA749213-8DFB-4CF6-8EE0-C7F801E6F8B5 (retrieved June 25, 2002).
6. *Global Economic Prospects and Developing Countries 2002* (Washington, D.C.: The World Bank, 2002): 71.
7. *World Development Indicator 2002* (Geneva, Switzerland: World Trade Organization, 2002), Table 4.2, 210.
8. Peter F. Drucker, "Knowledge-Worker Productivity: The Biggest Challenge," *California Management Review* 41, no. 2 (Winter 1999): 79–94; A. D. Amar, *Managing Knowledge Workers* (Westport, Conn.: Quorum, 2002); Cynthia C. Froggat, *Work Naked: Eight Essential Principles for Peak Performance in the Virtual Workplace* (New York: John Wiley and Sons, 2002); Mary Ann Roe, "Cultivating the Gold-Collar Worker," *Harvard Business Review* 79, no. 5 (May 2001): 32–33. See also D. P. Lepak and S. A. Snell, "The Human Resource Architecture: Toward a Theory of Human Capital Development and Allocation," *Academy of Management Review* 24, no. 1 (1999): 31–48.
9. "Industry Report 1998: Information-Technology Training," *Training* 35, no. 10 (October 1998): 63–68; Barb Cole-Gomolski, "Recruiters Lure Temps with Free IT Training," *Computerworld* 33, no. 31 (August 2, 1999): 10; Ben Worthen, "Measuring the ROI of Training," *CIO* 14, no. 9 (February 15, 2001): 128–36.
10. Scott A. Snell, Donna Stueber, and David P. Lepak, "Virtual HR Departments: Getting Out of the Middle," in R. L. Heneman and D. B. Greenberger (eds.), *Human Resource Management in Virtual Organizations* (Columbus, OH: Information Age Publishing, forthcoming); Samuel Greengard, "How to Fulfill Technology's Promise," *Workforce* (February 1999): HR Software Insights Supplement, 10–18.
11. Marilyn Linton, "Human Resource Queries Handled with Jet Speed," *Financial Post*, February 23, 2004, FE4.
12. Jill Vardy, "Web Use to Reach Employees on the Rise," *Financial Post*, January 17, 2002, FP9.
13. "Line Managers Who Use Web-Based Manager Self-Service Cut Costs and Increase the Effectiveness of Their Departments," *Web-Based Human Resources News*, Issue 3, http://www.towers.com/TOWERS/webhrnewsletter_3.htm (retrieved March 22, 2002).
14. Todd Humber, "With HR Slashed, Calgary Turns to Technology," *Canadian HR Reporter*, March 8, 2004, G6.
15. Peter MacDonald, "Heroes for Hard Times," *Profit 100*, http://www.profitguide.com/profit100/2002/features.asp?ID=950 (retrieved July 22, 2002).
16. Chad Terhune, "Home Depot's Home Improvement—Retail Giant Aims to Spur Sales with Less-Cluttered Stores, Increased Customer Service," *The Wall Street Journal*, March 8, 2001, B1.
17. Thomas A. Stewart, "Intellectual Capital," *Fortune* (October 3, 1994): 68–74. David Lepak and Scott Snell, "Knowledge Management and the HR Architecture," in S. Jackson, M. Hitt, and A. DeNisi (eds.), *Managing Knowledge for Sustained Competitive Advantage*: Designing Strategies for Effective Human Resource Management (SIOP Scientific Frontiers Series, forthcoming); David Lepak and Scott Snell, "Examining the Human Resource Architecture: The Relationship among Human Capital,

Employment, and Human Resource Configurations," *Journal of Management*, forthcoming; Steve Bates, "Study Links HR Practices with the Bottom Line," *HRMagazine* 46, no. 12 (December 2001): 14.

18. Gary S. Becker, *Human Capital* (New York: Columbia University Press, 1964); Charles A. O'Reilly III and Jeffrey Pfeffer, "Cisco Systems: Acquiring and Retaining Talent in Hypercompetitive Markets," *Human Resource Planning* 23, no. 3 (2000): 38–52.

19. Pam Withers, "Birth of a Leader," *BCBusiness* (January 2000): 38.

20. For more on Buckman Labs and its approach to managing human capital, visit its Web site at www.buckman.com/. The company is also well-known for its knowledge management initiatives, called Knowledge Nurture, as well as its knowledge management system, called K'Netix; see www.knowledge-nurture.com/; Nick Bontis, "There's a Price on Your Head: Managing Intellectual Capital Strategically," *Business Quarterly*, Summer 1996, 41–47.

21. Joseph E. McCann, *Managing Intellectual Capital: Setting the Agenda for Human Resource Professionals* (New York: Human Resource Planning Society, 1999); Benoit Guay, "Knowledge Management Is a Team Sport," *Computing Canada* 27, no. 3 (July 13, 2001): 23; Pimm Fox, "Making Support Pay," *Computerworld* 36, no. 11 (March 11, 2002): 28.

22. Debbie Murray and Michael Bloom, "Solutions for Employers: Effective Strategies for Using Learning Technologies in the Workplace," *The Conference Board of Canada*, March 15, 2000, Ottawa, 24–25.

23. Alan Toulin, "Skilled Labour Scarce: Employers," *Financial Post*, June 18, 2002, FP9.

24. Dave Ulrich, Steve Kerr, and Ron Ashkenas, *The GE Work-Out: How to Implement GE's Revolutionary Method for Busting Bureaucracy & Attacking Organizational Problems* (New York: McGraw-Hill Professional Publishing, 2002).

25. *The Evolving Workplace*, Catalogue No. 71-583-XPE, Statistics Canada, 2.

26. The term Six Sigma is a registered trademark of Motorola. It is based on the Greek letter sigma, used as a symbol of variation in a process (the standard deviation). For more information see Peter S. Pande, Robert P. Neuman, and Roland R. Cavanagh, *The Six Sigma Way: How GE, Motorola, and Other Top Companies Are Honing Their Performance* (New York: McGraw-Hill, 2000).

27. Charles R. Greer, Stuart A. Youngblood, and David A. Gray, "Human Resource Management Outsourcing: The Make or Buy Decision," *Academy of Management Executive* 13, no. 3 (August 1999): 85–96; T. Wagar, "The Death of Downsizing—Not Yet!" *Research Forum, HR Professional* 16, no. 1 (February–March 1999): 41–43.

28. Gene Koretz, "Hire Math: Fire 3, Add 5," *Business Week Online*, March 13, 2000, http://www.businessweek.com/archives/2000/b3672052.arc.htm (retrieved October 15, 2004).

29. Peter Diekmeyer, "Contracting-out Is In," *The Vancouver Sun*, December 14, 2002, E5.

30. James Brian Quinn, "Strategic Outsourcing: Leveraging Knowledge Capabilities," *Sloan Management Review* (Summer 1999): 9–21; William C. Byham and Sheryl Riddle, "Outsourcing: A Strategic Tool for a More Strategic HR," *Employment Relations Today* 26, no. 1 (Spring 1999): 37–55; Grover N. Wray, "The Role of Human Resources in Successful Outsourcing," *Employment Relations Today* 23, no. 1 (Spring 1996): 17–23.

31. "Ontario Hydro to Transfer Workers to Private Sector," *The Vancouver Sun*, February 14, 2002, D7.

32. David Brown, "Manufacturers Pressed to Improve Productivity," *Canadian HR Reporter* 16, no. 3 (July 14, 2003): 1 and 13; Jim Balsillie and Roger Martin, "We're Number 8: So What?" *Toronto Star*, August 5, 2003.

33. www.statcan.ca/english/labour/CANSIM Table 179-002.

34. 2001 Census, Statistics Canada, Analysis Series, http://www12.statcan.ca/english/census01/Products/Analytic/companion/age/canada.cfm (retrieved July 22, 2002).

35. Claudia Cattaneo, "Looking for Future Workers," *Financial Post*, February 6, 2002, FP10.

36. Shelley Donald Coolidge, "Retired. And Ready to Work. Selling Slow-Built Wisdom in a Churn-It-Out World, Senior Workers Get a Handle on the Hot Job Market," *Christian Science Monitor* (October 25, 1999): 11.

37. Peter Francese, "My, You've Grown: The Teen Economy Is Like Totally Awesome," *The Wall Street Journal*, June 28, 2000, S3.

38. Statistics Canada, Labour Force and Participation Rates, http://www.statcan.ca/english/Pgdb/People/Labour/labor05.htm (retrieved July 22, 2002).

39. Brigitte Bouchard and John Zhao, "University Education: Recent Trends in Participation, Accessibility and Returns," Statistics Canada, *Education Quarterly Review* 6, no. 4 (Summer 2000): 29.

40. Ross Finnie, "Employment and Earnings of Graduates," Statistics Canada, *Education Quarterly Review* 7, no. 1 (Summer 2000): 24–25.

41. Statistics Canada, "University Qualifications by Sex," http://www.statcan.ca/english/Pgdb/People/Education/educ21.htm; http://www.statcan.ca/english/Pgdb/People/Education/educ19.htm (retrieved July 23, 2002).

42. Sarah Schmidt, "One in Seven Struggles with Basic Reading," *National Post*, May 12, 2005, A8.

43. Organization for Economic Co-operation and Development, Statistics Canada, *Literacy in the Information Age: Final Report of the International Adult Literacy Survey*.

44. Statistics Canada, "Adult Literacy and Life Skills Survey," http://www.statcan.ca/Daily/English/050511/d050511b.htm (retrieved May 24, 2005).

45. Statistics Canada, "Full and Part-time Employment" http://www.statcan.ca/english/Pgdb/People/Labour/labor12.htm, and "Self-Employment" http://www.statcan.ca/english/Pgdb/People/Labour/labor64.htm (retrieved July 23, 2002).

46. Chris Conrath, "Complying with PIPEDA," *Computer World Canada* 18, no. 1, January 11, 2002.

47. Charlene Marmer Solomon, "Elder-Care Issues Shake the Workplace," *Workforce* (October 1999): 58–67.

48. Michael Porter, *Competitive Advantage* (New York: Free Press, 1985).

49. Lynda Gratton, Veronica Hope Hailey, Philip Stiles, and Catherine Truss, *Strategic Human Resource Management* (Oxford: Oxford University Press, 1999): 7.

50. The current author's late husband, Richard A. Robertson, was the key external resource assisting the President of Finning International in developing the HR strategy in 2002–03.

51. "Competency Management Delivers Spectacular Corporate Gains," *Workforce OnLine*, http://www.workforce.com/archive/article/22/06/06.php (retrieved March 21, 2002).

52. Edward E. Lawler III, and Susan Albers Mohrman, *Creating a Strategic Human Resources Organization* (Stanford: Stanford University Press, 2003): 36.

53. *Ibid*.

54. David E. Bowen and Cheri Ostroff, "Understanding HRM—First Performance Linkages: The Role of the 'Strength' of the HRM System," *Academy of Management Review* 29, no. 2, April 2004: 203–221.

55. Allan R. Cohen and David L. Bradford, "Building a New Partnership," *Resources in the 21st Century* (Hoboken, N.J.: John Wiley & Sons, Inc., 2003): 135–142.

56. Christopher A. Bartlett and Sumantra Ghoshal, "Building Competitive Advantage Through People," *MIT Sloan Management Review* (Winter 2002): 34–41.

57. Bowen and Ostroff, "Understanding HRM–First Performance Linkages."

CHAPTER 2

The Legal Framework of HRM

HRM
Close-Up

Denham Jolly, president and chief executive officer

"The best advice I can give a young manager is to be firm but fair."

When FLOW 93.5 FM hit the Toronto airwaves in the spring of 2001, Denham Jolly knew it had been worth the 14-year wait. With what he calls "the hottest music and spoken-word programming" and a "dynamic, talented workforce" that reflects Toronto's diversity, Jolly says FLOW has already landed a loyal audience. He and his partners at Milestone Radio have long had three goals for Canada's only urban Black radio station—to be economically viable, socially responsible, and a voice for the Black community. "We are committed to providing [an] alternative, supporting up-and-coming artists, and giving voice to the hopes and aspirations of our communities."

FLOW is hardly Jolly's first foray into business. With over 25 years experience, he's been a newspaper publisher and still owns and operates a nursing home in Mississauga. But radio offers unique challenges—it has to foster a creative environment, yet still adhere to broadcast standards and business practices. And with the average age of employees under 30, the learning curve, says Jolly, can be steep. Much of his job is to ensure that on-air personalities follow the conditions of FLOW's federal licence and know basic broadcast laws and regulations, such as "a broadcaster shall not broadcast any abusive comment that [may] expose an individual or class of individuals to hatred or contempt on the basis of race, ethnic origin, colour, religion, sex, sexual orientation, age, or mental or physical disability." Obscene and profane language is prohibited—so is broadcasting false or misleading information. And open-line programming has its own legalities—all callers, for example, must give their consent to being put on the air. There's an industry code of ethics that Jolly must guarantee—on-air language can't be gender-specific, and controversial issues must be treated fairly. FLOW also has its own programming and operations policy, and Jolly makes sure all staff have a copy.

And then there are the basics—the *Employment Standards Act, the Human Rights Code,* and occupational health and safety legislation. Jolly says that managers are responsible for knowing all "legislation and policies related to the human resource process—from recruitment to termination, pay and benefits, workplace harassment, parental leave, and employment equity." He takes complaints of harassment and discrimination "very seriously," and investigates and documents them thoroughly. But experience has shown that "if fairness is your guide," most situations can be settled amicably. Firing an employee depends "on the severity of the offence," but Jolly also uses reprimands or suspensions when appropriate. Overall, he tries to preempt problems through the hiring process itself and by creating the right workplace climate. "We are inclusive; we promote a spirit of cooperation and camaraderie; we encourage open communication between management and staff; and we stay focused on our goal of being Number 1."

He consults a labour lawyer or human resources specialist when the occasion demands and uses meetings and e-mail updates to keep staff abreast of any significant change, particularly regarding policy and legislation that affect the broadcast industry. Mostly, he says, experience has been his classroom. "The best advice I can give a young manager is to be firm but fair." He also includes in his advice the following: aim to be respected; build on an employee's strengths; clarify expectations; give positive feedback; be patient; be a mentor. In summary, then, "Create a work environment in which people can learn, grow, achieve their potential, and contribute fully to the organization."

INTRODUCTION

As the HRM Close-Up shows, there is no doubt that employment laws affect line managers and what they are expected to do to successfully manage the people they are responsible for. Laws have been written to protect the employer and the employees; these laws reflect the values of society and in some situations laws have been enacted because of poor management practices. Therefore, it is important for supervisors to understand the legal context in which they have to operate. Managers, supervisors, and employees can no longer behave and act in certain ways without severe consequences. When managers ignore the legal aspects of HRM, they risk incurring costly and time-consuming litigation, negative public attitudes, and damage to organization morale.

And some of the laws address not just legal issues; the issues can also be emotional. For example, human rights legislation is paramount over other laws and concerns all individuals regardless of their gender, race, religion, age, marital status, disability, family status, sexual orientation, national origin, colour, or position in an organization. As Denham Jolly indicates, he takes any complaint of harassment or discrimination very seriously. All employees, including supervisors and managers, should be aware of their personal biases and how these attitudes can influence their dealings with each other. It should be emphasized that whether the supervisor unintentionally or intentionally acts a certain way, the supervisor is responsible for any illegal actions. Being ignorant of the law is not a valid excuse. This chapter will focus on the various employment laws at both the federal and provincial levels that affect how a manager practises human resources management.

Beyond legislation, there is also an expectation in today's society that treating employees in certain ways is just "good business." Thus, the concept of diversity management in a multicultural society is gaining momentum simply because it makes good business sense. It is important to remember that we have gone beyond what is required by law in our human resources management practices.

THE LEGAL FRAMEWORK OF HRM

Canada has two distinct sets of legislation: federal and provincial. Federal laws apply to everyone who resides in Canada. For example, everyone must pay income taxes. Other laws are handled at the provincial level. For example, the provinces are responsible for determining who can get a driver's licence. While this chapter will discuss specific employment laws, other kinds of laws, such as common law (our body of law that is developed as a result of judicial decisions), contract law (the laws that relate to legal and binding agreements, such as the purchase of a car), and government regulations (called statutory law), can also have an impact on HR. For example, common law establishes the basic employee–employer relationship of trust. Contract law governs a person engaged in a fee-for-service activity for a company. Statutory law creates employment conditions, such as providing minimum wages or holidays with pay (i.e., Canada Day on July 1).

Federal legislation applies to only about 10% of Canadian workers who are employed by the federal government departments and agencies, Crown corporations, and other businesses and industries under federal jurisdiction, such as banks, airlines, railway companies, and insurance and communications companies. Examples of these companies are CIBC, Scotiabank, Air Canada, WestJet, and the Canada Revenue Agency.

In addition, each province and territory has its own legislation that covers employment standards, human rights, labour relations, and worker health and safety. Companies covered under provincial legislation would include the corner 7 Eleven, the local McDonald's, and others such as Inco Steel. Although there is a great deal of similarity across provinces and territories, there are some notable variations in minimum wage and vacation entitlement, for example. Also, some aspects of human rights legislation differ from one jurisdiction to another. Some provinces and territories have employment equity legislation, and others do not. For example, Ontario and Manitoba have stringent pay equity legislation. However, in Alberta and British Columbia, there is no such legislation. Therefore any pay equity adjustments are the decision of the organization.

Although both Employment Insurance (EI) and the Canada Pension Plan (CPP) are regulated by federal law, all employers and employees are covered, not just federal employees. EI provides for wage payment should you lose your job, and CPP provides for a small pension when you retire. Quebec has its own pension plan, which is similar to the Canada Pension Plan. Recent changes to EI (January 2004) have had an impact on human resource practices in organizations. Specifically, compassionate care leave is now available for employees. They can take up to six weeks off (with partial pay) to care for a dying family member.[1]

Canada Labour Code

laws.justice.gc.ca/en/
L-2/index.html

**Canadian Human
Rights Act**

laws.justice.gc.ca/en/
h-6/31147.html

**Personal Information
Protection and Electronic
Documents Act (PIPEDA)**

laws.justice.gc.ca/en/
P-8.6/92607.html

Federal Employment Laws

For companies that are federally regulated, there are two basic employment laws: the **Canada Labour Code** and the **Canadian Human Rights Act**. The Labour Code covers basic employment conditions, labour relations, and health and safety in the federal sector. This law is administered by the Canada Industrial Relations Board.

Like the Labour Code, the Canadian Human Rights Act applies to all federal government departments and agencies, Crown corporations, and businesses and industries under federal jurisdiction, such as banks, airlines, railway companies, and insurance and communications companies. It is administered by the Canadian Human Rights Commission, which makes decisions on complaints involving discrimination and harassment. The concept of a certain level of basic human rights is part of the very fabric of Canadian society. And it is an area that is constantly expanding. In order to ensure that the laws fit changing expectations, the federal government embarked on a year-long review of the Canadian Human Rights Act in 1999. The purpose of the review was to consider adding new grounds for discrimination and finding ways to streamline the complaint and resolution process. The review was completed in mid-2000 with many recommendations to the government of Canada in areas such as the complaints procedures and ensuring that modern human rights and equality principles were addressed. However, as of 2004, the recommended changes had not been made.[2]

Of increasing concern for managers and HR professionals is the recent privacy legislation. There are two primary laws—one that applies to only federally regulated companies (e.g., banks, airlines, etc.) and one that extends the federal legislation to provinces and businesses within the provinces. These laws are the **Personal Information Protection and Electronics Documents Act (PIPEDA)** and the Personal Information Privacy Act (PIPA). PIPEDA came into effect in late 2001 and PIPA came into existence on January 1, 2004. These acts have a direct influence on how companies and managers handle employee information and the rights of employees regarding this information.

Both acts enhance the protection granted to employees on their personal information that a company retains. Organizations can only use the information (such as social insurance number) for its intended purpose (to remit premiums to the Canada Pension Plan). Organizations can no longer collect personal information without disclosing the full use to employees. Further, organizations must seek written permission from the employee to disclose personal information. For example, if you want to get a car loan, your employer is obliged to seek your written authorization to disclose your pay to the lending agency.

These acts have been most noted in the monitoring of e-mails and Web site visits of employees while at the worksite. More information on this will be covered in Chapter 9, Management Rights, Employee Rights, and Discipline.

Recent changes to the Immigration and Refugee Protection Act will have implications for organizations when they wish to recruit and hire people who are not citizens or permanent residents of Canada. These changes will be discussed in Chapter 4, Human Resource Planning, Recruitment, and Selection.

Provincial Employment Legislation

Each province and territory has relatively similar legislation that provides certain rights and guarantees regarding employment. For example, each province has maximum limits regarding hours per day or hours per week that a person can work before the organization is obliged to pay overtime wages. Similarly, the health and safety of workers are also covered by provincial legislation. In addition, provinces and territories have legislation dealing with human rights and legislation that covers unions and their relationships with employers. In the following sections, you will get information about these major types of employment laws whether they are provincial or federal. Figure 2.1 provides a summary of the various federal and provincial employment laws referred to in the previous two sections.

HUMAN RIGHTS LEGISLATION

The legislation that has had the most far-reaching impact on employment conditions has been in the area of human rights. Although the original human rights legislation was at the federal level, all provinces have instituted similar laws. The basic foundation of human rights legislation is that every person has an equal opportunity and should not be discriminated against on the grounds of race, ethnic or national origin, colour, religion, age, sex, disability, or family or marital status.[3] Human rights legislation is enforced through human rights commissions (or tribunals). Since human rights legislation is paramount over other employment laws, the decisions of these commissions have a huge influence over all types of employment issues. Importantly, commission decisions have changed expectations regarding the proper treatment of employees. Thus, organizations now have higher standards to meet.

Since this legislation has had a profound effect on the employment landscape, the latter part of this chapter will discuss the impact of the legislation in more detail. Web sites for accessing the legislation can be found in the Appendix at the end of this chapter.

FIGURE 2.1 Major Employment Laws in Canada

Jurisdiction	Basic Employment Conditions	Labour Legislation	Occupational Health and Safety and Workers' Compensation	Human Rights
Federal	Canada Labour Code	Canada Labour Code	Canada Labour Code	Canadian Human Rights Act
Alberta	Employment Standards Code	Labour Relations Code	Occupational Health and Safety Code	Human Rights Citizenship and Multiculturalism Act
British Columbia	British Columbia Employment Standards Act	Labour Relations Code	Workers' Compensation Act	Human Rights Code
Manitoba	Employment Standards Code	Labour Relations Act	Workplace Safety and Health Act	Human Rights Code
New Brunswick	Employment Standards Act	Industrial Relations Act	Occupational Health and Safety Act	Human Rights Act
Newfoundland and Labrador	Labour Standards Act	Labour Relations Act	Occupational Health and Safety Act	Human Rights Code
Nova Scotia	Labour Standards Code	Industrial Standards Act	Occupational Health and Safety Act	Human Rights Act
Nunavut	Public Service Act	Public Service Act	Health and Safety/Workers' Compensation Act	Canadian Human Rights Act
Ontario	Employment Standards Act	Labour Relations Act, 1995	Occupational Health and Safety Act/Workplace Safety and Insurance Act	Human Rights Code
Prince Edward Island	Employment Standards Act	Labour Act	Occupational Health and Safety	Human Rights Act
Quebec	Act Respecting Labour Standards	Labour Code	Act Respecting Occupational Health and Safety	Quebec Charter of Human Rights and Freedoms
Saskatchewan	Labour Standards Act	Trade Union Act	Occupational Health and Safety Act	Saskatchewan Human Rights Code

Note: Web sites for legislation can be found in the Appendix at the end of this chapter.

Discrimination

Objective 3

The essence of human rights legislation is to prohibit discrimination on the basis of race, religion, gender, age, national or ethnic origin, disability, or family or marital status. The majority of provincial human rights legislation also covers sexual orientation. Figure 2.2 provides a listing of prohibited grounds of discrimination in employment for federal, provincial, and territorial jurisdictions. Note that some jurisdictions include pardoned convictions (e.g., federal, British Columbia, Ontario, and Quebec) and records of criminal convictions (British Columbia, Quebec, Prince Edward Island, and the Yukon Territory) as prohibited grounds. A person's political beliefs are protected only in British Columbia, Manitoba, Quebec, Prince Edward Island, Nova Scotia, and the Yukon Territory.

Employers may be permitted to discriminate if employment qualifications are based on a **bona fide occupational qualification (BFOQ)** or bona fide occupational requirement (BFOR). For example, in certain situations it has been justified that people must not have a substance abuse problem when operating equipment.[4] A BFOQ is justified if the employer can establish its necessity for business operations. Business necessity is a practice

Bona fide occupational qualification (BFOQ)
A justifiable reason for discrimination based on business reasons of safety or effectiveness

FIGURE 2.2   Prohibited Grounds of Discrimination in Employment

Prohibited	Fed.	B.C.	Alta.	Sask.	Man.	Ont.	Que.	N.B.	P.E.I.	N.S.	Nfld.	N.W.T.	Y.T.
Race or colour	•	•	•	•	•	•	•	•	•	•	•	•	•
Religion or creed	•	•	•	•	•	•	•	•	•	•	•	•	•
Age	•	•	•	•	•	•	•	•	•	•	•	•	•
		(19–65)	(18+)	(18–64)		(18–65)					(19–65)		
Sex (includes pregnancy or childbirth)	•	•[1]	•	•	•[2]	•	•	•	•[1]	•	•[1]	•[1]	•
Marital status	•	•	•	•	•	•	•[3]	•	•	•	•	•	•
Physical/Mental handicap or disability	•	•	•	•	•	•	•	•	•	•	•	•	•
Sexual orientation	•	•	•	•	•	•	•	•	•	•	•	•	
National or ethnic origin (includes linguistic background)	•			•[4]	•	•[5]	•	•	•	•	•	•[4]	•
Family status	•	•	•	•[6]	•	•	•[3]	•	•			•	•
Dependence on alcohol or drugs	•	•[7]	•[1]	•[1]	•[1]	•[1]	•[8]	•[1,7]	•[1]	•[7]	•		
Ancestry or place of origin		•	•	•	•			•				•	
Political belief		•				•	•	•	•	•	•[9]		•
Based on association						•	•	•	•	•			•
Pardoned conviction	•	•				•						•	
Record of criminal conviction		•				•	•			•			•
Source of income		•		•[10]	•		•[11]	•	•				
Assignment, attachment, or seizure of pay												•	
Social condition/origin							•					•	
Language							•[12]	•					•

Notes

1. Complaints accepted on policy.
2. Includes gender-determined characteristics.
3. Quebec uses the term "civil status."
4. Defined as nationality.
5. Ontario's Code includes citizenship and ethnic origin.
6. Saskatchewan defines a parent-child relationship.
7. Previous dependence only.
8. Included in "handicap ground."
9. Prohibition on basis of political opinion.
10. Defined as "receipt of public assistance."
11. Included under social condition.
12. Complaints accepted on grounds of ancestry, ethnic origins, place of origin, race.

Harassment on any of the prohibited grounds is considered a form of discrimination.

Source: *Human Resources Management in Canada,* eds. N.C. Agarwal et al.; Vol. 2, Human Rights: Issues in Employment, Employment Law and Discrimination, Human Rights Laws, Table 50-1 Selected Prohibited Grounds of Discrimination by Jurisdiction—1996, by Harish C. Jain. Reprinted by permission of Carswell, a division of Thomson Canada Limited.

that includes the safe and efficient operation of an organization. In other words, differential treatment is not discrimination if there is a justifiable reason. However, it should be pointed out that it is difficult for many employers to establish legitimate BFOQs. Therefore, a supervisor will probably be asked to carefully examine job requirements and demonstrate that a certain characteristic is absolutely essential. For example, the federal government has been allowed to hire only women as guards in prisons for women; however, a retail store specializing in women's fashions would not be allowed to hire only women. Frequently, the HR professional and the line manager would work together to review job requirements to determine if the qualifications met the BFOQ requirement. For recruitment and hiring purposes, it is important that job requirements not create a discriminatory situation. Likewise, even the process of hiring can be considered discriminatory if inappropriate questions are asked. This area will be discussed more fully in Chapter 4.

Most of the decisions made by the Supreme Court of Canada, human rights tribunals, and arbitrations have looked at whether the discrimination was "intentional" or "unintentional." Intentional discrimination is very clear and direct, such as a requirement that only males five feet nine inches and taller could apply for a certain job. On the other hand, some discriminatory employment situations were unintentional. An example of unintentional discrimination is the requirement that a firefighter be able to run a certain distance within a fixed amount of time.

A Supreme Court decision in October 1999 changed this approach and deviated from 14 years of jurisprudence.[5] The case involved a female forest firefighter in British Columbia who was terminated after performing successfully on the job for three years. As a consequence of a coroner's report, new fitness standards had been instituted requiring that all firefighters be able to run 2.5 km in 11 minutes. The person failed the standard on four attempts and was terminated, even though she had been doing the work successfully. The Court decided that the test was discriminatory since females have a lower aerobic capacity than males and would therefore not be able to meet the standard. The decision went on to establish a new approach to BFOQ that will require employers to demonstrate that it is impossible to accommodate individuals discriminated against without undue hardship. This means that whatever the standard is, it must provide for individual accommodation, if possible. Ethics in HRM 2.1 describes how legal interpretations of discrimination can vary from one province to another.

Another concept that has arisen from human rights decisions is that of reasonable accommodation. **Reasonable accommodation** involves adjusting employment policies and practices so that no individual is denied benefits, is disadvantaged with respect to employment opportunities, or is blocked from carrying out the essential components of a job because of race, colour, sex, or disability. Since the decision in 1999 (mentioned above), other subsequent decisions have clarified expectations for employers regarding accommodation. Specifically, an employer needs to thoroughly consider methods by which the employee's characteristic (gender, race, etc.) can be accommodated in the workplace, including whether the specific tasks can be organized in a way to deal with the characteristic.[6] For example, if someone does not have the necessary degree of hand-eye coordination to do detailed electronics work, the employer may be obliged to reconfigure the tasks so that the person can do the work. Whether an employer can accommodate the work to fit the individual needs is a decision made by human rights tribunals.

It is no longer acceptable for employers to simply assume that all employees will "fit in" no matter what their special needs. Employers must find the means to alter systems to meet the needs of their employees as long as this does not cause "undue hardship to the employer." However, undue hardship may be something different for a small organization compared with a large organization. For example, it may be a hardship for a small firm to

Reasonable accommodation
Attempt by employers to adjust the working conditions and employment practices of employees to prevent discrimination

ethics **in HRM 2.1** ethics in HRM 2.1

LAWS MAY NOT ALWAYS BE RIGHT

Two human rights cases in 2002 demonstrate that the same prohibited grounds for discrimination can be interpreted differently. The cases dealt with the "marital status" prohibited grounds in employment.

The Saskatchewan Human Rights Commission determined that a woman was not discriminated against when the employer fired her because she was married to an inmate in prison. The commission made its decision on the basis that being singled out because she was married to a particular person was not discrimination based on marital status.

On the other hand, the Ontario Human Rights Commission dealt with a case in which a man was fired while working for his wife's brother. Very serious accusations of inappropriate behaviour had been made by the man's (employee's) daughter against the brother-in-law. The man (employee) had 26 years of a perfect work record but the brother-in-law decided that the man would not be able to work for him since he (the brother-in-law) had been accused by the man's daughter of wrong-doing. The commission determined that the employer (the brother-in-law) discriminated against the man due to his marital status.

Were these ethical decisions?

Source: "Marital Status Treatment Varied Across Canada," *Workplace Today®*, January 2002, 17.

Neil Squire Foundation
www.neilsquire.ca

Abilities Magazine
www.enablelink.org

WorkAble Solutions
www.workablesolutionsbc.ca

modify a washroom to accommodate a person in a wheelchair. However, it may be reasonable to expect a large organization, with its own building, to renovate or install a washroom that can accommodate a wheelchair.

Reasonable accommodation may include redesigning job duties; adjusting work schedules; providing technical, financial, and human support services; and upgrading facilities. The City of Toronto developed award-winning facilities in its Barrier Free Access program, which was designed to allow people with disabilities accessible passage throughout city facilities. There are several Canadian not-for-profit organizations that support and encourage employment opportunities for people with disabilities. Among those are The Neil Squire Foundation (**www.neilsquire.ca**) and Abilities (**www.enablelink.org**). Also, in October 2004, CIBC sponsored a symposium to provide additional support and training for people with disabilities to access employment opportunities.[7] Lastly, a new initiative was launched in December 2004 between the Province of British Columbia and the BC Human Resources Management Association to create and sponsor an interactive job site to make it easier for employers to recruit people with disabilities (**www.workablesolutionsbc.ca**).

Reasonable accommodation benefits all employees. The provision of allowances for childcare expenses when employees take company-sponsored courses not only removes a barrier that blocks many women but also may assist any employee with sole parenting responsibilities. The flexible work schedules adopted by some companies in northern Canada benefit First Nations employees who are prepared to work unusual hours in exchange for significant breaks away from the worksite in order to take part in traditional hunting and fishing activities. Many other employees also benefit from these flexible work schedules. At Work with HRM 2.1 on page 50 provides two accommodation cases that were decided by human rights commissions.

Businesses today are actively seeking skilled and capable people with physical challenges.

Reverse Discrimination

Reverse discrimination
Giving preference to members of certain groups such that others feel they are the subjects of discrimination

In pursuing initiatives to avoid discrimination, employers may be accused of **reverse discrimination**, or giving preference to members of certain groups such that others feel they are being discriminated against. For example, if a company feels that it has too few women employees, it may take active steps to hire more women. However, by hiring more women, the company may hire fewer men, opening itself to criticisms that it is discriminating against men. When these charges occur, organizations are caught between attempting to correct past discriminatory practices and handling present complaints that they are being unfair. If an organization is required to comply with any type of employment equity legislation (discussed later), it can be quite legal to discriminate and hire certain individuals.

In some cases, organizations may identify the need to hire a certain proportion of people from certain groups, such as visible minorities. While these organizations may state that they wish to find a larger pool of qualified applicants from a particular group, the organizations may in fact create a type of quota system for hiring. If it is perceived that there are hard numbers attached to hiring, then it is easy for individuals not in a targeted group to feel that they are being discriminated against. Charges of reverse discrimination have occurred in the fire and police services as those organizations try to achieve a workforce that is more reflective of the residents in their communities.

at work **with HRM 2.1** at work with HRM 2.1

THE DUTY TO ACCOMMODATE

- Two employees of the Ford Motor Company of Oakville, Ontario, became members of a religious group that observed its Sabbath from Friday sunset to Saturday sunset. Both employees were required to work two Friday nights out of four, which they refused to do. They tried, but failed, to make alternative arrangements with other workers. They were disciplined and ultimately terminated for unauthorized absenteeism. After a 71-day hearing, the Human Rights Commission decided it would constitute undue hardship on Ford to accommodate the religious absences of these employees.

- The Ontario Human Rights Commission found that the City of Ancaster, Ontario,

had discriminated against a part-time firefighter when they turned him down for a full-time job because he had partial vision in one eye. As such, he was unable to obtain a class F driver's licence, a job requirement for driving ambulances that are driven by firefighters. The tribunal felt that the city should have accommodated him by assigning him to firefighter duties exclusively.

CRITICAL THINKING QUESTION

Do you think the commission made the correct decisions? Why or why not?

Sources: D. Brown, "Law Takes Tough Stand on Accommodation," *Canadian HR Reporter* 14, no. 4 (February 26, 2001): 1 and 5; P. Israel, "How Far Does an Employer Have to Go to Accommodate Religious Beliefs?" *Canadian HR Reporter* 15, no. 22 (December 16, 2002): 5.

Harassment

Objective 4

Sexual harassment
Unwelcome advances, requests for sexual favours, and other verbal or physical conduct of a sexual nature in the working environment

Besides prohibiting discrimination, human rights legislation also prohibits harassment. Some provinces protect only against sexual harassment, while other provinces prohibit any type of workplace harassment. Harassment is behaviour in the workplace that is not acceptable. Harassment can take many forms. It is not acceptable, for instance, for one co-worker to strike another, and it is not acceptable to display a calendar containing a nude female. When dealing with harassment in the workplace, a manager needs to ask whether a "reasonable person" would consider a certain behaviour harassment. If the answer is yes, then the supervisor is expected to act accordingly. It is interesting to note that what is considered harassment in today's workplace, was sometimes considered acceptable behaviour not long ago. For example, it was acceptable at one point to have a nude female calendar hanging on the wall.

For a number of years, discussions of harassment have focused on **sexual harassment**. Currently, 64% of women reported that they have experienced some form of sexual harassment throughout their working lives.[8] This belief is reinforced by such cases as the one involving a female Sears employee who was shot to death by her manager. Fifteen months earlier, she had complained to her employer that she was being sexually harassed by her manager. The company maintained that his behaviour did not constitute sexual harassment and that he was merely a "persistent pursuer." In keeping with this position, they made no effort to stop the manager's behaviour.[9] HRM and the Law 2.1 describes the consequences of sexual harassment.

HRM and **the law 2.1** HRM and the law 2.1

HARASSMENT CAN BE COSTLY

Comfort Suite Hotels in Ontario was fined $30,000 in February 2003 for alleged sexual harassment. The complaint, which was supported by evidence from a co-worker, stated that one of the owners had repeatedly made sexual advances and sexual solicitations. When the advances were rejected by the employee, the owner fired the employee for reporting the alleged harassment to the supervisor. The Ontario Human Rights Tribunal stated that a poisoned work environment had been created and ordered the hotel chain to implement a comprehensive workplace anti-harassment and anti-discrimination policy. Further, it ordered the owners to take educational programs on the principles of anti-discrimination and sexual harassment. In June 2002, the Canadian Human Rights Tribunal decided that a manager at a Manitoba cable company had sexually harassed four women. These women had launched complaints stating that they

were forced to quit their jobs due to the ongoing derogatory and inappropriate comments and sexual advances. The decision is particularly important as the manager was the supervisor of the women and he was held personally liable. The ruling stated that while this type of behaviour was acceptable in the past, no individual needs to endure it in the contemporary workplace. The tribunal ordered the manager to pay the four women various amounts in lost wages, ranging from approximately $700 to $14,000 and compensation for hurt feelings from $6,000 to $8,000 each plus $10,000 each in special compensation for reckless or wilful conduct—a total of $100,000. Finally, he was ordered to follow training and counselling and provide a letter of apology to three of the complainants.

Do you think the decisions were fair?

Sources: Extracts from Ontario Human Rights Commission, http://www.ohrc.on.ca/english/cases/summary-2003 .shtml (retrieved October 17, 2004); and Canadian Human Rights Commission, http://www.chrc-ccdp.ca/news-comm/ 2002/NewsComm061902_2.asp?l=e and "$100,000 compensation ordered for harassment," *The Vancouver Sun*, June 22, 2002, F1.

Many organizations are developing policies to deal with sexual harassment in the workplace. Some organizations have put policies in place to attempt to deal with the issue. For example, the sexual harassment policy at BC Hydro focuses on avoidance and resolution rather than punishment after the fact. In another organization, the Canadian Armed Forces, 90,000 members have been trained to recognize and avoid harassment of all kinds.

Sexual situations in the work environment are not new to organizational life. Sexual feelings are a part of group dynamics, and people who work together may come to develop these kinds of feelings for one another. Unfortunately, these encounters are often unpleasant and unwelcome, as evidenced by the many reported instances of sexual harassment. And it doesn't have to be explicit behaviour to be sexual harassment: a person can give someone "a look" that can be suggestive and be seen as harassment.

The Ontario Human Rights Code identifies three kinds of sexual harassment:

1. Someone says or does things of a sexual nature and the recipient does not want or welcome it. This includes behaviour that a person should know is not wanted or welcome. For example, a supervisor makes an employee feel uncomfortable

by talking about sex all the time. When the employee shows that the remarks or actions are not welcome or wanted, the Human Rights Code says that the supervisor must stop doing those things right away.

2. A person who has authority or power to deny something such as a promotion or a raise makes sexual suggestions or requests that the employee does not want or welcome. For example, a teacher says a student must have sex with the teacher or the student will not pass the course. Even if the recipient does not complain about a sexual suggestion or request, it still constitutes sexual harassment unless it is clear that it is welcomed or wanted.

3. A person with authority or the power to deny something important punishes or threatens to do something to the employee for refusing a sexual request. For example, an employer fires or threatens to fire an employee for refusing to go on a date.

In recent years, a great deal of attention has centred on general harassment in the workplace. Specifically, organizations have developed policy statements and guidelines for dealing with harassment in the workplace. The Canadian Human Rights Commission defines harassment as follows:

> Harassment is any unwanted physical or verbal conduct that offends or humiliates you. Such conduct can interfere with your ability to do a job or obtain a service. Harassment is a type of discrimination. It can take many forms, such as

> - threats, intimidation, or verbal abuse;
> - unwelcome remarks or jokes about subjects like your race, religion, disability or age;
> - displaying sexist, racist or other offensive pictures or posters;
> - sexually suggestive remarks or gestures;
> - inappropriate physical contact, such as touching, patting, pinching, or punching;
> - physical assault, including sexual assault.

> Harassment will be considered to have taken place if a reasonable person ought to have known that the behaviour was unwelcome.[10]

What this means for supervisors is that they are expected to work with employees to ensure they are behaving and acting in an acceptable fashion. And while supervisors are expected to handle things a certain way, employees are also expected not to harass.

A company's policies on harassment must be broad. For example, the Treasury Department of the federal government has the following guideline:

> Every employee must be treated fairly in the work place in an environment free of harassment. Harassment of another employee constitutes a disciplinary infraction subject to penalties up to and including discharge.[11]

In another example, Mohawk College's harassment policy states

> The primary purpose of the Mohawk College Human Rights Policy is to prevent harassment and discrimination in its employment, education, and business environments. The Policy provides a resolution-oriented process for receiving and investigating complaints when it is believed that the policy has been contravened.[12]

Its policy defines harassment as

> Comments or conduct related to a prohibited ground known or ought reasonably to be known to be unwelcome, unwanted, offensive or intimidating. Single acts of sufficient severity may constitute harassment.[13]

Mohawk's policy is very far-reaching as it applies to students, faculty and staff, and visitors to the campus as well as corporations and vendors who do business with the college.

For harassment policies to succeed, confidentiality is necessary, and so is a method for filing complaints. Without organizational commitment to zero tolerance of harassment, such policies are meaningless. It is also important to remember that harassment is against the law. As the Province of Saskatchewan reminds people

> As an employer, you must provide a discrimination-free workplace. It's up to you to protect your employees from harassment. A good way to do this is to set up a code of conduct and an anti-harassment policy.[14]

Manager's Toolkit 2.1 presents some suggestions for an effective harassment policy.[15]

The concepts of harassment in the workplace are being broadened to include psychological harassment, such as bullying. A new law in Quebec bans psychological harassment, which is defined as any repeated, hostile, or unwanted conduct, or verbal comments, actions, or gestures that affect an employee's dignity or psychological or physical integrity. This protection, the first of its kind in Canada, requires employers to create policies to prevent this type of harassment.[16]

Manager's Toolkit **2.1** Manager's Toolkit 2.1

GUIDELINES FOR EFFECTIVELY DEALING WITH HARASSMENT

1. Develop a written policy and explain what harassment is.
2. Involve and educate all employees.
3. Have clear procedures in place for complaints.
4. Treat all complaints seriously and investigate promptly.
5. Resolve instances of harassment as soon as you are aware there has been a complaint.
6. Do your best to mitigate effects of harassment, for example, by restoring sick leave used.
7. Take appropriate action with the person(s) who did the harassing.
8. Take action, such as human rights training, to prevent a reoccurrence.

Additional resources from the various human rights commissions are available at the following Web sites:

- www.albertahumanrights.ab.ca (Province of Alberta)
- www.bchrcoalition.org/ (Province of British Columbia)
- www.gov.mb.ca/hrc (Province of Manitoba)
- www.ohrc.on.ca (Province of Ontario)
- www.gov.sk.ca/shrc (Province of Saskatchewan)

**Canadian Human Rights
Commission (CHRC)**
www.chrc-ccdp.ca

Enforcement of Human Rights Legislation

The federal government and each province and territory have a commission or similar agency to deal with complaints concerning discriminatory practices covered by legislation. For example, the Canadian Human Rights Commission (CHRC) (**www.chrc-ccdp.ca**) deals with complaints from those employees and businesses covered by the *Canadian Human Rights Act*. These commissions can act on their own if they feel there are sufficient grounds for a finding of discrimination. The agencies also have the ability to interpret the act. Figure 2.3 presents a flowchart of the complaints process at CHRC. Other human rights commissions operate in a similar fashion.

FIGURE 2.3   Canadian Human Rights Commission Enforcement

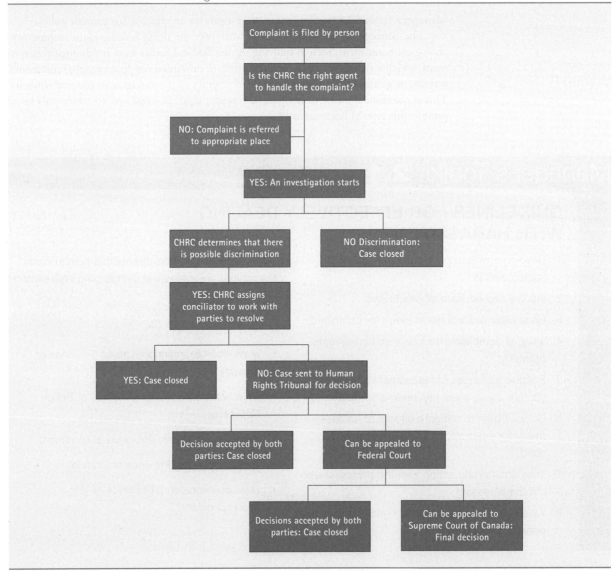

The steps are as follows:

1. Individuals have a right to file a complaint if they feel they have been discriminated against. (The CHRC may refuse to accept a complaint if it has not been filed within a prescribed period of time, if it is deemed trivial, or if it was filed in bad faith.) The complainant must first complete a written report describing the discriminatory action.
2. A CHRC representative reviews the facts and determines if the claim is legitimate.
3. Once a complaint has been accepted by the CHRC, an investigator is assigned the task of gathering more facts from both the complainant and the violator.
4. The investigator submits a report to the CHRC recommending a finding of either discrimination or no discrimination. If the determination is discrimination, a settlement may be arranged in the course of the investigation.
5. If the parties are unable to reach agreement, a human rights tribunal consisting of up to three members may be appointed to further investigate the complaint.
6. If the tribunal finds that a discriminatory practice did take place, or that the complainant's feelings or self-respect have suffered as a result of the practice, it may order the person or organization responsible to compensate the person. For example, Air Canada was recently ordered to compensate a man for thousands of dollars in lost wages. The man stated that he had not been hired due to his ethnic background. The airline was unable to provide any evidence that the decision not to hire him had been made in a nondiscriminatory fashion. The tribunal concluded that the man had been discriminated against.[17]

Any person who obstructs an investigation or a tribunal, or fails to comply with the terms of a settlement, can be found guilty of an offence that may be punishable by a fine and/or jail sentence. If the guilty party is an employer or an employee organization, the fine might be as high as $50,000 and up to $5,000 for individuals.[18]

Provincial human rights laws are enforced in a similar manner to that used in the federal system. The majority of cases are resolved at the investigation stage. If no agreement can be reached, the case is presented to the province's human rights commission. The members of the commission study the evidence and then submit a report to the minister in charge of administering human rights legislation. The minister may appoint an independent board of inquiry, which has similar powers to a tribunal at the federal level. Failure to comply with the remedies prescribed by the board of inquiry may result in prosecution in provincial court. Individuals may be fined between $500 and $1,000, and organizations or groups between $1,000 and $10,000. These levies may vary across provinces.

EMPLOYMENT STANDARDS LEGISLATION

Both federal, provincial, and territorial jurisdictions have passed employment standards laws specifying the minimum obligations of employers. The names of the laws usually include the words "employment standards" or something similar. However, the minimum obligations for federal companies are covered under the Canada Labour Code.

Usually included in this type of legislation are items such as hours of work, minimum wages, overtime pay, vacation pay, public holidays, and who is covered by the legislation. Standards vary between provinces. In Manitoba, for instance, "domestic workers" are covered. However, a person is defined as a domestic worker only if the person works more than 24 hours per week for a family doing cooking, cleaning, and childcare, for the entire family. The legislation also typically reflects the views of the respective government

Ontario Employment Standards

www.gov.on.ca/LAB/es/ese.htm

Manitoba Employment Standards

www.gov.mb.ca/labour/standards/

New Brunswick Employment Standards

www.gnb.ca/0062//deplinks/ENG/ted.htm

with regard to their social policy. For example, British Columbia's legislation provides the right for a person to take a limited number of days off to tend to childcare needs. Other jurisdictions, such as Ontario, have no such provision. In British Columbia, the legislation provides nine statutory holidays; in Ontario, there are only eight. There is usually a separate branch or agency that administers and interprets the legislation for both employers and employees. All the Web sites are listed in the Appendix at the end of this chapter but you can look at several of the following: **www.gov.on.ca/LAB/es/ese.htm**, **www.gov.mb.ca/labour/standards/**, and **www.gnb.ca/0062//deplinks/ENG/ted.htm**.

This is important legislation as it applies to all employers, whether they are unionized or not. And because it specifies minimum obligations of employers, every employer— large and small—needs to be aware of the legislation.

The legislation is administered by an agency or commission that both interprets and enforces the law. For example, if employees feel that they are not receiving the right amount of vacation pay, they can contact the agency and find out what the right amount should be. If they are getting the wrong amount, then the agency can contact the employer and start an investigation.

LABOUR RELATIONS LEGISLATION

Labour relations legislation governs both the process by which a trade union acquires bargaining rights and the procedures by which trade unions and employers engage in collective bargaining. In some jurisdictions, such as Ontario, the legislation (Labour Relations Act 1995) applies primarily to workplaces in the private sector but also to certain parts of the public sector (municipal workers, hospital employees, school boards, etc.). Ontario also has separate legislation for certain types of employers in the public sector, such as hospitals and Crown corporations.[19] However, in other jurisdictions, such as British Columbia, the legislation can apply to any workplace—whether it is in the public or private sector. Labour relations legislation only applies to unionized employees and to employers with unionized employees. Currently, approximately 4 million employees (or 30% of the workforce) in Canada belong to a union, primarily in the private sector although over 30% of the unionized workers are in the public sector.[20]

Labour relations legislation is usually administered through an agency called the Labour Relations Board, which is responsible for administering and enforcing the legislation. This board makes decisions on a variety of complaints from either a union or an employer. An employer might complain about the location of a trade union's picket or union members might complain that the union has not fairly represented them. The people making these decisions are hired by the board and are usually lawyers or have some type of legal training.

More information on labour relations legislation will be covered in Chapters 10 and 11.

HEALTH AND SAFETY LEGISLATION AND WORKERS' COMPENSATION

As you will see later in this book, the health and safety of employees is a responsibility of employers. This responsibility is governed by legislation that describes the expected standards for health and safety in the workplace, as well as outlining the role and

Construction workers must adhere to strict guidelines in order to meet workplace safety regulations.

involvement of employees in health and safety. Recent changes to this type of legislation have not only increased responsibility for employers, but have also placed more onus for a healthy and safe work environment on employees.[21] Violations of health and safety statutes are administered through a government agency, frequently called the Workers' Compensation Board. As part of the legislation, workers can receive a monetary payment if they are injured at work. Thus the employer is responsible not only for the health and safety of the workplace but also for financial compensation if the worker is injured on the job.

Additional information on health and safety legislation will be covered in Chapter 8.

EMPLOYMENT AND PAY EQUITY

Objective 6

Central to Canada's economic growth and prosperity in a highly competitive global marketplace will be a barrier-free environment in which all Canadians can fully explore and develop their career potential. Labour force statistics, described in Chapter 1, indicate changing patterns of immigration, the rising labour force participation rates of women, and an aging population with a proportionately higher incidence of disabilities. Women, visible minorities, First Nations, and people with disabilities make up over 60% of Canada's labour force, and their numbers continue to rise. These designated-group members entering Canada's labour pool constitute a vital resource, and their full participation in the workplace will be fundamental to an organization's ability to understand and respond to the needs of a rapidly changing marketplace.

Employment Equity

Equity by definition means fairness or impartiality. In a legal sense, it means justice based on the concepts of ethics and fairness and a system of jurisprudence administered by courts and designed primarily to decrease the rigidity of common law. The implementation of **employment equity** has involved the establishment of policies and practices designed to ensure equitable representation in the workforce and to redress past discriminations as they relate to employment and employment practices.

Employment equity
The employment of individuals in a fair and nonbiased manner

The Law on Employment Equity

The Employment Equity Act requires that the federal government, federal agencies, and Crown corporations with 100 employees or more and that are regulated under the Canada Labour Code must implement employment equity and report on their results. Some of the companies that are covered by the Employment Equity Act are the Royal Bank, Ahearn and Super Inc., Canadian Waste Services Inc., Bombardier, Johnson and Johnson, and Onyx Industries.[22] Under the act the employer is required to develop plans to better represent certain designated groups (women, First Nations people, visible minorities, and people with disabilities). In creating the plan, the employer must identify and remove any employment barriers, such as a keyboarding test for jobs in which no keyboarding is required. Further, the plan must have a timetable for achieving these changes. While this law does not extend to the provinces, the federal government, through its Federal Contractors Program, expects organizations that do business with the federal government to implement employment equity principles.

While there are no specific provincial acts pertaining to employment equity, the concept of employment equity is rooted in federal and provincial employment standards legislation, human rights codes, and the Canadian Charter of Rights and Freedoms. Employment equity involves the identification and removal of systemic barriers to employment opportunities that adversely affect designated groups, women, visible minorities, First Nations people, and people with disabilities. Employment equity also involves the implementation of special measures and reasonable accommodation (which was discussed earlier under "Discrimination").

Designated groups
Women, visible minorities, First Nations peoples, and persons with disabilities who have been disadvantaged in employment

The legislation identified four **designated groups** in Canada that had not received equitable treatment in employment: women, First Nations peoples, visible minorities, and people with disabilities faced significant but different disadvantages in employment. Some of the disadvantages included high unemployment, occupational segregation, pay inequities, and limited opportunities for career progress. While there has been progress, some of the original concerns have not been advanced very far.

Employment for women tends to be concentrated in retail trade, education, and health care (58%). On the other hand, while women represent approximately half of workforce participants, only 12% hold managerial positions.[23] Women tend to be underrepresented in forestry, mining, and construction, but they are close to being equally represented (4.1%) with men (5.3%) in labouring jobs.[24]

While the number of First Nations people is about 3% of the population, the numbers of young Aboriginal workers will increase, and in western Canada they will account for a substantial portion of labour market growth. However, many First Nations people face major employment barriers, which may be compounded by low educational achievement and lack of job experience, as well as language and cultural

at work **with HRM 2.2** at work with HRM 2.2

EMPLOYMENT EQUITY VISION AWARD

Human Resources Development Canada awarded Manitoba Hydro the Vision award for creativity and innovation in its employment equity programs. Currently, Aboriginal people make up 8.3% of Manitoba Hydro's workforce. In northern Manitoba, where there is a greater concentration of Aboriginal people, 27.4% of the corporation's workforce is Aboriginal. The goal is to get the overall corporate representation of Aboriginal people up to 10% by 2005, and up to 33% in the north. The creative ways in which these goals are being reached include the following:

- A zero tolerance policy of workplace harassment and discrimination.

- An outreach and partnership program with Aboriginal organizations to provide information about employment and training opportunities.

- Partnerships with postsecondary institutions to provide educational programs and career information and to brand Manitoba Hydro as an employer of choice.

- A review of training programs to ensure that there are no systemic barriers.

- Systematic recruitment efforts to introduce Aboriginals by means of internships, co-op placements, summer employment, and part-time work.

The most successful program is the pre-employment training designed to facilitate the entry of Aboriginals into Manitoba Hydro's training programs, which are more like apprenticeship programs. The pre-employment training provides academic upgrading, a rotation through three trades to familiarize candidates with these jobs, and workshops to deal with the concerns and issues about being away from home.

CRITICAL THINKING QUESTIONS

1. What has the company you are working for (or recently worked for) done to assist visible minorities, people with disabilities, and First Nations people in getting hired?
2. Is there more that they could do?

Source: Cheryl Petten, "Manitoba Hydro Recognized for Employment Equity Efforts," *Windspeaker* 20, no. 4 (August 2002): 31.

barriers. In urban centres, many First Nations workers are concentrated in low-paying, unstable employment. Economic self-sufficiency and participation in the economy are seen as essential to First Nations development. At Work with HRM 2.2 describes the success of Manitoba Hydro in assisting First Nations people to become an integral part of its workforce.

Visible-minority groups vary in their labour force profiles and in their regional distributions. Toronto and Vancouver have large visible-minority populations. Studies have shown that Latin Americans and Southeast Asians experience lower-than-average incomes, higher rates of unemployment, and reduced access to job interviews, even for those persons with the same qualifications as other candidates. Systemic barriers that have a negative employment impact on visible minorities can include culturally biased aptitude tests, lack of recognition of foreign credentials, and excessive levels of language

Systemic discrimination
The exclusion of members of certain groups through the application of employment policies or practices based on criteria that are not job-related

requirements. Recent statistics indicate that although visible minorities, 73% of whom are immigrants, possess higher educational achievements, they also have the highest unemployment rates.[25]

The unemployment rate (11.4%) for employable people with disabilities is much higher than the 7.1% unemployment rate in effect in 2004. People with disabilities face attitudinal barriers, physical demands that are unrelated to actual job requirements, and inadequate access to the technical and human support systems that would make productive employment possible.

Many employment barriers are hidden, unintentionally, in the rules and procedures that organizations use in their various human resources management practices. These barriers, referred to as **systemic discrimination**, have prevented the progress of these designated groups. Inequity can result if these barriers discourage individuals based on their membership in certain groups rather than on their ability to do a job that the employer needs done. An example of systemic discrimination would occur when an employer's workforce represents one group in our society and the company recruits new employees by posting job vacancies within the company or by word of mouth among the employees. This recruitment strategy is likely to generate a candidate similar to those in the current workforce, thereby unintentionally discriminating against other groups of workers in the labour market. A better approach might be to vary recruitment methods by contacting outside agencies and organizations.

Manager's Toolkit 2.2 gives examples of suggested solutions to systemic barriers.

Manager's Toolkit **2.2**

EXAMPLES OF EMPLOYMENT PRACTICES

1. *Word-of-mouth recruiting.* Supplementing this practice with other external recruitment methods, such as use of employment agencies, community groups, and advertising, can help to ensure that all groups of people have every opportunity to apply for available jobs.

2. Inflated job requirements may screen out designated group members. Avoid this by determining minimum job-specific requirements and by eliminating any that are not. For instance, do not request that employees be available to travel if only a small portion of the

time is spent travelling—this could cause many applicants not to apply when short trips could be arranged.

3. Sometimes designated group members do not participate in all training and development at the same rate as other employees. This could be a result of the jobs initially assigned to them. Employers may wish to keep records of designated-group participation in training events to determine if programs, policies, and procedures exclude designated-group members.

Source: Excerpted from *Guideline 6: Employment Systems Review*, Human Resources Development Canada, Labour Program. Available at http://info.load-otea.hrdc-drhc.gc.ca/workplace_equity/downloads/guide/gdln6.pdf. Reproduced with permission of the Minister of Public Works and Government Services Canada, 2002.

Benefits of Employment Equity

Employment equity makes good business sense since it contributes to the bottom line by broadening the base of qualified individuals for employment, training, and promotions, and by helping employers to avoid costly human rights complaints. Some of the benefits derived from implementing employment equity include ability to retain the best performers, ability to relate to a diverse customer base, ability to compete in a global marketplace, perception of being community leaders and therefore aligned with changing societal values.[26] Organizations such as Atlantic Tractors and Equipment in Nova Scotia and New Brunswick find that through employment equity initiatives they are able to attract young women to work for them.

Human Resources and Skills Development Canada administers the Employment Equity Act and as part of that administration recognizes organizations that have made special efforts to achieve a workforce that is representative of our population. Awards are given annually, and Pelmorex and The Weather Network were the recipients of the 2003 Vision Award for Workplace Equity. As stated by The Weather Network, "We believe in respect for all individuals, meeting and exceeding client expectations, and having a winning attitude."[27] The Weather Network has achieved this by creating an environment that is accessible by people with disabilities. Likewise, Pelmorex hosts holiday events for its employees and their families and friends.

For additional information on the Employment Equity Act, visit HRDC's Web site at **www.hrdc-drhc.gc.ca**.

W W W

**Human Resources
Development Canada
(HRDC)**

www.hrdc-drhc.gc.ca

First Nations University is a unique university in Canada that focuses on the educational needs of First Nations people.

Pay Equity

As a result of a 1978 amendment to the Canadian Human Rights Act, pay equity became law. Federal pay equity law makes it illegal for federally regulated employers to discriminate against individuals on the basis of job content. The focus of pay equity legislation is to narrow the wage gap between men and women, on the basis that women's work historically has been undervalued and therefore underpaid relative to work primarily done by men. For example, the average salary of males who worked full-time in 2002 was $60, 806, compared with $47, 481 for women.[28] Currently, eight provinces and the Yukon Territory have policies dealing with pay equity.

According to the federal definition, **pay equity** means equal pay for work of equal value, while in Ontario the definition is "equal pay for work of equal or comparable value." Pay equity is based on two principles. The first is equal pay for equal work. Equal pay for equal work means that if a woman and a man are doing substantially the same work for the same organization or company, they must receive the same wage unless the difference in pay is due to seniority or merit.[29] Equal pay for equal work is regulated through basic employment conditions legislation, usually called an Employment Standards Act.

The second principle of pay equity is equal pay for work that may be comparable in value to the organization. Pay equity compares the value of and pay of different jobs. This means that male and female workers must be paid the same wage rate for jobs of comparable value, such as a nurse (historically female-dominated work) to an electrician (historically male-dominated).

Implementation of pay equity is based on comparing jobs performed mostly by women with jobs performed mostly by males. Comparisons require the use of a gender-neutral, comparison system to evaluate the jobs in the organization.[30] The value of the work is based on the skills and effort required, the responsibilities of the job and the conditions under which the work is performed. It is important to remember that the comparisons are made on job content, not on the performance of the employee. The comparison must be done in such a way that the characteristics of "male" jobs, such as heavy lifting, are valued fairly in comparison with the characteristics of "female" jobs, such as keeping offices organized or exposure to communicable diseases.[31] For example, under pay equity, Canadian National Railways would need to compare the work of an accounts payable clerk with that of a person who repaired the train cars. Under provincial pay equity legislation in Ontario, the City of Toronto would compare the work of a clerk in the building department with that of a person repairing city roads.

The federal pay equity legislation applies to the workforce under its jurisdiction and covers all organizations regardless of number of employees. The federal pay equity system is complaint-based, meaning that complaints can be raised by an employee, a group of employees, or a union.[32]

In Ontario the legislation covers public- and private-sector employers with 10 or more employees. Like the federal legislation, Ontario's legislation is complaint-based. There is no pay equity legislation in either Alberta or British Columbia.

For more information on pay equity, check the following Web sites:

- **www.gov.on.ca/lab/pec**
- **www.chrc-ccdp.ca**
- **www.gov.ns.ca/enla/pequity**

Pay equity is not just an issue in Canada. See Around the World with HRM 2.1 for large organizations that are experiencing pay equity claims.

Pay equity
The practice of equal pay for work of equal value

Ontario Pay Equity Commission
www.gov.on.ca/lab/pec

Canadian Human Rights Commission
www.chrc-ccdp.ca

Nova Scotia Pay Equity Commission
www.gov.ns.ca/enla/pequity

around the world **with HRM 2.1** around the world

PAY EQUITY IN THE U.S.

Large organizations, such as Boeing and Wal-Mart, are experiencing class action lawsuits claiming gender discrimination in relation to pay and promotions. Boeing recently settled a claim for $72.5 million before the trial started, whereas Wal-Mart maintains that there is no discrimination.

Approximately 29,000 female employees at Boeing's three Washington plants were affected. Boeing has agreed to change its pay practices and will make managers more accountable for fairness in any pay decisions. The company further indicated that it is committed to creating a work environment in which all employees are treated fairly and have opportunities to build successful careers.

Wal-Mart has 1.6 million female employees who are involved in the class action lawsuit, making it the largest challenge in the history of gender discrimination cases. Even though Wal-Mart is denying the claim, observers feel that every major employer will be reviewing how it handles pay-related practices for all employees.

Source: Adapted from Pham-Duy Nguyen and Margaret Cronin Fisk, "Pay Equity Settlement to Cost Boeing US$72 Million" *Financial Post*, July 17, 2004, FP3," and "Wal-Mart's Women Problem," *Fortune*, July 12, 2004, 28.

DIVERSITY

Objective **7**

Diversity management
The optimization of an organization's multicultural workforce in order to reach business objectives

Managing diversity goes beyond Canadian employment equity legislation's four designated groups in addressing the need to create a fair work environment. The terms "diversity management" and "employment equity" are often used interchangeably, but there are differences. **Diversity management** is voluntary; employment equity is not. Managing diversity is a broader, more inclusive concept encompassing such factors as religion, personality, lifestyle, and education. By managing diversity, organizations hope to gain a strategic and competitive advantage by helping all employees perform to their full potential.[33]

According to the Statistics Canada census, over 13% of our total population is classified "visible minority."[34] In this context, diversity management is not merely a legal obligation but rather a business requirement for company success. Diversity is also not just about racial and cultural background. It is also about people with physical disabilities. One of the more progressive firms dealing with physical disabilities, as well as ethnic backgrounds, is Ekkon Global—a relatively new Web applications firm. The owners and several staff have significant disabilities. But the company has viewed this as another aspect of bringing together very talented people with the right skills for Web development work.[35] Further, organizations such as CN, Bank of Montreal, and Warner-Lambert are pioneers in the diversity movement. See At Work with HRM 2.3 for a fuller description of the work the Bank of Montreal (BMO) is doing in the diversity arena.

Statistics show that the ethnocultural profile of Canada has been changing since the 1960s and will continue to change dramatically over the next 20 years. It has been estimated that by the year 2016 visible minorities will account for 17% of the Canadian population.[36] The top five nonofficial languages (i.e., neither French nor English) spoken by Canadians in 2001 were, in ranked order, Chinese, Italian, German, Spanish, and Portuguese.[37]

BMO FINANCIAL GROUP

BMO Financial Group, well known throughout the Canadian marketplace as an exemplary leader in diversity and workplace equity issues, won the Catalyst Award for promoting women's careers. It was the first time a Canadian organization had won the award. (Catalyst recognizes organizations in North America for outstanding achievements in employment equity.) In 2002 and 2003, BMO was the only major Canadian bank to be cited by *Maclean's* magazine as one of Canada's top 100 employers. BMO has also won the Vision Award from Human Resources Development Canada twice. Rose M. Patten, senior executive vice-president, human resources, and head of Office of Strategic Management, oversees the equity campaign from her Toronto office.

"One of BMO's keys to success is the ability to integrate our programs into the fabric of the organization. At BMO Financial Group, our commitment to fostering a diverse and equitable workplace is reflected not only in our corporate values and part of our cultural fabric; it is how we do business. We don't just talk about values; we live them. BMO's people strategies focus on the importance

of talented, engaged, and high-performing employees. An important element of this is maintaining an equitable and supportive workplace, which reflects the diversity of the communities in which we do business. These objectives are explicitly aligned with strategic initiatives from the top, and, subsequently, are carefully measured and connected to performance. As part of this, diversity is seen as a strategic imperative at BMO. Today, BMO's commitment to diversity and workplace equity continues to be supported by a comprehensive system of goal setting, monitoring, and evaluation processes using clear metrics and benchmarks. As our progress towards the goal of a diverse workforce and an equitable and supportive workplace continues to be recognized, we at BMO will continue to be trailblazers pushing ourselves to new heights."

CRITICAL THINKING QUESTION

Can you think of other initiatives organizations can use to help create a positive work environment that supports diversity?

CEOs in Canada recognize that ethnic groups possess expertise, such as language skills and knowledge of foreign cultures and business practices, and natural trade links with overseas markets that can be used to capture market share in emerging economies and new Canadian markets.[38] Ebco Industries Ltd., a manufacturing company in Richmond, British Columbia, which has won awards for excellence in race relations, is doing business in Germany and Taiwan because it was able to tap the networks and skills of its employees, who trace their origins to 48 different countries. Besides the business reasons for hiring ethnic groups, the spending power of these groups is another motivating factor.

Creating an Environment for Success

Transforming an organizational culture into one that embraces diversity can be a complex and lengthy process. Diversity initiatives should be taken slowly so that everyone can understand that this change is an evolutionary process and that expectations should be realistic.

Leadership is one of the most important variables in an organization's ability to successfully incorporate the value of diversity into its business strategy. Good management is key to creating a workplace that values all employees and the talents and skills that they bring.[39]

As part of its mission statement, Ebco Industries Ltd. (mentioned above) has identified the "value of diversity" as one of its corporate values. Likewise, Petro-Canada's vision is to treat every customer as a guest and as an opportunity to build long-term relationships in the community in which it does business.[40]

Diversity initiatives should be linked directly to the business objectives and goals of the most senior level of management. At Work with HRM 2.4 describes how cultural diversity has become a way of doing business at Xantrex Technology Inc.

Organizations seeking to incorporate the value of diversity into their corporate philosophies must adopt appropriate internally and externally focused communications. For example, a variety of municipalities and health-care agencies provide important information in a number of different languages.[41]

at work **with HRM 2.4** at work with HRM 2.4

DIVERSITY: A WAY OF BUSINESS

"Cultural diversity is a fact of life for us," says Karen Hall, vice-president of human resources for Xantrex Technology Inc. "To win in today's market, we believe we need to be market-focused and results-oriented. We also believe we can achieve none of this without mutual respect and successful interdependence among all employees. We have a zero tolerance policy regarding prejudice—last year we trained every employee in harassment prevention. All Xantrex employees know that they have the right to work in an environment in which they feel safe and comfortable."

Xantrex's advanced power electronic and control products convert raw electrical power from any power source into high-quality power required by electronic and electrical equipment. Xantrex is a significant player in the renewable energy industry and is very excited about the opportunities its products can bring to people who are currently without electricity. Xantrex has received a number of business awards in recent years, among them an award of distinction from the Quality Council of British Columbia for the "People Focus" category as well as a nomination for the "Ethics in Action" award for social responsibility.

"Xantrex has customers, and employees, around the globe. As we have built these connections,

particularly in Europe and Central/South America, we have learned just how different it is to operate in some of these other cultures. Having a culturally diverse team, with people who understand both the language and the culture, is of critical importance to our business," Hall says.

"A while back," she notes, "an employee had raised a concern that employees were being hired based on their ethnicity and not on their ability. Although no evidence of such a practice was found, Xantrex implemented a team-based hiring process. This was done to minimize any employee concerns that biases were playing a role in hiring decisions. This approach continues to be an essential part of our recruiting process, and managers will attest to the contribution a diverse team of interviewers makes to our overall recruiting success."

CRITICAL THINKING QUESTIONS

1. What are the similarities between BMO (At Work with HRM 2.3) and Xantrex in relation to their diversity initiatives?
2. Which are the diversity initiatives at BMO that might be useful to consider at Xantrex?

Source: Interview with Karen Hall, April 2002.

Training is essential to the success of diversity implementation. A number of companies, including Imperial Oil and Connaught Laboratories, have incorporated diversity training. Cultural etiquette is an important aspect of diversity training that aims to explain the differences, or diversity, in people. The Department of National Defence includes diversity training in its basic officer training course.[42] Recently, the Yukon government established a diversity employment office. The goal of this office is to promote a public service that is reflective of the people it serves.[43] A consortium of European and North American businesses is attempting to develop a global diversity standard, by which companies will be able to use software to rate the success of their diversity programs.[44]

An added advantage of establishing a diversity initiative is its impact on employee retention. Keeping well-qualified and skilled employees is an important goal, considering the amount of resources, both in time and money, spent on recruiting and hiring new employees.

When establishing diversity initiatives, an overall review of policies and employment practices must be considered. The use of an employee attitude survey may prove beneficial in finding areas of systemic or perceived discrimination. The success indicators used most often by Canadian organizations are changes in staff attitudes, increases in promotions for minority employees, reduction in turnover of minority employees, reduction in number of harassment suits, improved recruitment statistics for minorities, and improvements in productivity. A final element in achieving success in the implementation of diversity initiatives is to monitor progress and provide qualitative and quantitative evidence of change.[45]

Measuring management's performance with regard to diversity initiatives will instill those values in the minds of all employees and demonstrate that valuing diversity is part of day-to-day business. Key to achieving success in diversity objectives is setting an example and creating an atmosphere that respects and values differences. Canadian organizations have recognized the competitive advantage gained by embracing diversity within their business strategies. Businesses have recognized that with a global economy and world-wide customers, it is important to have a workforce that understands people in other countries.[46]

SUMMARY

1. Explain the impact of laws on the behaviour and actions of supervisors and managers.
   - Accepted practices and behaviours of supervisors and managers toward their employees are governed through a variety of employment legislation at both the provincial and federal levels.
   - Various laws establish certain minimum requirements regarding working conditions as well as providing protection of basic human rights.

2. Discuss the legal framework of HRM in Canada.
   - There are two distinct sets of legislation—federal and provincial.
   - The Canadian Charter of Rights and Freedoms is the cornerstone of contemporary employment legislation.

3. Explain and describe discrimination and harassment in the workplace.
   - Discrimination is denying someone something because of race, ethnic background, marital status, or other prohibited grounds under human rights legislation.
   - Harassment is any behaviour that demeans, humiliates, or embarrasses a person.
   - Discrimination and harassment are illegal under human rights legislation.

4. Describe the line manager's role in creating a work environment that is free from harassment and discrimination.
   - Supervisor or manager needs to ensure that unacceptable behaviours are dealt with.
   - Supervisor is expected to work with employees to ensure that they are behaving and acting in an acceptable fashion.
   - Line manager is key link in creating an appropriate work environment.

5. Identify the general types of employment laws in Canada.
   - Employment standards legislation describes the basic obligations of employers.
   - Labour legislation governs both the process by which a trade union acquires bargaining rights and the procedures by which trade unions and employers engage in collective bargaining.
   - Health, safety, and Workers' Compensation legislation describes the expected standards for health and safety in the workplace and the impact if an employee is injured.
   - Human rights legislation prohibits discrimination on the basis of such areas as race, ethnic origin, marital status, and gender.
   - Human rights legislation is paramount over other employment laws.
   - Human rights legislation also protects individuals from sexual and other types of harassment.

6. Explain and describe the difference between employment equity and pay equity.
   - Employment equity refers to the employment of individuals in a fair and unbiased manner.
   - Four groups in Canada (women, visible minorities, First Nations peoples, and people with disabilities) have been designated as those needing help to fix past wrongs.
   - The federal government and some provinces have legislation to help achieve a more equitable workforce.
   - Pay equity means equal pay for work of equal value.
   - Pay equity examines job content and compares dissimilar work in an organization.

7. Describe the differences between diversity and employment equity.
   - Managing diversity not only incorporates but also goes beyond employment equity.
   - The goal of diversity management is to make optimal use of an organization's multicultural workforce in order to realize strategic business advantages.

Need to Know

- Relationship of Charter of Rights and Freedoms to employment laws
- Names of employment laws and what they do
- Definition of harassment and discrimination
- Purpose and definition of employment and pay equity
- Definition of diversity

Need to Understand

- Impact of legislation on managerial actions
- Relationship of bona fide occupational requirements to discrimination
- Impact of reasonable accommodation on managerial action
- Relationship of managerial behaviours to harassment and discrimination
- Impact of employment practices and managerial decisions on fair employment opportunities
- The link between diversity and business strategy

Key Terms

bona fide occupational qualification (BFOQ) 45

designated groups 58

diversity management 63

employment equity 58

pay equity 62

reasonable accommodation 47

reverse discrimination 49

sexual harassment 50

systemic discrimination 60

REVIEW QUESTIONS

1. What are three employment laws in your province? Provide examples.
2. Which of the laws described pertain to providing minimum standards in relation to hours of work before overtime pay is required?
3. How would you react to a comment that a company discriminates against women by having a height requirement to do certain types of work?
4. Explain why employment equity is needed in organizations. What are the arguments for and against it?
5. Describe the purpose of the Employment Equity Act and discuss some of its provisions.
6. Describe the process involved in implementing an employment equity plan. How would you evaluate its success?
7. Define pay equity and discuss how it is related to discrimination.
8. Describe the ways in which an organization can optimize the use of a multicultural workforce.

CRITICAL THINKING QUESTIONS

1. Assume you are a person who is less than 1.5 m tall. You apply for work where there is occasional shelving of merchandise. The top shelf is 2.5 m from the ground and the merchandise weighs 10 kg. Can the company justify a BFOR? If so, what is it?
2. Here are some myths about employment equity:

   • It leads to hiring unqualified workers.
   • It causes an overnight change in the workforce makeup.
   • It's a plan that would make Calgary's workforce look like Toronto's.
   • This program lays off white males to make room for designated group members.
   • It's a program mainly for racial minorities.
   • Employers who implement the plan can destroy hard-won seniority provisions that protect all workers.
   • It's the end of hiring for white males.

   In groups, determine if group members share these beliefs. Go to the Web site of the Alliance for Employment Equity (**www.web.net/~allforee/empeqity.htm**), and compare your answers.

3. You have recently been hired to work in a small retail operation. The owner wants your help in developing a work environment that celebrates diversity. What would you suggest?

4. A friend of yours has heard you are taking a human resources course and wants some help. Your friend is a single parent with three children under the age of seven. The bus schedule has just changed and your friend won't be able to get the children to school and daycare and still be on time for work. Is this a case for reasonable accommodation?

5. Can you legally discriminate against the following:

   a. A person with a poor driving record for a bus driver position?
   b. A non-Baptist for the position of secretary in a Baptist private school?
   c. A person who is colour-blind for an electrician position?
   d. A person whose religious beliefs prevent them from working Saturday at a retail store?
   e. A person with a criminal record for a position of cashier?
   f. A person in a wheelchair for a server in a restaurant?

6. After receiving several complaints of sexual harassment, the senior manager of a city library decides to establish a sexual-harassment policy. What should be included in the policy? How should it be implemented?

7. "Discrimination against older persons does not generate the same degree of moral outrage as other forms of discrimination." Do you agree? If you find this quote offensive, read the full text of the Human Rights Commission's discussion paper on human rights for the aging (**www.ohrc.on.ca**).

DEVELOPING YOUR SKILLS

1. Over the past decade, the problem of sexual harassment has captured the attention of all managers and employees. While it is widely known that sexual harassment is both unethical and illegal, the incidents of sexual harassment continue to plague business. Unfortunately, when these cases arise, they cause morale problems among employees, embarrassment to the organization, and costly legal damages. Consequently, all managers and supervisors play a central role in preventing sexual harassment complaints. It is important that managers understand the definition of sexual harassment, who is covered by sexual harassment guidelines, and how to prevent its occurrence.

   a. Working in teams of five or six members, develop an outline for a sexual harassment training program. Assume that the organization has 1,500 employees who work with both internal and external customers.

      As a minimum your training outline should consider (1) who should attend the training sessions, (2) the content outline for the training program (the list of materials your team wants to teach), (3) specific examples to illustrate the training materials, and (4) how to investigate sexual harassment complaints.
   b. Present your training outline to other class members.

2. Contact your student services office, or the human resources department where you work, and determine if it has a discrimination policy. If there is one, review the policy, including the manner in which it is enforced, and write a one-page analysis of how useful it is. If there is no policy, write a one-page summary indicating what the employer might do if there was a complaint about discrimination.

3. On an individual basis, identify which of the following statements are true and which are false:

    a. Most people with disabilities do not require special work arrangements.
    b. The real problem for people with disabilities is holding a job, not getting one.
    c. Employees with disabilities tend to have more accidents than other employees.
    d. People with the most severe impairments are likely to be at the top in job performance.
    e. Turnover tends to be higher among employees with disabilities than among other employees.
    f. Employees with disabilities are less likely to have a record of absenteeism.
    g. Other employees tend to respond negatively when accommodations (e.g., wheelchair ramps) are made for employees with disabilities.

    Working in groups of three to five students, share your individual responses. Review the correct answers (based on statistical evidence) at the end of the chapter (page 74). For each item you answered incorrectly, ask yourself, "Where did I get that idea?" Discuss any incorrect answers including why you gave the answer you did.

    The Canadian Council on Rehabilitation and Work shares knowledge and attempts to influence attitudes for equitable employment for people with disabilities; visit their Web site at **www.ccrw.org**.

4. Using any search engine, conduct a search using the phrase "sexual harassment" or the word "discrimination." Note the number of matches. Review the first 10 matches and determine if these would be a helpful resource site. Prepare a one- to two-page summary of the results of your search, indicating whether the sites were useful.

5. Access the Web sites of the employment laws in your province and review the home page of each and at least one other link. Identify which site would be the most helpful to you as an employee. Prepare a one- to two-page summary describing which site was useful and why.

6. By using the Web sites of at least three provincial employment standards laws, determine the minimum wage for each of those provinces. Are they higher or lower than the minimum wage in your province?

7. With reference to the employment standards legislation in your province, determine the following:

    a. Minimum wage
    b. Overtime hours and payment
    c. Paid holidays
    d. Maternity/parental leave

Case Study 1

But Was It Harassment?

Bill Smith, plant superintendent in a commercial laundry, was in his office reviewing a handwritten note that had just arrived. He was both surprised and concerned about the contents. The note indicated that Bob Jones had been making comments of a sexual nature to several of the female staff. What was disturbing about this was that Bob was Bill's best supervisor and had been involved in a relationship with one of the plant staff. Bill decided that he must investigate the allegation.

Bill decided to meet with Bob and bring the matter to his attention. During the meeting, Bob got very angry and accused his former girlfriend of spreading rumours. When pressed further, Bob confirmed that he had been joking with one of the junior secretaries and said that he would help her get a new computer if she treated him nicely. Bob also confirmed that while he knows the company has a policy about this sort of thing, he wasn't sure exactly what was expected.

After meeting with Bob, Bill decided that the company needed to have a training program on harassment and discrimination. As part of the training, Bill suggested a role-play exercise to explore workplace behaviours that might be construed as harassment. All supervisors in the plant were expected to attend.

Several days after the training, Bill got a phone call from one of his top production people. She expressed concern that Bob had just put up a calendar in his office that showed a scantily clad girl. The worker said that she approached Bob and asked him to remove the calendar as it didn't seem to comply with what was described in the training. She then described how Bob laughed and said, "Who cares about that kind of stuff? This is just some phase we are going through, and it will fade out soon." Bill also discovered that Bob had left the training session before it was over.

Questions

1. Are these two incidents harassment? Why or why not?
2. Who is more responsible for this situation—Bob or Bill?
3. If you were Bill, what would you do now?

Case Study 2

Developing New Job Requirements

Jesse Wong, owner/operator of a commercial and residential cleaning business, has been very concerned about the high incidence of back injuries and accidents involving cleaning solutions. The company employs approximately 300 people with the following profile:

65% female

35% male

30% who immigrated to Canada within the last year

80% with English as a second language

The company has been very successful, with revenues growing on a yearly basis, particularly in the commercial sector. Currently, the typical job duties include vacuuming floors; emptying trash and recycling containers, some of which are quite heavy; dusting furniture; mopping floors; disinfecting and cleaning bathroom and kitchen fixtures; waxing floors and furniture; and the occasional window washing.

In a meeting with the company's human resources practitioner, Jesse expresses a desire to change the skill requirements for all new employees. He feels that if the skills are different, the company will be able to reduce the accident and injury rates. His proposal for the skills level is

a. able to read and speak English to a Grade 8 level,

b. able to lift 25 kg, and

c. able to handle chemicals safely.

During the discussions, the HR person expresses some concern about whether these new skill requirements would be considered *bona fide occupational qualifications.* There have been a number of recent complaints to the provincial human rights agency from employees at other cleaning companies when those companies changed the skill requirements. While the human rights agency hadn't made any decisions yet, the complaints revolved around English speaking and reading levels and lifting heavy objects.

Questions

1. What would you say to Jesse to explain the concept of BFOQ?
2. In your understanding of BFOQ, would any of these skill requirements stand up to a challenge? If so, why? If not, why not?
3. What would you say to Jesse about his proposal?

APPENDIX

WEB SITES FOR EMPLOYMENT LEGISLATION

1. Federal Government
   - Canada Labour Code: http://laws.justice.gc.ca/en/L-2/16598.html
   - Canadian Human Rights Act: http://laws.justice.gc.ca/en/H-6/28526.html
2. Province of Alberta
   - Employment Standards Code: http://www3.gov.ab.ca/hre/employmentstandards/regs/index.html
   - Labour Relations Code: http://www3.gov.ab.ca/alrb/guidecontents.html
   - Occupational Health and Safety Act: http:// www3.gov.ab.ca/hre/whs/law/index.asp
   - Human Rights, Citizenship and Multiculturalism Act: http://www.albertahumanrights.ab.ca/legislation/
3. Province of British Columbia
   - Employment Standards Act: http://www.qp.gov.bc.ca/statreg/stat/E/96113_01.htm
   - Labour Relations Code: http://www.qp.gov.bc.ca/statreg/list_statreg_l.htm
   - Workers' Compensation Act: http://www.qp.gov.bc.ca/statreg/stat/W/96492_00.htm
   - Human Rights Code: http://www.qp.gov.bc.ca/statreg/stat/H/96210_01.htm
4. Province of Manitoba: electronic versions of the legislation can be accessed by downloading PDF files from http://www.gov.mb.ca/chc/statpub/free/
5. Province of New Brunswick
   - Employment Standards Act: http://www.gnb.ca/acts/acts/e-07-2.htm
   - Industrial Relations Act: http://www.gnb.ca/acts/acts/i-04.htm
   - Occupational Health and Safety Act: http://www.gnb.ca/acts/acts/o-00-2.htm
   - Human Rights Code: http://www.gnb.ca/acts/acts/h-11.htm

6. Province of Newfoundland and Labrador: all statutes are accessible through http://www.gov.nf.ca/hoa/sr/ with links to each law
7. Province of Nova Scotia: all statutes are accessible through http://www.gov.ns.ca/legislature/legc/ with links to each law
8. Province of Ontario: all statutes are accessible through http://www.e-laws.gov.on.ca/tocStatutes_E.asp?lang=en with links to each law
9. Province of Prince Edward Island: electronic versions of the legislation can be accessed by downloading PDF files from http://www.gov.pe.ca/law/statutes/index.php3
10. Province of Quebec: all statutes are accessible through http://www.formulaire.gouv.qc.ca/ with links to each law
11. Province of Saskatchewan: electronic versions of the legislation can be accessed by downloading PDF files from http://www.qp.gov.sk.ca/publications/index.cfm?fuseaction=home&c=1577&id=2

NOTES AND REFERENCES

1. Sari Sanders, "Policy Initiatives Augur a Busy Year for Canadian Lawmakers, Employers" *Canadian HR Reporter*, April 19, 2004, 6.
2. Telephone call placed to Minister's office, November 15, 2004.
3. *Canadian Human Rights Act*, Canadian Human Rights Commission, 1978, Paragraph 2, Subsection (a).
4. *Alberta (Human Rights and Citizenship Comm.) v. Elizabeth Metis Settlement* (2003), 46 C.H.R.R. D/283, 2003 ABQB 342, CHRR Online www.cdn-hr-reporter.ca (retrieved December 3, 2004).
5. *BC (PSERC) v. BCGEU (BC Forest Fighters)* (SCC, 1999), reference materials acquired during a seminar sponsored by Russell and DuMoulin, Vancouver, B.C., October 22, 1999.
6. Ron LeClair, "The Evolution of Accommodation," *Canadian HR Reporter*, February 24, 2003, 7.
7. CIBC Career Symposium for People with Disabilities, www.enablelink.org/employment.html?showemployment=1 (retrieved October 17, 2004).
8. Laura Cassiani, "Sexual Harassment Persists Despite Workplace Fallout," *Canadian HR Reporter*, April 9, 2001, http://www.hrreporter.com/loginarea/members/viewing.asp?ArticleNo=832&viewwhat=Print&subscriptionType=PRINT&callerpage=whoswho (retrieved July 23, 2002), 12.
9. "Inquest Probes Murder-Suicide Involving Harassment Victim," *Sexual Harassment, Workplace Diversity Update* 5, no. 3 (March 1997): 4.
10. "Discrimination and Harassment—Harassment: What Is It?" www.chrc-ccdp.ca/discrimination/what_is_it-en.asp (retrieved October 17, 2004).
11. Treasury Board of Canada, "Harassment in the Workplace," http://www.tbs-sct.gc.ca/Pubs_pol/hrpubs/TB_851/HARAE1.html#sta (retrieved January 19, 2000).
12. Mohawk College, Human Resources Division, "Human Rights Information," www.mohawkc.on.ca/dept/hrd/HRWEB/Rightshome.html (retrieved January 19, 2000).
13. *Ibid.*
14. Saskatchewan Human Rights Commission, "A Guide to Human Rights for Employers," www.gov.sk.ca/shrc/ (retrieved October 17, 2004).
15. Adapted from "Anti-Harassment Policies for the Workplace: An Employer's Guide."
16. Katherine Harding, "Taking Aim at Bullies," *The Globe and Mail*, March 19, 2003, C1.
17. Michael Friscolanti, "Right Board Gives Employers 'Warning Call,'" *National Post*, February 6, 2002, A16.
18. *Canadian Human Rights Act*, Paragraphs 53 and 54.
19. Ontario Ministry of Labour, Labour Management Services, "Legislation and Regulations," www.gov.on.ca/lab/english/about/leg/lr_leg.html (retrieved December 3, 2004).
20. "Study: The Union Movement in Transition," Statistics Canada, www.statcan.ca/Daily/English/040831/d040831b.htm (retrieved December 3, 2004).
21. For more detailed information on changes to health and safety legislation, refer to the discussion papers from British Columbia and Ontario ("British Columbia Royal Commission Report on Workers Compensation," "Preventing Illness and Injury,"), www.gov.on.ca/LAB/ohs/.
22. Labour Program, *2003 Annual Report, Employment Equity Act*, Human Resources and Skills Development Canada, http://www.hrsdc.gc.ca/asp/gateway.asp?hr=en/lp/lo/lswe/we/ee_tools/reports/annual/index-we.shtml&hs=wzp (pdf format, retrieved November 25, 2004).
23. Marie Drolet, "The 'Who, What, When, and Where,' of Gender Pay Differentials," *The Evolving Workplace Series*, Statistics Canada (June 2002): 25.

24. Drolet, "The 'Who, What, When, and Where,' of Gender Pay Differentials," 27.

25. Statistics Canada Web site, "Designated Minority Representation," http://www.statcan.ca/english/IPS/Data/96F0030XIE2001008.htm.

26. "Road to Equity," www.gov.sk.ca/psc/equity/Road/need.htm (retrieved November 27, 2004).

27. *Ibid.*

28. *Ibid.*

29. Ontario Pay Equity Commission, *Pay Equity Act*, "Pay Equity and Equal Pay: What Is the Difference?" www.gov.on.ca/lab/pec/peo/english/pubs/difference.html (retrieved October 23, 2004).

30. Ontario Pay Equity Commission, "10 Steps to Pay Equity," www.gov.on.ca/lab/pec/peo/english/pubs_10steps.html (retrieved October 23, 2004).

31. Ontario Pay Equity Commission, "Commonly Overlooked Features of Work," www.gov.on.ca/lab/pec/peo/english/pubs/overlooked.html (retrieved October 23, 2004).

32. "Making a Complaint," www.workrights.ca/Make+a+complaint/Making+A+Complaint.htm (retrieved October 23, 2004).

33. Rosemary Barnes, "Encouraging Diversity Key to Success," *The Globe and Mail*, September 11, 2004, B13.

34. Statistics Canada, 1996 Census Nation Table, Visible-minority population, 1996, www.statcan.ca/english/Pgdb/People/Population/demo40a.htm (retrieved November 24, 1999).

35. Maurice Bridge, "Disability No Barrier for This Firm," *The Vancouver Sun*, March 9, 2002, C1.

36. Statistics Canada, *Canada's Ethnocultural Portrait: The Changing Mosiac*, Cat. no. 96F0030XIE 2001008, Analysis Series, 2001; Erin Anderson, "Immigration Shifts Population Kaleidoscope," *The Globe and Mail*, January 22, 2003, A6.

37. Statistics Canada, 2001 Census, "Chinese Reaffirmed as Canada's Third Most Common Mother Tongue," www12.statcan.ca/english/products/analytic/companion/lang/Canada.cfm (retrieved December 12, 2002).

38. Statistics Canada, *Canada's Ethnocultural Portrait*; Anderson, "Immigration Shifts Population Kaleidoscope."

39. Barnes, "Encouraging Diversity Key to Success."

40. *2003 Annual Report*, www.petro-canada.ca (retrieved October 23, 2004).

41. *Current*, a publication by the Vancouver Coastal Health Authority and notices sent to residents of the City of Vancouver.

42. P. Lungen, "Military Addresses Racism Issue," *Canadian Jewish News* 30, no. 7 (February 17, 2000): 6.

43. "Workforce Diversity Office Established," www.hrreporter.com, February 18, 2004 (retrieved October 23, 2004).

44. L. Young, "Global Diversity Standard in Works," *Canadian HR Reporter*, April 5, 1999.

45. Susan Black, "What Gets Measured Gets Done: Using Metrics to Support Diversity," www.hrreporter.com, December 16, 2002 (retrieved October 23, 2004).

46. "Facing Diversity," *SHRM Weekly Survey*, August 3, 2004.

ANSWERS TO DEVELOPING YOUR SKILLS, QUESTION 3

a. True
b. False
c. False
d. True
e. False
f. True
g. False

PART 2

Attracting and Selecting People for the Organization

Chapter 3: Defining and Designing the Work

Chapter 4: Human Resource Planning, Recruitment, and Selection

CHAPTER 3

Defining and Designing the Work

OBJECTIVES

After studying this chapter, you should be able to

1 Explain the supervisor's role in defining and designing work.

2 Discuss the relationship between job requirements and HRM processes.

3 Explain the relationship between job analysis and a job description.

4 Define and describe the sections in a job description.

5 Describe the uses of information gained from job analysis.

6 Define employee contribution and describe the relationship of job design to employee contributions.

7 Discuss the different types of work designs to increase employee contribution.

8 Describe the role of the line manager in job design and employee contribution.

HRM
Close-Up

Daniel Speck, Vice-President, Sales and Marketing, Henry of Pelham Family Estate Winery, St. Catharines, Ontario

"If you don't know what your strengths and weaknesses are, how do you formulate a plan?"

Daniel Speck loves his job. And this was unexpected. "I never thought I'd love sales," he says. But he's not just Vice-President, Sales and Marketing, at Henry of Pelham Family Estate Winery, he's also an owner—one of three, in fact, who are brothers. "We started the company with my father in the early eighties. As kids we ripped out the vineyards that Henry, our ancestor, had planted, and replanted with wine grapes." While he's proud that their Chardonnay, Riesling, Sauvignon Blanc, Cabernet-Merlot, Pinot Noir, Baco Noir, sparkling wines, and ice wines are raking in awards, Speck is prouder still that they're 100% Ontarian. Like most premium wineries, Pelham is "vertically integrated"—meaning the growing, producing, bottling, marketing, and selling of the wine is all done in-house.

Though the company has grown by double digits over the past decade, the brothers remain very much "self-taught." And that's been the biggest challenge. "We've been in the industry for two decades and the first ten years were brutal. Initially, we knew nothing about winemaking. In this industry, you live and die by the weather. Plus, making good wine is not easy," explains Speck. "Like most family businesses we were long on hard work but short on skill." And there was no division of labour. Paul, the oldest, would be "talking to the banks, fighting for our life," then be in the fields farming or on the road selling. Matthew and Daniel did much the same during breaks from university and high school. "Everybody did everything. I was like an indentured servant on the farm."

The delineation of roles began as the company grew and each brother developed an expertise—Paul with administration and finance, Matthew with production, Daniel with sales and marketing. "Over time it became easy to tell who was going to fill which role," says Speck, though he admits it was also a matter of timing and circumstance. In the beginning, Paul was the only full-timer, and when Matthew came along, "it was just a big relief that [Paul] didn't have to sit on a tractor any more." They also needed people who did nothing but sell the wine. With "zero desire to be on the farm," Daniel hit the road. "Pretty soon I was handling most of the [sales] territories, and the best ones."

Sometimes, Speck has learned, it's just the "sheer momentum" of business that moves things along or gets things decided. But the brothers did recognize that a lack of knowledge about winemaking—about yeast strains, temperature effects, and chemistry—was a big obstacle. That's when they made their most critical hire—Ron Giesbrecht, professional winemaker. More important than his education in food science is his "incredible palate." Ron now works alongside the three brothers with Matthew and Ron discussing vineyard science and Daniel letting them know what's popular in stores. The key is to "know thyself," says Speck. "If you don't know what your strengths and weaknesses are, how do you formulate a plan?"

In fact, they have mapped out a company plan complete with tactics and strategy. Speck says the process helped identify the positions and people Pelham needed. A marketing manager, a seasoned professional, was the next big hire. "We got to a point where the company was doing well and the next question became 'Where are we lacking?'" The brothers believe a written plan is essential in family businesses, where agreements can be made on a handshake. "Without it, people may feel they've been taken advantage of." Employees should also understand where they fit in. "They don't want to live with a tyrant whose actions change with the weather."

INTRODUCTION

Just as Henry of Pelham Family Estate Winery evolved and the brothers had to determine who was going to do what, other organizations are looking at how work is arranged to make them more competitive.

Organizations are "re-engineering" themselves in an attempt to become more effective. Companies like Bell Canada and Sunnybrook Health Sciences Centre are breaking into smaller units and getting flatter. There is emphasis on smaller scale, less hierarchy, fewer layers, and more decentralized work units. As organizations reshape themselves, managers want employees to operate more independently and flexibly to meet customer demands. To do this, managers require that decisions be made by the people who are closest to the information and who are directly involved in the product or service delivered. The objective is to develop jobs and basic work units that are adaptable enough to thrive in a world of high-speed change.

This chapter will discuss how jobs can be designed to best contribute to the objectives of the organization and at the same time satisfy the needs of employees who perform them. You will learn about the role of the line manager in defining and designing work and the terminology used in the workplace that describes how jobs are defined. Several innovative job design and employee contribution techniques that increase job satisfaction while improving organizational performance are discussed. Teamwork and the characteristics of successful teams are highlighted. The chapter concludes by briefly discussing the importance of integrating other HR processes to strengthen employee contributions.

THE LINE MANAGER'S ROLE IN DEFINING WORK

Objective **1**

The line manager or supervisor is the primary individual who determines what tasks and activities need to be performed, and in what order, to reach the company's goals or objectives. Therefore, it is critical that the line manager understand what steps need to occur to maximize organizational performance. The line manager will take an active role in determining what skills and abilities are needed to successfully perform the work. The line manager is the most knowledgeable person about the work to be done and the skills necessary to do the work. Therefore, the line manager will play an integral role in developing and/or writing a job description.

RELATIONSHIP OF JOB REQUIREMENTS AND HRM PROCESSES

Objective **2**

Job
A group of related activities and duties

Position
Specific duties and responsibilities performed by only one employee

A number of HRM processes, such as recruitment or training, make use of information about the work or job. A **job** consists of a group of related activities and duties. Ideally, the duties of a job should consist of natural units of work that are similar and related. They should be clear and distinct from those of other jobs to minimize misunderstanding and conflict among employees and to enable employees to recognize what is expected of them. For some jobs, several employees may be required, each of whom will occupy a separate position. A **position** consists of the specific duties and responsibilities performed by only one employee. In a city library, for example, four employees (four positions) may be involved in reference work, but all of them have only one job (reference librarian).

In many ways, the words "job" and "position" are relics of the industrial age. As organizations need to be more flexible and adaptable and utilize their people resources well for a competitive advantage, managers also need to think in terms of "work." William Bridges, author of *Job Shift*, states, "Today's organization is rapidly being transformed from a structure built out of jobs to a field of 'work needing to be done.'"[1] By thinking of "**work**," employers have more flexibility to define what needs to be done and when and to change employee assignments on a short-term basis. You will recall from Chapter 1 that you were introduced to the concept of "competencies"—characteristics or behaviours that are necessary for successful work performance in an organization. Competencies become very important when focusing on "work" compared to job. Instead of organizations focusing on job descriptions, companies will use "work profiles" or "contract work" to describe the work to be done. Further, the concept of "roles" is also linked to competencies. Your "role" is the part you play in the organization, and it will have certain expected behaviours. For example, your role as a customer service representative includes active listening as an expected behaviour. You will continue to see more references to work and work processes, project management, tasks and task analysis rather than "job."

Whether thinking in terms of "job" or "work," a manager needs to describe what tasks need to be done, in what order, the skills a person needs to successfully perform the work requirements, and the role a person plays in the company. This is the essence of organizational success. For all HR processes you will need to have this type of information.

Job Analysis

Job analysis is sometimes called the cornerstone of HRM because the information it collects serves so many HRM processes. **Job analysis** is the process of obtaining information about jobs (or work) by determining what the duties, tasks, or activities of those jobs are and the necessary skills, knowledge, training, and abilities to perform the work successfully. The procedure involves undertaking a systematic approach to gathering specific job information, such as equipment used, individual tasks performed, and skills needed. When completed, job analysis results in a written report (job description) summarizing the information obtained from the analysis of 20 or 30 individual job tasks or activities.[2] The ultimate purpose of job analysis is to improve organizational performance and productivity. Figure 3.1 illustrates how job analysis is done and what the information is used for.

Job analysis is concerned with objective and verifiable information about the actual requirements of a job (compared to "job design" which reflects subjective opinions about the ideal requirements of the job). The outcome of a job analysis is a written job description. It should be as accurate as possible if it is to be of value to those who make HRM decisions. These decisions may involve any of the HR processes—from recruitment to termination of employees. Job analysis is not done in a vacuum: it is important that the organization's goals and strategies be known and understood. Without the organizational context or an understanding of the organization as a whole, the requirements identified may not reflect foreseeable future requirements.

Job analysis is typically undertaken by trained HR people; however, it can also be done by a line manager who has good analytical abilities and writing skills. The HR professional can provide assistance to the manager in gathering the relevant information by ensuring that appropriate questions are asked and that the job is not inflated. It is also valuable to have the person doing the work (and the supervisor or team leader) review the data gathered to ensure it is accurate and complete.

Work
Tasks or activities that need to be completed

Job analysis
Process of obtaining information about jobs by determining the duties, tasks, or activities and the skills, knowledge, and abilities associated with the jobs

Objective 3

FIGURE 3.1   The Process of Job Analysis

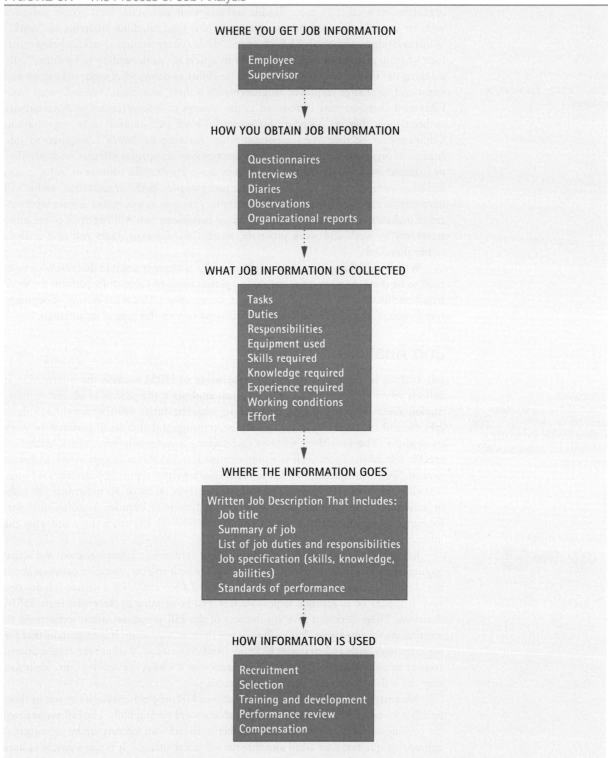

WHERE YOU GET JOB INFORMATION

- Employee
- Supervisor

HOW YOU OBTAIN JOB INFORMATION

- Questionnaires
- Interviews
- Diaries
- Observations
- Organizational reports

WHAT JOB INFORMATION IS COLLECTED

- Tasks
- Duties
- Responsibilities
- Equipment used
- Skills required
- Knowledge required
- Experience required
- Working conditions
- Effort

WHERE THE INFORMATION GOES

Written Job Description That Includes:
- Job title
- Summary of job
- List of job duties and responsibilities
- Job specification (skills, knowledge, abilities)
- Standards of performance

HOW INFORMATION IS USED

- Recruitment
- Selection
- Training and development
- Performance review
- Compensation

HR Gopher
http://www.hrgopher.com/
category/270.php

Job-Analysis.Net work
http://www.job-analysis.net/

Objective 4

Job data can be collected through interviews (asking questions, such as "What duties do you perform every day?" or "What tools do you use to complete these duties?"), questionnaires (forms that ask you to write down tasks performed, purpose of job, equipment and materials used, etc.), observation of someone doing the work, an employee log (a diary of work activities during a specified period of time), or any combination of these methods. Review the Manager's Toolkit 3.1 for some sample questions that could be either in an interview or on a questionnaire.

Frequently, in larger organizations a uniform approach is used to collect the data, such as asking people to fill out a questionnaire that requests only a list of work activities. Ethics in HRM 3.1 describes what can happen if a job is inflated.

For links to a variety of resources on writing job descriptions, go to **http://www.hrgopher.com/category/270.php**.

Job Descriptions

Once all the information on a particular job has been collected, it is organized into a **job description**—a written document. This description includes the types of duties or responsibilities, and the skills, knowledge, and abilities or competencies (job specifications)

Manager's Toolkit **3.1** Manager's Toolkit 3.1

JOB ANALYSIS QUESTIONS

Here are some sample questions when conducting a job analysis for a clerical job.

1. In a brief statement (three to four sentences), describe the basic purpose of your position. Do it in a way that answers "Why does my position exist?"

2. What are the most important responsibilities of your position, and how much time do you spend on each of these? Please list each main responsibility in order of importance. Start each statement with an action verb; some examples are "provides," "determines," "verifies."

3. What are the key tasks for each of the above responsibilities? What percentage of your time each month do you spend on each task?

4. What are the physical surroundings and/or hazards of your position? (This can include travel, exposure, danger, environmental risks, etc.)

5. Describe the mental and/or physical effort you expend in performing your work. For example, do you have long periods of intense concentration? Do you keyboard for long periods of time? Is there a lot of routine? Is the position physically demanding? Please include the frequency of the effort.

6. What are the knowledge and basic skills required to successfully fulfill the responsibilities?

7. Describe two or three of the more difficult problems you must solve to get your job done. Include situations which are a constant challenge as well as situations which require judgment and time to consider alternative solutions before problems can be resolved.

ethics **in HRM 3.1** ethics in HRM 3.1

INFLATING THE JOB

At some point in your working life, you will be asked to describe your job, perhaps when being interviewed by a job analyst or by answering questions on a form. Most employees have a reasonable expectation that their answers will affect their lives in significant ways. The information obtained may be used to reclassify the job to either a higher or lower pay level. Most employees believe that standards of performance may change, and the employer will expect them to work faster or to do more, although that is not the goal of job analysis. As a result of these beliefs and expectations, employees have a vested interest in "inflating" their job descriptions, by making the job sound very important and very difficult. Thus, night clerks in hotels become auditors and receptionists become administrators. Making a job sound more important than it is may reflect an employee's sincere belief in the significance of his or her contribution, or it may be an attempt to lobby for higher pay.

Job description
A document that lists the tasks, duties, and responsibilities of a job to be performed along with the skills, knowledge and abilities, or competencies needed to successfully perform the work

needed to successfully perform the work. Since there is no standard format for job descriptions, they tend to vary in appearance and content from one organization to another. However, the typical headings are the following:

1. Job title
   Provides an indication of what the duties might be or the nature of the work. For example, the title might be "night supervisor," "salesperson," "lab assistant," or "team leader."
2. Summary of job
   Two to three sentences describing the overall purpose of the job; it answers the question "Why does this job exist?"
3. List of duties and responsibilities
   Individual statements, usually listed in order of importance, of the key duties and responsibilities; you would expect to see between 10 and 15 statements.
4. Job specification
   Two to three sentences describing the knowledge, skills, and abilities.

Sometimes organizations might indicate that the employee's or job incumbent name ought to be included. This is not relevant nor appropriate as the description is of the job, not the person.

Job specifications
Statement of the needed knowledge, skills, and abilities of the person who is to perform the position. The different duties and responsibilities performed by only one employee

The specific skills, knowledge, and abilities that are required to successfully perform the job become the **job specifications**. Skills relevant to a job can include education and experience, specialized training, and specific abilities, such as manual dexterity. If there are any physical demands to the job, such as walking long distances or reaching high shelves, these would also be part of the job specifications. Many organizations now view job specifications as including "employability" skills and knowledge, such as problem-solving abilities. For a more complete list of employability skills, see Figure 5.1 in Chapter 5.

The Manager's Toolkit 3.2 provides an example of a job description for the manager of retail operations at a sports arena. Note that this particular job description includes specific HR responsibilities, as noted in the first section under "People Management."

Manager's Toolkit **3.2** Manager's Toolkit 3.2

SAMPLE JOB DESCRIPTION

Position: Manager, Retail Operations
Reports to: Director, Retail Operations

Summary

The manager, retail operations, is responsible for all aspects of retail operations for game nights and events. The manager ensures the store, booths, and kiosks are staffed with well-trained sales and service professionals and are visually attractive with appropriate merchandise for the customer environment. While staff development, sales, and service are primary focus areas, administrative activities such as payroll and scheduling are also part of this role.

Essential Duties and Responsibilities

People Management

1. Recruit, train, motivate, and develop a professional and knowledgeable part-time and on-call service and sales workforce.

2. Coach and communicate with employees in a fair and consistent manner (i.e., mentoring sessions, performance evaluations).

3. Work closely with senior retail management and human resources regarding disciplinary and other sensitive employee issues.

4. Identify and implement employee recognition and incentive programs.

5. Ensure staff are trained in all key areas of the business.

Business Management

1. Ensure selling areas are open for business on time and are clean and visually attractive.

2. Identify opportunities for increasing revenue.

3. Create sales and promotional programs.

4. Work with marketing staff regarding event details, such as expected attendance levels, merchandise deals, internal and external event contacts.

5. Produce sales reports.

Administration

1. Schedule staff in a fair and consistent manner.

2. Input payroll information into payroll time-management system.

3. Monitor payroll against budget and sales.

4. Develop and maintain an employee manual.

Required Experience and Qualifications (Job Specifications)

1. Four to six years' retail experience, with at least two years' supervisory experience.

2. Degree or diploma in business administration or related field.

3. Excellent leadership skills with the ability to coach, mentor, and motivate a sales service team.

4. Excellent communication, interpersonal, and problem-solving skills.

5. A solid understanding of the business and customer environment.

6. Must be able to identify and implement new business opportunities and promotions.

7. Flexible and adaptable.

8. Computer literate with a working knowledge of MS Word, MS Excel, point-of-sale software, and electronic mail systems.

9. Must be able to work evenings and weekends.

Standards of Performance

1. Meets on a weekly basis with all staff to review sales results.

2. Orients new staff during the first shift on customer-service requirements.

3. Meets or exceeds monthly sales targets.

4. Submits sales within 24 hours of each event.

5. Trains staff on any new procedures within one week.

6. Keeps customer satisfaction levels at 80% or above.

This sample job description includes both job duties and job specifications and should satisfy most of the job information needs of managers who must recruit, interview, and orient a new employee. While this job description does not have any signature lines, many job descriptions will have a place for the supervisor (and/or HR person) to sign and date as an indication that the information in the document is accurate and complete as of the date on the description.

Job descriptions are of value to both the employees and the employer. From the employees' standpoint, job descriptions that include standards of performance can be used to help them learn their job duties and to remind them of the results they are expected to achieve.

Problems with Job Descriptions

While many managers consider job descriptions a valuable tool for performing HRM activities, several problems are frequently associated with these documents, including the following:

1. If they are poorly written, using vague rather than specific terms, they provide little guidance to the jobholder (e.g., "other duties as assigned").
2. They are sometimes not updated as job duties or specifications change.
3. They may violate the law by containing specifications not related to job success (e.g., "must be single between the ages of 25 and 35").
4. They can limit the scope of activities of the jobholder.
5. They do not contain standards of performance, which are essential for selecting, training, evaluating, and rewarding jobholders.
6. They can be the basis for conflict, including union grievances, when expected behaviours are not included.

Writing Clear and Specific Job Descriptions

When writing a job description, it is essential to use statements that are concise, direct, and simply worded. Unnecessary words or phrases should be eliminated. Typically, the sentences that describe job duties begin with a present-tense and action-oriented verb, with the implied subject of the sentence being the employee performing the job. An example for an accounting clerk for a small company might read "Deposits cheques on a daily basis" or "Prepares month-end financial statements by the 10th of the following month." (Note that these two statements include performance standards.) The term "occasionally" is used to describe those duties that are performed once in a while. The term "may" is used in connection with those duties that are performed only by some workers on the job. Other examples of action-oriented, present-tense verbs include "coordinates," "handles," "researches," "conducts," "generates," and "evaluates." You can also get a list of verbs used in job descriptions at **http://www.job-analysis.net/G053.htm**).

Even when set forth in writing, job descriptions and specifications can still be vague. To the alarm of many employers, however, today's legal environment has created what might be called an "age of specifics." Human rights legislation requires that the specific performance requirements of a job be based on valid job-related criteria. Decisions that involve either job applicants or employees and are based on criteria that are vague or not job-related are increasingly being challenged successfully. Managers

Human rights legislation requires that specific job requirements be based on valid job-related criteria. For example, pilots must have a certain level of eyesight.

of small businesses, where employees may perform many different job tasks, must be particularly concerned about writing specific job descriptions. Or in a very small business, such as PowerTrader Software in British Columbia, the focus is not so much on writing a job description but identifying the core activities and then describing the attributes needed to be successful.[3]

When preparing job descriptions, managers must be aware of human rights legislation. Written job descriptions must match the requirements of the job. Position descriptions may need to be altered to meet reasonable accommodation. Reasonable accommodation is used most frequently to match religious or disability needs. The 1998 case *MacMillan Bloedel and Communications, Energy and Paperworkers Union of Canada, Local 76* made it clear that reasonable accommodation for physical-disability reasons is valid.[4] Job descriptions written to match the needs for reasonable accommodation reduce the risk of discrimination. The goal is to match and accommodate human capabilities to job requirements. For example, if the job requires the jobholder to read extremely fine print, to climb ladders, or to memorize stock codes, these physical and mental requirements should be stated within the job description.

Standards of Performance

Standards of performance
Set out the expected results of the job

This is the section least likely to be included in a job description; however, it often provides the most valuable data for both the manager and employee. **Standards of performance** set out the expected results of the job—what you are expected to accomplish, as well as how much and how fast. Look again at the sample job description above—it has several performance standards. From the employer's standpoint, written job descriptions can serve as a basis for minimizing the misunderstandings that occur between managers and their subordinates concerning job requirements. They also establish management's right to take corrective action when the duties covered by the job description are not performed as required by performance standards.

JOB ANALYSIS IN A CHANGING ENVIRONMENT

The traditional approach to job analysis assumes a static job environment and large organizations in which jobs remain relatively stable even though incumbents who might hold these jobs perform them differently. Here, jobs can be meaningfully defined in terms of tasks, duties, processes, and behaviours necessary for job success. This assumption, unfortunately, discounts technological advances that are often so accelerated that jobs, as they are defined today, may be obsolete tomorrow.[5]

Furthermore, downsizing, the adoption of teams, the demands of small organizations, or the need to respond to global change can alter the nature of jobs and the requirements of individuals needed to perform them successfully. In a dynamic environment where job demands rapidly change, job analysis data can quickly become inaccurate, and outdated job analysis information can hinder an organization's ability to adapt to change. Likewise, large organizations can find that the job information is outdated if it is not regularly reviewed and adjusted as needs change.

For organizations that operate in a fast-moving environment, several novel approaches to job analysis may accommodate needed change. First, managers might adopt a future-oriented approach to job analysis where managers have a clear view of how jobs should be restructured to meet future organizational requirements. Second, organizations might adopt a competency-based approach to job analysis in which emphasis is placed on characteristics or behaviours of successful performers rather than on standard job duties and tasks.[6] As was described in Chapter 1, these competencies might include such things as interpersonal communication skills, decision-making ability, conflict-resolution skills, adaptability, and self-motivation.[7] This technique of job analysis serves to enhance a culture of TQM and continuous improvement since organizational improvement is the stable concern. Neither of these

Determining the tasks to be done often involves seeking input from the people who actually do the work.

two approaches is without concerns, including the ability of managers to predict future job needs accurately, and the need for job analysis to comply with human rights legislation. A third and perhaps more practical method might be to have a "living job description" that is updated as the job changes. The line manager and employee would then ensure that substantial changes in duties, responsibilities, skills, and other work characteristics are documented on an ongoing basis. A type of "living job description" is a behavioural job description: one that describes how the work is to be done and what results are expected. Often these descriptions also describe typical issues and problems that may occur and the results that can be expected in dealing with the issues. By doing this, the manager and employee can also establish standards of performance.

In order to have the "right people with the right skills at the right time," contemporary managers must take the time to think about the work and the skills required to do the work. Organizational success depends on capable people. Managers want to be sure that they have the correct number of employees and the correct skills mix. Clearly identifying the work duties and the skills needed to perform the work can help managers achieve that objective.

USES OF INFORMATION FROM JOB ANALYSIS

Objective 5

As stated earlier in the chapter, a variety of HRM processes make use of the output of job analysis: recruitment, selection, training and development, performance reviews, and compensation. These are discussed below.

Recruitment

Recruitment is the process of locating and encouraging potential applicants to apply for job openings. Because job specifications establish the qualifications required of applicants for a job opening, they serve an essential role in the recruiting function as they define "who" will be successful doing the job and provide a basis for attracting qualified applicants.

Selection

After you have located individuals who are interested in working for you, you must now hire someone. Selection is the process of choosing the individual who has the relevant qualifications and who can best perform the job. Therefore, a manager will use the information on the job description as a basis to compare the skills and abilities of each applicant.

Legal Issues

In the past, job specifications used as a basis for selection sometimes bore little relation to the duties identified in the job description. Many examples can be cited of job requirements that do not match the actual duties of a job: the requirement that applicants for a labourer's job have a high school diploma; the requirement that firefighters be at least six feet tall; the requirement that applicants for the job of truck driver be male. These kinds of job specifications serve to discriminate against members of certain designated groups, many of whom have been excluded from these jobs.

Given changes to our society and the various employment laws, employers must be able to show that the job specifications used in selecting employees for a particular job relate specifically to the duties of that job. Because line managers usually help define the job specifications, they must ensure that the job requirements recruit the best candidate and do not discriminate. Managers must be careful to ensure that they do not hire employees on the basis of "individualized" job requirements that satisfy personal whims but bear little relation to successful job performance. Read HRM and the Law 3.1 to understand more about the legal implications of inappropriate job requirements.

Training and Development

Any discrepancies between the knowledge, skills, and abilities (referred to as KSAs) demonstrated by a jobholder and the requirements contained in the description and specification for that job provide clues to training needs. Also, if the job specification section contains competencies (such as "focus on customer" or "demonstrated excellent customer service skills"), these competencies could provide the basis for training. As line managers are often responsible for training the new employee, accurate job specifications and descriptions are essential. Also, as career development is often a concern for both the

HRM and **the law 3.1** HRM and the law 3.1

JOB REQUIREMENTS THAT DISCRIMINATE

In 2002, charges of discrimination were brought against Takamatsu Bonsai Design for its requirement that all employees be able to use pesticide chemicals. A pregnant woman requested that she be reassigned to other work and not be required to do work which required using pesticide. The woman had a doctor's report that indicated she ought not to be using pesticides. The B.C. Human Rights Tribunal that heard the case determined that in this circumstance the job requirement was unreasonable. The tribunal further indicated that there were sufficient other types of tasks and duties that the person could be accommodated.[8]

In 1998 an Ontario case involved the unsuccessful attempts of a school vice-principal to be

promoted to principal or to have his position reclassified to a more senior-level vice-principal. The Durham Board of Education had denied his reclassification requests for over 10 years and approved less time away from teaching for administrative duties than other vice-principals. The person launched a complaint through the Ontario Human Rights Commission, alleging that the Durham Board's denials were based on his race. After an investigation and hearing, the commission determined that discrimination had occurred, pointing to inconsistencies in how promotions were made and how decisions regarding administrative duties and courses required for promotion were arrived at.[9]

manager and the employee, the formal qualification requirements set forth in higher-level jobs serve to indicate how much more training and development are needed for employees to advance to those jobs.

Performance Reviews

The requirements contained in the job description provide the criteria for evaluating the performance of the jobholder. Evaluating an employee's performance is a major responsibility of the line manager. The results of the performance evaluation may reveal, however, that certain requirements established for a job are not completely valid. For example, the job description may require an employee to keyboard at the rate of 60 words per minute (wpm), but the performance evaluation may determine that 30 wpm is satisfactory. As already stressed, these criteria must be specific and job-related. If the criteria used to evaluate employee performance are vague and not job-related, employers may find themselves being charged with unfair discrimination. Evaluating employees fairly and objectively requires standards of performance that determine how the job should be done—how fast, how well, how timely, and so on.

Compensation

Job descriptions are often used solely for compensation purposes. In determining the rate at which a job is paid, the relative worth of the job is one of the most important factors. This worth (*pay rate*) is based on what the job demands of an employee in skill, effort, and responsibility, as well as on the conditions and hazards under which the work is performed. Systems that measure the worth of jobs are called *job evaluation systems* (see Chapter 7). Job descriptions and job specifications are used as sources of

Job analysis can be used to determine the type of training required to perform the job.

information in evaluating jobs. Often these job evaluation systems are designed by the HR department. Ultimately, however, it is the line manager who makes pay decisions based on performance relative to the standards of performance that have been established.

DESIGNING THE JOB

 Objective **6**

Job design
Process of defining and organizing tasks, roles, and other processes to achieve employee goals and organizational effectiveness

An outgrowth of job analysis, **job design** is the process of defining and arranging tasks, roles, and other processes to achieve employee goals and organizational effectiveness. For example, organizations engaged in continuous improvement or process re-engineering may revamp their jobs in order to eliminate unnecessary job tasks or find better ways of performing work.[10] Job design should facilitate the achievement of organizational objectives and at the same time recognize the capabilities and needs of those who are to perform the job. Well-designed jobs can assist in helping an organization be successful. Job design can also include job rotation (in which people move from one job to another to learn new tasks), job enlargement (in which a person's job expands in the types of tasks he or she is expected to perform), and job enrichment (in which a person's job takes on higher-order responsibilities).

As Figure 3.2 illustrates, job design is a combination of four basic considerations: (1) the organizational objectives the job was created to fulfill; (2) industrial engineering considerations, including ways to make the job technologically efficient; (3) ergonomic concerns, including workers' physical and mental capabilities; and (4) employee contributions. Employee contributions are reflected in the participation of employees in making job improvements or enhancing operational decisions.

FIGURE 3.2   Basis for Job Design

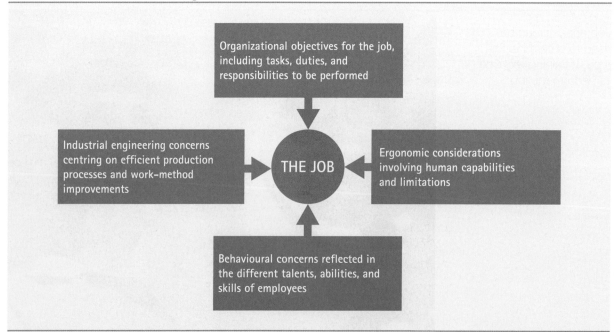

Job Design and Job Characteristics

Job design studies explored a new field when behavioural scientists focused on various job dimensions that would improve simultaneously the efficiency of organizations and the job satisfaction of employees. The **job characteristics model** proposes that three psychological states of a jobholder result in improved work performance, internal motivation, and lower absenteeism and turnover. The motivated, satisfied, and productive employee is one who (1) experiences meaningfulness of the work performed, (2) experiences responsibility for work outcomes, and (3) has knowledge of the results of the work performed. When these three psychological states are achieved, the employee is more strongly motivated to continue doing the job well.

There are five job characteristics in this model:

1. *Skill variety.* The degree to which a job entails a variety of different activities, which demand the use of a number of different skills and talents by the jobholder.
2. *Task identity.* The degree to which the job requires completion of a whole and identifiable piece of work—that is, doing a job from beginning to end with a visible outcome.
3. *Task significance.* The degree to which the job has a substantial impact on the lives or work of other people, whether in the immediate organization or in the external environment.
4. *Autonomy.* The degree to which the job provides substantial freedom, independence, and discretion to the individual in scheduling the work and in determining the procedures to be used in carrying it out.
5. *Feedback.* The degree to which carrying out the work activities required by the job results in the individual being given direct and clear information about the effectiveness of his or her performance.

The job characteristics model seems to work best when certain conditions are met. One of these conditions is that employees must have the psychological desire for the autonomy, variety, responsibility, and challenge of enriched jobs. When this personal characteristic is absent, employees may resist the job redesign effort. Also, job redesign efforts almost always fail when employees lack the physical or mental skills, abilities, or education needed to perform the job. Forcing enriched jobs on individuals who lack these traits can result in frustrated employees.

Designing Work for Group Contributions

Although a variety of group techniques has been developed to involve employees more fully in their organizations, all these techniques have two characteristics in common— enhancing collaboration and increasing synergy. By increasing the degree of collaboration in the work environment, these techniques can improve work processes and organizational decision making. By increasing group synergy, they underline the adage that the contributions of two or more employees are greater than the sum of their individual efforts. Research has shown that working in a group setting strengthens employee commitment to an organization's goals, increases employee acceptance of decisions, and encourages a cooperative approach to workplace tasks. Two collaborative techniques are discussed below: employee involvement groups and employee teams.

Job characteristics model
An approach to job design that recognizes the link between motivational factors and components of the job to achieve improved work performance and job satisfaction

Role of Management

Leadership issues arise at several levels when employees are involved in decision making. At both the executive and management levels, there needs to be clear support for employee involvement and teams as there may be changes required in processes and actions to support this new way of doing business. For many years, managers and supervisors have played the role of decision maker. Thus, organizations will need to redefine the role of supervisor when employees are participating more in the operations of the company. As stated by Carolyn Clark, vice-president of human resources for Fairmont Hotels and Resorts (Toronto), "People will stay where they have the ability to contribute and be developed, to grow. They want to know that their ideas are listened to, that they can make a difference."[11]

Therefore, when designing work for either individual or group contributions, it is critical that the organization be very clear on what is expected of managers and supervisors and the skills necessary to be successful. Further, the organization needs to carefully consider its overall design and structure. Research has demonstrated that the organizational structure is the key determinant of behaviours in the organization.[12] This means that if the organization wants a more committed and engaged workforce, then the way in which it is structured—who reports to whom and who makes decisions—will greatly influence the effectiveness of the leaders.

Organizations such as American Express and Reebok International have found that the success of employee involvement depends on first changing the roles of managers and team leaders. With fewer layers of management and a focus on team-based organizations, the role of managers and supervisors is substantially different. Managers and supervisors are seen more as coaches, facilitators, and integrators of team efforts.[13] Rather than autocratically imposing their demands on employees and closely watching to make sure that the workers comply, managers share responsibility for decision making with employees. Typically, the term "manager" has been replaced by "team leader." In a growing number of cases, leadership is shared among team members. Kodak, for example, rotates team leaders at various stages in team development. Alternatively, different individuals can assume functional leadership roles when their particular expertise is needed most.

A clear example of the role senior managers play in creating an involved organization is described in At Work with HRM 3.1.

Employee Empowerment

Objective 7

Employee empowerment
Granting employees power to initiate change, thereby encouraging them to take charge of what they do

Job enrichment, job characteristics, and creating work groups are specific ways that managers or supervisors can follow to formally change the jobs of employees. A less structured method is to allow employees to initiate their own job changes through the concept of empowerment. **Employee empowerment** is a technique for involving employees in their work through a process of inclusion. Empowerment encourages employees to become innovators and managers of their own work, and involves them in their jobs in ways that give them more control. Empowerment has been defined as "pushing down decision-making responsibility to those close to internal and external customers."

While defining empowerment can become the first step to achieving it, in order for empowerment to grow and thrive, organizations must encourage these conditions:

- *Participation.* Employees must be encouraged to take control of their work tasks. Employees, in turn, must care about improving their work process and interpersonal work relationships.

at work **with HRM 3.1**

EMPLOYER OF CHOICE

Would you like to work for the number-one Employer-of-Choice company? "Yes" is the answer most of us would give. Flight Centre Ltd., an international travel agency with offices throughout Canada, earned that distinction in 2002 in both the *Report on Business* magazine's "Top 50 Companies" and *Canada's Top 100 Employers* authored by Richard Yerema. But what led to that honour?

According to both publications, it is employers who go out of their way to meet the needs of their employees. For example, Flight Centre stresses the motto that no one has any privileges unless everyone has them, including no individual offices. The senior manager in Canada states that

it is critical for staff to feel that he appreciates them for who they are—respect is a two-way street. Since 75% of the staff are women, there is also a plan to build a safe and affordable daycare that stays open to at least 10:00 p.m.—which is when shifts end.

Check out *Report on Business* magazine (www.robmagazine.com) for current information on the Top 50 Companies.

CRITICAL THINKING QUESTION

What would your company need to do to "go out of its way to meet the needs of the employees"?

Sources: Adapted from *Report on Business* magazine, January 2002, and Asha Tomlinson, "Top Shops Deliver More Than Flashy Perks," *Canadian HR Reporter*, http://www.hrreporter.com/loginarea/members/viewing.asp?ArticleNo=1676&subscriptionType=WEB (retrieved July 23, 2002).

- *Innovation.* The environment must be receptive to people with innovative ideas and must encourage people to explore new paths and to take reasonable risks at reasonable costs. An empowered environment is created when curiosity is as highly regarded as technical expertise.
- *Access to information.* Employees must have access to a wide range of information. Involved individuals make decisions about what kind of information they need to perform their jobs.
- *Accountability.* Empowerment does not involve being able to do whatever you want. Empowered employees should be held accountable for their behaviour toward others. They must produce agreed-upon results, achieve credibility, and operate with a positive approach.

Additionally, employee empowerment succeeds when the culture of the organization is open and receptive to change. An organization's culture is created largely through the philosophies of senior managers and their leadership traits and behaviours. In an empowered organization, effective leadership is exemplified by managers who are honest, caring, and receptive to new ideas, and who treat employees with dignity and respect and as partners in organizational success.

However, some organizations will have difficulty instilling the concept of empowerment as managers are sometimes unwilling to give up power or actually give employees the authority to make decisions.

Manager's Toolkit 3.3 gives some additional examples of employee empowerment.

Manager's Toolkit 3.3 Manager's Toolkit 3.3

EXAMPLES OF EMPLOYEE EMPOWERMENT

Many types of organizations have successfully empowered their employees. Examples include such diverse companies as DuPont, Wal-Mart, Costco, and Home Depot. Empowered employees have made improvements in product and service quality, reduced costs, increased productivity, and modified or, in some cases, designed products.

- WestJet Airlines encourages employees to be free-thinking when it comes to solving customer problems. The success of WestJet's financial performance is attributed to the employees being empowered.

- Rand Merchant Bank is rated as being the best company to work for in South Africa and outperforms based on earnings.

- PanCanadian Petroleum, an Alberta oil and gas company, decided to increase productivity through employee involvement. Operators at one site knew that the field had additional reserves and assumed that management knew about this. So, when given the opportunity, the employees asked why management wasn't using the resource. The company acted on this information, which resulted in a dramatic increase in gas production and profits for PanCanadian.

Sources: Steven L. McShane, *Canadian Organizational Behaviour*, 5th ed. (Toronto: McGraw-Hill Ryerson, 2004), 184–186; and Stephen P. Robbins and Nancy Langton, *Organizational Behaviour: Concepts, Controversies and Applications*, Canadian Edition (Toronto: Prentice Hall, 1999), 460–61.

Hewitt Associates
www.hewitt.com

Employee Engagement

A somewhat newer concept resulting from employee empowerment is that of employee engagement—the employee who is committed and dedicated to the organization—where the organization has truly captured the total person in achieving organizational outcomes. A recent study by Hewitt Associates (**http://www.hewitt.com**), a worldwide human resources outsourcing and consulting firm, found that that employee engagement levels at high-growth companies exceed those of lower-growth companies by more than 20%. The study also suggests that higher-growth organizations focus more energy and attention on employee engagement than their counterparts. In addition, the study found that high-performing companies typically have better communication about career paths and opportunities for personal growth, and managers who are more focused on helping employees meet career goals. Employees at rapidly growing organizations are 18% more likely to feel that there are sufficient opportunities to obtain the skills necessary for advancement, 16% more likely to feel that they have a chance to improve their skills, and 16% more likely to know what skills they need to develop in order to advance.[14]

Employee Involvement Groups

Employee involvement groups (EIs)
Groups of employees who meet to resolve problems or offer suggestions for organizational improvement

Groups of five to ten employees doing similar or related work who meet together regularly to identify, analyze, and suggest solutions to shared problems are often referred to as **employee involvement groups (EIs)**. Also known as *quality circles (QCs)*, EIs are used

Employee involvement: leveraging the full capabilities of all employees. This group is working on a way to improve their product delivery system.

principally as a means of involving employees in the larger goals of the organization through their suggestions for improving product or service quality and cutting costs.[15] Generally, EIs recommend their solutions to management, which decides whether to implement them.

Although EIs have become an important employee contribution system, they are not without their problems and their critics. First, in order to achieve the results desired, those participating in EIs must receive comprehensive training in problem identification, problem analysis, and various decision-making tools, such as statistical analysis and cause-and-effect diagrams. Comprehensive training for EIs is often cited as the most important factor leading to their success. Second, managers should recognize the group when a recommendation is made, regardless of whether the recommendation is adopted. It is also important that management give its reasons for either accepting or rejecting the recommendation. This approach encourages the group to continue coming up with ideas even when they are not all implemented by management. This also helps EIs to gain a better understanding of the "big picture" or context in which decisions are made. Third, some organizations have found that EIs run out of ideas, and management must feed them suggestions to keep the process going. At Work with HRM 3.2 tells the story of how BC Hydro involved employees in identifying and finding solutions to employee concerns.

Employee Teams

During the past decade perhaps one of the more radical changes to how work is done is the introduction of **employee teams**. Employee teams are a logical outgrowth of employee involvement and of the philosophy of empowerment. While many definitions of teams exist, we define an employee team as a group of employees working together toward a common purpose, whose members have complementary skills, the

Employee teams
An employee-contributions technique in which work functions are structured for groups rather than for individuals, and team members are given discretion in matters traditionally considered management prerogatives, such as process improvements, product or service development, and individual work assignments

at work **with HRM 3.2** at work with HRM 3.2

EMPLOYEE INVOLVEMENT: NEW TOOLS FOR NEW PROBLEMS

BC Hydro, the Crown corporation that produces and distributes electricity throughout British Columbia, made a business decision to establish a number of call centres for better customer service. This meant that over 30 offices around the province would be consolidated into four regional call centres where agents would handle the vast majority of customer servicing needs through telephones. It also meant employees would have to relocate their families and work in a shift environment.

To make the transition for employees as smooth as possible, BC Hydro created a "call centre transition team" that was charged with identifying employee issues, developing solutions, and making recommendations to their managers. In doing so, Hydro allowed and encouraged employees to be involved in a way they hadn't experienced before and to have more control over the transition.

A team of eight people from the major regions in the province met one day a week for a period of three months, during which time they learned how to work together and develop solutions to the problems identified. The effort was successful, providing both the organization and the employees with a feeling of success in this new way of doing work. Some of the issues raised were how shifts would be determined, how vacations would be scheduled, and where people would sit. The team created practical and workable solutions that were eagerly accepted by management.

The success of this project would not have happened if the operating managers had not understood and supported the concept of allowing and encouraging employees to participate in decision making.

CRITICAL THINKING QUESTION

Would you like to work in a self-directed team? Why?

Employee Involvement Association

www.eianet.org/

work of the members is mutually dependent, and the group has discretion over tasks performed. Furthermore, teams seek to make members of the work group share responsibility for their group's performance. Inherent in the concept of employee teams is that employees, not managers, are in the best position to contribute to workplace improvements. With work teams, managers accept the notion that the group is the logical work unit, and then apply resources to resolve organizational problems and concerns.[16] Teamwork also embraces the concept of synergy. Synergy occurs when the interaction and outcome of team members is greater than the sum of their individual efforts. Teams also fulfill the expectations of today's workforce—meaningful and interesting work that allows for ability and skill development.[17]

An example of a very successful use of work teams is at Peregrine Inc. in Oshawa, Ontario. As a manufacturer of auto parts, it was organized in the traditional manufacturing mode: supervisor and worker with the supervisor telling the worker what to do. However, in 2000, the company created a work team of several employees involved in the productive process from engineer to assembly line worker to solve a particular problem. This was so successful that at any one time approximately 20 work teams are operating on a variety of problems and issues. A solution was found for a mechanical problem that saved the company over $500,000 per year. The company says that the secret to the effectiveness of these teams is the type of training provided for workers to take on this new type of work arrangement.[18]

Teams can operate in a variety of structures, each with different strategic purposes or functional activities. Figure 3.3 describes common team forms. One form, self-directed teams, also called *autonomous work groups* or *self-managed teams*, consists of employees who are accountable for a "whole" work process or segment that delivers a product or service to an internal or external customer. Team members acquire multiple skills that enable them to perform a variety of job tasks. Typical team functions include setting work schedules, dealing directly with external customers, training team members, setting performance targets, budgeting, and purchasing equipment and services.[19]

Regardless of the structure or purpose of the team, here are a few of the characteristics that have been identified in successful teams:

- Commitment to shared goals and objectives
- Consensus decision making
- Open and honest communication
- Shared leadership
- Climate of cooperation, collaboration, trust, and support
- Valuing of individual for their diversity
- Recognition of conflict and its positive resolution[20]

Unfortunately, not all teams succeed or operate to their full potential. Therefore, in adopting the work team concept, organizations must address several issues that could present obstacles to effective team function, including overly high expectations, group compensation, training, career movement, and power.[21] For example, new team members must be retrained to work outside their primary functional areas, and compensation systems must be constructed to reward individuals for team accomplishments. Since team membership demands

FIGURE 3.3 Forms of Employee Teams

Cross-functional teams

A group staffed with a mix of specialists (e.g., marketing, production, engineering) and formed to accomplish a specific objective. Cross-functional teams are based on assigned rather than voluntary membership.

Project teams

A group formed specifically to design a new product or service. Members are assigned by management on the basis of their ability to contribute to success. The group normally disbands after task completion.

Self-directed teams

Groups of highly trained individuals performing a set of interdependent job tasks within a natural work unit. Team members use consensus decision making to perform work duties, solve problems, or deal with internal or external customers.

Task force teams

A task force is formed by management to immediately resolve a major problem. The group is responsible for developing a long-term plan for problem resolution that may include a charge for implementing the solution proposed.

Process-improvement teams

A group made up of experienced people from different departments or functions and charged with improving quality, decreasing waste, or enhancing productivity in processes that affect all departments or functions involved. Team members are normally appointed by management.

Virtual teams

A group, usually from a mix of specialty areas that uses technology so that the teams can operate across time, space, and physical boundaries.

more general skills, and since it moves an employee out of the historical career path, new career paths to general management must be created from the team experience. Finally, as the team members become capable of carrying out functions, such as strategic planning, that were previously restricted to higher levels of management, managers must be prepared to utilize their newfound expertise.

Another difficulty with work teams is that they alter the traditional manager–employee relationship. Managers often find it hard to adapt to the role of leader rather than supervisor and sometimes feel threatened by the growing power of the team and the reduced power of management.[22] Furthermore, some employees may have difficulty adapting to a role that includes traditional supervisory responsibilities.

Objective 8

It is important for line managers to understand employee empowerment, employee involvement, and employee teams as they will be asked to help create and support these types of work relationships. And since such arrangements can change the role of line managers, they need to be comfortable with and accepting of the changes. Increasingly, the role of the line manager is to find ways to help, support, and expand employee involvement within the company. Without the manager's support and encouragement in creating employee involvement opportunities, there is little chance that such initiatives will succeed.

INTEGRATING HUMAN RESOURCE POLICIES AND PRACTICES

Even though we have stressed the importance of the line manager or supervisor in the successful implementation of employee empowerment and teams, all HR processes and systems in an organization need to be integrated. Work redesign, in and of itself, does not

FIGURE 3.4 A Model of Linking HR Processes for Employee Involvement

HR Process	Focus/Outcomes for Employee Involvement
Job or work design	Enabling employee empowerment Creating teams, including self-directed teams Allowing employee involvement groups Creating flexible work designs Providing alternative work arrangements Decentralizing management control

Training	Providing a variety of training, including
	    Formal vocational training
	    Team training
	    Problem-solving skills
	    Cross-skills training
	Providing an increased level of training

Performance management	Developing processes that link team to customer Seeking performance input from others Installing performance-based pay Providing different forms of recognition
Health and safety	Creating joint employee/employer committees Being proactive Able to make improvements

create a team environment. Neither does TQM or re-engineering. Other supporting elements of HRM are necessary to achieve success. Figure 3.4 presents a model of linking HR processes and employee involvement.[23] For example, recruitment and selection practices need to be particular.

Recruitment tends to be both broad and intensive in order to get the best pool of candidates from which to choose. Then, by selecting skilled individuals with the ability to learn continuously and work cooperatively, organizations are likely to make up for the time and expense they invested in selection. Likewise, training is focused on ensuring that employees have the skills needed to assume greater responsibility in this type of work environment.

As can be seen from the above, an organization cannot simply redesign work in order to have a successful company. There are many other aspects of HRM that must be aligned.

SUMMARY

1. Explain the supervisor's role in defining and designing work.
   - Line manager or supervisor is the primary individual who determines what work needs to be done.
   - Line manager takes an active role in determining what skills and abilities are needed to successfully perform the work.

2. Discuss the relationship between job requirements and HRM processes.
   - HRM processes, such as recruitment or training, make use of information about the work or job.
   - A job consists of a group of related activities and duties.
   - A position consists of the specific duties and responsibilities performed by only one employee.

3. Explain the relationship between job analysis and a job description.
   - Job analysis is the process of obtaining information about jobs (or work) by determining what the duties, tasks, or activities are.
   - The outcome is a job description—a written document that contains a number of elements.
   - A job description is a written description listing the types of duties and the skills (job specifications) needed to successfully perform the work.

4. Define and describe the sections in a job description.
   - Job title—indication of what the duties might be or the nature of the work.
   - Summary of job—two to three sentences describing the overall purpose of the job.
   - List of duties and responsibilities—statements of the key duties and responsibilities.
   - Job specifications—statement of the needed knowledge, skills, and abilities or competencies of the person who is to perform the work.

5. Describe the uses of information gained from job analysis.
   - Job specifications establish the qualifications required of applicants for a job opening and play an essential role in the recruiting function.

- Information on the job description is used as a basis for comparing the skills and abilities of each applicant in the selection process.
- Managers must be careful to ensure that they do not hire employees on the basis of "individualized" job requirements that satisfy personal whims but bear little relation to successful job performance.
- Requirements contained in the job description and specifications provide clues to training needs.
- The pay of a job is based on what the job demands in skill, effort, and responsibility, as well as the conditions and hazards under which the work is performed.

6. Define employee contribution and describe the relationship of job design to employee contributions.
   - Job design is the process of defining and arranging tasks, roles, and other processes to achieve the employee's goals and organizational effectiveness.
   - Employee contribution is the degree to which employees are involved in making critical work-process or organizational decisions.
   - Job design can enhance or take away from the employee's ability to participate in decision making.

7. Discuss the different types of work designs to increase employee contribution.
   - Employee empowerment is a method of involving employees in their work and encouraging them to take charge of what they do.
   - Employee involvement groups are groups of five to ten employees doing similar or related work who meet together regularly to identify, analyze, and suggest solutions to shared problems.
   - Employee teams are groups of employees who assume a greater role in the production or service process.

8. Describe the role of the line manager in job design and employee contribution.
   - Managers are asked to help create and support design of work to allow employee contributions.
   - The line manager finds ways to help, support, and expand employee involvement within the company.

Need to Know

- Definition of job analysis, job description, job specification, and standards of performance
- Definition of employee contribution
- Definition of employee involvement and empowerment

Need to Understand

- Relationship of job requirements to recruitment, selection, training, performance evaluation, and compensation
- Relationship between job analysis, job descriptions, job specifications, and standards of performance
- Role of line manager in designing job for maximum employee contributions
- Ways to encourage employee involvement
- Importance of integrated HRM practices for employee involvement

Key Terms

employee empowerment 92

employee involvement groups (EIs) 94

employee teams 95

job 78

job analysis 79

job description 82

job design 90

job specifications 82

position 78

standards of performance 85

work 79

REVIEW QUESTIONS

1. Explain the difference between job analysis and job description.
2. List the problems associated with a written job description.
3. Describe the way in which information from job analysis is used.
4. What are the types of employee and group contribution?
5. What are the different forms of team?

CRITICAL THINKING QUESTIONS

1. You have just been hired as a customer service representative at a branch of a very large bank. The branch manager is considering creating a non-traditional work schedule for everyone. The manager has asked for your advice about what to consider to ensure its success—and the continued strong performance of the branch. What would you say?
2. Assume you are a new supervisor in a hotel and you've been asked to prepare a job description for room attendant. What would you include as five key duties and what would you list as three key skills? Would you involve the current cashier in the preparation of the job description? Why?
3. You are working for a company that has recently created a number of work teams. Your boss has been assigned to head up one of the teams. What advice would you give so that the team and your boss create a high-performing team?
4. You are working for a new recreational resort that has no written job descriptions. From your observation it appears that many of the employees are not always sure what to do, and sometimes there is overlap in tasks and activities between employees. What arguments would you use to convince your boss to develop written job descriptions?
5. You are a small business owner in the catering business. What might be some of the work design issues you would need to consider to recruit and keep top performers?
6. How often should a job description be reviewed and/or revised? Why?
7. What methods would you use to collect job information for the following jobs:

   a. Production employee
   b. Police officer
   c. Customer service representative (answering telephone enquiries)
   d. College teacher

DEVELOPING YOUR SKILLS

**Human Resources and
Skill Development Canada**
www.hrsdc.gc.ca/

HRIM Mall
www.hrimmall.com

1. In groups of four to five students, identify the job specifications (knowledge, skills, and abilities) for the position of college instructor. (You will have approximately 20 minutes to complete the exercise.) Each group will then present its findings to the rest of the class. Discuss and compare the requirements and develop a single list of job specifications.
2. Working in groups of three to four students, identify what the group believes are successful characteristics of groups. Prepare a list of seven to eight significant characteristics that the group agrees upon. Share the results with the rest of the class.
3. Working in groups of four to five students, identify the tasks of a customer service person in a retail clothing store. How could the work be re-designed to keep employees and minimize turnover?
4. Access the Web page of the National Occupation Classification system that is managed by Human Resources and Skill Development (**www.hrsdc.gc.ca**). Click the link on "Career Planning" and then click "National Occupational Classification." Search through the various job titles and find a job description that interests you. Prepare a one- to two-page summary describing the key duties and skills, and explain what training and experience you would need in order to be hired.
5. Each student will access the HRIM Mall Web site (**www.hrimmall.com**) and click "HR Resource" link and then the "Job Descriptions" link. Once you are into the site, pick a job description, download it, and print it. Using the printed job description, assess the content from a legal-compliance perspective. Bring the job description and evaluation to class. Your instructor will ask you to share your results with each other.

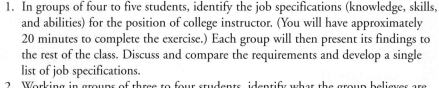

Case Study 1

Employee Contributions—Canadian Red Cross

The 1990s were not easy years for the Canadian Red Cross Society or for its many employees and volunteers across the country. In that decade, the organization experienced a significant decrease in its financial support as a result of decreased government funding, an increase in the number of not-for-profit organizations vying for donor dollars, and reduced confidence in the organization due to its handling of the Canadian blood supply. In 1998, the Canadian Blood Services was created for the collection of blood, while the Canadian Red Cross had to redefine its services. As a result, morale was low despite the dedication of the volunteers and employees. This problem was magnified due to constant structural change as the organization attempted to minimize its overhead. Wage freezes were in place for many years. Downsizing, centralizing, and layoffs were commonplace.

During this time Andrew Martin, a program manager, became aware of one of the greatest challenges facing the organization: its ability to attract and retain qualified staff. One of his tasks was to hire two individuals to fill two relatively interesting positions. "These were full-time, ongoing positions with full benefits and offered the incumbents an opportunity to interact with a variety of people and take on a wide array of interesting responsibilities. I was quite confident I would be able to find suitable candidates simply by word of mouth," explains Andrew. However, after a month, he had not received any communication from anyone who was even remotely interested in the positions. Eventually, he placed a newspaper advertisement and anticipated a flood of applications. However, he received only five applications. The response to the ad was far less than expected. "I was about 395 short!" exclaimed Andrew.

Although a few of the applicants were strong contenders, Andrew was uncomfortable with the fact that there were so few to choose from and decided to do a bit of investigation. He contacted a few individuals whom he thought would be interested in the position (and had the skills and abilities to be successful) to find out why they had not applied for the positions. "The response I received surprised me," stated Andrew. "I was very proud of my work and the work of the organization. Despite the difficulties, it was a great place to work, with wonderful opportunities to do different things and work with dedicated and talented people." However, public opinion of the Canadian Red Cross as an employer was very different. One of these contacts said, "Why would I leave my present organization, which provides me with a similar level of compensation, greater promotional opportunities, and more stability?" The Red Cross was no longer seen as a stable employer.

Although successful candidates were eventually hired for the positions, Andrew realized that one of the most challenging obstacles facing the Red Cross would be its ability to attract and retain an effective staff complement. This will be a challenging task as organizations are still competing for limited qualified human capital.

Source: Andrew Martin, Research Assistant; revised May 2005.

Questions

1. How might the Red Cross define the work in order to attract qualified candidates?
2. What could the Red Cross do to increase interest among internal candidates?
3. Would creating a "task force team" to provide suggestions on ways to overcome some of the public perception problems help? If so, how? If not, why not?

Case Study **2** | # Ducks Unlimited

Ducks Unlimited Canada, a private, not-for-profit environmental organization, conserves, restores, and manages wetlands and associated habitats in Canada. Relying on its 150,000 members, 7,700 volunteers, and 350 employees, this charitable organization has conserved over 18 million acres in Canada. Ducks Unlimited Canada has no problem attracting staff that includes biologists, habitat specialists, and accountants, because its recruits are committed to a conservation ethic and are dedicated to protecting the environment. It has also helped recruitment that Ducks Unlimited Canada has reorganized itself to flatten its management structure. The goal was to empower the employees and facilitate decision making. People working in the field no longer have to go up and down the power ladder to obtain approvals at every step. Field employees feel more in control of what they are doing.

The human resources administrator cites many advantages to an empowered workforce: increased retention, increased motivation, and decreased absenteeism and sick days.

Source: Adapted from Anonymous, "Taking Care of People," *Canadian Health Care Manager* 6, no. 3, April–May 1999, 5–9.

Questions

1. What arguments could be advanced both for and against the use of employee empowerment?
2. Empowerment is mainly a motivational tool, but at Ducks Unlimited Canada the employees arrive dedicated and committed to the environmental cause. Does Ducks Unlimited Canada need to implement empowerment?
3. How might a manager at a traditional organization react to the implementation of empowerment?

NOTES AND REFERENCES

1. William Bridges, *Job Shift* (New York: Addison-Wesley, 1994).
2. Richard Henderson, *Compensation Management*, 8th ed. (Englewood Cliffs, N.J.: Prentice Hall, 2000).
3. Excerpts from term paper prepared by Yonas Jongkind, April 1999.
4. J.M. MacIntyre, Q.C., *MacMillan Bloedel and Communications, Energy and Paperworkers Union of Canada, Local 76* [Indexed as MacMillan Bloedel (Powell River) and C.E.P.], file no. A-227/98, British Columbia, Heard: April 22 and 23, May 14 and July 15, 1998.
5. For a thought-provoking article on the future of jobs, see William Bridges, "The End of the Job," *Fortune*, September 19, 1994, 62–74.
6. Steven T. Hunt, "Generic Work Behavior: An Investigation into the Dimensions of Entry-Level, Hourly Job Performance," *Personnel Psychology* 49, no. 1 (Spring 1996): 51–83.
7. Kenneth P. Carson and Greg L. Stewart, "Job Analysis and the Sociotechnical Approach to Quality: A Critical Examination," *Journal of Quality Management 1*, no. 1 (1996): 49–56.
8. *Sidhu v. Broadway Gallery (2002), 42 C.H.R.R. D/215, 2002 BCHRT 9*, CHRR Online, www.cdn-hr-reporter.ca/ (retrieved December 3, 2004).
9. *Maxwell Nelson v. Durham Board of Education*, and Don Peel Board of Inquiry, August 28, 1998, 1998 Legal Decisions, Ontario Human Rights Commission, www.ohrc.on.ca/lsb.htm (retrieved January 24, 2000).
10. Gail L. Rein, "Feel It—A Method for Achieving Sustainable Process Changes," *Business Horizons*, May/June 2004, 47, no. 3, 75–81.
11. "How to Succeed at Recruitment and Retention," *The Globe and Mail*, January 17, 2000, E1.
12. Sheila M. Puffer, "Changing Organizational Structures: An Interview with Rosebeth Moss Kanter," *The Academy of Management Executive* 18, no. 2, May 2004, 96–105.
13. Jonathan P. Doh, "Can Leadership Be Taught? Perspectives from Manager Educators," *Academy of Management Learning and Education* 2, no. 1, March 2003, 54–67.
14. http://was4.hewitt.com/hewitt/resource/newsroom/pressrel/2004/05-18-04.htm (retrieved October 30, 2004).
15. Christopher M. Avery, "Individual-Based Teamwork," *Training and Development* 56, no. 1 (January 2002): 47–49.
16. Debra J. Housel, *Team Dynamics* (Mason, OH: South-Western Publishing Co., 2002).
17. "Job Design," Canadian Policy Research Networks, http://www.jobquality.ca/indicator%5Fe/des.stm (retrieved July 24, 2002).
18. Marissa Nelson, "Plant Gains Decision-Making Edge," *The Globe and Mail*, October 8, 2001, B8.
19. Bob Carroll, "Using Focus Activities to Drive a Self-Managed Team to High Performance," *National Productivity Review* 19, no. 2 (Spring 2000): 43–50. See also Kimball Fisher, *Leading Self-Directed Work Teams* (New York: McGraw-Hill, 2000).

20. Mel Silberman, "Smells Like Team Spirit," *Training and Development* 55, no. 2 (February 2001): 66–67.

21. Paul F. Levy, "When Teams Go Wrong," *Harvard Business Review* 79, no. 3 (March 2001): 51–67.

22. Rudy M. Yandrick, "A Team Effort," *HR Magazine* 46, no. 6 (June 2001): 136–41. See also Nancy Nelson, "The HR Generalists Guide to Team Building," SHRM Information Centre at www.shrm.org.

23. Developed from Pradeep Kumar, "Rethinking High Performance Work Systems," Queen's University: paper presented to Commission of Labour Cooperation, February 2000.

CHAPTER 4

Human Resource Planning, Recruitment, and Selection

After studying this chapter, you should be able to

1. Discuss the steps in human resource planning.

2. Describe the relationship between planning and recruiting people to work with the organization.

3. Explain the advantages and disadvantages of recruiting from within the organization.

4. Explain the advantages and disadvantages of external recruitment.

5. Explain the objectives of the selection process.

6. Describe the typical steps in the selection process.

7. Identify the various sources of information used for selection decisions.

8. Discuss the different approaches to conducting an employment interview.

9. Explain the value of different types of employment tests.

OUTLINE

HRM
Close-Up

"I really hire for attitude and train for skills, placing less emphasis on credentials and more on the person."

Sean Frisky is fond of dirt and contamination. The more dirt, the messier the spill, the more complex the contaminant, the better—better for the niche service he offers in the field of contaminant clean-up.

Frisky was a university engineering student and was in the midst of a co-op work term at an oil and gas refinery in Saskatchewan when he began to observe an unreliable and poorly designed piece of machinery. He envisioned a new design with fewer moving parts and better run times. His innovative thinking and determination to respond to a market that was just waking up to the need for environmental care and clean-up led to the small business he runs today called Ground Effects Environmental Services.

Based in Regina, Saskatchewan, Frisky's team of engineers, millwrights, welders, electricians, drillers, field technicians, office administrators, and skilled labourers has together created 70 new technologies used in the methodologies and manufacturing of equipment used to clean up contaminants.

Frisky worked alone for the first two years as he developed his business in his home garage. His first hires included an engineer, a field technician, and an office administrator. Over the next five years, his business grew to include over 40 people, as Frisky added staff based on the demand for his services. When the manufacturing of equipment was more intermittent than it is today, Frisky often used subcontractors to keep overhead low. "Our approach is to let the market drive our need to add staff, rather than ramping up in order to accommodate something we think is on the horizon," explains Frisky.

As his business grows, Frisky often sees the need for another level of staff. For instance, when he found himself with four welders on staff, it made sense to hire a welder foreman to help manage the area. He is now considering hiring a chief financial officer to take over the financial management he and a chartered accountant are currently responsible for.

Sean Frisky (right), owner of Ground Effects Environmental Services, consults with one of his field staff.

Frisky feels lucky that he has been able to recruit primarily within the province where he operates his business. "The best responses we've had when we have a new position to hire for is the response from family and friends of our current employees," says Frisky. "These people are acquainted with the company and come in understanding our approach to work and they seem to just fit the mould." Typically, Frisky places a newspaper ad and an Internet ad, and at the same time asks his staff for leads. These personal referrals from his own staff have netted some of his best new recruits.

When interviewing, Frisky has discovered that most strong candidates have anticipated the questions he's going to ask and have prepared what they know to be the right answers. He therefore tries to get to know the individual's personality and asks questions to understand how they would react in certain situations. "I really hire for attitude and train for skills, placing less emphasis on credentials and more on the person," comments Frisky.

Finding people who work well on the team is also a priority. "I use the analogy of a hockey team. We can't all be Wayne Gretzkys, but if we are diligent, hard-working, and really focus on all of our strengths, we can have a strong team," Frisky explains. As the company expands and the number of employees grows, he has been able to start hiring from within. "The best guy is usually the one who knows the ropes, and it's great to be able to recognize employees with a promotion or a new challenge. It's one of the key benefits of being part of a growing company."

INTRODUCTION

In earlier chapters we stressed that the structure of an organization and the design of the jobs (and work) within it affect the organization's ability to reach its objectives. These objectives, however, can be achieved only through the efforts of people. It is essential that jobs (and work) within the organization be staffed with people who are qualified to perform them. To achieve this, defining the core competencies for any work is critical to the recruitment and selection processes. And this starts with the line manager, who is also encouraged to think about current and future people requirements. Sean Frisky clearly understands the importance of planning and finding the right person for his company. He uses a variety of ways to find (recruit) and then pick (select) the people who have the attitudes desired to make the firm successful. And it is important that this process supports both operational and strategic planning.

Employment recruiting and selection have acquired a new importance for managers since almost all organizations are finding it increasingly difficult to secure qualified applicants to fill job openings. According to a recent study, most employers have entered a period in which jobs ranging from the unskilled to the professional and highly technical are harder to staff; this condition is not likely to improve in the near future.[1] No longer can managers rely solely upon unsolicited applications to fill openings nor can they be sloppy in making hiring decisions. This chapter will discuss the process of planning for staffing requirements, and then finding, attracting, and selecting applicants.

HUMAN RESOURCE PLANNING

You will recall from Chapter 1 that a company becomes competitive by means of its people. Therefore, it is essential that an organization look strategically at its people and the skills they require to accomplish the strategic and operational goals of the organization.

But what is meant by "strategic"? While strategy has many definitions, we will use the one you might have learned in a management course. Basically, a company's strategy lies in determining its key goals and the actions it needs to take to achieve those goals. Strategic HRM, as noted in Chapter 1, includes all the HR policies, processes, and practices that help the company achieve those goals through its employees. Therefore, it is important that the line manager link the goals of the company to the skills of the people employed.

In linking goals to skills, the line manager will need to anticipate the current and future needs of the company and develop the road map to get there. What the manager is really doing is ensuring that the right people with the right skills are in the right place at the right time.[2] This is called **human resource planning**. Human resource planning is a process to ensure that the people required to run the company are being used as effectively as possible, where and when they are needed, in order to accomplish the organization's goals. Depending on the organization, the process might also be called manpower planning or employment planning. No matter which phrase is used, the purpose is still the same: to have the right people with the right skills in the right jobs at the right time.

Human resource planning
Process that the people required to run the company are being used as effectively as possible, where and when they are needed, in order to accomplish the organization's goals

Linking HR Planning to Strategic Planning

Organizations will undertake strategic planning where major objectives are identified and comprehensive plans are developed to achieve the objectives. Because strategic planning involves the allocation of resources, including the people resources of the organization, HR planning is aligned to ensure the objectives are met. And from the overall organizational objectives, divisions and/or departments will also set objectives that support the attainment of organizational objectives. Thus, the line manager will need to make plans not only for business objectives but plans for the necessary staffing resources. For example, if the organization has strategically decided to enter a new market, it needs to ensure that it has the people with the right skill sets to gain a foothold in that market. Consequently, the HR plan must have an activity that assesses the skill of current employees and possibly a recruitment activity that attracts new employees with the necessary skills.

Likewise, through HR planning, all HR processes, systems, and practices can be aligned to the overall business strategy. In doing this, the organization ensures that it has the people capabilities to adjust to changes in the environment. One area of strategic HR planning that is receiving more and more attention is succession planning. Organizations are concerned about developing leaders for the future and are focusing efforts on training and development programs so that the leaders have the competencies necessary that can keep pace with the direction of the organization.[3] In the best companies, such as Fairmont Hotels, BMO, and IBM, there is virtually no distinction between strategic planning and HR planning; the planning cycles are the same and HR issues are seen as inherent in the management of the business. Lucent Canada, with 800 employees, links planning and HR and uses the acronym GROWS to summarize these behaviours: G for growth; R for results; O for the obsession with customers and competitors; W for a workplace that is open, supportive, and diverse; and S for speed to market.[4]

Importance of Planning for Staffing Needs

Why is it important for the line manager to be involved in human resource planning? Consider these facts about the Canadian labour force:

- In 2002, about 17 million Canadians were in the labour force out of a population of about 32 million. The workforce is aging. About one-third of the workforce is over forty-five. By 2030, the last of the baby boomers will be sixty-five, and the elderly will account for one-quarter of the population.
- The fastest-growing segments of the workforce are women and Asian Canadians, the latter mainly as a result of immigration.
- Around 18 percent of Canadians were born in another country.
- Labour shortages are predicted in manufacturing industries, and employers will be forced to recruit overseas for engineers, tool and die makers, machinists, and other trades people.
- Today, nearly one-third of workers are part-timers, temporary workers, or self-employed. Five percent of Canadians hold two or more jobs. The number of self-employed is around 18 percent of total employment.[5]

These dramatic shifts in the composition of the labour force require that managers become more involved in planning their staffing needs, since such changes affect not only employee recruitment but also methods of employee selection, training, compensation, and motivation. To illustrate the impact of changes in the workforce, companies, such as Akita, Precision Drilling Corporation, and Ensign Resource Services, have actively sought women and immigrants to move into Canada's drilling industry.[6] Without doing their own workforce planning, they would not have known there was a problem. An organization may incur several intangible costs as a result of inadequate or no people planning. For example, inadequate planning can cause vacancies to remain unfilled. The resulting loss in efficiency can be costly, particularly when lead-time is required to train replacements. Situations also may occur in which employees are laid off in one department while applicants are hired for similar jobs in another department.

Realistically, planning occurs more systematically in medium and larger organizations. Small, entrepreneurial organizations tend to approach HR staffing needs on a more short-term basis. For example, Dymaxium Inc., a Toronto firm that specializes in CD-based drug marketing tools, has fewer than 50 employees. It has been very vulnerable to the ups and downs in both the pharmaceutical and technology sectors and has had to respond very quickly to either hiring or downsizing.[7]

Statistics Canada provides a variety of different reports that can be helpful in HR planning. The "Population Pyramid" Web site at **http://www.statcan.ca/english/kits/animat/pyone.htm** is animated to demonstrate the changes in population from which organizations can determine their own trends in relation to their staffing needs.

HR Planning Approaches

Since the overall outcome of HR planning is to have the right people with the right skills at the right time in the right job, there is a need to forecast the demand for employees. Forecasting can be done through quantitative approaches, such as a **trend analysis**, or through qualitative approaches, such as **management forecasts**.

A trend analysis will forecast employment requirements on some type of organizational index, such as sales or units of production. Previous years' experiences will be analyzed and projections will be made for the future. In management forecasts, the

Statistics Canada Population Pyramids

http://www.statcan.ca/english/kits/animat/pyone.htm

Objective **1**

Trend analysis
Quantitative approach to forecasting labour demand on an organizational index

A research scientist has knowledge and company-specific skills that are directly linked to the company's strategy.

Management forecasts
Opinions and judgments of supervisors or managers and others that are knowledgeable about the organization's future employment needs

Staffing table
Graphic representations of organizational jobs along with the numbers of employees currently occupying those jobs and future employment needs

Markov analysis
Method for tracking the pattern of employee movements through various jobs

opinions and judgments of people who are knowledgeable about the organization's future needs will develop scenarios that can be used for planning purposes.

Besides forecasting the demand for employees, an organization will also need to look at the supply of employees. This includes looking both internally, in the organization, and externally, to the larger labour market. Two techniques to assess the internal supply are **staffing tables** and **Markov analysis**. Staffing tables are graphic representations of all organizational jobs, along with the numbers of employees currently occupying those jobs (and perhaps also future employment requirements derived from demand forecasts). Markov analysis shows the percentage (and actual number) of employees who remain in each job from one year to the next, as well as the proportions of those who are promoted, demoted, or transferred, or who leave the organization. While staffing tables and Markov analysis focus on numbers of employees, another technique focuses on the skill mix. When assessing the organization's supply, organizations will identify the key skills or core competencies necessary for organizational success. Without knowing the core competencies required for business success, the other HR processes may not be successful. All other HR needs are based on the identified competencies of employees to ensure good organizational performance. Organizations such as Hewlett-Packard and DuPont Canada use computers and special programs to perform this task. Figure 4.1 describes the steps in the planning process.

Results of HR Planning

The outcome of HR planning is to achieve a useable balance between the demand for and supply of employees. It is here that organizations can see the results of good HR planning. The demand for and supply of labour is very much a function of the economic environment. For example, during the sluggish economy in late 2001 and early 2002, many

FIGURE 4.1   The HR Planning Steps

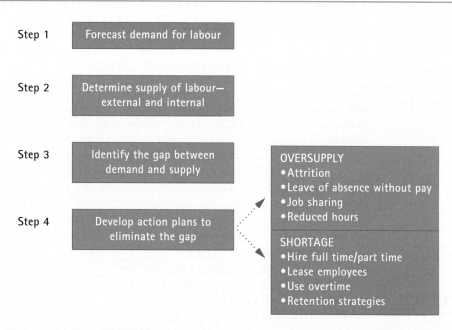

organizations found that they had to modify their plans and did not need as many people. However, there were new graduates (high school, college, and university) who were looking for employment.[8]

But HR planning is not a guarantee that there might not come a time when the organization has too many employees for its immediate or long-term needs. This can be the result of severe economic conditions (such as the aftermath from September 11, 2001) or major company collapses, such as Enron or Nortel Networks. In either case, a company may be faced with terminating or laying off employees. However, there are other ways that an organization can balance its employee complement without having to terminate people or hire more staff.

Ways to Deal with an Oversupply of Labour

Some organizations have decided that since employees are key to its success, any need to reduce employee numbers would be done by attrition. Attrition is the natural departure of employees through people quitting, retiring, or dying. Usually organizations can estimate how many people leave and for what reasons. Therefore, an organization may be able to avoid downsizing because it knows that people will leave.

Not all attrition is good. If too many people leave—high turnover—it can cost the company more money than intended. Replacing an employee is a costly and time-consuming activity. It is currently estimated that it costs about two to three times the person's salary.[9] One of the more serious business issues of the 21st century has been the concern with retaining key employees.

If the organization can predict that the excess supply of employees is more short-term, it may suggest that some employees take a leave of absence (without pay), that they job-share, reduce working hours (and pay) or the organization can redeploy people to units that have a need. Generally speaking, most organizations do not stop hiring just because of economic pressures. Frequently, it may mean that there are too many people in one area of the business and not enough in another area. By utilizing a number of strategies an organization can minimize the need to terminate employees.

Ways to Deal with Shortages of Labour

Even though human resource planning frequently focuses on the surplus of employees, there are many times when organizations have too few employees for the work that is necessary. Further, the need for additional employees may be short-term or temporary, and, therefore, the organization will not want to hire for the longer term. Therefore, the organization may request that employees work extra hours, such as during peak periods.

As mentioned in Chapter 1, the number of part-time employees has increased a great deal. Therefore, it is not unusual for companies to hire part-time staff to cover for absences of regular, full-time employees. Likewise, organizations will utilize the services of a temporary employment agency to acquire short-term staff, particularly in areas where a certain type of expertise is required, such as software programmers. In addition, an organization could increase the use of overtime, enhance retention strategies, and, as mentioned in Chapter 1, employees could be leased.

For more information on HR planning, see The HRM Guide Network at **www.hrmguide.net/canada/**.

Once a manager knows what work is to be done and the skills required to do the work successfully, the task of finding and selecting the right people begins.

The HRM Guide Network
www.hrmguide.net/canada/

RECRUITMENT

Once an organization has determined its needs, it must then recruit potential employees. The line manager, together with available HR professionals, will identify where a company might look for these candidates. **Recruitment** is the process of locating and encouraging potential applicants to apply for existing or anticipated job openings. The purpose of recruitment is to have a large pool of potentially qualified applicants. Figure 4.2 provides an overview of the recruitment process.

This process informs the applicants about the qualifications required to perform the job and the career opportunities the organization can offer its employees. Whether or not a particular job vacancy will be filled by someone within the organization or from outside will, of course, depend on the availability of people, the organization's HR practices, and the requirements of the job to be staffed.

One of the biggest challenges for organizations is to continue the recruitment process even during difficult economic times. As mentioned in the section on HR planning, and in Chapter 1 regarding the business environment and demographics, there is still a shortage of people with certain skill sets for certain types of industries. Therefore, it is important to focus on employee retention as well as focusing on accessing new talent. In some cases there is a need for the organization to consider its "branding" from a future employer perspective. For those of you who have not had a course in marketing, "branding" refers to the need to have a total and holistic approach to how the marketplace sees the company and/or products. There is a desire to have a uniform image come into the consumer's mind when the company or product is visible. Many companies are

FIGURE 4.2   The Recruitment Process

now transferring the concept of "branding" to its employment framework—to have a uniform image come into prospective employees' minds (and existing employees) when the company name is mentioned. By using a branding approach to all aspects of employment, contemporary organizations can create an opportunity to retain their key talent.

Recruiting Within the Organization

Objective 3

Most public sector organizations, and many private sector organizations, try to follow a policy of filling job vacancies above the entry-level position through promotions and transfers. By filling vacancies in this way, an organization can capitalize on the investment it has made in recruiting, selecting, training, and developing its current employees. Promotion-from-within policies at CIBC and Canada Mortgage and Housing Corporation have contributed to the companies' overall growth and success.

Advantages of Recruiting from Within

Promotion serves to reward employees for past performance and is intended to encourage them to continue their efforts. Promoting from within makes use of the people who already know the organization and the contribution they have made. It also gives other employees reason to anticipate that similar efforts by them will lead to promotion, thus improving morale within the organization. This is particularly true for members of designated groups who have encountered difficulties in finding employment and have often faced even greater difficulty in advancing within an organization. Most organizations have integrated promotion policies as an essential part of their employment equity programs.

Transfers can also serve to protect employees from layoff or to broaden their job experiences. This becomes more noticeable as organizations become flatter with fewer layers between the frontline employees and the executives. Furthermore, the transferred employee's familiarity with the organization and its operations can eliminate the

By filling job vacancies from within, organizations can capitalize on investments made in developing current employees.

orientation and training costs that recruitment from the outside would entail. Most important, the transferee's performance record is likely to be a more accurate predictor of the candidate's success than the data gained about outside applicants.

Methods of Locating Qualified Internal Job Candidates

The effective use of internal sources requires a system for locating qualified job candidates and for enabling those who consider themselves qualified to apply for the opening. Qualified job candidates within the organization can be located by using computerized record systems, and by internal job postings.

Human Resource Information Systems   Information technology has made it possible for organizations to create databases that contain the complete records and qualifications of each employee within an organization. Combined with increasingly user-friendly search engines, managers can access this information and identify potential candidates for available jobs. Organizations have developed résumé-tracking systems that allow managers to query an online database of résumés. Companies such as PeopleSoft and SAP are leaders in developing automated staffing and skills management software. Similar to the skills inventories mentioned earlier, these information systems allow an organization to rapidly screen its entire workforce to locate suitable candidates to fill an internal opening. These data can also be used to predict the career paths of employees and to anticipate when and where promotion opportunities may arise. Since the value of the data depends on its being kept up to date, the systems typically include provisions for recording changes in employee qualifications and job placements as they occur.[10]

Succession Planning   It is quite likely that many organizations have done some succession planning—the process of identifying, developing, and tracking key employees for future promotions. Therefore, when a job opening occurs in a particular part of the organization, it might make use of the succession plan and put the employee into the vacancy. Succession plans rely upon the organization identifying its long-term goals, outlining the competencies required to achieve those goals, and making sure the employee is developed in order to assume other roles and take on other responsibilities.

Internal Job Posting   Organizations may advertise about job openings through a process referred to as **internal job posting**. In the past, this process has consisted largely of posting vacancy notices on company employment boards in an HR department or common area, such as lunchroom. In addition, internal advertising can also be done through a company's intranet, e-mails, or other types of internal memos, and company newsletters. Increasingly, companies such as Xerox are developing computerized job posting systems and maintaining voluntary lists of employees looking for upgraded positions. As a position becomes available, the list of employees seeking that position is retrieved from the computer, and the records of these employees are reviewed to select the best-qualified candidate.[11]

Internal job posting can provide many benefits to an organization. However, these benefits may not be realized unless employees believe the process is being administered fairly. Furthermore, it is more effective when internal job posting is part of a career development program in which employees are made aware of opportunities available to them within the organization. For example, the organization may provide new employees with literature on job progression that describes the lines of job advancement, training requirements for each job, and skills and abilities needed as they move up the job-progression ladder.

Internal job posting
Method of communicating information about job openings

Limitations of Recruiting from Within

Sometimes certain jobs that require specialized training and experience cannot be filled from within the organization and must be filled from the outside. This is especially common in small organizations. Also, for certain openings it may be necessary to hire individuals from the outside who have gained the knowledge and expertise required for these jobs from another employer.

Even though the company may encourage that job openings be filled from within the organization, potential candidates from the outside should be considered in order to prevent the inbreeding of ideas and attitudes. Applicants hired from the outside, particularly for certain technical and managerial positions, can be a source of new ideas and may bring with them the latest knowledge acquired from their previous employers. Indeed, excessive reliance on internal sources can create the risk of "employee cloning." Furthermore, it is not uncommon for firms in competitive fields, such as high technology or retailing, to attempt to gain secrets and managerial talent from competitors by hiring away their employees.

Recruiting Outside the Organization

Objective 4

Frequently, organizations will decide to fill positions by bringing people in from outside the organization. Thus, when a mid-level manager of the organization leaves, a chain reaction of promotions may subsequently occur. This creates other openings throughout the organization. The question, therefore, is not whether to bring people into the organization, but rather at which level they are to be brought in.

Usually, external recruitment is organized and coordinated by an HR department with the line manager frequently giving suggestions about where to recruit, such as an ad in a newspaper or professional journal. However, if there is no HR department, the line manager will perform this function. These people need to be aware of such things as labour market conditions and where to recruit.

In the past few years, organizations such as Air Canada, the Toronto Maple Leafs, and Weyerhaeuser have brought in outsiders to be their new CEOs. In fact, a very high percentage of Fortune 500 companies who replace their CEOs do so by hiring executives from outside their companies. In many of these cases, hiring someone from the outside is seen as essential for revitalizing the organization.[12]

Advantages and Disadvantages of External Recruitment

Like recruiting from within, external recruitment has advantages and disadvantages. One advantage of bringing someone in from outside the organization is that the individual brings certain unique skills that the company needs now. Likewise, it is possible to bring in people with a variety of different experiences and perspectives.

A disadvantage to external recruitment is the lack of solid information about the person's performance on the job. That information is available only through second-hand sources, such as what the applicant volunteers and what references might say. Also, the person may not know the industry or organization, necessitating more extensive orientation and training. Further, there may be constraints in the organization, such as salary levels, that prevent the organization from accessing a large pool of applicants. In addition, there are usually significant costs associated with external recruitment. These costs include the amount of time, the cost of advertising (sometimes as much as $9,000 per newspaper), and the cost of familiarizing the person with the organization. Lastly, there may be legislative requirements, such as employment equity, that lead to certain applicant pools.

The Labour Market

Labour market
Area from which applicants are recruited

The **labour market**, or the area from which applicants are recruited, will vary with the type of position to be filled and the amount of compensation to be paid. Recruitment for executives and technical personnel who require a high degree of knowledge and skill may be national or even international in scope. Most colleges and universities, for example, conduct national employment searches to fill top administrative positions. Recruitment for jobs that require relatively little skill, however, may encompass only a small geographic area. The reluctance of people to relocate may cause them to turn down offers of employment, thereby eliminating them from employment consideration beyond the local labour market.

The condition of the labour market may also help to determine which recruiting sources an organization will use. During periods of high unemployment, organizations may be able to maintain an adequate supply of qualified applicants from unsolicited résumés alone. A tight labour market, one with low unemployment, may force the employer to advertise heavily and/or seek assistance from local employment agencies. How successful an organization has been in reaching its employment equity goals may be still another factor in determining the sources from which to recruit. Typically, an employer at any given time will find it necessary to utilize several recruitment sources.[13]

For a number of years, Canada has relied on immigration to assist in meeting the demand for labour. However, with the changes to the federal *Immigration and Refugee Protection Act* in June 2002, some employers may have more difficulty, while others may have a more readily available source of skilled applicants. For example, more weight is given to people with trade certificates or a second degree. Likewise, the weighting for experience has shifted so that people with fewer years of experience will now be considered.[14] These changes are intended to allow younger, educated applicants into Canada. As mentioned in Chapter 1, Canada has an aging population with insufficient younger workers to fill the work requirements in the future. Organizations that have relied on recruiting outside Canada will need to pay particular attention to the new Act. Further, as more and more individuals become part of a global talent pool, companies will seek a number of ways to recruit beyond one's home country. See Around the World with HRM 4.1 for examples of worldwide recruiting.

Outside Sources of Recruitment

The outside sources from which employers recruit will vary with the type of position to be filled. A computer programmer, for example, is not likely to be recruited from the same source as a machine operator. Trade schools can provide applicants for entry-level positions, though these recruitment sources are not as useful when highly skilled employees are needed. Networking, referrals from previous and existing staff, information from customers/clients, and being involved in the community are a few ways that organizations seek people outside the organization. A variety of new and creative recruitment approaches is emerging For example, the Government of Alberta has a "Careers in Motion" motor home that travels across the province providing information about

around the world **with HRM 4.1** around the world

THE GLOBAL TALENT POOL

With the spread of a global community, organizations from the manufacturing to the service sectors are finding that they are competing in an international labour market. This is particularly true of organizations that have worldwide operations such as KPMG (accounting/consulting firm), Royal Dutch/Shell Group of Cos., and Boston Consulting. But what are they looking for? Typically, these organizations are looking for people with a mix of academic and work experiences, languages, and interpersonal skills. These are all assessed against the culture of company and the geographic setting of the employing company. For example, employers in southeast Asia place more emphasis on academic achievements.

This isn't just a one-way path of what employers are looking for. Potential employees from around the world are also looking at the nature of the organization to ensure it meets their needs. For example, particularly for employees from North America, there is a desire to have a work-life balance. Thus, when considering an opportunity in another country, the potential employees will want to know about the ability to work from home or to have time to pursue other interests.

Sources: Adapted from Alicia Clegg, "Top Companies Trawl for Global Talent Pool," *The Financial Post*, July 7, 2004, FP8; and Gillian Shaw, "Top Gamers Kept on the Job with Array of Sweet Deals," *The Vancouver Sun*, March 25 2004, D1.

Careers in Motion
www3.gov.ab.ca/hre/
careersinmotion

employment opportunities. The motor home is equipped with online resources and the ability to e-mail, fax, or telephone prospective employers (**www3.gov.ab.ca/hre/ careersinmotion**).

Some of the major outside sources of recruitment are described below.

Advertisements   One of the most common methods of attracting applicants is through advertisements. While newspapers and trade journals are the media used most often, radio, television, billboards, posters, and electronic mail are also utilized. Advertising has the advantage of reaching a large audience of possible applicants. Some degree of selectivity can be achieved by using newspapers and journals directed toward a particular group of readers. Professional journals, trade journals, and publications of unions and various fraternal or nonprofit organizations fall into this category.

As Manager's Toolkit 4.1 illustrates, the preparation of recruiting advertisements requires creativity in developing design and message content. Well-written advertisements highlight the major assets of the position while showing the responsiveness of the organization to the job and career needs of the applicants. Among the information typically included in advertisements is a statement that the recruiting organization is an equal-opportunity employer.

**Human Resources
Development Canada**
www.hrdc-drhc.gc.ca

Canada's Human Resources Development (HRD) Centres (**www.hrdc-drhc.gc.ca**) are responsible for administering the Employment Insurance program and can be found in most communities. Individuals who become unemployed must register at one of these offices and be available for "suitable employment" in order to receive their weekly employment insurance cheques. Consequently, public employment agencies

Manager's Toolkit **4.1** Manager's Toolkit 4.1

Manager's Toolkit **4.1**

A different kind of Workplace

At Shell Canada we offer you work/life balance, flexible working arrangements, and a number of employee development programs to help foster career satisfaction. We also give you the opportunity, on an annual basis, to evaluate both your supervisor and your work environment. We are currently looking for:

IT ERP Project Leads & Analysts, Calgary

Business ERP Project Leads & Analysts, Calgary

Accountants & Financial Analysts

Contracts Engineer, Calgary and/or Fort McMurray

Buyer – Muskeg River Minesite, Fort McMurray

Learn more, and view all our current job postings at shell.ca.

Shell Canada Limited
400 - 4th Avenue S.W., Calgary, AB T2P 2H5
Email: **recruitment-hr@shell.com (MS Word)**
Fax: (403) 691-3350

Shell is an equal opportunity employer and encourages applications from all qualified individuals.
Only those individuals legally entitled to work in Canada will be considered.

We thank all applicants for their interest; however, only those selected for an interview will be contacted.
No telephone inquiries please.

Source: Courtesy of Shell Canada.

are able to refer to employers with job openings those applicants with the required skills who are available for employment. Applicants for jobs can access the Employment Telemessage system via the telephone, or review online information at the centre itself. There is also a national job bank that lists information about jobs across the country.

Internet   Perhaps the most significant influence of technology on recruitment has been the growth of the Internet. Many employers will use an intermediary, such as Workopolis, Monster, or Jobshark in order to post jobs. At Work with HRM 4.1 describes how Jobshark links companies with people who have the necessary skills.

at work **with HRM 4.1** at work with HRM 4.1

JOBSHARK.COM—DREAM MAKER

Jobshark.com is an online recruitment company that helps link job seekers with jobs that match their needs and skills. According to Matt Von Teichman, co-founder and president of Jobshark, the process is fast and effective, and very, very simple for those with little time to pursue jobs.

The job seeker spends about 20 minutes completing an online application form, giving information on skills, experience, and interests, and filling out a brief personality test. Once the personality profile is entered into the system, the form is considered active. Recruiting companies post jobs, listing skills required, again using a standardized format. About 1,000 new jobs are posted each month, with spring and fall being the busiest recruitment times. Within minutes of a company posting a job, the application-matching software sends a notification by e-mail to the job seekers whose profiles match it, giving a detailed job description, salary, etc. The job seeker can reply by e-mail or by an internal messaging system.

In replying and indicating interest, the candidate must answer questions the company has posted. For example, a company might ask, "What was the last project you managed?" Jobshark.com has a bank of about 500 questions, including such diverse ones as "Who is your favourite action hero and why?"

The company then receives the résumé and responses (again, often within minutes) and determines whether any close matches have been made (95% would be considered close). The company can then communicate with the applicants by e-mail or call to arrange a face-to-face or telephone interview.

The service is free for job seekers, but the companies pay a fee based on the number of jobs advertised. "In general, online recruitment is a great tool," says Von Teichman. "It allows someone who is overloaded with work or school to be connected actively to the job market. Many people have found their dream job in this way."

Jobshark.com is a Canadian company with offices throughout Canada, the United Kingdom, and South America.

CRITICAL THINKING QUESTIONS

1. What do you think is making Internet recruiting so popular?
2. What are the potential problems that can happen with Internet recruiting?

Jobshark
www.jobshark.ca

Monster.ca
www.monster.ca

Workopolis
www.workopolis.ca

Further, many companies use their Web sites to announce job openings. For example, the networking company Cisco Systems posts detailed information about hundreds of job openings at its Web site. Likewise, Bombardier Aerospace, headquartered in Montreal, and CIBC actively use their company Web sites to encourage people to consider working for them. Canadian recruiting sites include Monster.ca (**www.monster.ca**), Workopolis (**www.workopolis.ca**), NiceJob (**www.nicejob.ca**), and working.com (**http://working.canada.com**), a site that provides information about job opportunities listed in the major Canadian newspapers. In addition, Human Resources Development Canada (HRDC) has an Internet site that is a "virtual" library of career and employment information (**www.workinfonet.ca**).

Employers claim that the Internet is faster (with some job applicants responding within 30 minutes of the job posting); that it generates higher-quality candidates; and that it is cheaper (by as much as 80%) than traditional advertising media. An

NiceJob

www.nicejob.ca

working.com

http://working.canada.com

Workinfonet

www.workinfonet.ca

Internet posting can be as low as $50 per month compared to a newspaper ad of $6,000 per day, with Monster and Workopolis being about $500 per month. And there is a higher rate of success of hiring from Web sites: organizations in a recent study indicated that 16 percent of those hired were recruited through their Web site.[15] For example, a company using Workopolis can search over 500,000 résumés from Canadian applicants.[16] In addition, Workopolis.ca has a competency questionnaire that assesses whether the candidate meets the minimum requirements of the position. If the candidate does, then the résumé is forwarded to the hiring company. This is used as a screening tool and narrows the résumé review of the hiring company.[17] Estimates are that more than 2,500 Web sites exist that contain job postings, and more than 1.5 million résumés are currently online.[18] A capability like this can help companies find the people with the competencies that are required in today's dynamic business environment.

But online recruiting has become more than just matching candidates with companies. The next generation of Web-based tools includes online job fairs in which companies can "meet" candidates in a virtual environment and chat with them online. The method is often cost-effective as well. The Employee Management Association estimates that the cost per hire is about $377, compared to $3,295 using print media.[19]

There is also a need to prepare Internet advertisements in a careful way so that the Web site does attract the qualified people you are seeking. Manager's Toolkit 4.2 provides tips for creating such a Web site. But having a Web-based ad is not sufficient. The organization must also have the means to easily and quickly process the number of applications that can come from this tool. Therefore, more and more companies are providing opportunities for you to transmit your résumé directly to the company through the company Web site. Once this has happened, companies will often have software that automatically sorts and categorizes applicants by skill sets. It is through the use of technology that companies are better able to handle the volume of applications being submitted as well as effectively screen to get the people with the right skill sets.[20]

Manager's Toolkit **4.2** Manager's Toolkit 4.2

DEVELOPING EFFECTIVE WEB SITE ADVERTISEMENTS

1. Design your company Web site so that it is a site visited not only by customers but also by potential employees. Work as hard building the "employer" brand as you do the product brand.

2. Market the company—don't sell a job. Talk about the vision and the opportunities.

3. Create job information that talks about what the employee will be doing and the potential for the future. Don't simply say what the employee needs to bring to the job.

4. Link your site to other sites, anything from career sites and trade sites to game sites—anywhere your potential employee might surf.

5. Once candidates have entered your employment site, let them join forums or connect with an employee similar to them. Give them a reason to return.

Sources: Adapted from L. Adler, "Tips for Successful Recruiting on Your Company Web Site," *Canadian HR Reporter*, April 19, 1999: 10; and J. Carrol, "Hook a Job with On-Line Resume," *The Globe and Mail*, June 19, 2000, B5.

Companies, such as Finning International and Hydro One, and organizations, such as the federal government and the Government of Ontario, use the Internet to attract people. Employers indicate that the reason is to increase the opportunity to attract the people with the right skill sets for their organizations.

Employment Agencies and Executive Search Firms Employment agencies and executive search firms attempt to match applicants with the specific needs of a company. Charging a fee enables these agencies to tailor their services. It is common for such agencies to specialize in serving a specific occupational area, such as office staff or technical computer people. Private agencies usually focus on clerical, technical, and junior–middle management whereas executive search firms tend to focus on senior and executive management. These agencies may charge an employer 25 to 30 percent of the annual salary if they find a candidate who gets hired. Since these agencies differ in the services they offer, job seekers would be wise to take the time to find a recruiter who is knowledgeable, experienced, and professional. When talking with potential recruiters, individuals should discuss openly their philosophies and practices with regard to recruiting strategies, including advertising, in-house recruiting, screening procedures, and costs for these efforts. They should try to find a recruiter who is flexible and who will consider their needs and wants.[21]

Check out the Web site of Angus One Professional Recruiters (**www.angusone.com**) and Olsten Staffing Services (**www.olsten.com**) to find out more about employment agencies.

Angus One Professional Recruiters

www.angusone.com

Olsten Staffing Services

www.olsten.com

Headhunters In contrast to employment agencies, which help job seekers find the right job, headhunters help employers find the right person for a job. They seek out candidates with qualifications that match the requirements of the positions their client firm is seeking to fill. The fees charged by these firms may range from 30 to 40 percent of the annual salary for the position to be filled. The client firm pays this fee.

As noted earlier, it is an increasingly common occurrence to bring in new chief executive officers (CEOs) from outside the organization. A large number of these new CEOs are placed in those positions through the services of an executive search firm or headhunter. Since high-calibre executives are in short supply, a significant number of the nation's largest corporations, including the Government of Alberta and Molson Canada, use search firms to fill their top positions.

Educational Institutions Educational institutions are a source of young applicants with formal training but relatively little full-time work experience. High schools are usually a source of employees for clerical and blue-collar jobs. Community colleges, with their various types of specialized training, can provide candidates for technical jobs. These institutions can also be a source of applicants for a variety of white-collar jobs, including those in the sales and retail fields. Some management-trainee jobs are also staffed from this source. Humber College in Etobicoke, Ontario, and the BC Institute of Technology offer a Human Resource Management post-diploma program. For technical and managerial positions, universities are generally the primary source. Some employers fail to take full advantage of college and university resources because of a poor recruitment program.[22] Consequently, their recruitment efforts fail to attract many potentially good applicants. Another common weakness is the failure to maintain a planned and continuing effort on a long-term basis. Furthermore, some recruiters sent to college campuses are not sufficiently trained or prepared to talk to interested candidates about career opportunities or the requirements of specific openings. Attempts to visit too many campuses instead of concentrating on selected institutions and the inability to use the campus placement office effectively are other recruiting weaknesses. Mismanagement of applicant visits to the organization's headquarters and the failure to follow up on individual prospects or to obtain hiring commitments from higher management are among other mistakes that have caused employers to lose well-qualified prospects.

Open Houses and Job Fairs   Organizations may also use open houses and job fairs to recruit new employees—particularly if the organization is expanding or is looking for particular types of skills. For example, with the shortage of skilled trades, an organization might participate in a job fair at an educational institution that graduates tradespeople. Or the organization might have an open house where potential applicants are encouraged to visit the company and see what might be available. Season resort operations such as Whistler/Blackcomb in British Columbia use open houses at the start of each ski season as a way to attract people with a variety of skills.

Employee Referrals   The recruitment efforts of an organization can be aided by employee referrals or recommendations made by current employees. Managers have found that the quality of employee-referred applicants is normally quite high, since employees are generally hesitant to recommend individuals who might not perform well. The effectiveness of this recruitment effort can be increased by paying commissions to employees when they make a successful "recruitment sale." Playdium, entertainment complexes in Burnaby, British Columbia, and Mississauga, Ontario, pay up to $1,000 as a bonus when a referral is hired. Other types of incentives include complimentary dinners, discounts on merchandise, and all-expense-paid trips.[23] An organization, however, needs to ensure in utilizing employee referrals that it is not creating a situation of systemic discrimination.

Unsolicited Applications and Résumés   Many employers receive unsolicited applications and résumés from individuals who may or may not be good prospects for employment.[24] Even though the percentage of acceptable applicants from this source may

Many applicants were recruited at a job fair in Markham, Ontario, for positions at IBM.

not be high, it is a source that cannot be ignored. Many job search strategies suggest that individuals use this method to introduce themselves to organizations that are of interest to them.[25]

Good public relations dictates that any person contacting an organization for a job be treated with courtesy and respect. If there is no possibility of employment in the organization at present or in the future, the applicant should be tactfully and frankly informed of this fact.

Professional Organizations   Many professional organizations and societies offer a placement service to members as one of their benefits. Listings of members seeking employment may be advertised in their journals or publicized at their national meetings. A placement centre is usually established at national meetings for the mutual benefit of employers and job seekers.

Unions   Unions can be a principal source of applicants for blue-collar (such as welders, electricians, plumbers) and some professional jobs. Some unions, such as those in the maritime, printing, and construction industries, maintain hiring halls that can provide a supply of applicants, particularly for short-term needs. Employers wishing to use this recruitment source should contact the local union under consideration for employer eligibility requirements and applicant availability.

Temporary Help Agencies   The temporary services industry is one of the fastest-growing recruitment sources. Companies such as Imperial Oil Ltd., International Forest Products, and SaskTel use temporary employees extensively. "Temps" are typically used for short-term assignments or to help when managers cannot justify hiring a full-time employee, such as for vacation fill-ins, for peak work periods, or during an employee's parental or sick leave.

Increasingly, temps are being employed to fill positions once staffed by permanent employees. At Hydro-Québec, for example, "long-term temporaries" have replaced permanent hires as a staffing practice. Employees are hired for one- to three-year terms. This practice is growing because temporaries can be laid off quickly, and with less cost, when work lessens. The use of temporaries thus becomes a viable way to maintain proper staffing levels. Also, the employment costs of temporaries can often be lower than those of permanent employees because temps are usually not provided with benefits and can be dismissed without the need to file employment insurance claims.

The drawbacks of contract employees are that their commitment to the company is lower than that of full-time employees, and they may take confidential information to their next employer, possibly a competitor.

To get more information about the types of work available through temporary agencies, look at the Web site of Manpower, one of Canada's largest temporary agencies at **www.manpower.ca**.

Manpower
www.manpower.ca

Recruitment of Designated-Group Members

In meeting their legal obligation to provide equal employment opportunity, employers often develop a formal employment equity program. An essential part of any employment equity policy must be an effort to recruit members of the designated groups. These legislated designated groups are women, visible minorities, people with disabilities, and First Nations people.

However, beyond satisfying the legislated requirements, many companies are seeking the business success of having a diverse workforce. As indicated in a recent study of the

S&P 500 over the last five years, companies that aggressively sought and supported a diverse workforce outperformed the other companies in the study. According to Rajesh Subramaniam, CEO of FedEx Canada, "We have a tendency to reject what is different. And at the time, we need what is different. Because what is different is the only way we can grow. Sameness is suicide in the business world—particularly now as we operate in the global economy."[26] Therefore, it will be important for line managers and supervisors to be knowledgeable about and supportive of their organization's objective to have employees with diverse ethnic and cultural backgrounds. Managers may also be actively involved in recruitment "outreach" programs, where they speak at ethnic community centres to let people know about employment opportunities with their company. Other avenues for recruiting designated groups include ethnic community newspapers and TV stations.

There is a cautionary note regarding whether the recruitment program is perceived as a quota system leading to reverse discrimination. The entire organization needs to ensure that the values and behaviours of the organization support a diverse workforce and that the organization is not just going through the motions.

SELECTION

Objective **5**

Once the recruitment process has yielded applicants whose qualifications appear to fit the organization's requirements, you then must assess those qualifications and make a decision on whom to hire—which individual or individuals will perform best on the job. It is usually the line manager's responsibility to make the final selection decision. If there is an HR department, it will usually play a supporting role by arranging interviews, doing reference checking, administering employment tests, and so on. However, if there is no HR professional to help, the line manager needs to know these steps and their importance.

Matching People and Jobs

Making hiring decisions is not a scientific process, and, therefore, it cannot be structured to achieve perfect results. However, by being systematic in the selection process, there is a greater possibility of getting the right person for the right job at the right time.[27] **Selection** is the process of choosing individuals who have relevant qualifications to fill existing or projected job openings. Those responsible for making selection decisions should have adequate information on which to base their decisions. Information about the jobs to be filled, and as much relevant information as possible about the applicants themselves, is essential for making sound decisions. The objective is to have information that will predict job performance of the candidate in the organization.

Prior to the selection process, it is important to reconfirm the necessary knowledge, skills, and abilities for the job. As mentioned in Chapter 3, these job requirements are identified through job analysis. Managers can then use selection methods, such as interviews, references, psychological tests, and the like, to measure the applicant's knowledge, skills, and abilities (KSAs), more currently referred to as "competencies," and match these against the requirements of the job and the needs of the organization.[28]

Ordinarily, managers are well acquainted with the requirements pertaining to skills, physical demands, and other factors for jobs in their respective departments. If the interview

Selection
The process of choosing individuals who have relevant qualifications and who will best perform on the job to fill existing or projected job openings

step includes professionals from the HR department, the HR professional will need to maintain a close liaison with the various departments to become thoroughly familiar with the jobs and competencies needed to perform them.

The Selection Process

Objective 6

In most organizations, selection is a continuous process. Turnover inevitably occurs, leaving vacancies to be filled by applicants from inside or outside the organization or by individuals whose qualifications have been assessed previously. In some situations, organizations will have a waiting list of applicants who can be called when permanent or temporary positions become available.

The number of steps in the selection process and their sequence will vary, not only with the organization but also with the type and level of jobs to be filled. Each step should be evaluated on its contribution. The steps that typically make up the selection process are shown in Figure 4.3. Not all applicants will go through all these steps. Some may be rejected after a review of their application form or résumé, or after a preliminary interview.

As shown in Figure 4.3, organizations use several different means to obtain information about applicants. These include application forms and résumés, interviews, tests, and reference checks. Regardless of the method used, it is essential that it conform to accepted ethical standards, including privacy and confidentiality, as well as legal requirements. Above all, it is essential that the information obtained be sufficiently reliable and valid.

Obtaining Reliable and Valid Information

Reliability
The degree to which interviews, tests, and other selection procedures yield comparable data over time and alternative measures

The degree to which interviews, tests, and other selection procedures yield comparable data over a period of time is known as **reliability**. For example, unless interviewers judge the capabilities of a group of applicants to be the same today as they did yesterday, their judgments are unreliable (i.e., unstable). Likewise, a test that gives widely different scores when it is administered to the same individual a few days apart is unreliable.

FIGURE 4.3 Steps in the Selection Process

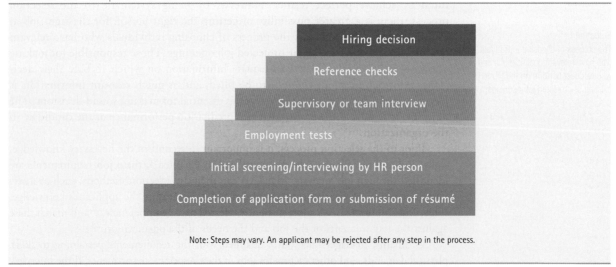

Note: Steps may vary. An applicant may be rejected after any step in the process.

Validity
How well a test or selection procedure measures a person's attributes

In addition to having reliable information pertaining to a person's suitability for a job, the information must be as valid as possible. **Validity** refers to what a test or other selection procedure measures and how well it measures it. In the context of employee selection, validity is essentially an indicator of the extent to which data from a procedure (interview or test, for example) predict job performance. However, whether something is valid depends upon the selection tool's overall reliability. Therefore, whatever selection procedures or tools are used—whether an interview or an employment test—they must be both reliable and valid in order to provide useful information about predicting the applicant's performance in the organization. For example, companies that screen job applicants for values will not get good information about a person's overall capability to perform the job successfully; the best overall predictor for job success is the person's intelligence.[29]

Sources of Information about Job Candidates

Objective **7**

Many sources of information are used to provide as reliable and valid a picture as possible of an applicant's potential for success on the job. This section looks at the usefulness of application forms and résumés, reference checks, employment tests, and interviews.

Application Forms and Résumés

Most organizations require application forms to be completed because they provide a fairly quick and systematic means of obtaining a variety of information about the applicant. Application forms serve several purposes:

- They provide information for deciding whether an applicant meets the minimum requirements for experience, education, and so on.
- They provide a basis for questions the interviewer will ask about the applicant's background.
- They also offer sources for reference checks. For certain jobs, a short application form is appropriate.

The McDonald's form reproduced in Manager's Toolkit 4.3 is quite brief but asks for information that is highly relevant to job performance. It also provides information regarding the employer's conformity with various laws and regulations. For scientific, professional, and managerial jobs, a more extended application form or a résumé is likely to be used.

Individuals frequently exaggerate or overstate their qualifications on a résumé. However, the consequences of falsifying information on applications and résumés are frequently severe, such as termination. But candidates not only exaggerate; in a tight labour market, candidates sometimes delete advanced qualifications, as described in Ethics in HRM 4.1. Other cases highlight the importance of integrity in job applications. Some observers estimate that at least 33% of applicants "stretch" the truth on their résumés. Ethics in HRM 4.1 also describes these situations. One technique for anticipating problems of misrepresentation is to ask applicants to transcribe specific résumé material onto a standardized application form. The applicant is then asked to sign a statement that the information contained on the form is true and that he or she accepts the employer's right to terminate the candidate's employment if any of the information is subsequently found to be false.[30]

Résumés are prepared by the applicant and provide job-related information about the job seeker. A résumé will usually contain sections on work experience, education, volunteer activities, and personal interests. In preparing and presenting résumés, applicants can display their creativity in how they present themselves.

Manager's Toolkit **4.3** Manager's Toolkit 4.3

McDONALD'S APPLICATION

McDONALD'S RESTAURANTS
EMPLOYMENT APPLICATION

Date: _____
           D   M   Y

PERSONAL INFORMATION

Name: _____ Phone:(_____) _____
              Last   First   Middle

Present
address: _____ How long
              No. & Street   City   Province   Postal Code   there? _____

Position Applied for: _____ Are you presently employed? ☐ Yes ☐ No Date of availability: _____

Have you ever worked for McDonald's before? ☐ Yes ☐ No   If so, where? _____

If you are under 16, please state your age*: _____   Referred by: _____
*Please Note: You may be required to provide proof of age prior to hire.

Have you ever been convicted of a criminal   ☐ Yes ☐ No   Are you legally entitled to work in Canada? ☐ Yes ☐ No
offense for which you have not been pardoned?   (You may be required to provide proof of employment status prior to hire.)

AVAILABILITY

HOURS AVAILABLE	MONDAY	TUESDAY	WEDNESDAY	THURSDAY	FRIDAY	SATURDAY	SUNDAY
FROM							
TO							

EMPLOYMENT BACKGROUND
List your present or last position first

DATE MONTH & YEAR	COMPANY NAME & ADDRESS	TELEPHONE NUMBER INCLUDING AREA CODE	NAME AND POSITION OF SUPERVISOR	YOUR POSITION	SALARY/WAGE START I END	REASON FOR LEAVING
FROM						
TO						
FROM						
TO						
FROM						
TO						

I declare that the information contained in this application is correct to the best of my knowledge and understand that any omission or incorrect information is just cause for the rejection of my application or dismissal in accordance with the Company policy. If hired, I understand that I may be transferred to another restaurant because of promotions, training or staffing requirements. I also agree that, at all times, I will follow the rules and regulations of the Company. I authorize the Company, or its agents, to verify the information provided, and to obtain any other information relevant to this application. This information may be obtained by telephone or in writing from educational institutions, my current or former employers, financial institutions, personal information agents and my personal references. This consent is valid during the consideration of my application for employment, and if I am hired, for the duration of my employment.

SIGNATURE: _____   DATE: _____

To the applicant:
Your application will be considered active for 90 days, after which you must submit a new application. The information which you have supplied, and any other information obtained, will be used solely for the assessment of your application for employment. Your application will be kept by the Management Team and, if you are hired, it will become part of your employee file. Your file will be retained in the Manager's office, and may be accessed by Management. You may access your file by appointment with a representative of the Company. If there are mistakes in your file, you have the right to ask for them to be corrected.

Source: Reprinted with permission of McDonald's Restaurants of Canada Limited.

ethics **in HRM 4.1** ethics in HRM 4.1

WRITING IT WRONG

Most candidates for white-collar jobs prepare a résumé and submit it to prospective employers. They also complete the application form, answering questions required by employers for comparison purposes. Some recruitment agencies noticed during the last recession that résumé padding increased. Applicants were "stretching" the dates of their employment, misleading employers about the nature of their duties, and misrepresenting their salaries. While you are writing a résumé, adding three months to your previous employment, saying you were a night auditor instead of clerk, and adding $950 to your last salary seem like relatively harmless lies.

What are the facts? Studies of "creative" résumé writing indicate that about 30% of résumés report incorrect dates, 11% misrepresent reasons for leaving, and others exaggerate education attainments or omit criminal records. The probability is that about two-thirds of employers check references. Some former employers give only dates of employment and previous salary ranges.

Most organizations require you to sign a statement saying that the information you supply is true, and that if it is not you will be dismissed. Some cases of résumé padding have been heavily publicized. A Toronto Stock Exchange manager was dismissed for lying about having a master's degree. A Member of Parliament listed an ILB on his résumé, which normally stands for International Baccalaureate of Law, but which he claimed stood for Incomplete Baccalaureate of Law. In one heart-wrenching case, a person who was ready to retire was found to have lied about his age decades earlier to get a job. On discovery, he was dismissed and lost his pension. In another case, a Canadian businessman was sentenced to eight months in jail in New Zealand for lying on his résumé, by listing false qualifications, such as an MBA.

In a labour market where there are too many people chasing too few jobs, candidates will also lie on their résumés, but do so by dropping experience and educational qualifications. This practice, called "stripping," is used because job seekers are ready to take any job in order to survive or to hold them over until the jobs they really want are available.

Source: E. Urquhart, "Should We Edit Our Job Skills?" *The Globe and Mail*, June 20, 2003: C1; P. Waldie, "Davy Sentenced to Eight Months in N. Z. Court," *The Globe and Mail*, May 30, 2002: B6.

10MinuteResume.com
www.10minuteresume.com

University of Waterloo
www.adm.uwaterloo.ca/ infocecs/CRC/manual/ resumes.html

Career Magazine
www.careermag.com

JobSearchTech
http://jobsearchtech.com

Students can practise reading and analyzing résumés online at these sites:

- **www.10minuteresume.com**
- **www.adm.uwaterloo.ca/infocecs/CRC/manual/resumes.html**
- **www.careermag.com**
- **http://jobsearchtech.com**

Many managers remain unclear about the questions they can ask on an application form. While most know they should steer clear of such issues as age, race, marital status, and sexual orientation, other issues are less clear. The following are some suggestions for putting together an application form:

- *Application date.* The applicant should date the application. This helps managers know when the form was completed and gives them an idea of the time limit (for example, one year) that the form should be on file.
- *Educational background.* The applicant should also provide grade school, high school, college, and university attendance—but not the dates attended, since that can be connected with age.

- *Experience.* Virtually any questions that focus on work experience related to the job are permissible.
- *Arrests and criminal convictions.* Questions about arrests, convictions, and criminal records are to be avoided. If bonding is a requirement, ask if the individual can be bonded.
- *Country of citizenship.* Such questions are not permitted. It is allowable to ask if the person is legally entitled to work in Canada.
- *References.* It is both permissible and advisable that the names, addresses, and phone numbers of references be provided. (References are covered in more detail below.)
- *Disabilities.* Employers should avoid asking applicants if they have physical disabilities or health problems, if they have ever received psychiatric care or have been hospitalized, or if they have received workers' compensation.[31]

The Employment Interview

Traditionally, the employment interview has played a very important role in the selection process—so much so that it is rare to find an instance where an employee is hired without some sort of interview. Depending on the type of job, applicants may be interviewed by one person, by members of a work team, or by other individuals in the organization. While researchers have raised some doubts about its validity, the interview remains a mainstay of selection because (1) it is especially practical when there are only a small number of applicants; (2) it serves other purposes, such as public relations; and (3) interviewers maintain great faith and confidence in their judgments. Nevertheless, the interview can be plagued by problems of subjectivity and personal bias. In such cases, some interviewers' judgments are more valid than those of others in the evaluation of applicants. Remember, the purpose of the interview is to gather relevant information to determine if the candidate has the skills, abilities, and knowledge to be successful on the job in the organization. However, it is also critical that the interview questions are based on the work requirements (as determined through the job analysis) and specific knowledge required for the job. Further, the interviewer needs to have good training and use a consistent approach to questions and the rating used for responses to the questions.[32]

Interviewing Methods

Objective 8

Employment or selection interviews differ according to the methods used to obtain information and to find out an applicant's attitudes, feelings, and behaviours. Organizations have a variety of methods to choose from. Further, depending on the number of interviews, more than one method may be used.

One-on-One   Most often, the first face-to-face interview occurs between the applicant and the interviewer. The interviewer could be an HR professional or a supervisor. Questions are asked and observations are made of both the interviewer and the applicant. The structure of the questions could be behavioural description interview (BDI), situational, or non-directive. (The different types of questions are explained below.)

Panel or Group Interview   This type of interview involves a panel of interviewers who question and observe a single candidate. In a typical **panel or group interview**, the candidate meets with several interviewers who take turns asking questions. After the interview, the interviewers pool their observations to reach a consensus about the suitability of the candidate. It is reported that panel interviews provide several significant advantages over traditional one-to-one interviews, including a better measure of the

Panel interview
An interview in which a board of interviewers questions and observes a single candidate

candidate's attributes, greater acceptance of the decision, and shorter decision time.[33] During the interview, the panel may use structured questions, situational questions, BDI questions, or a combination of all three.

Telephone Interview   Generally, organizations are doing more interviews today than they have done in the past. Much of this is caused by the need to make a better hire decision than in the past. Companies have assessed that a poor decision can be very costly and want to minimize the costs. Therefore, many companies use a telephone interview as the first interview in the screening process. This interview can be conducted by someone from the company, or with the advent of technology, companies can use software where applicants are asked to respond to questions by touching a keypad.

Internet-based Interview   The increased use of technology has not only helped in creating a way to recruit job applicants, technology has also enabled organizations to pre-screen or assess applicants online. A growing number of organizations have been using online assessment tools to help with the interview process. Some companies will assess online using the GMA (general mental ability) tool or personality profiles. Other companies might use online information to conduct background checks. Blockbuster and Home Depot use a variety of assessment tools. In order to make maximum use of online assessment, some organizations have developed video-based simulations that can assess how a candidate would handle a particular situation. A company may wish to assess the selling skills of applicants by having a computer screen that shows two people engaged in a conversation with several captions to choose from. The responses can then be processed against desired responses to assess the fit of the candidate.[34]

In addition to the benefits of objectivity, some research evidence suggests that applicants may be less likely to engage in "impression management" in computerized interviews than in face-to-face interviews. So far, organizations have used the computer mainly as a complement to rather than as a replacement for conventional interviews.[35]

Types of Interview Questions

Regardless of the type of interview method used, questions must be asked of the applicant. In addition, for an interview to be reliable, the questions must be stated in such a way that the same questions are asked of each applicant. Listed below are the types of interview questions typically used.

The Behavioural Description Interview   The leading type of interview question being used is a **behavioural description interview (BDI)**. A BDI question focuses on real work incidents, not hypothetical situations as a situational interview question does. The BDI format asks job applicants what they actually did in a given situation. For example, to assess a potential manager's ability to handle a problem employee, an interviewer might ask, "Tell me about the last time you disciplined an employee." Or the format might be this sequence:

1. Describe a situation when you disciplined an employee.
2. What was the action taken?
3. What were the results?

Manager's Toolkit 4.4 provides an example of a BDI question and approach for interviewing someone for a front-desk position in a hotel.

Such an approach to interviewing is based on solid research that past performance is the best predictor of future performance. You will notice that with this type of interview, the

Behavioural description interview (BDI)
Question about what a person actually did in a given situation

Manager's Toolkit **4.4** Manager's Toolkit 4.4

SAMPLE BDI INTERVIEW QUESTION

You are being considered for work in our hotel. As we encounter difficult situations with our customers, please describe a time you had to tell a customer that there was no reservation for a room. What action did you take? What were the results?

Some additional clarification might be gained from the following questions:

Was there any aspect of your decision that you were uncertain about?

Did the customer have information that you didn't have?

Could anyone overhear the customer?

What decision did you finally make?

---

questions can produce a variety of responses. The interviewer usually will clarify or ask further questions to get the necessary information. Many more organizations are using BDI questions to better assess the applicant's ability to perform successfully in the organization's environment. If you have recently looked for work, you may have encountered BDI questions.

This type of interview question is being used more for a number of reasons:

1. Questions are based on the job and are directly related to the skills necessary.
2. Answers are more easily rated against established criteria.
3. Information can be readily integrated with other screening tools such as tests.[36]

Recent research indicates the behavioural description interview is more effective than the situation interview for hiring higher-level positions, such as general managers and executives.[37]

Structured question
Question which has an established set of answers

The Structured Question   More attention is being given to using **structured questions** as a result of employment equity requirements and a concern for increasing the validity of selection decisions.[38] Because a structured question is based on job requirements and an established set of answers against which applicant responses can be rated, they provide a more consistent basis for evaluating job candidates.

Structured questions are more likely to provide the type of information needed for making sound decisions. They also help to reduce the possibility of legal charges of discrimination. Employers must be aware that any interview is highly vulnerable to legal attack and that more challenges (human rights and grievances) in this area can be expected in the future.

Situational question
Question in which an applicant is given a hypothetical incident and asked how he or she would respond to it

The Situational Question   One variation of a structured question is called a **situational question**. With this type of question, an applicant is given a hypothetical incident and asked to respond to it. The applicant's response is then evaluated relative to pre-established benchmark standards. Interestingly, many organizations are using situational questions to select new college graduates. Manager's Toolkit 4.5 shows a sample situational question used to select systems analysts at a chemical plant.

Guidelines for Employment Interviewers

There have been several reviews of research studies on the employment interview.[39] Each review discusses and evaluates numerous studies concerned with such questions as "What traits can be assessed in the interview?" and "How do interviewers reach their decisions?" Manager's Toolkit 4.6 presents some of the major findings of these studies. It shows that information is available that can be used to increase the validity of interviews.

Manager's Toolkit **4.5** Manager's Toolkit 4.5

SAMPLE SITUATIONAL INTERVIEW QUESTION

Question:

It is the night before your scheduled vacation. You are all packed and ready to go. Just before you get into bed, you receive a phone call from the plant. A problem has arisen that only you can handle. You are asked to come in to take care of things. What would you do in this situation?

Record Answer:

_____
_____
_____

Scoring Guide:

Good: "I would go in to work and make certain that everything is okay. Then I would go on vacation."

Good: "There are no problems that only I can handle. I would make certain that someone qualified was there to handle things."

Fair: "I would try to find someone else to deal with the problem."

Poor: "I would go on vacation."

Training has been shown to dramatically improve the competence of interviewers.[40] If not done on a continuing basis, training should at least be done periodically for managers, supervisors, and HR representatives who conduct interviews. Interviewer training programs should include practice interviews conducted under guidance. Some variation in technique is only natural. However, the following list presents ten ground rules for employment interviews that are commonly accepted and supported by research findings.

1. *Establish an interview plan.* Determine the areas and specific questions to be covered. Review job requirements, application or résumé data, test scores, and other available information before seeing the applicant.
2. *Establish and maintain rapport.* This is accomplished by greeting the applicant pleasantly, by explaining the purpose of the interview, by displaying sincere interest in the applicant, and by listening carefully.
3. *Be an active listener.* Strive to understand, comprehend, and gain insight into what is only suggested or implied. A good listener's mind is alert, and facial expressions and posture usually reflect this fact.
4. *Pay attention to nonverbal cues.* An applicant's facial expressions, gestures, body position, and movements often provide clues to that person's attitudes and feelings. Interviewers should be aware of what they themselves are communicating nonverbally.
5. *Provide information as freely and honestly as possible.* Answer the applicant's questions fully and frankly. Present a realistic picture of the job.
6. *Use questions effectively.* To obtain a truthful answer, questions should be phrased as objectively as possible, giving no indication of what response is desired.
7. *Separate facts from inferences.* During the interview, record factual information. Later, record inferences or interpretations of the facts. Compare inferences with those of other interviewers.
8. *Recognize biases and stereotypes.* One typical bias is for interviewers to consider strangers who have interests, experiences, and backgrounds similar to their own to be more acceptable. Stereotyping involves forming generalized opinions of how

Manager's Toolkit 4.6 Manager's Toolkit 4.6

MAJOR FINDINGS FROM RESEARCH STUDIES ON THE INTERVIEW

1. Structured interviews are more reliable than unstructured interviews.

2. Interviewers are influenced more by unfavourable than by favourable information.

3. Inter-rater reliability is increased when there is a greater amount of information about the job to be filled.

4. A bias is established early in the interview, and this tends to be followed by either a favourable or an unfavourable decision.

5. Intelligence is the trait most validly estimated by an interview, but the interview information adds nothing to test data.

6. Interviewers can explain why they feel an applicant is likely to be an unsatisfactory employee but not why the applicant may be satisfactory.

7. Factual written data seem to be more important than physical appearance in determining judgments. This increases with interviewing experience.

8. An interviewee is given a more extreme evaluation (positive/negative) when preceded by an interviewee of opposing value (positive/negative).

9. Interpersonal skills and motivation are probably best evaluated by the interview.

10. Allowing the applicant time to talk makes rapid first impressions less likely and provides a larger behaviour sample.

11. Nonverbal as well as verbal interactions influence decisions.

12. Experienced interviewers rank applicants in the same order, although they differ in the proportion that they will accept. Experienced interviewers tend to be more selective than less experienced ones.

Canadian Human Rights Commission

www.chrc-ccdp.gc.ca

people of a given gender, race, or ethnic background appear, think, feel, and act. Also, interviewers will sometimes rate one competency very high, such as leadership, and assume that all other competencies are equally as high (halo effect). Likewise, an interviewer may consider all competencies average even though there is evidence of either poor or excellent job performance (central tendency).

9. *Control the course of the interview.* Stick to the interview plan. Provide the applicant with ample opportunity to talk, but maintain control of the situation in order to gather the information required.

10. *Standardize the questions asked.* To increase reliability and avoid discrimination, ask the same questions of all applicants for a particular job. Keep careful notes; record facts, impressions, and any relevant information, including what was told to the applicant.

Employers have found it advisable to provide interviewers with instructions on how to avoid potentially discriminatory questions in their interviews. The examples of appropriate and inappropriate questions shown in Figure 4.4 may serve as guidelines for application forms as well as pre-employment interviews. Complete guidelines may be developed from current information available from the office of the Canadian Human Rights Commission (or check the Web site at **www.chrc-ccdp.gc.ca**). Once the individual is hired, the information needed but not asked in the interview may be obtained if there is a valid need for it and if it does not lead to discrimination.

FIGURE 4.4 Appropriate and Inappropriate Interview Questions

	Appropriate Questions	Inappropriate Questions
National or ethnic origin	Are you legally entitled to work in Canada?	Where were you born?
Age	Have you reached the minimum or maximum age for work, as defined by the law?	How old are you?
Sex	How would you like to be referred to during the interview?	What are your child-care arrangements?
Marital status	As travel is part of the requirement of our position, would you foresee any problems meeting this obligation?	What does your spouse do for a living? Is there travel involved? Who takes care of the children when you are away?
Disabilities	Do you have any conditions that could affect your ability to do the job?	Do you use drugs or alcohol?
Height and weight	(Ask nothing.)	How tall are you? How much do you weigh?
Address	What is your address?	What were your addresses outside Canada?
Religion	Would you be able to work the following schedules?	What are your religious beliefs?
Criminal record	Our job requires that our employees be bonded.	Are you bondable? Have you ever been arrested?
Affiliations	As an engineer, are you a member of the engineering society?	What religious associations do you belong to?

As a final helpful hint for interviews, applicants need to be provided with all aspects of the job, both desirable and undesirable (called a realistic job preview), so that the applicants may self-select out of the selection process if they feel they would not be satisfied with the job. This helps avoid production losses and costs associated with low job satisfaction that can result in the person leaving the organization.

Employment Tests

An employment test is an objective and standardized way to assess a person's KSAs, competencies, and other characteristics in relation to other individuals.[41] When an organization decides to use a particular employment test, it is critical that the attribute or skill being tested is used in the work. For example, if someone's keyboarding skills are tested and yet the job doesn't have any tasks that require keyboarding, it would be inappropriate to use that test. Again, the purpose of tests is to gather additional information on the candidate so that job performance in the organization can be predicted.

More and more organizations are using tests as part of the information-gathering activity on applicants.[42] Employers are less fearful about legal challenges to the use of employment tests since it has become easier to demonstrate the validity of those tests.[43] If a good test is used and it measures the person's capabilities in relation to the work, it is a better source of information than interviewing.[44]

Types of Employment Tests

Aptitude tests
Measures of a person's capacity to learn or acquire skills

Achievement tests
Measures of what a person knows or can do right now

Employment tests may be classified in different ways. Generally, they are viewed as measuring either **aptitude** (capacity to learn or acquire skills) or **achievement** (what a person knows or can do right now).

Cognitive Ability Tests   Cognitive ability tests measure mental capabilities, such as general intelligence, verbal fluency, numerical ability, and reasoning ability. A variety of paper-and-pencil tests measure cognitive abilities, including the General Aptitude Test Battery (GATB), the Graduate Management Aptitude Test (GMAT), and the Bennett Mechanical Comprehension Test. Figure 4.5 shows some items that could be used to measure different cognitive abilities.

Although cognitive ability tests can be developed to measure very specialized areas such as reading comprehension and spatial relations, many experts believe that the validity of cognitive ability tests simply reflects their connection to general intelligence. Measures of general intelligence (e.g., IQ) have been shown to be good predictors of performance across a wide variety of jobs.[45]

Personality and Interest Inventories   Whereas cognitive ability tests measure a person's mental capacity, personality tests measure personal characteristics such as extroversion, agreeableness, and openness to experience. While the ability for such tests to predict job performance has been quite low, recent research indicates that if used with cognitive ability tests, the predictive value increases.[46] Personality tests can be problematic if they inadvertently discriminate against individuals who would otherwise perform effectively. Therefore, it is generally not recommended that personality tests be used for background information when selecting employees.

Physical Ability Tests   In addition to learning about a job candidate's mental capabilities, employers may need to assess a person's physical abilities as well. Particularly for demanding and potentially dangerous jobs like those held by firefighters and police officers, physical abilities such as strength and endurance tend to be good predictors not only of

Some employers use tests, such as keyboarding, to provide additional information for making a selection decision.

FIGURE 4.5   Sample Measures of Cognitive Ability

Verbal	1. What is the meaning of the word "surreptitious"?

      a. covert   c. lively
      b. winding   d. sweet

    2. How is the noun clause used in the following sentence? "I hope that I can learn this game."

      a. subject   c. direct object
      b. predicate nominative   d. object of the preposition

Quantitative   3. Divide 50 by 0.5 and add 5. What is the result?

      a. 25   c. 95
      b. 30   d. 105

    4. What is the value of 144^2?

      a. 12   c. 288
      b. 72   d. 20736

Reasoning   5. _____ is to boat as snow is to _____ .

      a. Sail, ski   c. Water, ski
      b. Water, winter   d. Engine, water

    6. Two women played 5 games of chess. Each woman won the same number of games, yet there were no ties. How can this be?

      a. There was a forfeit.   c. They played different people.
      b. One player cheated.   d. One game is still in progress.

Mechanical   7. If gear A and gear C are both turning counterclockwise, what is happening to gear B?

      a. It is turning counterclockwise.   c. It remains stationary.
      b. It is turning clockwise.   d. The whole system will jam.

A   B   C

Answers: 1. a, 2. c, 3. d, 4. d, 5. c, 6. c, 7. b

performance, but of accidents and injuries.[47] A physical ability test is not the same as a medical exam. Some organizations may still require a medical exam prior to actually starting employment to ensure there is no medical condition that could preclude the employee from successfully performing the work. However, more and more organizations are no longer doing medical exams due to privacy issues or potential challenges of discrimination.

Job Sample Tests   Job sample tests, or work sample tests, require the applicant to perform tasks that are actually a part of the work required on the job. Like job knowledge tests, job sample tests are constructed from a carefully developed outline that experts agree includes the major job functions; the tests are thus considered content-valid. They are often used to measure skills for office and clerical jobs. Job sample tests

Certain jobs require people who can cope with potentially dangerous situations. The aftermath of this Alberta tornado put workers to the test.

have also been devised for many diverse jobs: a map-reading test for traffic control officers, a lathe test for machine operators, a complex coordination test for pilots, an in-basket test for managers, a group discussion test for supervisors, a judgment and decision-making test for administrators, to name a few.

Drug Testing The Canadian Human Rights Commission and some of its provincial counterparts have issued policies on employment-related drug testing. Addiction to drugs or alcohol is considered a handicap, and the employer is to be guided by legislation and by practices such as workplace accommodation. Syncor Canada, a world leader in mining and extracting crude oil, feels that drug testing of heavy equipment operators could be justified on safety grounds, but not for those in an office environment.[48]

If the employer has established that drug testing is job-related—typically, this involves safety issues—the candidate must be informed that job offers are conditional on the successful passing of a drug test and that this test will be required during the course of employment. The employer then has the right to demand a medical examination. If an employee refuses, he or she can be dismissed. Toronto-Dominion Bank, Imperial Oil, and the Federal Transport Department all use drug testing as part of the selection process.

Reference Checks

Organizations use both the mail and the telephone to check references. But while references are commonly used to screen and select employees, they have not proved successful for predicting employee performance. Written letters of reference are notoriously inflated, and this limits their validity. Generally, telephone checks are preferable because they save time and provide for greater candour. At Intuit, the Edmonton, Alberta, software company that produces Quicken, managerial applicants are asked to provide between five and nine references who are then called and asked specific job-related questions.

An employer has no legal obligation to provide a former employee with a reference. To avoid liability, many employers are providing a perfunctory letter of reference, which supplies only the name, employment dates, last position with the company, and final salary. New privacy legislation being enacted by provinces will make employers even more cautious. However, inadequate reference checking can contribute to high turnover, employee theft, and white-collar crime. By using sources in addition to former employers, organizations can obtain valuable information about an applicant's character and habits. Telephone interviews are most effective and one key question that is particularly effective in screening is to ask "Would you re-hire this employee?" Some employers prefer to outsource reference checking to professional firms, such as Intelysis Employment Screening Services in Toronto, Ontario. The most common problems found by reference checkers, in about 40 percent of the cases, are candidates listing family members as former supervisors, gaps in employment not shown on the résumé, incorrect start and end dates, false academic credentials, and incorrect job titles.[49]

Those individuals supplying references must do so in a responsible manner without making statements that are damaging or cannot be substantiated. To aid employers in ensuring appropriate reference checks are done, a new association (National Association of Professional Background Screeners) was formed to create and promote standards when screening job applicants.[50]

Inadequate reference checking can contribute to high turnover or difficulties with the employee. Further, organizations could face legal liability issues if inadequate reference checks were done (see Chapter 9). Remember, the reference check is to get relevant information to predict whether the person will be a good match with the organization and is capable of performing the work successfully. Manager's Toolkit 4.7 provides some sample questions to use when doing reference checks.

Reaching a Selection Decision

While all of the steps in the selection process are important, the most critical step is the decision to accept or reject applicants. Because of the cost of placing new employees on the payroll, the short probationary period in many organizations, and human rights considerations, the final decision must be as sound as possible. Thus it requires systematic

Manager's Toolkit **4.7** Manager's Toolkit 4.7

SAMPLE REFERENCE CHECK QUESTIONS

1. How long has the person been employed in your organization?

2. Describe their attendance pattern.

3. What are the person's strengths?

4. What are some areas the person needs to develop?

5. Would you rehire?

6. Describe the person's ability to work with others or in a team.

consideration of all the relevant information about applicants. It is common to use summary forms and checklists to ensure that all the pertinent information has been included in the evaluation of applicants.

Summarizing Information about Applicants

Fundamentally, an employer is interested in what an applicant both can do and will do. An evaluation of candidates on the basis of assembled information should focus on these two factors, as shown in Figure 4.6. The "can-do" factors include knowledge and skills, as well as the aptitude (the potential) for acquiring new knowledge and skills. The "will-do" factors include motivation, interests, and other personality characteristics. Both factors are essential to successful performance on the job. The employee who has the ability (can do) but is not motivated to use it (will not do) is little better than the employee who lacks the necessary ability.

Specific criteria must be established under the various factors, especially for the "can-do" factors. For example, if a person is being hired as a call-centre agent, one of the abilities might be to "input data quickly on a computerized system." In most call centre environments, there are performance standards regarding the amount of time it would take to input the average call centre information. The standard would also identify extremely poor performance. This would then be a specific level below which an applicant would not be deemed suitable for the job.

A useful approach to ensuring the criteria is appropriate and conforms to legal requirements is the OUCH test: Objective, Uniform in application, Consistent in effect, Has job relatedness.

Making a selection decision is no different than making any other type of management decision: identifying criteria and weighting of the criteria needs to be done. For practice on this, see the exercise at the end of this chapter in "Developing Your Skills."

It is much easier to measure what individuals can do than what they will do. The can-do factors are readily evident from test scores and verified information. What the individual will do can only be inferred. Responses to interview and application-form questions may be used as a basis for obtaining information for making inferences about what an individual will do.

Decision Strategy

The strategy used for making personnel decisions for one category of jobs may differ from that used for another category. The strategy for selecting managerial and executive personnel, for example, will differ from that used in selecting clerical and technical personnel.

FIGURE 4.6 "Can-Do" and "Will-Do" Factors in Selection

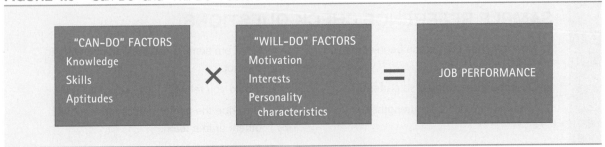

While many factors are to be considered in hiring decisions, the following are some of the questions that managers must consider:

1. Should the individuals be hired according to their highest potential or according to the existing needs of the organization?
2. At what grade or wage level should the individual be started?
3. Should initial selection be concerned primarily with an ideal match of the employee to the job, or should potential for advancement in the organization be considered?
4. To what extent should those who are not qualified but are qualifiable be considered?
5. Should overqualified individuals be considered?
6. What effect will a decision have on meeting employment equity plans and diversity considerations?

The Final Decision

The line manager makes the decision as to who gets hired. Therefore, it is important that the manager understand the importance of the steps necessary to make a good decision. In large organizations, notifying applicants of the decision and making job offers is often the responsibility of the HR department. This department will confirm the details of the job, working arrangements, wages, and so on, and specify a deadline by which the applicant

HRM and **the law 4.1** HRM and the law 4.1

LEGAL IMPLICATIONS OF HIRING PROCESS

When making a hiring decision, managers must ensure that facts are used when assessing qualifications. In a case between the National Bank of Canada and an applicant, it was determined by the Canadian Human Rights Commission that this was not done.

Specifically, an applicant who identified herself as a transgendered individual applied for part-time work in the bank's call centre, TelNat. TelNat continually recruited new staff as it had a 20 to 30% turnover rate. During the initial application review stage, the TelNat staff noted that the applicant had a broad and varied background—including a law degree and an MBA, and had had a successful career as a management consultant. All of her work and education, however, had occurred as a male. The applicant indicated during the interview that she wished to

reorient her life and career. She also wished a prospective employer to know the full background and provided information to TelNat representatives on how other large North American financial institutions had developed policies and practices for hiring such individuals.

The various stages of the screening process went well, including three interviews, until the call centre manager made a final decision. At that point, a decision was made that the person lacked experience in customer sales and service. The commission in analyzing the facts of the information determined that she had extensive background in customer sales and service. Further, notes on the résumé by TelNat indicated that it agreed she had the necessary background.

The commission concluded that the applicant had not been hired based on sex.

Source: Canadian Human Rights Tribunal, Tribunal canadien des droits de la personne Micheline Montreuil, Complainant, and Canadian Human Rights Commission, and National Bank of Canada, 2004 CHRT 72004/02/05.

must reach a decision. In smaller organizations without an HR practitioner, the manager will notify the candidates. Therefore, if there is an HR department, it is valuable to forge a strong partnership with HR in order to gain their valuable technical and legal assistance.

To better understand the implications of a poor hiring process, read HRM and the Law 4.1.

SUMMARY

1. Discuss the steps in human resource planning.
   - Forecast demand for labour in the organization.
   - Determine the supply of labour—both external and internal to the organization.
   - Identify the gap between demand and supply.
   - Develop action plans to close or eliminate the gap.

2. Describe the relationship between planning, recruiting, and selecting people to work with the organization.
   - As organizations plan for their future, supervisors and managers at all levels must play an active role in planning for future people requirements.
   - It is critical that the organization have the right number and type of employees available to implement a chosen business plan.
   - Managers play a key role in planning for the human resources necessary to achieve the business plan.

3. Explain the advantages and disadvantages of recruiting from within the organization.
   - By recruiting from within, an organization can capitalize on previous investments made in recruiting, selecting, training, and developing its current employees.
   - Internal promotions can reward employees for past performance and send a signal to other employees that their future efforts will pay off.
   - A disadvantage can be the inbreeding of ideas and attitudes.

4. Explain the advantages and disadvantages of external recruitment.
   - External recruitment can bring in new ideas and acquire people with specialized skills.
   - Constraints on the organization, such as a legislated employment equity plan, may lead to a different pool of applicants than what the manager may want.

5. Explain the objectives of the selection process.
   - The selection process attempts to get the right person with the right skills at the right time in the right job.

6. Describe the typical steps in the selection process.
   - Typical steps start with the receipt of an application form, then an initial interview, possible employment tests, an interview with the supervisor, reference checks, and then a hiring decision.

7. Identify the various sources of information used for selection decisions.
   - Interviews
   - Application forms or résumés
   - References
   - Employment tests

8. Discuss the different approaches to conducting an employment interview.
   - Unstructured, wherein the interviewer is free to pursue whatever approach and sequence of topics might seem appropriate.
   - Structured, wherein each applicant receives the same set of questions, which have pre-established answers.
   - Situational, in which candidates are asked about hypothetical situations and how they would handle them.
   - Behavioural descriptions of previous work experiences.
   - Interviews can be conducted by a single individual, a panel, or via a computer interface.
9. Explain the value of different types of employment tests.
   - More objective than the interview.
   - Can provide a broader sampling of behaviour and skills.

Need to Know

- Purpose of human resource planning
- Definition of recruitment
- Various recruitment sources
- Definition and purpose of selection
- Typical steps in selection process
- Types of interview methods

Need to Understand

- Advantages and disadvantages of internal or external recruitment
- Use of tests and interviews in selection decision
- Applications and interview questions in relation to human rights legislation
- Importance of good decision making in hiring

Key Terms

achievement tests 136	recruitment 113
aptitude tests 136	reliability 126
behavioural description interview (BDI) 131	selection 125
human resource planning 108	situational question 132
internal job posting 115	staffing table 111
labour market 117	structured question 132
management forecasts 111	trend analysis 110
Markov analysis 111	validity 127
panel interview 130	

REVIEW QUESTIONS

1. Distinguish between the quantitative and qualitative approaches to forecasting human resource requirements.
2. What are the comparative advantages and disadvantages of filling openings from internal sources? From external sources?

3. If you were looking to hire for the following jobs, where might you recruit? (List both internal and external sources.)

   - Data entry clerk
   - Computer technician
   - Supervisor for retail store
   - Welder
   - Pharmacist
   - Plumber

4. Discuss some of the employment problems faced by members of the designated groups.
5. What are some of the problems that arise in checking references furnished by job applicants? Are there any solutions to these problems?
6. What characteristics do job knowledge tests and job sample tests have that often make them more acceptable to the examinees than other types of tests?
7. Personality tests, like other tests used in employee selection, have been under attack for several decades. What are some of the reasons applicants find personality tests objectionable? On what basis could their use for selection purposes be justified?
8. Compare briefly the major types of employment interviews described in this chapter. Which type would you prefer to conduct? Why?

CRITICAL THINKING QUESTIONS

1. You have recently applied for work at a large accounting firm as a junior accounting clerk. Part of the screening process will include a panel interview with the people you would be working with. What questions do you think they will ask you? What questions would you ask of them?
2. You are starting your own company and need the following positions filled:

   - Receptionist
   - Sales people
   - Information technology people

   Identify two or three key job requirements for each position and then develop the selection criteria for each requirement. What selection tools or techniques would you use to assess each criterion?
3. You have just been asked to assist in hiring a new administrative assistant for a medium-sized manufacturing company. However, before starting the process, the owner of the company wants to know how much time it will take and what the cost will be. Estimate the number of staff hours and how many dollars that might be spent on this hiring.
4. Identify the steps that were used to hire you for a job that you either have now or had recently. What steps, if any, do you feel ought to have been included?

DEVELOPING YOUR SKILLS

jobsearchtech.com

http://jobsearchtech.com

CareerInfoNet

www.careernet.org

1. Working in small groups of five or six, develop an advertisement for an instructor in your college. Ensure that you identify the skills, knowledge, and abilities required. Debrief with the entire class, share results, and identify common themes.

2. Working in groups of four to five students, list three recent times you have been interviewed. Working with this list, identify the type of interview conducted. Determine if the interview was valid and whether or not it was effective in attracting you to work for the organization.

3. Access **http://jobsearchtech.com** and click onto the link "Résumé." Pick one of the related links with sample résumés. Review the sample résumé and then prepare your résumé. Bring your résumé to class and then working in pairs, critique each other's and identify what is similar and what is different in the formatting of each. Share your findings with the rest of the class.

4. Access **www.careernet.org**; click the link "Explore Careers." Identify at least three careers (be as specific as you can) that might interest you. Prepare a one- to two-page summary explaining why each career is interesting to you. Also explain how useful each Web site was in helping you explore those possible careers.

Case Study

Filling the Shoes

Bata Ltd. is a multinational shoe company, headquartered in Canada. It has more than 55,000 employees worldwide, located in 67 subsidiaries. Every single subsidiary has a succession plan in place. Each senior position has three possible successors: a person who could fill the job immediately; a second who could be ready in two years; and a third who could be considered in five years. There are developmental plans for each employee on the chart; these plans are contained in a master file that lists such things as the highest position the employee can be expected to attain, the training programs completed, and areas that need improvement.

The methods for developing these senior managers are varied. For example, Bata has four levels of management training: (1) for high-potential middle managers; (2) for potential company managers; (3) for executive managers who are ready to lead the company now; and (4) for existing company managers. Employees know who is on the chart.

For those not currently part of the management succession plan, there are annual opportunities to earn a place. Formal appraisal programs identify those who are doing well and make recommendations for further training. Another method for developing managers is to offer them temporary "testing" assignments. Managers can replace people on vacation for trial periods to test and upgrade their skills. A system like this one runs the risk of simply repeating the managerial styles and thinking of the previous generation. So Bata, very conscious of the need to look for new blood (i.e., new ways of thinking and acting), also identifies people who have suggested new business opportunities and who are open to divergent perspectives.

Source: Adapted from D. Brown, "You Have to Become Deputy Before You Become Sheriff," *Canadian HR Reporter,* February 14, 2000: 9.

Questions

1. Bata Ltd. has a plan for replacing senior managers. Should this plan be extended to lower levels? Would the plan be similar, or does the training of supervisors and middle managers require different selection criteria and developmental methods?
2. What are the advantages and disadvantages of making employees aware of who is part of the succession chart?

Case Study 2

Aptitude Tests at an Electronics Corporation

An electronics plant in Midland, Ontario, has begun using aptitude tests as part of its selection process. Before they will be considered for new job openings and for promotions, new candidates must pass eight different aptitude tests. One test for manual dexterity requires applicants to move small metal pegs from holes on one side of a board to holes on the other side as fast as they can. In another test, employees are shown pictures of two cows—one white and the other spotted—and asked, "Which cow would be easier to see from an airplane?"

The company's employees see no relationship between their jobs and the cow test; they also find it humiliating to have to move pegs on a board in order to qualify for jobs they have been doing for years. In one testing session, 80% of employees failed. The price of failure is exclusion from higher-paying and more desirable jobs. Even more shameful is the fact that people with less seniority and little plant experience are passing the aptitude tests.

The dispute is deeply rooted. The union feels that the tests are allowing management to replace experienced workers with new hires who work for less pay. The fact that test results are almost always confidential has led to suspicions that the results are being manipulated in some way. After seeing their colleagues fail the tests, some workers are so discouraged that they don't even try for new jobs or promotions. Other changes that have been introduced along with the tests include 12-hour rotating shifts, the "flexible" replacement of workers, and new computerized inspection systems.

Management defends the testing, claiming that new plants and new work methods require aptitudes such as problem solving and flexible thinking. These skills are not usually associated with the stereotype of the senior blue-collar worker. In the past, young people had no need to even graduate from high school if there was a plant in town offering big paycheques for manual labour. The tests that have been introduced discriminate against older workers with less formal education. In demand today are employees who can do many jobs, solve problems, make decisions, provide creative solutions, and function effectively as part of an empowered work team.

Source: Reprinted by permission of the author Megan Terepocki.

Questions

1. Do you see any problems with the way the company's testing program is being managed? Discuss.
2. Suggest how the program might be modified.
3. The union is fighting to eliminate the testing. On what grounds could the union base its arguments?
4. If an employee files a complaint with the Ontario Human Rights Commission on the grounds that the test discriminated against him as an older worker, what kinds of information will have to be gathered to determine the validity of the claim?

NOTES AND REFERENCES

1. Roger Moncarz and Azure Reaser, "The 2000–10 Job Outlook in Brief," *Occupational Outlook Quarterly* 46, no. 1 (Spring 2002): 2–47.
2. Kenneth J. McBey, *Strategic Human Resources Planning* (Scarborough, Ont.: Thomson Nelson Learning, 2000), 14.
3. Presentation to the HRMA Leadership Forum by Mark Jackson, Hay Group, November 2001.
4. Carol Stephenson, "Corporate Values Drive Global Success at Lucent Technologies," *Canadian Speeches* 13, no. 5 (November–December 1999): 23–7.
5. Statistics Canada, CANSIM II, table 282-0002, http://www.statcan.ca/english/Pgdb/labor20a.htm; Laura Cassiani, "Labour Shortages Stunts Manufacturing Growth," *Canadian HR Reporter* 13, no. 18 (October 23, 2000): 2.
6. "Bridging the Oilpatch Labour gap," *Financial Post,* March 16, 2004, FP8.
7. Peter MacDonald, "Heroes for Hard Times," *Profit 100,* http://www.profitguide.com/profit100/2002/features.asp?ID=950 (retrieved July 22, 2002).
8. David Brown, "When the War for Talent Gounds to a Halt," *Canadian HR Reporter,* April 22, 2002, 7; Kira Vermond, "Grads Find Job Hunt Tough Assignment," *The Globe and Mail,* January 30, 2002.
9. "The Retention Challenge," *Turning the Tide,* Corporate Leadership Council, Presentation Materials in June 1999 to the HRMA Leadership Forum: 8.
10. Interested readers can check out the Web sites of these companies at http://www.peoplesoft.com and http://www.sap.com.
11. Gillian Flynn, "Texas Instruments Engineers a Holistic HR," *Workforce* 77, no. 2 (February 1998): 30–35; Gillian Flynn, "Internet Recruitment Limits Demographic Scope," *Workforce* 79, no. 4 (April 2000): 85–87; Vivian Marino, "A Traffic Jam of Resumes," *The New York Times,* December 16, 2001, 3, 10.
12. Rekha Balu and L. Amante, "Kellogg Co. Shakes Up Management: Financial Officer among Those Quitting," *The Wall Street Journal,* March 4, 1999, B14; George Lazarus, "Pepsi Bottlers May Look Outside for New Chief," *Chicago Tribune,* February 12, 1999, 3; Joann S. Lublin, "Albertsons Picks an Outsider—GE Veteran Johnston—for Top Posts," *The Wall Street Journal,* April 24, 2001, B1.
13. Gary Reamey, "HR Strategies to Attract and Keep Top Talent the Edward Jones Way," *Canadian HR Reporter,* November 9, 2000, www.hrreporter.com/loginarea/members/viewing.asp? ArticleNo=364&subscriptionType=WEB (retrieved June 20, 2002).
14. "Canada's New Immigration and Refugee Protection Regulations Finalized," news release, www.hrreporter.com/loginarea/members/viewing.asp?ArticleNo=364&subscriptionType=WEB,Citizenship and Immigration Canada (retrieved June 11, 2002).
15. Karen Francola, "Better Recruiting on Corporate Web Sites," *Workforce Online,* http://www.workforce.com/archive/article/23/22/30.php (retrieved May 26, 2002).
16. Paul Lima, "Talent Shortage? That Was Yesterday," *Profit,* February–March 2002, 65.

17. President, Workopolis, HRPAO Annual Conference, 2001.

18. Sarah Fister Gale, "Internet Recruiting: Better, Cheaper, Faster," *Workforce* 80, no. 12 (December 2001): 74–77.

19. Samuel Greengard, "Putting Online Recruiting to Work," *Workforce* 77, no. 8 (August 1998): 73–76; Richard Ream, "Rules for Electronic Resumes," *Information Today* 17, no. 8 (September 2000): 24–25; Pat Curry, "Log On for Recruits," *Industry Week* 249, no. 17 (October 16, 2000): 46–54.

20. "Recruitment and Staffing," *Canadian HR Reporter*, February 11, 2002.

21. Michelle Neely Martinez, "Working With an Outside Recruiter? Get It in Writing," *HRMagazine* 46, no. 1 (January 2001): 98–105.

22. Audrey Bottjen, "The Benefits of College Recruiting," *Sales and Marketing Management* 153, no. 4 (April 2001): 12; Rhea Nagel and Jerry Bohovich, "College Recruiting in the 21st Century," *Journal of Career Planning & Employment* 61, no. 1 (Fall 2000): 36–37.

23. Monica Belcourt et al., *Managing Human Resources* (Scarborough, Ont.: Thomson Nelson, 2002), 144.

24. For additional sources on writing résumés, see Martin Yates, *Knock 'Em Dead 2002* (Avon, MA: Adams Media Corporation, 2001); Arthur Rosenberg and David Hizer, *The Résumé Handbook: How to Write Outstanding Résumés and Cover Letters for Every Situation,* 3rd ed. (Avon, MA: Adams Media Corporation, 1996); Joyce Lain Kennedy, *Résumés for Dummies* (New York: John Wiley and Sons, 2000).

25. "Top Ten Job Search Strategies," www.jobwavebc.com/jobseekers/top10.asp (retrieved May 28, 2005); "Job Search Strategies," http://youth.ednet.ns.ca/development/jobsearch.htm (retrieved May 28, 2005); "Job Search Strategies," http://www.sasknetwork.ca/html/ JobSeekers/lookingforwork/searchstrategies.htm (retrieved May 28, 2005); and other similar resources on job search techniques.

26. Uyen Vu, "FedEx Holds Managers Accountable for Diversity," *Canadian HR Reporter*, November 8, 2004, 3.

27. Claudio Fernandez-Araoz, "Hiring without Firing," *Harvard Business Review*, July–August 1999, 108–20.

28. Allison Stein Wellner, "EDS Reinvents Its Workforce," *Workforce Management Online,* http://www.workforce.com/archive/article/23/88/96.php (retrieved November 20, 2004).

29. Sara L. Rynes, Kenneth G. Brown, and Amy E. Colbert, "Seven Common Misconceptions about Human Resource Practices: Research Findings versus Practitioner Beliefs," *Academic of Management Executive*, 2002, 16, no. 3, 92–103.

30. Tammy Prater and Sara Bliss Kiser, "Lies, Lies, and More Lies," *A.A.M. Advance Management Journal* 67, no. 2 (Spring 2002): 9–14.

31. Victor M. Catano et al., *Recruitment and Selection in Canada*, 2nd ed. (Scarborough, Ont.: Thomson Nelson Learning, 2001): 48.

32. Cynthia Kay Stevens, "Antecedents of Interview Interactions, Interviewers' Ratings, and Reactions," *Personnel Psychology* 51, no. 1 (Spring 1998): 55–85; Laura Gollub Williamson, James E. Campion, Stanley B. Malos, and Mark V. Roehling, "Employment Interview on Trial: Linking Interview Structure with Litigation Outcomes," *Journal of Applied Psychology* 82, no. 6 (December 1997): 900–12; Richard A. Posthuma, Frederick Morgeson, and Michael Campion, "Beyond Employment Interview Validity: A Comprehensive Narrative Review of Recent Research and Trends over Time," *Personnel Psychology* 55, no. 1 (Spring 2002): 1–8; Frank Schmidt and Mark Rader, "Exploring the Boundary Conditions for Interview Validity: Meta-Analytic Validity Findings for a New Interview Type," *Personnel Psychology* 52, no. 2 (Summer 1999): 445–64.

33. Amelia J. Prewett-Livingston, John G. Veres III, Hubert S. Field, and Philip M. Lewis, "Effects of Race on Interview Ratings in a Situational Panel Interview," *Journal of Applied Psychology* 81, no. 2 (April 1996): 178–86; Philip L. Roth and James E. Campion, "An Analysis of the Predictive Power of the Panel Interview and Pre-Employment Tests," *Journal of Occupational and Organizational Psychology* 65 (March 1992): 51–60.

34. Igor Kotlyar and Kim Ades, "E-selection: Advancements in Assessment Technology," *Canadian HR Reporter*, April 8, 2002, 15–19.

35. Dan Hanover, "Hiring Gets Cheaper and Faster," *Sales and Marketing Management* 152, no. 3 (March 2000): 87; Linda Thornburg, "Computer-Assisted Interviewing Shortens Hiring Cycle," *HRMagazine* 43, no. 2 (February 1998): 73–79; Jessica Clark Newman et al., "The Differential Effects of Face-to-Face and Computer Interview Modes," *American Journal of Public Health* 92, no. 2 (February 2002): 294; David Mitchell, "ijob.com Recruiting Online," *Strategic Finance* 80, no. 11 (May 1999): 48–51.

36. "Guidelines for Best Practice in Selection Interviewing," SHL Group Inc., United Kingdom, 2001, 7.

37. Todd Maurer, Jerry Solamon, and Deborah Troxtel, "Relationship of Coaching with Performance in Situational Employment Interviews," *Journal of Applied Psychology* 83, no. 1 (February 1998): 128–36; Allen Huffcutt, Jeff Weekley, Willi Wiesner, Timothy Degroot, and Casey Jones, "Comparison of Situational and Behavior Description Interview Questions for Higher-Level Positions," *Personnel Psychology* 54, no. 3 (Autumn 2001): 619–44.

38. Schmidt and Rader, "Exploring the Boundary Conditions for Interview Validity: Meta-Analytic Validity Findings for a New Interview Type"; Williamson, Campion, Malos, and Roehling, "Employment Interview on Trial"; Jennifer R. Burnett and Stephan J. Motowidlo, "Relations between Different Sources of Information in the Structured

Selection Interview," *Personnel Psychology* 51, no. 4 (Winter 1998): 963–83. See also Geoffrey Colvin, "Looking to Hire the Very Best? Ask the Right Questions. Lots of Them," *Fortune* (June 21, 1999): 192–94; "Recruiting Practices That Get the EEOC's Attention," *HRMagazine* 42, no. 11 (November 1997): 60.

39. Posthuma, Morgeson, Campion, "Beyond Employment Interview Validity"; Schmidt and Rader, "Exploring the Boundary Conditions for Interview Validity."

40. Burnett and Motowidlo, "Relations between Different Sources"; Allen Huffcutt and David Woehr, "Further Analysis of Employment Interview Validity: A Quantitative Evaluation of Interviewer-Related Structuring Methods," *Journal of Organizational Behavior* 20, no. 4 (July 1999): 549–60; "LIMRA Offers New Recruiting, Assessment, and Retention Technologies," *LIMRA's MarketFacts* 19, no. 3 (May/June 2000): 15. See also Mike Frost, "Interviewing ABCs," *HRMagazine* 42, no. 3 (March 1997): 32–34.

41. For books with comprehensive coverage of testing, including employment testing, see Anne Anastasi and Susana Urbina, *Psychological Testing*, 7th ed. (Upper Saddle River, N.J.: Prentice Hall, 1997); Lee J. Cronbach, *Essentials of Psychological Testing*, 5th ed. (New York: HarperCollins, 1990).

42. Edward Prewitt, "Personality Tests in Hiring: How to Do It Right," *Harvard Management Update*, October 1998.

43. Kathryn Tyler, "Put Applicants' Skills to the Test," *HRMagazine* 45, no. 1 (January 2000): 74–80. For a counterargument, see Kevin R. Murphy and Ann Harris Shiarella, "Implications of the Multidimensional Nature of Job Performance for the Validity of Selection Tests: Multivariate Frameworks for Studying Test Validity," *Personnel Psychology* 50, no. 4 (Winter 1997): 823–54.

44. Catano et al., *Recruitment and Selection in Canada*, 2nd ed., Chapter 9.

45. Linda S. Gottfredson, "Why g Matters: The Complexity of Everyday Life," *Intelligence—A Multidisciplinary Journal*, January/February 1997, 79–132.

46. Gregory Hurtz and John Donovan, "Personality and Job Performance: The Big Five Revisited," *Journal of Applied Psychology* 85, no. 6 (December 2000): 869–79.

47. Walter C. Borman, Mary Ann Hanson, and Jerry W. Hedge, "Personnel Selection," *Annual Review of Psychology* 48 (1997): 299–337; Charles Sproule and Stephen Berkley, "The Selection of Entry-level Corrections Officers: Pennsylvania Research," *Public Personnel Management* 30, no. 3 (Fall 2001): 377–418.

48. T. Humber, "Name, Rank and Serial Number," *Canadian HR Reporter* 15, no. 10 (May 19, 2003): 1.

49. "Alberta's Suncor Says It's Reviewing Drug Testing after Human Rights Ruling," *Canada Press Newswire*, January 12, 2002.

50. Nancy Dunne, "Screeners Wanted," *Financial Post*, May 3, 2004, FE5.

PART 3

Developing People in the Organization

Chapter 5: Orientation, Training, and Development

Chapter 6: Managing Performance

Chapter 7: Compensation: Recognizing
and Rewarding Employees

CHAPTER 5

Orientation, Training, and Development

OBJECTIVES

After studying this chapter, you should be able to

1 List some of the characteristics of an effective orientation process.

2 Discuss the systems approach to training and development.

3 Describe the components of a training-needs assessment.

4 Identify the principles of learning and how they facilitate training.

5 Identify the types of training and development methods used for all levels of employees.

6 Describe the special training programs that are currently popular.

7 Explain how a career development program integrates individual and organizational needs.

8 Discuss specialized career development needs.

OUTLINE

Introduction
Orientation
Benefits of Orientation
Continuous Process
Cooperative Endeavour
Careful Planning
Follow-up and Evaluation
The Scope of Training and Development
Investments in Training
A Systems Approach to Training and Development
Phase 1: Conducting the Needs Assessment
Phase 2: Designing the Training Program
Phase 3: Implementing the Training Program
Phase 4: Evaluating the Training Program

Special Topics in Training and Development
Basic Skills Training
Team Training
Diversity Training
Career Development—Individual and Organizational Needs
Creating Favourable Conditions
Changes in HRM Practices
Specialized Development Needs
Mentoring
Specialized Career Development for a Diverse Workforce
Keeping a Career in Perspective

HRM
Close-up

Francisco Del Cueto, Chief Technology Officer, Toon Boom Animation Inc., Montreal

"Managers must give their employees time to learn the things they need to know."

Francisco Del Cueto has a cool job—he oversees 25 people who develop animation software for feature films, television, and the Internet. Winner of the 2005 Primetime Emmy Engineering Award, Toon Boom Animation of Montreal has been in business for more than a decade and has clients all over the world. Originally, the company bought USAnimation, a high-end 2D animation software now marketed as Opus, and invested significantly in research and development to bring this enterprise to its current level of quality and efficiency. Today, Toon Boom offers both consumer-level animation software used by animation hobbyists, creative professionals, and schools, and higher-end professional-level software used by both small and large studios and independent filmmakers.

Like many companies, Toon Boom uses in-house training as part of its orientation program for staff. This is where software developers, technical support experts, technical writers, and client service representatives learn about animation production and the animation software the company sells. Del Cueto finds that experienced staff make the best educators. "These people are our 'demo artists' and regularly give demonstrations for clients," he explains. "They make very effective teachers for fellow staff."

Training and development in the tech industry bring unique challenges. "There is constant change with clients always looking for products that are faster, cheaper, and offer more performance," says Del Cueto. Software developers must keep up with new technology, including new versions of the operating system and new computer hardware. The company finds that external classes, even at universities, are often not advanced enough for the company's needs. "But luckily," says Del Cueto, "our developers tend to be self-learners who prefer reading a manual and practising on a computer." Because of this, Toon Boom has a budget for books. "We also find that visits to client sites prove to be very instructive since developers can see how the technology is actually used in the context of a real production," he adds.

Toon Boom allows employees to take one class a year during business hours and will reimburse half the cost if completed successfully. As an example, an employee pursued her master's degree in building e-learning tools for advanced technical writing. When she graduated, she was reimbursed for half the tuition. The benefit was that she brought new ideas and new ways of doing things back to the company.

One big challenge Toon Boom faced was adapting its animation software to a Macintosh platform. "People really wanted to use all our products on the Mac but we didn't have the expertise in-house," explains Del Cueto. "So we hired an instructor to teach the developers and allowed them time to become adept at it. The developers then became the in-house experts and held a seminar to teach other staff." As it turned out, the group approach to learning was highly effective: "This kind of learning is also a team-building exercise. When people learn the same thing at the same time, they tend to exchange what they learn."

As far as identifying the type of training needed, Del Cueto takes his cues from the developers, technical writers, technical support experts, and service reps. He lets them tell him what training they need and how best to do it. "We go from bottom to top, definitely," he says, adding that "managers must give their employees *time* to learn the things they need to know."

INTRODUCTION

Training
The acquisition of skills, behaviours, and abilities to perform *current* work

Development
The acquisition of skills, behaviours, and abilities to perform *future* work or to solve an organizational problem

The ability for an organization to ensure its people continue to learn, grow, and develop has become critical to business success. As we noted in Chapter 1, organizations often compete on competencies—the core sets of knowledge and expertise that give them an edge over their competitors. Frequently, organizations refer to "intellectual capital," which is the combination of the "human capital" (the competencies) and the organizational support that enables the human capital to flourish.[1] Further, as individuals learn (i.e., the human capital increases), the organization has the potential to learn. It is only through individuals that the organization gains knowledge.[2] Orientation, **training**, and **development** play a central role in enabling, nurturing, and strengthening the human capital in the organization. In addition, rapidly changing technologies require that employees continuously hone their knowledge, skills, and abilities (KSAs), or "competencies," to cope with new processes and systems. As Francisco Del Cueto describes in the HRM Close-Up, his company is providing more training so that the company remains competitive. Jobs that require little skill are rapidly being replaced by jobs that require technical, interpersonal, and problem-solving skills. And, as described, the business world is constantly changing, requiring improved skills and abilities. The manager/supervisor plays a key role in ensuring that the training and development efforts are appropriate and reinforced for the individuals for whom they are responsible. Without the managers' involvement, organizational growth, success, and sustainability could be at risk. Other trends toward empowerment, total-quality management, teamwork, and international business make it necessary for managers as well as employees to develop the skills that will enable them to handle new and more demanding assignments.

ORIENTATION

 Objective   1

Orientation
Formal process of familiarizing new employees with the organization, their jobs, and their work unit and embedding organizational values, beliefs, and accepted behaviours

The first objective in the orientation process is to get new employees off to a good start. This is generally accomplished through a formal orientation program. **Orientation** is the formal process of familiarizing new employees with the organization, their job, and their work unit and embedding organizational values, beliefs, and accepted behaviours. The benefit for new employees is that it allows them to get "in sync" so that they become productive members of the organization. Orientation is a process—not a one-day event. Further, it is important to remember that orientation is a socialization process, and that how employees are treated when they first join the organization makes a huge impact on their views of their supervisors, managers, and the organization.

Benefits of Orientation

In some organizations a formal new-hire orientation process is almost nonexistent or, when it does exist, is performed in a casual manner. Some readers may remember showing up the first day on a new job, being told to work, and receiving no instructions, introductions, or support. This is unfortunate, since a number of practical and cost-effective benefits can be derived from conducting a well-run orientation. Benefits frequently reported by employers include the following:

1. Lower turnover
2. Increased productivity
3. Improved employee morale

Video-streams and video-conferencing are frequently used in remote locations to orient new employees.

4. Lower recruiting and training costs
5. Facilitation of learning
6. Reduction of the new employee's anxiety

The more time and effort an organization devotes to making new employees feel welcome, the more likely they are to identify with the organization and become valuable members of it. Unlike training, which emphasizes the "what" and "how," orientation stresses the "why." It is designed to develop in employees a particular attitude about the work they will be doing and their role in the organization. It defines the philosophy behind the rules and provides a framework for their work in that organization.

Continuous Process

**Online Orientation
Program**

http://onlineorientation.com/

Since an organization is faced with ever-changing conditions, its plans, policies, and procedures must change with these conditions. Unless current employees are kept up to date with these changes, they may find themselves embarrassingly unaware of activities to which new employees are being oriented. While the discussion that follows focuses primarily on the needs of new employees, it is important that all employees be continually reoriented to changing conditions. Many companies are using intranets (internal Web sites) and online orientation modules to keep new and current employees up to date. For an example of online orientation, check out **http://onlineorientation.com/** (Deliver the Promise Complete On-Line Orientation).

Cooperative Endeavour

For a well-integrated orientation process, cooperation between line and staff is essential. The HR department is ordinarily responsible for coordinating orientation activities and for providing new employees with information about conditions of employment, pay, benefits, and other areas not directly under a supervisor's direction. However, the supervisor has the most important role in the orientation process. New employees are interested primarily in what the supervisor says and does and what their new co-workers are like. Before the arrival of a new employee, the supervisor should inform the work group that a new worker is joining the unit. It is also common practice for supervisors or other managerial personnel to recruit co-workers to serve as volunteer "sponsors" or "buddies" for incoming employees. In addition to providing practical help to newcomers, this approach conveys an emphasis on teamwork.

Careful Planning

An orientation process can make an immediate and lasting impression on an employee that can mean the difference between the employee's success and failure at work. Thus, careful planning—with emphasis on goals, topics to be covered, and methods of organizing and presenting them—is essential Successful orientation processes emphasize the individual's needs for information, understanding, and a feeling of belonging.

To avoid overlooking items that are important to employees, many organizations devise checklists for use by those responsible for conducting the orientation. Orientation information can also be printed and given to the new employee. Companies are also beginning to use their intranets to make the information more readily available to their employees. The Manager's Toolkit 5.1 suggests items to include in an orientation checklist for supervisors. Orientation should focus on matters of immediate concern, such as important aspects of the job and organizational behaviour expectations (e.g., attendance and safety). Since orientation focuses on helping the new employee become familiar, comfortable, and productive, it is important not to overwhelm or provide too much information at one time. At Work with HRM 5.1 describes how Intuit Canada approaches the orientation process.

Manager's Toolkit **5.1** Manager's Toolkit 5.1

SUPERVISORY ORIENTATION CHECKLIST

1. A formal greeting, including introduction to colleagues

2. Explanation of job procedures, duties, and responsibilities

3. Training to be received (when and why)

4. Supervisor and organization expectations regarding attendance and behaviour norms

5. Job standards and production and service levels

6. Performance appraisal criteria, including estimated time frame to achieve peak performance

7. Conditions of employment, including hours of work, pay periods, and overtime requirements

8. Organization and work unit rules, regulations, and policies

9. Overview of health and safety expectations, as well as when specific training will occur

10. Those to notify or turn to if problems or questions arise

11. Chain of command for reporting purposes

12. An overall explanation of the organization's operation and purpose

13. A review of the organizational chart or structure indicating departments and work flow

14. Offers of help and encouragement, including a specific time each week (in the early stages of employment) for questions or coaching

at work **with HRM 5.1** at work with HRM 5.1

WOWING THE CANDIDATE

Intuit Canada, headquartered in Edmonton, Alberta, is a leading developer of financial software, including personal finance management, small business accounting, and tax preparation, with products, such as Quicken. Intuit is a top employer; it is ranked number two in Canada by the *Globe and Mail* survey and 45th of the 100 best companies to work for in America by *Fortune* magazine in 2002. What makes Intuit special is its success in a highly competitive industry. There are many factors, but evidence of its success is its low attrition rate of 3%, which is remarkable in a sector where the average turnover is 20%. Ninety-four percent of its employees report that Intuit is a "great place to work," according to their annual surveys.

Intuit is very careful about the first few days of a new employee's work life. There are too many stories about employees in other organizations showing up very excited about their new job, only to discover that no one remembers they are hired, supplies and offices are not ready, and the reporting manager is absent. Intuit is committed to wowing the candidate—now employee—on the first day. Upon arriving at work, new employees are greeted by name by the receptionist who gives them a stainless steel coffee mug engraved with their name. The hiring manager is called and arrives promptly. He knows the candidate and takes him to the workstation, showing him the computer, telephone, and office supplies. The next step is to introduce the new employee to colleagues and other team members and a "buddy" who has volunteered to guide the new employee and answer all questions for the next three weeks. New employees often struggle with simple questions, such as how does the photocopier work? Do most people bring their lunches to work? Next, the IT person arrives and helps set up voice mail, e-mail, Internet access, etc. Intuit considers it vital that when the new employee goes home that night, he should be able to answer the universal question "How was your first day on the job?" with "Wow, am I ever glad that I took this job!"

This informal orientation is completed by a formal session, in which information about the strategy, vision, plans, and history, including war stories and all the successes, is shared. A key part of this session is a discussion of Intuit values. At the end of the first week, and again at the end of the first month, feedback about the new employee's experiences is solicited on what worked, what was frustrating, and how the orientation can be improved.

CRITICAL THINKING QUESTIONS

1. What else might Intuit do to ensure that the orientation process is successful?
2. How does the orientation process at Intuit compare with an orientation process you experienced at your last job?

Source: M. Belcourt and S. Taggar, "Making Government the Best Place to Work: Building Commitment," IPAC, New Directions Series, no. 8, 2002.

Those planning an orientation process should take into account the anxiety employees feel during their first few days on the job. It is natural to experience some anxiety, but if employees are too anxious, training costs, turnover, absenteeism, and even production costs may increase. Early in the orientation, steps should be taken to reduce the anxiety level of new employees. This anxiety reduction can be accomplished by establishing specific times in which the supervisor will be available for questions or coaching.

Work911
www.work911.com/articles/
orient.htm

Furthermore, reassuring newcomers that the performance levels they are observing among their co-workers will be attained within a predetermined time frame, based on experiences with other newcomers, can decrease anxiety. This reassurance is particularly important for employees with limited work experience who are learning new skills. For additional information and tips about planning an orientation, read the article entitled "A Quick Guide to Employee Orientation" at **www.work911.com/articles/orient.htm**.

Follow-up and Evaluation

Supervisors should always check with their new employees after the first day and frequently throughout the first several weeks on the job. When all the items on the orientation checklist have been addressed, both the supervisor and the employee should sign it, and the record should then be placed in the employee's personnel file to document what has been covered. After the employee has been on the job for six months to one year, the supervisor or the HR professional should follow up to determine how effective the orientation has been. Evaluations can be conducted through in-depth interviews, questionnaires, or discussion groups.

THE SCOPE OF TRAINING AND DEVELOPMENT

Many new employees come equipped with most of the skills and capabilities needed to start work. Others may require extensive training before they are ready to make much of a contribution to the organization. All employees need some type of training and development on an ongoing basis to maintain effective performance or to adjust to new ways of work.

The term "training" is often used casually to describe any effort initiated by an organization to foster learning among its members. However, many experts make a distinction between training and development. Training tends to be more focused and oriented toward acquiring skills, behaviours, and abilities to perform current work, while development tends to be oriented more toward acquiring skills, behaviours, and abilities to perform future work or to solve an organizational problem. These terms tend to be combined into a single phrase—"training and development"—to recognize the combination of activities used by organizations to increase the abilities and capabilities of their employees.

Lastly, you often hear the word "learning." Learning refers to an ongoing change in behaviour and thinking—which is ultimately the goal of training and development.

The primary reason that organizations train new employees is to bring their KSAs up to the level required for satisfactory performance. As these employees continue on the job, additional training and development provide opportunities for them to acquire new knowledge and skills. As a result of this training, employees may be even more effective on the job and may be able to perform other jobs in other areas or at higher levels. To understand the importance of training in today's business environment, Figure 5.1 lists the skills that many employers seek.

**Conference Board of
Canada**
www.conferenceboard.ca

Investments in Training

According to a Conference Board of Canada survey, Canadian businesses spend about $859 per employee each year on formal training.[3] Overall, the average expenditure in Canada on training and development was 1.8% of payroll, and organizations

FIGURE 5.1   Workplace Skills and Capabilities

Employees want to know what employers are looking for today in skill sets. The Conference Board of Canada researched this topic and has prepared the following broad list. While all employers do not look for all of these skills, many employers look for many of these skills.

Fundamental Skills

- Read and understand information presented in different forms (e.g., words, graphs)
- Write and speak so that others understand
- Use relevant knowledge and skills (scientific, technological) to explain and clarify
- Identify the root cause of a problem
- Evaluate solutions to make a decision
- Use numbers to complete tasks, such as making estimates and verifying calculations
- Manage information by locating, gathering, and organizing information using appropriate technology and systems

Personal Management Skills

- Be flexible and adaptable
- Be honest and ethical
- Be responsible for setting goals
- Be able to work safely
- Demonstrate positive attitudes and behaviours, such as dealing with people with honesty and integrity
- Be willing to keep learning

Teamwork Skills

- Understand and contribute to the organization's goals
- Understand and work within the dynamics of the group
- Plan and make decisions with others and support the outcomes
- Respect the thoughts and opinions of others
- Adapt to changing requirements
- Understand the role of conflict in group dynamics and resolve as appropriate

Source: Adapted from Employability Skills 2000+ PDF 2000 E/F (Ottawa: The Conference Board of Canada, 2000, pdf file). Reprinted with permission of The Conference Board of Canada.

annually provided about thirty hours of training per employee.[4] The BMO Financial Group is one organization that does better than the average—it has an annual training budget of $71 million, which is 2.5% of payroll. Its employees receive on average 41 hours of annual training.[5] Ethics in HRM 5.1 describes the debate surrounding decisions to force organizations to provide training and to force employees to take training. Consistent with the trend toward recognizing employees as the source of competitive advantage, nearly half the respondents in the Conference Board survey reported that their training budgets are increasing. As well, another Conference Board of Canada report indicated that leading-edge companies considered training an investment, not a cost.[6]

In addition to formal training, more than $180 billion is spent on informal instruction that goes on every day in organizations everywhere. More and more organizations are also providing training on an "as need" basis and ensuring that it is linked to actual work experiences. For example, team training would be done as part of a team project that might be designing a new product. The types of training range from computer application skills to customer service.

A question always asked by organizations is "Will training improve organizational performance?" The answer is an unqualified yes. A study in 2000 conducted

ethics **in HRM 5.1** ethics in HRM 5.1

MANDATORY OR VOLUNTARY?

There is only one payroll training tax in North America. The Quebec government program that forces employers to spend 1% of payroll on training may not have the intended consequences of increasing training investments in employees. Using data from a Statistics Canada survey, Alan Saks of the University of Toronto and Robert Haccoun of the Université de Montréal matched Quebec employers with Ontario employers and found that there were no differences in amounts spent on training. The paperwork is so cumbersome that many employers prefer to pay the 1% tax rather than go through the thick guidebooks necessary to report the training.

If there is little effect gained by forcing employers to provide training, are there benefits forcing employees to attend training? The answer is not clear: some studies report some slight benefits in outcomes (such as improved job performance) when employees voluntarily attend courses; other studies see no differences.

There may be more serious problems than performance results created by forcing employees to attend courses. Half of the 24 employees of SaskTel who participated in a training program on process re-engineering required psychological counselling, or stress leave, or both in its aftermath. Trainees said they were subjected to a greenhouse environment: windows were papered over, employees were not allowed to communicate

with one another, and all were subjected to verbal abuse from the training consultants. As the president of the Ontario Society for Training and Development commented: "That's not training, that's assault."

Seagulls Pewter and Silversmiths of Pugwash, Nova Scotia, sent its employees to seminars based on the controversial Est therapy. Employees complained to their union that the seminars, in which participants were encouraged to delve into painful emotions, often drove participants to break down. In another example, a large insurance company hired a consultant to conduct management training for hundreds of supervisors and managers. The company did not realize that the consultant was a member of L. Ron Hubbard's Church of Scientology and was teaching management principles developed by Scientologists. Critics contend that Scientology is a cult, not a religion. Employees resented being subjected to psychological concepts based on "tones" that catalogue emotions; to the ruthless devotion to ferreting out and firing problem employees; and to "religious scriptures." The employees in these organizations were required to participate in programs that caused them undue stress and sometimes violated their moral or religious beliefs. Those who organized the programs believed that employees with the "right" attitudes would be more effective.

Sources: K. Harding, "A Taxing Way to Train Staff," *The Globe and Mail*, June 4, 2003: C1; D. Brown, "Legislated Training, Questionable Results," *Canadian HR Reporter* 15, no. 9, May 6, 2002: 1; A. Thomlinson, "Mandatory or Voluntary?" *Canadian HR Reporter* 15, no. 6 (March 25, 2002): 1.

jointly by the ASTD (American Society for Training and Development) and Saba Software found the following:

- When ranked according to how much the organizations spent on training, those firms in the top half had a total shareholder return that was 86% higher than firms in the bottom half, and 45% higher than the market average.
- Firms in the top quarter had a 24% higher profit margin.
- Firms in the top quarter had a price-to-book ratio that was 26% higher.[7]

A SYSTEMS APPROACH TO TRAINING AND DEVELOPMENT

Objective 2

Since the primary goal of training and development is to contribute to the organization's overall goals, training and development programs should be structured with an eye to organizational goals and strategies. Unfortunately, many organizations never make the connection between their strategic objectives and their training programs. Instead, fads, fashions, or "whatever the competition is doing" can sometimes be the main drivers of an organization's training agenda. As a result, much of an organization's investment can be wasted—training programs are often misdirected, poorly designed, inadequately evaluated—and these problems directly affect organizational performance.

To make certain that investments in training and development have the maximum impact on individual and organizational performance, a systems approach to training should be used. The systems approach involves four phases: (1) needs assessment, (2) program design, (3) implementation of training, and (4) evaluation of training.

Phase 1: Conducting the Needs Assessment

Objective 3

Managers and HR professionals should stay alert to the kinds of training that are needed, where they are needed, who needs them, and which methods will best deliver increased abilities to employees. If workers consistently fail to achieve productivity objectives, this might be a signal that training is needed. Likewise, if organizations receive an excessive number of customer complaints, this too might suggest inadequate training. To make certain that training is timely and focused on priority issues, and that training is the right solution for the concern, managers should approach a needs assessment systematically. You can also think of this as trying to identify the actual training problem.

Determining the specific training needs of individuals helps determine their abilities before entering a training program.

A needs assessment can be done by asking (and answering) four questions:

1. How important is this issue to the success of the organization?

   If it is important, then proceed to answer the next three questions: Questions 2, 3, and 4.

2. What competencies or knowledge, skills, and abilities do employees *need*?
3. What competencies or knowledge, skills, and abilities do the employees currently *have*?
4. What is the gap between the desired (need) and the actual (have)?

Once answers have been determined, then specific action plans can be developed to address the gap. For example, since the September 11, 2001, attacks, training of airport

---

Manager's Toolkit 5.2

NOTES ON RAPID NEEDS ASSESSMENT

Note 1: Look at Problem Scope. Common sense suggests that small, local matters may require less information gathering than big problems with a major impact on the organization. Ask managers a series of questions about the nature of the problem and its impact on the organization and gear your analysis accordingly.

Note 2: Do Organizational Scanning. Stay connected with what is going on in the organization in order to anticipate upcoming training needs. If a new technology is about to be launched, the need for training should take no one by surprise. In short, needs assessment isn't an event with a start-and-stop switch. It is the process of being engaged in your business.

Note 3: Play "Give and Take." Get the information you need, but don't drag your feet with excessive analysis before reporting back to managers. Show them that you are sensitive to their need for action by giving them updates on the information you have collected. If necessary, explain that better value may be gained by further analysis.

Note 4: Check "Lost and Found." Often, information gathered for a different purpose may bear on your training issue. Performance data (such as errors, sales, customer complaints) and staffing data (such as proficiency testing, turnover, absenteeism) can be very helpful as a starting point.

Note 5: Use Plain Talk. Instead of using clinical terms, such as "analysis" or "assessment," use straight talk with managers that tells them what you are doing: (1) Identify the problem, (2) identify alternative ways to get there, (3) implement a solution based on cost/benefit concerns, and (4) determine the effectiveness and efficiency of the solution.

Note 6: Use the Web. Information technology allows you to communicate with others, perhaps setting up an electronic mailing list to post questions, synthesize responses, share resources, get feedback, gather information on trends, and the like.

Note 7: Use Rapid Prototyping. Often the most effective and efficient training is that which is "just-in-time, just enough, and just for me." Create a rapid prototype of a training program, evaluating and revising as you implement and learn more about the problems.

Note 8: Seek Out Exemplars. Find those in the organization who currently demonstrate the performance the organization wants. Bring others together with them to talk about the performance issues, and let the exemplars share their experiences and insights. This avoids the risk of packaging the wrong information, and people learn just what they need to know from each other.

Source: Condensed from Ron Zemke, "How to Do a Needs Assessment When You Think You Don't Have Time," *Training* 35, no. 3 (March 1998): 38–44. Bill Communications, Inc., Minneapolis, MN.

security personnel has increased substantially. It has also increased for flight crews of airlines, employees in the transportation industry, workers in nuclear power plants, and even security staff at theme parks.

Manager's Toolkit 5.2 provides some suggestions for rapidly assessing training needs.

According to Chris Rogers, senior consultant for loss control at Aon Corporation's National Entertainment Practices Group, there is an emphasis today on training theme park security in a tactic called "aggressive hospitality," which calls for staff to greet people and look them in the eye and offer to assist, rather than waiting to be approached by visitors. "This is one of the best and simplest security measures," he says. When staff members engage visitors, they become more aware of them. This heightened level of attention also discourages troublemakers from coming to the facility, because they generally go where they can remain anonymous.[8]

Other training issues tend to revolve around the strategic initiatives of an organization. Mergers and acquisitions, for example, frequently require that employees take on new roles and responsibilities and adjust to new cultures and ways of conducting business. Nowhere is this more prevalent than in grooming new leaders within organizations. Other issues, such as technological change, globalization, re-engineering, and total quality management, all influence the way work is done and the types of skills needed to do it. A study of 6,000 Canadian organizations reported that about one-third had adopted new technology and about 40% had implemented an organizational change, primarily by re-engineering and downsizing.[9] Still other concerns may be more tactical but no less important in their impact on training. Organizational restructuring, downsizing, empowerment, and teamwork, for example, have immediate training requirements. Finally, trends in the workforce itself have an impact on training needs. As we mentioned in Chapter 1, employees increasingly value self-development and personal growth, and with this has come an enormous desire for learning. At the same time, as older workers near retirement, younger workers need to focus on gaining the skills and knowledge needed to take their place. Because no company in the private sector can count on stable employment levels, organizations as diverse as Inco and Boeing are facing situations in which they need to prepare the next generations of employees as the current groups approach retirement.

At Work with HRM 5.2 describes how the province of New Brunswick used training to improve its overall economic performance.

It is important that the supervisor or manager be knowledgeable about the organization's needs, the requirements of the work, and the capabilities of the person in order to assess that training is the right solution. Training efforts (and dollars) can be wasted if the supervisor has not adequately determined whether training is appropriate. The question to ask here is "If Joe receives more training on how to handle customer complaints, will his performance improve?" If performance issues are due to ability problems, training may likely be a good intervention. However, if performance issues are due to poor motivation or factors outside an employee's control, training may not be the answer. Ultimately, managers have to sit down with employees to talk about areas for improvement so that they can jointly determine the developmental approaches that will have maximum benefit.[10]

Phase 2: Designing the Training Program

Once the training needs have been determined, the next step is to design (or buy) appropriate training programs. The success of training programs depends on more than the organization's ability to identify training needs. Success hinges on taking the information gained from the needs analysis and utilizing it to design first-rate training programs.

at work **with HRM 5.2** at work with HRM 5.2

BREATHING NEW LIFE INTO A DYING ECONOMY

In the early 1990s, the province of New Brunswick decided that the future looked poor for its traditional economic base: mining, fishing, and lumber. However, as jobs were lost in the resource-based industries, people did not have the skills to move into the information-age economy. Unemployment was climbing and a quick solution had to be found. Enter the then premier: Frank McKenna. He recognized the need to break the economy's dependency on government dollars.

McKenna felt that for the economy to improve, there had to be a new industry that could quickly become a leader where geographic location didn't matter. He decided that the emerging information technology field would be the answer. But at the core of New Brunswick's economic problem was an HR problem: people did not have the right skills for working with technology. He

needed to find a way to train many people throughout the province efficiently and effectively. He found a way to do this by using emerging distance learning technology and by providing support to learners to adjust to a new work culture.

And the result? In the year 2002, New Brunswick's unemployment rate was low—5%—and over 20,000 people were employed in the information-technology sector. Further, the province is now considered a global leader in distance learning and online corporate training.

CRITICAL THINKING QUESTION

Could the people of New Brunswick have transitioned to the new economic base without the support of the province? Why or why not?

Sources: Adapted from "Searching for New Ways," Atlantic Institute for Market Studies, December 1997, www.aims.ca/Archive/1997/prdec97.html (retrieved September 27, 2002); Patrick J. Kiger, "Training Transforms a Region's Economy"; and "Reinvent Yourself With Training Strategy," *Workforce*, July 2002, 46–50.

Experts believe that training design should focus on at least four related issues: (1) instructional objectives, (2) trainee readiness and motivation, (3) principles of learning, and (4) characteristics of instructors.

Instructional Objectives

Instructional objectives
Desired outcomes of a training program

As a result of conducting organization, task, and person analyses, managers will have a more complete picture of the company's training needs. On the basis of this information, they can more formally state the desired outcomes of training through written **instructional objectives**. Generally, instructional objectives describe the desired outcomes of the training: the skills and knowledge the company wants people to have and the behaviours employees should acquire and/or change. For example, a stated objective for one training program might be "Employees trained in team methods will be able to demonstrate the following skills within six months: Problem-solving, conflict resolution, and effective team meetings."

Frequently, managers will seek external resources to design the training program and write the learning objectives. However, this is done with the help and guidance of the manager. Therefore, it is important for managers to be able to describe what they want the person to do or how they want the person to act after completing a training program.

Trainee Readiness and Motivation

Trainee readiness
The consideration of a trainee's maturity and experience when assessing him or her

Two preconditions for learning affect the success of those who are to receive training: readiness and motivation. **Trainee readiness** refers to both maturity and experience factors in the trainee's background. Prospective trainees should be screened to determine that they have the background knowledge and the skills necessary to absorb what will be presented to them. The other precondition for learning is trainee motivation. For optimum learning to take place, trainees must recognize the need for new knowledge or skills, and they must maintain a desire to learn as training progresses. By focusing on the trainees themselves rather than on the trainer or training topic, managers can create a training environment that is conducive to learning. Six strategies can be essential:

1. Use positive reinforcement.
2. Eliminate threats and punishment.
3. Be flexible.
4. Have participants set personal goals.
5. Design interesting instruction.
6. Break down physical and psychological obstacles to learning.[11]

While most employees are motivated by certain common needs, they differ from one another in the relative importance of these needs at any given time. Training objectives that are clearly related to trainees' individual needs will increase the motivation of employees to succeed in training programs. Again, the manager plays a vital role in ensuring that the training is suitable for the person and that the person is ready to take on the training initiative.

Principles of Learning

Objective 4

As we move from needs assessment and instructional objectives to employee readiness and motivation, we are shifting from a focus on the organization to a focus on employees. Ultimately, training has to build a bridge between employees and the organization. One important step in this transition is giving full consideration to the psychological principles of learning, that is, the characteristics of training programs that help employees grasp new material, make sense of it in their own lives, and transfer it back to the job.

Because the success or failure of a training program is frequently related to certain principles of learning, managers as well as employees should understand that different training methods or techniques vary in the extent to which they utilize these principles. When investing in effective and efficient training programs, it is important that they incorporate the following principles of learning (see Figure 5.2):

Goal Setting   It is important that the goals and objectives for the training are clear.

Individual Differences   People learn at different rates and in different ways.

Active Practice and Repetition   Trainees should be given frequent opportunity to practise their job tasks in the way that they will ultimately be expected to perform them.

Whole-versus-Part Learning   Most jobs and tasks can be broken down into parts that lend themselves to further analysis. Determining the most effective manner for completing each part then provides a basis for giving specific instruction.

Massed-versus-Distributed Learning   Another factor that determines the effectiveness of training is the amount of time devoted to practice in one session. Should trainees be given training in five two-hour periods or in ten one-hour periods? It has been found in most cases that spacing out the training will result in faster learning and longer retention.

FIGURE 5.2   Principles of Learning

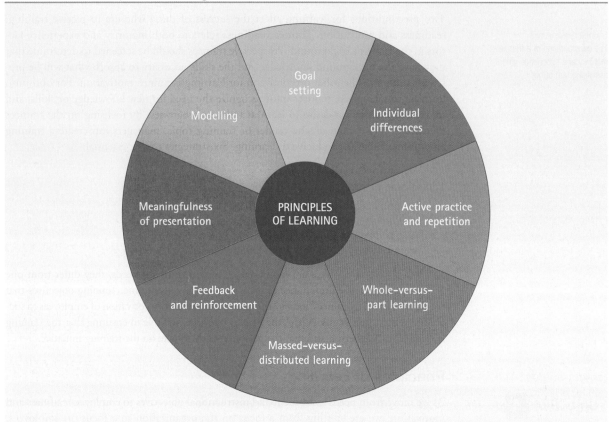

Feedback and Reinforcement   Can any learning occur without feedback? Some feedback comes from self-monitoring while other feedback comes from trainers, fellow trainees, and the like. As an employee's training progresses, feedback serves two related purposes: (1) knowledge of results, and (2) motivation.

Meaningfulness of Presentation   The material to be learned must be presented in as meaningful a manner as possible so that the trainees can connect the training with things that are already familiar to them.

Modelling   The old saying "A picture is worth a thousand words" applies to training. Quite simply, we learn by watching.

Behaviour modification
Technique that if behaviour is rewarded it will be exhibited more frequently in the future

In recent years some work organizations have used **behaviour modification**. This technique operates on the principle that behaviour that is rewarded—positively reinforced—will be exhibited more frequently in the future, whereas behaviour that is penalized or unrewarded will decrease in frequency. For example, in safety training it is possible to identify "safe" behavioural profiles—that is, actions that ensure fewer accidents—as well as unsafe profiles. As a follow-up to training, or as part of the training itself, managers can use relatively simple rewards to encourage and maintain desired behaviour. However, the idea with behaviour modification is that behaviour can be motivated and gradually shaped toward the desired profile using reinforcement.[12]

Characteristics of Trainers

The success of any training activity will depend in large part on the skills and personal characteristics of those responsible for conducting the training. Good trainers, whether staff persons or line managers, need to be knowledgeable about the subject, be well-prepared, have good communication skills, and be enthusiastic with a sense of humour.

Phase 3: Implementing the Training Program

Despite the importance of needs assessment, instructional objectives, principles of learning, and the like, choices regarding instructional methods are where "the rubber meets the road" in implementing a training program. A major consideration in choosing among various training methods is determining which ones are appropriate for the KSAs to be learned. For example, if the material is mostly factual, methods such as lecture, classroom, or programmed instruction may be fine. However, if the training involves a large behavioural component, other methods, such as on-the-job training, simulation, or computer-based training, might work better.[13]

Training and Development Methods

Objective 5

A wide variety of methods are available for training and developing employees at all levels. Some of the methods have a long history of usage. Newer methods have emerged over the years as the result of a greater understanding of human behaviour, particularly in the areas of learning, motivation, and interpersonal relationships. More recently, technological advances, especially in computer hardware and software, have resulted in training devices that in many instances are more effective and economical than the traditional training methods.

On-the-Job Training   The most common method used for training employees is **on-the-job training (OJT)**. OJT has the advantage of providing hands-on experience under normal working conditions and an opportunity for the trainer—a manager or senior employee—to build good relationships with new employees. As time becomes a critical resource—and "just-in-time training" is needed most—OJT is viewed by some to be potentially the most effective means of facilitating learning in the workplace.[14]

On-the-job training (OJT)
Method by which employees are given hands-on experience with instructions from their supervisor or other trainer

Although all types of organizations use it, OJT is often one of the most poorly implemented training methods. Three common drawbacks include (1) the lack of a well-structured training environment, (2) poor training skills of managers, and (3) the absence of well-defined job performance criteria. To overcome these problems, training experts suggest the following:

1. Develop realistic goals and/or measures for each OJT area.
2. Plan a specific training schedule for each trainee, including set periods for evaluation and feedback.
3. Help managers to establish a non-threatening atmosphere conducive to learning.
4. Conduct periodic evaluations, after training is completed, to prevent regression.[15]

Manager's Toolkit 5.3 shows the basic steps of an OJT program.

The following are other types of training approaches:

Apprenticeship Training   **Apprenticeship training** is used extensively where individuals entering an industry, particularly in the skilled trades, such as machinist, laboratory technician, or electrician, are given thorough instruction and experience, both on and off the job, in the practical and theoretical aspects of the work. Many former fishermen left the declining East Coast fishery to join in a seafarers' training program funded by several

Apprenticeship training
System of training in which a worker entering the skilled trades is given thorough instruction and experience, both on and off the job, in the practical and theoretical aspects of the work

Manager's Toolkit **5.3** Manager's Toolkit 5.3

THE PROPER WAY TO DO ON-THE-JOB TRAINING

P *Prepare.* Decide what employees need to be taught. Identify the best sequence or steps for training. Decide how best to demonstrate these steps. Have materials, resources, and equipment ready.

R *Reassure.* Put each employee at ease. Learn about his or her prior experience, and adjust accordingly. Try to get the employee interested, relaxed, and motivated to learn.

O *Orient.* Show the employee the correct way to do the job. Explain why it's done this way. Discuss how it relates to other jobs. Let him or her ask lots of questions.

P *Perform.* When employees are ready, let them try the job themselves. Give them an opportunity to practise the job and guide them through rough spots. Provide help and assistance at first, then less as they continue.

E *Evaluate.* Check the employees' performance, and question them on how, why, when, and where they should do something. Correct errors, repeat instructions.

R *Reinforce and Review.* Provide praise and encouragement, and give feedback about how the employee is doing. Continue the conversation and express confidence in his or her doing the job.

companies, the federal government, and the Nova Scotia government to learn new skills working in the engine rooms of larger vessels. Magna International, the auto parts giant, pays students $8 to $15 per hour to train as millwrights and tool and die makers. Learning is offered variously in shops, laboratories, and classrooms. Recently, employers in the oil industry in Alberta have started to establish an apprenticeship approach to ensure that oil-patch workers have the appropriate training. With advanced technology, high-school dropouts and drifters won't provide the necessary skills to ensure quality work. Finning Canada has taken a similar approach.[16]

Cooperative Training and Internship Programs   Similar to apprenticeships, **cooperative training** and **internship programs** combine practical on-the-job experience with formal education. Typically, co-op programs are offered at universities where students work for an entire semester as part of their education. While they don't get course credit, they do graduate with an indication that they have been involved in a co-op program. This gives them the ability to demonstrate to prospective employers that they have work experience. The pioneer in co-op education is the University of Waterloo, but there are now co-op programs throughout Canada. Syncrude Canada, Harley-Davidson, and Canadian Microelectronics Corporation are among the many companies that have formed partnerships with education. Further, organizations benefit by getting student-employees with new ideas, energy, and eagerness to accomplish their assignments. Humber College in Toronto, British Columbia Institute of Technology (BCIT) in Burnaby, and many other colleges allow students to earn college credits on the basis of successful job performance and fulfillment of established program requirements.

Classroom Instruction   Classroom instruction enables the maximum number of trainees to be handled by the minimum number of instructors. This method lends itself particularly to training in areas where information can be presented in lectures,

Cooperative training
Training program that combines practical on-the-job experience with formal education

Internship programs
Programs jointly sponsored by colleges, universities, and other organizations that offer students the opportunity to gain real-life experience while allowing them to find out how they will perform in work organizations

demonstrations, films, and videotapes or through computer instruction. Where it is not possible to obtain videotapes, audiotapes can be very valuable.

A special type of classroom facility is used in vestibule training. Trainees are given instruction in the operation of equipment like that found in operating departments. The emphasis is on instruction. For example, a check-out clerk in a supermarket first learns how to use the cash register.

Self-Directed Learning   Self-directed learning occurs when individuals work at their own pace at programmed instruction. This typically involves the use of books, manuals, or computers to break down subject matter content into highly organized, logical sequences that demand continuous response on the part of the trainee.

Audio-Visual   Audio-visual methods are used to teach the skills and procedures required for a number of jobs. An example would be golf and tennis coaches using video or camcorders so that their students can see their mistakes. RBC Financial Group uses video-conferencing extensively, broadcasting about 40 hours of programming per month. All 1,300 branches across Canada are hooked by satellite, and the employees can listen to the keynote speaker, see slides and video presentations, ask questions, and take multiple-choice tests.[17]

Simulation   Simulation is used when it is either impractical or unwise to train employees on the actual equipment used on the job. An obvious example is training employees to operate aircraft, spacecraft, and other highly technical and expensive equipment. The simulation method provides realism in equipment and its operation. For example, before the launch of its first edition, the *National Post* used simulations to train a new workforce by requiring them to produce a mock newspaper with real content and headlines.

Computer-Based Training and E-Learning   Computer-based training and e-learning have been increasing in industry, schools, and the military as development of technology proceeds at a rapid pace and the cost of computers continues to decline. In 2001, about four out of ten organizations were using e-learning, and there are estimates that 90% of all new training would be Internet-based by 2005. Forty percent of employees said they preferred e-learning to classroom training. E-learning has helped cut Bell Nexxia's annual training budget by about 40%, largely because of savings in the cost of developing courses, and paying for travel and accommodations. Courses that once consumed eight hours of class time can be taught in 90 minutes, leaving employees more time to spend at work.[18] Further, there are systems available that can track the progress of learners. For example, go to **www.webct.com** and see how CMI systems are used in educational institutions to track student progress.

WebCT
www.webct.com

E-learning is a term used to describe many types of online learning. More and more organizations are looking to the Internet as a vehicle to not only deliver training but also connect the learner to a variety of other resources. Because Web pages can be revised rapidly, the Internet has the potential to provide continuously updated training material, thereby making it easier and cheaper to revise training curricula. In addition, analysts believe that use of the Internet can save travel and classroom costs. The downside for training might be that Internet users tend to "surf." Given the sometimes non-direct format of the Internet, it may be a challenge to focus trainee interaction. Of course, this could be an advantage as well. The Internet requires that users become adept at searching, comparing, and making sense of a large amount of information. These skills are particularly important for building other skills: troubleshooting, problem solving, and analytical thinking.

When combined with e-mail capabilities, e-learning may be a very useful resource.[19] Through corporate universities and learning centres, organizations such as Magna, General Motors, and CIBC through their corporate universities and learning centres have been able to customize training and development to fit each organization and the employees. Some organizations take the relationship of training and technology so seriously that they have partnered with educational institutions to ensure that technological skills for tomorrow's workforce are being delivered today. A pioneer in this area is Cisco Systems when it created its Cisco Networking Academy with relationships to the Southern Alberta Institute of Technology (SAIT), McGill University, and Centennial College.[20] The program is delivered online with components on new ways of learning as well as allowing students to pace themselves.

Providing online learning is not just for those organizations in more traditional industries. New service companies, such as Teranet, also use e-learning to enable their growing workforce to stay current.[21] Teranet is an e-service solutions company and was faced with needing to find better and more flexible ways in training its younger workforce. It succeeded by thoroughly investigating how best to make use of e-learning and then ensuring that its senior management endorsed the approach.

A review of training media can be found at Training Media Review (**www .tmreview.com**). This is a good resource for managers who want to find out about current effective training approaches.

On-the-Job Experiences   On-the-job experiences present managers with the opportunities to perform under pressure and to learn from their mistakes. Such experiences are some of the most powerful and commonly used techniques. However, just as on-the-job training for first-level employees can be problematic if not well planned, on-the-job management development should be well organized, supervised, and challenging to the participants. Methods of providing on-the-job experience include the following:

a. *Coaching* involves a continuing flow of instructions, comments, and suggestions from the manager to the subordinate.
b. *Mentoring* usually involves an informal relationship in which an executive coaches, advises, and encourages a more junior employee. Some organizations have formal mentorship programs in which someone being considered for upward movement is

Training Media Review
www.tmreview.com

Mentors—Peer Resources
www.mentors.ca

Canadian businesses are increasing their training budgets in efforts to increase employee effectiveness. Computers and Web-based training are exploding.

assigned to another employee in the organization. A good mentor will focus on goals, opportunities, expectations, and standards and assist people in fulfilling their potential.[22]

c. *Understudy assignments* groom an individual to take over a manager's job by helping the individual gain experience in handling important functions of the job.

d. *Job rotation* provides, through a variety of work experiences, the broadened knowledge and understanding required to manage more effectively.

e. *Lateral transfer* involves horizontal movement through different departments, along with upward movement in the organization.

f. *Special projects* and *junior boards* provide an opportunity for individuals to become involved in the study of current organizational problems and in planning and decision-making activities.

g. *Action learning* gives managers release time to work full-time on projects with others in the organization. In some cases, action learning is combined with classroom instruction, discussions, and conferences.

h. *Staff meetings* enable participants to become more familiar with problems and events occurring outside their immediate areas by exposing them to the ideas and thinking of other managers.

i. *Planned career progressions* utilize all these different methods to provide employees with the training and development necessary to progress through a series of jobs requiring higher and higher levels of knowledge and/or skills.

The Canadian Federation of Independent Businesses (CFIB) report that the most effective form of training for businesses of fewer than 50 employees is on-the-job coaching.[23]

American Management Association
www.amanet.org

Seminars and Conferences   Seminars and conferences are useful for bringing groups of people together for training and development. In management development, seminars and conferences can be used to communicate ideas, policies, or procedures, but they are also good for raising points of debate or discussing issues (usually with the help of a qualified leader) that have no set answers or resolutions. In this regard, seminars and conferences are often used when attitude change is a goal. Check out **www.amanet.org** for a variety of conferences geared toward managers.

Case Studies   Case studies use documented examples, which may have been developed from the actual experiences of participants in their own organizations. Cases help managers learn how to analyze (take apart) and synthesize (put together) facts, become conscious of the many variables on which management decisions are based, and, in general, improve their decision-making skills.

This textbook uses case studies as a way for students, with the help of the instructor, to better understand and integrate the information covered in each chapter.

Management Games   Management games are valuable for bringing a hypothetical situation to life. Many games have been designed for general use. For example, TD Bank uses a simulation called Desert Kings to encourage more open communication, to increase levels of team performance, and to increase commitment to both internal and external customer service. One of the newer approaches is to use endurance-style athletic competitions, such as adventure racing, to help managers learn risk-taking and innovation.[24]

Role Playing   Role playing consists of assuming the attitudes and behaviour—that is, playing the role—of others, often a supervisor and a subordinate who are involved in a particular problem. By acting out another's position, participants in the role playing can improve their ability to understand and cope with others. Role playing can also help participants learn how to counsel others by helping them see situations from a different point of view. Role playing is used widely in training health-care professionals to be empathic and sensitive to the concerns of patients. It is also used widely in training managers to handle employee issues relating to absenteeism, performance appraisal, and conflict situations. At the end of this chapter, Developing Skills provides an opportunity for students to practise role playing.

Phase 4: Evaluating the Training Program

Training, like any other HRM process, should be evaluated to determine its effectiveness. A variety of methods are available to assess the extent to which training and development programs improve learning, affect behaviour on the job, and have an impact on the bottom-line performance of an organization. Unfortunately, few organizations adequately evaluate their training programs. In many ways, this goes beyond poor management; it is poor business practice. Given the substantial monetary stake that organizations have in training, it would seem prudent that managers would want to maximize the return on that investment.

There are four basic methods to evaluate training: (1) reactions, (2) learning, (3) behaviour, and (4) results. Some of these are easier to measure than others, but each is important in that it provides different information about the success of the programs. The combination of these can give a total picture of the training program in order to help managers decide where problem areas lie, what to change about the program, and whether to continue with a program.[25]

At Work with HRM 5.3 provides an example of how a Saskatchewan company uses all four ways to evaluate its training.

Method 1: Reactions

One of the simplest and most common approaches to training evaluation is assessing participant reactions. Happy trainees will be more likely to want to focus on training principles and to utilize the information on the job. However, participants can do more than say whether they liked a program or not. They can give insights into the content and techniques they found most useful. They can critique the instructors or make suggestions about participant interactions, feedback, and the like.

While evaluation methods based on reactions are improving, too many conclusions about training effectiveness are still based on broad satisfaction measures that lack specific feedback. Furthermore, it should be noted that positive reactions are no guarantee that the training has been successful. It may be easy to collect glowing comments from trainees, but gratifying as this information is to management, it may not be useful to the organization unless it somehow translates into improved behaviour and job performance. In the final analysis, reaction measures should not stop with assessing the training's entertainment value.[26]

Method 2: Learning

Beyond what participants *think* about the training, it might be a good idea to see whether they actually learned anything. Testing knowledge and skills before a training program gives a baseline standard on trainees that can be measured again after training to determine improvement.

at work **with HRM 5.3**

A CLASSIC FOUR-LEVEL EVALUATION

CONEXUS is the largest credit union in Saskatchewan with assets of $1.1 billion. According to Gayle Johnson, CHRP, EVP Human Resources and Corporate Secretary, its training and development budget for its 465 employees is 6% of payroll. Three percemt is spent on university education, and the other 3% is spent on training. Its largest training program is one that develops financial service representatives (their title is to be changed to "relationship managers"). The training consists of several steps and each is measured.

In-house and classroom-based modules teach content, such as computer literacy, cash duties, and introduction to CONEXUS's products and services, and progresses through to more advanced training, such as consumer lending practices, estates, and minimal mortgage lending. Each three- to five-day module is followed by a work period of three to twelve months, so that employees can apply their knowledge. The four levels of measurement of the effectiveness of training are as follows:

1. *Reaction*: "Smile sheets" are completed by each participant at the end of the classroom training, asking questions such as "What did you get from this session?"

2. *Comprehensive Review*: Exams are given after each module and the results are fed back to the employees and managers.

3. *Employee Performance Competencies*: Every job family has a number of job-specific competencies, and managers are asked to rate the participants on these performance competencies. The changes in ratings are tracked.

4. *Results*: These vary by module. For example, after the cash-lending module, the performance tracked would be the number of call-outs to customers and the number of sales.

CRITICAL THINKING QUESTIONS

1. If the annual payroll for CONEXUS is $18,750,000, what is the annual dollar amount budgeted for training and development?

2. Are there other ways that CONEXUS could use to ensure that the training and development expenditures are worthwhile?

Method 3: Behaviour

Much of what is learned in a training program never gets used back on the job. It's not that the training was necessarily ineffective. In fact, on measures of employee reactions and learning, the program might score quite high. But for several reasons, trainees may not demonstrate behaviour change back on the job. **Transfer of training** refers to the effective application of principles learned to what is required on the job. While it may not be necessary to measure the extent of the behaviour change, it is important for the supervisor to expect the behaviour change and to reinforce the changes.

Transfer of training
Effective application of principles learned to what is required on the job

Method 4: Results

Training managers are coming under additional pressure to show that their programs produce "bottom-line" results. Some of the results-based criteria used in evaluating training include increased productivity, fewer employee complaints, decreased costs and waste, and profitability.[27] Manager's Toolkit 5.4 provides some resources and examples of organizations focusing on ROI.

Increasingly, organizations with sophisticated training systems look to training to support long-term strategy and change more than they look for short-term financial returns from their investments. For example, Motorola found that for every $1 spent on training, $33 was returned to the company.[28] Instead of looking for a "payback," organizations view training in relation to its "pay-forward," the extent to which the training provides knowledge and skills that create a competitive advantage and a culture that is ready for continuous change.[29]

As training and development are increasingly viewed from a strategic standpoint, there is heightened interest in benchmarking developmental services and practices against those of recognized leaders in industry. While no single model for exact benchmarking exists, the simplest models are based on the late W. Edwards Deming's classic four-step process. The four-step process advocates that managers do the following:

1. *Plan.* Conduct a self-audit to define internal processes and measurements; decide on areas to be benchmarked; and choose the comparison organization.
2. *Do.* Collect data through surveys, interviews, site visits, and/or historical records.
3. *Check.* Analyze data to discover performance gaps and communicate findings and suggested improvements to management.
4. *Act.* Establish goals, implement specific changes, monitor progress, and redefine benchmarks as a continuous-improvement process.

Benchmarking
Process of measuring one's own services and practices against the recognized leaders in order to identify areas for improvement

To use **benchmarking** successfully, managers must clearly define the measures of competency and performance and must objectively assess the current situation and identify areas for improvement.

Manager's Toolkit **5.4**

RETURN ON TRAINING INVESTMENT

Organizations spend about 2% of payroll on training, an estimated $750 billion around the globe. Most organizations (four out of five) do not measure the ROI on their training dollars, citing barriers, such as the difficulty of doing so, the cost, lack of training, and lack of experience. However, at TD Bank, which has 1,500 branches, 45,000 employees, and 30 different businesses, a focus on measuring the ROI of training captures results, such as revenues and profitability. TD has a front-end process—that is, the business units determine the business results expected, the job performance that will generate these results, and the role that training plays.

According to the Conference Board of Canada, a positive relationship exists between formal training expenditures and performance indicators, such as employee productivity and company profitability. A useful tool for developing Return on Training Investment (ROTI) can be found at the Web site of FutureEd Inc. (www.futured.com/audited/returned.htm).

Sources: S. Carrigan, "Training: Investment in the Future," *Canadian HR Reporter* 14, no. 11 (June 4, 2001): G1; "What Should You Expect from Your Investment in Training?" Strategis, Industry Canada, "Canadian Training Solutions," www.strategis.gc.ca.

**American Society of
Training and Development**
www.astd.org/

The American Society for Training and Development (ASTD) and its Institute for Workplace Learning have established a project that allows organizations to measure and benchmark training and development activities against each other. This benchmarking forum, which shares findings from over 800 companies, compares data on training costs, staffing, administration, design, development, and delivery of training programs. Not only do initiatives such as these help organizations evaluate their training programs, but the process serves as a feedback loop to reinitiate needs assessment and design of future training.[30]

Other helpful articles and publications on training and development can be found through the Canadian Society for Training and Development at **http://www.cstd.ca/**.

**Canadian Society for
Training and Development**
http://www.cstd.ca/

SPECIAL TOPICS IN TRAINING AND DEVELOPMENT

Objective　6

While this chapter has focused almost exclusively on the processes underlying a systems model of training (needs assessment, principles of learning, implementation methods, evaluation), it may be useful to discuss some of the more popular topics that are covered in these training programs. As noted in Figure 5.1, there is a wide variety of skills and capabilities required in today's workplace. In addition to the training that addresses the competencies associated with a particular job, many employers develop training programs to meet the needs of a broader base of employees. This section summarizes some of these programs, including basic skills training, team training, and diversity training.

Basic Skills Training

The National Literacy Secretariat and Human Resources Development Canada finds that 42% of Canadians have literacy skills below the level they need to succeed. Experts define an illiterate individual as one having a sixth-grade education or less. Working adults who improve their literacy skills gain better pay and more promotions and are employed for longer periods of time. Employers launch literacy training in order to improve productivity. Avon Foods in Nova Scotia and Palliser's Furniture in Manitoba created workplace education programs to give workers easy access to skills upgrading.[31]

These figures have important implications for society at large and for organizations that must work around these skill deficiencies. Never has this been truer, given tight labour markets on the one hand, and increasing skill requirements (related to advances in technology) on the other. Basic skills have become essential occupational qualifications, having profound implications for product quality, customer service, internal efficiency, and workplace and environmental safety. According to the ABC Canada Literacy Foundation, 26% of adult Canadians have problems understanding a simple document like an owner's manual.[32] Canadian employers report that the top five skills they need in employees today are the ability to

- read and understand information
- listen, ask questions, and understand
- work in teams
- assess situations and identify problems
- share information orally and work with others

But grown-ups don't learn the way kids do, so many of the traditional basic skills training techniques are not successful with adults. To implement a successful program in basic and remedial skills, managers should do the following:

1. Explain to employees why and how the training will help them in their jobs.
2. Relate the training to the employees' goals.
3. Respect and consider participant experiences, and use these as a resource.
4. Use a task-centred or problem-centred approach so that participants "learn by doing."
5. Give feedback on progress toward meeting learning objectives.

At Work with HRM 5.4 provides additional information about what some other organizations are doing to improve workplace literacy.

Team Training

As discussed in Chapter 3, organizations rely on teams to attain strategic and operational goals. Whether the team is an air crew, a research team, or a manufacturing or service unit, the contributions of the individual members of the team are not only a function of

---

at work **with HRM 5.4** at work with HRM 5.4

WORKPLACE LITERACY SUCCESSES

There are a variety of success stories in Canada dealing with workplace literacy. Dofasco, a Hamilton, Ontario, steel company, recently had to acknowledge that the skills needed to help improve organization performance were missing. Through an assessment, it was determined that employees were lacking in basic reading skills, computer skills, and numerical skills. But it wasn't just the inability to read and write that needed improvement—it also included the ways in which information was presented to be understood. The design of the program included input from the employees as well as buy-in and support from senior management. Dofasco indicates it is having huge success and sees the skills of the employees improving.

Ekati Diamond Mine in the Arctic Circle can no longer rely upon employees who just have good physical capabilities. Most of the mining equipment is now computerized with complicated manuals. Even the warehouse and distribution functions have trucks that use GPS. The mine also wanted to hire as many Aboriginal employees as it could. In order to achieve these goals, Ekati created a literacy program that uses materials found on the job as teaching aids. This ensured that employees not only learned what they needed to be able to perform their job, but it helped employees learn to read, get a high-school credential, and learn a trade. Approximately $500,000 is spent by Ekati each year on this program.

CRITICAL THINKING QUESTION

Do you think the investment of $500,000 per year for basic skill training is a worthwhile expense? Explain your reasoning.

Source: Adapted from Andy Holloway, "Get a Proper Read," *Canadian Business*, November 22–December 5, 2004, 105; and Sandra Mingail, "Tackling Workplace Literacy a No-Brainer," *Canadian HR Reporter*, November 22, 2004, G3.

the skills and capabilities (competencies) of each individual but also of the interaction of the team members. To give an example of how important this can be to an organization, Dofasco had 6,700 employees participate in four-day workshops on interpersonal and group skills over a three-year period. The company wanted all its employees to learn to work with each other in new and different ways.

Teamwork behaviours that characterize effective teams are shown in Figure 5.3. They include both process skills and behavioural skills. The fact that these behaviours are observable and measurable provides a basis for training team members to function more effectively in the pursuit of their goals.[33]

Managers who want to design team training for their organization should keep the following points in mind:

1. Team building is a difficult and comprehensive process. Since many new teams are under pressure to produce, there is little time for training. Everything cannot be covered in a 24-hour blitz. Team training works best when it is provided over time and parallels team development.
2. Team development is not always a linear sequence of "forming, storming, norming, and performing." Training initiatives can help a team work through each of these stages, but managers must be aware that lapses can occur.
3. Additional training is required to assimilate new members. Large membership changes may result in teams reverting to a previous developmental stage.
4. Behavioural and process skills need to be acquired through participative exercises. Team members cannot internalize subjects like conflict resolution through passive listening. Hands-on experiences are much better.[34]

FIGURE 5.3   Team Training Skills

Process Skills	**Behavioural Skills**
(Operational Tools/Techniques)	(Interpersonal Skills)
• Meeting skills	• Member communications
• Problem solving	• Conflict resolution
• Brainstorming	• Trust building
• Decision making	• Establishing norms
• Negotiation skills	• Handling difficult members (for example, overbearing participants)
• Goal setting	
• Presentation skills	• Diversity awareness
• Process analysis	• Stages of team development
• Task evaluation	• Team issues and concerns
• Customer and supplier analysis	• Team benefits
• Project planning	• Characteristics of effective team members
• Business information management	• Negotiations
• Creativity	

Source: George Bohlander and Kathy McCarthy, "How to Get the Most from Team Training," *National Productivity Review*, Autumn 1996, 25–35. This material is used by permission of John Wiley & Sons, Inc.

Employees are more diverse and expect to be involved in decision making.

HRM and **the law 5.1** HRM and the law 5.1

DISCRIMINATION IN TRAINING HAS ORGANIZATIONAL IMPLICATIONS

The complainant worked for the federal government and wished to enter the full-time French-language training program. She wished to have the training so that she would have the skills necessary to be promoted into a more senior management position—one that required the incumbent to be bilingual. She was denied the request because an assessment had revealed that she was dyslexic and had difficulty processing auditory information.

Through the human rights hearing, it was discovered that the actual assessment process was discriminatory and had not considered some of the newer methods that have been successful with these types of learning disabilities. Specifically, new adaptive learning technology, if used by the complainant, would have enabled her to learn French and therefore be qualified for a more senior management position.

The Canadian Human Rights Tribunal ordered an immediate appointment to the more senior management position, a lump-sum payment for lost wages, plus an additional $5,000 for special compensation in recognition of the poor way in which she was treated.

Source: *CHRR Online*, Canada (Attorney General) v. Green (No. 1) (2000), 38 C.H.R.R. D/1 (F.C.T.D.), www.cdn-hr-reporter.ca, December 4, 2004; and Natalie C. Macdonald "Workplace Discrimination Prohibited—and That Includes Training," *Canadian HR Reporter*, November 22, 2004, G3.

Diversity Training

Many large organizations sponsor some sort of diversity training. This emphasis is sparked by an awareness of the varied demographics of the workforce, the challenges of employment equity, the dynamics of stereotyping, the changing values of the workforce, and the potential competitive payoffs from bringing different people together for a common purpose.

There are basically two types of diversity training: (1) awareness building, which helps employees appreciate the benefits of diversity, and (2) skill building, which provides the capabilities necessary for working with people who are different. For example, a skill-building diversity program might teach managers how to conduct performance appraisals with people from different cultures or teach male supervisors how to coach female employees toward better career opportunities. All the diverse dimensions—race, gender, age, disabilities, lifestyles, culture, education, ideas, and backgrounds—should be considered in the design of a diversity training program.[35]

To understand the implications of training and diversity, read HRM and the Law 5.1.

CAREER DEVELOPMENT—INDIVIDUAL AND ORGANIZATIONAL NEEDS

Objective **7**

Career development programs, with their greater emphasis on the individual, introduce a personalized aspect to the term "development." Most training and development programs have a career development component. Most career development programs should be viewed as a dynamic process that attempts to meet the needs of managers, their employees, and the organization.

Career planning, on the other hand, is a systematic approach where you would assess your values, interests, abilities, goals, and identify the path(s) you would need to take to realize your career goals. It would then be through career development programs that you would journey along the career path.

Ultimately, in today's organizations, individuals are responsible for initiating their own career planning. It is up to individuals to identify their knowledge, skills, abilities, interests, and values and seek out information about career options in order to set goals and develop career plans. Managers should encourage employees to take responsibility for their own careers, by offering continuing assistance in the form of feedback on individual performance and making available information about the organization, the job, and career opportunities that might be of interest.

The organization should be responsible for supplying information about its mission, policies, and plans and for providing support for employee self-assessment, training, and development. Significant career growth can occur when individual initiative combines with organizational opportunity. Career development programs benefit managers by giving them increased skill in managing their own careers, greater retention of valued employees, increased understanding of the organization, and enhanced reputations as people developers. Some organizations make use of leadership career development programs. For more information about the types of programs available for leadership development, visit the Web site of the Center for Creative Leadership at **www.ccl.org**.

Center for Creative Leadership
www.ccl.org

FIGURE 5.4   Balancing Individual and Organizational Needs

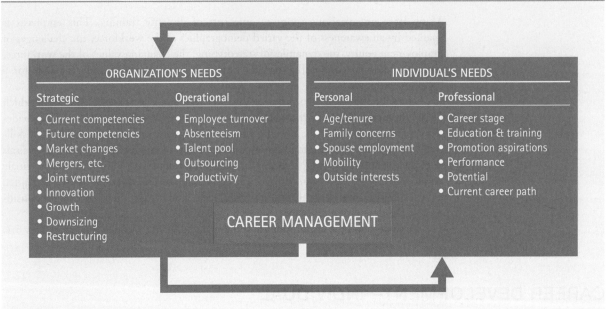

As shown in Figure 5.4, organizational needs should be linked with individual career needs in a way that joins personal effectiveness and satisfaction of employees with the achievement of the organization's strategic objectives.

Creating Favourable Conditions

While a career development program requires many special processes and techniques, some basic conditions must be present if it is to be successful. These conditions create favourable conditions for the program.

Management Support

If career development is to succeed, it must receive the complete support of top management. The system should reflect the goals and culture of the organization, and the people philosophy should be woven throughout. A people philosophy can provide employees with a clear set of expectations and directions for their own career development. For a program to be effective, managerial staff at all levels must be trained in the fundamentals of job design, performance appraisal, career planning, and coaching.

Goal Setting

Before individuals can engage in meaningful career planning, they must not only have an awareness of the organization's philosophy but also a clear understanding of the organization's more immediate goals. Otherwise, they may plan for personal change and growth without knowing if or how their own goals match those of the organization. For example, if the technology of a business is changing and new skills are needed, will the organization retrain to meet this need or hire new talent? Is there growth, stability, or decline in the number of employees needed? How will turnover affect this need? Answers to these kinds of questions are essential to the support of individual career planning.

Changes in HRM Practices

Transfer
Placement of an individual in another job for which the duties, responsibilities, status, and remuneration are approximately equal to those of the previous job

To ensure that its career development program will be effective, an organization may need to alter its current HRM practices. For example, a practice of job rotation can counteract obsolescence and maintain employee flexibility. Another practice that can aid development involves job transfers and promotions. A **transfer** is the placement of an employee in another job for which the duties, responsibilities, status, and remuneration are approximately equal to those of the previous job (or work requirements). A transfer may require the employee to change work group, workplace, work shift, or organizational unit; it may even necessitate moving to another geographic area. Transfers make it possible for an organization to place its employees in jobs where there is a greater need for their services and where they can acquire new knowledge and skills. A downward transfer, or demotion, moves an individual into a lower-level job that can provide developmental opportunities, but such a move is usually considered unfavourable by the individual who is demoted.

Promotion
Change of assignment to a job at a higher level in the organization

A **promotion** is a change of assignment to a job at a higher level in the organization. The new job (or work) normally provides an increase in pay and status and demands more skill or carries more responsibility. Promotions enable an organization to utilize the skills and abilities of its staff more effectively, and the opportunity to gain a promotion serves as an incentive for good performance. The two principal criteria for determining promotions are merit and seniority. Often the problem is to determine how much consideration to give to each factor.

As organizations continue to change, including their structure and number of employees, the ability to promote people as part of career development is becoming more difficult. The issues of balancing work and family, mentioned in Chapter 1, can become paramount when considering a promotion. Organizations are using "transfer" or "job rotation" more frequently.

Transferring people to other areas of the organization can also be a way of minimizing a business disruption. Around the World with HRM 5.1 describes how the Westin Bayshore Hotel in Vancouver transferred employees to other locations when it closed for renovations, thereby providing employees with growth assignments.

Specialized Development Needs

Objective **8**

As mentioned earlier in this chapter, "development" is a long-term approach for acquiring and utilizing new skills. Since the purpose of a development program is to give employees enhanced capabilities, there are a number of ways in which this can occur. The responsibility to develop the talent lies with all managers in the organization—not just the person's immediate supervisor or team leader.

Mentoring

When one talks with men and women about their employment experiences, it is common to hear them mention individuals at work who influenced them. They frequently refer to immediate managers who were especially helpful as career developers. But they also mention others at higher levels in the organization who provided guidance and support to them in the development of their careers. These executives and managers who coach, advise, and encourage employees of lesser rank are called **mentors**.

Generally, the mentor initiates the relationship, but sometimes an employee will approach a potential mentor for advice. Most mentoring relationships develop over time on an informal basis. However, proactive organizations emphasize formal mentoring plans that assign a mentor to those employees considered for upward movement in the organization. Under a good mentor, learning focuses on goals, opportunities, expectations, standards, and assistance in fulfilling one's potential.[36]

In order to form an effective mentoring relationship, individuals should follow a few general guidelines:

1. *Research the person's background.* Do your homework. The more you know about your potential mentor, the easier it will be to approach him or her and establish a relationship that will work for both of you.
2. *Make contact with the person.* Have a mutual friend or acquaintance introduce you, or get involved with your potential mentor in business settings. That will help the mentor see your skills in action.
3. *Request help on a particular matter.* Let the mentor know that you admire him or her, and ask for help in that arena. For example, you might say, "You're good at dealing with customers. Would it be okay if I came to you for advice on my customers?" Keep your request simple and specific.

Mentors
Executives who coach, advise, and encourage individuals of lesser rank

---

around the world **with HRM 5.1** around the world

WESTIN HOTEL SENDS STAFF OFF IN SEARCH OF KNOWLEDGE

The Westin Bayshore Hotel, located on Vancouver's waterfront, had to be very creative with staff during its 10-month closure while the hotel was being renovated and updated. As Daphne Hampson, the hotel's general manager, explained, they needed to find a way to keep staff during the shutdown. "If we had to lay them off, they would go job hunting elsewhere and ultimately leave the Westin Bayshore. We wanted to keep these key people; every hotel lives and dies by its staff."

About 20 managers were relocated to other Westin properties in Canada and in other parts of the world. "We're taking advantage of the 10-month closure to give our staff the opportunity to learn different ways of doing things so they can bring back the best practices," Hampson explained.

Providing a learning and living experience in another location not only broadens employees' perspectives but also encourages them to bring back new and innovative practices. Westin solved a difficult situation in a positive and exciting way.

Source: Adapted from Wing Chow, "Managers Moved as Bayshore Renovates," *The Vancouver Sun*, August 18, 1999, D1.

Mentoring helps people at all levels in the organization develop their special skills and talents.

4. *Consider what you can offer in exchange.* Mentoring is a two-way street. If you can do something for your potential mentor, then by all means, tell him or her.

5. *Arrange a meeting.* Once your specific request has been accepted, you're ready to meet with your potential mentor. Never go into this meeting cold. Set goals, identify your desired outcomes, and prepare a list of questions. Listen attentively. Then ask your prepared questions and request specific suggestions.

6. *Follow up.* After the meeting, try some of your potential mentor's suggestions and share the results. Express appreciation by identifying something in particular that was significant to you.

7. *Ask to meet on an ongoing basis.* After your potential mentor has had a chance to not only meet and interact with you, but also to see the value of what he or she can provide, you're in a good position to request an ongoing relationship. Suggest that you meet with him or her regularly, or ask permission to get help on an ad hoc basis.[37]

Manager's Toolkit 5.5 provides guidelines for some of the qualities an individual should look for in a mentor.

Organizations with formal mentoring programs include Shell International, Sun Microsystems, Johnson & Johnson, and the Bank of Montreal. Alternatively, given the importance of the issue, a number of mentoring organizations have begun to spring up. About 70% of Canadian organizations have formal or informal mentoring programs.[38] When done well, the mentoring process is beneficial for both the pupil and the mentor. A new form of mentoring, sponsored by the MS Foundation for Women, provides an opportunity for girls nine to fifteen years old to spend a day with mothers or friends on the job. The program is designed to give young women more attention and to provide them with career role models. Many large organizations, including Nike, DuPont, Ford, and Valvoline, have participated in this program, and it has grown to include boys of the same age.

Manager's Toolkit 5.5 Manager's Toolkit 5.5

MENTOR GUIDELINES

Successful mentoring is built on a common understanding of interests and "ground rules." Here are some to consider before establishing a mentor–protégé relationship:

1. Formalize the expectations with a written agreement that outlines the behaviours of each person.

2. Understand that either party can withdraw from the relationship at any time, and it is not necessary to provide an explanation.

3. All documents exchanged, such as company plans or résumés, will be treated as confidential.

4. The mentor cannot be solicited for a job. Doing so is grounds for breaking the relationship.

5. Respect each other's time. Arrive on time and prepared with a list of questions or topics to be discussed.

6. Provide feedback honestly. For example, the protégé could state, "This is not the kind of information I need at this stage" or the mentor might advise, "You should not skip meetings just because they are tedious; it is an important part of this company's culture to be visible at these meetings."

Society for Canadian Women in Science and Technology

www.harbour.sfu.ca/scwist/links.html

National Mentoring Partnership

www.mentoring.org

There are a number of resources on the Internet for mentoring. A few examples include the following:

- *Society for Canadian Women in Science and Technology (SCWIST)* is an association that has assembled thousands of women in technology fields who act as online mentors to visitors to its Web site.
- *National Mentoring Partnership* is an online site for a variety of different resources for mentors and mentees, including information about how to find a mentor.

Specialized Career Development for a Diverse Workforce

Today, some organizations offer extensive career development programs geared to special groups, such as women, minorities, youth, and/or dual-career couples. For example, male managers have traditionally had an informal network of interpersonal relationships that has provided a means for senior (male) members of the organization to pass along news of advancement opportunities and other career tips to junior (male) members. Women have typically been left outside this network, lacking role models to serve as mentors. To combat their difficulty in advancing to management positions, women in several organizations have developed their own women's networks. At the Bank of Montreal, a women's network serves as a system for encouraging and fostering women's career development and for sharing information, experiences, and insights.

Another example is an organization actively creating conditions that recognize and reward performance on the basis of objective, nondiscriminatory criteria. Many organizations are taking the position that their employees should reflect the communities in which they function. At the Bank of Montreal, each manager is required to set diversity targets.

Keeping a Career in Perspective

It is important in any training and development program to keep everything in perspective. While work is a very important part of someone's life, it is only a part. Organizations want people who maintain an appropriate balance between their work life and their personal life, and therefore can continue to grow and develop for personal satisfaction and success for the organization.

Some of the other areas of life that must be considered are the following:

1. Off-the-job interests can provide a break from the demands of a career while allowing employees to gain satisfaction from non-work-related activities.
2. Family life can be negatively affected if the organization does not provide recognition of a person's life outside of work. Conflict between work and family may arise over such issues as number of hours worked per week, the need to relocate for career advancement, and the amount of overtime that may be required.
3. Planning for retirement is an important consideration given the aging workforce. Many companies are now providing pre-retirement programs to allow an employee to be productive in the organization while minimizing problems that can arise in the retirement years.

It is important to maintain a balance. According to a 2003 survey of Canadians, an appropriate work-life balance was the top indicator of personal career success.[39]

SUMMARY

1. List some of the characteristics of an effective orientation process.
   - Familiarizing new employees with the organization, their job, and their work unit.
   - Embedding organizational values, beliefs, and accepted behaviours.
   - Active involvement and participation from the supervisor.
2. Discuss the systems approach to training and development.
   - Training and development need to be linked to the organization's goals and objectives.
   - A systems approach to training and development creates this link.
   - A systems approach consists of five phases: needs analysis, training program design, implementation, evaluation, and transfer to work environment.
3. Describe the components of a training-needs assessment.
   - Contributes to the organization's overall goals.
   - Involves five phases: needs assessment, program design, implementation, evaluation, and transfer of training.
4. Identify the principles of learning and how they facilitate training.
   - Goal setting.
   - Meaningfulness of presentation.

- Modelling.
- Individual differences.
- Active practice and repetition.
- Feedback.
- Rewards and reinforcement.

5. Identify the types of training and development methods used for all levels of employees.
   - On-the-job.
   - Apprenticeship.
   - Cooperative and internship programs.
   - Computer-based.
   - Seminars and conferences.
   - Role playing and management games.

6. Describe the special training programs that are currently popular.
   - Basic skills training (such as literacy) where people learn basic reading and math.
   - Team work where people learn new behaviours and skills to work in teams.
   - Diversity where people develop an appreciation of the benefits of diversity.

7. Explain how a career development program integrates individual and organizational needs.
   - It blends employee effectiveness and satisfaction with the achievement of the organization's strategic objectives.
   - HRM practices must fit so that both individual and organization needs can be achieved.

8. Discuss specialized career development needs.
   - Mentoring programs where more senior individuals coach and encourage more junior staff.
   - Specialized career programs for diverse workforce where the organization gears the development to special groups, such as women, youth, etc.

Need to Know

- Definition of training, development, and learning
- Definition of orientation
- Definition of employee involvement and empowerment
- Variety of training methods
- Ways to reinforce training in the work environment
- Basic approaches to development

Need to Understand

- Importance of the line manager in identifying training needs
- Relationship of orientation to organizational performance
- Importance of ensuring appropriate method is used to enhance learning
- Role supervisor or line manager plays in helping the trainee use the new skills and behaviours
- Organizational and individual responsibility in a person's development

Key Terms

apprenticeship training 167

behaviour modification 166

benchmarking 174

cooperative training 168

development 154

instructional objectives 164

internship programs 168

mentors 182

on-the-job training (OJT) 167

orientation 154

promotion 181

trainee readiness 165

training 154

transfer of training 173

transfer 181

REVIEW QUESTIONS

1. What are the benefits of a well-designed orientation process?
2. Describe the steps in developing a training and development program.
3. Describe and define the principles of learning.
4. What are the various methods for training and development?
5. Describe five process skills for teams and five behavioural skills.
6. Explain mentoring.
7. List the four issues in evaluating training programs and describe why each is important.
8. Give some reasons for the trend toward increased emphasis on career development programs.

CRITICAL THINKING QUESTIONS

1. Sukh has just been promoted to a managerial role in a small auto parts company in Southern Ontario. She immediately noticed that the company had no orientation process for new employees. A decision was made to implement a new orientation process for all employees. What might be included and over what period of time?
2. Your employer has approached you to assume a supervisory role. While this flatters you, you are also concerned about your ability to carry out the role successfully. What type of training or development might you want to help you succeed?
3. Sally was recently hired as a cashier for a fast-food restaurant. The shift leader gave her a very brief introduction to the food and cash handling procedures. Unfortunately, at the end of Sally's shift, there was a lot of food waste and the cash count was short. Detail the training Sally needs in order to perform the work successfully.
4. "Mentorship programs are a waste of time and money." Why might an employer say this? What might you say to the employer to counter the employer's thinking?

5. You have recently joined an organization as a customer service representative. The company places high value on satisfied customers. Specifically describe the type of training you ought to have in order to ensure customers receive a high level of customer satisfaction. What would be the "hard skills" and the "soft skills"?

6. What contributions can a career development program make to an organization that is forced to downsize its operations?

7. You work in an organization that focuses on sales. Recently, there have been a number of complaints about a particular sales representative in terms of accuracy of orders and timeliness of work being completed. Complete the four steps in the systems approach to training and development. Specifically, (1) how will you determine if training is the answer? (2) identify a possible learning or training objective; (3) what methods would you use to implement training? (4) how would you evaluate if the training was effective?

DEVELOPING YOUR SKILLS

1. Role Playing. In class, working in pairs, determine which role each person will play from the following scenario. Play the role for 15 to 20 minutes. After the time period, the class will discuss how they felt, what worked, what could have been done better, and how they might use role play if they were a supervisor.

Scenario

Role 1: Hotel Manager   You are getting ready for a quarterly review of the performance of your front-desk supervisor. You are halfway through the performance year. You have had weekly discussions about the service levels and have reviewed results against the targets. You have also discussed specific training needs of the supervisor and the staff who report to the supervisor.

In setting objectives at the beginning of the year, you and the supervisor had agreed that the supervisor's style of management needed to change. The company is moving toward empowering front-line staff, and managers need to have a different approach and relationship with employees. It is in this area that your supervisor is struggling. Employees have complained that the supervisor tells them what to do, is very abrupt in interactions, and at times says things in a way that people feel is disrespectful. You have discussed this behaviour before, but you are not seeing the improvement you'd like to see. On the other hand, you are confident the supervisor can modify the behaviour and become the kind of leader the company wants. You want this interview to be positive and constructive and you want to find the right training program to help the supervisor.

Role 2: Front-Desk Supervisor   You are getting ready for the quarterly review of your performance with your boss. You are pleased with the results of service levels as targets have been exceeded every week for the last six months.

You are certain your boss will want to discuss your management style. This is an area where you are still having difficulty. You want to act differently with your employees but you aren't sure exactly what to do. You have read some articles but that doesn't seem to help when you try to put some of the suggestions into practice. You'd like to have some training but you aren't sure if the hotel will support you.

Motorola University
www.motorola.com
(mu.motorola.com)

GE's Business School
www.gecareers.com

Royal Bank's Career Edge
www.rbc.com/careers/
index.html

Training Media Review
www.tmreview.com

2. In groups of three to four students, develop a list of behaviours or skills that would improve your performance as a team member. For each behaviour or skill, identify one or two training methods that would be appropriate for learning that behaviour or skill.

3. Providing training to employees is a significant retention tool in a tight labour market. In groups of four to five students, discuss the benefits of training for individuals and organizations. Prepare a response to the following statement: "Employees should be required to repay the cost of any training if they leave the organization before one year."

4. In groups of three to four students, access the following Web sites for major corporations that use a number of different techniques for training and development. Write a one- to two-page paper describing the similarities and the differences:

   Motorola University, **www.motorola.com** (**mu.motorola.com**)
   GE's Business School, **www.gecareers.com**
   Royal Bank's Career Edge, **www.rbc.com/careers/index.html**

5. Each student will search **www.tmreview.com** and find one item that might be a valuable training resource in the future. Students are to print the description and describe in approximately one-half page why this is a good training resource.

Case Study   1

Service at the Chateau Whistler

The Chateau Whistler in Whistler, British Columbia, is one of the world's leading hotels and has been named the number one ski resort in North America for the past eight years. The 557-room hotel opened in 1989 and currently has 650 full-time employees.

The orientation program for new employees at the Chateau Whistler reflects the same standards that guests enjoy at the hotel. New recruits have raw talents, such as energy and enthusiasm but have to be trained quickly in the art of excellent service.

On Day One of the orientation program, an "Orientation Game" is played; then the employees are introduced to the hotel (the types of rooms, the amenities, etc.). Then the following are discussed:

- Salary and benefits, including health care, pension plan, discounted ski passes, staff meals, food discounts, discounted rates at other properties, and health club access
- Employment standards, human rights, and labour relations (although the hotel is not unionized)
- Health and safety, including WHMIS (Workplace Hazardous Material Information System) and MSDS (Material Safety Data Sheets) and the environmental program
- Harassment policy
- The wellness program
- The incentive program

New employees also receive a tour of the town of Whistler, so that they can talk to guests about the key attractions and establish a network of friends.

Day Two is devoted to the Service Plus Program. The Service Plus Code is spelled out this way:

S	support
E	empathy
R	responsiveness
V	valuing differences
I	interdependence
C	caring
E	expectations

The Day Two program focuses on the guest–employee interaction and strives to teach employees how to provide excellent service, deal empathetically and effectively with problems reported by guests, and solve problems creatively. Training consists of role plays, such as "handling the difficult guest." Specifically, the new recruits gain an understanding of the CP Hotel's mission statement and commitment to service, the changing service culture, and the high service expectations of the guests.

The third component of the orientation program is "Guest for a Night," during which employees who have been working at the hotel for three months eat at the restaurants, enjoy the facilities, and spend one night in the hotel as a guest. According to David Roberts, the hotel's general manager, the goal of the Guest for a Night program is to ensure that employees can talk knowledgeably about guest rooms, restaurants, and other facilities, and understand the level of quality that the hotel provides.

As part of this program, employees are asked to fill out a feedback survey, just like a guest. Also at this time, employees are invited to be part of a focus group to express concerns and provide feedback about their work experiences.

Through these orientation and training programs, employees develop knowledge and skills in service excellence. More importantly, they develop a commitment to the company. At a ten-year reunion party given for 600 people, 599 said it was the best working experience of their lives.

Questions

1. Why does the Chateau Whistler invest so much time, money, and energy into its orientation process?
2. Describe the activities in the orientation and training programs that would ensure a high degree of transfer of training to the job.
3. Design an approach to evaluating the effectiveness of these programs using all four levels of results.

Case Study 2

People Development Strategies at Credit Union Central of Saskatchewan

There are 128 credit unions in Saskatchewan, with assets ranging from less than $1 million to more than a billion dollars. All of these are affiliated with Credit Union Central of Saskatchewan, which facilitates cooperation among credit unions and provides consulting services, trade association functions, and liquidity management.

Credit Union Central, together with the four largest Saskatchewan credit unions, developed a plan to implement a comprehensive human resource management system to produce, first, a better alignment of employee performance to organizational objectives, and, second, more focused training to produce desired business results and an enhanced ability to retain employees through opportunities for professional development. Working with Hay Management Consultants, the first step was to develop a competency glossary, followed by performance management processes and tools, selection and staffing tools, and then succession planning.

Competencies can be defined as attitudes, skills, knowledge or behaviours that are essential to perform at work and that differentiate superior performers. The competency glossary defines core competencies, which apply to all roles within the organization, and role-specific competencies. Competency target levels indicating superior performance are set for each role.

An example of a core competency, based on the key values and strategies of the organization, is "results orientation."

When your employee tried to improve his/her own performance he/she

1. Identified areas of waste or inefficiency but didn't take any action
2. Made some changes to work methods in order to reach particular goals that had been set for him/her
3. Made specific changes in the system and his/her own work methods in order to improve performance beyond goals set
4. Set own challenging goals that were accomplished with a significant amount of planning, analysis, and effort
5. Set individual goals by thinking through the costs and benefits, and explicitly considered potential profits, risks, and return on investment, in order to make decisions that ended up having a positive organizational impact
6. Took a calculated entrepreneurial risk and committed significant organizational resources to act on an idea that ended up significantly improving performance.

A role-specific competency might be "concern for order, quality, and compliance" defined as follows.

When your employee demonstrated attention to detail in his/her work, he/she

1. Checked on the work to ensure it was accurate, complied with all relevant regulations, and followed all standard practices and procedures.
2. Monitored the accuracy and quality of his/her own work and others' work consistently and systematically and kept a detailed record of work when it was necessary.
3. During the project, monitored the progress of the project against milestones and deliverables, took action to ensure the procedures put in place were effective, and quickly corrected any weaknesses or deficiencies.
4. Established and utilized a procedure and/or system to facilitate work efficiency and ensure high-quality output; modified and improved the procedure and/or system when a weakness was identified, in order to ensure that high-quality work was being produced.

Managers work with employees to assess competency levels. The competency glossary and a competency assessment questionnaire enable managers and employees to discuss skills, abilities, and behaviours using a common framework. Training and development plans are based on gaps between target performance and actual performance. A developmental resource kit, which includes training courses, seminars, books, and work opportunities, all classified by competency, assists with building development plans.

This approach has resulted in clear direction on performance and development plans to move employees toward optimum performance levels.

Questions

1. Describe the advantages and disadvantages of the approach used to identify performance gaps.
2. Why would managers resist or support this approach? Explain your answers.

NOTES AND REFERENCES

1. Mark A. Youndt and Scott A. Snell, "Human Resource Configurations, Intellectual Capital, and Organizational Performance," *Journal of Managerial Issues* XVI, no. 3 Fall 2004, 337–60.
2. *Ibid.*
3. Asha Tomlinson, "T & D Spending Up in U.S. as Canada Lags Behind," *Canadian HR Reporter*, March 25, 2002, 1.
4. Asha Thomlinson, "T & D Spending up in U.S. as Canada Lags Behind," *Canadian HR Reporter* 15, no. 6 (March 25, 2002): 1; Industry Canada, "Canadian Training Solutions," http://strategix.ic.gc.ca/epic/internet.
5. Training Magazine, "Feature Stories," www.trainingmag.com. March 2003.
6. Debbie Murray and Michael Bloom, "Solutions for Employers: Effective Strategies for Using Learning Technologies in the Workplace," The Conference Board of Canada, March 15, 2000, 8.
7. Laurie J. Bassi, Jens Ludwig, Daniel P. McMurrer, and Mark Van Buren, "Profiting from Learning: Do Firms' Investments in Education and Training Pay Off?" ASTD, Washington, D.C., September 2000, 3–4.
8. Tracy Mauro, "Helping Organizations Build Community," *Training and Development* 56, no. 2 (February 2002): 25–29; Liam Lahey, "RFIDs Touted as Standard for Airport Security," *Computing Canada* 28, no. 13 (June 21, 2002): 21; Caroline Wilson, "Ensuring a Smooth Ride," *Security Management* 46, no. 8 (August 2002): 92.
9. N. Leckie, A. Leonard, J. Turcotte, and D. Wallanc, *The Evolving Workplace Series: Employer and Employee Perspectives on Human Resources Practices,* Statistics Canada/Human Resources Development Canada, September 2001.
10. Elwood Holton, Reid Bates, and Sharon Naquin, "Large-Scale Performance-Driven Training Needs Assessment: A Case Study," *Public Personnel Management* 29, no. 2 (Summer 2000): 249–67.
11. Jason A. Colquitt and Marcia J. Simmering, "Conscientiousness, Goal Orientation, and Motivation to Learn during the Learning Process: A Longitudinal Study," *Journal of Applied Psychology* 83, no. 4 (August 1998): 654–65; Sherry Ryan, "A Model of the Motivation for IT Retraining," *Information Resources Management Journal* 12, no. 4 (October–December 1999): 24–32; Kimberly A. Smith-Jentsch, Florian G. Jentsch, Stephanie C. Payne, and Eduardo Salas, "Can Pretraining Experiences Explain Individual Differences in Learning?" *Journal of Applied Psychology* 81, no. 1 (February 1996): 110–16.
12. Don Hartshorn, "Reinforcing the Unsafe Worker," *Occupational Hazards* 62, no. 10 (October 2000): 125–28; Jean M. Patterson, "Smart Training," *Occupational Health& Safety* 68, no. 10 (October 1999): 216–21; Fred Luthan and Alexander Stajkovic, "Reinforce for Performance: The Need to Go beyond Pay and Even Rewards," *Academy of Management Executive* 13, no. 2 (May 1999): 49–57.
13. Eduardo Salas and Janis Cannon-Bowers, "The Science of Training: A Decade of Progress," *Annual Review of Psychology* 52 (2001): 471–99.
14. Diane Walter, *Training on the Job* (Alexandria, VA: American Society for Training and Development, 2001); Toni Hodges, *Linking Learning and Performance: A Practical Guide to Measuring Learning and On the Job Application* (Burlington, MA: Butterworth-Heinemann, 2001); Gary Sisson, *Hands-On Training: A Simple and Effective Method for On-the-Job Training* (San Francisco: Barrett-Koehler, 2001).
15. Alison Booth, Yu-Fu Chen, and Gylfi Zoega, "Hiring and Firing: A Tale of Two Thresholds," *Journal of Labor Economics* 20, no. 2 (April 2002): 217–48; Sherrill Tapsell, "Train to Retain," *New Zealand Management* 46, no. 7 (August 1999): 49–53; Gary Sisson, "HOT Training," *Executive Excellence* 19, no. 3 (March 2002): 15; Holly Ann Suzik, "On-the-Job Training: Do It Right!" *Quality* 38, no. 12 (November 1999): 84.

16. Charlie Gillis, "Drillers Hope to Get 'Rig Pigs' an Education," *National Post*, November 5, 2002, A3 and David Brown, "Western Thirst for Skilled Labour," *Canadian HRReporter*, June 14, 2004, 1.

17. S. Wintroe, "Satellites Present Cost Savings," *Financial Post*, June 16, 2003, FE 6.

18. "What Is the Impact of Learning Technologies," Industry Canada, at Strategis.gc.ca; R. Ray, "Employers, Employees Embrace E-Learning," *The Globe and Mail*, May 25, 2001, E2.

19. Laura Moushey and James Kirk, "Retooling for E-Learning," ASTD Learning Circuits, http://www .learningcircuits.org/2002/jan2002/kirk.html (retrieved April 12, 2002).

20. "Technology and Education: Learning From Each Other," *Canadian Business*, September 27–October 10, 2004.

21. Laura Micks, "A Lesson in E-Learning," *Canadian HR Reporter*, November 18, 2002, G9.

22. Peer Resources—The Mentors Corporation, www.mentors.ca (retrieved November 26, 2004).

23. Virginia Galt, "The Task of Getting Workers Up to Speed," *The Globe and Mail*, April 22, 2004, B15.

24. Anne Marie Owens, "Corporate Leaders Taking to the Hills," *National Post*, April 2, 2002, A3.

25. Donald Kirkpatrick, "Great Ideas Revisited: Revisiting Kirkpatrick's Four-Level Model," *Training and Development* 50, no. 1 (January 1996): 54–57; Martin Delahoussaye, "Show Me the Results," *Training* 39, no. 3 (March 2002): 28–29; Reinout van Brakel, "Why ROI Isn't Enough," *Training and Development* 56, no. 6 (June 2002): 72–74.

26. James Pershing and Jana Pershing, "Ineffective Reaction Evaluation," *Human Resource Development Quarterly* 12, no. 1 (Spring 2001): 73–90.

27. Martin Delahoussaye, Kristine Ellis, and Matt Bolch, "Measuring Corporate Smarts," *Training* 39, no. 8 (August 2002): 20–35; Daniel Crepin, "From Design to Action: Developing a Corporate Strategy," *Quality Progress* 35, no. 2 (February 2002): 49–56; Brad Miller, "Making Managers More Effective Agents of Change," *Quality Progress* 34, no. 5 (May 2001): 53–57.

28. Earl Honeycutt, Kiran Karande, Ashraf Attia, and Steven Maurer, "A Utility Based Framework for Evaluating the Financial Impact of Sales Force Training Programs," *Journal of Personal Selling and Sales Management* 21, no. 3 (Summer 2001): 229–38.

29. Richard Lee, "The 'Pay-Forward' View of Training," *People Management* 2, no. 3 (February 8, 1996): 30–32; Terry Sloan, Paul Hyland, and Ron Beckett, "Learning as a Competitive Advantage: Innovative Training in the Australian Aerospace Industry," *International Journal of Technology Management* 23, no. 4 (2002): 341–52.

30. Ellen Drost, Colette Frayne, Keven Lowe, and J. Michael Geringer, "Benchmarking Training and Development Practices: A Multi-Country Comparative Analysis," *Human Resource Management* 41, no. 1 (Spring 2002): 67–86; Daniel McMurrer, Mark Van Buren, and William Woodwell, "Making the Commitment," *Training and Development* 54, no. 1 (January 2000): 41–48.

31. A. Thomlinson, "Math, Reading Skills Holding Employees Back," *Canadian HR Reporter* 15, no. 8 (October 21, 2002).

32. Advertisement, *The Financial Post*, February 12, 2002.

33. "What Makes Teams Work?" *HRFocus* 79, no. 4 (April 2002): S1–S3; John Annett, David Cunningham, and Peter Mathias-Jones, "A Method for Measuring Team Skills," *Ergonomics* 43, no. 8 (August 2000): 1076–94; Alan Auerbach, "Making Decisions under Stress: Implications for Individual and Team Training," *Personnel Psychology* 52, no. 4 (Winter 1999): 1050–53.

34. George W. Bohlander and Kathy McCarthy, "How to Get the Most from Team Training," *National Productivity Review*, Autumn 1996, 25–35; Howard Prager, "Cooking Up Effective Team Building," *Training and Development* 52, no. 12 (December 1999): 14–15.

35. Gary Stern, "Small Slights Bring Big Problems," *Workforce* 81, no. 8 (August 2002): 17; Bill Leonard, "Ways to Tell If a Diversity Program Is Measuring Up," *HRMagazine* 47, no. 7 (July 2002): 21.

36. Matt Starcevich and Fred Friend, "Effective Mentoring Relationships from the Mentee's Perspective," *Workforce*, supplement, July 1999, 2–3; Kenn Fracaro, "Mentoring: Tool for Career Guidance," *SuperVision* 63, no. 9 (September 2002): 10–12.

37. Kathleen Barton, "Will You Mentor Me?" *Training and Development* 56, no. 5 (May 2002): 90–92.

38. Suzan Butyn, "Mentoring Your Way to Improved Retention," *Canadian HR Reporter* 16, no. 2 (January 27, 2003): 13.

39. Katherine Harding "Balance Tops List of Job Desires," *The Globe and Mail*, May 7, 2003, C1.

CHAPTER 6

Managing Performance

After studying this chapter, you should be able to

1   Define a performance management system.

2   Explain the purpose of a performance management system.

3   Describe the management practices necessary for a good performance management system.

4   Identify the steps in an effective performance management system.

5   Describe the different sources of performance review information.

6   Explain the various methods used for performance reviews.

7   Outline the characteristics of an effective performance review interview.

OUTLINE

HRM
Close-Up

Patricia Gallagher, marketing and promotions manager for the Maritime provinces, Global Television, Halifax

"Communicating with staff, working as a team, and maintaining strong lines of communication are key."

As a 25-year management veteran, Patricia Gallagher has overseen as many as 55 employees, and, as marketing and promotions manager for the Maritime provinces at Global Television, as few as five. Based in Halifax, Nova Scotia, and Saint John, New Brunswick, Gallagher's staff sets the local programming schedule and ensures all Canadian-content regulations are met. While Global's basic schedule is planned in Toronto, "our time zone allows for some unique situations," says Gallagher. "We can simulcast programs because of the time that American networks air them." Her staff also produces the promos for local shows, newscasts, and community events; answers media calls and viewer complaints; and oversees aspects of public relations. Gallagher herself handles the things that most managers do—namely, people performance. "A lot of that is learning what it is that people hear—and how best to say it, so that they do hear it!"

Communicating with staff, working as a team, and maintaining strong lines of communication are key to Gallagher's management strategy. "So if I give them a project where the time line is too short, they feel comfortable bringing those concerns forward." While she manages performance by checking in with her staff daily, she also allows them to work independently—a necessity for the creative process. "I just assigned a major project to my news producer. I gave him some criteria in terms of what we needed in the promos, then let him go to it!" While her staff often seeks her guidance, she also prefers them to think for themselves. When asked about a problem, she often answers with a question: "What do you think we should do?"

Managing performance sometimes means pulling people back "when they're going off path," Gallagher says. At times it entails pointing out errors. "Sometimes I say, 'That's not your best work.' And they don't like to hear that." Analyzing poor outcomes or mistakes are opportunities for growth, says Gallagher, who also believes that problems should be nipped in the bud. "I'm more comfortable when people communicate with me, so I assume others are more comfortable when I communicate with them." Performance evaluations take place every fall and include setting goals for each employee for the coming year. Progress is reviewed at the six-month mark.

The downside of managing a smaller staff, says Gallagher, is the same as its upside: being up-close and personal. "If something happens in their personal life, you get drawn into it." Balancing this intimacy against the need to oversee performance is likely her biggest daily challenge. Developing a professional detachment is essential, she says, to retaining authority and managing effectively. If the business environment or job function were to change, "you might have to make a difficult decision." According to Gallagher it is important to be sure to draw firm boundaries with staff. "If you believe everybody is your friend, you may be sharing things that are inappropriate." So while she enjoys her role as manager, Gallagher remains fully aware of her responsibility. At times she holds "a bit of a hammer"—and at times, she says, "I have to use it!"

INTRODUCTION

In the preceding chapters, we discussed how an organization hires and develops a productive workforce. In this chapter, we turn to performance management, which is one of the most critical processes that managers use to maintain and enhance productivity and facilitate progress toward strategic goals. While we will focus mainly on a formal system, the processes of managing and reviewing performance can be informal as well. All managers monitor the way employees work and assess how this matches organizational needs. Supervisors and managers form impressions about the relative value of employees to the organization and seek to maximize the contribution of every individual. Yet while these ongoing informal processes are vitally important, most organizations also have a system that includes a formal review of the person's performance once or twice a year, or on an ongoing basis. In the HRM Close-Up, it was noted that Patricia Gallagher informally checks in with her staff on a daily basis although she formally reviews the progress of their goals every six months.

The success or failure of a performance management system depends on the philosophy underlying it, its connection with business goals, the attitudes and skills of those responsible for using it, and the individual components of the system. A performance management system is more than the actual review—it is an overall approach to getting the maximum contribution from each individual.

WHAT IS A PERFORMANCE MANAGEMENT SYSTEM?

Objective 1

Performance management system
A set of integrated management practices

Objective 2

A **performance management system** is a set of integrated management practices. While the formal review of employees' performance is a key component, a good performance review program does not make a good performance management system. A systems approach to performance management (1) allows the organization to integrate the management functions in order to maximize employee potential, and (2) helps increase employees' satisfaction with their work and with the organization.

Formal programs for reviewing performance are by no means new to organizations. Performance review programs are used in large and small organizations in both the public and private sectors. Advocates see these programs as among the most logical means to review, develop, and thus effectively utilize the knowledge and abilities of employees. However, a growing number of observers point out that performance reviews frequently fall short of their potential.[1] In a recent book entitled *Performance Management*, Robert Bacal argues that one of the primary reasons performance management systems fail is that they have conflicting purposes.[2] Not only do they communicate how work is performed but also reflect values and organizational culture. For example, an organization that employs a team-based structure might have a performance management system that focuses on reviewing individual performance. This gives mixed messages about who owns the responsibility for the results.

There is no doubt that managing performance is not always easy. Managers and supervisors frequently avoid discussing employee performance—whether it is good or poor. McKinsey & Company, a worldwide consulting firm that specializes in helping organizations develop practical solutions, conducted a survey of 6,900 managers in 56 organizations. The survey identified that top performers can increase organizational effectiveness by as much as 130%.[3] However, this same study indicated that while 89% felt candid feedback was critical to both individual and company success, only 39% had received it.[4]

Performance management is not an added activity in the busy supervisor's life—it is central to the everyday work of managers.[5] However, supervisors and managers have struggled for years to find ways to make such an important activity more meaningful and helpful to employees.

MANAGEMENT PRACTICES

Objective 3

The following management practices are essential for an effective performance management system:

1. Setting and communicating clear performance expectations for all work and all jobs.
2. Ensuring clear and specific performance objectives (or standards of performance) for all work.
3. Providing supportive and helpful coaching by the supervisor to enable staff to reach their objectives.
4. Focusing on the accomplishment of objectives during performance reviews.
5. Recognizing and celebrating good performance.

As shown, the actual review step (item 4) is only one component of the system. However, the vast majority of performance management systems focus primarily on the review and typically use that step for making compensation decisions.[6] The practice of "pay for performance" is found in all types of organizations. For example, at PMC-Sierra, a company that designs and develops Internet chips, pay is linked to individual and team performance and can include stock purchase plans.[7]

Purposes of Managing Performance

There are several purposes for performance reviews, all intended to benefit both the organization and the employee and to ensure that any decisions are based on objective information.

Administrative Purposes

A performance management system also integrates a number of other major HR processes, such as promotion, transfer, and layoff decisions. Further, it can be used as part of HR planning—particularly when the organization has a succession plan. As well, the system provides a "paper trail" for documenting HRM processes that may result in legal action. For example, if a person were being disciplined regarding very poor customer service, the system would be able to identify what the goals were, how well the person met the goals, and the discussions and coaching sessions to improve performance in relation to customer service.

Measurement of Performance

In order to assess the overall success of the organization, it is important to be able to measure the accomplishments of the employees. Thus, you want to know how the employees performed compared to the established goals. A well-designed performance management system will be able to measure the performance of the organization and the employees. A performance management system also has the capability to influence employee behaviour, thereby leading directly to improved organizational performance.[8]

Developmental Purposes

From the standpoint of individual development, a performance system provides the feedback essential for discussing strengths and areas where performance needs improving—at both the individual and organizational levels. For example, if, through setting objectives, many supervisors identify that people have to improve their computer literacy skills, then the organization can provide a solution that meets those needs. From this information, the organization may set up a formal training program for all employees. This can be a better solution than having each supervisor deal with each person on an individual basis. Without such a step in the system, the manner in which developmental needs are identified can be hit-and-miss.

Regardless of the employee's level of performance, the system provides an opportunity to identify issues for discussion, eliminate any potential problems, and work on ways of achieving high performance. Newer approaches to performance management emphasize training as well as development and growth plans for employees. A developmental approach recognizes that the purpose of a manager is to support and help the person (or team) achieve results for good organizational performance. Having a sound basis for identifying performance goals, coaching, reviewing, and recognizing performance leads to successful organizations.

Figure 6.1 provides a summary of the purposes of managing performance.

Why Performance Management Systems Sometimes Fail

In actual practice, formal performance management systems sometimes yield disappointing results. Figure 6.2 shows that the primary reasons include keeping objectives secret (the supervisor knowing what the employee ought to achieve but not informing the employee),

FIGURE 6.1   Purposes for Managing Performance

Administrative

- Promotion decisions
- Salary increases
- Transfer decisions
- Layoff decisions
- Succession planning
- Paper trail for documenting HRM actions

Measurement of Performance

- Determine accomplishment of goals
- Influence employee behaviour
- Improve organizational performance

Developmental

- Feedback for discussing strengths and areas for improvement
- Eliminate potential problems
- Identify training needs

FIGURE 6.2 Top 10 Reasons Performance Management Systems Can Fail

1. Objectives were not linked to business objectives.
2. Objectives did not represent the entire job.
3. Objectives were kept a secret from individual and teams; for example, you were expected to call back all customers within 24 hours but that standard was not disclosed.
4. Feedback was usually one-way, from the manager to the employee, and frequently was negative.
5. Training and development needs were frequently overlooked.
6. Measurable goals were lacking.
7. Necessary resources (such as equipment and time) were not provided.
8. Objectives were impossible to meet.
9. Infrequent discussions of performance took place.
10. Yearly reviews were done in a haphazard fashion.

Sources: Adapted from Anne Stephen and Tony Roithmayr, "Escaping the Performance Management Trap," *Re-Inventing HR: Changing Roles to Create the High-Performance Organization* (Toronto: John Wiley and Sons, 1999), 233; and Donald J. Mills, "Setting Objectives: Avoid Missed Deadlines," *Workplace Today* (November 1999): 36–37.

imposing objectives on the employee, and not having constructive feedback. For example, if a review is used to provide a written assessment for salary action and at the same time to motivate employees to improve their work, the administrative and developmental purposes may be in conflict. As a result, the actual review interview may become a discussion about salary in which the manager seeks to justify the action taken. In such cases, the discussion might have little influence on the employee's future job performance.

As with all HR processes and systems, if the support of top management is lacking, the system will not be successful. Even the best-conceived process will not work in an environment where managers are not encouraged by their superiors to take their responsibilities seriously in managing performance. To underscore the importance of this responsibility, top management should ensure that managers and supervisors are also part of the overall performance management system and that their performance will be reviewed for how well they are managing their employees' performance. At Work with HRM 6.1 describes how the performance system at Mountain Equipment Co-Op (MEC) evolved.

Other reasons performance management systems can fail include the following:

1. Managers feel that little or no benefit will be derived from the time and energy spent on the process.
2. Managers dislike the face-to-face discussion and performance feedback.
3. Managers are not sufficiently adept in setting goals and performance measures, in coaching and supporting, or providing performance feedback.
4. The judgmental role of a review can conflict with the helping role of developing employees.

Performance management in many organizations is a once-a-year activity in which the review interview becomes a source of friction for both managers and employees. An important principle of performance management is that continual feedback and employee coaching must be a positive regular activity—be it daily or hourly. The annual or semiannual performance review should simply be a logical extension of the day-to-day supervision process. For example, Mead Johnson Canada, a subsidiary of Bristol-Myers Squibb, a large pharmaceutical firm, changed its performance management system so that employees received ongoing reviews. This system now has a future growth and expectations focus with immediate and specific feedback.

at work **with HRM 6.1** at work with HRM 6.1

PERFORMANCE MANAGEMENT AT MEC

It was a decision by the executive team in the late 1990s that led to the development of a performance management system. The executive created a vision for MEC for the 21st century and wanted to ensure that its HR processes supported that vision.

The performance management system was designed around competencies with a developmental focus. The purpose of the system was to help the employees self-manage, identify any training needs, and enable MEC to provide the training to meet their needs. In developing the system, HR staff met with MEC staff in all its locations across Canada.

In designing the system around competencies, the feedback from staff identified which competencies would be used in performance reviews. The following six clusters of competencies were chosen:

1. Vision
2. Planning
3. Communication
4. Problem solving and decision making

5. Staff hiring, coaching, and attitudes
6. Values and attributes.

Each of the competencies was further defined with behaviours, skills, and knowledge. For example, under "vision," a knowledge component is understanding the external environment and its impact on MEC. Proficiency levels were then developed for the various competencies, such as 0 for introductory and 4 for ability to be a mentor.

Built into the system is a focus on people, identifying their needs with an ongoing review of competencies. Through such an approach, MEC's performance management system links individual performance to organizational goals as well as empowering the employees to be self-managing.

CRITICAL THINKING QUESTIONS

1. Do you think that MEC has captured the appropriate competencies? Are there others that ought to be included?
2. What are some of the difficulties that could be encountered by allowing employees to self-manage?

Sources: Adapted from Karen Aplin-Payton, "Work in the Fast Lane! How to Rev Up Employee Performance," *People Talk*, Winter 2000, 8–17; and Nancy Neil, "Competing Competencies," *People Talk*, Summer 2000, 10–12.

One of the main concerns of employees is the fairness of the performance management system, since the process is central to so many HRM decisions. Employees who believe the system is unfair may consider the review interview a waste of time and leave the interview with feelings of anxiety or frustration. Also, they may view compliance with the system as mechanical and thus play only a passive role during the interview process. By addressing these employee concerns during the planning stage of the system, the organization will help the performance management system succeed in reaching its goals. Employees can help ensure that the review is fair by being well prepared. This can include keeping track of positive (and negative) feedback from the supervisor and keeping records of courses, workshops, and any other training activities.

Finally, organizational politics can introduce a bias even in a well-run system.[9] For example, managers may inflate reviews because they desire higher salaries for their employees or because higher subordinate ratings make them look good as managers. Alternatively, managers may want to get rid of troublesome employees, passing them off to another department by inflating their ratings. Supervisors and managers have to be watchful for the same types of errors in performance reviews as in selection interviews. The supervisor may make decisions about a person's performance based on recent events (recency error) or judging performance favourably or unfavourably overall by putting emphasis on only one area that is important in the supervisor's mind (halo error). Likewise, the supervisor may be unwilling to give either extremely low or extremely high assessments and decide to rate everyone as "above average" (central tendency). A supervisor can also be biased by comparing one employee's performance to another (contrast error) instead of assessing the employee against a set of standards.

For a sample performance review form, go to **www.performanceappraisal.com**.

Performance Appraisal
www.performanceappraisal
.com

STEPS IN AN EFFECTIVE PERFORMANCE MANAGEMENT SYSTEM

Objective 4

About.com
http://humanresources
.about.com/

MAP for Nonprofits
http://mapnp
.nonprofitoffice.com/

Development Dimensions International
www.ddiworld.com/

The HR department ordinarily has the primary responsibility for overseeing and coordinating the performance management system. HR may also design or select a performance management system to use. Managers from the operating departments must also be actively involved, particularly in helping to establish the objectives for the system. Furthermore, employees are more likely to accept and be satisfied with the performance management system when they have the chance to participate in its development. Their concerns about fairness and accuracy in determining raises, promotions, and the like tend to be alleviated somewhat when they have been involved at the planning stage and have helped develop the performance standards themselves. This section describes five steps that are key to an effective performance management system. In addition, other useful information on performance management can be found at About.com (**http://humanresources.about.com/**), MAP for Nonprofits (**http://mapnp.nonprofitoffice.com/**), and Development Dimensions International (**www.ddiworld.com/**).

Clarifying the Work to Be Done

Before any goals can be established or any performance standards identified, it is important to clarify the work to be accomplished. And this is done by identifying the expected outcomes or results and determining how those results will be measured. For example, an expected result for a cook at a fast-food restaurant may be "no food wastage." The supervisor and cook would then decide how this will be measured. It could be measured by determining the number of kilograms of food in the garbage pail or the number of voided customer orders. Note that the clarification step is done jointly with the supervisor and the employee. The key to a good performance management system is the involvement of the employee in the entire process.

Setting Goals and Establishing a Performance Plan

Once the supervisor and employee (or team) are clear on expected results and how those results will be measured, goals must be set. And for the system to really work, these goals must be linked to overall business objectives. For example, an overall business objective

Setting specific, measurable performance goals is a key step in a performance management system.

for the fast-food restaurant is to reduce costs. Since food costs are a large proportion of overall costs, the restaurant may decide to focus on reducing food costs. Therefore, for the individual employee, the ability to cut down on wasted food will reduce the overall food costs and the goal may be "to reduce food waste by 10% within the next three months." You will note that this is a very specific goal that includes a time frame.

To ensure that there is a strong link to business goals, the supervisor may also need to establish "softer measures" such as customer satisfaction or customer loyalty.[10] With the use of both financial results (e.g., cost of food) and soft measures (e.g., customer satisfaction), the results are more strongly linked to the overall restaurant outcomes. This step also involves discussion between both the supervisor and the employee, which leads to greater involvement and commitment to the specific goals.

There are other types of methods, such as trait and behavioural, in addition to goals, which can be used in establishing the performance plan. These will be discussed later in the chapter.

Regular and Frequent Coaching

Coaching sessions are designed to help employees achieve their results. Coaching should not involve fault-finding or blaming. Most people want to do a good job, and, therefore, it is important that a supervisor approach coaching in a helpful and supportive way. If the employee is having difficulty reaching a goal, the supervisor and employee can explore together the reasons why and what can be done to fix the difficulty. Coaching is also a good way to avoid costs of firing employees and hiring new employees. It is very difficult for employees to improve on mistakes if the supervisor does not take the time to help them understand what they need to do.

Conducting a Formal Review of Performance

Most performance management systems include an annual formal review of the employee's overall performance. This allows both the supervisor and employee to consider the employee's accomplishments and to discuss development areas for the next year. It is also usually at this point that the organization uses the results of the annual performance review for salary adjustments.

Since the employee was involved in the original goal setting, and since there has been regular and frequent feedback and coaching, this step is more of a review—there shouldn't be any surprises.

Recognizing and Rewarding Performance

No system will be effective without recognition of accomplishments. Although we usually think of recognition in monetary terms, some nonfinancial rewards for the employee include the following:

1. Being considered for a promotion.
2. Being given the opportunity to work on a special project.
3. Being praised by the supervisor.
4. Being profiled in a business journal about a particular achievement or receiving an award of excellence.

These types of rewards cost little or no money. People like to know that their good work and achievements are noticed. Appropriate rewards can be a great tool in helping the organization be successful.[11] Around the World with HRM 6.1 describes the performance management systems in other countries.

Complying with the Law

Since performance assessments are used as a basis for HRM actions, they must meet certain legal requirements. The legality of any performance management system is measured against criteria of reliability, fairness, and validity. *Reliability* refers to whether performance is measured consistently among the employee participants. *Fairness* refers to the extent to which the system avoids bias caused by any factors unrelated to performance. *Validity* refers to the extent to which the system is job-related and accurate. Under the Charter of Rights and Freedoms, and other federal and provincial human rights requirements, performance management systems must be, above all, valid. Worker performance must be assessed on the basis of job requirements to ensure legal compliance.

Although currently there is little litigation pertaining to performance management systems in Canada, the spillover effect of litigation in the United States has prompted organizations to try to eliminate vagueness in descriptions of traits, such as attitude, cooperation, dependability, initiative, and leadership. For example, the trait "dependability" can be made much less vague if it is spelled out as employee tardiness and/or unexcused absences. In general, reducing room for subjective judgments will improve the entire performance review process.

Employers might face legal challenges to their performance management systems when reviews indicate acceptable or above-average performance but employees are later passed over for promotion, disciplined for poor performance, discharged, or laid off from the organization. In these cases, the performance reviews can undermine the legitimacy

around the world **with HRM 6.1** around the world

ALIGNING THE PERFORMANCE MANAGEMENT SYSTEM

Ensuring that an employee's performance is linked to organizational performance is not just an issue in Canada. Throughout the world, all types of organizations are striving to make this happen. Here are some specific examples.

Through the World Bank, member countries such as Malta are provided performance management systems for use in government offices which are results-focused, participative and linked to organizational outcomes.

The U.S. government and all its agencies, both at home and abroad, use a system that creates a "line of sight" between the individual and organizational goals, fosters a results-oriented culture, and links pay to performance.

In 2004, the New Zealand Ministry of Foreign Affairs and Trade, which is responsible for managing New Zealand's business with foreign countries and international organizations, implemented a performance management framework that directly aligns and reinforces the Ministry's key objectives, and links level of competency with compensation.

Source: Adapted from "Individual Performance Management," *The World Bank*, http://www1.worldbank.org/ publicsector/civilservice/individual.htm (retrieved May 29, 2005); "Results-Oriented Cultures: Using Performance Management Systems in U.S. Agencies and Abroad," http://unpan1.un.org/intradoc/groups/pulic/documents/ ASPA/UNPAN006701.pdf (retrieved May 28, 2005); "Annual Report 30 June 2004: Report of the Ministry of Foreign Affairs and Trade," http://www.mfat.govt.nz/about/oppu/annualreport/annreport3.html (retrieved May 29, 2005).

of the subsequent decision. And legal challenges can be very costly. For example, if an organization terminated someone due to a downsizing, but then subsequently said it was for poor performance, the company would not be successful in defending its action if the personnel file did not contain a poor performance review.

Therefore, performance reviews should meet the following guidelines:

- Performance ratings must be job-related, with performance standards related to the work as identified through job analysis.
- Employees must be given a written copy of their performance standards in advance of any formal performance review.
- Managers who conduct the review must be able to observe the behaviour they are assessing. This implies having a measurable standard with which to compare employee behaviour.
- Managers and supervisors should be trained to understand their role in managing performance, specifically on (1) how to set goals and performance standards; (2) how to coach and conduct a formal review session; and (3) how to write a review report or use any other written materials associated with the performance system.
- Reviews should be discussed openly with employees and coaching or corrective guidance offered to help poor performers improve their performance.
- An appeals procedure should be established to enable employees to express disagreement with the formal evaluation.

Employers must ensure that managers and supervisors document reviews and reasons for subsequent HRM actions. This information may prove decisive should an employee

HRM and **the law 6.1** HRM and the law 6.1

LACK OF PERFORMANCE DOCUMENTATION

The National Bank of Canada made newspaper headlines in February 2000 after being accused of terminating a person without just cause. The individual launched a lawsuit claiming that he was terminated because he had AIDS; the bank said the employee was terminated because of poor performance and bad behaviour. The company defended the termination on the fact that the person had been demoted about two years before the termination. The bank president indicated that co-workers and customers had complained about the person's unreliability and poor judgment, and that the demotion ought to have sent a strong and clear message about the employee's performance and behaviour problems. However, during the trial, there was no clear evidence that any of the problems had been documented or reviewed with the employee. During the trial the employee maintained that there had been no discussions regarding performance.

How do you think the court ruled on this case?

Source: Adapted from an article by Allan Swift, "National Bank Boss Defends Firing," *The Vancouver Sun*, February 2, 2000, D16. Reprinted with permission of the Canadian Press.

take legal action. An employer's credibility is strengthened when it can support performance results by documenting instances of poor performance. Read HRM and the Law 6.1 to get an understanding of what can happen when performance issues are not clearly documented.

Deciding Who Should Provide Performance Information

Objective 5

For many years, the traditional approach to reviewing an employee's performance was based solely on information the supervisor gathered through first-hand knowledge of the person. However, given the complexity of today's jobs, it is often unrealistic to presume that one person can fully observe and assess an employee's performance. Also, there may be a desire to gather information directly from those who are best acquainted with the person's performance, such as a customer. Consequently, information about a person's performance may come from supervisors, the employee being reviewed, peers, team members, subordinates, and customers. The Canadian Institute of Chartered Accountants and the Ontario Ministry of Northern Development and Mines have begun using information gathered from a number of sources. Since supervisors spend much of their time on gathering data for and conducting the performance review, the remainder of this section will focus on that portion of the performance management system.

Manager and/or Supervisor Review

Manager and/or supervisor review
Performance review done by the employee's supervisor

Manager and/or supervisor review has been the traditional approach to assessing an employee's performance. In most instances, supervisors are in the best position to perform this function, although it may not always be possible for them to do so. Managers often complain that they do not have the time to fully observe the performance of employees.

These managers must then rely on performance records to review an employee's performance. For example, Istonish, a customer service centre in Canada, uses telephone monitors to assess the quality of the communication between a service centre representative and a customer. Employees are aware that they are being monitored for developmental purposes. If such reliable and valid measures are not available, the review may be less than accurate.

Where a supervisor reviews employees independently, provision is often made for an analysis of the reviews by the supervisor's superior. Having reviews examined by a supervisor's superior reduces the chance of superficial or biased reviews. Reviews by superiors generally are more objective and provide a broader perspective of employee performance than do reviews by immediate supervisors.

Self-Review

Sometimes employees are asked to assess themselves on some or all aspects of their performance. **Self-review** is beneficial when managers seek to increase an employee's involvement in the review process. Such an approach may require an employee to complete a review form prior to the performance interview. At a minimum, this gets the employee thinking about strengths and areas for improvement and may lead to discussions about barriers to effective performance. During the performance interview, the manager and the employee discuss job performance and agree on a final assessment. This approach also works well when the manager and the employee jointly establish future performance goals or employee development plans.

Critics of self-review argue that employees are more lenient than managers in their assessments and tend to present themselves in a highly favourable light. However, one of the authors has found through personal experience that people tend to underrate their overall performance. Research also suggests that people may understate their performance due to lack of skills or lack of self-confidence.[12] Therefore, managers are able to build on employees' views of themselves and make employees feel better about their performance. When used in conjunction with other input sources, self-reviews can be a valuable source of information.[13]

Subordinate Review

Some organizations use **subordinate appraisal** to give managers feedback on how their subordinates view them. Subordinates are in a good position to provide feedback on their managers since they are in frequent contact with their superiors and occupy a unique position from which to observe many performance-related behaviours. Those performance dimensions judged most appropriate for subordinate input include leadership, oral communication, delegation of authority, coordination of team efforts, and interest in subordinates. The manager at Victoria-based B.C. Buildings Corporation appreciated the specific feedback received from her subordinates that she could be providing them with more guidance.[14] However, dimensions related to managers' specific job tasks, such as planning and organizing, budgeting, creativity, and analytical ability, are not usually appropriate for subordinate feedback.

Since subordinate feedback gives employees power over their bosses, the managers themselves may be hesitant to endorse such an approach, particularly when it might be used as a basis for compensation decisions. However, when the information is used for developmental purposes, managers tend to be more open to the idea. Available evidence suggests that when managers heed the advice of their subordinates, their own performance can

Self-review
Performance review done by the employee being assessed, generally on a form completed by the employee prior to the performance interview

Subordinate review
Performance review of a superior by an employee, which is more appropriate for developmental than for administrative purposes

improve substantially. Nevertheless, to avoid potential problems, subordinate appraisals should be submitted anonymously and combined across several individual raters.[15]

Peer Review

Individuals of equal rank who work together are increasingly asked to assess each other. A **peer review** provides information that differs to some degree from information by a superior, since peers often see different dimensions of performance. Peers can readily identify leadership and interpersonal skills along with other strengths and weaknesses of their co-workers. A superior asked to provide input about a server in a restaurant on a dimension such as "dealing with the public" may not have had much opportunity to observe it. Fellow servers, on the other hand, have the opportunity to observe this behaviour regularly.

One advantage of peer input is the belief that these assessments furnish more accurate and valid information than assessments by superiors. The supervisor often sees employees putting their best foot forward, while those who work with their fellow employees on a regular basis may see a more realistic picture. With peer input, co-workers are asked to provide input on specific areas, usually in a structured, written format. The forms are then compiled into a single profile, which is given to the supervisor for use in the final review.[16]

Despite evidence that peer reviews are possibly the most accurate method of judging employee behaviour, there are reasons why they are not used more often.[17] These reasons are commonly cited:

1. Peer reviews are simply a popularity contest.
2. Managers are reluctant to give up control over the assessment process.
3. Those receiving low ratings might retaliate against their peers.
4. Peers rely on stereotypes in ratings.

When peers are in competition with one another (e.g., sales associates), peer reviews may not be advisable for administrative decisions, such as those relating to salary or bonuses. Also, employers who use peer reviews must make sure to safeguard confidentiality in handling the review forms. A breach of confidentiality can create interpersonal rivalries or hurt feelings and foster hostility among fellow employees.

Team Review

An extension of the peer assessment is the **team review**. While peers are on equal standing with one another, they may not work closely together. In a team setting, it may be nearly impossible to separate out an individual's contribution. Advocates of team review argue that, in such cases, individual reviews can be dysfunctional since they detract from the critical issues of the team. To address this issue, organizations ranging from Chevron to Xerox to Harley-Davidson have been using team reviews to assess the performance of the team as a whole.[18]

A company's interest in team reviews is frequently motivated by its commitment to TQM principles and practices. At its root, TQM is a control system that involves setting standards (based on customer requirements), measuring performance against those standards, and identifying opportunities for continuous improvement. In this regard, TQM and performance reviews are perfectly complementary. However, a basic tenet of TQM is that performance is best understood at the level of the system as a whole, whereas performance reviews traditionally have focused on individual performance. Team reviews represent one way to break down barriers between individuals and encourage their collective effort.[19] Organizations such as Casino Windsor (Ontario), NorskeCanada (British Columbia), and Town of Canmore (Alberta) have successfully implemented performance management systems that link individuals' performance to organizational standards.[20]

Customer Input

Also driven by TQM concerns, an increasing number of organizations use internal and external **customer input** as a source of performance review information. While external customers' information has been used for some time to review restaurant, hotel, and car rental company personnel, companies such as Federal Express, AT&T, UPS, and Sears have begun utilizing external customers as well. For example, Sears customers receive a coupon asking them to call a 1-800 number within the next week. In exchange for answering prerecorded questions on a touch-tone phone, they receive $5 off their next purchase. Each call can be linked to a particular transaction (and sales associate) based on the receipt number. With 468 million transactions a year, enough survey data are generated for each sales associate to provide meaningful feedback on such performance measures as service and product knowledge. Customer information can also tell an organization if employees are following procedures. Secret shoppers at the Radisson Hotel Saskatoon provided feedback to hotel management that employees were failing to provide accurate accounting on some customers' bills.

Managers establish customer service measures (CSMs) and set goals for employees that are linked to company goals. Often the CSM goals are linked to employee pay through incentive programs. Customer survey data are then incorporated into the performance evaluation. By including CSMs in their performance reviews, managers hope to produce more objective evaluations, more effective employees, more satisfied customers, and better business performance.[21]

In contrast to external customers, internal customers include anyone inside the organization who depends on an employee's work output. For example, managers who rely on the HR department for recruitment and training services would be candidates for seeking internal customer feedback of that department. For both developmental and administrative purposes, internal customers can provide extremely useful feedback about the value added by an employee or team of employees.

Putting It All Together: 360-Degree Review

As mentioned previously, many companies are combining various sources of performance appraisal information to create multi-person—or 360-degree—appraisal and feedback systems. Jobs are multifaceted, and different people see different things. As the name implies, 360-degree feedback is intended to provide employees with as accurate a view of their performance as possible by getting input from all angles: supervisors, peers, subordinates, customers, and the like. Although in the beginning, 360-degree systems were purely developmental and were restricted mainly to management and career development, they have migrated to performance appraisal and other HR purposes. Over 90% of Fortune 1000 companies have implemented some form of 360-degree feedback for career development, performance review, or both.

Because the system combines more information than a typical performance appraisal, it can become administratively complex. For that reason, organizations have recently begun using Web technology (Internet, intranet) to compile and aggregate the information.[22] For example, PerformancePro.net is an online system developed by Exceed that provides managers and employees with the ability to develop performance plans, goals, and objectives, and then track progress over time. The planning process includes an online "wizard" that helps users establish SMART goals (Specific, Measurable, Achievable, Results-oriented, and Time-bound) and then allows employees to submit revised goals and action steps for approval. Using the tracking module, managers can see all of an employee's goals and action steps on a single screen. The program then combines self-appraisal and multiple-rater inputs in a 360-degree format. After rating an employee's performance on each goal, raters can provide summary comments in three categories: victories and accomplishments, setbacks and frustrations, and general comments. To ensure security, a user ID and password are required and all the data are captured and saved in the employee's history file.[23]

Figure 6.3 is a graphical depiction of 360-degree input sources.

Software used to help prepare 360-degree feedback systems is available from a number of companies. The Web sites for the Center for Employee Development (**www .halogensoftware.com/**) and Survey connect (**www.surveyconnect.com/**) not only give a list of resources for anyone interested in using 360-degree systems but also provide information about "best practices."

Figure 6.4 lists the pros and cons of 360-degree feedback.

Halogen Software
www.halogensoftware.com/

Survey Connect
www.surveyconnect.com

FIGURE 6.3   360-Degree Review Information

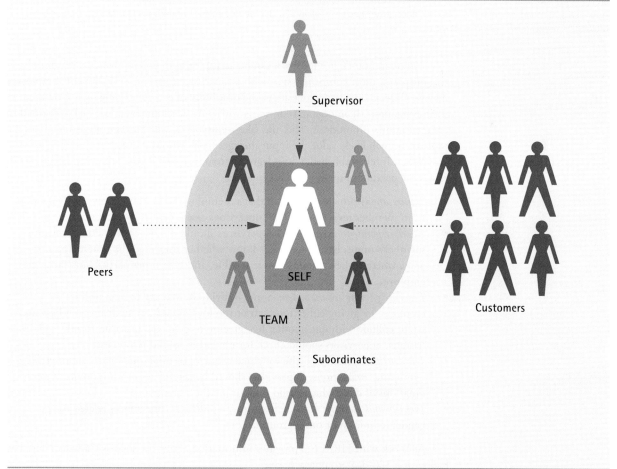

FIGURE 6.4   Pros and Cons of 360-Degree Feedback

Pros

- The system is more comprehensive in that responses are gathered from multiple perspectives.
- The quality of information is better. (Quality of respondents is more important than quantity.)
- It provides better data for developmental purposes.
- It complements TQM initiatives by emphasizing internal and external customers and teams.
- It may lessen bias and prejudice since feedback comes from more people, not one individual.
- It provides more consistent information on behaviours and actions.
- Feedback from peers and others may increase employee self-development.

Cons

- The system is administratively complex in combining all the responses.
- Feedback can be intimidating and cause resentment if the employee feels the respondents have "ganged up."
- It can be seen as a popularity contest.
- There may be conflicting opinions, though they may all be accurate from the respective standpoints.
- People can feel overwhelmed and in shock from the information.
- The system requires training to work effectively.
- Employees may collude or "game" the system by giving invalid evaluations of one another.

Sources: Compiled from Carol Orsag Madigan, "Full Circle Feedback," *Business Finance*, May 1999, www.businessfinancemag.com/archives/appfiles/Article.cfm?IssueID=154&ArticleID=5519, retrieved July 31, 2002; Dayton Fandray, "New Thinking in Performance Appraisals," *Workforce*, May 2001, 36–40; and Larry Shetzer, "Online 360-degree Feedback Encourages Bottom-Up Decision-Making," *Canadian HR Reporter*, November 6, 2000.

Although 360-degree feedback can be useful for both developmental and administrative purposes, most companies start with an exclusive focus on development. Employees may be understandably nervous about the possibility of everyone "ganging up" on them in their evaluations. If an organization starts with only developmental feedback—not tied to compensation, promotions, and the like—employees will become accustomed to the process and will likely value the input they get from various parties.

When Intel established a 360-degree system, it observed the following safeguards to ensure its maximum quality and acceptance:

- *Ensure anonymity.* Make certain that no employee ever knows how any evaluation-team member responded. (The supervisor's assessment is an exception to this rule.)
- *Make respondents accountable.* Supervisors should discuss each evaluation-team member's input, letting members know whether they used the system appropriately, whether their responses were reliable, and how other participants rated the employee.
- *Prevent "gaming" of the system.* Some individuals may try to help or hurt an employee by giving either too high or too low an evaluation. Team members may try to collude with one another by agreeing to give each other uniformly high evaluations. Supervisors should check for obviously invalid responses.
- *Use statistical procedures.* Use weighted averages or other quantitative approaches to combining evaluations. Supervisors should be careful about using subjective combinations of data, which could undermine the system.
- *Identify and quantify biases.* Check for prejudices or preferences related to age, gender, ethnicity, or other group factors.[24]

At Work with HRM 6.2 provides information about the success Canadian Tire has had with a 360-degree approach.

at work **with HRM 6.2** at work with HRM 6.2

CANADIAN TIRE 360-DEGREE MATRIX

"Accentuate the positive; build on leadership strengths" is the principal theme of leadership performance evaluation and development conducted by the Canadian Tire Corporation as described by Janice Wismer, vice-president of Human Resources. Canadian Tire is a network of interrelated businesses with retail, financial, and petroleum interests. About 45,000 employees work in 1,000 retail stores across Canada.

The customized 360-degree feedback process used at Canadian Tire is research based and designed to build a cadre of great leaders. The first step in the design of the 360-degree feedback instrument was to benchmark other organizations that had effective 360-degree feedback processes. Twenty-seven key employees at Canadian Tire were interviewed to identify the attributes of their great leaders as measured by the standards of the organization. These key leadership attributes were then discussed and evaluated in workshops with important stakeholders. A total of 16 competencies were identified: 7 related to "who one is"—characteristics, such as trustworthy, passionate, and curious. Nine others focused on "what one can do for the team, business, and enterprise," such as make strategic choices, motivate and celebrate, communicate authentically.

To date, about 170 managers have been assessed by an average of nine colleagues, including peers, subordinates, and bosses. Colleagues complete a self-survey, and all feedback assessment is analyzed relative to their own organization and to industry standards, which are maintained in a database. A confidential feedback report is given to each individual.

According to Ed Haltrecht, Ph.D., CHRP, who specializes in measurement and organizational leadership development, in most organizations when performance feedback is presented, both the employee and the manager focus on the reds—the weaknesses—and try to work out methods of development to improve this area. What is unique about Canadian Tire is that the focus is on the positive. It has found that improvements in weak areas (provided it is not a fundamental flaw) do not affect overall performance, while improvements in areas of strength bring managers from good to extraordinary. The goal is to identify and strengthen attributes so employees will distinguish and present themselves as extraordinary. Individuals first address any "fundamental flaws"—either a very weak attribute of the individual or, more importantly, elements regarded as critical to the organization.

Canadian Tire's leadership development system also recognizes two other significant research findings: first, extraordinary leaders have about three competencies that they excel at and developing a few strengths to very high performance levels has a greater impact than improving several competencies from poor to average. Second, competencies travel together and improvement in one leads to significant progress in others. Identifying these companion competencies has proven to be extremely worthwhile. In a nutshell, these are the findings: start with the right set of competencies or attributes; focus on strengths; eliminate any fundamental flaws; and pay attention to companion attributes.

The assessment feedback process at Canadian Tire is seen as a tool for dialogue and for focusing on what makes a great company and what matters in leadership. Those employees who try to improve are given a developmental opportunities guidebook. Canadian Tire has discovered that the best development methods are stretch challenging assignments, coaching and mentoring, personal feedback, talks with consultants, and training programs.

CRITICAL THINKING QUESTION

What would be your reaction to this approach if you were working for Canadian Tire? Explain your answer.

Manager's Toolkit **6.1** Manager's Toolkit 6.1

SAMPLE 360-DEGREE STATEMENTS WITH DESCRIPTORS

Based on interaction that you have had with the individual, select the level that best describes their performance in each competency area.

Level 4: Consistently demonstrates the behaviour.

Level 3: Usually demonstrates the behaviour.

Level 2: Sometimes demonstrates the behaviour.

Level 1: Rarely demonstrates the behaviour.

Competency 1: Teamwork—Works effectively with others within own department and across departments for benefit of company. Specifically, displays an openness to ideas, works collaboratively with team members, participates in development of the team, celebrates team successes, and treats team members with respect.

Competency 2: Customer service—Shows a commitment to understanding customer needs and strives to exceed their expectations. Specifically, displays knowledge of customer needs, provides exceptional service to customers, exhibits knowledge of products, shows steady gains in response time without sacrificing positive interaction.

Based on the experiences of companies like Celestica, Allstate Insurance, and Canadian Tire, it appears that 360-degree feedback can provide a valuable approach to performance review. Its success, as with any performance review method, depends on how managers use the information and how fairly employees are treated. Manager's Toolkit 6.1 provides sample competency descriptors and how they might be assessed on a 360-degree performance review.

Training Reviewers

A weakness of many performance management systems is that managers and supervisors are not adequately trained for setting performance goals or assessing performance and therefore provide little meaningful feedback to subordinates. Because they lack precise standards for reviewing subordinates' performance and have not developed the necessary observational and feedback skills, their reviews often become general, unspecific, and meaningless. Therefore, training people who will conduct performance reviews can vastly improve the overall performance management system. Thus it is important that supervisors and managers be trained in how to conduct performance reviews. The training needs to help remove the barriers of time constraints, lack of knowledge, and interpersonal conflicts. By overcoming these barriers, the performance review process will be more effective.

PERFORMANCE REVIEW METHODS

Objective **6**

Since the early years of their use by the federal government, methods of reviewing staff have evolved considerably. Old systems have been replaced by new methods that reflect technical improvements and legal requirements and are more consistent with the purposes of a performance management system. In the discussion that follows, you will be introduced to those methods that have found widespread use; methods that are used less frequently will be touched on briefly. Performance review methods can be broadly classified as measuring traits, behaviours, or results; many organizations may incorporate all three into their system.

Trait Methods

Trait approaches to performance reviews are designed to measure the extent to which an employee possesses certain characteristics—such as dependability, creativity, initiative, and leadership—that are viewed as important for the job and the organization in general. Trait methods are popular as they are easy to develop but can be notoriously biased.

Frequently in the trait method, the supervisor is asked to numerically rate the person on the specific characteristics. For example, on the characteristic of "dependable," the supervisor might be asked to rate the person on a scale of 1 to 5, with 1 being unsatisfactory and 5 being exceptional. This is called a **graphic rating scale**, a sample of which is shown in Manager's Toolkit 6.2. The supervisor may also be asked to provide a short paragraph commentary on the person's dependability.

Graphic rating scales
A trait approach to performance review whereby each employee is rated according to a scale of characteristics

When using the trait method of performance review, a customer service representative may be reviewed on being friendly and helpful.

Manager's Toolkit **6.2** Manager's Toolkit 6.2

GRAPHICS RATINGS SCALE WITH PROVISION FOR COMMENTS

Appraise employee's performance in PRESENT ASSIGNMENT. Check (✔) most appropriate square. Appraisers are *urged to freely use* the "Remarks" sections for significant comments descriptive of the individual.

1. KNOWLEDGE OF WORK:
Understanding of all phases of his/her work and related matters

Needs instruction or guidance		Has required knowledge of own and related work	Has exceptional knowledge of own and related work	
☐	☐	☐	✔	☐

Remarks: *Is particularly good on gas engines.*

2. INITIATIVE:
Ability to originate or develop ideas and to get things started

Lacks imagination		Meets necessary requirements		Unusually resourceful
☐	✔	☐		☐

Remarks: *Has good ideas when asked for an opinion, but otherwise will not offer them. Somewhat lacking in self-confidence.*

3. APPLICATION:
Attention and application to his/her work

Wastes time Needs close supervision		Steady and willing worker		Exceptionally industrious
☐	☐	✔		☐

Remarks: *Accepts new jobs when assigned.*

4. QUALITY OF WORK:
Thoroughness, neatness, and accuracy of work

Needs improvement		Regularly meets recognized standards		Consistently maintains highest quality
☐	☐	☐	✔	

Remarks: *The work he turns out is always of the highest possible quality.*

5. VOLUME OF WORK:
Quantity of acceptable work

Should be increased		Regularly meets recognized standards		Unusually high output
☐	☐	✔		☐

Remarks: *Would be higher if he did not spend so much time checking and rechecking his work.*

Behavioural Methods

As mentioned above, one of the potential drawbacks of a trait-oriented performance review is that traits tend to be vague and subjective. Behavioural methods have been developed to specifically describe which actions should (or should not) be exhibited on the job. Since behavioural methods are becoming more common, this section describes three approaches that use them: the behavioural checklist method, the behaviourally anchored rating scale (BARS), and the behaviour observation scales (BOS).

Behavioural Checklist Method

This method consists of having the supervisor check those statements on a list that are believed to be the characteristics of the employee's performance or behaviour. A checklist developed for computer salespeople might include a number of statements like the following:

_____ Is able to explain equipment clearly
_____ Keeps abreast of new developments in technology
_____ Tends to be a steady worker
_____ Reacts quickly to customer needs
_____ Processes orders correctly

Behaviourally Anchored Rating Scale (BARS)

Behaviourally anchored rating scale (BARS)
A behavioural approach to performance review that consists of a series of vertical scales, one for each important dimension of job performance

The **behaviourally anchored rating scale (BARS)** approach consists of a series of five to ten vertical scales—one for each important dimension or component of performance. These components are then given a numerical scale based on critical incidents of on-the-job performance. Manager's Toolkit 6.3 displays an example of this for an employee in a service-based industry such as hospitality.

Manager's Toolkit **6.3** Manager's Toolkit 6.3

EXAMPLE OF BARS FOR SERVICE-BASED INDUSTRY

Communications: This area of performance concerns the ability of the person to exchange information in all forms including demonstration of active listening.

High	7	Consistently demonstrates exceptional verbal and written communication skills. Demonstrates exceptional sensitivity and empathy. Improves lines of communication throughout hotel.
	6	
	5	Frequently demonstrates exceptional verbal and written communication skills. Correctly assesses and responds to sensitive situations.
Average	4	Facilitates the clear, concise communication of information in appropriate forms in a timely fashion. Adapts communication style to meet the needs of others.
	3	Inconsistent ability to communicate effectively or in a timely manner. Does not always adapt communication style to meet the needs of others.
Low	2	Receives and imparts information inaccurately.
	1	

Behaviour Observation Scales (BOS)

A behaviour observation scale (BOS) is similar to a BARS in that both are based on critical incidents. The value of BOS is that it enables the reviewer to play the role of observer rather than judge. In this way, he or she can more easily provide constructive feedback to the employee.

Results Methods

Rather than look at the traits of employees or the behaviours they exhibit on the job, many organizations review employee accomplishments—the results they achieve through their work. Advocates of results methods argue that they are more objective and empowering for employees. Looking at results, such as sales figures, production output, and the like, involves less subjectivity and therefore this method may be less open to bias. Furthermore, this approach often gives employees responsibility for their outcomes, while giving them discretion over the methods they use to accomplish them (within limits). This is empowerment in action.

Productivity Measures

A number of results measures are available to review performance. Salespeople are reviewed on the basis of their sales volume (both the number of units sold and the dollar amount in revenues). Production workers are reviewed on the basis of the number of units they produce and perhaps the scrap rate or number of defects that are detected. Customer service people are reviewed on the number of customers handled. Executives are frequently reviewed on the basis of company profits or growth rate. Each of these measures directly links what employees accomplish with results that benefit the organization. In this way, results reviews can directly align employee and organizational goals.

Results methods may inadvertently encourage employees to "look good" on a short-term basis, while ignoring the long-term ramifications. Line supervisors, for example, may let their equipment suffer to reduce maintenance costs. Further, in any job involving interaction with others, it is not enough to simply look at production or sales figures. Factors such as cooperation, adaptability, initiative, and concern for human relations may be important to job success. If these factors are important job standards, they should be added to the review. Thus, to be realistic, both the results and the method used to achieve them should be considered.[25]

Management by Objectives

Management by objectives (MBO) Philosophy of management that rates performance on the basis of employee achievement of goals

Accel-Team
www.accel-team.com

One method that attempts to overcome some of the limitations of results-oriented reviews is **management by objectives (MBO)**. MBO is a philosophy of management that has employees establish objectives (e.g., production costs, sales per product, quality standards, profits), through consultation with their superiors and then uses these objectives as a basis for review.[26] MBO is a useful approach to an overall performance management system. As shown in Figure 6.5, MBO begins with setting the organization's common goals and objectives and ultimately returns to that step. For additional information on Management by Objectives, review the article on improving productivity at **www.accel-team.com**.

As the figure illustrates, a significant feature of the cycle is the establishment of specific goals by the employee. However, since those goals are based on a broad statement of employee responsibilities prepared by the supervisor, situations can arise in which unrealistic expectations can be agreed to.

FIGURE 6.5 Performance Management Using an MBO Approach

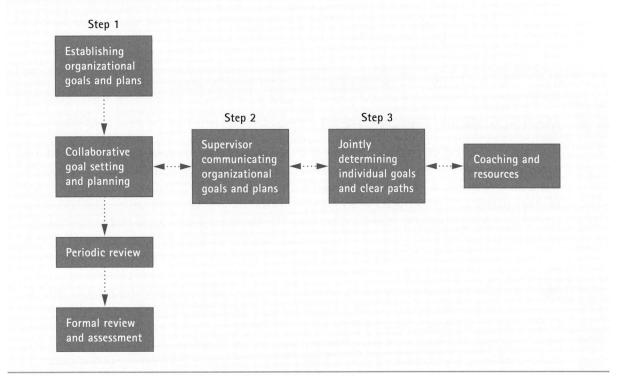

Source: From *Management*, 5th Edition, by Ricky W. Griffin and Jan B. Singh, Copyright © 2000. Reprinted with permission of Nelson, a division of Thomson Learning: www.thomsonrights.com. Fax 800-730-2215.

To ensure success, MBO programs should be viewed as part of a total system for managing, not as merely an addition to the manager's job. Managers must be willing to empower employees to accomplish their objectives on their own, giving them discretion over the methods they use (but holding them accountable for outcomes). The following guidelines may be especially helpful:

1. Managers and employees must be willing to establish goals and objectives together.
2. Objectives should be quantifiable and measurable for the long and short term.
3. Expected results must be under the employee's control.
4. Managers and organizations must be supportive and provide necessary resources in order for employees to reach the expected outcomes.
5. Goals and objectives must be consistent for each level (top executive, manager, and employee).
6. Managers and employees must establish specific times when goals are to be reviewed and evaluated.

With the recent concern about business ethics, more and more organizations are including standards of performance related to ethics and reviewing ethical behaviour as part of the performance management system. Ethics in HRM 6.1 discusses how this might be done. Manager's Toolkit 6.4 presents a sample goal-setting worksheet used in organizations. You will note the column titled "Key Results." This is a description of what the goal will look like when it has been achieved. For example, a key result might be "Increased customer satisfaction." This would be measured by the percentage of satisfied customers and the goal might be "To increase the customer satisfaction level from 75% to 80%."

ethics **in HRM 6.1** ethics in HRM 6.1

MEASURING ETHICAL PERFORMANCE

How do you distinguish between ethical and nonethical behaviour and performance at work? The answer frequently is "It depends." Since the business scandals of recent years more organizations are looking at ways to review and assess ethical behaviours.

Much has been written on "corporate responsibility" over the last several years—the behaviour of organizations that believe their responsibility extends beyond the shareholder to the employees, customers, and community at large. Many of the companies that take this view have also developed codes of ethics—a set of statements that indicate correct behaviour and actions in the organization. It is from this code that specific and measurable

behaviours of performance can be established. For example, frequently in a code of ethics there is a statement about "being respectful to each other." Therefore, the performance measure might be "Demonstrates respect for all staff and customers." This particular measure would also need to have very clear definitions for respect, as this word can mean different things different people.

With a more diverse workforce with different values and expectations, it is even more important to ensure people in the organization are clear on organizational values and ethics. To help with that clarity, reviewing employees' performance on ethical behaviours will go a long way to ensure employees are behaving appropriately.

Sources: Adapted from "What Is Corporate Social Responsibility?" EthicsScan Canada, Ltd., www.ethicscan.ca; Industry Canada, "The Cross-Cultural Marketing Edge," strategis.ic.gc.ca/SSG/sc01691e.html; and R.W. Dye, "Who's Minding the Store?" *CMA Management*, June 2002, 18–20.

Manager's Toolkit **6.4** Manager's Toolkit 6.4

SAMPLE GOAL-SETTING WORKSHEET

Performance Management System

Name   Performance Period

Key Results	Measure	Goal	By When

The Balanced Scorecard

One of the most enthusiastically adopted performance management innovations over the past decade has been the Balanced Scorecard (BSC). Developed by Harvard professors Robert Kaplan and David Norton, the BSC is a measurement framework that helps managers translate strategic goals into operational objectives. The generic model, shown in Manager's Toolkit 6.5, has four related categories: (1) financial, (2) customer, (3) processes, and (4) learning. The logic of the BSC is that learning and people management help organizations improve their internal processes. These internal

Manager's Toolkit **6.5**

THE BALANCED SCORECARD

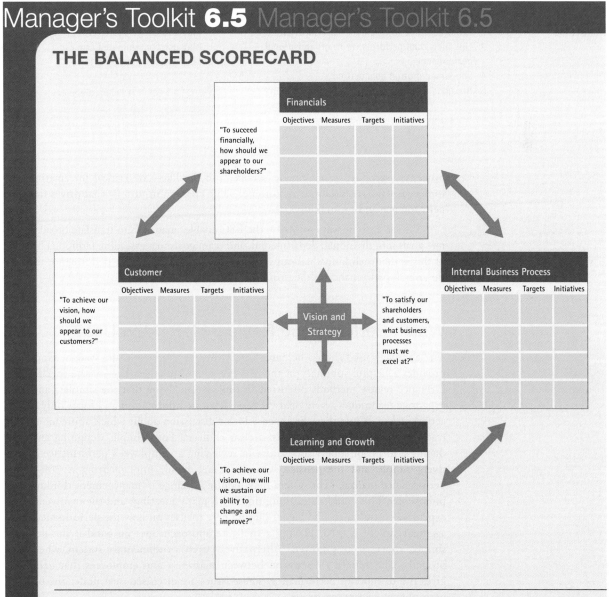

Source: Robert Kaplan and David Norton, "Strategic Learning and the Balanced Scorecard," *Strategy & Leadership* 24, No. 5 (Sept/Oct 1996): 18–24.

FIGURE 6.6 Summary of Various Review Methods

	Advantages	Disadvantages
Trait Methods	1. Are inexpensive to develop 2. Use meaningful dimensions 3. Are easy to use	1. Have high potential for rating errors 2. Are not useful for employee counselling 3. Are not useful for allocating rewards 4. Are not useful for promotion decisions
Behavioural Methods	1. Use specific performance dimensions 2. Are acceptable to employees 3. Are useful for providing feedback 4. Are fair for reward and promotion decisions	1. Can be time-consuming to develop/use 2. Can be costly to develop 3. Have some potential for rating error
Results Method	1. Have less subjectivity bias 2. Are acceptable to employees and superiors 3. Link individual performance to organizational performance 4. Encourage mutual goal setting 5. Are good for reward and promotion decisions	1. Are time-consuming to develop/use 2. May encourage short-term perspective 3. May use contaminated criteria 4. May use deficient criteria

processes—product development, service, and the like—are critical for creating customer satisfaction and loyalty. Customer value creation in turn is what drives financial performance and profitability.

Similar in some ways to MBO, the BSC enables managers to translate broad corporate goals into divisional, departmental, and team goals in a cascading fashion. The value of this is that each individual can see more clearly how his or her performance ties into the overall performance of the firm.

Which Performance Review Method to Use?

The approach used should be based largely on the purpose of the system. Figure 6.6 provides a helpful summary of the advantages and disadvantages of the specific performance review methods discussed in this section. Note that the simplest and least expensive techniques often yield the least accurate information and focus only on the actual review. While there has been a lot of discussion about which approach to use, research has not always supported a clear choice.[27] For example, designing and producing a form for supervisors to use in reviewing an employee's performance is relatively simple and inexpensive. On the other hand, implementing a 360-degree performance management system may require a change in management thinking and philosophy. This could take a long time with many meetings and the involvement of expensive consultants. The bigger picture here focuses on how the performance management system is used. Having a first-rate approach does no good if the manager simply "shoves it in a drawer." Alternatively, even a rudimentary system, when used properly, can initiate a discussion between managers and employees that genuinely gives rise to superior performance. These issues are discussed next under the topic of performance review interviews.

PERFORMANCE REVIEW INTERVIEWS

The coaching and review discussions are perhaps the most important parts of the entire performance management process. These discussions give a manager the opportunity to discuss a subordinate's performance record and to explore areas of possible improvement and growth. They also provide an opportunity to identify the subordinate's attitudes and feelings more thoroughly and thus to improve communication.

The format for the coaching sessions and the formal performance review interview will be determined in large part by the purpose of the interview, the type of system used, and the organization of any interview form. Most performance interviews attempt to give feedback to employees on how well they are performing their jobs and on planning for their future development. Interviews should be scheduled far enough in advance to allow the interviewee, as well as the interviewer, to prepare for the discussion. Usually ten days to two weeks is a sufficient amount of lead-time.

Conducting the Formal Performance Interview

Objective 7

While there are no hard-and-fast rules for how to conduct a formal review, there are some guidelines that may increase the employee's acceptance of the feedback, satisfaction with the interview, and intention to improve in the future. Many of the principles of effective interviewing discussed in Chapter 4 apply to performance review interviews as well. Here are some other guidelines that should also be considered.

1. *Ask for a self-assessment.* As noted earlier in the chapter, it is useful to have employees review their own performance prior to the interview. Recent research evidence suggests that employees are more satisfied and view the performance management system as providing more procedural justice when they have input into the process. The interview can then be used to discuss those areas where the manager and the employee have reached different conclusions—not so much to resolve the "truth," but to work toward a resolution of problems.[28]

2. *Invite participation.* The basic purpose of a performance interview is to initiate a dialogue that will help employees improve their performance. Research evidence suggests that participation is strongly related to an employee's satisfaction with the review feedback as well as that person's intention to improve performance.[29] During the conversation, it is important that the supervisor actively listens to the employee's comments and responses to questions.

3. *Express appreciation.* Praise is a powerful motivator, and in a performance interview, particularly, employees are seeking positive feedback. Start the interview by expressing appreciation for what the employee has done well. In this way, the employee may be less defensive and more likely to talk about aspects of the job that are not going so well.

4. *Minimize criticism.* If an employee has many areas in need of improvement, managers should focus on those few objective issues that are most problematic or most important to the job.

People in retail are frequently assessed on their customer service interactions.

5. *Change the behaviour, not the person.* Avoid suggestions about personal traits to change; instead, suggest more acceptable ways of performing. For example, instead of focusing on a person's "unreliability," a manager might focus on the fact that the employee "has been late to work seven times this month."

6. *Focus on solving problems.* In addressing performance issues, it is frequently tempting to get into the "blame game" in which both manager and employee enter into a potentially endless discussion of why a situation has arisen. The interview should be directed at devising a solution to the problem.

7. *Be supportive.* One of the better techniques for engaging an employee in the problem-solving process is for the manager to ask, "What can I do to help?" By being open and supportive, the manager conveys to the employee that the manager will try to eliminate external roadblocks and work with the employee to achieve higher standards.

8. *Establish goals.* Since a major purpose of the performance review is to make plans for further growth and development, it is important to focus the interviewee's attention on the future rather than the past.

9. *Follow up day to day.* Ideally, coaching and ongoing feedback should be a regular part of a manager's job. Feedback is most useful when it is immediate and specific to a particular situation.

There may be times that the performance interview is very difficult—either because the manager is uncomfortable or the employee is not willing to take responsibility. Therefore, it is very important that the supervisor remain calm and is very clear on what the problem is and what specifically needs to be done differently. For further tips on handling this type of interview, view the video clip produced by trainingABC at **www.trainingabc.com/screeningroom.htm**.

trainingABC
www.trainingabc.com/
screeningroom.htm

Improving Performance

In many instances, the performance interview will provide the basis for noting deficiencies in employee performance and for making plans for improvement. Unless these deficiencies are brought to the employee's attention, they are likely to continue until they become quite serious. Sometimes underperformers do not understand exactly what is expected of them. However, once their responsibilities are clarified, they are in a position to take the corrective action needed to improve their performance.

Identifying Sources of Ineffective Performance

There are many reasons why an employee's performance might not meet the standards. First, each individual has a unique pattern of strengths and weaknesses that play a part. In addition, other factors—such as the work environment, the external environment (including home and community), and personal problems—have an impact on job performance. To provide a better understanding of possible sources of ineffective performance related to these environments, the comprehensive list shown in Figure 6.7 has been devised.

It is recommended that a diagnosis of poor employee performance focus on three interactive elements: skill, effort, and external conditions. For example, if an employee's performance is not up to standard, the cause could be a skill problem (knowledge, abilities, technical competencies), an effort problem (motivation to get the job done),

FIGURE 6.7 Sources of Ineffective Performance

Organization Policies and Practices
- Ineffective placement
- Insufficient job training
- Ineffectual employment practices
- Permissiveness with enforcing policies or job standards
- Heavy-handed management
- Lack of attention to employee needs or concerns
- Inadequate communication within organization
- Unclear reporting relationships

Job Concerns
- Unclear or constantly changing work requirements
- Boredom with job
- Lack of job growth or advancement opportunities
- Management–employee conflict
- Problems with fellow employees
- Unsafe working conditions
- Unavailable or inadequate equipment or materials
- Inability to perform the job
- Excessive workload
- Lack of job skills

Personal Problems
- Marital problems
- Financial worries
- Emotional disorders (including depression, guilt, anxiety, fear)
- Conflict between work demands and family demands
- Physical limitations, including disabilities
- Low work ethic
- Other family problems
- Lack of effort
- Immaturity

External Factors
- Industry decline or extreme competition
- Legal constraints
- Conflict between ethical standards and job demands
- Union–management conflict

and/or some problem in the external conditions of work (poor economy). Any one of these problem areas could cause performance to suffer.

Managing Ineffective Performance

Once the sources of performance problems are known, a course of action can be planned. This action may lie in providing training in areas that would increase the knowledge and/or skills needed for effective performance. A transfer to another job or department might give an employee a chance to become a more effective member of the organization. In other instances, greater attention may have to be focused on ways to motivate the individual.

If ineffective performance persists, it may be necessary to transfer the employee, take disciplinary action, or discharge the person from the organization. Whatever action is taken to cope with ineffective performance, it should be done with objectivity, fairness, and a recognition of the feelings of the individual involved.

SUMMARY

1. Define a performance management system.
   - Set of integrated management practices.

2. Explain the purpose of a performance management system.
   - Allows the organization to get the right things done.
   - Helps increase employees' satisfaction with their work and the organization.

3. Describe the management practices necessary for a good performance management system.
   - Setting and communicating clear performance expectations.
   - Clear and specific performance objectives.
   - Supportive and helpful coaching by the supervisor.
   - Focusing on accomplishment of objectives during performance appraisals.
   - Recognizing and celebrating good performance.

4. Identify the steps in an effective performance management system.
   - Clarifying the work (job) to be done.
   - Setting goals and establishing a performance plan.
   - Regular and frequent coaching.
   - Conducting formal review of performance.
   - Recognizing and rewarding performance.

5. Describe the different sources of performance information.
   - Manager or supervisor who is able to provide feedback on contribution.
   - Self—provides a personal review of accomplishments.
   - Subordinate—provides a perspective on certain behaviours such as leadership.
   - Peers and team members—who are able to describe how the person works with others.
   - Customers—provides input about the quality of service.

6. Explain the various methods used for performance reviews.
   - Trait approaches are designed to measure the extent to which an employee possesses certain characteristics.
   - Behavioural methods specifically describe which actions should (or should not) be exhibited on the job.

- Productivity measures look at results or outputs.
- Management by objectives (MBO) is a philosophy of management that has employees establish objectives (e.g., production costs, sales per product, quality standards, profits), through consultation with their superiors and then uses those objectives as a basis for appraisal.

7. Outline the characteristics of an effective performance review interview.
   - Ask the employees to review and assess their own performance prior to the interview.
   - Invite and encourage active participation by employees in the discussion of their performance.
   - Express appreciation for what the employee has done well.
   - Minimize criticism.
   - Change the behaviour, not the person.

Need to Know

- Definition of performance management system
- Purpose and reasons for introducing a performance management system
- The characteristics of an effective performance management system
- Various methods used to gather performance information
- Advantages and disadvantages of various performance review methods
- Guidelines for conducting a performance appraisal interview

Need to Understand

- Link of management practices with performance management systems
- Relationship of organizational performance with performance management systems
- Role supervisor or line manager plays in the effectiveness of any system
- Relationship of methods to the overall system and the style of management
- Importance of good coaching and interviewing skills for appraising overall performance

Key Terms

behaviourally anchored rating scale (BARS) 215	peer review 207
customer input 208	performance management system 196
graphic rating scales 213	self-review 206
management by objectives (MBO) 216	subordinate review 206
manager and/or supervisor review 205	team review 207

REVIEW QUESTIONS

1. What are the major purposes of a performance management system?
2. Describe the relationships among performance management systems and selection, training, and development.
3. How can a performance management system be adjusted to include the principles of total-quality management (TQM)?
4. Describe the steps of an effective performance management system.

5. Discuss the guidelines that performance evaluations should meet in order to be legally defensible.
6. Who could evaluate the performance of people working in the following jobs?

   a. Sales representative
   b. Air traffic controller
   c. Room attendant in a hotel
   d. Activity coordinator in an eldercare centre
   e. Customer service representative in a financial institution

7. In many organizations, evaluators submit the reviews of their subordinates to their immediate superiors for review before discussing them with the individual employees they have evaluated. What advantages are there to this procedure?
8. What are the pros and cons of trait, behaviour, and results evaluations?
9. What are the suggested guidelines for conducting an effective performance review?

CRITICAL THINKING QUESTIONS

1. Your study group at school has been asked to develop a set of performance standards by which you could measure your performance. What would you include and why?
2. Assume you have just been hired as a customer service representative in a call centre for a bank. Your supervisor has asked that you work with a small task force to develop an appropriate performance appraisal approach. What method would you recommend and why?
3. An autopart's purchasing department is responsible for ordering and receiving all deliveries, including rush deliveries. Recently the person who checked the orders received failed to check that an urgent part had been received for a key client. When discovered by the supervisor after the client complained, the person confirmed that this was not checked. This was not the first time that a shipment had not been properly checked. The supervisor was also aware that during the employee's vacation the replacement worker had been able to perform all the duties without any difficulty. Explain how a performance management system might have prevented such a situation.
4. Discuss how you would diagnose poor performance in an accounting clerk's job. List several factors to consider.
5. Do you think students ought to be able to provide input into their instructor's performance? Why or why not? Explain your reasoning.

DEVELOPING YOUR SKILLS

1. On an individual basis, use the worksheet shown in Manager's Toolkit 6.4 to establish goals in relation to either this course or a job you are currently doing. After completing the worksheet, pair up with another student. Review and critique each other's work. In particular, look for realistic measurements and dates of completion.

2. Working in pairs, identify three to four performance characteristics on which your instructor ought to be reviewed. Share your responses with the entire class. Develop a single list of three to four performance characteristics. Discuss as an entire class. Determine whether the instructor agrees with your list; if not, enquire as to what ought to be on the list.

3. Working in groups of three to four students, review the following descriptions of three different employees. Describe the potential causes of poor performance in each case. And for each potential cause, identify appropriate solutions to enhance performance.

   a. *Carl Spackler* is the assistant greens-keeper at Bushwood Country Club. Over the past few months, members have been complaining that gophers are destroying the course and digging holes in the greens. Although Carl has been working evenings and weekends to address the situation, the problem persists. Unfortunately, his boss is interested only in results, and because the gophers are still there, he contends that Carl is not doing his job. He has accused Carl of "slacking off" and threatened his job.

   b. *Sandeep Dhillon* works in research and development for a chemical company that makes non-nutritive food additives. His most recent assignment has been the development of a nonstick aerosol cooking spray, but the project is way behind schedule and seems to be going nowhere. CEO Frank Shirley is decidedly upset and has threatened that if things don't improve, he will suspend bonuses again this year like he did last year. Sandeep feels dejected, because without the bonus he won't be able to take his family on vacation.

   c. *Soon Tan* is the host of a local television talk show called *Morning Winnipeg*. Although she is a talented performer and comedian, Soon has an unacceptable record of tardiness. The show's producer, David Bellows, is frustrated, because the problem has affected the quality of the show. On several occasions, Soon was unprepared when the show went on the air. Bellows has concluded that Soon is not a morning person and has thought about replacing her with a different host.

Panoramic Feedback

www.panoramicfeedback .com

4. Access **www.panoramicfeedback.com**. Click the link "Demo" and develop a 360-degree feedback survey, respond to it, and receive the report. Print the report. In groups of four to five students, compare the survey instrument and the reports.

5. Access the following two Web sites:

   • **www.performance-appraisal.com/anpas.htm**
   • **www.knowledgepoint.com**

   Each of these sites has a sample performance assessment tool. Try each tool, using information about yourself. As you go through the samples, identify features that are useful for the supervisor and ones that might not be as useful. Write a one-page summary of the tools, explaining which you would use and why.

Archer North's Performance Appraisal

www.performance-appraisal .com/anpas.htm

KnowledgePoint

www.knowledgepoint.com

6. Access the Government of Canada's Web site for small business (**www.employers.gc.ca**) and click the link titled "Employee and Labour Relations." Follow the link to "employee motivation and performance." Review one of the documents and prepare a one-page summary explaining how the information would help a small business owner deal with performance management.

Government of Canada

www.employers.gc.ca

Case Study ┃ **1**

Workload Worries

A hotel's receiving department is responsible for checking deliveries of food and beverages, checking what has been received against what has been ordered, and verifying the quality of the merchandise received. In May 2000 an employee of the Westin Ottawa failed to check a case of vegetables, which had started to rot. The receiver, who had been with the hotel for seventeen years, admitted that he had not checked the vegetables. As a result, his supervisor gave him a written warning. The employee grieved, stating that he was too busy because the work load was excessive.

There was an investigation, which indicated that the grievor had not worked any overtime, nor had he requested permission to work any overtime. It was also noted that during the receiver's vacation period, the replacement worker had been able to perform the job without any difficulty. There was also evidence that the receiver was taking excessive breaks.

As a result of this investigation, the grievance was denied. In addition, the employee was sent a letter reminding him of his job responsibilities and of the need to restrict himself to the scheduled breaks. As a last step he was given a procedure to follow if he believed that the work was becoming excessive.

Questions

1. Discuss how a performance appraisal system might have prevented this grievance.
2. Which performance appraisal method would you recommend for this type of job?

Case Study ┃ **2**

The Bank of Montreal's Balanced Scorecard

In 1990, when Matthew W. Barrett became the Bank of Montreal's chairman and Tony Comper became its president, they had one main goal: to focus the entire workforce on success. It's a simple idea, but not so easy to execute. How would they get entry-level tellers to think of their work not just as a means to a paycheque, but as a direct contribution to BMO shareholders? How would they remind corporate executives that their jobs were not just to boost the bottom line, but to charm entire communities?

The answer was a balanced scorecard approach. To be competitive, executives decided, the bank had to meet the needs of four stakeholders: BMO shareholders, customers, employees, and communities.

Executives translated that idea into four goals: shareholders needed a return on equity, customers needed good service, employees needed to feel loyal and satisfied, and communities needed to feel that the bank made a difference in their neighbourhoods. Return on investment would determine satisfaction for shareholders; surveys and feedback would determine satisfaction for customers, employees, and communities. So far, so good. But every single department and every employee in every department had to understand how their work contributed to achieving those four goals. Now, each employee and department performance rating is dependent on contributions toward each goal. Employees in the customer service department, for instance, are rated by their return on equity (judged by their cost-effectiveness), their customer satisfaction (judged by customer feedback), and their community involvement (judged by any outreach programs or increase in customers). Departments may be assigned a specific stakeholder.

At the end of the year, the scores from everyone's performance ratings are translated into indexes, with ratings from 1 to 10. The index for the employee stakeholder piece is determined by ratings for competency, commitment, and cost-effectiveness. The four indexes—for BMO shareholders, customers, employees, and communities— are then rolled up into one figure of merit. At the end of each year, these results are presented to the board of directors, who use them to determine bonuses.

Source: "How the Bank of Montreal Keeps Score on Success" by Gillion Flynn, copyright December 1997. ACC Communications/Workforce, Costa Hesa, CA. http://www .workforce.com.

Questions

1. What are the strengths and weaknesses of a balanced scorecard approach to performance review?
2. Do you think such an approach would integrate well with an MBO system? Explain.

NOTES AND REFERENCES

1. David Brown, "Re-evaluating Evaluations," *Canadian HR Reporter*, April 8, 2002, www.hrreporter.com/loginarea/ members/viewing.asp?ArticleNo=1751&viewwhat=Print& subscriptionType=PRINT&callerpage=whoswho (retrieved July 31, 2002); Dayton Fandray, "The New Thinking in Performance Appraisals," *Workforce*, May 2001, 36–40.
2. Robert Bacal, *Performance Management*, chap. 1: www.perform.8m.com/art.htm (retrieved September 29, 1999).
3. Elizabeth L. Axelrod, Helen Handfield-Jones, and Timothy A. Welsh, "The War for Talent, Part Two," *The McKinsey Quarterly, 2001, Number 2*, http://www.mckinseyquarterly .com/article_page.aspx?ar=1035&L2=18&L3=31 (retrieved May 29, 2005).
4. *Ibid.*
5. Anne Stephen and Tony Roithmayr, "Escaping the Performance Management Trap," *Re-Inventing HR: Changing Roles to Create the High-Performance Organization* (Toronto: John Wiley & Sons, 1998): 229–48.

6. Matt Bloom, "The Performance Effects of Pay Dispersion on Individuals and Organizations," *Academy of Management Journal* 42, no. 1 (February 1999): 25–40; Donald J. Campbell, Kathleen M. Campbell, and Ho-Beng Chia, "Merit Pay, Performance Appraisal, and Individual Motivation: An Analysis and Alternative," *Human Resource Management* 37, no. 2 (Summer 1998): 131–46; Janet Wiscombe, "Can Pay for Performance Really Work?" *Workforce* 80, no. 8 (August 2001): 28–34.
7. Nancy Neill, "Competing with Compensation: The High Tech Challenge," *PeopleTalk* 3, no. 1 (Autumn 1999): 8–16.
8. David Zweig and Jane Webster, "Validation of Multidimensional Measure of Goal Orientation," *Canadian Journal of Behavioural Science* 36, no. 3, July 2004, 232–43; David Allen and Rodger Griffeth, "Test of a Mediated Performance-Turnover Relationship Highlighting the Moderating Roles of Visibility and Reward Contingency," *Journal of Applied Psychology* 86, no. 5 (October 2001): 1014–21; Charles Pettijohn, Linda Pettijohn, and Michael D'Amico, "Characteristics of

Performance Appraisals and Their Impact on Sales Force Satisfaction," *Human Resource Development Quarterly* 12, no. 2 (Summer 2001): 127–46; Scott and Einstein, "Strategic Performance Appraisal in Team-Based Organizations."

9. Robert Bookman, "Tools for Cultivating Constructive Feedback," *Association Management* 51, no. 2 (February 1999): 73–79; Clinton O. Longnecker and Dennis A. Gioia, "The Politics of Executive Appraisals," *Journal of Compensation and Benefits* 10, no. 2 (September/October 1994): 5–11; John Newman, J. Mack Robinson, Larry Tyler, David Dunbar, and Joseph Zager, "CEO Performance Appraisal: Review and Recommendations/Practitioner Application," *Journal of Healthcare Management* 46, no. 1 (January/February 2001): 21–38.

10. Accenture Business Services, *The Point* 3, no. 5, 2004, www.accenture.com/fs (retrieved December 4, 2004).

11. Richard Kantor, "Managing Global Total Rewards," *Human Resources in the 21st Century* (New Jersey: John Wiley & Sons, 2003): 157–67.

12. Stephen and Roithmayr, "Escaping the Performance Trap," 241.

13. Adrian Furnham and Paul Stringfield, "Congruence in Job-Performance Ratings: A Study of 360-Degree Feedback Examining Self, Manager, Peers, and Consultant Ratings," *Human Relations* 51, no. 4 (April 1998): 517–30; Bob Rosner, "Squeezing More Respect out of Your Team," *Workforce* 79, no. 7 (July 2000): 80; Dick Grote, "The Secrets of Performance Appraisal: Best Practices from the Masters," *Across the Board* 37, no. 5 (May 2000): 14–20.

14. Paddy Kamen, "360-Degree Review a New Spin for Managers," *The Globe and Mail*, September 22, 2002, B13.

15. Alan G. Walker and James W. Smither, "A Five-Year Study of Upward Feedback: What Managers Do with Their Results Matters," *Personnel Psychology* 52, no. 2 (Summer 1999): 393–423; Joan Brett and Leanne Atwater, "360-Degree Feedback: Accuracy, Reactions, and Perceptions of Usefulness," *Journal of Applied Psychology* 86, no. 5 (October 2001): 930–42.

16. Donald B. Fedor, Kenneth L. Bettenhausen, and Walter Davis, "Peer Reviews: Employees' Dual Roles as Raters and Recipients," *Group & Organization Management* 24, no. 1 (March 1999): 92–120.

17. Vanessa Urch Druskat and Steven B. Wolff, "Effects and Timing of Developmental Peer Appraisals in Self-Managing Work Groups," *Journal of Applied Psychology* 84, no. 1 (February 1999): 58–74; John Drexler, Jr., Terry Beehr, and Thomas Stetz, "Peer Appraisals: Differentiation of Individual Performance on Group Tasks," *Human Resource Management* 40, no. 4 (Winter 2001): 333–45.

18. Mohsen Attaran and Tai T. Nguyen, "Creating the Right Structural Fit for Self-Directed Teams," *Team Performance Management* 6, no. 1/2 (2000): 25–33.

19. Bradley Kirkman and Benson Rosen, "Powering Up Teams," *Organizational Dynamics* 28, no. 3 (Winter 2000): 48–66; Matthew Valle and Kirk Davis, "Teams and Performance Appraisal: Using Metrics to Increase Reliability and Validity," *Team Performance Management* 5, no. 8 (1999): 238–43.

20. Client testimonials, JPS Management Consulting, Calgary, Alberta, www.jpsmanagement.com/ (retrieved August 1, 2002).

21. Michael Cohn, "Best Buy Beefs Up Customer Value at the Call Center," *Internet World* 8, no. 6 (June 2002): 42–43; Joe Kohn, "Isuzu Has IDEA for Boosting Sales," *Automotive News* 76, no. 5973 (March 4, 2002): 41; D. L. Radcliff, "A New Paradigm of Feedback," *Executive Excellence* 19, no. 4 (April 2002): 20.

22. Bruce Pfau, Ira Kay, Kenneth Nowak, and Jai Ghorpade, "Does 360-Degree Feedback Negatively Affect Company Performance?" *HRMagazine* 47, no. 6 (June 2002): 54–59; Maury Peiperl, "Getting 360-Degree Feedback Right," *Harvard Business Review* 79, no. 1 (January 2001): 142–47; Jack Kondrasuk, Mary Riley, and Wang Hua, "If We Want to Pay for Performance, How Do We Judge Performance?" *Journal of Compensation and Benefits* 15, no. 2 (September/October 1999): 35–40; Matt Graybill, "From Paper to Computer," *The Human Resource Professional* 13, no. 6 (November/December 2000): 18–19.

23. David W. Bracken, Lynn Summers, and John Fleenor, "High-Tech 360," *Training and Development* 52, no. 8 (August 1998): 42–45; Gary Meyer, "Performance Reviews Made Easy, Paperless," *HRMagazine* 45, no. 10 (October 2000): 181–84.

24. David A. Waldman, Leanne E. Atwater, and David Antonioni, "Has 360-Degree Feedback Gone Amok?" *Academy of Management Executive* 12, no. 2 (May 1998): 86–94.

25. Daniel Bachrach, Elliot Bendoly, and Philip Podsakoff, "Attributions of the 'Causes' of Group Performance as an Alternative Explanation of the Relationship between Organizational Citizenship Behavior and Organizational Performance," *Journal of Applied Psychology* 86, no. 6 (December 2001): 1285–93; Susan Leandri, "Measures That Matter: How to Fine-Tune Your Performance Measures," *Journal for Quality and Participation* 24, no. 1 (Spring 2001): 39–41.

26. Peter F. Drucker, *The Practice of Management* (New York: Harper & Brothers, 1954). Reissued by HarperCollins in 1993.

27. Deloris McGee Wanguri, "A Review, an Integration, and a Critique of Cross-Disciplinary Research on Performance Appraisals, Evaluations, and Feedback," *Journal of*

Business Communications 32, no. 3 (July 1995): 267–93; Aharon Tziner, Christine Joanis, and Kevin Murphy, "A Comparison of Three Methods of Performance Appraisal with Regard to Goal Properties, Goal Perception, and Ratee Satisfaction," *Group & Organization Management* 25, no. 2 (June 2000): 175–90.

28. David E. Bowen, Stephen W. Gilliland, and Robert Folger; "HRM and Service Fairness: How Being Fair with Employees Spills Over to Customers," *Organizational Dynamics* 27, no. 3 (Winter 1999): 7–23; Audrey M. Korsgaard and Loriann Roberson, "Procedural Justice in Performance Evaluation: The Role of Instrumental and Non-Instrumental Voice in Performance Appraisal Discussions," *Journal of Management* 21, no. 4 (1995): 657–69; Susan M. Taylor, Kay B. Tracy, Monika K.

Renard, J. Kline Harrison, and Stephen J. Carroll, "Due Process in Performance Appraisal: A Quasi-Experiment in Procedural Justice," *Administrative Science Quarterly* 40, no. 3 (September 1995): 495–523; Fran Rees, "Reaching High Levels of Performance through Team Self-Evaluation," *Journal for Quality and Participation* 22, no. 4 (July/August 1999): 37–39.

29. Martin Geller, "Participation in the Performance Appraisal Review: Inflexible Manager Behavior and Variable Worker Needs," *Human Relations* 51, no. 8 (August 1998): 1061–83; Cawley, Keeping, and Levy, "Participation in the Performance Appraisal Process"; Douthitt and Aiello, "The Role of Participation and Control in the Effects of Computer Monitoring on Fairness Perceptions, Task Satisfaction, and Performance."

CHAPTER 7

Compensation: Recognizing and Rewarding Employees

HRM
Close-Up

Dave Taillefer (third from left) with members of his Code Shoppe team.

"I think that's the ultimate compensation—having a piece of the pie!"

Although he was schooled in biology, Dave Taillefer chose a completely different field when he began his business in 2000 at the age of 30. He pursued a Web-site development and hosting business because he saw a lot of demand for the services especially in Calgary. "I feel like Calgary is an MBA playground," he says. "There is incredible potential for the services we are offering and the economy is strong. It's allowing us to learn from our mistakes and keep learning as we grow."

The people who work for Dave Taillefer at The Code Shoppe have been motivated by his dream of providing Web development and hosting services based on a standardized methodology. Taillefer hopes to keep his business centred in Calgary but able to offer services from various locations across Canada with everyone on his team working from the same set of standard practices and to the same level of quality control. Compensation for the people who work with Taillefer is partly to do with money and partly to do with being part of this dream. "Everyone who works for me believes that our company will grow, and they want to be part of it," explains Taillefer.

At start-up, Taillefer did all the work himself and was soon able to confirm the potential for new business. But without the revenue or capital reserves to offer secure full-time employment to employees, Taillefer chooses to work with people on retainer or two-year contracts. "Each member of my team also has other clients. I happen to be their best client, but they do work outside of my shop." Taillefer feels that this makes for the best employee–employer relationship possible. "The best employee is a business owner," he says. "They have gone through the ropes, they know when something needs to be done, and they do it."

Taillefer seeks people who are highly competent and self-starters. He expects them to manage themselves since there are no levels of management in his seven-person company. "When I hire, it's 50% skill and 50% personality," he explains. "It has to be a good fit, someone who meshes with everyone else and can share the vision we have."

The specialists bring their own computers to his premises and they work in an open, creative environment that they are free to set up as they please. A two-storey loft with no cubicles and plenty of glass and cement, the space is conducive to the creative design and development taking place there. Because Taillefer is the up-front salesperson and is generally hands-off during project development, he allows his people to run their department as they see fit. "They have the freedom to make decisions and apply their unique skills. I try to create an environment where people are free to be themselves—provided of course that our clients are happy," he says. "We do have a lot of fun with jokes, videos, and watching TV occasionally. It's all part of the deal with the team." It's this kind of freedom that attracts the young high-tech people working at The Code Shoppe.

Taillefer's server administrator is one of the experts necessary for this shop. "Keith runs this department better than I ever could. He does things differently, and it has taken our clients a while to adapt, but everyone now sees the logic and intelligence in his way of doing it," says Taillefer.

Aware that his compensation structure with his workforce is unconventional, Taillefer explains that the structure is open to change in the future. "I set salaries based on instinct and with the knowledge of what it would take to do it myself," Taillefer comments. He regularly shares revenue and expense numbers with staff and feels it establishes trust and ensures that everyone continues to have common goals as the company grows. "I'm confident that everyone understands the vibe," he explains. "I would one day like to offer shares because I'm not able to pay a lot of money at this stage of our company's growth. I think that's the ultimate compensation—having a piece of the pie!"

INTRODUCTION

You will note from the HRM Close-Up that compensation is a big issue not just for employees but also for the managers of those employees and the owner of the company. Although companies may set guidelines about how much each position or job is worth, it is the manager who has to implement those guidelines. It is the manager who will make decisions about who gets paid what. Therefore, it is important for the manager and supervisor to have an understanding of compensation and its link to the success of the organization. It is also important for the manager to understand how compensation is derived, and what factors influence the setting of the wage and benefits structure.

Literature and research indicates that important work-related variables leading to job satisfaction include challenging work, interesting job assignments, equitable rewards, competent supervision, and rewarding careers.[1] It is doubtful, however, that many employees would continue working were it not for the money they earn. Employees want compensation systems that are fair and commensurate with their skills and expectations. Pay, therefore, is a major consideration in HRM because it provides employees with a tangible reward for their services, as well as a source of recognition and livelihood. As mentioned earlier, the effectiveness of the manager has a large impact on the employee's job satisfaction and it is usually the manager who is the first one to deal with any concerns or issues regarding compensation. While an HR professional in the organization may be responsible for gathering compensation information and developing approaches to how compensation is managed, it is the manager who typically makes decisions on how much a person is compensated. Further, a recent study conducted by Towers Perrin, a global management consulting firm, reinforces that while managers play a key role in the above factors that lead to job satisfaction, they also play a critical role in ensuring that employees are rewarded for the contributions they make to the success of the organization.[2]

It is important to know that employee compensation includes all forms of pay and rewards received by employees for the performance of their jobs. **Direct compensation** encompasses employee wages and salaries, incentives, bonuses, and commissions. **Indirect compensation** comprises the many benefits supplied by employers, such as dental plans, life insurance coverage, and *nonfinancial compensation* includes employee recognition programs, rewarding jobs, and flexible work hours to accommodate personal needs. Direct and indirect compensation are referred to as "total compensation" or "total rewards approach." This latter phrase helps communicate to employees that their compensation doesn't have just a monetary value but that it includes other forms of recognition and reward.

Both managers and scholars agree that the way compensation is allocated among employees sends a message about what management believes is important and the types of activities it encourages. Furthermore, for an employer, total compensation constitutes a sizable operating cost. In manufacturing firms, compensation is seldom as low as 20% of total expenditures, and in service enterprises it often exceeds 80%. A strategic compensation program, therefore, is essential so that pay can serve to motivate employee production sufficiently to keep labour costs at an acceptable level.

While the focus of this chapter is on salary and benefits, it is important to state that more organizations are beginning to think about and create "reward strategies." The thrust of this approach is to develop an organizational mind-set to recognize and reward people based on performance.[3] Further, it is important to ensure that the

Towers Perrin
www.towers.com/towers

Direct compensation
Employee wages and salaries, incentives, bonuses, and commissions

Indirect compensation
Benefits, such as dental plans and life insurance, supplied by employers

recognition and rewards are seen as valuable to the employees.[4] In doing so, organizations will tend to have components of direct compensation that are tied to the success of the organization and to the contributions of that success through individual (or team) performance.

COMPENSATION AS PART OF COMPANY STRATEGY

Objective 1

Companies structure their compensation in ways that enhance employee motivation and growth while aligning the employees' efforts with the objectives, philosophies, and culture of the organization. Designing the compensation system goes beyond determining what market rates to pay employees—although market rates are one element of compensation planning. Companies that link reward strategy to business strategy tend to deliver higher shareholder return.[5] This makes a compelling argument to ensure that the organization takes into consideration what employees see as important in the reward equation.

Looking at the compensation system in a strategic fashion serves to mesh the monetary payments made to employees with specific HR, and, therefore, business objectives. For example, in the recruitment of new employees, the rate of pay for jobs can increase or limit the supply of applicants. Employers have adopted special pay strategies to attract job applicants with highly marketable skills, such as high-tech workers, and engineers and scientists with financial knowledge and good people skills. Organizations also use compensation to retain scarce skills. According to a Conference Board of Canada study of 294 Canadian companies, the following retention strategies are used: cash bonus/incentive (90%); profit-sharing/gain-sharing (20%); and team-based incentives (11%).[6] Of the organizations surveyed, 62% link individual performance to the organization's performance.

If rates of pay are high, creating a large applicant pool, then organizations may choose to raise their selection standards and hire better-qualified employees. This in turn can reduce employer training costs. When employees perform at exceptional levels, their performance assessments may justify an increased pay rate. For these reasons and others, an organization should ensure it has a systematic way to manage employee compensation and that it is linked to business performance. For example, a recent survey conducted by Watson Wyatt, a large consulting firm in Canada and the rest of the world, has demonstrated that there is a link between rewarding top performers and achieving strong business results.[7] A summary of this and other similar compensation reports can be found at Watson Wyatt's Web site (**www.watsonwyatt.com**).

At Work with HRM 7.1 discusses the importance of communicating the overall strategy and the total value of compensation.

Watson Wyatt
www.watsonwyatt.com

Linking Compensation to Organizational Objectives

Compensation has been revolutionized by heightened domestic competition, globalization, increased employee skill requirements, and new technology. Therefore, an outcome of today's dynamic business environment is that managers have needed to change their pay philosophies from paying for a specific position or job title to rewarding employees

at work **with HRM 7.1** at work with HRM 7.1

COMMUNICATING THE VALUE OF COMPENSATION

Many organizations include a communications plan as part of the overall compensation strategy. Why? As employers compete in an international market for employees, it is important to ensure that people understand the value the organization places on their employment. Many employees do not fully understand what it might cost the company in terms of total rewards nor what that employment is worth. And without providing the information, employees might undervalue some key components of the compensation plan. Information that would form part of the plan could include annual salary, detailed information on benefits coverage, and the employer/employee portion of the cost of premiums for those benefits.

In developing the communications plan, there are several key things to keep in mind.

1. Set clear goals regarding the purpose of the communications.
2. Make it easy for employees to understand.
3. Involve line managers in developing the communications and ensure they understand the components.
4. Communicate frequently.
5. Keep information fresh.
6. Ensure components of the compensation plan are consistent with overall rewards philosophy.

A leader in developing and communicating a total rewards program has been InSystems, a Markham, Ontario, business automation software firm. The company has found that a good rewards strategy directly relates to employee satisfaction, which in turn relates to customer satisfaction that translates into company revenues. Therefore, a very high priority has been placed on ensuring that the components of the reward program are valued by the employees and that the employees have information on the value.

Laurie McRae, vice-president human resources, says that the changes occurred after an employee satisfaction survey was conducted in 2002. The feedback from employees indicated that some of the components were not known and/or valued. As McRae says, "We really hadn't effectively bundled and marketed our offerings."

CRITICAL THINKING QUESTIONS

1. If you are working, do you know the value of your total compensation? Would you think differently about the organization if you did?
2. Providing information about the value of compensation does take resources that could be used differently. Would you want to know the total value of your compensation? Why or why not?

Sources: Adapted from Barry Gros, "Communication Is King When It Comes to Employees Valuing Remuneration," *Canadian HR Reporter*, November 8, 2004, www.hrreporter.com (retrieved December 11, 2004); and David Brown, "Soft Side of Rewards Has Hard Impact," April 5, 2004, www.hrreporter.com (retrieved December 12, 2004).

on the basis of their individual competencies or group contributions to organizational success. A recent study showed that 81% of responding organizations listed *improving employee's focus on achieving business goals* as a significant objective influencing reward changes (see Figure 7.1). A compensation program, therefore, must be tailored to the needs of the organization and its employees.

It is not uncommon for organizations to establish specific goals for aligning their organizational objectives with their compensation program.[8] Formalized compensation

FIGURE 7.1   Significant Goals Driving Pay and Reward Changes

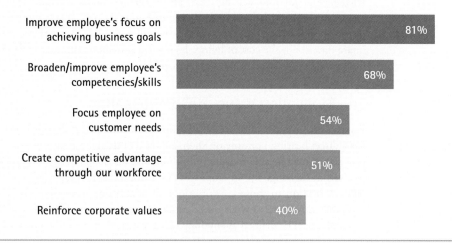

Source: Towers Perrin and Duncan Brown, "Reward Strategies for Real: Moving from Intent to Impact," *World at Work Journal 10*, No.3, 2001, p.43. Used with permission.

goals serve as guidelines for managers to ensure that wage and benefit policies achieve their intended purpose. Some of the more common goals are the following:

1. To reward employees' past performance.
2. To remain competitive in the labour market.
3. To maintain salary equity among employees.
4. To mesh employees' future performance with organizational goals.
5. To control the compensation budget.
6. To attract new employees.[9]
7. To reduce unnecessary turnover.[10]

To achieve these goals, specific actions or steps must be taken. Three areas of action are discussed below.

The Pay-for-Performance Standard

To raise productivity and lower labour costs in today's competitive economic environment, organizations are increasingly setting compensation objectives based on a **pay-for-performance standard**.[11] It is agreed that managers must tie at least some reward to employee effort and performance. Without this standard, motivation to perform with greater effort will be low, resulting in higher wage costs to the organization.

The term "pay for performance" refers to a wide range of direct compensation options, including merit-based pay, bonuses, salary commissions, job and pay banding, team or group incentives, and gainsharing programs.[12] Each of these compensation systems seeks to differentiate between the pay of average performers and that of outstanding performers. In 2000, when Pfizer acquired Warner-Lambert Company, creating the world's largest pharmaceutical company, it created a pay-for-performance compensation strategy that linked an employee's pay level to performance of the company, their division, their team, and to personal contributions.[13] Interestingly, productivity studies show that employees will increase their output by 15 to 35% when an organization installs a pay-for-performance program.

Unfortunately, designing a sound pay-for-performance system is not easy. Considerations must be given to how employee performance will be measured, what

Pay-for-performance standard
Standard by which managers tie compensation to employee effort and performance

monies will be allocated for compensation increases, which employees will be covered, what payout method will be used, and when payments will be made. A critical issue concerns the size of the monetary increase and its perceived value to employees, as a pay-for-performance program will lack its full potential when pay increases only approximate the rises in the cost of living. Figure 7.2 provides a summary of the advantages and disadvantages of different pay-for-performance systems.

The Motivating Value of Compensation

Pay is a quantitative measure of an employee's relative worth. For most employees, pay has a direct bearing not only on their standard of living, but also on the status and recognition they may be able to achieve both on and off the job. Since pay represents a reward received in exchange for an employee's contributions, it is essential that the pay be equitable in relation to those contributions. It is also important that an employee's pay be equitable in relation to what other employees are receiving for their contributions.

Equity can be defined as anything of value earned through the investment of something of value. Equity theory is a motivation theory that explains how employees respond to situations in which they feel they have received less (or more) than they deserve.[14] Central to the theory is the role of perception in motivation and the fact that individuals make comparisons. It states that individuals form a ratio of their inputs (abilities, skills, experiences) in a situation to their outcomes (salary, benefits) in that situation. They then compare the value of that ratio with the value of the input/output ratio for other individuals in a similar class of jobs either internal or external to the organization. If the value of their ratio equals the value of another's, they perceive the situation as equitable and no tension exists. However, if they perceive their input/output ratio as inequitable relative to others', this creates tension and motivates them to eliminate or reduce the inequity. The strength of their motivation is

FIGURE 7.2　Advantages and Disadvantages of Pay-for-Performance Systems

Type of System	Advantages	Disadvantages
Individual	• Simple to compute • Clearly links pay to organizational outcomes • Motivates employees • Are variable costs • Employees focus on clear performance targets • Distributes success among those responsible for producing success	• Standards of performance may be difficult to establish • May not be an effective motivator • Difficult to deal with missed performance targets • Available money may be inadequate • Employees may be unable to distinguish merit pay from other types of pay increases
Team	• Support group planning • Builds team culture • Can broaden scope of contribution that employees are motivated to make • Tends to reduce jealousies and complaints • Encourage cross-training	• Individuals may perceive efforts contribute little to group success • Intergroup social problems can limit performance • Can be difficult to compute and therefore difficult to understand
Organization	• Creates effective employee participation • Can increase pride in organization • Can be structured to provide tax advantages • Are variable costs	• Difficult to handle if organization's performance is low • Can be difficult to compute and therefore difficult to understand • More difficult for individual effort to be linked to organizational success

proportional to the magnitude of the perceived inequity. If a person feels that someone is getting more compensation for similar work, this can negatively affect that employee's view of the value of the employee's own work. HR practitioners who specialize in compensation systems are particularly concerned not only that employees are paid fairly for the work they do but also that they are paid equitably relative to other people in the organization.

For employees, pay is **equitable** when the compensation given is perceived to be equal to the value of the work performed. Research clearly demonstrates that employees' perceptions of equity, or inequity, can have dramatic effects on their work behaviour and productivity.[15] Although line managers do not design compensation systems, they do have to respond to employee concerns about being paid equitably. Compensation policies are internally equitable when employees believe that the wage rates for their jobs approximate the job's worth to the organization. Perceptions of external equity exist when the organization is paying wages and benefits that are relatively equal to what other employers are paying for similar types of work. At Work with HRM 7.2 provides an interesting perspective on pay-for-performance and equity.

Equitable pay
Compensation received is perceived to be equal to the value of the work performed

at work **with HRM 7.2**

INCENTIVE COMPENSATION

Yvonne Blaszczyk, FCHRP, publisher of *Strategic Human Resources Compensation News*, suggests that when the economy is unstable, organizations look to control basic compensation and motivate employees through incentive compensation. Because markets are fragile, organizations are not achieving the profit performances that were expected, and so incentive compensation payouts for individual performers are variable and declining. How can incentive plans be structured so that not only employee results and organizational outcomes are rewarded, but so are contribution and efforts? These softer and less objective measures of contribution and effort can be measured and are important to the survival and ultimate success of organizations. For example, one company that deals with the financing and leasing of equipment has to work closely with another company that is selling the equipment. The first company cannot influence sales and therefore cannot be rewarded on the sales results. However, the company does have to service the leases and ensure customer retention. The incentive program for this company recognizes the importance of maintaining good relations with the sales company and so rewards employees based on the number of contacts, number of successfully resolved conflicts, and success in renewal of difficult contracts.

The other major change is that of the decline of merit compensation. A fixed pool of money usually distributed at the rate of 3 to 4% per employee is not motivating. The most common complaint heard by Blaszczyk is from high-producing employees who receive the same salary increases as average-performing employees. So companies are taking the merit money and distributing it at larger rates to only the top performers. In the next decade we can expect to see companies bravely embarking on heavily weighted incentive pay, with lower base compensation. The base salary pays for day-to-day work; the incentives pay for making sure the company stays in business and is profitable. But there may be legal issues. Current employees may perceive this as a change in the implicit agreement about how they are paid.

CRITICAL THINKING QUESTION

Would you like to have your pay tied directly to your performance? Why or why not?

The Bases for Compensation

Hourly work
Work paid on an hourly basis

Piecework
Work paid according to the number of units produced

Work performed in most private, public, and not-for-profit organizations has traditionally been compensated on an hourly basis. This is referred to as **hourly work**, in contrast to **piecework**, in which employees are paid according to the number of units they produce. Hourly work, however, is far more prevalent than piecework as a basis for compensating employees.

Employees compensated on an hourly basis are classified as *hourly employees*, or wage earners. Those whose compensation is computed on the basis of weekly, biweekly, or monthly pay periods are classified as *salaried employees*. Hourly employees are normally paid only for the time they work. Salaried employees, by contrast, are generally paid the same for each pay period, even though they occasionally may work more hours or fewer than the regular number of hours in a period. They also usually receive certain benefits not provided to hourly employees.

DETERMINING COMPENSATION

 Objective 2

A combination of *internal* and *external* factors can influence, directly or indirectly, the rates at which employees are paid, as shown in Figure 7.3.

Internal Factors

The internal factors that influence wage rates are the employer's compensation policy, the worth of a job, an employee's relative worth in meeting job requirements, and an employer's ability and willingness to pay.

Employer's Compensation Strategy

Organizations will usually state objectives regarding compensation for their employees. For example, a public-sector employer may wish to pay fairly and at the market average. (Remember: "market" means the geographical area in which the organization typically finds qualified candidates for work.) On the other hand, a software development company may wish to pay fairly but be the industry leader to attract and retain high-calibre staff.

Usually both large and small employers set pay policies reflecting (1) the internal wage relationship among jobs and skill levels, (2) the external competition or an employer's pay position relative to what competitors are paying, (3) a policy of rewarding employee performance, and (4) administrative decisions concerning elements of the pay system, such as overtime premiums, payment periods, and short- or long-term incentives.[16]

Worth of a Job

Organizations without a formal compensation program generally base the worth of jobs on the subjective opinions of people familiar with the jobs. In such instances, pay rates may be influenced heavily by the labour market or, in the case of unionized employees, by collective bargaining. Organizations with formal compensation programs, however, are more likely to rely on a system of job evaluation to aid in rate determination. Even when rates are subject to collective bargaining, job evaluation can assist the organization in maintaining some degree of control over its wage structure.

FIGURE 7.3 Factors Affecting the Wage Mix

Job evaluation
Systematic process of determining
the relative worth of jobs in order
to establish which jobs should be
paid more than others within an
organization

Job evaluation is the systematic process of determining the *relative* worth of jobs in order to establish which jobs should be paid more than others within the organization. Job evaluation helps to establish internal equity between various jobs. Job worth is measured by the following criteria: level of skill, effort, responsibility, and working conditions of the job. The relative worth of a job is then determined by comparing it with others within the organization using these criteria. Furthermore, each method of comparison may be made on the basis of the jobs as a whole or on the basis of the parts that constitute the jobs. Four methods of comparison will be explored starting on page 244.

Employee's Relative Worth

In both hourly and salaried jobs, employee performance can be recognized and rewarded through promotion and with various incentive systems. Superior performance can also be rewarded by granting merit raises on the basis of steps within a rate range established for a job class. If merit raises are to have their intended value, however, they must be determined by an effective performance appraisal system that differentiates between those employees who deserve the raises and those who do not. This system, moreover, must provide a visible and credible relationship between performance and any raises received. Unfortunately, too many so-called merit systems provide for raises to be granted automatically. As a result, employees tend to be rewarded more for merely being present than for being productive on the job.

In some situations, supervisors will also compare the performance of one employee to another. While proponents of performance stress that a person is to be assessed against standards of performance, there is a tendency to compare employees against each other. This is particularly true in the absence of any performance management system.

Employer's Ability and Willingness to Pay

In the public sector, the amount of compensation (pay and benefits) employees can receive is limited by the funds budgeted for this purpose and by the willingness of taxpayers to provide them. Federal government employees had their pay frozen for six years, in response to the drive to balance the budget and because of the public's perception of highly paid government workers. In the private sector, profits and other financial resources available to employers often limit pay levels. Economic conditions and competition faced by employers can also significantly affect the rates they are willing to pay. Competition and recessions can force prices down and reduce the income from which compensation payments are derived. In such situations, employers may have little choice but to reduce wages and/or lay off employees, or, even worse, to go out of business.

External Factors

The major external factors that influence wage rates include labour market conditions, area wage rates, cost of living, collective bargaining if the employer is unionized, and legal requirements.

Labour Market Conditions

The labour market reflects the forces of supply and demand for qualified labour within an area. These forces help to influence the wage rates required to recruit or retain competent employees. It must be recognized, however, that counterforces can reduce the full impact of supply and demand on the labour market. The economic power of unions, for example, may prevent employers from lowering wage rates even when unemployment is high among union members. Employment laws also may prevent an employer from paying at a market rate less than an established minimum.

Area Wage Rates

A formal wage structure should provide rates that are in line with those being paid by other employers for comparable jobs within the area. Data pertaining to area wage rates may be obtained at minimal cost from local area wage surveys. Wage-survey

An employee's contribution to the organization (relative worth) is often considered when making salary decisions.

data also may be obtained from consulting firms, such as Towers Perrin and Watson Wyatt. Smaller employers use government or local board of trade surveys to establish rates of pay. Many organizations conduct their own surveys. Others engage in a cooperative exchange of wage information or rely on various professional associations, such as the Professional Engineering Association of Ontario or British Columbia, for these data.

Cost of Living

Consumer price index (CPI)
Measure of the average change in prices over time in a fixed "market basket" of goods and services

Statistics Canada
www.statcan.ca/start.html

Because of inflation, compensation rates tend to be adjusted upward periodically to help employees maintain their purchasing power. To do this, organizations frequently use the **consumer price index (CPI)**. The CPI is a measure of the average change in prices over time in a fixed "market basket" of goods and services.[17] The index is based on prices of food, clothing, shelter, and fuels; transportation fares; charges for medical services; and prices of other goods and services that people buy for day-to-day living. Statistics Canada collects price information on a monthly basis and calculates the CPI for Canada as a whole and various Canadian city averages. Figure 7.4 illustrates wage increases for unionized and nonunionized employees, compared with the inflation rate.

FIGURE 7.4   Inflation and Wage Increases (1993–2005)

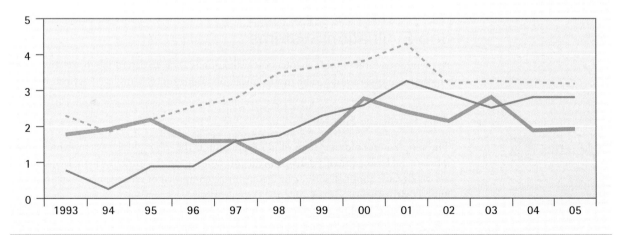

Source: Compensation Planning Outlook 2005, The Conference Board of Canada, Ottawa, 2004. Reproduced with permission from the Conference Board of Canada. Note: figures given for 2005 are forecasts.

Using the CPI to determine changes in pay rates can also compress pay rates within a pay structure, thereby creating inequities among those who receive the wage increase. For example, an increase of 50 cents an hour represents a 10% increase for an employee earning $5 an hour, but only a 5% increase for someone earning $10 per hour.

Collective Bargaining

Real wages
Wage increases larger than rises in the consumer price index; that is, the real earning power of wages

One of the primary functions of a labour union is to bargain collectively over conditions of employment, the most important of which is compensation. The union's goal in each new agreement is to achieve increases in **real wages**—wage increases larger than the increase in the CPI—thereby improving the purchasing power and standard of living of its members. This goal includes gaining wage settlements that equal if not exceed the pattern established by other unions within the area.

The agreements negotiated by unions tend to establish rate patterns within the labour market. As a result, wages are generally higher in areas where organized labour is strong. To recruit and retain competent personnel and avoid unionization, nonunion employers must either meet or exceed these rates. The "union scale" also becomes the prevailing rate that all employers must pay for work performed under government contract. The impact of collective bargaining therefore extends beyond that segment of the labour force that is unionized.

Legal Requirements

As discussed in Chapter 2, legislation is in place that either influences or requires certain pay rates. For example, most provinces have a legislated minimum hourly wage. This means that an employer cannot pay any worker less than the per-hour rate. In addition, pay equity legislation obliges certain companies to pay the same wage rate for jobs of a dissimilar nature and is based on comparing jobs performed mostly by men to jobs performed mostly by women. Under pay equity, a company must use a "gender-neutral" system, comparing jobs based on the amount and type of skill, effort, and responsibility needed to perform the job and on the working conditions in which the job is performed. Some provinces also consider male–female pay rates under human rights legislation. Read HRM and the Law 7.1 for a recent human rights decision that involved what a person was paid.

Job Evaluation Systems

As mentioned earlier in this chapter, job evaluation is a way to determine the relative worth of jobs in an organization. The most typical job evaluation systems are described below.

Job Ranking System

Objective 3

The simplest and oldest system of job evaluation is the job ranking system, which arrays jobs on the basis of their relative worth. Job ranking can be done by a single individual knowledgeable about all jobs or by a committee composed of management and employee representatives.

The basic weakness of the job ranking system is that it does not provide a very refined measure of each job's worth. Since the comparisons are normally made on the basis of the job as a whole, it is quite easy for one or more of the factors of a job to bias the ranking given to a job, particularly if the job is complex. Its simplicity, however, makes it ideal for use by smaller employers.

HRM and **the law 7.1** HRM and the law 7.1

DIFFERENT PAY RATES CAN CAUSE COMPLAINTS OF DISCRIMINATION

In a recent case in Alberta, a female electrician claimed that she was paid $1 less an hour than a male employee performing similar work. The law in Alberta forbids employers from discriminating on the basis of gender and stipulates that men and women working in the same establishment and performing "similar or substantially similar work" must be paid at the same rate of pay. However, companies may pay employees different rates of pay based on other factors, such as experience, education, and merit.

The Alberta Human Rights and Citizenship Commission concluded that work in the shop was not the same as work in the field. It also concluded that the female electrician had less work experience than the male electrician even though she had been certified as a journeyman electrician in 1990. The panel stated that she was paid appropriately and that she had not been discriminated against.

What do you think?

Source: Adapted from *Cathy Paul v. PowerComm Inc.*, Commission Panel Decisions, Alberta Human Rights and Citizenship Commission, www.albertahumanrights.ab.ca (retrieved February 13, 2000).

Job Classification System

In the job classification system, jobs are classified and grouped according to a series of predetermined grades. Successive grades require increasing amounts of job responsibility, skill, knowledge, ability, or other factors selected to compare jobs. For example, the position of Aquatic Leader I for the municipality of West Vancouver is classified as follows:

> This is an introductory leadership position with responsibilities involving staff supervisor, lifeguarding and swim instruction in the provision of a safe leisure environment to all users of Municipal indoor and outdoor aquatic facilities. An incumbent will perform life-saving functions, provide instruction to all age groups in aquatic programs, and perform general maintenance duties. The work is performed under general supervision.

The Aquatic Leader II position is described as follows:

> This is a supervisory leadership position involving responsibility for the safety and instruction of users at the centres, guarded beaches and in the Backyard Pool Program. An Aquatic Leader II participates in program development, special events, lesson supervision, and lifeguard training. As well, tasks include involvement with staff in a leadership role, staff motivation and general supervision. Work is reviewed by a supervisor to ensure conformance with established standards and procedures for safe swimming and instruction.[18]

As you can see, the Leader II position has both more complexity and more responsibilities—including supervision of other staff.

While this system has the advantage of simplicity, it is less precise than the point and factor comparison systems (discussed in the next sections) because the job is evaluated as a whole.

Point System

The point system is a quantitative job evaluation procedure that determines a job's relative value by calculating the total points assigned to it. It has been successfully used by high-visibility organizations, such as Boeing and Honeywell, and by many other public and private organizations, both large and small. Although point systems are rather complicated to establish, once in place they are relatively simple to understand and use. The principal advantage of the point system is that it provides a more refined basis for making judgments than either the ranking or classification systems and thereby can produce results that are more valid and less easy to manipulate.

The point system permits jobs to be evaluated quantitatively on the basis of factors or elements—commonly called *compensable factors*—that constitute the job. The skills, efforts, responsibilities, and working conditions that a job usually entails are the more common major compensable factors that serve to evaluate the worth of a job as more or less important than another.

Factor Comparison System

The factor comparison system, like the point system, permits the job evaluation process to be accomplished on a factor-by-factor basis. A factor comparison system is typically used for legislated pay equity purposes. It differs from the point system, however, in that the compensable factors of the jobs to be evaluated are compared against the compensable factors of key jobs within the organization that serve as the job evaluation scale.

What system would you use to determine the worth of a rescue worker's job?

University of British Columbia

www.hr.ubc.ca

Key jobs are evaluated against five compensable factors—skill, mental effort, physical effort, responsibility, and working conditions—resulting in a ranking of the different factors for each key job. An example of a factor comparison system can be found on the University of British Columbia Web site (**www.hr.ubc.ca**), where the HR unit has posted its job evaluation program.

Regardless of the methodology used, it is important to remember that all job evaluation methods require varying amounts of judgment made by individuals. Supervisors or managers make decisions on the components of any job. Also, supervisors will make decisions on how much responsibility and authority any particular job may have. Therefore, as careful an organization is in having objective ways of measuring the value of a job, subjective decisions are made regarding the content of the job. As mentioned previously, organizations frequently use a committee or panel for job evaluation assessments to help ensure objectivity in the process.

Whatever system a company uses, it will frequently make use of the companies HRMS to actually collect the data, assess the data, and to record the final decision. This is particularly true if the organization is medium to large and is using either a point or factor comparison system. Manager's Toolkit 7.1 describes what needs to be considered if an HRMS is used to administer the job evaluation system in any organization.

Manager's Toolkit **7.1** Manager's Toolkit 7.1

MAKING GOOD USE OF AN HRMS IN JOB EVALUATION

Organizations that have an HRMS sometimes only have minimal information with which to make decisions. In many cases, the HRMS may only store the final decision while manual systems are used for the decision making. The outcome of this is a sense of secrecy around the entire process. However, with careful planning and attention, an HRMS can provide valuable assistance in the overall job evaluation process. Here are some key things to consider:

- Ensure employees can use online questionnaires from their desktops through self-service and be able to view job description information.

- Create a Web-based job evaluation on a global basis.

- Supervisor approvals and routing information to the job analyst and the committee are done via technology.

- Ensure there is an online capability to highlight any inconsistent evaluations.

- Ensure system can store evaluation notes and other relevant documents.

- Electronically provide job evaluation results to the manager and employee and ensure system information is updated.

- Support a variety of different evaluation approaches within the organization.

Source: John Johnston, "The Achilles Heel of HR Systems," *Canadian HR Reporter*, www.hrreporter.com (retrieved December 12, 2004).

THE COMPENSATION STRUCTURE

Job evaluation systems provide for internal equity and serve as the basis for wage-rate determination. *They do not in themselves determine the wage rate.* The evaluated worth of each job based on its rank, class, points, or monetary worth must be converted into an hourly, daily, weekly, or monthly wage rate. The compensation tool used to help set wages is the wage and salary survey.

Wage and Salary Surveys

Wage and salary survey
Survey of the wages paid to employees of other employers in the surveying organization's relevant labour market

The **wage and salary survey** is a survey of the wages paid by employers in an organization's relevant labour market—local, regional, or national, depending on the job. The labour market is frequently defined as that area from which employers obtain certain types of workers. The labour market for office personnel would be local, whereas the labour market for engineers would be national. It is the wage and salary survey that permits an organization to maintain external equity—that is, to pay its employees wages equivalent to the wages similar employees earn in other establishments.

Collecting Survey Data

Watson Wyatt
www.watsonwyatt.com

Hewitt Associates
was4.hewitt.com/hewitt/

Mercer Human Resource Consulting
www.mercerHR.com

Hay Management Consultants
www.haygroup.com

Although many organizations conduct their own wage and salary surveys, a variety of "pre-conducted" pay surveys are available to satisfy the requirements of most public, not-for-profit, or private organizations. For example, you might want to see what the average hourly rate is for an accounting clerk in the Toronto area. Or you might want to know the average hourly rate for a Web designer anywhere in Canada. Companies such as Watson Wyatt (**www.watsonwyatt.com**), Hewitt Associates (**was4.hewitt.com/hewitt/**), Mercer Human Resource Consulting (**www.mercerHR .com**), and Hay Management Consultants (**www.haygroup.com**) conduct annual surveys.

The Wage Curve

The relationship between the relative worth of jobs and their wage rates can be represented by means of a wage curve. This curve may indicate the rates currently paid for jobs within an organization, the new rates resulting from job evaluation, or the rates for similar jobs currently being paid by other organizations within the labour market. Figure 7.5 provides an example of a wage curve.

Pay Grades

Pay grades
Groups of jobs within a particular class that are paid the same rate or rate range

From an administrative standpoint, it is generally preferable to group jobs into **pay grades** and to pay all jobs within a particular grade the same rate or rate range. When the classification system of job evaluation is used, jobs are grouped into grades as part of the

FIGURE 7.5 Wage Curve

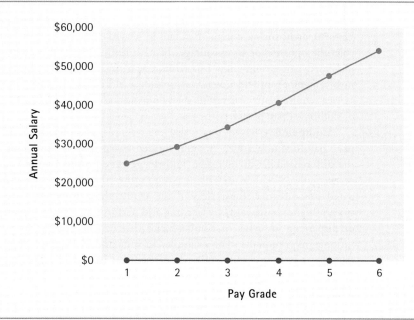

evaluation process. When the point and factor comparison systems are used, however, pay grades must be established at selected intervals that represent either the point or the evaluated monetary value of these jobs.

Rate Ranges

Although a single rate may be created for each pay grade, it is more common to provide a range of rates for each pay grade. The rate ranges may be the same for each grade or proportionately greater for each successive grade, as shown in Figure 7.6. Rate ranges constructed on the latter basis provide a greater incentive for employees to accept a promotion to a job in a higher grade.

FIGURE 7.6 Salary Structure with Increasing Rate Ranges

Pay Grade	Minimum	Mid-Point	Maximum
6	$49,120	$53,970	$58,830
5	43,220	47,500	51,770
4	36,750	40,375	44,000
3	31,250	34,320	37,400
2	26,600	29,200	31,800
1	22,600	24,820	27,050

Trends in Wage Determination

The predominant approach to employee compensation is still the job-based system.[19] Unfortunately, such a system often fails to reward employees for their skills or the knowledge they possess or to encourage them to learn a new job-related skill. Additionally, job-based pay systems may not reinforce an organizational culture stressing employee involvement or provide increased employee flexibility to meet overall production or service requirements. Therefore, many organizations have introduced competency-based or skill-based pay plans.

Competency-based pay
Pay based on how many capabilities employees have or how many jobs they can perform

Competency-based pay—also referred to as knowledge-based pay, skill-based pay, pay-for-knowledge, or multiskilled-based pay—compensates employees for the different skills or increased knowledge they possess or the collective behaviours or characteristics that they demonstrate rather than for the job they hold in a designated job category. Regardless of the name, these pay plans encourage employees to earn higher base wages by learning and performing a wider variety of skills (or jobs) or displaying an array of competencies that can be applied to a variety of organizational requirements. For example, in a manufacturing setting, new tasks might include various assembly activities carried out in a particular production system or a variety of maintenance functions. Within service organizations, employees might acquire new knowledge related to advanced computer systems or accounting procedures.[20] Organizations will grant an increase in pay after each skill or knowledge has been mastered and can be demonstrated according to a predetermined standard.[21]

Competency-based pay systems represent a fundamental change in the attitude of management regarding how work should be organized and how employees should be paid for their work efforts. The most frequently cited benefits of competence-based pay include greater productivity, increased employee learning and commitment to work, improved staffing flexibility to meet production or service demands, and the reduced effects of absenteeism and turnover, since managers can assign employees where and when needed. Competency-based pay also encourages employees to acquire training when new or updated skills are needed by an organization.

For example, the National Research Council recently introduced a competency-based pay system in order to promote career self-management, support an entrepreneurial and participative culture, develop staff, and attract and retain the best employees.[22]

Broadbanding   Organizations that adopt a skill-based pay system frequently use broadbanding to structure their compensation payments to employees. Broadbanding simply collapses many traditional salary grades into a few wide salary bands. Broadbands may have midpoints and quartiles or they may have extremely wide salary ranges or no ranges at all.[23] Banding encourages lateral skill building while addressing the need to pay employees performing several jobs with different skill-level requirements. Additionally, broadbands help eliminate the obsession with grades and, instead, encourage employees to move to jobs where they can develop in their careers and add value to the organization. Paying employees through broadbands enables organizations to consider job responsibilities, individual skills and competencies, and career mobility patterns in assigning employees to bands.

Current trends in compensation are discussed further in At Work with HRM 7.3.

at work **with HRM 7.3** at work with HRM 7.3

TRENDS IN COMPENSATION

The Conference Board of Canada annually reviews and describes trends in compensation. According to the 2004 research, though the Canadian economy is growing, companies are hesitant to provide large pay increases in a low-inflation environment. Part of the reluctance relates to the significant cost pressures of competing in a world market. Another reason is that while there is still a shortage of certain skills, generally speaking, organizations are having better success in attracting new employees as the overall labour market has some surpluses. Further, the rising cost of employee benefits means that there is less money available for pay adjustments.

But what are employers planning to do in 2005? Employers are making careful decisions about the manner in which pay increases are distributed. More and more organizations are creating a pay structure that ties a portion (can be large or small) to performance. Over 80% of the companies in the research indicated that they seek to drive organizational and individual performance through variable pay plans. And approximately 73% state that the performance objectives are being realized. The average variable pay plan indicates that front-line employees have approximately 5.6% of their compensation in this form whereas executives can have as much as 40% of their compensation at risk, depending on performance—both of the organization and the person.

CRITICAL THINKING QUESTIONS

1. Would you like to have part of your compensation "at risk" depending on your performance? Why or why not?
2. If you would like to have part of your pay tied to your performance, what would be a reasonable amount for you? Why?

Source: *Compensation Planning Outlook 2005*, Ottawa: The Conference Board of Canada, 2004.

INCENTIVE PLANS

Objective 5

A clear trend in compensation management is the growth of incentive plans, also called variable pay programs, for employees throughout the organization. As noted earlier in this chapter, a Conference Board of Canada study of compensation practices in 294 organizations indicated that 83% of the companies had established one or more variable pay plans.[24] By far the most prominent incidence of variable pay is in the private sector (90%), but 53% of public sector organizations now have such plans.

Incentive plans emphasize a shared focus on organizational objectives by broadening the opportunities for incentives to nontraditional groups while operating outside the merit (base pay) increase system.[25] Incentive plans create an operating environment that champions a philosophy of shared commitment through the belief that every individual contributes to organizational performance and success.

By linking compensation with organizational objectives, managers believe that employees will assume "ownership" of their jobs, thereby improving their effort and overall job performance. Incentives are designed to encourage employees to put out more effort to complete their job tasks—effort they might not be motivated to expend under hourly and/or seniority-based compensation systems. Financial incentives are therefore offered to improve or maintain high levels of productivity and quality, which in turn improves the market for Canadian goods and services in a global economy.

Do incentive plans work? Various studies have demonstrated a measurable relationship between incentive plans and improved organizational performance. A recent study also indicated that organizations that encouraged employee participation and involvement had both competency-based pay and incentive plans and improved organizational performance.[26]

A variety of individual and group incentive plans exists for both hourly and salaried employees. These include the following:

1. *Individual bonus*—an incentive payment that supplements the basic pay. It has the advantage of providing employees with more pay for exerting greater effort, while at the same time giving employees the security of a basic wage. Bonuses are common among managerial employees but as indicated earlier, organizations are increasingly providing bonuses to front-line staff.
2. *Team or group-based incentive*—a plan that rewards team members with an incentive bonus when agreed-upon performance standards are exceeded. Figure 7.7 provides the pros and cons of team incentive plans.
3. *Merit raises*—an incentive, used most commonly for salaried employees, based on achievement of performance standards. One of the problems with merit raises is that they may be perpetuated year after year even when performance declines.
4. *Gainsharing*—a plan in which both employees and the organization share the financial gains according to a predetermined formula that reflects improved productivity and/or decreased labour costs.[27]
5. *Profit-sharing*—any plan by which an employer pays special sums based on the profits of the organization.
6. *Employee stock ownership plans (ESOPs)*—stock plans in which an organization contributes shares of its stock to an established trust for the purpose of stock purchases by its employees.

But do incentive plans work? Read At Work with HRM 7.4, which provides some insights.

FIGURE 7.7   The Pros and Cons of Team Incentive Plans

Pros	Cons
• Team incentives support group planning and problem solving, thereby building a team culture. • The contributions of individual employees depend on group cooperation. • Unlike incentive plans based solely on output, team incentives can broaden the scope of the contribution that employees are motivated to make. • Team bonuses tend to reduce employee jealousies and complaints over "tight" or "loose" individual standards. • Team incentives encourage cross-training and the acquiring of new interpersonal competencies.	• Individual team members may perceive that "their" efforts contribute little to team success or to the attainment of the incentive bonus. • Intergroup social problems—pressure to limit performance (for example, team members are afraid one individual may make the others look bad) and the "free-ride" effect (one individual puts in less effort than others but shares equally in team rewards)—may arise. • Complex payout formulas can be difficult for team members to understand.

at work **with HRM 7.4** at work with HRM 7.4

ORGANIZATIONAL BENEFITS OF INCENTIVE PLANS

Incentive pay is a strategic tool used most often to attract and retain employees and to improve organizational outcomes. Organizations pay an average of 9% of total payroll dollars on variable compensation programs. Is this money well spent?

1. Four out of five organizations report that incentive compensation is an effective tool for attracting and retaining employees.

2. About one-third of employers reported that compensation had a positive effect on operating results. In another study, retail stores that used the Scanlon Plan had higher sales performance, more favourable customer satisfaction scores, and lower turnover than a control group. Higher-performing companies are more likely to provide stock options and feel strongly that these options influence behaviour among professional ranks. The offering of stock options is associated with improved company performance, as a Watson Wyatt study found that the more a CEO makes, the better the company performs financially.

Sources: D. Scott, WorldatWork, "Survey of Compensation Policies and Practices," www.worldatwork.org/research (March 2003); D. Scott, J. Floyd, P. G. Benson, and J. W. Bishop, "The Impact of the Scanlon Plan on Retail Store Performance," *WorldatWork Journal* 11, no. 3 (Third Quarter, 2002); D. J. Gherson, "Getting the Pay Thing Right," *Workspan* 43, no. 6 (June 2000); K. H. Van Neek and J. E. Smilko, "Variable Pay Plans," *WorldatWork Journal* 11, no. 4 (Fourth Quarter 2002).

EMPLOYEE BENEFITS

Objective **6**

Employee benefits constitute an indirect form of compensation intended to improve the quality of the work and personal lives of employees. Benefits typically represent 40%[28] of total payroll costs to employers. In return, employers generally expect employees to be supportive of the organization and to be productive. Since employees have come to expect an increasing number of benefits, the motivational value of these benefits depends on how the benefits program is designed and communicated. Once viewed as a gift from the employer, benefits are now considered rights to which all employees are entitled.

Too often a particular benefit is provided because other employers are doing it, because someone in authority believes it is a good idea, or because there is union pressure. However, the contributions that benefits will make to the compensation package (and therefore to organizational performance) depend on how much attention is paid to certain basic considerations.

Linking Benefits to the Overall Compensation Program

Like any other component of the compensation plan, an employee benefits program should be based on specific objectives. The objectives an organization establishes will depend on many factors, including the size of the firm, its profitability, its location, the degree of unionization, and industry patterns.

The chief objectives of most benefits programs are to improve employee satisfaction, to meet employee health and security requirements, to attract and motivate employees, to reduce turnover, and to maintain a favourable, competitive position. Ensuring that the company is competitive can take many different forms. For example, the Ford Motor Company recently started a computers-at-home program that gives employees a computer, a colour printer, and Internet access for a nominal monthly fee. The company believes that this type of benefit will help them reach their goal of being on the leading edge of technology.[29] In a 2002 survey of job candidates who were hired, about half stated that the benefits plan was a factor in their decision to join the company, mainly because they did not want to worry about paying for health benefits not covered by their provincial plan.[30] Furthermore, these objectives must be considered within the framework of cost containment—a major issue in today's programs. And, as with other good HR practices, it is a good idea to consult with employees when a new benefit is being considered. Many organizations establish committees made up of managers and employees to administer, interpret, and oversee their benefits policies. Opinion surveys are also used to obtain employee input. Having employees participate in designing benefits programs helps to ensure that management is satisfying employee wants.

Cost Concerns

Organizations typically spend about 25% of their annual payroll costs on benefits such as group health plans.[31] When you then add in other costs such as pensions, EI premiums, CPP premiums, and WCB premiums, the total costs can increase to 35 to 45%. The increasing costs, particularly of health-care provisions, have made more and more organizations strive to manage those costs.

Since many benefits represent a fixed rather than a variable cost, management must decide whether it can afford this cost under less favourable economic conditions. As

Providing medical benefits will be a growing burden on employers in years to come.

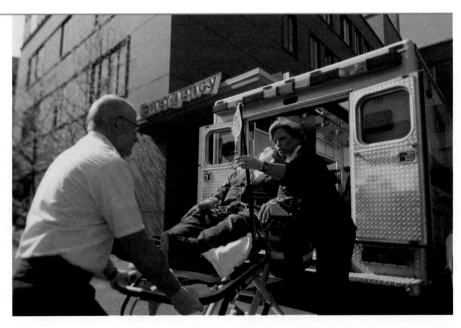

managers can readily attest, if an organization is forced to discontinue a benefit, the negative effects of cutting it may outweigh any positive effects that accrued from providing it.

To minimize negative effects and avoid unnecessary expense, many employers enlist the cooperation of employees in evaluating the importance of particular benefits. Increasingly, employers are requiring employees to pay part of the costs of certain benefits (e.g., through co-payments or higher deductibles). At all times, benefit plan administrators are expected to select benefit service vendors who have the most to offer for the best cost.

The escalating cost of health-care benefits is a major concern to employers, who must strike an appropriate balance between offering quality benefits and keeping costs under control. Increasing deductibles and imposing caps on specific health-care benefits, such as eyeglasses and prescription drugs, are among the cost-containing strategies that have been proposed.[32] At Work with HRM 7.5 describes the steps taken by organizations such as RBC Financial Institution to manage these costs. For additional articles on managing the cost of health care, check out the Web site of Benefits Canada (**www.benefitscanada.com**).

Benefits Canada
www.benefitscanada.com

---

at work **with HRM 7.5** at work with HRM 7.5

MANAGING THE COSTS OF BENEFITS

Mandatory benefits cost employers a minimum of 12% of payroll; when voluntary benefits are included, these costs may rise to 50% of payroll, up from 15% in the 1950s. These costs continue to increase at rates higher than inflation. For example, drug costs have been rising by 16% annually (higher than any other country) and drug costs represent as much as 70% of health-care costs (excluding dental and vision care costs). These benefits represent a fixed rather than a variable cost, so management must decide whether it will be able to afford this cost in bad economic times. As managers can readily attest, if an organization is forced to discontinue a benefit, the negative effects of cutting it often outweigh any positive effects that accrued from providing it.

A current trend (and one not universally liked by employees) is for employers to require employees to pay part of the costs of certain benefits (e.g., through co-payments or higher deductibles). The

Royal Bank used to pay 100% of benefits but now requires employees to pay a small deductible. At all times, benefit plan administrators are expected to select vendors of benefit services that have the most to offer for the cost. Furthermore, besides the actual costs of employee benefits, there are the costs of administering them, including direct labour costs, overhead charges, office space, and technology. But a big part of the escalating costs is the employee attitude of entitlement. Employees think that they are "entitled" to 12 days of sick leave, so they take them, or they feel that since they have paid $50 for $600 of vision care, they should use it.

CRITICAL THINKING QUESTION

Do you think that you are "entitled" to benefits as part of your compensation? Provide reasons for your answer.

Sources: D. Brown, "Runaway Drug Costs Make Benefit Upgrades Impractical," *Canadian HR Reporter,* 16, no. 12 (June 16, 2003); S. Felix, "Gimme Gimme," *Benefits Canada* 24, no. 7 (July 2000): 20–21.

BENEFITS REQUIRED BY LAW

Legally required employee benefits cost over 12% of an organization's annual payroll.[33] These benefits include employer contributions to Canada/Quebec pension plans, unemployment insurance, workers' compensation insurance (covered in Chapter 8), and, in some provinces, provincial medicare.

Canada and Quebec Pension Plans (CPP/QPP)

The Canada and Quebec pension plans cover almost all Canadian employees between the ages of 18 and 70. Both plans require employers to match the contributions made by employees. The revenues generated by these contributions are used to pay three main types of benefits: retirement pensions, disability benefits, and survivors' benefits. With Canada's population aging, funds from the CPP will not be able to meet the needs of retirees unless those currently working, and their employers, significantly increase their contributions.

Employment Insurance (EI)

Employment insurance (EI) benefits have been available for over 50 years and were provided as income protection to employees who were between jobs. Employees and employers both contribute to the Employment Insurance fund. The amount of benefit paid is a formula (which can change) based on the number of hours of employment in the past year and the regional unemployment rate.

Provincial Hospital and Medical Services

Most provinces fund health-care costs from general tax revenue and federal cost sharing. Ontario, Quebec, and Newfoundland also levy a payroll tax, while other provinces, such as Alberta and British Columbia, charge premiums that are payable by the resident or an agent, usually the employer (subsidies for low-income residents are provided).

The cost of providing health care has escalated to the point where major reform in Canada's health-care system is occurring. As of 2004, almost 24% of the Canadian population is over 55 with those over 80 comprising 4%.[34] As has been discussed by policy makers, politicians, and journalists, the increasing longevity of people and the major health problems that do occur mean that our health-care system will need significant redesign to be sustainable in the future.[35]

Leaves without Pay

Most employers grant leaves of absence to employees who request them for personal reasons. In some provinces, these types of leaves must be granted by law. These leaves are usually taken without pay, but also without loss of seniority or benefits.

Other Required Benefits

In addition to the ones described, through provisions in employment standards legislation, provinces do require employers to pay for statutory holidays, minimum vacation pay, premiums when people work overtime, and in some provinces a severance payment when employees are terminated.

VOLUNTARY EMPLOYEE BENEFITS

Objective 7

International Foundation of Employee Benefit Plans
www.ifebp.org

In addition to the benefits that are required by legislation, employers can choose to provide additional benefits as part of the overall compensation package. Organizations do this to ensure that they are able to attract and retain the kind of employees they want. These benefits are called "voluntary benefits." While there can be many of these types of benefits, we will look at the more typical ones. You can review some of the other voluntary benefits at the International Foundation of Employee Benefit Plans Web site (**www.ifebp.org**).

Health and Welfare Benefits

The benefits that receive the most attention from employers today, due to sharply rising costs and employee concern, are health-care benefits. In the past, health insurance plans covered only medical, surgical, and hospital expenses. Today, employers include prescription drugs as well as dental, optical, and mental health-care benefits in the package they offer their workers. As mentioned earlier in this chapter, employers are attempting to ensure that the benefit provided will be of value to the person. Listed below is a brief description of typical health and welfare benefits.

Dental Coverage

Dental plans are designed to help pay for dental-care costs and to encourage employees to receive regular dental attention. Typically, the insurance pays a portion of the charges and the employee pays the remainder.

Many employers offer additional health benefits, such as dental coverage.

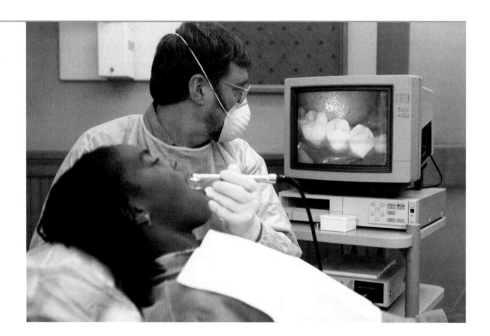

Extended Health Coverage

This benefit provides for additional payments beyond the basic provincial medical coverage. It typically provides such things as semi-private or private hospital rooms, prescription drugs, private nursing, ambulance services, out-of-country medical expenses that exceed provincial limits, and vision care. In an effort to better manage these costs, a number of larger employers, such as Caterpillar, have formed an employers association to negotiate lower drug prices directly with the manufacturers instead of through the companies that manage the extended health coverage. In doing so, they are hoping to reduce their yearly prescription drug costs of $4 billion.[36]

It should be noted that there can be duplication of coverage if both partners in a relationship have access to health coverage. In some cases, if there is better coverage in one plan than in another, the partner with the better coverage will enroll and include the partner.

Life Insurance

One of the oldest and most popular employee benefits is group term life insurance, which provides death benefits to beneficiaries and may also provide accidental death and dismemberment benefits.

Retirement and Pension Plans

Retirement is an important part of life and requires sufficient and careful preparation. In convincing job applicants that theirs is a good organization to work for, employers usually emphasize the retirement benefits that can be expected after a certain number of years of employment.

Pension plans are classified into two primary categories: (1) defined benefit, and (2) defined contribution. In a *defined benefit plan*, a person receiving benefits receives a specific amount (usually based on years of service and average earnings), regardless of the amount of contributions. On the other hand, a *defined contribution plan* provides to the recipient an amount that is based on the amount of accumulated funds and how much those funds can purchase (at the time of retirement) for retirement benefits.

Since defined benefit plans have to provide the specific payment whether or not the employee has made sufficient contributions, the organization becomes liable for the difference. With the aging workforce, more and more organizations and employees are expressing concern about whether their plan will be able to fund what has been promised. Much of the discontent of employees at Air Canada during its potential bankruptcy had to do with the pension plan. Air Canada wanted to reduce the shortfall in the funding by either reducing pensions or having employees contribute more. Had Air Canada not had such a large amount of unfunded liability with its pension plans, it may not have had the financial problems—or at least not to the extent it did. The potential impact of poorly funded pension plans has the Canadian government so concerned that on May 26, 2005, it announced that it was reviewing the rules companies must follow regarding how retirement benefits are handled.[37] There is a suggestion that people be encouraged to work beyond age 65 in order to retain skilled workers and to minimize stress on pension plans.[38] With the increase in a person's expected life span, retirees could live longer and potentially have insufficient pension income. In fact, with the recent discussions regarding eliminating mandatory retirement, concern is being expressed that removing any age limits will jeopardize a person's ability to collect the pension value to which the worker has contributed.[39] This is coupled with more firms moving to pension

ethics **in HRM 7.1** ethics in HRM 7.1

PENSIONS IN A DYNAMIC MARKET

When the headlines were focusing on the decrease in Nortel's stock price, very few people thought about what that decrease might mean for employees. You might have thought about the people who were laid off and the people who wouldn't get hired since Nortel was contracting out some of its business ventures. But what about the people still employed?

One of the significant results of the decrease in Nortel's stock value was the impact on the employee pension plan. By mid-2002, Nortel's pension plan had lost $1.5 billion (CDN) because Nortel had invested the assets of the employee pension plan in its own stock. While the employees chose to invest the money in Nortel stock, Nortel contributed to the purchase so that employees could have an investment with a higher value. Unfortunately, with the decline in value of the stock, employees lost approximately one-third of their investment.

Was it ethical for Nortel to invest pension plan contributions in its own stock?

Sources: Adapted from Derek DeCloet, "US $1B Loss at Nortel Pension Plan," *Financial Post*, July 5, 2002, FP1; and John Hobel, "Ethics, Enron and Intrigue," *Canadian HR Reporter*, June 3, 2002, 4.

plans that cost less to fund.[40] These concerns are magnified when financial scandals, such as WorldCom and Enron, affect the pensions of future retirees. Ethics in HRM 7.1 discusses the dilemma of pensions when Nortel's stock price decreased significantly.

Pay for Time Not Worked

The "pay for time not worked" category of benefits includes statutory holiday pay, vacation pay (above any legislated minimum), bereavement, rest periods, coffee breaks, sick leave, and parenting benefits (salary continuance). These benefits typically account for a large portion of overall benefit costs.

Vacations with Pay

It is generally agreed that vacations are essential to the well-being of an employee. Eligibility for vacations varies by industry, locale, and organization size. To qualify for longer vacations of three, four, or five weeks, one may expect to work for seven, fifteen, and twenty years, respectively.

As shown in Around the World with HRM 7.1, European professional and managerial personnel tend to receive more vacation time than do their Canadian, U.S., and Japanese counterparts. Although most countries have government mandates for employers to guarantee vacation time to workers, the United States and United Kingdom do not.

Paid Holidays

Both hourly and salaried workers can expect to be paid for statutory holidays as designated in each province. The standard statutory holidays in Canada are New Year's Day, Good Friday, Canada Day (Memorial Day in Newfoundland), Labour Day, and Christmas Day. Other

around the world **with HRM 7.1** around the world

VACATION DAYS: A GLOBAL LOOK

Employees of these countries are entitled to the following average vacation days:

Austria	25	
Sweden	25	Collective agreements may improve this provision.
Germany	24	Minimum statutory entitlement based on a 6-day work week.
United Kingdom	23	Fixed by collective agreement. Typical practice is 4–6 weeks. Figure is an average.
Belgium	20	For 1 year of service, based on a 5-day work week.
Ireland	20	Most employees entitled to a 4-week leave.
Canada	10	Federal provisions; 2–4 weeks depending on jurisdiction.
United States	5	1 week leave for 6 months–1 year service; 2 weeks after 1–5 years.

Note: These comparisons are intended as general guidelines and do not take into consideration age, length of service, employee level, or salary unless otherwise stated.

Source: *Worldwide Benefit & Employment Guidelines 2003/2004*, Mercer Human Resource Consulting LLC.

holidays that are recognized by various provinces are Victoria Day, Thanksgiving Day, and Remembrance Day. Additionally, each province may designate special holidays important to that province only. Many employers give workers an additional one to three personal days off.

Sick Leave

Employees may be compensated in several ways during periods when they are unable to work because of illness or injury. Most public employees, as well as many in private firms (particularly in white-collar jobs), receive a set number of sick-leave days each year to cover such absences. Where permitted, sick leave that employees do not use can be accumulated to cover prolonged absences. Accumulated vacation leave may sometimes be used as a source of income when sick-leave benefits have been exhausted. Group insurance that provides income protection during a long-term disability is also becoming more common. As discussed earlier in the chapter, income lost during absences resulting from job-related injuries may be reimbursed, at least partially, through workers' compensation insurance.

According to a recent Statistics Canada report, sick-leave benefits cost Canadian businesses over $10 billion annually.[41] Much of this amount is due to the aging workforce. Workers aged 55 to 64 missed 12 days of work on average each year, while workers aged 25 to 44 missed only 1.5 days.

Wellness Programs

In recent years, new types of services have been offered to make life at work more rewarding and to enhance employee well-being. "Wellness is good for business," says Ann Coll of Husky Injection Molding Systems Ltd. Employees at the Bolton, Ontario, facility enjoy a subsidized cafeteria with organic vegetarian meals, a $500 stipend for vitamins, and a fitness centre that is open around the clock.

Employee Assistance Programs

To help workers cope with a wide variety of problems that interfere with the way they perform their jobs, organizations have developed employee assistance programs (EAPs). An employee assistance program typically provides diagnosis, limited counselling, and referral for advice or treatment when necessary for problems related to substance (alcohol, drug) abuse, emotional difficulties, and financial or family difficulties. (EAPs will be discussed in detail in Chapter 8.) Approximately 49% of Canadian employers have an EAP for their employees and families.[42] The main intent of these programs is to help employees solve their personal problems or at least to prevent problems from turning into crises that affect their ability to work productively.

Educational Assistance Plans

One of the benefits most frequently mentioned in literature for employees is the educational assistance plan. The primary purpose of this plan is to help employees keep up to date with advances in their fields and to help them get ahead in the organization. Usually the employer covers—in part or totally—costs of tuition, books, and related fees, while the employee is required to pay for meals, transportation, and other expenses.

Childcare and Eldercare

Consider these statistics:

- About 32% of Canadians have eldercare responsibilities.
- Employees spend an average of twenty-three hours each month on eldercare.[43]

In the past, working parents had to make their own arrangements with sitters or with nursery schools for pre-school children. Today, benefits may include financial assistance, alternative work schedules, and family leave. For many employees, on-site or near-site childcare centres are the most visible, prestigious, and desired solutions.

A growing benefit offered employees with children experiencing a short illness is called mildly ill childcare. Medical supervision is the primary difference between these facilities and traditional day care arrangements. See At Work with HRM 7.6 for the benefits of these arrangements as cited by CIBC.

Eldercare
Care provided to an elderly relative by an employee who remains actively at work

Responsibility for the care of aging parents and other relatives is another fact of life for more and more employees. The term **eldercare**, as used in the context of employment, refers to situations where an employee provides care to an elderly relative while remaining actively at work. Most caregivers are women. In 2001, four million Canadians were 65 or older, of which close to 25% were over 80.[44] One-fifth of this number will have some type of disability. As a consequence of the expected shortfall in eldercare facilities, the responsibility for the care of these seniors will be borne by their children and other relatives. The majority of caregivers are women.

To reduce the negative effects of caregiving on productivity, organizations may offer eldercare counselling, educational fairs and seminars, printed resource material, support groups, and special flexible schedules and leaves of absence.

at work **with HRM 7.6** at work with HRM 7.6

CIBC CARES

CIBC was the first Canadian corporation to open an employer-sponsored centre dedicated to backup childcare. Every parent has faced the hardship of finding emergency care, when regular childcare arrangements break down due to a caretaker's illness, or when schools are closed for professional development days or snow days. The CIBC Children's Centre offers special play areas for children of different ages and is licensed under the *Day Nurseries Act*. The centre is operated by ChildrenFirst, which designs, develops, and operates innovative backup childcare facilities in North America. Nearly 600 parents used the CIBC Children's Centre in the first six months of operation, with a resultant saving of 760 employee days. At an average daily rate of about $200, the productivity saving was estimated to be about $150,000. The projected savings over five years are $1,400,000. The intangible benefits include increased attraction and retention of employees and allowing them to achieve better work-life family balance. CIBC discovered through surveys that 90% of Canadians want organizations to focus on more than profits, 60% form an impression of a company based on its social responsibility, and 17% have avoided a company's products because of its lack of social responsibility.

Sources: ChildrenFirst, www.childrenfirst.com; CIBC, www.cibc.com; presentation made by Joyce M. Phillips, executive vice-president human resources, CIBC in April 2003.

Many organizations recognize the needs of working parents and ensure appropriate childcare is available.

at work **with HRM 7.7** at work with HRM 7.7

PERKS AT INTUIT

Intuit Canada, which develops financial software, employs about 400 employees at its Edmonton offices and is rated one of Canada's top employers. The benefits it offers employees is one of the reasons for its success. First, Intuit offers the standard benefits package, for which it pays 100% of the premiums. Then the fun stuff begins. There is a staff lounge with pool table, foozball, ping pong, and a gas fireplace. Down the hall, employees work out in the company gym, playing volleyball, basketball, and floor hockey. A complete fitness centre, with a free towel service, is greatly valued by employees. For the long hours and stress, Intuit even provides three nap rooms after listening to employees who said they just wanted a place to crash for an hour or two. Intuit pays for employees and their families to relax at the annual corporate retreat at Alberta's Jasper Park Lodge. For Intuit, the benefit of these benefits is the ability to attract and retain the best people.

CRITICAL THINKING QUESTION

Do you think these special benefits are reasonable? Why or why not?

Source: T. Humber, "Perquisites No Longer a Prerequisite," *Canadian HR Reporter* 16, no. 3 (February 10, 2003): G7–G9.

Interest in and demand for eldercare programs is increasing dramatically as the Canadian population ages and lives longer. The typical profile of an eldercaregiver is a 40-something employed female.[45] One of the authors of this text (Stewart) found herself in just this situation: raising a young child and having to care for aging parents at a distance.

Other Services

The variety of benefits and services that employers offer today could not have been imagined a few years ago. Some are fairly standard, and we will cover them briefly. Some are unique and obviously grew out of specific concerns, needs, and interests. Some of the more creative and unusual benefits are group insurance for employee pets, free baseball tickets for families and friends, summer boat cruises, and subsidized haircuts for MPs. At Work with HRM 7.7 describes the perks at Intuit Canada.

CURRENT COMPENSATION ISSUES

Objective **8**

As with other HR matters, compensation management operates in a dynamic environment. For example, as managers strive to reward employees in a fair manner, they must consider controls over labour costs, legal issues regarding male and female wage payments, and internal equity concerns. Each of these concerns is highlighted in four important compensation issues: equal pay for comparable value, wage-rate compression, low salary budgets, and two-tier wage systems.

Equal Pay for Comparable Value (Pay Equity)

Comparable value
The concept that male and female jobs that are dissimilar, but equal in value or worth to the employer, should be paid the same

One of the most important gender issues in compensation is equal pay for work of equal value. The issue stems from the fact that jobs performed predominantly by women are paid less than those performed by men. This practice results in what critics term *institutionalized sex discrimination*, causing women to receive less pay for jobs that may be different from but comparable in worth to those performed by men. The issue of **comparable value** goes beyond providing equal pay for jobs that involve the same duties for women as for men. It is not concerned with whether a female secretary should receive the same pay as a male secretary. Rather, the argument for comparable value is that jobs held by women are not compensated the same as those held by men, even though both job types may contribute equally to organizational success.

Advocates of comparable value argue that the difference in wage rates for predominantly male and female occupations rests in the undervaluing of traditional female occupations. To remedy this situation, they propose that wages should be equal for jobs that are "somehow" equivalent in total value or compensation to the organization. Unfortunately, there is no consensus on a comparable value standard by which to evaluate jobs, nor is there agreement on the ability of current job evaluation techniques to remedy the problem.[46] Indeed, organizations may dodge the comparable value issue by using one job evaluation system for clerical and secretarial jobs and another system for other jobs. Furthermore, the advocates of comparable value argue that current job evaluation techniques simply serve to continue the differences in pay between the sexes. However, others believe that job evaluation systems can be designed to measure different types of jobs.

The argument over comparable value is likely to remain an HR issue in the future. Unanswered questions, such as the following, will keep the issue alive:

1. If comparable value is adopted, who will determine the value of jobs, and by what means?
2. How much would comparable value cost employers?
3. Would comparable value reduce the wage gap between men and women caused by labour market supply-and-demand forces?
4. Would comparable value reduce the number of employment opportunities for women?

Cost Containment of Health and Welfare Benefits

The approaches used to contain the costs of health-care benefits include reductions in coverage, increased deductibles or co-payments, and increased coordination of benefits to make sure the same expense is not paid by more than one insurance reimbursement. Cost-containment strategies must be subject to a cost–benefit analysis. Also, many organizations are developing communication strategies to help employees understand the costs of benefits and who pays for what.[47]

Some organizations are entering into relationships with pharmacies with a goal to educate people about proper usage of medication and alternatives to more expensive drugs. Falconbridge and Inco, both steel manufacturing companies, have been successful in reducing their costs by creating a drug-plan monitoring program.[48] Employee assistance programs and wellness programs may also allow an organization to cut the costs of its health-care benefits.

Pension Portability

For a long time, most pension plans lacked portability; in other words, employees who changed jobs were unable to maintain equity in a single pension. Unions addressed this concern by encouraging multiple-employer plans. These plans cover the employees of two or more unrelated organizations in accordance with a collective agreement. They are governed by boards of trustees on which both the employers and the union are represented. Multiple-employer plans tend to be found in industries in which few companies have enough employees to justify an individual plan. They are also often found in industries in which employment tends to be either seasonal or irregular. These plans are common in the following manufacturing sectors: apparel, printing, furniture, leather, and metalworking. They are also common in nonmanufacturing industries, such as mining, construction, transport, entertainment, and private higher education.

Employees who leave an organization can leave their locked-in funds in their current pension plan, or they can transfer those funds into a locked-in RRSP, or into their new employer's pension plan (if one exists).

Flexible Benefit Plans

Flexible benefit plans
Plans that enable individual employees to choose the benefits that are best suited to their particular needs

To accommodate the individual needs of employees, many organizations are embracing **flexible benefits plans**, also known as cafeteria plans. Over 90% of employers who responded to a survey were interested in offering flexible benefits.[49] These plans enable individual employees to choose the benefits that are best suited to their particular needs. They also prevent certain benefits from being wasted on employees who have no need for them. Typically, employees are offered a basic or core benefits package of life and health insurance, sick leave, and vacation. Requiring a core set of benefits ensures that employees have a minimum level of coverage to protect against unforeseen financial hardships. Employees are then given a specified number of credits that they may use to "buy" whatever other benefits they need. Other benefit options might include prepaid legal services, financial planning, or long-term care insurance.[50] Compensation specialists often see flexible benefits plans as ideal. Employees select the benefits of greatest value to them, while employers manage benefits costs by limiting the dollars employees have to spend.

Honeywell Canada considered three types of flexible benefits programs: cafeteria-style, whereby employees could choose any benefits they wanted; a module approach, whereby employees could select among prepackaged sets of benefits; and a core-plus-options plan, whereby employees could choose among options to augment a basic level of protection. Employees were able to select health and dental benefits that suited their life stages and that matched well with the plans their spouses had.

Because cafeteria plans increase the complexity of administering the entire benefits programs, organizations may elect to outsource the handling of this function to a professional benefits vendor. About a third of Canadian firms rely on third parties to perform these types of transactional services for their plans.[51] Paying a service or contract fee to these firms may be particularly cost-effective for the smaller employer. Furthermore, benefits programs must be flexible enough to accommodate the constant flow of new laws and regulations that affect them. A number of consulting firms specializing in benefits can help managers track changes in all phases of the programs they oversee.

One of the more innovative approaches to flexibility in benefits is to focus on the needs of women in the workplace. Whether the woman is single or married, there is a recognition that women have a higher proportion of responsibility in family matters outside the work environment. Therefore, employers in businesses with a greater proportion of female employees are discovering that such plans are a good way to attract and retain female staff.[52] Of particular note in this situation is that over 75% of users of EAP services are women and the single most common issue is work-life balance. The impact of stress from an imbalance is costing the Canadian marketplace between $3 billion and $5 billion annually.[53] Therefore, it makes good business sense to ensure that the benefits programs provided to female employees meet their needs.

SUMMARY

1. Explain an organization's concerns in developing a strategic compensation program.
   - Companies structure compensation in ways that enhance employee motivation and growth.
   - Compensation must be tailored to fit the needs of the company and its employees.
   - Companies are concerned that employees believe the compensation to be equitable.

2. Identify the various factors that influence the setting of pay levels.
   - There are internal and external factors.
   - Internal factors include the organization's compensation policy, the perceived worth of the job, the performance of the employee, and the employer's willingness to pay.
   - The external factors include labour market conditions, cost of living, collective bargaining, and legal considerations.

3. Describe the major job evaluation systems.
   - Job ranking system, which groups jobs on the basis of their relative worth.
   - Job classification system, where jobs are grouped according to a series of predetermined grades based on a number of factors.
   - Point system, which determines a job's relative worth by using a quantitative system of points.
   - Factor comparison system, where a job is evaluated on a factor-by-factor basis; this type of system is typically used for legislated pay equity purposes.

4. Describe the compensation structure.
   - Wage and salary survey, which provides information about average wage rates external to the organization.
   - Developing a wage curve, which indicates the rates currently paid for jobs within the organization.
   - Development of pay rates for paying individuals based on the job.

5. List the types of incentive plans.
   - Individual bonus.
   - Team- or group-based.
   - Merit raises.
   - Gainsharing.
   - Profit-sharing.
   - Employee stock ownership plan.

6. Explain the employee benefits that are required by law.
   - Canada and Quebec pension plans, which provide for a pension for all employees working in Canada.
   - Employment insurance, which provides income protection to employees who are between jobs.
   - Workers' compensation insurance, which pays people for work-related accidents or illnesses.

7. Describe voluntary benefits.
   - Benefits which are considered indirect compensation.
   - Benefits an organization chooses to provide.
   - Can include health and welfare coverage, pay for time not worked (vacation, sick leave), wellness programs, and childcare assistance.

8. Discuss the current compensation and benefits issues.
   - Equal pay for work of equal value, which attempts to remedy the situation of undervaluing traditionally female occupations.
   - Organizations are using a variety of methods to contain the costs of benefits—which are increasing every year.
   - Employees are expecting to have pension plans that are portable from one employer to another.
   - Flexible benefit plans, in which individuals can choose benefits that best fit their needs.

Need to Know

- Definition of compensation and compensation management
- Internal and external factors that affect compensation
- Types of incentive plans
- Types of voluntary and mandatory benefits

Need to Understand

- Relationship of compensation and organizational objectives
- Complexity of factors in relation to compensation decisions
- Role of line manager in making individual employee pay decisions
- Impact of benefits costs on costs of running business

Key Terms

comparable value 264

competency-based pay 250

consumer price index (CPI) 243

direct compensation 234

eldercare 261

equitable pay 239

flexible benefit plans 265

hourly work 240

indirect compensation 234

job evaluation 241

pay grades 248

pay-for-performance standard 237

piecework 240

real wages 244

wage and salary survey 248

REVIEW QUESTIONS

1. List the common goals of a compensation strategy.
2. Explain the motivational value of pay.
3. What are the internal and external factors used in determining compensation levels?
4. What is job evaluation? Describe the various methods of job evaluation.
5. Explain incentive plans.
6. What are some of the problems of developing a pay system based on equal pay for comparable value?
7. What are some of the advantages of team-based pay? The disadvantages?
8. List the benefits required by law.
9. Describe some the types of benefits that employers voluntarily provide for employees.

CRITICAL THINKING QUESTIONS

1. You have been asked to prepare a report for your company regarding a policy on a mandatory retirement age. What would you identify as the advantages and disadvantages? What factors might influence the decision of an employee to retire before the mandatory age?
2. You work for a retail store in your community that is part of a large national chain of retail stores. The store manager has approached you about your thoughts on introducing a bonus based on the sales each person generates. How would you respond and why?
3. A fast-food restaurant in your community has a large number of part-time employees, primarily in the 16- to 18-year age range. The owner of the restaurant knows that you are taking an introductory course in human resource management and has approached you to give some ideas about the restaurant's benefits package. What items would you suggest be included and why?
4. You have recently been promoted to supervisor. Your company is in the hardware business and has a policy that supervisors are paid on a salary instead of an hourly wage basis. Why would the company do this? What are the advantages and disadvantages to you and your company?
5. One of the objections to granting wage increases on a percentage basis is that the lowest-paid employees, who are having the most trouble making ends meet, get the smallest increase, while the highest-paid employees get the largest increase. Is this objection a valid one? Explain.
6. Because of competitive forces within your industry, you have decided to implement a profit-sharing plan for your employees. Discuss the advantages of profit-sharing and identify specific characteristics that will assure success for your plan.
7. Many organizations are concerned about the rising cost of employee benefits and question their value to the organization and to the employees.

   a. In your opinion, what benefits are of greatest value to employees? To the organization? Why?
   b. What can management do to increase the value to the organization of the benefits provided to employees?

8. Do you think that compensation is the only way of rewarding employees? What other methods can organizations use that will prove effective motivators for employees?

9. Access your province's employment standards legislation and determine the current minimum wage.

DEVELOPING YOUR SKILLS

1. Since pay-for-performance is an important factor governing salary increases, managers must be able to defend the compensation recommendations they make for their employees. Merit raises granted under a pay-for-performance policy must be based on objective appraisals if they are to achieve their intended purposes of rewarding outstanding employee performance. As managers know, however, other factors that can affect salary recommendations must be dealt with. These may include the opinions of the employee's peers or extenuating circumstances, such as illness or family responsibilities. The purpose of this exercise is to provide you with the experience of granting salary increases to employees based on their work performance and other information.

ASSIGNMENT

1. Following are the work records of five employees. As their supervisor, you have just completed their annual appraisal reviews, and it is now time to make recommendations for their future salaries. Your department budget has $8,000 allocated for salary increases. Distribute the $8,000 among your employees based on the descriptions for each subordinate.

   a. Janet Jenkins currently earns $35,000. Her performance appraisal rating was very high. She is respected by her peers and is felt to be an asset to the work group. She is divorced and has three young children to support.

   b. Russell Watts earns a salary of $32,000. His annual performance appraisal was average. Several members of the work group have spoken to you about the difficulty involved in Russell's job. They feel that it is a tough and demanding job and that he is doing his best.

   c. Jack Perkins earns $33,000. His performance appraisal was below average and he seems to have difficulty adjusting to his co-workers. Jack has had a difficult time this past year. His wife passed away early in the year and his father has recently been diagnosed as terminally ill.

   d. Rick Jacobson earns $32,000. His performance appraisal was above average. He is respected by his peers and is generally considered to be a "good guy."

   e. Paula Merrill earns $32,000. Her performance appraisal was very high. Her peers are upset because they feel that she is working only to provide a second income. Moreover, her peers see her as trying to "show them up."

   Share your results with other class members. Be prepared to explain your allocation of money.

2. Working in groups of four to five students, pick an organization that is relatively familiar to all students in the group—this could even be the college/university in which you are taking this course. Develop two to three compensation objectives for the organization and decide whether you would include an incentive program and give your reasons. Share your results with the class, including an explanation of your results.

3. Working in teams of three or four, list and discuss the various benefits offered by your employer (or former employer). How were the costs of these benefits paid for?

4. Assume your team has been hired as a benefits consultant by a small business with 50 to 60 employees. What benefits do you believe this employer should offer given its limited resources? Explain why you would offer these benefits.

5. On an individual basis, search the URL **www.shrm.org**. Find a link that references or deals with "compensation" and/or "benefits." Pick two to three specific online resource sites that would be useful to you as a line manager. Print the first page of the site; bring it to class and share the information with your fellow students—including a description of why the site is valuable to you.

6. In pairs, access the Employee Benefit Research Institute at **www.ebri.org**. Select one of its current news releases. Review the contents and do a comparison with materials presented in this chapter. Share the results of your comparison with others in the class.

**Society for Human
Resource Management**
www.shrm.org

**Employee Benefit
Research Institute**
www.ebri.org/

Case Study **1**

Pay-for-Performance: The Merit Question

In January 2000, Central Hospital implemented a formal performance review program for its 127 staff nurses. The program originally met with some resistance from a few nurses and supervisors, but generally the system was welcomed as an objective way to appraise nursing performance. Complaints centred on the increase in time it took to complete the appraisal review process and the fact that supervisors disliked having to confront nurses who disagreed with their performance review. Nursing supervisors are required to appraise employee performance annually and to forward to the HR department a copy of each appraisal form.

In July 2004, Thomas Chen, HR manager for the hospital, reviewed all nurses' assessments on file since the beginning of the program. From this study he concluded that the large majority (82%) of nurses were assessed as performing at an "average" level, as indicated by a global rating at the bottom of the form. Approximately 10% were rated "above average" or "superior," and the remainder received "below standard" performance reviews. As a response to these findings, Chen decided to base the annual raise for all nurses on the consumer price index for the hospital's metropolitan area. This, he concluded, would allow the nurses to maintain their standard of living while guaranteeing all nurses a yearly raise.

As part of the hospital's employee involvement program, Chen holds quarterly meetings with groups of employees to solicit their feelings regarding hospital policy and their jobs. Both positive and negative opinions are expressed at these gatherings. These opinions are used to modify hospital policy. At meetings in the past year, a number of both junior and senior nurses have expressed dissatisfaction with the across-the-board pay policy for annual raises. The biggest complaint concerns the lack of motivation to increase output, since all nurses are paid the same regardless of individual performance. These comments have been numerous enough that Chen has considered changing the nurses' compensation policy. During the past seven months, nine of the better nurses have quit to take jobs with area hospitals that award annual increases on a merit or pay-for-performance basis.

Questions

1. What are the advantages of adopting a merit pay plan for hospital nurses? Are there any disadvantages to starting a merit pay program?
2. What problems might arise with a supervisor's assessment of nurses?
3. Develop a merit pay guideline chart based on the following levels of performance evaluation: superior, above average, average, below average, and poor. Use current cost-of-living figures for your area or salary survey data available to you to guide your merit percentage increases.
4. It is not uncommon for hospital nurses to work in teams. Explain how a team-based incentive program for nurses might be developed. What criteria might be used to evaluate team performance?
5. Should the hospital give higher starting salaries for nurses with unique skill sets that are in high demand (such as operating room nurses) where such salaries may be higher than more senior nurses? Why or why not?

Case Study 2

True North Family-Friendly Benefits: The Backlash

True North Consulting Services, a provider of HR software application systems, prides itself on the variety of benefits it offers employees. In addition to extra health-care, pension, and vacation benefits, the company also offers an attractive family-friendly benefits package including flexible schedules, child and eldercare assistance, counselling services, adoption assistance, and extended parental leave. Unfortunately, in recent months, the company's progressive work-life policy has experienced a backlash from several employees, as the following case illustrates.

In March 2002, Teresa Wheatly was hired by True North as a software accounts manager. With excellent administrative and technical skills, as well as four years of experience at Adaptable Software, True North's main competitor, Teresa became a valued addition to the company's marketing team. As a single mother with two grade-school children, Teresa received permission to take Fridays off. She was also allowed to leave work early or come in late to meet the demands of her children. Teresa is one of eleven software account managers at True North.

The problem for True North, and particularly Janis Blancero, director of marketing, began in the fall of 2002. On September 15, Dorothy McShee, citing "personal reasons"—which she refused to discuss—requested a four-day work week for which she was willing to take a 20% cut in pay. When Dorothy asked for the reduced work schedule, she sarcastically quipped, "I hope I don't have to have kids to get this time off." On October 3, Juan Batista, a world-class marathon runner, requested a flexible work hours arrangement in order to accommodate his morning and afternoon training schedule. Juan is registered to run the London,

England, marathon in May 2005. Just prior to Juan's request, Susan Woolf asked for, and was granted, an extended maternity leave to begin after the birth of her first child in December. If these unexpected requests were not enough, Blancero has heard comments from senior account managers about how some employees seem to get "special privileges," while the managers work long hours that often require them to meet around-the-clock customer demands. Janis has adequate reason to believe that there is hidden tension over the company's flexible work hours program. Currently, True North has no formal policy on flexible schedules. Furthermore, the company's growth in business combined with the increasing workload of software account managers and the constant service demands of some customers has made Blancero realize that she simply cannot grant all the time-off requests of her employees.

Source: Adapted from Alden M. Hayashi, "Mommy-Track Backlash," *Harvard Business Review* 79, no. 3 (March 2001): 33–42.

Questions

1. Do managers like Janis Blancero face a more complicated decision when evaluating the personal requests of employees rather than evaluating employees' individual work performance? Explain.
2. a. Should True North establish a policy for granting flexible work schedules? Explain.
   b. If you answered yes, what might that policy contain?
3. If you were Janis Blancero, how would you resolve this dilemma? Explain.

NOTES AND REFERENCES

1. Paul W. Mulvey, Gerald E. Ledford, Jr., and Peter V. LeBlanc, "Rewards of Work," *WorldatWork Journal* 9, no. 3 (Third Quarter 2000): 6–18.
2. "Workforce Realities Remain in a Sputtering Economy," *Towers Perrin Monitor*, November 2001, www.towers.com/towers_publications/publications/pubs_frame_towers.asp?target=Monitor/mon.htm (retrieved April 24, 2002).
3. Carolyn Baarda, *Compensation Planning Outlook 2005*, The Conference Board of Canada, 2004.
4. "Reward Programs Offer Organizations a Competitive Edge," *The Galt Global Review*, September 2, 2003, www.galtglobalreview.com/careers/reward_programs.html (retrieved December 11, 2004).
5. *Ibid.*
6. Baarda, *Compensation Planning Outlook 2005*.
7. *Human Capital as a Lead Indicator to Shareholder Value*, Watson Wyatt, 2002, www.watsonwyatt.com/canada-english/research/resrender.asp?id=W-488&page=1 (retrieved August 2, 2002).
8. Robert L. Heneman and Katherine E. Dixon, "Reward and Organizational Systems Alignment: An Expert System," *Compensation and Benefits Review* 33, no. 6 (November–December 2001): 18–28.
9. Kenneth F. Clarke, "What Businesses Are Doing to Attract and Retain Employees—Becoming an Employer of Choice," *Employee Benefits Journal* 26, no. 1 (March 2001): 21–23.
10. Claudia Zeitz Poster, "Retaining Key People in Troubled Companies," *Compensation and Benefits Review* 34, no. 1 (January–February 2002): 7–11.
11. "The Future of Salary Management," *Compensation and Benefits Review* 33, no. 4 (July–August 2001): 7–13.
12. Michelle Brown and John S. Heywood, *Paying for Performance: An International Comparison* (Armonk, NY: M. E. Sharpe, 2002).
13. Randolph W. Keuch, "Pay-for-Performance Is Alive and Well," *WorldatWork Journal* 10, no. 3 (Third Quarter 2001): 18–23.

14. Steven J. McShane, *Canadian Organizational Behaviour*, 5th ed. (Toronto: McGraw-Hill Ryerson, 2004): 152–154.

15. Ramon J. Aldag and Loren W. Kuzuhara, *Organizational Behavior and Management* (Mason, OH: South-Western Publishing, 2002): 266–70.

16. George T. Milkovich and Jerry M. Newman, *Compensation*, 7th ed. (Chicago: Irwin, 2002): 12–16.

17. *CPI Detailed Report*, December 2001 (Washington, DC: U.S. Department of Labor, Bureau of Labor Statistics). Published monthly.

18. Classification provided by Moira Penwill and Susan Ney, District of West Vancouver, August 2002.

19. Edward E. Lawler, "Pay Strategy: New Thinking for the New Millennium," *Compensation and Benefits Review* 32, no. 1 (January–February 2000): 7–12.

20. James R. Thompson and Charles W. LeHew, "Skill-Based Pay as an Organizational Innovation," *Review of Public Personnel Administration* 20, no. 2 (Winter 2000): 20–38.

21. David A. Hofrichter and Todd McGovern, "People, Competencies and Performance: Clarifying Means and Ends," *Compensation and Benefits Review* 33, no. 4 (July–August 2001): 34–38.

22. Ken Gibson, "Building a Competency-Based HRM System at NRC," National Research Council presentation, September 30, 1999.

23. Michael Enos and Greg Limoges, "Broadbanding: Is That Your Company's Final Answer?" *WorldatWork Journal* 9, no. 4 (Fourth Quarter 2000): 61–68.

24. Baarda, *Compensation Planning Outlook 2005*, 5.

25. Katie Lematre and Larry Retssman, "Managing Performance: Achieving Outstanding Performance through a Culture of Dialogue," Hay Group Working Paper, 2002.

26. Richard Long, "Your Compensation System: To KISS or Not," Research Forum, *HR Professional*, June/July 2002.

27. Robert Mangel and Michael Useen, "The Strategic Role of Gainsharing," *Journal of Labor Research* 21, no. 2 (Spring 2000): 327–43.

28. The Canadian Payroll Association, "Compensation Planning 2003," *Dialogue* [online magazine] www.payroll.ca. November/December 2002: 14–17.

29. John Tompkins and Sarah Beech, "Do Benefit Plans Attract and Retain Talent," *Benefits Canada* 26, no. 10 (2002): 49–56.

30. "Ford to Put PCs in the Homes of Its Workforce," *National Post*, February 3, 2000, A14.

31. Baarda, *Compensation Planning Outlook 2005*, 19.

32. Anna Sharratt, "Employers Lack Health Care Strategies," *Benefits Canada*, July 30, 2002, www.benefitscanada.com/news/2002/07-02/july30_02.html (retrieved August 2, 2002).

33. Jacqueline Taggart, "No Easy Answer for Cost Conundrum," *Canadian HR Reporter*, April 19, 2004, 11.

34. Statistics Canada, "Population by Sex and Age Group, www.statcan.ca/english/Pgdb/demo10a.htm (retrieved December 13, 2004).

35. Information gathered by the current author on a consulting assignment to Vancouver Coastal Health Authority, 2004–2005.

36. Milt Freudenheim, "Big Employers Join Forces in Effort to Negotiate Lower Drug Prices," *The New York Times*, June 12, 2004, B1.

37. Sandra Cordon, "Crisis in Corporate Pension-Plan Funding Prompts Look at Federal Rule Changes," *Business Centre*, www.canada.com/businesscentre/story.html?id=791f80a7-7114-4-bbe-96c8-d04464fb1446 (retrieved May 29, 2005).

38. David Brown, "What's So Special about 65?" *Canadian HR Reporter*, September 20, 2000.

39. April Lindgren, "Retirement Change 'Threat to Pensions,'" *Financial Post*, August 19, 2004, FP6.

40. Jonathan Chevreau, "More Firms Opt for Cheaper Pensions," *Financial Post*, April 22, 2004, FP4.

41. "As Age Increases, So Does a Worker's Sick Time Off," *The Vancouver Sun*, July 20, 1999, A4.

42. John Butler, "You've Invested in an EAP, Now Learn How to Use It," *Canadian HR Reporter*, June 3, 2002, 7.

43. A. Tomlinson, "Trickle Down Effect of Retiring Boomers," *Canadian HR Reporter* 15, no. 11 (June 3, 2002): 1, 12.

44. 2001 Census, Statistics Canada, www12.statcan.ca/english/census01/products/analytic/companion/age/canada.cfm (retrieved August 2, 2002).

45. Ann Vincola, "Eldercare: What Firms Can Do to Help," *Canadian HR Reporter*, www.hrreporter.com/loginarea/members/viewing.asp?ArticleNo=247&subscriptionType=WEB (retrieved August 2, 2002).

46. Marie Drolet, "The Who, What, When, and Where of Gender Pay Differentials," Statistics Canada, *The Evolving Workplace Series*, June 2002.

47. Jason Billard, "Communication Can Ease the Pain of Rising Benefit Costs," *Canadian HR Reporter*, June 17, 2002, G3.

48. Anna Sharratt, "The Feasibility of Falconbridge," *Benefits Canada*, November 2004, 21.

49. J. Taggart, "Guide to Pension and Benefits," *Canadian HR Reporter* 15, no. 21 (December 2, 2002): G3.

50. Ronald W. Perry and N. Joseph Cayer, "Cafeteria Style Health Plans in Municipal Govt.," *Public Person Management* 28, no. 1 (Spring 1999): 107–17;

Jon J. Meyer, "The Future of Flexible Benefit Plans," *Employee Benefits Journal* 25, no. 2 (June 2000): 3–7. See also Carolyn Hirschman, "Kinder, Simpler Cafeteria Rule," *HRMagazine* 46, no. 1 (January 2001): 74–79.

51. L. Byron, L. and R. Dawson, "Flex Benefits Are More Popular than Ever with Employers and Employees," *Benefits*, Benefits Canada, http://www.benefitscanada.com/magazine/article.jsp?content=20030624_134506_4312, April 2003, (retrieved May 28, 2005).

52. Tom Buller, "A Flexible Combination," *Benefits Canada*, November 2004, 99–101.

53. *Ibid.*

PART 4

Employee Relations

CHAPTER 8

Creating a Safe and Healthy Work Environment

OBJECTIVES

After studying this chapter, you should be able to

1 Describe what supervisors and managers can do to create a safe and healthy work environment.

2 Cite the measures that should be taken to control and eliminate health and safety hazards.

3 List the current workplace health and safety issues.

4 Describe the organizational services and programs for building better health.

5 Explain the role of employee assistance programs.

6 Describe the ways in which supervisors can support work groups on health and safety matters.

OUTLINE

Holly O'Rourke with her staff at Saint Andrews Physiotherapy Clinic

"I have a direct and personal interest in the health and safety of my staff."

When your business is physiotherapy, you're about as close as possible to the real reason for health and safety programs in the workplace. "We've been in business 12 years without accidents or injuries," explains Holly O'Rourke, owner of the Saint Andrews Physiotherapy Clinic in Saint Andrews, New Brunswick. "I attribute that to the nature of our work and our knowledge of proper body mechanics."

O'Rourke works as a physiotherapist in addition to running the business. "About half of our clients are being treated for workplace injuries, and many of them have repetitive strain injuries. It didn't take long for me to realize that we needed ergonomically correct computers and chairs for the staff using them," says O'Rourke. She also believes in getting feedback and ideas from the staff when it comes to improving safety at the clinic. Most problems are solved with common sense and creativity. "Because we all work in the same area, it's in our best interest to keep the work area safe."

The majority of people treated at the clinic are outpatient orthopedic patients with soft tissue injuries. Patients typically use the exercise stations and equipment within the clinic to do their physiotherapy programs. Because the clinic is quite busy, O'Rourke is watchful that a clear pathway for staff and patients is always maintained. For example, she placed different exercise stations along the periphery of the clinic allowing a central passage. There are also many electric machines in the clinic, so O'Rourke installed extra electrical outlets to avoid having cords run across the floor. She also built plastic rings to hold the clinic's large exercise balls to prevent them from rolling around on the floor.

O'Rourke is conscious of her own staff's exposure to repetitive strain—for example, when they move large pieces of equipment from cubicle to cubicle. O'Rourke introduced rolling carts to move equipment around in order to ease the strain on staff. She placed outlets at waist height to limit the amount of bending required to plug in and unplug equipment, and she organized supply shelves at waist height in order to reduce the amount of reaching required.

Many health professionals are injured when assisting patients. Therefore, when a patient is weak, needs help transferring from a chair to bed, or is starting to walk again, O'Rourke encourages staff to ask for assistance from another physiotherapist or the office manager.

As the business owner, O'Rourke feels personally responsible for keeping the workplace a safe and happy environment. Putting the right physical safeguards in place is one thing; keeping the staff happy and content with their jobs is another concern. "Because we are such a small business, we become like family. Not only is it a cost benefit to keep all staff happy and healthy, but it would be upsetting to me if a staff member was injured on the job, especially if the injury could have been prevented," explains O'Rourke. "I have a direct and personal interest in the health and safety of my staff."

And for O'Rourke, mental health is as important in the workplace as physical health. As a mother of three children herself, she respects parents who may need to receive or make phone calls pertaining to important family matters. "It's one of the reasons I started the business," she explains. "I wanted flexibility with my own kids and family and now I'm happy to be able to extend that to my staff. It's one more thing I can do to make this a happy and pleasant work environment."

INTRODUCTION

You will note from the HRM Close-Up that health and safety concerns have a significant impact on managers. Occupational health and safety accidents are both numerous, costly to employers, and can even result in criminal charges. For example, in 2004, a supervisor with Vista Construction was charged with criminal negligence causing death. This was the consequence of a worker being crushed to death when a trench collapsed. The police noted that the required safety supports were not in place—an expectation of supervision.[1] To prevent accidents such as these, employers are required by law to provide working conditions that do not impair the safety or health of their employees.

Although the laws safeguarding employees' physical and emotional well-being are certainly an incentive to provide desirable working conditions, many employers are motivated to comply by virtue of their sensitivity to human needs and rights. The more cost-oriented employer recognizes the importance of avoiding accidents and illnesses wherever possible. Costs associated with sick leave, disability payments, replacement of employees who are injured or killed, and workers' compensation far exceed the costs of maintaining a safe and healthy workplace. Accidents and illnesses attributable to the workplace may also have pronounced effects on employee morale and on the goodwill that the organization enjoys in the community and in the business world.

While managers at all levels are expected to know and enforce health and safety standards throughout the organization, in reality it is the supervisor who has the biggest role. The supervisor must ensure a work environment that protects employees from physical hazards, unhealthy conditions, and unsafe acts of other personnel. Through effective safety and health practices, the physical and emotional well-being of employees may be preserved and even enhanced. This chapter will discuss health and safety in the workplace, including the responsibilities of employers, supervisors, and workers. You will also be presented with information about how to create a safe and healthy work environment and culture.

HEALTH AND SAFETY: THE LAW

Consider these facts:

- In 2002, over 1,000,000 workplace injuries occurred.
- In 2002, 934 employees died in work-related accidents.
- Workers' compensation boards throughout Canada pay out over $5 billion in benefits each year.
- Work-related injuries result in over 16 million lost workdays per year.
- The annual cost of occupational injuries to the Canadian economy is over $12 billion.
- Approximately 17,000 young adults between the ages of 15 and 19 are injured each year in Canada.[2]

The burden on the country's commerce as a result of lost productivity and wages, medical expenses, and disability compensation is staggering. HRDC estimates that every minute worked costs the Canadian economy about $80,000 in compensation payments to workers for accidents and injuries.[3] And there is no way to calculate the human suffering involved.

Occupational health and safety is regulated by the federal, provincial, and territorial governments. While statutes and standards differ slightly from jurisdiction to jurisdiction, attempts have been made to harmonize the various acts and regulations. Health and safety legislation has had an impact on workplace injuries and illnesses. The number of workplace accidents in Canada has declined even though there has been an increase in the number of workers.

An **occupational injury** is any cut, fracture, sprain, or amputation resulting from a workplace accident or from an exposure involving an accident in the work environment. An **occupational illness** is any abnormal condition or disorder, other than one resulting from an occupational injury, caused by exposure to environmental factors associated with employment. It includes acute and chronic illnesses or diseases that may be caused by inhalation, absorption, ingestion, or direct contact. With regard to parts of the body affected by accidents, injuries to the back occur most frequently, followed by leg, arm, and finger injuries.

Occupational injury
Any cut, fracture, sprain, or amputation resulting from a workplace accident

Occupational illness
Abnormal condition or disorder resulting from exposure to environmental factors in the workplace

Acts and Regulations

All supervisors, managers, and HR professionals should become familiar with the occupational health and safety legislation governing the jurisdiction under which their organization operates. The applicable legislation for each jurisdiction, the Web addresses, and the agency that administers the legislation is shown in Manager's Toolkit 8.1.

Duties and Responsibilities

The fundamental duty of every employer is to take every reasonable precaution to ensure employee safety. The motivating forces behind workplace legislation were effectively articulated in the landmark case *Regina v. Wholesale Travel Group*, which dealt with the legal liability and obligation of employers to behave in accordance with legislation:

> Regulatory legislation is essential to the operation of our complex industrial society; it plays a legitimate and vital role in protecting those who are most vulnerable and least able to protect themselves. The extent and importance of that role have increased continuously since the onset of the Industrial Revolution. Before effective workplace legislation was enacted, labourers—including children—worked unconscionably long hours in dangerous and unhealthy surroundings that evoke visions of Dante's inferno. It was regulatory legislation with its enforcement provisions which brought to an end the shameful situations that existed in mines, factories and workshops in the nineteenth century.

Duties of Employers

Objective 1

In addition to providing a hazard-free workplace and complying with the applicable statutes and regulations, employers must inform their employees about safety and health requirements. Employers are also required to keep certain records, to compile an annual summary of work-related injuries and illnesses, and to ensure that supervisors are familiar with the work and its associated hazards (the supervisor, in turn, must ensure that workers are aware of those hazards). Organizations with large numbers of employees may have a full-time health and safety officer. In At Work with HRM 8.1, the health and safety manager at the Vancouver International Airport Authority talks about the health and safety issues that apply to any airport.

Manager's Toolkit **8.1** Manager's Toolkit 8.1

WORKERS' COMPENSATION REFERENCE CHART

Jurisdiction	Body of Legislation	Administration Agency	Web Site
Canada			www.canoshweb.org
Alberta	Occupational Health and Safety Code	Workers' Compensation Board of Alberta	www.wcb.ca
British Columbia	Workers' Compensation Act	Workers' Compensation Board of British Columbia	www.worksafebc.ca
Manitoba	Workplace Safety and Health Act	Workers' Compensation Board of Manitoba	www.wcb.mb.ca
New Brunswick	Occupational Health and Safety Act	Workplace Health, Safety and Compensation Commission (New Brunswick)	www.whscc.nb.ca
Newfoundland and Labrador	Occupational Health and Safety Act	Workplace Health, Safety and Compensation Commission (Newfoundland)	www.whscc.nf.ca
Northwest Territories	Workers' Compensation Act	Workers' Compensation Board	www.wcb.nt.ca/
Nova Scotia	Occupational Health and Safety Act	Workers' Compensation Board of Nova Scotia	www.wcb.ns.ca
Nunavut	Workers' Compensation Act	Workers' Compensation Board	www.wcb.nt.ca/
Ontario	Occupational Health and Safety Act/Workplace Safety and Insurance Act	Workplace Safety and Insurance Board (Ontario)	www.wsib.on.ca
Prince Edward Island	Occupational Health and Safety Act	Workers' Compensation Board of Prince Edward Island	www.wcb.pe.ca
Quebec	Act Respecting Occupational Health and Safety	Commission de la santé et de la sécurité du travail of Quebec	www.csst.qc.ca
Saskatchewan	Occupational Health and Safety Act	Workers' Compensation Board of Saskatchewan	www.wcbsask.com
Yukon	Consolidated Workers' Compensation Act and Consolidated Occupation Health and Safety Act	Workers' Compensation Health and Safety Board of the Yukon	www.wcb.yk.ca

at work **with HRM 8.1** at work with HRM 8.1

WALKING AND OBSERVING

John Beckett, manager of health and safety with the Vancouver Airport Authority, describes three key areas—communicating, correcting, and observing—that all managers must observe in order to ensure a healthy and safe work environment. Ensuring safety involves a process similar to that applied to implementing an organization's financial or maintenance systems. The big difference between a safety system and other systems is that it deals with employee perceptions. Creating an environment where employees perceive that the employer cares for their safety is an ongoing, never-ending process. "The first responsibility for any supervisor is to see that employees are oriented to safety expectations. And this doesn't just apply to new employees," Beckett says. He goes on to say that a change in operating procedures can mean a new safety requirement that must be communicated to all employees.

"Second," Beckett says, "managers need to correct employees' behaviour if they are not working safely. For example, at the airport, if a supervisor sees a millwright lifting pieces of a baggage system into place without proper lifting devices, then the supervisor has an obligation to

speak to the millwright about how to do this in a safe manner. There is no doubt that supervisors play an incredible role in helping employees behave and act safely."

Finally, "in order to determine if employees are behaving and acting in a healthy and safe manner, the supervisor must walk around and observe work practices. If the supervisor isn't able to see what people are doing, then they are not able to either praise good safety practices or correct poor safety practices."

As you can see, the person who has the most influence on health and safety in the workplace is the supervisor or manager.

This approach at Vancouver Airport not only ensures the health and safety of airport workers but also lets passengers know they are being serviced by people who understand the importance of a healthy and safe environment.

CRITICAL THINKING QUESTION

Can you identify some of the safety issues at your place of work or your school?

Source: Interview with John Beckett, May 2005.

**WSIB-Young Worker
Awareness Program**

www.youngworker.ca

In all jurisdictions, employers are required to report any accidents that cause injuries and diseases to the Workers' Compensation Board. Accidents resulting in death or critical injuries must be reported immediately; the accident must then be investigated and a written report submitted. Finally, employers must provide safety training and be prepared to discipline employees for failing to comply with safety rules. The high incidence of youth injuries is attributable to lack of work experience and insufficient training. To help build the awareness of safety at work in young people, the Ontario agency has created a separate Web site as a resource for young people (**www.youngworker.ca**). Its objective is to help younger workers protect themselves and others in the workplace. The poster in Manager's Toolkit 8.2 depicts young people, one of whom has had a workplace injury.

Manager's Toolkit **8.2** Manager's Toolkit 8.2

MAKING YOU THINK ABOUT SAFETY

Source: Courtesy of Workers' Compensation Board of British Columbia, www.worksafebc.com.

The more complex and diverse your workplace, the more difficult managing safety can be.

Duties of Workers

Employees are required to comply with all applicable acts and regulations, to report hazardous conditions or defective equipment, and to follow all employer safety and health rules and regulations, including those prescribing the use of protective equipment, such as wearing hard hats or steel-toed boots at a construction site or protective eyewear in a laboratory.

Workers have many rights that pertain to requesting and receiving information about safety and health conditions. They also have the right to refuse unsafe work without fear of reprisal. (Some professionals, such as police, firefighters, teachers, and health-care workers have only a limited right of refusal in the sense that their work is inherently dangerous.) For example, in Ontario, an employee who suspects hazardous work conditions may refuse to do the work but must immediately report this concern to the supervisor, triggering an investigation by the supervisor and a worker representative.

A work-refusal investigation can result in either the employee's return to work in a safer environment or the employee's continued refusal. In the latter case, the appropriate ministry is notified and an investigator is dispatched to the job site to provide a written decision. If a replacement worker is used, that individual must be notified of the previous employee's refusal to work. Employees cannot be suspended, fired, or docked pay for refusing unsafe work and can continue to refuse the work until the situation is corrected.[4] For more information on the standards in Ontario, check out the province's agency responsible for workplace safety (**www.wsib.on.ca**).

Workplace Safety and Insurance Board

www.wsib.on.ca

Duties of Supervisors

A *supervisor* is generally defined as a person (with or without a title) who has charge of a workplace and authority over a worker. Occupational health and safety laws require supervisors to advise employees of potential workplace hazards; ensure that workers use or wear safety equipment, devices, or clothing; provide written instructions where applicable; and take every reasonable precaution to guarantee the safety of workers.

Duties of Joint Health and Safety Committees

Most jurisdictions require the formation of health and safety committees operated jointly by employee and management representatives. This arrangement is intended to create a nonadversarial climate in which labour and management work together to create a safe and healthy workplace. In Ontario, at least one management committee member and one worker representative must be certified. The certification program provides training in such subjects as safety laws, sanitation, general safety, rights and duties, and indoor air quality.

In addition, the legislation in British Columbia requires that a joint worker–employer committee must be formed in a company with 20 or more employees. Further, the employer is obligated to provide at least eight hours of annual educational leave for training and upgrading on health and safety issues.[5]

Figure 8.1 summarizes the legally required duties and responsibilities of those directly involved in health and safety issues.

FIGURE 8.1 Health and Safety Duties and Responsibilities

Employers

- Provide a hazard-free workplace
- Comply with laws and regulations
- Inform employees about safety and health requirements
- Keep records
- Compile annual summary of work-related injuries and illnesses
- Ensure supervisors are familiar with work and associated hazards
- Report accidents to WCB
- Provide safety training

Workers

- Comply with all laws and regulations
- Report hazardous conditions or defective equipment
- Follow employer safety and health rules
- Refuse unsafe work

Supervisors

- Advise employees of potential workplace hazards
- Ensure workers use or wear safety equipment
- Provide written instructions
- Take every reasonable precaution to guarantee safety of workers

Joint Health and Safety Committees

- Advise employer on health and safety matters
- Create nonadversarial climate to create safe and healthy work environment
- Investigate accidents
- Train others in safety obligations

Penalties for Employer Noncompliance

Penalties for violations of occupational health and safety regulations vary across provinces and territories. The Ontario Health and Safety Act provides for fines of up to $500,000, and offenders can be sent to jail. For example, Dominion Bridge was fined $100,000 when a worker was fatally injured while operating a crane. In May 2002, the government of Alberta fined Hy-Mark Builders $138,000 for an accident that resulted in the death of the owner's nephew. Included in the decision was a reference that there had been numerous stop orders issued on various construction sites for safety infractions.[6] Also in May 2002, the United Steelworkers began lobbying the federal government to change the Criminal Code to charge executives and managers of organizations for negligent health and safety acts.[7] And the lobbying was successful. Effective March 31, 2004, the Criminal Code was changed to make it easier to bring criminal charges against co-workers, supervisors, executives, and employers when a worker is killed or injured on the job.[8] The legislation was a direct result of a public inquiry into the Westray Mine disaster in 1992 that killed 26 workers. Numerous safety infractions occurred at Westray, and it was determined that senior managers and executives knew of the infractions but did nothing to fix them. There is no doubt that violations of health and safety laws can have significant consequences. Look at some other examples in HRM and the Law 8.1.

Workers' Compensation

Under workers' compensation, injured workers or workers who become ill as a result of their work environment can receive benefits in the form of a cash payout (if the disability is permanent) or wage-loss payments (if the worker can no longer earn the same

HRM and **the law 8.1** HRM and the law 8.1

CHARGES UNDER HEALTH AND SAFETY ACT

In early 2005, an owner of a Regina snow-clearing business was charged under the Saskatchewan law with failing to ensure the health, safety, and welfare of employees, failing to ensure the provision and maintenance of a safe workplace, and failing to ensure elevated equipment was securely blocked. An employee was killed when the loader arm on the snow-clearing equipment came down on him.

Even more dramatically, on May 26, 2005, a truck driver in Guelph, Ontario, was sentenced to 20 days in jail for two violations under Ontario's Health and Safety Act. The driver was found responsible for the death of a co-worker when the driver was backing up the truck in a manner that put the co-worker in danger.

Companies also face severe consequences of safety violations. In May 2005, Quebecor World Inc., a Montreal-based printing company with operations in Ontario, was fined $130,000 for not providing sufficient instructions to an employee on how to safely handle a situation where a machine was not operating properly. The unsafe action by the employee resulted in serious leg injuries to the employee.

Source: Adapted from *OH&S News*, OHS Canada, http://www.ohscanada.com/, January 21, 2005; "Truck Driver Jailed 20 Days for Health and Safety Violations," May 31, 2005, www.ohscanada.com/article.asp?id=43695&issue=05302005&lid=43695&lpos=dailyNews; and "Quebecor World Inc. Fined $130,000 for Health and Safety Violation," May 31, 2005, www.ohscanada.com/article.asp?id=43512&issue=05242005&lid=43512&lpos=dailyNews.

amount of money). Unlimited medical aid is also provided, along with vocational rehabilitation, which includes physical, social, and psychological services. The goal is to return the employee to the original job (or some modification thereof) as soon as possible. Sun Life Assurance Company of Canada has a return-to-work awards program, which will give premium credits to employers that allow injured workers to change jobs or duties to enable these employees to return to work. A person who has been off work for six months has a 50% chance of returning; after twelve months, a 20% chance; and after two years, a 10% chance. Return-to-work models are being developed by Canadian Pacific Railway and Weyerhaeuser Canada Ltd. of Kamloops, British Columbia.[9]

Equally problematic is compensation for stress, which is discussed in more detail later in the chapter. Stress-related disabilities are usually divided into three groups: physical injuries leading to mental disabilities (e.g., clinical depression after a serious accident); mental stress resulting in a physical disability (ulcers or migraines); and mental stress resulting in a mental condition (anxiety over work load or downsizing leading to depression). Most claims, it should be pointed out, result from accidents or injuries.

In some industrial sectors, employers are working together to establish rules and training programs to further the cause of accident prevention. For further information on the specific objectives of each provincial and territorial workers' compensation agency, visit the Web sites listed in Manager's Toolkit 8.1.

Industrial disease
A disease resulting from exposure relating to a particular process, trade, or occupation in industry

Compensation has become a complex issue. Workers are now able to receive payment if they have contracted an **industrial disease**. An industrial disease is a disease resulting from exposure to a substance relating to a particular process, trade, or occupation in industry. Cause and effect can be difficult to determine. Consider, for example, the case of a mine worker who has contracted a lung disease, but who also smokes heavily.

With 1.1 million Canadians injured at work every year, the cost of these injuries is $8.5 billion in compensation claims, but less is collected from employers.[10] This has left workers' compensation boards with a huge deficit to pay existing claims. To encourage employers to introduce better prevention and claims management practices, the emphasis on workers' compensation has been shifting from assessments and payments to the creation of a safety-conscious environment intended to reduce the number of work-related accidents, disabilities, and diseases. Figure 8.2 lists some ways in which employers can reduce their workers' compensation costs.

FIGURE 8.2 Ways to Reduce Workers' Compensation Costs

1. Perform an audit to assess high-risk areas within a workplace.
2. Prevent injuries by proper ergonomic design of the job (such as position of keyboard) and effective assessment of job candidates.
3. Provide quality medical care to injured employees by physicians with experience and preferably with training in occupational health.
4. Reduce litigation by effective communication between the employer and the injured worker.
5. Manage the care of an injured worker from the injury until return to work. Keep a partially recovered employee at the work site.
6. Provide extensive worker training in all related health and safety areas.

CREATING A SAFE WORK ENVIRONMENT

Objective

We have seen that employers are required by law to provide healthy and safe working conditions for their employees. To achieve this objective, the majority of employers have a formal safety program. The success of a safety program depends largely on managers and supervisors of operating departments, even though an HR department may have responsibility for coordinating the safety communication and training programs, and maintaining safety records required by occupational health and safety regulations.

Organizations with formal safety programs generally have an employee-management safety committee that includes members from management, each department or manufacturing or service unit, and the pool of employees. Committees are typically involved in investigating accidents and helping to publicize the importance of safety rules and their enforcement.

The Canada Safety Council Web site (**www.safety-council.org**) provides resources to assist in the development of a safe work environment.

Canada Safety Council
www.safety-council.org

Promoting Safety Awareness

Probably the most important role of a safety program is motivating managers, supervisors, and subordinates to be aware of safety considerations. While there is a requirement by law to do this, success comes when a manager/supervisor willingly promotes a safe work environment. If managers and supervisors fail to demonstrate awareness, their subordinates can hardly be expected to do so. Unfortunately, most managers and

In certain workplaces, safety standards require the use of protective clothing.

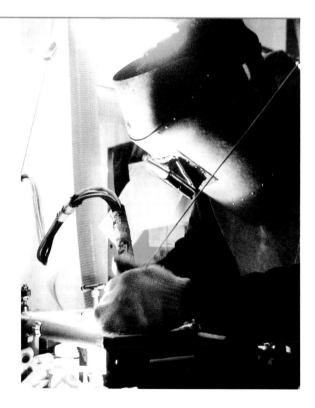

supervisors wear their "safety hats" far less often than their "production, quality control, and methods improvement hats."

While discipline may force employees to work safely, the most effective enforcement of safety expectations occurs when employees willingly obey and "champion" safety rules and procedures. This can be achieved when management actively encourages employees to participate in all aspects of the organization's safety program and the organization provides incentives to do so. The Procter & Gamble plant in Belleville, Ontario, won an award for its novel approach to incentives. The plant manager calculated that P & G would receive a refund from workers' compensation of about $200,000 a year if injuries were eliminated at the plant. He then set up a plan that would allow this refund to go to the local hospital if the target of zero injuries was achieved. With this community-based incentive, P & G employees met the target and the hospital received a large donation.[11] Also, in 2002, a joint labour/management task force, which had been commissioned by the Government of Alberta, found that provincial economic and societal costs of safety incidents was $3 billion annually.[12] Manager's Toolkit 8.3 provides some steps in setting up a safety incentive program.

Safety Awareness Programs

Most organizations have a safety awareness program that entails the use of several different media. Safety lectures, commercially produced films, specially developed videocassettes, and other media, such as pamphlets, are useful for teaching and motivating employees to follow safe work procedures. A poster from a safety awareness program is shown in Manager's Toolkit 8.4. Posters have been found to be very effective because they

Manager's Toolkit **8.3** Manager's Toolkit 8.3

STEPS TO A SUCCESSFUL SAFETY INCENTIVE PROGRAM

- Obtain the full support and involvement of management by providing cost benefits.

- Review current injury and health statistics to determine where change is needed.

- Decide on a program of action and set an appropriate budget.

- Select a realistic safety goal, such as reducing accidents by a set percentage, improving safety suggestions, or achieving a length of time without a lost-time injury. Communicate your objectives to everyone involved.

- Select incentive rewards on the basis of their attractiveness to employees and their fit with your budget.

- Develop a program that is both interesting and fun. Use kickoff meetings, posters, banners, quizzes, and/or games to spark employee interest. Give all employees a chance to win.

- Communicate continually the success of your program. Provide specific examples of positive changes in behaviour.

- Reward safety gains immediately. Providing rewards shortly after improvements reinforces changed behaviour and encourages additional support for the safety program.

Manager's Toolkit 8.4
Manager's Toolkit **8.4**

POSTER FROM WSIB YOUNG WORKER AWARENESS PROGRAM

Source: Workplace Safety and Insurance Board.

can be displayed in strategic locations where workers will be sure to see them. For example, a shipyard found that placing posters at the work site helped reduce accidents by making employees more conscious of the hazards of using scaffolds.

The Key Role of the Supervisor

One of a supervisor's major responsibilities is to communicate to an employee the need to work safely. Beginning with new employee orientation, safety should be emphasized continually. Proper work procedures, the use of protective clothing and devices, and potential hazards should be explained thoroughly. Furthermore, employees' understanding of all these considerations needs to be verified during training sessions, and employees encouraged to take some initiative in maintaining a concern for safety. Since training by itself does not ensure continual adherence to safe work practices, supervisors must observe employees at work and reinforce safe practices. Where unsafe acts are detected, supervisors should take immediate action to find the cause. Supervisors need to foster a team spirit of safety among the work group. Again, it is important to identify that while this is a legal requirement, the success of any safety awareness depends on the willingness of the supervisor to actively support the employees in creating a safe work environment.

Proactive Safety Training Program

What are the most popular subjects in safety training programs? One study found the most frequent topics to be (1) first aid, (2) defensive driving, (3) accident prevention techniques, (4) hazardous materials, and (5) emergency procedures.[13]

Most programs emphasize the use of emergency first-aid equipment and personal safety equipment. Furthermore, many organizations provide training in off-the-job safety—at home, on the highway, and so on—as well as in first aid. Injuries and fatalities away from the job occur much more frequently than do those on the job and are reflected in employer costs for insurance premiums, wage continuation, and interrupted production.

HR professionals and safety directors, in particular, advocate employee involvement when designing and implementing safety programs.[14] Employees can offer valuable ideas regarding specific safety and health topics to cover, instructional methods, and proper teaching techniques. Furthermore, acceptance for safety training is heightened when employees feel a sense of ownership in the instructional program. The Industrial Accident Prevention Association (IAPA) offers six diploma programs for workers, supervisors, managers, and health and safety representatives. Course topics include health and safety legislation, hazard identification, and workplace inspection. Visit the Web site of the IAPA (**www.iapa.on.ca**).

Industrial Accident Prevention Association (IAPA)
www.iapa.on.ca

Information Technology and Safety Awareness and Training

Several reasons are advanced for the use of the Internet and information technology in safety and health training. First, enhanced delivery modes facilitate the development of both managers and employees.[15] Videos, PowerPoint presentations, and interactive CD-ROM training are ideal methods for standardized safety, environmental, and health instruction. Second, information technology allows organizations to customize their safety and health training needs.[16] At Stanley Works, Inc., the company's Internet is the number one tool for reducing health and safety problems. According to Kevin Nelson, employee health and safety director, "The Internet functions as the organization's SWAT team to develop and implement timely and efficient health and safety programs."[17]

Enforcement of Safety Rules

Specific expectations and standards concerning safety are communicated through supervisors, bulletin-board notices, employee handbooks, and signs attached to equipment. Safety rules are also emphasized in regular safety meetings, at new employee orientations, and in manuals of standard operating procedures. Such rules typically refer to the following types of employee behaviours:

- Using proper safety devices
- Using proper work procedures
- Following good housekeeping practices
- Complying with accident and injury reporting procedures
- Wearing required safety clothing and equipment
- Avoiding carelessness or horseplay

Penalties for violation of safety rules are usually stated in the employee handbook. In a large percentage of organizations, the penalties imposed on violators are the same as those imposed for violations of other standards and expectations. They include an oral or written warning for the first violation, suspension or disciplinary layoff for repeated violations, and, as a last resort, dismissal. However, for serious violations—such as smoking around volatile substances—even the first offence may be cause for termination.

Sometimes the consequences of poor safety behaviours result in serious injuries. For example, a young person died because of a design flaw in an ice-surfacing machine. No one, including the worker, had stood back to see if it was operating safely—it exploded when it was started.[18]

Safety begins with preparedness, as these employees demonstrate in a practice situation.

Accident Investigations and Records

Every accident, even those considered minor, should be investigated by the supervisor and a member of the safety committee. Such an investigation may determine the factors contributing to the accident and may reveal what corrections are needed to prevent it from happening again. Correction may require rearranging workstations, installing safety guards or controls, or, more often, giving employees additional safety training and ensuring that they understand the importance of safe work practices.

Employers are also required to keep certain records and to compile and post an annual summary of work-related injuries and illnesses. From these records, organizations can compute their *incidence rate*, the number of injuries and illnesses per 100 full-time employees during a given year. The standard formula for computing the incidence rate is shown by the following equation, where 200,000 equals the base for 100 full-time workers who work 40 hours a week, 50 weeks a year:

$$\text{Incidence rate} = \frac{\text{Number of injuries and illnesses} \times 200{,}000}{\text{Total hours worked by all employees during period covered}}$$

It should be noted that the same formula can be used to compute incidence rates for (1) the number of workdays lost because of injuries and illnesses, (2) the number of nonfatal injuries and illnesses without lost workdays, and (3) cases involving only injuries or only illnesses.

Incidence rates are useful for making comparisons between work groups, between departments, and between similar units within an organization. They also provide a basis for making comparisons with other organizations doing similar work. Occupational health and safety departments in each province and Human Resources Development Canada compile data that an organization can use as a basis for comparing its safety record with those of other organizations. Progressive organizations can also use this information to benchmark "best practices." As Ethics in HRM 8.1 indicates, reporting and investigating accidents can make an organization subject to more inspections, higher insurance premiums, and possible lawsuits.

CREATING A HEALTHY WORK ENVIRONMENT

Occupational health and safety legislation was clearly designed to protect the health, as well as the safety, of employees. Because of the dramatic impact of workplace accidents, however, managers and employees alike may pay more attention to these kinds of immediate safety concerns than to job conditions or work environments that may be dangerous to their health. It is essential, therefore, that health hazards be identified and controlled. Attention should also be given to nonwork-related illnesses and injuries and their impact on the organization and its members. Special health programs may also be developed to provide assistance to employees with health problems.

Largely because of the growing public awareness of the efforts of environmentalists, factors in the work environment affecting health are receiving greater attention. Unprecedented air and water pollution throughout the world has made everyone more conscious of the immediate environment in which they live and work. Articles about workers who have been exposed to potential dangers at work can frequently be found in

ethics **in HRM 8.1** ethics in HRM 8.1

SUPERVISOR AND EMPLOYEES BURY THE RECORD

A supervisor was instructing a group of new recruits in the cleaning of metal parts in an assembly plant. She was attempting to demonstrate the cleaning technique to two employees at one workstation, while at another workstation another new employee was trying to clean the parts himself. The cleaning liquid was highly toxic. The employee felt restricted by his safety gloves and so removed them. His eyes started to water, and instinctively he rubbed them with his solution-soaked hands. The pain was overwhelming, and no water was immediately available with which he could rinse his eyes. The employee suffered some temporary vision loss.

Who is to blame? The worker who started to clean without receiving full instructions and without using the issued gloves? The supervisor who could have forbidden the worker to start work until she explained the safety aspects? Or the company that failed to post warning signs about the hazardous nature of the cleaning solvent and to have an eye-washing facility available?

Because workplace accidents increase workers' compensation premiums and the number of inspections, the company had an interest in not reporting the accident. Furthermore, because the company had instituted a reward program that provided incentives to employees for accident-free days, even the employees did not want to report the accident. Thus the supervisor and the employees agreed to "bury the record." What are the consequences of this decision?

Canadian Centre for Occupational Health and Safety

www.ccohs.ca

Objective **3**

the newspapers. Pressure from the federal government and unions, as well as increased public concern, has given employers a definite incentive to provide the safest and healthiest work environment possible.

As part of "Developing Your Skills" at the end of this chapter, you will be asked to explore the Web site for the Canadian Centre for Occupational Health and Safety (**www.ccohs.ca**).

Health Hazards and Issues

At one time health hazards were associated primarily with jobs found in industrial processing operations, such as coal mining. In recent years, however, hazards in jobs outside the plant, such as in offices, health-care facilities, and airports, have been recognized and preventive methods adopted. Substituting materials, altering processes, enclosing or isolating a process, issuing protective equipment, and improving ventilation are some of the common methods to prevent problems. General conditions of health with respect to sanitation, housekeeping, cleanliness, ventilation, water supply, pest control, and food handling are also important to monitor.

Workplace Hazardous Materials Information Systems

Believing that workers have the right to know about potential workplace hazards, industry, labour, and government joined forces several years ago to develop a common information system for labelling hazardous substances. The Workplace Hazardous Materials Information Systems (WHMIS) is based on three elements:

1. *Labels.* Labels are designed to alert the worker that the container holds a potentially hazardous substance. The two types of labels (supplier labels and workplace labels) must contain specified and regulated information, including product identifiers and data on safe handling and material safety. WHMIS class symbols and subclass designations are shown in Figure 8.3.

FIGURE 8.3   WHMIS Class Symbols and Subclass Designations

CLASS & SUBCLASS DESIGNATIONS

COMPRESSED GAS

FLAMMABLE AND COMBUSTIBLE MATERIAL

Flammable Gas
Flammable Liquid
Flammable Solid
Flammable Aerosol
Reactive Flammable Material

OXIDIZING MATERIAL

DANGEROUSLY REACTIVE MATERIAL

POISONOUS AND INFECTIOUS MATERIAL

Materials Causing Immediate and Serious Toxic Effects

Materials Causing Other Toxic Effects

Biohazardous Infectious Material

CORROSIVE MATERIAL

The subclass designations are shown below the Class designation.

Source: *Solvents in the Workplace*, Cat. No. B01230 (Toronto: Industrial Accident Prevention Association, March 1990).

Material Safety Data Sheet (MSDS)
Documents that contain vital information about hazardous substances

2. *Material Safety Data Sheet (MSDS).* The **MSDS** identifies the product and its potentially hazardous ingredients, and suggests procedures for the safe handling of the product. The MSDS information must be comprehensive, current, and available in English and French.
3. *Training.* Workers must be trained to check for labels and to follow specific procedures for handling spills. Training workers is part of the due diligence required of employers; it also becomes an important factor in the event of a lawsuit. The Peel Board of Education in Ontario has developed a computer-based program to train workers in WHMIS, allowing illiterate workers to respond to audio commands by touching the screen, thus giving the right response.

Indoor Air Quality

As a consequence of energy concerns, commercial and residential construction techniques have been changed to increase energy efficiency of heating, ventilating, and air-conditioning systems. This has included sealing windows, reducing outside air intake, and in general "buttoning up" buildings—thus resulting in the "sick building syndrome" (SBS) and "building related illnesses" (BRI) that give rise to such employee complaints as headaches, dizziness, disorientation, fatigue, and eye, ear, and throat irritation.[19] Popular office equipment, including photocopying machines, computer terminals, fax machines, and laser printers, contributes to these health complaints.

Four basic ways to overcome polluted buildings are to (1) eliminate tobacco smoke, (2) provide adequate ventilation, (3) maintain the ventilating system, and (4) remove sources of pollution. It is now common practice in both office and industrial settings, as well as public facilities (airports, hotels, schools, and so on), to monitor and manage the quality of indoor air.[20]

Tobacco Smoke Probably the most talked-about workplace health issue in recent years is smoking. Nonsmokers, fuelled by studies linking "passive smoking" (inhaling other people's smoke) with disease and death and irritated by smoke getting in their eyes, noses, throats, and clothes, have been extremely vocal in demanding a smoke-free environment. The number of organizations restricting smoking in the workplace has risen dramatically, motivated by legislation in most provinces. Banning smoking releases employers from concerns about future lawsuits or being forced into installing ventilating systems for smokers.

In a study published in the *Journal of the American Medical Association*, findings showed that "in businesses that permitted smoking, more than 60% of the office air samples contained nicotine levels above the 'significant risk' level of 6.8 micrograms per cubic meter."[21] Because of findings such as these, smokers have been banned from lighting up on airplanes, at work, and in restaurants and hotels.

Technology

Initially, the concerns about the effects of technology on workers' health focused on computer monitors, or video display terminals (VDTs). However, many fears about computer terminals have proved to be unfounded. Although employers are learning ways to minimize the negative effects of desktop computers, serious health concerns remain an issue.

Cumulative Trauma Disorders

Cumulative trauma disorders
Injuries involving tendons of the fingers, hands, and arms that become inflamed from repeated stresses and strains

Meat cutters, cooks, dental hygienists, textile workers, violinists, flight attendants, office workers at computer terminals, and others whose jobs require repetitive motion of the fingers, hands, or arms are reporting injuries in growing percentages. Known as **cumulative trauma disorders** or repetitive motion injuries, these musculoskeletal disorders (MSDs) are injuries of the muscles, nerves, tendons, ligaments, joints, and spinal discs caused by repeated stresses and strains. One of the more common conditions is *carpal tunnel syndrome*, which is characterized by tingling or numbness in the fingers occurring when a tunnel of bones and ligaments in the wrist narrows and pinches nerves that reach the fingers and base of the thumb. This type of injury is the most prevalent and accounts for 17% of all workplace injuries.[22]

Ergonomics attempts to design equipment and systems that can be easily and efficiently used by people. As a result, ergonomics techniques are also successfully used to improve or correct workplace conditions that cause or aggravate cumulative trauma disorders.[23] Continuous developments in office furniture, video display terminals, tool design, computer keyboards, and adjustable workstations are all attempts to make the work setting more comfortable—and, hopefully, more productive—but also to lessen musculoskeletal disorders. Mini-breaks involving exercise and the changing of work positions have been found helpful. Importantly, these kinds of injuries often go away if they are caught early. If they are not, they may require months or years of treatment or even surgical correction. Also, when cumulative trauma disorders result from work activities, they serve to lower employee productivity, increase employers' health costs, and incur workers' compensation payments.[24]

Communicable Diseases

Communicable diseases, such as herpes simplex (cold sores), influenza, athlete's foot, and AIDS (acquired immune deficiency syndrome), are covered in public health legislation, not

Many employers were unprepared to deal with SARS issues, such as employee quarantines.

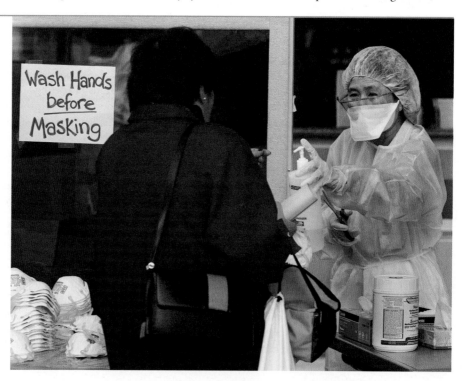

5

occupational health and safety legislation. In recent years, no issue has received as much attention as SARS (severe acute respiratory syndrome). SARS is a pneumonia-like and potentially fatal illness that, in 2003, infected areas such as Hong Kong, Taiwan, Singapore, and Toronto. The Centres for Disease Control advised business travellers to avoid these areas. Employers in Canada had to make decisions about travel bans, quarantines, the right to refuse work, and what constituted a safe work environment. Provincial legislation provides certain rights for employees affected by SARS, including job-protected leave, no penalties for emergency leave, payment for those not working because of quarantines, and work refusal processes. At Work with HRM 8.2 describes how some employers coped with this crisis.

at work **with HRM 8.2** at work with HRM 8.2

THE SARS CRISIS

Human resource professionals, particularly those working in hospitals, faced a crisis in the spring of 2003 that none had seen in their working lifetimes. For the first time in the memory of most hospital employees at Sunnybrook and Women's College Health Sciences Centre in Toronto and London Health Sciences Centre in London, Ontario, there was a code orange crisis—in other words, the most serious level. People looked to the HR team to initiate action plans to deal with sick employees, quarantined employees, and scared employees. Unlike crises such as the events of September 11, 2001, where there is one dramatic event, SARS was an escalating event, with every day creating new problems. At Sunnybrook, the HR director took every decision with the thought "What are the repercussions? Long after SARS ends, the employees and the unions will remember how they were treated." The escalating pace was difficult. HR people had to train employees to screen 12,000 people a day and had just one weekend to design the process and hire and train staff. Communication had to be objective and immediate, not only with employees but with their worried families. For the first time, health-care workers could not leave their work behind, with most having to wear masks at home and avoid contact with their families. To deal with these concerns, staff forums were held (employees had a need to talk about their concerns). The managers learned a lot and now crisis planning has become an ongoing activity in the organization.

The London Health Sciences Centre faced similar issues. Both vice-presidents of HR emphasized the need for visible leadership. One immediate problem that was soon evident was the folly of any absenteeism program that motivated employees to come to work sick, which of course increased the risk of communicable diseases spreading throughout the workforce. Some employees continued to come to work even when they weren't feeling well because they were worried they would lose income, so a policy that had to be developed immediately was a commitment to maintain the wages of workers in quarantine. Another unusual problem was that certain categories of workers, such as nurses, have limited rights to refuse work. When Mount Sinai Hospital in Toronto asked employees to staff screening stations, a librarian refused to do this work as she deemed it to be unsafe. A lesson learned is the importance of preparing for an emergency by stockpiling personal protective equipment and training all staff in its use.

It is not just hospitals that have to be prepared for outbreaks of communicable diseases. Hewlett-Packard has a workforce of 8,000 employees, with 3,200 of them at ten sites in the Greater Toronto Area. Two HP employees were hospitalized with SARS, and one site was forced to close. Fortunately, because the site had always required

(Continued)

employees and visitors to sign in, and access was controlled with a pass card, all those known to have been at the site were easy to trace and all pass cards were revoked. Also, because HP is a high-tech company, with all employees online all the time, communication with employees was not difficult. However, the nature of the highly mobile workforce posed problems for health-care officials. The public health department required lists of all employees who were absent, but HR does not track absences because most HP employees work from home or off site.

CRITICAL THINKING QUESTIONS

1. What are the potential problems when a hospital does not have enough skilled employees available to handle a public health crisis such as SARS?

2. What would be some of the impacts if many businesses in one city had to close down for a limited period of time due to a similar crisis?

Sources: B. Orr, "SARS Outbreak Teaches Valuable Lessons on a New 'Normal' State for HR Management," *Canadian HR Reporter* 16, no. 11 (June 2, 2003): 5; Ministry of Labour, "Workplace Laws and SARS," www.gov.on.ca/LAB; A. Picard, "Mommy Are You Going to Die?" *The Globe and Mail*, April 5, 2003; David Brown "One Year Later—The Invaluable Lessons of SARS," *Canadian HR Reporter*, March 8, 2004: 1.

Workplace Security

Perhaps the most significant event that has affected workplace security has been the events that occurred on September 11, 2001. From that day forward, organizations throughout Canada and the United States have placed renewed emphasis on personal safety and security at work. On a recent study tour, one author of this book was acutely aware of the heightened security measures to get into certain government buildings. In some cases, unless you were employed there, you could not enter. Further, if you were an employee, you had to go through substantive security checks, including metal detectors, prior to being authorized to enter.

And the concerns of employees are not restricted to those from terrorism or bomb threats. Employees are concerned about disaster preparedness and workplace violence.[25] In fact, changes to the Canadian Labour Code have provided an expanded definition of the reasons that employees can refuse work that they perceive as dangerous. Employees can now refuse on the basis of any "potential" condition that could reasonably be expected to cause injury or illness.[26] The legislation was tested recently when a group of maximum security prison guards in British Columbia challenged a prohibition from carrying handcuffs as a routine practice. The prison officials had banned the practice to remove an overt symbol of authority in daily dealings with prisoners, but the guards felt that a potential danger was created by doing so.[27]

Reducing Workplace Violence

The National Institute of Occupational Safety and Health (NIOSH) identified workplace homicide as one of the leading causes of workplace deaths. Manon Blanc at Queen's University and Kevin Kelloway, director of the CN Centre for Occupational Health and

Safety at St. Mary's University, have identified the job characteristics that put workers at risk for aggression and violence in the workplace:

- Interacting with the public.
- Making decisions that influence other people's lives (e.g., terminating an employee or assigning a failing grade) or denying the public a service or request.
- Supervising and/or disciplining others.
- Working nights, working alone.
- Handling cash, handling or guarding valuables, collecting or delivering items of value.
- Caring for the physical or emotional needs of others, going to clients' homes.
- Serving or selling alcohol, dealing with individuals under the influence of mind-altering substances.[28]

Currently, only Saskatchewan and British Columbia have implemented regulations dealing with workplace violence as part of their Occupational Health and Safety Regulations. Among the requirements of these regulations is a risk assessment, development of policies and procedures to handle the risks identified, instruction and training of workers in handling violence, and a requirement that incidents be reported.[29] To quote the B.C. regulations, "The requirements for risk assessment, procedures and policies, the duty to respond to incidents and to instruct workers are based on the recognition of violence in the workplace as an occupational hazard."[30]

Even without legislated requirements, employers can take specific actions to reduce workplace violence. For example, organizations can screen job applicants for histories showing a propensity to violence. Additionally, managers and employees can be trained to recognize violence indicators, such as those given in Figure 8.4. Proper training and reinforcement of security measures can help reduce the potential of workplace incidents.[31]

FIGURE 8.4   Warning Signs of Violence in the Workplace

Most people leave a trail of indicators before they become violent. Similarly, disgruntled former employees who commit acts of violence leave warning signs of their intent before and after termination. The following behaviours should be taken seriously when assessing situations of potential violence:

- Direct or veiled threatening statements
- Recent performance declines, including concentration problems and excessive excuses
- Prominent mood or behaviour changes
- Unexplained increase in absenteeism
- Noticeable decrease in attention to appearance and hygiene
- Depression and withdrawal
- Preoccupation with guns, knives, or other weapons
- Deliberate destruction of workplace equipment; sabotage
- Fascination with stories of violence
- Reckless or antisocial behaviour; evidence of prior assaultive behaviour
- Aggressive behaviour or intimidating statements
- Written messages of violent intent
- Serious stress in personal life
- Obsessive desire to harm a specific group or person

Sources: Adapted from Jurg W. Mattman, "Preventing Violence in the Workplace," Workplace Violence Research Institute, http://www.workviolence.com (retrieved May 3, 2002); and Christina McGovern, "Take Action, Heed Warnings to End Workplace Violence," *Occupational Health and Safety* 61, no. 3 (March 1999): 61–63.

Awareness of these threatening behaviours can provide an opportunity to intervene and prevent disruptive, abusive or violent acts. It is also critical that any violent behaviour is challenged and confronted. Employees need to know that violent behaviour, even if it is only an outburst on the shop floor, is not acceptable.[32] Finally, organizations can establish formalized workplace prevention policies, informing employees that aggressive employee behaviour will not be tolerated. Manager's Toolkit 8.5 lists violence-prevention measures that organizations can take.

Manager's Toolkit **8.5** Manager's Toolkit 8.5

WORKPLACE SECURITY MEASURES

Organizations that ignore workplace violence will experience a resulting decline in employee morale and productivity. There are four key pillars to creating an environment that makes employees feel safe and secure:

1. Management commitment and employee involvement
2. Worksite analysis
3. Hazard prevention and control
4. Training and education

   Here are some steps that help implement these pillars:

1. A written policy:
   - identifies the nature and extent of workers' risks of injury from violence
   - states the overall approach to preventing violent incidents and that violence is prohibited
   - clearly outlines the responsibilities of managers, supervisors, and workers
   - indicates the direction and support of senior management

2. Regular risk assessments:
   - identify the types and probability of risks of injury due to violent incidents
   - provide a means to document the risk assessments
   - help make the results available to workers

3. Prevention procedures:
   - include written instructions detailing the violence prevention procedures to be followed by workers and supervisors
   - explain the work environment arrangements implemented to prevent incidents of violence
   - provide direction to workers outlining safe response methods and procedures for reporting incidents
   - take all threats of violence seriously

4. Worker and supervisor training:
   - provides workers at risk and their supervisors with correct response procedures
   - helps to ensure that violence prevention procedures are understood and followed
   - allows for the maintenance of accurate records
   - look for signs of aggressive and/or bullying behaviour
   - learning to observe and report behaviours of explosive outbursts of anger or rage with no provocation

5. Procedures for reporting and investigating incidents: These procedures—including policies and documentation—should cover the following:
   - reporting incidents of violence
   - supervisors' actions to address reported incidents
   - investigating incidents of violence
   - implementing corrective action

6. Incident follow-up:
   - provides for a review of actions taken in response to violent incidents and an evaluation of their effectiveness

7. Other steps that can be taken include the following:
   - organize the physical facility to control the movement of people and manage crowds.
   - use physical protection devices, such as guards and screens
   - ensure that work areas are well lit and not isolated
   - increase security procedures so that access to the building is limited, high-risk areas are monitored by video cameras, security

escorts are provided, and cash-custody procedures are implemented
- create in-house emergency response teams
- develop emergency communication procedures, including emergency codes, overhead paging, and personal alarms
- park in well-lit areas, avoid alleys, wooded areas, and tunnels
- use caution in underground lots—stay in open, lit areas near exits (vehicle should be locked and windows rolled up as you enter the parking lot)
- provide safe escorts for after-hours work

Sources: "Workplace Violence," OHSA, U.S. Department of Labor, http://www.osha-slc.gov/ (retrieved May 3, 2002); James Montgomery and Kevin Kelloway, *Management of Occupational Health and Safety*, 2nd ed. (Toronto: Nelson Thomson, 2002), and "Spotting the Signs of Workplace Violence," Magellan Health Services, https://www.magellanassist.com/guest/tg/wv_spotting.asp (retrieved January 26, 2005).

Organizations are also using a number of different ways to inform employees about security issues. For example, Seneca College in Ontario uses its intranet as a communication tool to inform employees of internal security as well as external security issues in the surrounding geographic area of the college.

Crisis Management Teams

Some organizations have formal crisis management teams. Home Depot has a crisis management team that arrives within one hour of an incident. These teams, composed of both hourly and managerial employees, conduct initial risk assessment surveys, develop action plans to respond to violent situations, and, importantly, perform crisis intervention during violent, or potentially violent, encounters.[33] For example, a crisis management team would investigate a threat reported by an employee. The team's mandate would be to gather facts about the threat, decide if the organization should intervene, and, if so, to determine the most appropriate method of doing so.

When violent incidents, such as the death of a co-worker, happen at work, employees can experience shock, guilt, grief, apathy, resentment, cynicism, and a host of other

Effective handling of workplace violence involves intervention from specialists trained in handling workplace traumas.

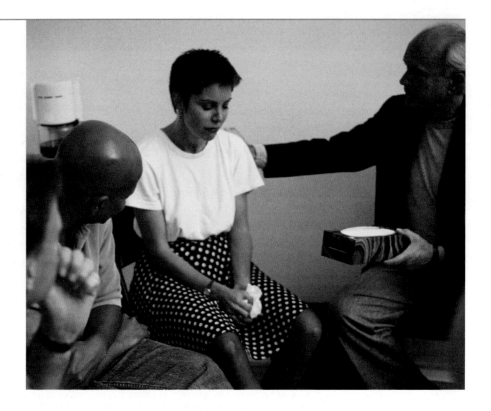

emotions.[34] Such incidents may require the violence response team to perform crisis intervention through positive counselling techniques.

Building Better Health

Objective 4

Along with improving working conditions that are hazardous to employee health, many employers provide health services and have programs that encourage employees to improve their health habits. It is recognized that better health benefits not only the individual but also the organization in reduced absenteeism, increased efficiency, and better morale. An understanding of the close relationship between physical and emotional health and job performance has made broad health-building programs attractive to employers as well as to employees.

Health Services

The type of health services employers provide is primarily related to the size of the organization and the importance of such services. Small organizations have only limited facilities, such as those needed to handle first-aid cases, while many larger firms offer complete diagnostic, treatment, and emergency medical services. Since employers are required to provide medical services after an injury, the larger firms may have nurses and physicians on full-time duty or certainly have arrangements with local physicians for preferred attention. Medium-sized and smaller organizations have one or more physicians on call.

Alternative Approaches

In a discussion of health services as well as health benefits, it should be emphasized that there are many nontraditional approaches to better health. These are typically referred to as alternative approaches. Many of the approaches differ from traditional medicine in that they are less invasive and they empower the patient by enlisting patient participation in health-care decisions.

Relaxation techniques, chiropractic, therapeutic massage, acupuncture, homeopathy, megavitamin and herbal therapy, special diets, and many other alternative approaches are used to treat a wide variety of health problems.

Similarly, changes to the physical structure of the work environment can also improve the overall effectiveness of employees. This is especially true if the organization is part of the information-age economy where there are many cross-functional interactions and creative approaches to the business. A physical layout that produces a silo effect (i.e., physical layouts that have lots of barriers) can diminish employee output.[35]

Wellness Programs

Many organizations have developed programs that emphasize regular exercise, proper nutrition, weight control, and avoidance of substances harmful to health. For example, the employee health management program at Xerox includes cardiovascular fitness through aerobic exercises, such as jogging, skipping rope, and racquet sports.

Wellness programs are not only popular, but they can produce measurable cost savings. Wellness efforts are particularly effective when organizations target their wellness initiatives at specific health risks, such as high cholesterol or blood pressure counts, high body-fat levels, or smoking. Every dollar invested in a wellness program produces a return of $1.95 to $3.75 per employee.[36] For example, Husky Oil believes that its program has enabled its absenteeism rate in its Canadian operations to be less than one-half of the manufacturing industry average (3.7 days per year versus 9.1).[37] Other success stories can be found in At Work with HRM 8.3. In addition, a 2002 study conducted on high-risk employees, such as smokers, indicated that for every $1 invested in a wellness program the organization could expect an overall saving of $4.[38]

However, not everyone is convinced of the effectiveness of wellness programs. Unions such as CUPE and the Canadian Union of Postal Workers (CUPW) express concern that too much attention is focused on a person's unhealthy lifestyle and that in doing so, potential workplace issues that are creating unhealthy employees are being ignored. There is also some evidence that suggests it is difficult to identify a wellness program being the variable in reducing absenteeism.[39]

Employee Assistance Programs

Objective 5

Employee assistance program (EAP)
Program to provide short-term counselling and referrals to appropriate professionals

A broad view of health includes the emotional as well as the physical aspects of one's life. While emotional problems, personal crises, alcoholism, and drug abuse are considered to be personal matters, they become organizational problems when they affect behaviour at work and interfere with job performance. It is estimated that psychological problems in the workplace cost Canadian companies approximately $16 billion each year.[40] **Employee assistance programs (EAPs)** can provide a useful way to deal with problems, such as stress and depression, which could lead to more serious mental

at work **with HRM 8.3** at work with HRM 8.3

INVESTING IN EMPLOYEE HEALTH

For the 2,800 employees at Husky Injection Molding Systems of Bolton, Ontario, work seems like play as they visit their children over lunch, eat fresh healthy cafeteria food, play table tennis on their breaks, and receive an extra vacation day for staying fit. Husky spends more than $4 million a year on employee benefits, but this investment more than pays for itself in higher productivity, lower turnover, and lower absenteeism. The voluntary turnover rate is about 15%, which is 5% below the industry average. The absenteeism rate is 4 days compared to 7.3 days for the industry average. Injury claims are 1.2 for every 200,000 hours worked, compared with an industry average of 5.8. The estimated savings are $8.4 million a year.

Husky is not the only company seeing returns on investments in workplace well-being. Organizations in Atlantic Canada found that employees who participated in a three-month wellness program reduced the risk of heart disease and stroke, for an estimated return on the investment of $1.64 for every dollar spent. In one of the largest studies done on ROI of health-care programs, the National Wellness program delivered wellness programs consisting of smoking cessation workshops, lifestyle and nutrition counselling, and on-site fitness to 90,000 employees in 30 locations. Those who participated had lower health-care costs of between $5 and $16 per month. Even a one-time inexpensive program can show returns. TELUS introduced a flu immunization program and saw absences due to respiratory illness drop from 33% to 22%. Overall, studies of wellness programs document cost–benefit ratios of between $3 and $8 for every dollar spent. The benefits to organizations include decreased lost workdays, decreased workers' compensation costs, increased employee morale and productivity, reduced overtime costs, and reduced workplace injuries.

CRITICAL THINKING QUESTION

If wellness programs can save a company money, why don't more organizations have them? Explain your answer.

Sources: T. Grant, "Husky Woos Workers with Unique Perks," *The Globe and Mail*, August 20, 2001; S. Kee, "The Bottom Line on Wellness," *Canadian Health Care Manager* 9, no. 1 (Fall 2002): 23; G. Lowe, "The Dollars and Sense of Health Promotion," *Canadian HR Reporter*, September 23, 2002.

EAP Directory

www.eap-sap.com

health problems. Indeed only about 7% of employees use employee assistance programs.[41] Supervisors are often given training and policy guidance in the type of help they can offer their subordinates. To be able to handle such problems, organizations such as RBC Financial Group and NCR in Waterloo and Mississauga, Ontario, offer an employee assistance program. Figure 8.5 outlines the type of programs offered to employees in Canada. The reasons most companies do not offer programs is the lack of resources and staff, and concerns over the cost benefits of such initiatives.[42] Research, however, has shown that 80% of mental health problems can be successfully treated with early detection and treatment.

For additional information on EAP service providers, access **www.eap-sap.com**.

FIGURE 8.5   Corporate Wellness Initiatives

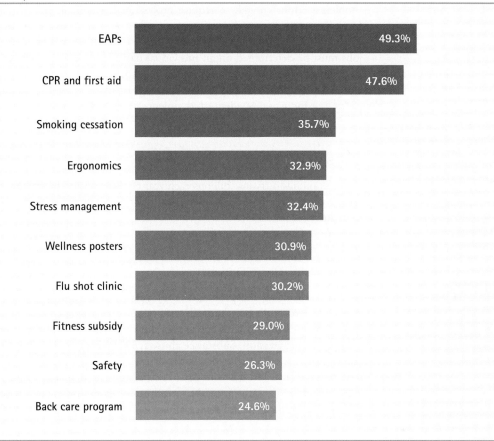

Source: J. Butler, "You've Invested in an EAP, Now Learn to Use It," *Canadian HR Reporter* 15, no. 11 (June 3, 2002): 7.

Personal Crises

The most prevalent problems among employees are personal crises involving marital, family, financial, or legal matters. Such problems often come to a supervisor's attention. In most instances, the supervisor can usually provide the best help simply by being understanding and supportive and by helping the individual find the type of assistance needed. In many cases, the person is referred to the EAP program. In recent years, crisis hotlines have been set up in many communities to provide counselling by telephone for those too distraught to wait for an appointment with a counsellor or for those organizations that do not have an EAP.[43]

Emotional Problems

Mental health claims are the fastest growing category of disability costs in Canada today, and the cost of lost productivity alone is approximately $8 billion a year.[44] While personal crises are typically fraught with emotion, most of them are resolved in a reasonable period of time, and the troubled individual's life reaches balance. There will, however, be a small percentage of employees—roughly 3% on average—who have emotional problems serious enough to require professional treatment. An estimated 1.4 million Canadians suffer from depression and only about 6% have been diagnosed and are receiving proper treatment.[45] Whether such individuals will be able to perform their jobs must be determined on an individual basis. In reviewing such cases, the organization should pay particular attention to workplace safety factors, since there is general agreement that emotional disturbances are primary or secondary factors in a large proportion of industrial accidents and violence.

Substance Abuse

Business and industry lose billions each year because of substance abuse. According to the most recent study by the Canadian Centre on Substance Abuse, the following productivity losses occur:

- $4.1 billion from alcohol abuse
- $823.1 million from illicit drugs
- $6.8 billion from tobacco[46]

In confronting the problem, employers must recognize that substance abuse is now considered a disease that follows a rather predictable course. Thus, they can take specific actions to deal with employees showing symptoms of the disease at particular stages of its progression. Substance abuse typically begins with social drinking or drug taking that gets out of control. As the disease progresses, the person loses control over how much to use and when to use. The person uses denial to avoid facing the problems created by the substance abuse and often blames others for these problems. The first step in helping the substance abuser is to awaken the person to the reality of the situation.

To identify substance abuse as early as possible, it is essential that supervisors monitor the performance, attendance, and behaviour of all employees regularly and systematically. A supervisor should carefully document evidence of declining performance, behaviour, and/or attendance and then bring the matter to the attention of the employee with evidence that the individual's work is suffering. The employee should be assured that help will be made available without penalty. In fact, through decisions of the court concerning substance abuse, the courts have confirmed that substance abuse is a disability, and employers are legally obliged to deal with the problem. This means that the employer can no longer terminate a person's employment simply because they have an abuse problem. Specifically, a supervisor needs to set clear expectations, be consistent, act, and follow any other health and safety regulations. Since the assessments are made solely with regard to poor job performance, attendance, or behaviour, a supervisor can avoid any mention of the abuse and allow such employees to seek aid as they would for any other problem. A supervisor cannot discipline an employee because a person is suspected of abusing a substance: discipline is dependent on the degree of problem with job performance, attendance, or behaviour. Between 70 and 80% of employees accept the offer to get help and resolve their problems. Therefore, it is important for supervisors and managers to recognize that any discipline, whether it is a verbal warning or a termination, has to be related to the job. Further, as mentioned in previous chapters, there are many constraints on employers to legally test to see if an employee is using any substance that might impair the work performance.

Job-Related Stress

Stress
Any adjustive demand caused by physical, mental, or emotional factors that requires coping behaviour

Many people use EAPs to help them deal with **stress**. But what is stress? People frequently talk about being stressed at work, yet they are often unable to explain what they mean. Stress is simply any demand on the physical or emotional self that requires a person to cope with that demand. For example, while running five kilometres an individual may become short-winded after three kilometres. Thus the body is "stressed" as the individual deals with being short of breath. Likewise, a student may have just received a special award at school and be excited about the recognition. Again, the student has to cope with this. Stress can be either positive or negative, and each person handles stress differently. Recent research indicates that more than 13% of all provincial government employees had sought some kind of help to deal with stress.[47]

Causes of workplace stress are many; however, high workloads, excessive job pressures, layoffs and organizational restructuring, and global economic conditions are identified as the primary causes of employee stress.[48] Additionally, disagreements with managers or fellow employees are a common cause of stress, along with little or no say about how a job is performed, lack of communication on the job, and lack of recognition for a job well done. Even minor irritations, such as lack of privacy, unappealing music, excessive noise, or other conditions, can be stressful to one person or another. Whatever the causes of workplace stress, the condition is now costing the Canadian health-care system more than $5.8 billion annually.[49]

Burnout is the most severe stage of distress. Career burnout generally occurs when a person begins questioning his or her own personal values. Quite simply, one no longer feels that what he or she is doing is important. Depression, frustration, and a loss of productivity are all symptoms of burnout. Burnout is due primarily to a lack of personal fulfillment in the job or a lack of positive feedback about performance. In organizations that have downsized, remaining employees can experience burnout since they must perform more work with fewer co-workers. Overachievers can experience burnout when unrealistic work goals are unattainable.[50]

Coping with organizational stress begins by having managers recognize the universal symptoms of work stress as well as the stressful situations particular to their work unit. Major stressors include the following:

- Responsibility without authority.
- Inability to voice complaints.
- Prejudice because of age, gender, race, or religion.
- Poor working conditions.
- Inadequate recognition.
- Lack of a clear job description or chain of command.
- Unfriendly interpersonal relationships.[51]

Many employers have developed stress management programs to teach employees how to minimize the negative effects of job-related stress. A typical program might include instruction in relaxation techniques, coping skills, listening skills, methods of dealing with difficult people, time management, and assertiveness. Organizational techniques, such as clarifying the employee's work role, redesigning and enriching jobs, correcting physical factors in the environment, and effectively handling interpersonal factors, should not be overlooked in the process of teaching employees how to handle stress.[52]

Even though the number and severity of organizational stressors can be reduced, everyone encounters situations that may be described as distressful. Those in good physical health are generally better able to cope with the stressors they encounter. Figure 8.6 describes several ways to reduce job-related stress.

Before concluding this discussion, we should observe that stress that is harmful to some employees may be healthy for others. Most managers learn to handle distress effectively and find that it actually stimulates better performance. However, there will always be those who are unable to handle stress and need assistance in learning to cope with it. The increased interest of young and old alike in developing habits that will enable them to lead happier and more productive lives will undoubtedly be beneficial to them as individuals, to the organizations where they work, and to a society where people are becoming more and more interdependent.

FIGURE 8.6   Tips for Reducing Job-Related Stress

- Build rewarding relationships with co-workers.
- Talk openly with managers or employees about job or personal concerns.
- Prepare for the future by keeping abreast of likely changes in job demands.
- Don't greatly exceed your skills and abilities.
- Set realistic deadlines; negotiate reasonable deadlines with managers.
- Act now on problems or concerns of importance.
- Designate dedicated work periods during which time interruptions are avoided.
- When feeling stressed, find time for detachment or relaxation.
- Don't let trivial items take on importance; handle them quickly or assign them to others.
- Take short breaks from your work area as a change of pace.

BUILDING A STRONG HEALTH AND SAFETY CULTURE[53]

Are the health and safety initiatives described in this chapter working? It is important for managers and supervisors to understand that effective health and safety needs must be part of the organizational culture. Merely having safety training programs or violence response teams will not create the overall healthy and safe work environment that employers and employees desire. The culture of the organization plays a critical role.

Building organizational processes and mechanisms is a difficult task at the best of times. They must be able to respond well to immediate needs as well as help propel the organization toward a desirable future. In addition, these mechanisms must be simple to manage and maintain. When this doesn't happen, the result is that too much time and attention and too many resources are spent going nowhere in a "vehicle" that is not working well. These processes and mechanisms can be grouped into two main categories: pull and push. "Pull" mechanisms are ones that motivate, encourage self-discipline and learning, are customer-focused, and build understanding of and commitment to the organization's purpose and direction. "Push" mechanisms, on the other hand, are based on control, rules, consistency, fairness, and forced discipline. These are often referred to as bureaucratic procedures.

The realities of organizational life and human nature dictate a mixture of both pull and push mechanisms. Many organizations tend to swing from one to the other, achieving some short-term benefit by focusing on one, until the absence of the other makes sustained performance very difficult.

It should be recognized that the better the pull, the less need there is for a push; that rules and control are often needed because individuals are low on understanding and commitment. Yet organizations seem to build push mechanisms. Part of the reason is that push mechanisms are easier to make. Pull mechanisms lend themselves less to precision and are based more on relationships, chance, and networking. Face-to-face events are hard to steer. When filling out reports, the expected outcome can be clearly defined. However, when people get together, who knows what will happen?

Health and safety programs in the workplace have primarily been based on the push approach: legislation, union pressure, regulations, and enforcement. Management has traditionally avoided taking an active role in health and safety (either push or pull), further encouraging other parties to push.

For push to have some effect, some pull has to be present. Where should this pull come from? The principal puller has to be the work group: the people who work together on a daily or hourly basis. They have to be the primary source of energy, knowledge, and commitment for a safe and healthy workplace. Without their commitment to and understanding of health and safety, all the pull and push in other places of the organization will not have much, if any, constructive impact on health and safety.

The goal, then, is to create a work environment where the pull comes from the work group, and all the others in the organization constructively support the work group to achieve its own health and safety goals and objectives. This will naturally have to happen within legislation, regulatory, union–management, and corporate frameworks. Yet the focus is to equip the work group both technically and organizationally to work safely in a healthy work environment.

Objective 6

The dynamic of this situation is shown in Figure 8.7 with the focus on the work group. It will need the support, skills, and desire to work safely and stay healthy. At a minimum, this means the work group, together with the supervisor, has

- health and safety goals,
- plans for their implementation,
- a process to assess their progress,
- the ability to learn from the experience, and
- a way to continually improve the quality of the work experience.

Without this capability at the work-group level, even the best of health and safety programs will have limited impact in the workplace. To bring this scenario into place, strong support is needed from the outer ring. A good deal of this support is expected to be of the pull kind.

The choice is quite clear. Organizations can carry on doing what they know, bringing in more rules and more referees, or they can challenge their direction, assess the nature of their relationships, and build the necessary mechanisms that will pull all employees and employers toward a better future.

FIGURE 8.7   The Framework for a Strong Health and Safety Culture

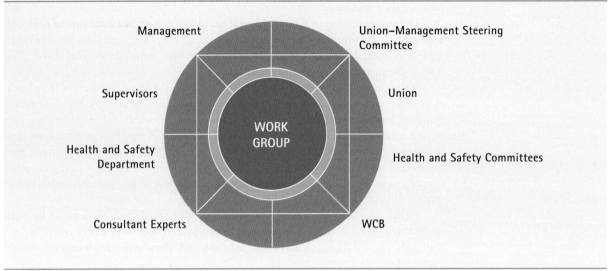

SUMMARY

1. Describe what supervisors and managers can do to create a safe and healthy work environment.
    *   Become familiar with the occupational health and safety legislation governing their operation.
    *   Enforce health and safety standards throughout the organization.
    *   Protect employees from physical hazards, unhealthy conditions, and unsafe acts of other employees.

2. Cite the measures that should be taken to control and eliminate health and safety hazards.
    *   Take every reasonable precaution to ensure employee safety.
    *   Inform and train employees about safety and health requirements in the organization.
    *   Keep records and investigate any accidents.
    *   Involve employees in identifying and eliminating health and safety problems.
    *   Provide safety training programs and emphasize the importance of health and safety in the workplace.
    *   Enforce safety procedures.

3. List the current workplace health and safety issues.
    *   Indoor air quality, including second-hand smoke
    *   Cumulative trauma disorders
    *   Communicable diseases
    *   Workplace violence

4. Describe the organizational services and programs for building better health.
    *   Wellness programs that emphasize regular exercise, proper nutrition, weight control, and avoidance of substances harmful to health.
    *   Employee assistance programs.

- Programs that deal with substance abuse.
- Stress management programs.

5. Explain the role of employee assistance programs.
   - Organizations recognize that personal problems can create organizational problems.
   - EAPs provide employees in need with appropriate resources.
   - EAPs typically cover financial, family, and emotional issues.

6. Describe the ways in which supervisors can support work groups on health and safety matters.
   - Create health and safety goals.
   - Plan for their implementation.
   - Develop a process to assess goal attainment.
   - Learn from experience.
   - Continually improve the quality of the work experience.

Need to Know

- Definition of WHMIS
- Types of health and safety concerns and issues in the workplace, such as air quality, technology
- Definition of employee assistance programs and what they handle

Need to Understand

- Role of legislation in occupational health and safety
- Duties and responsibilities of employer, supervisor, and employee regarding health and safety
- Role supervisor plays in creating a healthy and safe work environment
- Prevention and control of workplace violence
- Role supervisor can play in preventing burnout

Key Terms

cumulative trauma disorders 296

employee assistance program (EAP) 303

industrial disease 286

Material Safety Data Sheet (MSDS) 295

occupational illness 279

occupational injury 279

stress 307

REVIEW QUESTIONS

1. List the primary duties and responsibilities in relation to health and safety for each of the following:

   employers
   workers
   supervisors

2. What is the purpose of workers' compensation legislation?
3. What can employers do to reduce the cost of workers' compensation?
4. Identify some specific ways that an employer can create a safe work environment.
5. List the warning signs of violence in the workplace.
6. Explain the purpose of an employee assistance program and list some of the problems handled.
7. What is stress and what are the specific causes of workplace stress?

CRITICAL THINKING QUESTIONS

1. An unhealthy work environment can lower productivity, contribute to low morale, and increase medical and workers' compensation costs. Working individually or in teams, list specific ways managers can

   a. Improve indoor air quality
   b. Reduce the harmful effects of technology
   c. Reduce risks of violence in the workplace
   d. Accommodate the desires of smokers and nonsmokers

2. You've just been hired by ABC Auto Parts as a management trainee. Part of your responsibilities includes introducing a "Safety First" mindset. How would you approach this task and what elements would you want in the mindset?
3. Samir has recently joined a well-known retail clothing store in his community. On his first full shift he noticed a number of safety and health violations. What advice would you give him and why?
4. You work in the medical equipment and pharmaceutical department at a local hospital. Your department is responsible for dispensing medical supplies and prescriptions to patients. There have been some recent incidents in which patients have been quite vocal and threatening in their behaviour toward staff. As a consequence, you and four other staff have been appointed to a task group to undertake a workplace violence audit and then develop appropriate procedures. What steps could you take to do the audit and what might be some of the procedures you could use to minimize the possibility of workplace violence?

DEVELOPING YOUR SKILLS

1. Working in pairs, identify health and safety concerns at your school or work. Suggest ways in which these concerns could be addressed and how you would go about solving them. Share your responses with the rest of the class.
2. Access your provincial workers' compensation Web site. Identify five companies that violated health and safety regulations in your province. Prepare a one- to two-page summary describing the losses to the organizations in work (man-hours) and the dollar penalties.

3. Individually, think about a situation where employees follow the safety rules when the supervisor is watching yet violate the rules when the supervisor isn't watching. How would you motivate these employees to follow the rules when the supervisor isn't there? In groups of four to five students, develop a plan to improve safety under these conditions. Share your information with the rest of the class and identify any common approaches.

4. Visit the Web site of Human Resources and Skills Development Canada and access the link to Individuals/Labour and Workplace. Then choose Work/Life Balance and New Workplace Challenges (**www.hrsdc.gc.ca**). Select any of the topics and prepare a one-page summary of the key points. In the class setting, working in groups of four to five, share the information with each other.

5. Access the following Web sites:

- **www.safety-council.org** (Canada Safety Council)
- **www.ccohs.ca** (Canadian Centre for Occupational Health and Safety)

Compare the home page of each site. If you were an employee and needed information, which home page would appear to meet that need? If you were a supervisor? Select the one topic that is the same from each site. Compare the information from the supervisor's perspective. Which information is similar? Which information is different? Prepare a one- to two-page report outlining the similarities and differences.

Human Resources and Skills Development Canada
www.hrsdc.gc.ca

Canada Safety Council
www.safety-council.org

Canadian Centre for Occupational Health and Safety
www.ccohs.ca

Case Study 1 — Workplace Safety and Young Workers

Young workers are 70% more likely to have a workplace injury than any other group.

About 95% of these young workers are men. This means that one in eleven young men can expect to suffer a workplace injury. Typically, these young men are employed at small manufacturing businesses, fast-food restaurants, convenience stores, and warehouses. The accidents happen within the first six months on the job. These young men lose fingers while slicing meat at the deli counter, are crushed by equipment they do not know how to operate, are electrocuted on metal ladders that touch hydro poles, or are burned handling chemicals because they are not wearing protective equipment. The top five causes of injuries to young workers are slips and falls, overexertion, being struck by an object, exposure to toxic chemicals, and burns.

Young workers do receive some safety training, but it is not enough. About 30% of teenagers receive first aid and CPR in their safety training, but most learn nothing about the law, their rights, hazards on the job, or safety management. Young workers are especially vulnerable because they feel invincible and lack experience. Most will not ask for safety training because they are unaware of risks, are anxious to please, or are fearful of losing their jobs.

Many provinces, recognizing these risks, have added health and safety training to the high school curriculum. Most such programs discuss workplace hazards, employer rights and responsibilities, health and safety laws, and the workers' right of refusal. Alberta has the most advanced training course for young workers in Canada: Job Safety Skills, which consists of 75 hours of instruction, divided into three modules:

- personal safety management (first aid, back care, and safety and the law)
- workplace safety practices (ergonomics, confined space entry, transportation of dangerous goods, and farm safety)
- safety management systems (loss control, accident investigation, and a mock workshop in which students develop an entire safety program)

Sources: Adapted from L. Ramsay, "2000 Work Safely for a Healthy Future," Human Resources Development Canada; and WSIB-Young Workers Awareness Program, "Work Can Kill You," *National Post*, September 27, 1999, C12; L. Young, "Young Workers: Changing the Face of Safety," *Occupational Health and Safety* 14, no. 4, June–July 1998, 24–30; and Anonymous, "Workplace Safety," *The Globe and Mail*, Friday, May 12, 2000.

Questions

1. Why are there more workplace injuries among those aged 16 to 25?
2. By law, workplace safety is the responsibility of the employer and employee. Why have nearly all provinces created courses in occupational health and safety as part of the high school curriculum? Should these be mandatory courses or electives?
3. Consider the various places you have worked. What type of training program could the employer have undertaken to focus on the young worker?

Case Study 2

Safety Concerns at Majestic Hotel

Majestic Hotel has received many awards for its customer service approach. It has over 5,000 people staying at its hotel every year. Part of the success of the hotel has been its focus on training its staff to provide an exceptional experience for the hotel guest.

Recently the hotel general manager has noticed an increase in the number of reported accidents and workplace injuries. A hotel worker was so concerned about the number of back injuries and wrist strains that the worker contacted the local WCB officer and asked that there be a safety audit. However, the audit did not uncover anything unusual for the hotel industry.

Majestic Hotel has the following Health and Safety Policy:

Majestic Hotel is committed to the prevention of illness and injury through the creation of a healthy and safe work environment. The hotel endeavours to provide an environment that promotes health and safety practices that go beyond the minimum required by law. The hotel expects that health and safety, of both employees and guests, is primary in every area of operation.

New employees receive training on how to do their work safely with a special emphasis on lifting, carrying, and using items such as sheets and trash cans. Employees also receive reminders about safe work practices at monthly staff meetings. As new methods are identified to minimize the physical impact of the work, all employees receive training. To do anything more would mean more dollar resources than are currently allocated for all health and safety initiatives.

Last week the general manager received notification from the provincial agency that the hotel's workers' compensation premiums would be increased in the following calendar year as a result of the increased claims.

Questions

1. Why might the accident and injury claims be increasing?
2. By law, workplace safety is the responsibility of the employer and employee. What else can Majestic Hotel do to ensure that employees are doing their work in a safe and healthy way?
3. Develop a new health and safety approach that will improve the hotel's safety and health performance.
4. Suggest some ergonomic solutions, even at a cost, that might be considered.

NOTES AND REFERENCES

1. David Brown, "Criminal Charges Laid Under New Corporate Killing Law," *Canadian HR Reporter*, September 27, 2004, 1.
2. National Day of Mourning, http://www.clc-ctc.ca/web/ organizing/health_safety/day_mourning_en.html (retrieved January 20, 2005), and Tim Hearn, Chairman, Imperial Oil, "Putting Safety First," http://www.imperialoil.ca/ Canada-English/thisis/publications/2004Q2/pages/ safetyFirst.html (retrieved January 22, 2005).
3. HRDC, "Work Safely for a Healthy Future," *Research and Analysis*, March 2000.
4. "Your Health and Safety Rights and Responsibilities," Workplace Safety and Insurance Board, http://www.wsib .on.ca/wsib/wsibsite.nsf/Public/PreventionYHSRR (retrieved February 16, 2000).
5. "Occupational Health & Safety Amendments to the Worker's Compensation Act," Russell & DuMoulin bulletin, September 1999.
6. "Uncle Who Runs Edmonton Construction Company Fined for Nephew's Death on Site," *OH & S Canada*, http://www.ohscanada.com/news (retrieved May 3, 2002).
7. "Steelworkers Launch Westray Campaign," May 1, 2002, www.uswa.ca/eng/news_releases/westray.htm (retrieved August 6, 2002).
8. David Brown, "Criminal Charges Laid Under New Corporate Killing Law."
9. M. Basch Scott, "Insures, Support Services Focus on Enabling Return to Work from Disability," *Employee Benefits Plan Review* 54, no. 9 (March 2000): 16–21;

   V. Galt and K. Harding, "No Safety in the Numbers," *The Globe and Mail*, June 18, 2003, C1.
10. "Work Safely for a Healthy Future," Occupational Safety and Health and Fire Prevention Division, Human Resources Development Canada, March 6, 2000, 9.
11. Tara Neal, "Tools of the Trade," *Occupational Health and Safety* 18, no. 2 (March 2002): 60–68.
12. "Joint Industry and Government Strategy on Workplace Safety," July 2002, www3.gov.ab.ca/hre/whs/ws2point0/ pdf/ws20_strategy.pdf (retrieved May 29, 2005).
13. Todd Humber, "WCBs, Lawmakers Tackle Rising Death Toll," *Canadian HR Reporter*, April 19, 2004, 19.
14. Tim W. McDaniel, "Employee Participation: A Vehicle for Safety by Design," *Occupational Hazards* 6, no. 5 (May 2002): 71–76.
15. Andrew J. Sorine, Richard T. Walls, and Robert W. Trinkleback, "Safety Training Gets Wired through Web-Based E-Learning," *Occupational Hazards* 63, no. 2 (February 2001): 35–40.
16. G. C. Shah, "Five Steps to Digital Safety," *Occupational Health and Safety* 71, no. 3 (March 2002): 22–25.
17. Roger Brooks, "OSHA's E-Tool for Lockout/Tagout," *Occupational Health and Safety* 71, no. 4 (April 2002): 22–24.
18. "True Tales of Health and Safety," *Young Worker Awareness Program*, WSIB Young Worker Awareness, www .youngworker.ca (retrieved August 6, 2002).
19. Robert J. Grossman, "Out with the Bad Air," *HRMagazine* 45, no. 10 (October 2000): 37–44.

20. Brian Shockley, "Air Quality Management in Confined Spaces," *Occupational Hazards* 63, no. 9 (September 2001): 91–94. See also Michael Tesmer, "Avoiding the Air Monitoring Blues," *Occupational Hazards* 63, no. 4 (April 2001): 49–51.

21. "Smoke Gets in Your Lungs," *HRFocus* 73, no. 2 (February 1996): 19.

22. "Work Safely for a Healthy Future," 21.

23. Walt Rostykus, "Sustaining Ergonomic Success," *Occupational Hazards* 64, no. 2 (February 2002): 51–53.

24. Timothy Bland and Pedro P. Forment, "Navigating OSHA's Ergonomics Rules," *HRMagazine* 46, no. 2 (February 2001): 61–67.

25. Asha Tomlinson, "Re-Evaluating Your Workplace: Is It Safe and Secure?" *Canadian HR Reporter*, February 25, 2002, 3.

26. Uyen Vu, "Right to Refuse Dangerous Work Expands," *Canadian HR Reporter*, August 9, 2004: 1.

27. "Working Without Cuffs Unsafe: Guards," *Canadian HR Reporter*, August 9, 2004: 2.

28. NIOSH document, *Violence in the Workplace: Risk Factors and Prevention Strategies*, Bulletin #59, is available from Publications Dissemination, EID, National Institute for Occupational Safety and Health, 4676 Columbia Parkway, Cincinnati, OH 45226-1998, (800) 356-4674.

29. Part 4, General Conditions, Occupational Health and Safety Regulations, Workers' Compensation Board, British Columbia, http://regulation.healthandsafetycentre.org/s/Part4.asp#SectionNumber:4.27 (retrieved January 23, 2005).

30. Ibid.

31. Asha Tomlinson, "Re-evaluating Your Workplace: Is It Safe and Secure?"

32. William M. Glenn, "Workplace Violence: An Employee's Survival Guide," *OH & S Canada*, April/May 2002: 26–31.

33. Thomas Beck, "Set Up a Proactive Crisis Management Program," *HRFocus* 77, no. 1, January 2000, 13.

34. Claire Ginther, "A Death in the Family," *HRMagazine* 46, no. 5 (May 2001): 55–58.

35. Sharon VanderKaay, "Thinking Outside the Cubicle," *Canadian HR Reporter*, December 17, 2001, 22.

36. "Wellness for a Healthy Bottom Line," *Canadian Business*, January 17–30, 2005.

37. *Ibid.*

38. David Brown, "Wellness Programs Bring Healthy Bottom Line," *Canadian HR Reporter*, December 17, 2001, 1.

39. Anthony Pizzino, "Show Us the Link to OH & S," *Canadian HR Reporter*, May 9, 2005, 8.

40. "Addressing Mental Health in the Workplace," International Foundation Education, Benefits, Compensation, http://www.ifebp.org/knowledge/ichotcndis.asp (retrieved January 25, 2005).

41. S. Pinker, "SOS Call Your EAP," *The Globe and Mail*, December 11, 2002, C1.

42. F. Puchalksi, "On Site Health Care Brings Healthy Bottom Line," *Canadian HR Reporter* 13, no. 7 (October 9, 2000): 7.

43. Dale Masi and Michael Freedman, "The Use of Telephone and On-Line Technology in Assistance, Counseling and Therapy," *Employee Assistance Quarterly* 16, no. 3 (2001): 49–63.

44. Kathryn Dorrell, "Breaking Down the Barriers" *Benefits Canada* 24, no. 12 (December 2000): 36–38.

45. *Ibid.*

46. "Canadian Profile 1999: Substance Abuse and the Workplace: Highlights," Canadian Centre on Substance Abuse, www.ccsa.ca/cp99work.htm (retrieved October 28, 1999).

47. Nicholas Read, "Provincial Government Workers Are Most Stressed," *The Vancouver Sun*, July 13, 2004, A1.

48. William Atkinson, "When Stress Won't Go Away," *HRMagazine* 45, no. 12 (December 2000): 105–10.

49. Uyen Vu, "Stress Costs $5.8 Billion," *Canadian HR Reporter*, December 6, 2004, 1.

50. "Stop Burnout—Before It Stops Your Employees," *HRFocus* 79, no. 2 (February 2002): 3–4.

51. Merry Mayer, "Breaking Point," *HRMagazine* 46, no. 10 (October 2001): 111–16.

52. "The Key to Stress Management, Retention, and Profitability: More Workplace Fun," *HRFocus* 77, no. 9 (September 2000): 5–6.

53. This section is based on John Beckett, "Building a Strong Safety Culture," unpublished article, December 1999. Used with permission.

CHAPTER 9

Management Rights, Employee Rights, and Discipline

HRM
Close-Up

Stacey Sandison (centre), general manager, Customer and Marketing Services, SaskTel Mobility, Regina, Saskatchewan

"The time spent telling people what's expected of them, what their role is, and how much time their job will take translates into more settled and motivated employees,"

Disaster can sometimes be defined as "a breakdown in communications." Stacey Sandison takes this definition to heart—and to work—as the general manager of customer and marketing services for SaskTel Mobility, the wireless division of Saskatchewan's provincially owned telephone and telecommunications company. Based in Regina, Sandison is one of almost 70 managers at a company that boasts 300 employees, annual revenues of more than $200 million, and a strong position in an increasingly competitive industry. In such a high-stakes environment, it is imperative that staff know their rights, as well as SaskTel Mobility's own disciplinary procedures, from the outset. "The time spent telling people what's expected of them, what their role is, and how much time their job will take translates into more settled and motivated employees," says Sandison, who has a business administration degree from the University of Regina and 22 years' experience with the Crown corporation.

SaskTel Mobility measures what Sandison refers to as "employee effectiveness" with its annual performance rating system, Partnership for Excellence (PFE). PFE is designed to pinpoint areas where an employee is underachieving and to identify solutions to the problem. Gaps in performance, says Sandison, can often be reflected in an employee's sales record and overall financial results. Sandison's job involves recognizing and dealing with poor performers. "Sometimes it's a case of saying, 'Pull up your socks, or you'll have to leave.' But more often it's just a matter of speaking with the person to find out what's wrong, and why they're not reaching their potential."

Since all non-management staff at SaskTel Mobility are members of the Communications, Energy and Paperworkers Union of Canada (CEP), all disciplinary procedures and grounds for termination are laid out in a comprehensive and well-defined collective agreement. "One strike doesn't mean someone is out the door," says Sandison, whose own management philosophy is to "get a person to 'strike number ten.'" By that she means working with an employee to map out a plan to improve performance over the long term. "I want to give people the benefit of the doubt all the way through the [disciplinary] process."

For their part, managers must participate in what SaskTel calls "360-degree surveys" that get distributed annually to a cross-section of co-workers and peers. Disciplining managers falls into what Sandison admits is a bit of a grey area, but can be more black and white provided the rules of fairness are obeyed. For Sandison, this may involve showing a manager how the bottom line is being affected, or taking the person aside to deliver a discreet and friendly reprimand. After all, creating a nurturing environment—one that attracts talent and provides opportunities for growth and contribution—is what SaskTel Mobility is all about. "People don't feel loyalties to companies like they used to," says Sandison. "So we need to make sure that the HR support mechanisms motivate people to stay."

INTRODUCTION

In this chapter, employee rights, management rights, workplace privacy, and employee discipline are discussed. Managers note that these topics have a major influence on the activities of both employees and supervisors. Managers are discovering that the right to discipline and discharge employees—a traditional responsibility of management—is more difficult to exercise in light of the growing attention paid to employment protection rights.[1] In addition, disciplining employees is a difficult and unpleasant task for most managers and supervisors; many of them report that taking disciplinary action against an employee is the most stressful duty they perform. Balancing employee rights and employee discipline may not be easy, but it is a universal requirement and a critical aspect of good management. As Stacey Sandison expressed in the HRM Close-Up, the role of the supervisor is to help employees understand their rights as well as the company's disciplinary procedures.

Because the growth of employee rights issues may lead to an increase in the number of lawsuits filed by employees, this chapter includes a discussion of alternative dispute resolution as a way to foster a less legalistic approach to solving disagreements. As managers are the people who take disciplinary actions that are subject to challenge and possible reversal through governmental agencies or the courts, managers should make a positive effort to prevent the need for such action. Further, managers often avoid difficult performance reviews and thus may create a situation where disciplinary action is considered. When disciplinary action becomes impossible to avoid, however, that action should be taken in accordance with carefully developed HR policies and practices. Since ethics is an important element of good managerial practice, the chapter concludes with a discussion of organizational ethics in employee relations. The vast majority of this chapter applies to both nonunionized and unionized workplaces. Where a concept applies only to a nonunion workplace, this will be identified.

MANAGEMENT RIGHTS

The concept of "management rights" has evolved with the introduction of unions. Some of these rights include making decisions about how the business is run or how much the company should charge for its products or services. One of the more basic rights is that the company has the right to hire or terminate whomever it wants.

However, as discussed in both this chapter and in Chapter 10, those rights now have to be exercised in certain ways. Managers function as the representative of the organization and therefore have the legal responsibilities and liabilities that go with the managerial role. One illustration of this is "negligent hiring." Negligent hiring refers to a situation where a person is hired and then involved in job-related misconduct which could have been determined if the person's previous work background and behaviours were referenced.[2] While any claim would be against the employer, it is the action (or lack of action) of the manager that creates the situation. Think about a situation in a long-term residential care facility where a resident is physically assaulted by an employee who has a long (and verifiable) history of physical violence. Negligent hiring would occur if the manager did not do a thorough enough background check to identify the history or did and still hired the person.

In addition, supervisors and managers are expected to behave and act in ways that acknowledge that employees also have certain rights. Managers are no longer able to make decisions or take actions without being aware of their obligations as to how an employee must be treated in today's workplace.

EMPLOYEE RIGHTS

Employee rights
Expectations of fair treatment from employers

Various human rights laws, wage and hour regulations, and safety and health legislation have secured basic employee rights and brought numerous job improvements to the workplace. Now employee rights litigation has shifted to such workplace issues as employees' rights to protest unfair disciplinary action, to refuse to take drug tests, to have access to their personnel files, to challenge employer searches and surveillance, and to privacy protection.[3] All these things make it very important that managers act and behave in fair and objective ways.

The current emphasis on employee rights is a natural result of the evolution of societal, business, and employee interests. **Employee rights** refers to the expectation of fair treatment from employers in the employment relationship. These expectations become rights when they are granted to employees by the courts, legislatures, or employers. Employee rights frequently involve an employer's alleged invasion of an employee's right to privacy. Unfortunately, the difference between an employee's legal right to privacy and the moral or personal right to privacy is not always clear. The confusion is due to the lack of a comprehensive and consistent body of privacy protection, whether from laws or from court decisions.

There can be perceived invasion of privacy when the employer uses electronic monitoring or surveillance to observe or monitor employees while they are doing their work. Although such action is not illegal, employers are well advised to let employees know when and why they are doing it. For example, companies that have a call-centre operation frequently will use electronic means to monitor customer calls. However, employees are provided full information about the purpose and in some situations given guarantees that the data will be used only to help the employees learn and improve their customer-service skills.

Balanced against employee rights is the employer's responsibility to provide a safe workplace for employees while guaranteeing safe, high-quality goods and services to consumers. An employee who uses drugs may exercise a privacy right and refuse to submit to a drug test. But should that employee produce a faulty product as a result of drug impairment, the employer can be held liable for any harm caused by that product. Employers must therefore exercise *reasonable care* in the hiring, training, and assignment of employees to jobs. As mentioned earlier, without the exercise of reasonable care, employers can be held negligent by outside parties or other employees injured by a dishonest, unfit, or incompetent employee.[4] In law, **negligence** is the failure to use a reasonable amount of care where such failure results in injury to another person.

Negligence
Failure to provide reasonable care where such failure results in injury to consumers or other employees

It is here that employee rights and employer responsibilities can come most pointedly into conflict. The failure of employers to honour employee rights can result in costly lawsuits, damage the organization's reputation, and hurt employee morale. But failure to protect the safety and welfare of employees or consumer interests can invite litigation from both groups. At Work with HRM 9.1 discusses the practical implications

at work **with HRM 9.1** at work with HRM 9.1

EMPLOYEE RIGHTS LITIGATION

Kevin O'Neill is a lawyer specializing in employment and labour law with one of Canada's largest law firms, Fasken, Martineau, DuMoulin. For O'Neill, two court cases[5] demonstrate the shift in balance toward employee rights and employer responsibilities. "The Supreme Court of Canada (SCC) over the last decade has consistently given special recognition to the employer–employee relationship," states O'Neill. "Fair and individual treatment of each person is being stressed. This means that the manager must pay greater attention to the particular individual before, during, and at the conclusion of employment."

One of the cases, *Wallace vs. United Grain Growers*, points to the need for employers to pay more attention to the way in which people are terminated. "It is no longer just a matter of calculating how much notice or pay in lieu of notice someone is to get. Employees are now seeking damages if they feel they were poorly treated during the actual termination," says O'Neill. "Managers must be more thoughtful and be thoroughly prepared when conducting a termination." This means that the manager's behaviour during the process can have a bearing on how much the termination will cost the employer.

In another case, a female firefighter was terminated because she could not perform a physical test, even though she had been performing the job successfully for more than three years. The SCC ruled in favour of the employee. In its decision, the SCC stated that the employer must look at the "unique capabilities and inherent worth and dignity of every individual, up to the point of undue hardship." As O'Neill says, "Direct and indirect discrimination are gone—you now have to accommodate the individual to the point of undue hardship. The key question is to what degree has the focus shifted from job requirements to individual capabilities? Is the right to select the best candidate gone? Where does that leave job requirements, especially for physically or intellectually demanding work? In subsequent decisions, the SCC continues to reinforce that the context of the employment situation must be examined when a decision is made."

CRITICAL THINKING QUESTIONS

1. Do you believe that employees have too many rights? Why or why not?
2. Should an employee have the right to refuse a drug test?

Source: Interview with Kevin O'Neill, May 2005.

for managers of the balance between employee rights and employer responsibilities. The remainder of this section will discuss various rights employees have come to expect from their employers.

Employment Protection Rights

It is not surprising that employees should regard their jobs as an established right—a right that should not be taken away lightly. Without the opportunity to hold a job, our personal well-being would be greatly curtailed. This line of reasoning has led to the emergence of three legal considerations regarding the security of one's job: statutory rights, contractual rights, and due process.

Statutory Rights

Objective

Statutory rights
Rights that derive from legislation

Statutory rights are rights that derive from legislation. As we saw in Chapter 2, human rights legislation protects employees from discrimination on the basis of such grounds as age, sex, and race. For example, in Ontario a woman was terminated during her probationary period and the language in the collective agreement stated that she had no right to challenge such a termination. However, she felt she had been terminated due to her maternity leave and therefore it was a case of discrimination. The courts determined that the union and the employer could not have collective agreement language that prevented her from accessing human rights legislation.[6] Provincial employment standards acts establish basic rights for such things as overtime pay and minimum vacation pay, while occupational health and safety legislation attempts to ensure safe and healthy working conditions. Labour relations laws (discussed in Chapter 11) give employees the right to form and belong to unions, and to bargain for better working conditions. All these laws are "statutory" and grant certain rights to people.

Contractual Rights

Contractual rights
Rights that derive from contracts

While law establishes statutory rights, **contractual rights** are derived from contracts. A contract is a legally binding agreement; if one party breaches the contract, a remedy can be sought through an appeal to the courts. Although formal contracts between employers and full-time employees are rare, they are standard practice when it comes to contingent workers, a growing segment of the Canadian labour force. Such a contract is referred to as the "employment contract" and will contain such items as the type of work, length of work, the amount of pay for the work, including any benefits, and whether or not there is any obligation on the employer if the employee is terminated.

Not all contracts are written. An implied contract can occur when an employer extends to an employee a promise of some form of job security. Implied contractual rights can be based on either oral or written statements made during the pre-employment process or subsequent to hiring. Promises of job security are sometimes contained in employee handbooks, HR manuals, or employment applications. Whether explicit or implicit, promises of job security are generally ruled by the courts to be binding. The decision in *Wallace vs. United Grain Growers* was an important one. Jack Wallace had been induced by an assurance of job security until retirement to leave his employer of 25 years and join a Winnipeg printing firm owned by United Grain Growers. Then Wallace was abruptly dismissed by his new employer. He was later awarded damages by the Supreme Court of Canada.[7]

The following are circumstances in which an implied contract may become binding:

- Telling employees their jobs are secure as long as they perform satisfactorily and are loyal to the organization.
- Stating in the employee handbook that employees will not be terminated without the right of defence or access to an appeal procedure (that is, due process).
- Urging an employee to leave another organization by promising higher wages and benefits, and then reneging after the person has been hired.

To lessen their vulnerability to implied-contract lawsuits, employers can do the following:

1. Train supervisors and managers not to imply contract benefits in conversations with new or current employees.
2. Include in employment offers a statement that an employee may voluntarily terminate employment with proper notice, and the employee may be dismissed by the employer at any time and for a justified reason (just cause). The language in this statement must be appropriate, clear, and easily understood while conveying a tone of welcome to the company.
3. Explain the nature of the employment relationship in documents—for example, employee handbooks, employment applications, and letters of employment.
4. Have written proof that employees have read all documents pertaining to the employment relationship. This can be in the form of an offer-of-employment letter that the person signs or another type of sign-off document.

Due Process

Management has traditionally had the right to direct employees and to take corrective action when needed. Nevertheless, many individuals also believe that a job is the property right of an employee and that the loss of employment has such serious consequences that employees should not lose their jobs without the protection of due process. Managers normally define **due process** as the employee's right to a fair treatment in the handling of an employment matter.[8] However, proactive employers will additionally incorporate the following principles—or rights—in their interpretation of due process:

1. The right to know job expectations and the consequences of not fulfilling those expectations.
2. The right to consistent and predictable management action for the violation of rules.
3. The right to fair discipline based on facts, the right to question those facts, and the right to present a defence.
4. The right to appeal disciplinary action.
5. The right to progressive discipline—to be informed about an incident and be given a chance to improve.

Due process
Employee's right to a fair process in making a decision related to employment relationship

Employment Rights Not a Guarantee

It should be understood that although employees might have cause to regard their jobs as an established right, there is no legal protection affording employees a permanent or continuous job. Furthermore, in general, the concept of due process does not guarantee employees any assurance of employment. However, the concepts of due process and of job as a right do obligate management to act in a consistent and fair manner.

Employees *do* have the right to expect sound employment practices and to be treated respectfully as individuals. In Canada, in absence of a formal contract specifying the duration of employment, the employment relationship can be construed as ongoing. While employment is not considered necessarily to be permanent, the employer must provide reasonable notice and grounds for termination. Thus, Canada functions under statutory and common (contract) law.[9]

Canada Online

http://canadaonline.about.com/cs/hremployers/

Job Expectancy Rights

Objective **2**

Once hired, employees expect certain rights associated with fair and equitable employment. Employee rights on the job include those regarding substance abuse and drug testing, privacy, plant closing notification, and just-cause disciplinary and discharge procedures.

Substance Abuse and Drug Testing

Annual productivity losses in Canada due to substance abuse have been estimated at $4.1 billion for alcohol, $6.8 billion for tobacco, and $823.1 million for illicit drugs. Taken together, all forms of substance abuse account for $11.8 billion in productivity losses, representing 1.7 per cent of the gross domestic product or $414 per capita.[10] Most human rights commissions see drug and alcohol as dependencies; it follows that testing for these dependencies is a form of discrimination.[11]

According to a 2004 survey conducted by the Canadian Centre on Substance Abuse, 80% of the Canadian population reported that they drank alcohol and that one out of 10 drinkers reported experiencing harm from their drinking.[12] The trend in the general population continues to find daily and heavy drinking significantly higher for males than females, that the highest marijuana use levels are in the 18 to 39 age group, and approximately twice as many males are current marijuana users as females. Since illicit drugs are available and increasingly available in high quality throughout Canada, studies are finding cannabis use is up among Canadian adults, and recent student surveys in Ontario find use patterns increasing for most drug categories. Various studies have credited alcohol and other drug use with contributing to increased turnover, accidents, absenteeism, workers compensation, sick benefits and insurance claims, loss of productivity and human potential, low-quality products and services, theft and trafficking.[13]

As mentioned earlier in this chapter, the failure of an employer to ensure a safe and drug-free workplace can result in astronomical liability claims when consumers are injured because of a negligent employee or faulty product. Because of this, Canadian companies are ensuring that their occupational health and safety programs include policies on alcohol and other drugs.[14] Although the Canadian government has not introduced legislation on drug testing, such legislation exists south of the border. Companies with drug-testing policies report reductions in absenteeism, sick days, and accidents. Some of the issues surrounding drug testing are discussed in At Work with HRM 9.2.

Employee Searches and Surveillance

The Retail Council of Canada estimates that employee theft is costing Canadian retailers about $2 million a day.[15] Employees justify stealing by offering such excuses as "I'm underpaid and take what I deserve; everyone does it; the company expects it and just writes it off; the company makes huge profits and so they can afford it; the company makes me mad and I am getting even."[16] Air Canada estimates it is losing as much as 9% of cabin stock each year as a result of employee theft. Private investigators employed by Air Canada searched the rooms of flight crews for these missing items—and found them—after the crews had checked out of the hotels.[17]

WHEN IS DRUG AND/OR ALCOHOL TESTING DISCRIMINATORY?

Many employers express concern about the impact of an employee being impaired at work. The concerns range from loss of productivity to safety for customers and employees. While legislation exists in the U.S. to allow random and regular drug testing, there is no legislation in Canada that allows this. Further, since most human rights tribunals see drug or alcohol abuse as a disability, any testing for these substances can be a form of discrimination.

So what can an employer do? A recent case in the Ontario Court of Appeal has helped provide better guidelines for employers. The case, *Entrop vs. Imperial Oil*, challenged Imperial Oil's policy on drug and alcohol testing. Employees in safety-sensitive positions were subject to random testing and any positive result would lead to immediate termination. While the court re-affirmed that any abuser was considered disabled and therefore entitled to human rights' protections, this was not necessarily the case for casual or recreational users. The court did agree that freedom from impairment was a legitimate BFOQ and that the company had a right to assess that.

However, the court went on to say that drug testing could only identify if there had been previous usage and could not determine if the person was currently impaired. Therefore, drug testing was not a legitimate BFOQ. On the other hand, a breath sample test could assess a person to be currently impaired. Therefore, it was appropriate to use a breath sample test to assess current alcohol impairment.

Since this case, the Canadian Human Rights Commission has publicly stated that employers should not conduct random drug testing but that it is okay to do random alcohol testing if an employee is working where safety is a concern.

CRITICAL THINKING QUESTIONS

1. Do you think employers ought to have the right to test for drug or alcohol use? Why or why not?
2. Do you agree that drug and/or alcohol abuse ought to be considered a disability? Why or why not?
3. How would you feel if your employer did random drug and alcohol tests? Explain your answer.

Source: Adapted from Stuart Rudner, "Keep Drugs, Alcohol Out of the Workplace Without Violating Human Rights," *Canadian HR Reporter*, February 4, 2004 (retrieved February 12, 2005); and "Employers Should Not Conduct Random Drug Tests: CHRC," *Canadian HR Reporter*, July 11, 2002 (retrieved February 12, 2005).

(Employers can minimize the risk of employee theft by following the guidelines provided in Figure 9.1.)

Employees have no reasonable expectation of privacy in places where work rules that provide for inspections have been put into effect. They must comply with probable-cause searches by employers. And they can be appropriately disciplined, normally for insubordination, for refusing to comply with search requests. It is advisable that employers inform new employees through either the final employment interview or an orientation session that mandatory or random searches are done.

FIGURE 9.1   Tips for Reducing the Risk of Employee Theft

Employers lose over 1% of annual revenues as a result of "inventory shrinkage," that is, employee and customer theft. Thieves are like good customers: if they like what they get, they'll come back for more. The key to preventing loss through employee theft is to break up the employee dishonesty triangle—opportunity, rationalization, and financial need. Here are some strategies experts recommend for decreasing the risk of employee theft:

- Determine the extent of the loss—is it worth the effort.
- Use a point-of-sale system which has an inventory control link.
- Use closed-circuit television to monitor both customers and employees.
- Put more expensive goods in an easily monitored area.
- Scrutinize job application forms. Be on the alert for lack of references, skipped portions of the form, conflicting dates of employment, lack of explanation for leaving old jobs, and long gaps between jobs.
- Check references thoroughly.
- Implement a confidential hotline where employee theft can be reported by other employees.
- Use pre-employment screening instruments that help assess and identify people who might be prone to stealing from an employer.
- Ensure that management is perceived as acting ethically.

Sources: John Towler, "Dealing with Employees Who Steal," *Canadian HR Reporter*, September 23, 2002, Vol. 15, Issue 16: 4; Asha Tomlinson, "Small Crimes, Big Problem," *Canadian HR Reporter*, September 9, 2002, Vol. 15, Issue 15: 1; and Graham Cunningham, "Take Steps to Curb Five-Finger Discounts," *Pharmacy Post*, August 2003, Vol. 11, Issue 8: 33.

Managers must be diligent when conducting employee searches. Improper searches can lead to employee complaints under various privacy legislations (see Chapter 2) and possible lawsuits claiming defamation of character and negligent infliction of emotional distress.

It is not uncommon for employers to monitor the conduct of employees through surveillance techniques. Employers can use electronic surveillance equipment providing photographic or video images. General Electric employs tiny fish-eye lenses installed behind pinholes in walls and ceilings to observe employees suspected of crimes. DuPont uses long-distance cameras to monitor its loading docks. One of the most common means of electronic surveillance by employers is telephone surveillance to ensure that customer requests are handled properly or to prevent theft. With the *Personal Information Protection and Electronic Documents Act (PIPEDA)*, there is an expectation that employers are reasonable in their use of any type of surveillance technique. It is suggested that in determining the reasonableness, an employer asks the following questions:[18]

1. Is the measure demonstrably necessary to meet a specific need?
2. Is it likely to be effective in meeting that need?
3. Is the loss of privacy proportional to the benefit gained?
4. Is there a less invasive way of achieving the same end?

PIPEDA also entitles employees to examine their own personnel file—including any information that is stored in an electronic format. Employers have the right to monitor employees, provided they do it for compelling business reasons and employees have been informed that their calls will be monitored.[19] Employees can sue for invasion of privacy, but courts have held that to win damages, an employee must show that the reasonable expectation of privacy outweighs the organization's reason for surveillance.[20] An investigation of computer misuse (downloading pornography) by Yukon government employees resulted in a number of disciplinary actions, including terminations. The case was decided in favour of

Video monitoring is frequently used in retail operations.

the government citing that it was more important to protect the rights of employees to work in an environment free from exposure to harassing material than the privacy of employees who had misused the computers.[21] Ethics in HRM 9.1 highlights some of these issues.

Access to Employee Files

The information kept in an employee's official employment record or employee file can have a significant impact—positive or negative—on career development. The personnel file, typically kept by the HR department, can contain performance reviews, salary information, investigatory reports, credit checks, criminal records, test scores, and family data.

In compliance with legislation, most employers give their employees access to their employment files. There is virtually no organization that is exempt from privacy legislation. In addition, any personal information cannot be used or disclosed without the prior knowledge and consent of the employee. For example, if you are seeking a car loan and the company wants confirmation of your employment, only you can authorize release of that information from your employer. The most important legal principle with regard to data privacy is the concept of consent—ahead of time from the employee. Under PIPEDA, the person must be notified of the following before any information can be provided:

- That he or she is about to provide personal data
- The purposes for which the information is to be processed
- The people or bodies to whom the information might be disclosed
- The proposed transfer of information to other countries
- The security measures protecting the information

For example, one organization collected information about the birth country of employees in order to facilitate international transfers. However, collecting this information for clerks, who will not be transferred, is unnecessary and would not meet the new standards.[22] Sources of information from selection interviews and employee assessments may have to be made available to employees.[23]

ethics **in HRM 9.1** ethics in HRM 9.1

WHEN DOES EMPLOYEE MONITORING BECOME AN INVASION OF PRIVACY?

More and more employers are using a variety of electronic surveillance techniques to observe employees in the workplace. Several experts believe that this is increasing stress in the workplace for many people. The prevalence is high in both Canada and the U.S., where over 45% of employers indicated that some type of monitoring was used. Further, vendors in the "spying" business report a tremendous increase in sales. Many employers do this to reduce the recreational use of computers. But when does this become an invasion of one's privacy?

In late 2004, the federal privacy commissioner had some harsh words about companies that use Web cameras to monitor employee actions. The case arose when a former employee of an Internet-service provider complained that personal privacy had been breached when cameras were installed in 2003 to monitor performance. Representatives of the company stated that the cameras were necessary to (1) ensure the safety and security of staff, and (2) to monitor the productivity of employees.

In assessing the statements of the company, the commissioner did not accept the safety and security defence as the cameras were only located at interior work areas and not at employee entrances. With respect to the issue of employee productivity, it was determined that the company used any number of methods to assess performance, such as supervised telephone calls, monitored e-mail, and performance reviews. The commissioner also identified that the company was reluctant to have additional supervisory functions performed and wanted to rely upon the cameras when management was not present.

The commissioner ruled that the cameras were intrusive to all employees, particularly under the new PIPEDA legislation, and appeared to be intended to deal with a few troublesome employees.

Would you work differently if you knew that your performance was continually monitored? Is it ethical for employers to do this?

Sources: Adapted from Patricia MacInnis, "Don't Count on Privacy When You're at Work," *Computing Canada*, June 8, 1998, Vol. 24, Issue 22: 29; Joaquim Menezes, "More Employers Spying on Workers," *Computer Dealer News*, July 9, 1999, Vol. 15, Issue 27: 52; Lorna Harris, "Employee Video Surveillance Challenged Under New Privacy Law," *Canadian HR Reporter*, August 9, 2004, Vol. 17, Issue 14: 5; and "Privacy Commissioner Blasts Video Surveillance of Employees," *Canadian Employment Law Today*, November 10, 2004, Issue 425: 3325.

Because privacy law obliges organizations to obtain consent from the individual whose personal information is being gathered, professionals recommend that organizations develop a policy on employee files that includes, as a minimum, the points noted in Manager's Toolkit 9.1.[24]

Electronic Privacy

The benefits of e-mail and voice mail are many: they encourage openness and sharing of information; they diffuse power throughout the organization; and they allow more employees to participate in decision making.[25] Unfortunately, the growth of management and financial information systems can create privacy problems by making personnel information more accessible to those with prying eyes, or "hackers," who might use the information inappropriately. Messages can be read or heard, and deleted messages can be

Manager's Toolkit **9.1** Manager's Toolkit 9.1

POLICY GUIDELINES ON HANDLING PERSONNEL FILES

- Ensure compliance with legislation.

- Define exactly what information is to be kept in employee files.

- Ensure informed consent has been received from employees regarding types of information that will be collected and stored.

- Develop different categories of personnel information, depending on legal requirements and organizational needs.

- Specify where, when, how, and under what circumstances employees may review or copy their files.

- Ensure appropriate security measures are in place to safeguard information.

- Identify company individuals allowed to view personnel files.

- Prohibit the collection of information that could be viewed as discriminatory or could form the basis for an invasion-of-privacy suit.

- Audit employment records on a regular basis to remove irrelevant, outdated, or inaccurate information.

retrieved. Further, there is no way to verify that the "from" is really from the person listed.[26] Moreover, messages can be forwarded, replicated, and printed with ease. In addition, e-mail that exposes employees to inappropriate materials by co-workers can make for a hostile work environment, which creates a liability for organizations under human rights legislation.[27] A recent decision by the B.C. Supreme Court upheld the employer's right to dismiss someone for using e-mail to send disrespectful and untrue statements about the company president.[28]

Technology creates the need for a critical balance between employee privacy and the employer's need to know. Although employees may assume that their right to privacy extends to e-mail and voice-mail messages, it does not. The Freedom of Information and Protection of Privacy Act (federal legislation) applies only to records in the custody or control of public bodies, such as a Crown corporation, a school board, or a government ministry. This act does not apply to the employment relationship in many organizations. This means employers have the right to monitor materials created, received, or sent for business-related reasons.[29] Employers are strongly encouraged to develop clear policies and guidelines that explain to employees how any form of electronic communication is to be used, including when and under what conditions employees can be monitored (see Manager's Toolkit 9.2).[30] In addition, employees should be reminded of their responsibilities under the company's policy every time they log on to the company's computer system. More and more decisions by courts and arbitrators are re-affirming the organization's right to monitor e-mail or any other electronic transmission on the company-owned computers. This is also true for a company that monitors the Internet use of its employees. For example, if an employee subjects co-workers to inappropriate materials from a Web site (such as racial jokes or graphic sexual pictures), the employer has an obligation to protect the co-workers.[31]

Therefore, it is important for managers and supervisors, as well as employees, to understand that employers have the right to monitor any and all electronic transmissions at work. Where e-mail and voice-mail policies do exist, employees should be required to sign a form indicating that they have read and understand the policy. In most cases, courts will find disciplining an employee for Internet abuse to be a reasonable action.[32]

Employees often assume that they have a right to privacy on the company's telephone.

Employee Conduct outside the Workplace

Consider the following case. On Monday morning the owner of ABC Corporation reads in the newspaper that a company employee has been charged with robbery and assault on a local convenience store owner. The employee has been released pending trial. A phone call to the employee's supervisor reveals that the employee has reported to work. What should the owner do?

New technologies enable employers to monitor staff very closely, even on their personal time. While most courts uphold the right of the employer to monitor employees at the workplace, particularly if there is a justifiable reason to collect evidence, the monitoring of employees outside the workplace is more complex. For example, recent court cases have suggested that videotaping an employee inside his home is an unreasonable invasion of privacy. Videotaping in a public place was found reasonable in other cases. An employee of the City of Toronto who worked as an arborist claimed to have injured himself at work and yet was videotaped cutting and removing branches from trees while off duty, work that he claimed he could not do.[33] Another company hired a private investigator to follow a travelling sales representative and fired her for stealing company time and money because she was using a company car to pick up her husband and drive him to work when she was supposed to be

Manager's Toolkit **9.2** Manager's Toolkit 9.2

E-MAIL, INTERNET, AND VOICE-MAIL POLICY GUIDELINES

- Ensure compliance with any federal and provincial legislation.

- Specify that anything sent through the company's computer systems is the property of the employer, including any files and documents.

- Expressly prohibit accessing certain Internet sites, including storage of certain types of materials or posting on electronic bulletin boards.

- Expressly prohibit use of pirated software or any other potential copyright violations.

- Specify who has access and how it is acquired.

- Specify the circumstances, if any, under which the system can be used for personal use.

- Specify that confidential information is not to be sent electronically.

- Inform employees that the employer reserves the right to monitor and that employees must agree to the monitoring.

- Specify that electronic information be sent only to users who need it for business purposes.

- Prohibit use of any electronic means to harass others or send any inappropriate content to anyone.

- Advise employees that e-mail and computer use is not private and therefore may be reviewed by others.

- Specify that employees who violate the policy are subject to discipline, including dismissal.

Source: Adapted from materials presented at workshop sponsored by Fasken Martineau, February 22, 2002; and Stuart Rudner, "The High Cost of Internet, E-mail Abuse," *Canadian HR Reporter: Report on Employment Law*, January 31, 2005: R5.

visiting clients. Recently, a company fired its president after it discovered the reason for his absences during the day were fitness sessions at the gym.[34] Organizations that want to discipline employees for off-duty misconduct must establish a clear relationship between the misconduct and its negative effect on other employees or the organization. This might be established, for example, in cases where off-duty criminal misconduct (e.g., child molestation) creates a disruptive impact on the workplace. Another example might be where the public nature of the employee's job (e.g., police or fire department personnel) creates an image problem for the organization. Generally, however, an employer is encouraged to use caution when attempting to connect off-duty behaviour with discipline at work.[35]

In a recent case, searches were conducted of the home computers of flight attendants with Northwest Airlines. The company was looking for evidence that these employees had organized co-workers to call in sick for work. Critics have expressed concern, stating that searching a person's private home computer constitutes an invasion of privacy.[36]

Further legal resources on the topics discussed in this chapter can be found on the Web site of Canada Law Book (**www.canadalawbook.com**).

Canada Law Book
www.canadalawbook.com

With the Internet increasingly becoming a place where people's movements are tracked, logged, and bought and sold, a Montreal-based company, Zero-Knowledge Systems Inc., has launched a product that will prevent unauthorized users from tracking your usage.

DISCIPLINARY POLICIES AND PROCEDURES

Objective 3

The rights of managers to discipline and discharge employees are increasingly limited. There is thus a great need for managers at all levels to understand discipline procedures. Disciplinary action taken against an employee must be for justifiable reasons, and there must be effective policies and procedures to govern its use. Such policies and procedures serve to assist those responsible for taking disciplinary action and help to ensure that employees receive fair and constructive treatment. Equally important, these guidelines help to prevent disciplinary action from being voided or from being reversed through the appeal system.

If an organization has an HR department, it will have a major responsibility in developing the disciplinary policies and procedures. While the HR department will get top-management approval, it is also critical that supervisors and managers be involved in the development of the policies and procedures. It will be the supervisors and managers who carry out the policies, and therefore any of their experiences can contribute to more effective coordination and consistency in the use of disciplinary action throughout the organization. As part of the manager–HR partnership, the HR department will work with the manager to ensure that any actions taken against employees are consistent with any collective agreements and conform to current law.

The primary responsibility for preventing or correcting disciplinary problems rests with an employee's immediate supervisor. This person is best able to observe evidence of unsatisfactory behaviour or performance and to discuss the matter with the employee. Discussion is frequently all that is needed to correct the problem, and disciplinary action becomes

Office Depot Business Tools

www.officedepot.com/

CCH Business Owners' Toolkit

www.toolkit.cch.com/tools/ coach_m.asp

unnecessary. However, when disciplinary action is needed, the supervisor should strive to use a problem-solving attitude. Causes underlying the problem are as important as the problem itself, and any attempt to prevent recurrence will require an understanding of them.

Admittedly, it is often difficult for supervisors to maintain an objective attitude toward employee infractions. But if supervisors can maintain a problem-solving stance, they are likely to come up with a diagnosis that is nearer the truth than would be possible were they to use the approach of a trial lawyer. For example, if an employee is late for work several days in a row, the supervisor needs to discuss the situation with the employee and try to determine the reasons for the lateness. The supervisor needs to remember that the objective is to get the employee to get to work on time—not to discipline the individual for being late. Therefore, by attempting to find out the reasons for the lateness, the supervisor is in a better position to work with the employee to find an acceptable solution. For additional resources in disciplining employees, see Office Depot (**www.officedepot.com**; access the link Business Tools and then link to Small Business Handbook) and CCH Business Owners' Toolkit (**www.toolkit.cch.com/tools/coach_m.asp**).

Setting Organizational Rules

Clearly stating expectations of performance and behaviour is the foundation for an effective disciplinary system. These expectations govern the type of behaviour expected of employees. Since employee behaviour standards are established through the setting and communicating of organizational procedures and rules, the following suggestions may help reduce problems in this area:

1. Information about rules should be widely distributed and known to all employees. It should not be assumed that employees know what is expected of them.
2. Rules should be reviewed periodically—perhaps annually—especially those critical to work success.
3. The reasons for rules concerning performance and behaviour should always be explained. Acceptance is greater when employees understand the reasons behind rules.
4. Organization policies and rules should always be written. Ambiguity should be avoided, since this can result in different interpretations by different supervisors.
5. Rules must be reasonable and relate to the safe and efficient operation of the organization. These should not be made simply because of personal likes or dislikes.
6. If management has been lax in the enforcement of a policy or rule, it must be restated, along with the consequences for its violation, before disciplinary action can begin.
7. Have employees sign that they have read and understand the organizational rules regarding their behaviour and performance in that organization.

When seeking reasons for unsatisfactory performance, supervisors must keep in mind that employees may not be aware of certain expectations. Before initiating any disciplinary action, therefore, it is essential that supervisors determine whether they have given their employees careful and thorough orientation in what is expected of them in relation to their jobs. In fact, the proper communication of organizational expectations and policy is so important that labour arbitrators cite neglect in communicating workplace expectations and having clear policies as major reasons for reversing the disciplinary action taken against an employee.[37]

Defining Discipline

Objective

Discipline
1. Treatment that punishes;
2. Orderly behaviour in an organizational setting; or
3. Training that moulds and strengthens desirable conduct—or corrects undesirable. conduct—and develops self-control

In dictionaries, **discipline** normally has three meanings:

1. Treatment that punishes
2. Orderly behaviour in an organizational setting
3. Training that moulds and strengthens desirable conduct—or corrects undesirable conduct—and develops self-control

To some managers, discipline is synonymous with force. They equate the term with the punishment of employees who violate rules or regulations. Other managers think of discipline as a general state of affairs—a condition of orderliness where employees conduct themselves according to standards of acceptable behaviour. Discipline viewed in this manner can be considered positive when employees willingly practise self-control and respect organizational values and expectations.

The third definition considers discipline a management tool used to correct undesirable employee performance or behaviour. Discipline is applied as a constructive means of getting employees to conform to acceptable standards of behaviour and performance. Figure 9.2 provides examples of common disciplinary problems.

Many organizations, such as Goodyear Aerospace, define the term "discipline" in their policy manuals as training that "corrects, moulds, or perfects knowledge, attitudes, behavior, or conduct." Discipline is thus viewed as a way to correct poor employee performance rather than simply as punishment for an offence. As these organizations emphasize, discipline should be seen as a method of training employees to perform better or to improve their job attitudes or work behaviour. It is also interesting to note that the word "discipline" is derived from the word "disciple," which means follower or pupil. At least one group of researchers believes that the implication here is that good discipline is based on good supervisory leadership.[38] Figure 9.3 shows one disciplinary model, which consists of several steps that must be carried out to ensure that the termination is justifiable.

FIGURE 9.2 Common Disciplinary Problems

Attendance Problems

- Unexcused absence
- Chronic absenteeism
- Unexcused or excessive tardiness
- Leaving without permission

Dishonesty and Related Problems

- Theft
- Falsifying employment application
- Willfully damaging organizational property
- Punching another employee's time card
- Falsifying work records

Work Performance Problems

- Failure to complete work assignments
- Producing substandard products or services
- Failure to meet established production requirements

On-the-Job Behaviour Problems

- Intoxication at work
- Insubordination
- Horseplay
- Smoking in unauthorized places
- Fighting
- Gambling
- Failure to use safety devices
- Failure to report injuries
- Carelessness
- Sleeping on the job
- Using abusive or threatening language with supervisors
- Possession of narcotics or alcohol
- Possession of firearms or other weapons
- All forms of harassment, such as sexual innuendo or actions, teasing, racial slurs, inappropriate jokes, and bullying

---

FIGURE 9.3 A Disciplinary Model

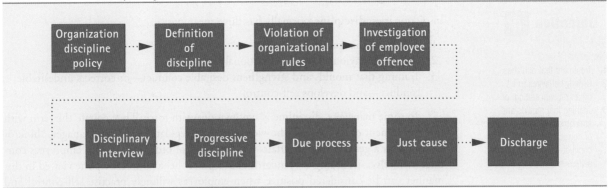

Investigating the Disciplinary Problem

It's a rare manager who has a good, intuitive sense of how to investigate employee misconduct. Too frequently, investigations are conducted in a haphazard manner; worse, they overlook one or more investigative concerns. In conducting an employee investigation, it is important to be objective and to avoid the assumptions, suppositions, and biases that often surround discipline cases. Manager's Toolkit 9.3 lists seven questions to consider in investigating an employee offence. Attending to each question will help ensure a full and fair investigation while providing reliable information free from personal prejudice.

When preparing documentation, it is important for a manager to record the incident immediately after the infraction takes place, when the memory of it is still fresh, and to ensure that the record is complete and accurate. Remember, a manager's records of employee misconduct are considered business documents, and as such they are admissible as evidence in arbitration hearings, administrative proceedings, and courts of law.[39]

The Investigative Interview

Before any disciplinary action is initiated, an investigative interview should be conducted to make sure employees are fully aware of the offence. This interview is necessary because the supervisor's perceptions of the employee's behaviour may not be entirely accurate. The interview should concentrate on how the offence violated the performance standards of the job. It should avoid getting into personalities or areas unrelated to job performance. Most important, the employee must be given a full opportunity to explain so that any deficiencies for which the organization may be responsible are revealed.

Approaches to Disciplinary Action

Objective 5

When taken against employees, disciplinary action should never be thought of as punishment. Discipline can embody a penalty as a means of obtaining a desired result; however, punishment should not be the intent of disciplinary action. Rather, discipline must have as its goal the improvement of the employee's future behaviour. To apply discipline in any other way—as punishment or as a way of getting even with employees—can only invite problems for management, including possible wrongful-dismissal suits. If a thorough

Manager's Toolkit **9.3** Manager's Toolkit 9.3

CONSIDERATIONS IN DISCIPLINARY INVESTIGATIONS

1. In very specific terms, what is the offence charged?

   - Is management sure it fully understands the charge against the employee?
   - Was the employee really terminated for insubordination, or did the employee merely refuse a request by management?

2. Did the employee know he or she was doing something wrong?

   - What rule or provision was violated?
   - How would the employee know of the existence of the rule?
   - Was the employee warned of the consequence?

3. Is the employee guilty?

   - What are the sources of facts?
   - Is there direct or only indirect evidence of guilt?
   - Has anyone talked to the employee to hear his or her side of the situation?

4. Are there extenuating circumstances?

   - Were conflicting orders given by different supervisors?
   - Does anybody have reason to want to "get" this employee?

   - Was the employee provoked by a manager or another employee?

5. Has the rule been uniformly enforced?

   - Have all managers applied the rule consistently?
   - What punishment have previous offenders received?
   - Were any other employees involved in this offence?

6. Is the offence related to the workplace?

   - Is there evidence that the offence hurt the organization?
   - Is management making a moral judgment or a business judgment?

7. What is the employee's past work record?

   - How many years of service has the employee given the organization?
   - How many years or months has the employee held the current job?
   - What is the employee's personnel record as a whole, especially his or her disciplinary record?

investigation shows that an employee has violated some organization rule, disciplinary action must be imposed. Two approaches to disciplinary action are progressive discipline and positive discipline.

Progressive Discipline

Progressive discipline
Application of corrective measures by increasing degrees

Generally, discipline is imposed in a progressive manner. By definition, **progressive discipline** is the application of corrective measures by increasing degrees. Progressive discipline is designed to motivate employees to correct their misconduct voluntarily. The technique is aimed at correcting unacceptable behaviour as soon as it starts, using only enough corrective action to remedy the shortcoming. However, the sequence and severity of the disciplinary action vary with the type of offence and the circumstances surrounding it. Since each situation is unique, a number of factors must be considered in determining how severe a disciplinary action should be. Some of the factors to consider were listed in Manager's Toolkit 9.3.

at work **with HRM 9.3** at work with HRM 9.3

CORRECTIVE DISCIPLINE APPROACHES

A number of organizations have readily available guidelines aimed at changing unwanted employee behaviour. Before discipline begins, it is expected that the supervisor can show that the employee is aware of desired behaviour and that he or she is choosing to act otherwise. Frequently all that is needed is to let employees know that a particular behaviour is not appropriate. Employees usually react positively to this. It definitely is not used as a way of punishing an employee. Typical steps in a discipline process are the following:

Step 1: Oral or verbal warning. This is a private discussion between the employee and the supervisor that takes place immediately after the incident. The supervisor describes the incident and ensures that all sides of the story are heard. Human Resources Development Canada's verbal warning step also states that the supervisor needs to be very clear on outlining the consequences if expectations are not met.

Step 2: Written warning. If the employee's behaviour continues, a meeting is held with the supervisor and the employee. At the meeting the supervisor describes the events, reviews expectations as discussed in Step 1, seeks solutions from the employee, and indicates what will happen if unacceptable behaviour continues. The meeting is summarized in writing and placed in the employee's personnel file. In the Canadian Media Guild's guidelines, a copy of the written document is also provided to the employee.

Step 3: Suspension. If the inappropriate behaviour continues, the supervisor will next consider suspension. A meeting is held, similar to the meeting in Step 2. At the conclusion of the meeting, a suspension may be imposed with a length that is linked to the nature of the problem. It can be for one day or for several days. A letter of suspension is written and placed in the employee's file.

Step 4: Dismissal. This is a very serious step and is taken only when all other options have been exhausted. Again, a meeting is held to review facts and expectations and to summarize previous meetings and actions. Even at this meeting it is important to provide an opportunity for the employee to explain. At the end of the meeting, a letter of dismissal is presented, which is also placed in the employee's file with a copy given to the employee.

CRITICAL THINKING QUESTION

Are there any other steps that ought to be taken in corrective discipline? Describe and explain.

Sources: Adapted from "Progressive Discipline," http://info.load-otea.hrdc-drhc.gc.ca/publications/labour_standards/progressive.shtml (retrieved November 13, 2002); "Discipline and Discharge," Canadian Media Guild, http://www.cmg.ca/disciplineanddischarge.htm (retrieved November 17, 2002); and "Code of Conduct," BC Hydro, November 2002.

The typical progressive discipline procedure includes four steps. From an oral warning (or counselling) that subsequent unsatisfactory behaviour or performance will not be tolerated, the action may progress to a written warning, to a suspension without pay, and ultimately to dismissal.[40]

The corrective discipline used by several organizations is described in At Work with HRM 9.3. The "capital punishment" of discharge is utilized only as a last resort. Organizations normally use lower forms of disciplinary action for less severe performance problems. It is important for managers to remember that three important things occur when progressive discipline is applied properly:

1. Employees always know where they stand regarding offences.
2. Employees know what improvement is expected of them.
3. Employees understand what will happen next if improvement is not made.

Positive Discipline

Although progressive discipline is the most popular approach to correcting employee misconduct, recently some managers have questioned its logic. They have noted that it has certain flaws, including its intimidating and adversarial nature, which prevent it from achieving the intended purpose. For these reasons, some organizations are using an approach called **positive**, or **nonpunitive, discipline**. Positive discipline is based on the concept that employees must assume responsibility for their personal conduct and job performance.[41]

Positive discipline requires a cooperative environment in which the employee and supervisor engage in joint discussion and problem solving to resolve incidents of employee irresponsibility. The approach focuses on the early correction of misconduct, with the employee taking total responsibility for resolving the problem. Management imposes nothing; all solutions and affirmations are jointly reached. While positive discipline appears similar to progressive discipline, its emphasis is on giving employees reminders rather than reprimands as a way to improve performance. Figure 9.4 illustrates the procedure for implementing the three-step positive discipline procedure.

> **Positive, or nonpunitive, discipline**
> System of discipline that focuses on the early correction of employee misconduct, with the employee taking total responsibility for correcting the problem

Compiling a Disciplinary Record

In applying either progressive or positive discipline, it is important for managers to maintain complete records of each step of the procedure. When employees fail to meet the obligation of a disciplinary step, they should be given a warning, and their manager should document the warning. A copy of this warning is usually placed in the employee's personnel file. After an established period—frequently six months—the warning is usually removed, provided that it has served its purpose. Otherwise it remains in the file to serve as evidence should a more severe penalty become necessary later.

An employee's personnel file contains the employee's complete work history. It serves as a basis for determining and supporting disciplinary action and for evaluating the organization's disciplinary policies and procedures. Maintenance of proper records also provides management with valuable information about the soundness of its rules and regulations. Those rules that are violated most frequently should receive particular attention, because the need for them may no longer exist or some change might be

FIGURE 9.4   Positive Discipline Procedure

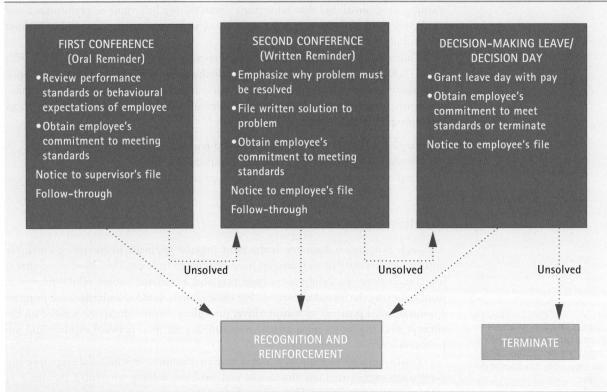

required to facilitate their enforcement. If the rule is shown to have little or no value, it should be revised or rescinded. Otherwise employees are likely to feel they are being restricted unnecessarily.

Documentation of Employee Misconduct

"It's too complicated." "I just didn't take time to do it." "I have more important things to do." These are some of the frequent excuses used by managers who have failed to document cases of employee misconduct. The most significant cause of inadequate documentation, however, is that managers have no idea what constitutes good documentation. Unfortunately, the failure of managers to record employee misconduct accurately can result in the reversal of any subsequent disciplinary action. Written records are key in discipline.[42] For documentation to be complete, the following eight items should be included:

1. Date, time, and location of the incident(s)
2. Negative performance or behaviour exhibited by the employee—the problem
3. Consequences of that action or behaviour on the employee's overall work performance and/or the operation of the employee's work unit
4. Prior discussion(s) with the employee about the problem
5. Disciplinary action to be taken and specific improvement expected

The final stage of discipline is termination.

About Human Resources
http://humanresources
.about.com

6. Consequences if improvement is not made, and a follow-up date
7. The employee's reaction to the supervisor's attempt to change behaviour
8. The names of witnesses to the incident (if appropriate)

It is critical that managers at all levels understand the guidelines for appropriate discipline. For additional resources on discipline, do a search on "discipline" at **http://humanresources.about.com**.

Grounds for Dismissal

No matter how helpful and positive a supervisor is with an employee who is not abiding by the organization's policies and rules, there may come a time when the employee must be dismissed. Since dismissal has such serious consequences for the employee—and possibly for the organization—it should be undertaken only after a deliberate and thoughtful review of the case.

Wrongful Dismissal

When an employer dismisses or terminates an employee for not performing as expected or not following the company's rules, this is called dismissal for "just cause." To do this, the employer must document and prove serious misconduct or incompetence on the part of the employee. In recent years, a growing number of employees have sued their former employers for "**wrongful dismissal**," claiming the termination was "without just or sufficient cause," implying a lack of fair treatment by management or insufficient reasons for the termination. Termination for cause also expects that the employee could to something different and had been informed of this prior to termination. This means that a termination resulting from a job redefinition/redesign, downsizing, restructuring, or lack of organizational fit is not just cause. However, poor performance, poor interpersonal relationships, and technical incompetence might be just cause if the employee had been informed of expectations and had been given a chance to improve but failed to conform. Figure 9.5 lists some "just-cause" reasons.

Many managers are faced with having to terminate someone when there are sufficient and legitimate grounds for doing so. Some companies may suggest that just cause includes the organization's financial difficulties. It is important for managers and supervisors to know that the economic hardship of the company is not a justifiable reason to terminate someone's employment. One comprehensive study of wrongful-dismissal suits found that employers won 40% of the time when the charge was dishonesty, theft, substance abuse, or abusive behaviour; 54% of the time when the charge was insubordination; 65% of the time when the charge was conflict of interest or competing with the employer; and just 25% of the time when the charge was poor performance.[43] HRM and the Law 9.1 gives two examples of unsuccessful wrongful dismissal cases. For additional information on wrongful dismissals, see **www.duhaime.org**.

Managers must be able to document that any performance problems have been brought to the attention of the employee and that sufficient time, training, and assistance have been given to improve the weak performance. If the organization has an HR professional, the line manager needs to work closely with the HR person to ensure that the appropriate type of documentation occurs. Other tips to prevent a challenge by a terminated employee are discussed later in the chapter.

If an employee termination is to be upheld for good cause, what constitutes fair employee treatment and valid reasons? This question is not easily answered, but standards governing just-cause dismissal have evolved from the field of labour arbitration. These standards are applied by arbitrators in dismissal cases to determine if management had just cause for the termination. These guidelines are normally set

Wrongful dismissal
Terminating an employee's employment without just cause

Duhaime Law
www.duhaime.org

FIGURE 9.5 Sample "Just-Cause" Reasons

- Excessive lateness or absenteeism
- Theft from the company
- Improper or wrong conduct, such as fighting with a co-worker

Depending on the seriousness of the wrongdoing, the individual may be terminated immediately, bypassing the steps of progressive discipline. For example, a hotel concierge who makes threatening statements to a guest could be terminated right away.

HRM and **the law 9.1** HRM and the law 9.1

EMPLOYERS DID NOT HAVE CAUSE TO TERMINATE

A recent Ontario Supreme Court decision dealt with an employee who was terminated after being with the employer for over 14 years. The employer stated that the employee had been absent for over 13 months due to an illness and that the employment relationship had become frustrated. The employee sued for wrongful dismissal. The court ruled in favour of the employee, saying that the employment relationship was not frustrated and awarded the employee 15 months' compensation. Further, the employer sought to have any compensation reduced by the amount of disability payment received by the employee. Again, the court ruled in favour of the employee by indicating that disability payments are simply insurance payments and therefore have nothing to do with the claim for wrongful dismissal.

In another case, the judge was quite harsh toward an investment firm that terminated its chief financial officer. The reasons given by the company, through the testimony of the president, was that the person was terminated because he was not carrying out his duties properly. This occurred after another person was hired as chief financial officer. The president testified that the terminated employee knew that another person was hired and that the two of them were to co-manage the corporate finance group. However, the company could not produce evidence to support the claim. Further, during the case, the judge determined that the president had also been untruthful in describing the performance of the terminated employee and had attempted to deceive the court through testimony. The judge ruled in favour of the terminated employee. The decision cost the company $4 million!

How would you have ruled?

Source: Adapted from "Research Capital CEO Blasted, Loses Wrongful Dismissal Case," by Paul Waldie, *The Globe and Mail*, November 29, 2002: B1, 14; "Deception Costs Big for Research Capital," by Andrew Willis, *The Globe and Mail*, November 29, 2002: B16; and "Claims for Wrongful Dismissal," by Norman Grosman, *workopolis.com*, April 4, 2002 (retrieved May 10, 2002).

forth in the form of questions, provided in the Manager's Toolkit 9.4. For example, before dismissing an employee, did the manager warn the person of possible disciplinary action in the past? A "no" answer to any of the seven questions generally means that just cause was not established and that management's decision to terminate was arbitrary, capricious, or discriminatory. These guidelines are being applied not only by arbitrators in dismissal cases but also by judges in wrongful-dismissal suits.

Constructive Dismissal

Constructive dismissal
Changing an employee's working conditions such that compensation, status, or prestige is reduced

Another type of dismissal is constructive. **Constructive dismissal** occurs when an employer changes an employee's working conditions such that compensation, status, or prestige is reduced. Even if the employee agrees to the changed conditions (the only other option might be unemployment) or resigns, the court considers the employee to have been dismissed.[44]

Manager's Toolkit 9.4 Manager's Toolkit 9.4

"JUST-CAUSE" DISMISSAL GUIDELINES

1. Did the organization forewarn the employee of the possible disciplinary consequences of his or her action?

2. Were management's requirements of the employee reasonable in relation to the orderly, efficient, and safe operation of the organization's business?

3. Did management, before changing the working conditions or discharging the employee, make a reasonable effort to establish that the employee's performance was unsatisfactory?

4. Was the organization's investigation conducted in a fair and objective manner?

5. Did the investigation produce sufficient evidence or proof of guilt as charged?

6. Has management treated this employee under its rules, orders, and penalties as it has other employees in similar circumstances?

7. Did the discharge fit the misconduct, considering the seriousness of the proven offence, the employee's service record, and any mitigating circumstances?

Two cases illustrate the concept. One involved a Royal Trust Co. regional manager, earning about $150,000 in base salary and commissions; his job was eliminated. He was offered the position of branch manager at the company's least profitable branch, where his income would have been based solely on commissions (he had held a similar position about four promotions earlier). The court ruled that he had been constructively dismissed and awarded him damages and legal costs. In another case, Embassy Cleaners changed the working conditions of a presser, resulting in a more physically demanding job, an earlier start time, a change in the work week from five to six days, and a change from hourly wages to piecework. The court ruled that these changes constituted a fundamental break of contract and resulted in constructive dismissal.[45] To access the latest information on constructive dismissals, *The Wrongful Dismissal Handbook*, 2nd Edition (Butterworth) is a helpful resource.

In a nonunion setting, employers can give notice of future changes in compensation (wages and benefits), working hours, location, and other similar items so long as they provide actual notice equivalent to that given for dismissal. For example, if the company wished to reduce the amount of paid sick leave, they could do so with sufficient notice.

Dismissing Employees

Regardless of the reasons for a dismissal, it should be done with personal consideration for the employee affected. Every effort should be made to ease the trauma a dismissal creates. The employee must be informed honestly, yet tactfully, of the exact reasons for the action. Such candour can help the employee face the problem and adjust to it in a constructive manner.

Managers need to discuss, and even rehearse, with their peers the upcoming termination meeting. Given the recent concerns over the implications of the *Wallace* case, the manager should have a script prepared. This practice can ensure that all important points are covered while giving confidence to the manager. Although managers agree that there is no single right way to conduct the dismissal meeting, the following guidelines will help to make the discussion more effective:

1. Hold the meeting early in the week and in a neutral meeting place.
2. Come to the point within the first two or three minutes, and list in a logical order all reasons for the termination.
3. Be straightforward and firm, yet tactful, and remain resolute in the decision; avoid debating reasons and decisions.
4. Make the discussion private, businesslike, and fairly brief; makes notes of the meeting.
5. Avoid making accusations against the employee and injecting personal feelings into the discussion; be courteous and respectful at all times.
6. Avoid bringing up any personality differences.
7. Provide any information concerning severance pay and the status of benefits and coverage.
8. Explain how employment inquiries from future employers will be handled.
9. Arrange a mutually agreed upon time for the employee to clear out personal belongings and for the return of any company property.
10. Have another manager present as a witness.

Termination meetings should be held in a neutral location, such as a conference room, so that the manager can leave if the meeting gets out of control. The prudent manager will also have determined, prior to the termination decision, that the dismissal does not violate any legal rights the employee may have.

Finally, when terminated employees are escorted off the premises, the removal must not serve to defame the employee. Managers should not give peers the impression that the terminated employee was dishonest or untrustworthy. Increasingly, terminated employees are pursuing lawsuits that go beyond the issue of whether their dismissal was for business-related reasons.[46]

Providing Career Transition Assistance

Employers often use career transition or outplacement agencies to assist employees who are being dismissed. This assistance is especially likely to be provided for managers of long tenure. Sometimes it is also provided for employees being laid off as a result of organizational right-sizing or restructuring, or because they don't fit a changed corporate identity.[47] These agencies not only provide job search technique help but also emotional support. While terminations do not have the negative stigma they once did, they are still traumatic for the employee.

Managers cite the following reasons for providing outplacement services: concern for the well-being of the employees, protection against potential lawsuits, and the psychological effect on remaining employees. Outplacement consultants assist employees being terminated by reducing their anger and grief and helping them regain self-confidence as they begin searching in earnest for a new job. Since many terminated workers have been out of the job market for some time, they may lack the knowledge and skills needed to look for a new job. Outplacement specialists can coach them in how to develop contacts, probe for job openings through systematic letter and telephone campaigns, and handle employment interviews and salary negotiations.

Job-site learning joins the electronic age. Nova Scotia's virtual apprenticeship program is a case in point: it allows those wanting to learn a certified trade to complete the classroom portions of their training via the Internet.

The Results of Inaction

Failure to act implies that the performance or behaviour of the employee concerned is acceptable. If disciplinary action is eventually taken, the delay will make it more difficult to justify the action if appealed. In defending against such an appeal, the employer is likely to be asked why an employee who had not been performing or behaving satisfactorily was kept on the payroll. Or an even more probing question might be "Why did that employee continue to receive pay adjustments if there was a question about the performance?"

Such contradictions in practice can only aid employees in successfully challenging management's corrective actions. Unfortunately, some supervisors try to build a case to justify their corrective actions only after they have decided that a particular employee should be dismissed. The following are common reasons given by supervisors for their failure to impose a disciplinary penalty:

1. The supervisor had failed to document earlier actions, so no record existed on which to base subsequent disciplinary action.
2. Supervisors believed they would receive little or no support from higher management for the disciplinary action.
3. The supervisor was uncertain of the facts underlying the situation requiring disciplinary action.
4. Failure by the supervisor to discipline employees in the past for a certain infraction caused the supervisor to forgo current disciplinary action in order to appear consistent.
5. The supervisor wanted to be seen as a likable person.

It is critical to remember that any grounds for discipline must be well-documented. Failure to do so can result in the disciplinary action being invalid.

APPEALING DISCIPLINARY ACTIONS

With growing frequency, organizations are taking steps to protect employees from arbitrary and inequitable treatment by their supervisors. A particular emphasis is placed on creating a climate in which employees are assured that they can voice their dissatisfaction with their superiors without fear of reprisal. This safeguard can be provided through the implementation of a formal procedure for appealing disciplinary actions.

Alternative Dispute-Resolution Procedures

Objective

Alternative dispute resolution (ADR)
Term applied to different types of
employee complaint or dispute-
resolution procedures

Arbitration and Mediation
Institute of Canada
www.amic.org

Mediation
The use of an impartial third party
to help facilitate a resolution to
employment disputes

Step-review system
System for reviewing employee
complaints and disputes by
successively higher levels
of management

In unionized workplaces, grievance procedures are stated in virtually all collective agreements. In nonunion organizations, however, **alternative dispute resolution (ADR)** processes are increasingly being used to keep employers out of court.[48] The employer's interest stems from the desire to meet employees' expectations for fair treatment in the workplace while guaranteeing them due process—in the hope of minimizing discrimination claims or wrongful-dismissal suits.

Some organizations prefer these procedures as an avenue for upward communication for employees and as a way to gauge the mood of the workforce. Others view these systems as a way to resolve minor problems before they mushroom into major issues, thus leading to improved employee morale and productivity.

The appeal procedures described in this chapter are mediation, the step-review system, the use of a hearing officer, the open-door policy, the use of an ombudsperson, and arbitration. A helpful resource for additional information on ADR can be found at **www.amic.org**.

Mediation

Mediation is fast becoming a popular way to resolve employee complaints and is discussed in detail in Chapter 11. The essence of mediation is facilitating face-to-face meetings so that the employee and manager can reach an agreement. Mediation is a flexible process that can be shaped to meet the demands of the parties.[49] Also, it can be used to resolve a wide range of employee complaints, including discrimination claims or traditional workplace disputes.[50] Employees like the process because of its informality. According to one authority, "Mediation might be described as a private discussion assisted by an impartial third party."[51] Settlements fashioned through mediation are readily accepted by the parties, thus promoting a favourable working relationship.

Step-Review Systems

As Figure 9.6 illustrates, a **step-review system** is based on a pre-established set of steps—normally four—for the review of an employee complaint by successively higher levels of management. These procedures are patterned after the union grievance systems, which will be discussed in Chapter 11. For example, they normally require that the employee's complaint be formalized as a written statement. Managers at each step are required to provide a full response to the complaint within a specified time period, perhaps three to five working days.

FIGURE 9.6 Step-Review Appeal Procedure

Use of a Hearing Officer

Hearing officer
Person who holds a full-time position with an organization but assumes a neutral role when deciding cases between management and the aggrieved employees

This procedure is ordinarily confined to large organizations, where unions may represent employees. The **hearing officer** holds a full-time position with the organization but assumes a neutral role when deciding cases between an aggrieved employee and management. Hearing officers are employed by the organization; however, they function independently from other managers and occupy a special place in the organizational hierarchy. Their success rests on being perceived as neutral, highly competent, and completely unbiased in handling employee complaints. They hear cases upon request, almost always made by the employee. After considering the evidence and facts presented, they render decisions or awards that are normally final and binding on both sides.

Open-Door Policy

Open-door policy
Policy of settling grievances that identifies various levels of management above the immediate supervisor for employee contact

The open-door policy is an old standby for settling employee complaints. In fact, most managers, regardless of whether their organization has adopted a formal open-door policy, profess to maintain one for their employees. The traditional **open-door policy** identifies various levels of management above the immediate supervisor that an aggrieved employee may contact; the levels may extend as high as a vice-president, president, or chief executive officer. Typically, the person who acts as "the court of last resort" is the HR director or a senior staff official.

Ombudsperson System

Ombudsperson
Designated individual from whom employees may seek counsel for the resolution of their complaints

An **ombudsperson** is a designated individual from whom employees may seek counsel for the resolution of their complaints. The ombudsperson listens to an employee's complaint and attempts to resolve it by mediating a solution between the employee and the supervisor. This individual works cooperatively with both sides to reach a settlement, often employing a clinical approach to problem solving. Since the ombudsperson has no authority to finalize a solution to the problem, compromises are highly possible and all concerned tend to feel satisfied with the outcome. To function successfully, ombudspersons must be able to operate in an atmosphere of confidentiality that does not threaten the security of the managers or subordinates who are involved in a complaint.

Arbitration

Private employers may require that employees submit their employment disputes for a binding resolution through arbitration. (Arbitration is fully explained in Chapter 11.) Arbitration is used primarily to resolve discrimination suits in areas of age, gender, sexual harassment, and race.[52]

ORGANIZATIONAL ETHICS IN EMPLOYEE RELATIONS

Objective   7

Throughout this textbook the legal requirements of HRM are emphasized. Laws and court decisions affect all aspects of the employment process—recruitment, selection, performance appraisal, safety and health, labour relations, and testing. Managers must comply with governmental regulations to promote an environment free from litigation.

Ethics

Set of standards of conduct and moral judgments that help to determine right and wrong behaviour

However, beyond what is required by the law is the question of organizational ethics and the ethical—or unethical—behaviour engaged in by managers. **Ethics** can be defined as a set of standards of acceptable conduct and moral judgment. Ethics provides cultural guidelines—organizational or societal—that help decide between proper and improper conduct. Therefore, ethics, like the legal aspects of HR, permeates all aspects of the employment relationship. For example, managers may adhere to the organization's objective of hiring more members of designated groups, but how those employees are supervised and treated once employed gets to the issue of managerial ethics. Compliance with laws and the behavioural treatment of employees are two completely different aspects of the manager's job. While ethical dilemmas will always occur in the supervision of employees, it is how employees are treated that largely distinguishes the ethical organization from the unethical one. An ethical organization recognizes and values the contributions of employees and respects their personal rights. And certainly the court cases mentioned earlier in this chapter are reinforcing this belief.

Many organizations have their own codes of ethics that govern relations with employees and the public at large. These codes are formal written statements of the organization's primary values and provide a basis for the organization, and individual managers, for behaviours and actions. In Canada, 90% of companies with revenues over $1 billion (all of which are operating on a world-wide basis) have a stated code of ethics.[53] Organizations now have ethics committees and ethics ombudspersons to provide training in ethics to employees. In addition, the Government of Canada has an ethics counsellor, reporting directly to the prime minister. As part of his work, he has already encouraged the federal government to enforce its own conflict of interest code.[54] The ultimate goal of ethics training is to avoid unethical behaviour and adverse publicity; to gain a strategic advantage; but most of all, to treat employees in a fair and equitable manner, recognizing them as productive members of the organization.

However, even with codes of ethics and ethics committees, people do not always behave ethically. When this happens, employees will sometimes report an organization's unethical practices outside the organization. This is referred to as "whistle-blowing." A recent court case in Richmond, B.C., reaffirmed that even if an employee is covered by a collective agreement, the employee has the right to use civil courts to defend allegations of whistle-blowing. The employee went public with allegations that that private asphalt contractors were delivering less material than had been contracted and that other city employees knew of this and benefited from it. The employee testified that he had been threatened and harassed. However, the City of Richmond management stated that this was a labour relations issue and ought to be handled through other challenges. The judge ruled that given how the person was treated, the employee had a right to be heard in civil court.[55]

As demonstrated above, organizations have frequently attempted to discipline or punish an employee for whistle-blowing. But with the renewed interest in business ethics, more and more companies are taking steps to ensure that any unethical behaviour or action by an employee is punished and that people are encouraged to report unethical actions. In order to ensure that employees understand the importance of dealing with unethical behaviour, top management needs to visibly support ethical actions by behaving ethically themselves and also openly encouraging their employees to report inappropriate behaviour, even as a whistle-blower.[56]

SUMMARY

1. Explain statutory rights, contractual rights, due process, and legal implications of those rights.
   - Statutory rights derive from legislation, such as human rights legislation.
   - Contractual rights are derived from contracts, such as an employment contract.
   - Due process is the employee's right to be heard through a complaint process.
   - Legal implications flow from how the employee is treated.

2. Identify the job expectancy rights of employees.
   - Fair and equitable treatment.
   - Ensuring that the workplace is safe and drug-free.
   - Reasonable treatment regarding privacy.
   - Access to employee's own personnel file.
   - Not being subject to discipline for off-duty behaviour.
   - Being notified of any plant closings.

3. Explain the process of establishing disciplinary practices, including the proper implementation of organizational rules.
   - The primary purpose of having disciplinary procedures is to prevent or correct discipline problems.
   - Failure to take disciplinary action only serves to aggravate a problem that eventually must be resolved.
   - Organizations need to clearly outline rules and expectations regarding performance and behaviour.

4. Discuss the meaning of discipline and how to investigate a disciplinary problem.
   - Discipline is action that results in desirable conduct or performance.
   - If a problem occurs, the supervisor needs to determine when the situation occurred and to have a full discussion with the employee to get the employee's view of the situation.

5. Explain the differences between progressive and positive discipline.
   - Progressive discipline is the application of corrective measures by increasing degrees.
   - Progressive discipline is designed to motivate an employee to correct misconduct.
   - Positive discipline is based on the concept that the employee must assume responsibility for personal conduct and job performance.
   - Positive discipline requires a co-operative environment for joint discussion and problem solving between the supervisor and the employee.

6. Identify the different types of alternative dispute-resolution procedures.
   - Step-review systems.
   - Peer-review systems.
   - Use of hearing officers.
   - Open-door system.
   - Ombudsperson system.
   - Arbitration.

7. Discuss the role of ethics in the management of human resources.
   - Ethics in HRM extends beyond the legal requirements of managing employees.
   - Managers engage in ethical behaviour when employees are treated in a fair and objective way and when an employee's personal and work-related rights are respected and valued.

Need to Know

- Definition of termination with cause, and wrongful dismissal
- Types of disciplinary approaches
- Types of discipline appeal mechanisms for nonunion staff
- Definition of ethics

Need to Understand

- How employee rights are protected
- How to conduct a discipline investigation
- How to dismiss an employee
- Factors used to determine if termination was for cause
- Relationship of organizational ethics to employee rights and expectations

Key Terms

alternative dispute resolution (ADR) 347	negligence 321
constructive dismissal 343	ombudsperson 348
contractual rights 323	open-door policy 348
discipline 335	positive, or nonpunitive, discipline 339
due process 324	progressive discipline 337
employee rights 321	statutory rights 323
ethics 349	step-review system 347
hearing officer 348	wrongful dismissal 342
mediation 347	

REVIEW QUESTIONS

1. What is meant by management rights? Employee rights?
2. Define statutory rights and contractual rights.
3. What are some of the guidelines for developing a policy on employee searches?
4. List several guidelines for inclusion in an employer's policy manual for e-mail, Internet, and voice-mail usage.
5. Why is documentation is so important to the disciplinary process? What constitutes correct documentation?
6. Describe progressive and positive discipline, noting the differences between these two approaches.
7. Define "just cause" dismissal and "wrongful dismissal."
8. Explain mediation.
9. What is a code of ethics?

CRITICAL THINKING QUESTIONS

1. Sara has recently been asked to develop a voice-mail and e-mail protocol for the home improvement company for which she is working. What specific items would she want in the protocol?
2. Pardeep works as a millwright in a sawmill. The company is considering redesigning its discipline procedures to be oriented toward positive discipline. What would be the advantages and disadvantages of this change? What would the company want to include in the new procedure?
3. You have recently been promoted to a supervisory position. One of your first tasks is to discipline one of your staff for an ongoing tardiness problem. What information do you need prior to the discipline meeting and how would you conduct the meeting?
4. Your professor is dealing with a case where a student was alleged to have cheated on a final exam. Would documentation be important? If so, what type of documentation would be necessary?
5. A new manager has recently joined a large financial institution. She has noticed that some staff are not following the code of ethics. What advice would you give her in dealing with this?

DEVELOPING YOUR SKILLS

1. Working in a group of four to five students, identify the ethical dilemmas that could arise in the areas of selection, performance reviews, health and safety, privacy rights, and compensation.
2. Individually read the following scenarios. Then in groups of four to five students, determine if the situations are or are not fair. Explain your reasons. Be prepared to share your information with the rest of the class.

   a. Jane was using the company network system to locate childcare facilities in her local community. Her supervisor observed this and then sought confirmation from the IT unit. Jane was given a written reprimand. Meanwhile, John used his desk telephone to do his personal banking and bill paying. John was not reprimanded.

   b. Sonita spent her lunch hour at the gym; she is following a strenuous workout program as she prepares for a triathlon event in the next several weeks. Meanwhile, Anthony met his friends for lunch, sharing several beers at the local pub. Both employees felt fatigued in the afternoon, and their work performance decreased, which was noted by their supervisor. Anthony was asked to meet with his supervisor to review performance expectations and received a verbal warning. Sonita did not.

3. Access the following Web sites, which discuss employee privacy rights in the workplace. Prepare a one- to two-page report summarizing what each site has to offer. Indicate if there are any areas of the site that might be more helpful to an employee rather than an employer.

   - **www.privcom.gc.ca/**
   - **www.privacyrights.org/**
   - **www.eff.org/Privacy/Workplace/**
   - **www.fairmeasures.com/privacy.html**

Privacy Commissioner of Canada

www.privcom.gc.ca/

Privacy Rights Clearing House

www.privacyrights.org/

Electronic Frontier Foundation

www.eff.org/Privacy

Workplace/Fair Measures

www.fairmeasures.com
privacy.html

**Alternative Dispute
Resolution Resources**

www.adrr.com/

ADR Institute of Ontario

www.adrontario.ca

**Conflict Resolution
Network**

www.crnhq.org/

4. Access the following Web sites on alternative dispute resolution:

    - **www.adrr.com/**
    - **www.adrontario.ca**
    - **www.crnhq.org/**

    In addition, conduct your own Internet search, using any search engine, under the heading of "alternative dispute resolution." Share with your classmates what you learned about alternative dispute resolution.

Case Study

Improving Performance through a Progressive Discipline Policy

Jennifer started her new job as vice-president, human resources at ABC Manufacturing— a manufacturer of state-of-the-art furniture products in Southern Ontario. She started in mid-2000. One of the first issues she faced was an unacceptable absenteeism rate. There were about 250 employees on the three assembly lines, operating two shifts a day. The average employee was absent fourteen days a year. The benchmark for other manufacturing sites was nine days. Jennifer calculated that the company was employing between 30 and 35 extra people to cover absences. This hurt the bottom line.

A related problem was punctuality. Employees were habitually five or ten minutes late for their shifts. In a white-collar environment with flextime, this would not have been as critical. But tardiness in this situation meant that the assembly line could not operate, and that the other employees on the three lines were forced to remain idle.

The solution was to develop a system of progressive discipline. Jennifer prepared a simple two-page policy. Page one dealt with behaviour in the control of employees, such as arriving late, leaving work without permission, calling in sick but playing golf, and so on. Page two dealt with legitimate absences, such as food poisoning, stomach flu, etc. Jennifer met with the unions and notified them that this policy would come into effect as of December 2000. All employees started with zero absences at this time.

The policy assumed that all absences were innocent. However, if an employee was absent five times in a 12-month period, the supervisor met with that employee to express concern over the absences and to identify any need for counselling or assistance. The goal of the meeting was to express legitimate concerns, reinforce that the employee was needed, and ensure that the employee accepted responsibility for managing his or her own attendance. Following this meeting, if the employee had fewer than two absences in the ensuing six months, the employee was no longer part of the program. However, if the pattern of absence continued, the employee was counselled a second and third time. If no improvements resulted, a level 4 employment status review was conducted. This was done on a case-by-case basis. For example, a frequently absent employee with 28 years of good service would be treated differently from another employee with the same absenteeism record but only two years of employment.

The results were impressive. About 70 employees entered the program. Of these, 8 to 10 advanced to step 2, 2 to step 3, and none to step 4. The absenteeism rate dropped to an average of less than 10 days, and punctuality was no longer an issue. Labour costs were reduced, because it meant that 20 fewer employees were needed.

Questions

1. "The policy assumed that all absences were innocent." What do you think this means?
2. The policy was active as of December 2002, and all employees were treated equally from that date, regardless of their previous absenteeism records. Was this fair? Why or why not?
3. Do you think that this policy will continue to get the results being sought? Why or why not?

Case Study **2**

Is This Whistle-Blowing?

A Health Canada scientist whose responsibilities included evaluating drugs for veterinary use spoke out publicly against the ban on Brazilian beef. In early 2002, there was a trade conflict between Canada and Brazil over Canada banning the import of canned beef produced in Brazil. The banning resulted from the Brazilian producers failing to address concerns from Canada about whether the meat could possibly be infected with mad cow disease. The ban lasted about three weeks. In the middle of the ban, two scientists publicly stated that there was no scientific basis for the ban and that the motivation for the ban was due to other trade disputes.

One of the scientists involved made her name known to the press. As a consequence of knowing who made the public statements, Health Canada suspended the scientist for 10 days indicating that the public comments helped fuel the international trade dispute. Her defence was that she did not approach the press but that a reporter contacted her to seek her comments. She appealed the suspension. During the appeal hearing, the scientist did admit that her comments were about political matters, not health and safety questions. While the adjudicator did reduce her suspension from ten days to five days, the adjudicator stated that she had lost her right to take her criticism to the media when she did not first deal with it internally. Her lawyer, in his comments on the ruling, stated that there was no route for such a discussion and that by upholding the suspension, other staff would be reluctant to be whistle-blowers in the future.

Source: Adapted from Tom Blackwell, "Suspension of Ottawa Whistle-blower Upheld," *National Post*, January 31, 2002: A4. Reprinted with permission of *National Post*.

Questions

1. Discuss all the possible consequences of reporting concerns about a banned product, including the possible consequences to the scientist's career.
2. Suggest a proper course of action the scientist could use in bringing health and safety matters to the attention of Health Canada.
3. Do you feel that the scientist was a whistle-blower? Explain your answer.

NOTES AND REFERENCES

1. Josh Bevins and Christian Weller, "Rights Make Might," *EPI Issue Brief #192,* The Economic Institute, April 9, 2003, www.epinet.org/content.cfm/Issuebriefs_ib192 (retrieved January 28, 2005).

2. "Pre-Employment Screening Services," www.dataresearch.com/services.htm (retrieved January 28, 2005).

3. Shawn Cohen and Adrienne V. Campbell, "It's Time to Face the Inevitable and Comply with Privacy Laws, *Canadian HR Reporter,* January 28, 2002, www.hrreporter.com/loginarea/members/ viewing.asp? ArticleNo=1690 &viewwhat=Print&subscriptionType=PRINT&callerpage= whoswho (retrieved January 28, 2005).

4. James N. Jorgensen, "Resume Certification Can Negate Liability," LawSight.com, www.lawsight.com/jjart12.htm (retrieved January 28, 2005).

5. *Wallace v. United Grain Growers* (1997, 152 DLR (4th) 1 (SCC); *BC(PSERC)* v. *BCGEU* (1999) SCJ No. 46 (SCC)).

6. *Parry Sound (District) Social Services Administration Board* v. *O.P.S.E.U., Local 324* Neutral citation: 2003 SCC 42. File No.: 28819. 2003: January 24; 2003: September 18, www.cdn-hr-reporter.ca/disccase.htm (retrieved January 28, 2005) and "Parry Sound The Supreme Court of Canada rules arbitrators must enforce human rights statutes," www.caut.ca/en/publications/ legalreview/ 5.1parry_sound.pdf (retrieved January 28, 2005).

7. Gwendoline C. Allison, R. David House, and Kristy J. Child, "Dismissal Planning, The Continuing Legal Education Society of British Columbia, April 11, 2002, http://www.cle.bc.ca/cle/utility+postings/ PRFanalysis?to_print-%7B65F7BDD5-4D1F-11D6-84D5-0002B33844C6%7D (retrieved January 28, 2005).

8. *The Online Ethics Center Glossary,* http://onlineethics.org/glossary.html (retrieved January 28, 2005).

9. "Employment at Will: A Foreign Concept in Canada," *Information,* Ogilvy Renault Labour and Employment Law Group, www.ogilvyrenault.com/en/data/pu/182e_g.pdf (retrieved May 10, 2002).

10. Stuart Rudner, "Keep Drugs, Alcohol out of Workplace without Violating Human Rights," *Canadian HR Reporter,* February 4, 2004, www.hrreporter.com (retrieved February 5, 2005).

11. "Policy on Drug and Alcohol Testing," Ontario Human Rights Commission, September 27, 2000, www.ohrc.on.ca/english/publications/index.shtml (retrieved February 5, 2005).

12. Canadian Executive Council on Addictions and Health Canada, "Canadian Addiction Survey, November 2004, www.ccsa.ca/index.asp?menu=Statistics&ID=118 (retrieved February 5, 2005).

13. Barbara Butler & Associates, "Who Is Responsible?—Employer Perspective Dealing with Alcohol and Drug Issues through a Comprehensive Approach," 2004, www.ccsa.ca/index.asp?menu=Topics&ID=16 (retrieved February 5, 2005): 2.

14, Barbara Butler & Associates, "Brief Analysis of Current Workplace Substance Abuse Issues and Activities in Canada," December 2004, www.ccsa.ca/index.asp?menu= Topics&ID=16 (retrieved February 5, 2005): 13.

15. J. Towler, "Dealing with Employees Who Steal," *Canadian HR Reporter* 15, no. 16 (September 23, 2002): 4.

16. Graham Cunningham, "Take Steps to Curb Five-Finger Discounts," *Pharmacy Post,* August 2003, no. 11, 8, 33.

17. "Air Canada Searches Employee Rooms," *Canadian HR Reporter* 16, no. 3 (February 3, 2003): 2.

18. Lorna Harris, "Employee Video Surveillance Challenged under New Privacy Law," *Canadian HR Reporter* (August 9, 2004): 5; and "*Personal Information Protection Act,*" November 4, 2003, seminar sponsored by Fasken Martineau.

19. "Privacy Issues in the Workplace," February 22, 2002, seminar sponsored by Fasken Martineau.

20. "2004 Labour, Employment & Human Rights Seminar," Vancouver, B.C. October 31, 2003. Fasken Martineau.

21. "Yukon's Computer Porn Scandal," *Guide to HR Technology (Canadian HR Reporter),* March 8, 2004, G4.

22. Shawn Cohen and Adrienne V. Campbell, "It's Time to Face the Inevitable and Comply with Privacy Laws," *Canadian HR Reporter* 15, no. 2 (January 28, 2002): 9–10.

23. David Brown, "10 Months to Get Ready," *Canadian HR Reporter* 16, no. 4 (February 24, 2003): 1, 11.

24. Shawn Cohen and Adrienne V. Campbell, "It's Time to Face the Inevitable and Comply with Privacy Laws."

25. Chantalle Bita Kudsi-Zadeh, "E-mail in the Workplace: The Potential for Increased Employee Participation," Industrial Relations Centre, Queen's University, 2000, www.industrialrelationscentre.com/infobank/ current_issues_series/e-mail_in_the_workplace.pdf (retrieved February 6, 2005): 1.

26. Bill Gates, "Preserving and Enhancing the Benefits of Email," Microsoft Executive Newsletter, June 28, 2004, www.ironport.com/press/pp_microsoft_en_06-28-2004.html (retrieved February 6, 2005).

27. "Privacy Issues in the Workplace," Fasken Martineau.

28. *Christensen v. Armtec,* 1996, B.C. Supreme Court.

29. "Privacy Issues in the Workplace," Fasken Martineau.

30. Stuart Rudner, "The High Cost of Internet, E-mail Abuse," *Canadian HR Reporter: Report on Employment Law,* January 31, 2005: R5; S. M. Entwisle, "E-Mail

and Privacy in the Workplace," www.ucalgary.ca/
~dabrent/380/webproj/privacy.html (retrieved
February 6, 2005).

31. "Privacy Issues in the Workplace," Fasken Martineau.

32. N.C. MacDonald, "You've Got E-Mail Problems,"
Canadian HR Reporter 16, no. 5 (March 10, 2003): 5, 10.

33. P. Israel, "Spying on Employees—and It's Perfectly Legal,"
Canadian HR Reporter 16, no. 8 (April 21, 2003): 5;
"What the Courts are Saying," *Canadian HR Reporter* 16,
no. 8 (April 21, 2003): 5.

34. Marjo Johne, "Is Someone Watching You?" *The Globe and
Mail*, January 10, 2003, C1.

35. Uyen Vu, "Off-Duty Behaviour, At-Work Reprisals,"
Canadian HR Reporter, June 14, 2004,
www.hrreporter.com (retrieved January 28, 2005).

36. Eric Wieffering and Tony Kennedy, "Court Authorizes
Search of Northwest Employees' Home Computers," *Star
Tribune*, February 18, 2000.

37. Peter Israel, "How to Tackle Poor Job Performance—and
Bring Down Legal Costs," *Canadian HR Reporter*,
www.hrreporter.com/loginarea/members/viewing.asp?
ArticleNo=2334&viewwhat=Print&subscriptionType=
PRINT&callerpage=whoswho (retrieved February 7,
2005).

38. Donald C. Mosley, Leon C. Megginson, and Paul H.
Pietri, *Supervisory Management: The Art of Developing and
Empowering People*, 4th ed. (Cincinnati, Ohio: South-
Western, 1997).

39. Rebecca K. Spar, "Keeping Internal Investigations
Confidential," *HRMagazine* 41, no. 1 (January 1996): 33–36.

40. Jeffrey A. Mello, "The Fine Art of the Reprimand: Using
Criticism to Enhance Commitment, Motivation, and
Performance," *Employment Relations Today* 22, no. 4
(Winter 1995): 19–27.

41. Readers interested in the pioneering work on positive dis-
cipline should see James R. Redeker, "Discipline, Part 1:
Progressive Systems Work Only by Accident," *Personnel*
62, no. 10 (October 1985): 8–12; James R. Redeker,
"Discipline, Part 2: The Nonpunitive Approach Works by
Design," *Personnel* 62, no. 11 (November 1985): 7–14. See
also Alan W. Bryant, "Replacing Punitive Discipline with a
Positive Approach," *Personnel Administrator* 29, no. 2
(February 1984): 79–87.

42. Peter Israel, "How to Tackle Poor Job Performance—and
Bring Down Legal Costs."

43. T. Wagar, "Wrongful Dismissal: Perception vs. Reality,"
Human Resources Professional 8, no. 10 (1996).

44. www.duhaime.org/dictionary/dict-c.aspx (retrieved
February 8, 2005).

45. J. Melnitzer, "Ciciretto vs. Embassy Cleaners," *Workplace
News* 5, no. 2 (February 1999): 1.

46. Andrew Willis, "Deception Costs Big for Research
Capital," *The Globe and Mail*, November 29, 2002, B16.

47. Dennis St. Amour, "Four Steps to Professional Terminations,"
Canadian HR Reporter (October 18, 1999): 7–8.

48. "Keep Your Company out of Court," *Canadian HR
Reporter*, www.hrreporter.com/loginarea/members/
viewing.asp?ArticleNo=1125&viewwhat=Print&
subscriptionType=PRINT&callerpage=whoswho (retrieved
February 10, 2005).

49. Brenda Paik Sunoo, "Hot Disputes Cool Down in Online
Mediation," *Workforce* 80, no. 1 (January 2001): 48–52.

50. Lamont E. Stallworth, Thomas McPherson, and Larry
Rute, "Discrimination in the Workplace: How Mediation
Can Help," *Dispute Resolution Journal* 56, no. 1
(February–April 2001): 35–44, 83–87.

51. "How Best to Avoid Mediation Mistakes," *HR Focus* 77,
no. 9 (September 2000): 2.

52. Stuart L. Bass, "Recent Court Decisions Expand Role of
Arbitration in Harassment and Other Title VII Cases,"
Labor Law Journal 46, no. 1 (January 1995): 38–46;
Patrick J. Cihon, "Recent Developments in the Arbitration
of Employment Discrimination Claims," *Labor Law
Journal* 46, no. 10 (October 1995): 587–96; Lamont E.
Stallworth and Linda K. Stroh, "Who Is Seeking to
Use ADR and Why Do They Choose to Do So?" *Dispute
Resolution Journal* 51, no. 1 (January–March 1996):
30–38; Kathryn M. Werdegar, "The Courts and Private
ADR: Partners in Serving Justice," *Dispute Resolution
Journal* 51, no. 2–3 (April 1996): 52–55.

53. Stephen P. Robbins, David A. DeCenzo, Robin Stuart-Kotze,
Eileen B. Stewart, *Fundamentals of Management* (Toronto:
Pearson Education Canada Inc., 2005): 38.

54. Andrew McIntosh, "Watchdog Urges Action on Ethics
Code," *The National Post*, January 17, 2002: A6.

55. Gerry Bellett, "Appeal Court to Hear Case of 'Whistle-
Blower' City Employee," *The Vancouver Sun*, February 12,
2005, B11.

56. Edward Keyserlingk, "Encouraging Whistle-Blowers,"
Canadian HR Reporter, August 11, 2003, www.hrreporter
.com/loginarea/members/viewing.asp?ArticleNo=2685&
viewwhat=Print&subscriptionType=PRINT&callerpage=
whoswho (retrieved February 10, 2005).

CHAPTER 10

Labour Relations

OBJECTIVES

After studying this chapter, you should be able to

1 Explain the supervisor's role in labour relations.

2 Explain the federal and provincial legislation that provides the framework for labour relations.

3 Cite the reasons employees join unions.

4 Describe the process by which unions organize employees and gain recognition as their bargaining agent.

5 Describe the functions labour unions perform at the national and local levels.

6 Describe the differences between private-sector and public-sector labour relations.

7 List some of the current challenges for labour organizations.

OUTLINE

Introduction
The Laws Governing Labour Relations
Labour Relations Legislation
Why Employees Unionize
Pay, Benefits, and Working Conditions
Dissatisfaction with Supervisors
    and Managers
Social and Status Concerns
How Employees Organize
Organizing Steps
Employer Tactics
Union Tactics
Certification Procedures
Voluntary Recognition
Regular Certification
Prehearing Votes
Contract Negotiations

Decertification
Impact of Unionization on Managers
How Unions Operate
Structure, Functions, and Leadership of International and
    National Unions
Structure and Functions of Local Unions
Union Leadership Approaches and Philosophies
Labour Relations in the Public Sector
Public-Sector Legislation
Political Nature of the Labour–Management Relationship
Strikes in the Public Sector
Current Challenges for Unions
Globalization
Technological Change
Changes to the Nature of Work
Demographics
Innovative Workplace Practices

HRM
Close-Up

Sharon Duggan, vice-president, Aliant customer service strategy, planning & development, St. John's, Newfoundland

"The best employer–employee relationships are collaborative ones built on respect. Having respect for the rights of employees and respect for the union is incredibly important for our managers."

Aliant is a telecommunications company serving Atlantic Canada. The company offers local and long-distance telephone service, Internet, e-commerce, and managed network services to over 2 million consumers and 80,000 businesses. The company has roots that trace back over one hundred years, but the Aliant of today was formed in 1999 with the merger of four Atlantic provincial telecom companies. With that merger came employees with nine bargaining units and separate collective agreements. "You can imagine the challenges of working with nine different sets of rules around employee relationships," explained Sharon Duggan, who was vice-president of human resources at the time of the merger. "Everything is covered including hours of work, benefits, vacation, and compensation, and so there were many variances across our business."

As a company operating in a federally regulated industry, Aliant was subject to a Labour Board ruling which determined the optimum union structure for the new company. In 2002, the company made its first attempt to negotiate a single collective agreement which resulted in a strike in 2004. That strike lasted five months. "There's always a tendency to want to hang on to all the good things about an existing agreement. Negotiations are extremely complex and take a great deal of effort. But now that we have a single agreement, everyone is happy to have this milestone behind us," said Duggan.

Probably the biggest challenge during negotiations is balancing the needs of the employees as represented by the union and the needs of the company. "A critical piece of the process is talking about business challenges and customer expectations," commented Duggan. In fact, the new agreement outlined a "joint consultative process" whereby a group of senior managers and union leaders meet regularly to better understand the business and its strategic direction. The company's CEO and vice-presidents also attend regularly, leading discussions about business direction. The process is helping to both strengthen the business and build strong working relationships, especially important following a labour disruption.

For the first 90 days following the strike, a priority for Duggan and the human resources division was to support staff during the transition back to work. "Our employee assistance program was key since staff had many issues, including financial stress and anxiety about returning to work. We also relied on new union–management teams to break the ice and get people working together again and focusing on the customer," said Duggan. All new managers also received special training on communication and relationships because, as Duggan explains, "the best employer–employee relationships are collaborative ones built on respect. Having respect for the rights of employees and respect for the union is incredibly important for our managers."

At the end of the day, Duggan feels that the agreement was fair and balanced and also achieved Aliant's business goals. She acknowledges many frustrating moments but is most appreciative of the fact that the team was able to build a good framework that will lead to success in the future. "Many elements of our agreement have a long-lasting impact on our business. That was incredibly motivating."

INTRODUCTION

Mention the word "union" and most people will have some opinion, positive or negative. To some, the word evokes images of labour–management unrest—grievances, strikes, picketing, boycotts. To others, the word represents fairness, opportunity, equal representation, and someone who will look after them. Many think of unions as simply creating an adversarial relationship between employees and managers, while others feel that unions are necessary to counterbalance the power employers have.

Regardless of how people feel about them, unions have been an important force shaping organizational practices, legislation, and political thought in Canada since the mid-1800s. Consider Sharon Duggan's statements in the HRM Close-Up. Some people might say that fears about unionization have helped employers become better at managing people. Today, unions remain of interest because of their influence on organizational productivity and competitiveness, the development of labour law, and HR policies and practices. Like business organizations themselves, unions are undergoing changes in both operation and philosophy. Labour–management co-operative programs, company buyouts by unions, and labour's increased interest in global trade are examples of labour's new role in society.

In spite of the long history of unions, the intricacies of labour relations are unfamiliar to many individuals. Therefore, this chapter describes government regulation of labour relations, the labour relations process, the reasons workers join labour organizations, the structure and leadership of labour unions, contemporary challenges to labour organizations, and the role a supervisor or manager plays in labour relations.

Objective 1

Unions and other labour organizations can significantly affect the ability of managers to direct and control the various HR processes. For example, union seniority provisions in the labour contract may influence who is selected for job promotions or training programs. Pay rates may be determined through union negotiations, or unions may impose restrictions on management's employee evaluation methods. Therefore, it is essential that managers understand how unions operate and familiarize themselves with the growing body of laws governing labour relations. It is also important for the supervisor to understand how unionization affects the actions of the union and those of the HR professional.

THE LAWS GOVERNING LABOUR RELATIONS

Unions have a long history in North America, and the regulations governing labour relations have evolved over time. Initially, employers strongly opposed union growth, using court injunctions (e.g., court orders forbidding various union activities, such as picketing and strikes) and devices, such as the "yellow-dog contract." A yellow-dog contract was an employer's anti-union tactic by which employees had to agree not to join a union while working for the employer's organization. Using strikebreakers, blacklisting employees (e.g., circulating the names of union supporters to other employers), and discriminating against those who favoured unionization were other anti-union tactics.

Today, the laws governing labour relations seek to create an environment in which both unions and employers can exercise their respective rights and responsibilities. Chapter 2 provided an overview of the various employment laws, including those governing labour relations. This chapter now looks at the laws in more detail.

Labour Relations Legislation

The first labour relations legislation, the Trades Unions Act, was passed by the federal Parliament in 1872. This act exempted unions from charges of criminal conspiracy, allowed them to pursue goals of collective bargaining without persecution, and gave them the ability to strike. Between 1872 and 1900, legislation to settle industrial disputes was enacted in a number of provinces, including Quebec, Ontario, British Columbia, and Nova Scotia. Although these acts are no longer in effect, they did mark Canada's early recognition of the rights of unions.

Several different laws at the federal and provincial levels currently regulate labour relations. These laws make up a labour relations "system" consisting of government, unions, and employers. The government makes the laws that regulate how unions and employers behave with each other.[1] In making laws, the government will determine who can unionize and where they can unionize. There are specific laws, or acts, for different sectors, industries, and workers. Canada's labour relations system is highly decentralized, whereas the U.S. system is highly centralized. For example, in Canada, the federal law governs interprovincial transportation and communications, while provincial legislation governs manufacturing and mining. However, 90% of the workforce is governed by provincial legislation. As mentioned earlier in this book, federally regulated companies such as Bell, Rogers, Sprint, and Telus are governed by the Canada Labour Code, whereas companies such as Molson Breweries are governed by the province in which they operate. Labour legislation, whether federal or provincial, has certain features in common:

- The right of people to join unions
- The right of unions to be granted authority to represent employees
- The requirement that employers recognize a certified union as the rightful and exclusive bargaining agent for that group of employees
- The requirement that unions and employers bargain in good faith
- The identification of unfair labour practices
- The right of unions to strike and right of employers to lock out workers[2]

However, as HRM and the Law 10.1 points out, it may take a decision by the Supreme Court of Canada to acquire rights to form a union.

The Canada Industrial Relations Board (CIRB) was established to administer and enforce the Canada Labour Code. Similarly, each province has a labour relations board (LRB) whose members are appointed by the provincial government and who administer the labour law. (The exception is Quebec, which has a labour court and commissioners.) The LRB is generally separate from the government and is composed of representatives from labour and management. The duties of the LRB include, but are not limited to

- developing administrative regulations that describe how people unionize;
- hearing complaints related to unfair labour practices;
- determining if bargaining was done in good faith; and
- remedying violations of collective-bargaining legislation.[3]

It is important to remember that the administrative regulations are greatly influenced by the politics of any provincial government. Therefore, the legislation can be relatively

HRM and **the law 10.1** HRM and the law 10.1

FARM WORKERS IN ONTARIO GET RIGHT TO UNIONIZE

In late 2001, the Supreme Court of Canada determined that a labour law in Ontario was unconstitutional. The *Ontario Labour Relations Act* has a section that prohibits farm workers from unionizing.

The United Food and Commercial Workers (UFCW) initiated the case, which eventually ended in the Supreme Court. The law in question was initially passed in the 1940s, and was repealed briefly during the NDP reign in Ontario. The Ontario government, in its submission to the court, indicated that labour legislation was the realm of the provinces and, as such, could structure the legislation to fit economic circumstances. For Ontario's farming industry, the legislation was intended to protect that industry in an increasingly global market. In its ruling, the Supreme Court stated that the "freedom to organize lies at the core of the *Charter's* protection of freedom of association."

After the ruling, the UFCW estimated that about 100,000 workers in Ontario could be affected by the decision. However, labour lawyers suggest that it wasn't that big a win. The union did not get a decision that there was a fundamental right under the *Charter* for people to bargain collectively and to strike.

What do you think of the decision?

Sources: Adapted from Thomas Schiller and Hugh Finnamore, "Supreme Court Out of Touch on Unions," *Financial Post*, January 4, 2002, FP 11, and Janice Tibbetts, "Supreme Court Knocks Down Ban on Farm Workers Union in Ontario," *The Vancouver Sun*, December 21, 2001, D1.

similar, but the interpretation of the law can vary greatly from one province to another. The law typically gets interpreted by the decisions made by the respective labour boards that then influence the actions a union or company can take in the future. To learn more about the administration of labour relations, Manager's Toolkit 10.1 lists the Web sites of the labour relations boards.

WHY EMPLOYEES UNIONIZE

 Objective 3

Labour relations process
Logical sequence of four events: (1) workers desire collective representation, (2) union begins its organizing campaign, (3) collective negotiations lead to a contract, and (4) the contract is administered

Employees frequently feel that individually they will be unable to exercise power regarding their employment conditions at any particular employer. The treatment and benefits they receive depend in large part on how their employers view their worth to the organization. Of course, if they believe they are not being treated fairly, they have the choice of quitting. However, another way to correct the situation is to organize and bargain with the employer collectively. When employees pursue this direction, the labour relations process begins. As Figure 10.1 illustrates, the **labour relations process** consists of a logical sequence of four events: (1) employees desire collective representation, (2) union organizers or employees begin the organizing campaign, (3) collective negotiations lead to a collective agreement, and (4) the collective agreement is administered. Laws and administrative rulings influence each of the separate events by granting special privileges to, or imposing defined constraints on, employees, employers, and union officials.[4]

Manager's Toolkit **10.1** Manager's Toolkit 10.1

LABOUR RELATIONS BOARDS

Labour relations boards are making it easier for employers and employees to access information. The following Web sites are a valuable resource for the supervisor and HR professional.

Jurisdiction	Name	Web Site
Federal government	Canada Industrial Relations Board	www.cirb-ccri.gc.ca
Alberta	Alberta Labour Relations Board	www.gov.ab.ca/alrb
British Columbia	Labour Relations Board	www.lrb.bc.ca
Manitoba	Manitoba Labour Board	www.gov.mb.ca/labour/labbrd
New Brunswick	Industrial Relations Branch	www.gnb.ca/0110/0001e.htm
Newfoundland and Labrador	Labour Relations Board	www.gov.nf.ca/lrb/
Nova Scotia	Labour Relations Board/ Construction Industry Panel	www.gov.ns.ca/enla/lrb/
Ontario	Ontario Labour Relations Board	www.gov.on.ca/lab/olrm
Prince Edward Island	Labour Relations Board	www.gov.pe.ca/commcul/ lair-info/index.php3
Quebec	The Labour Code is administered through investigations and commissions created at the time of a complaint.	
Saskatchewan	Labour Relations Board	www.sasklabourrelationsboard.com/

Union shop
Provision of the collective agreement that requires employees to join the union as a condition of their employment

Closed shop
Provision of the collective agreement that requires employers to hire only union members

Open shop
Provision of the collective agreement that allows employees to join or not join the union

The majority of research on why employees unionize comes from the study of blue-collar employees in the private sector. These studies generally conclude that employees unionize as a result of

1. economic need;
2. general dissatisfaction with managerial practices; and/or
3. a desire to fulfill social and status needs.

In short, employees see unionism as a way to get results they cannot achieve by themselves.[5]

It should be pointed out that some employees join unions because of the **union shop** provisions of the collective agreement that require employees to join as a condition of their employment. Others join because it is a **closed shop**—only members of a union will be hired or because they choose to under an **open shop** provision. Even when forced to

FIGURE 10.1   Labour Relations Process

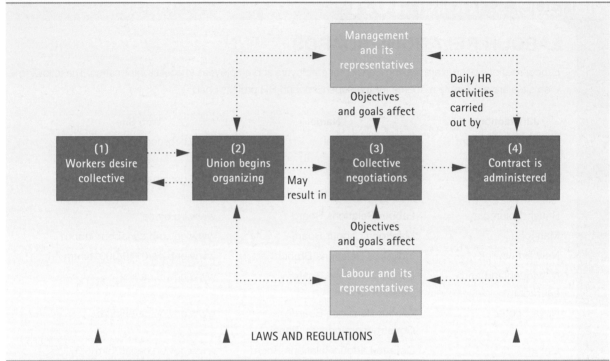

Winnipeg Strike of 1919, showing a group of strikers lining a downtown street in Winnipeg. In the centre of the photo is a burning streetcar. Metal workers started the strike to force their employers to improve their working conditions.

join, many employees eventually accept the concept of unionism. The sections that follow look at some of the more specific reasons people unionize and what role the supervisor and/or organization plays in the unionization process.

Pay, Benefits, and Working Conditions

Whether or not a union can become the bargaining agent for a group of employees will be influenced by the employees' degree of dissatisfaction, if any, with their overall employment conditions. For example, employees may feel their concerns about health and safety are ignored or they may be required to wear uniforms without being reimbursed for the cost. It will also depend on whether the employees perceive the union as likely to be effective in improving these conditions. However, unhappiness with wages, benefits, and working conditions appear to be the strongest reasons to join a union. Unions will generally try to convince potential members that they can deliver pay increases and benefits. Work restructuring issues, such as multi-skilling/multi-tasking and the use of part-time, temporary, and contract workers are faced by about two-thirds of the unions.[6]

Dissatisfaction with Supervisors and Managers

Employees may seek unionization when they perceive that managerial practices regarding promotion, transfer, shift assignment, or other job-related policies are decided unfairly. Employees cite favouritism shown by managers as a major reason for joining unions. This is particularly true when the favouritism concerns discipline, promotion, and wage increases. Unions will describe the structured complaint process in the collective agreement (the grievance or arbitration process) as a formal way in which employees can have their complaints heard and acted on.

This book has noted that today's employees are better educated than those of the past and often express a desire to be more involved in decisions affecting their jobs. Chapter 3 discussed the concept of employee empowerment and highlighted various employee involvement techniques. The failure of employers to give employees an opportunity to participate in decisions affecting their welfare may encourage union membership. It is widely believed that one reason managers begin employee involvement programs and seek to empower their employees is to avoid collective action by employees. For example, in one unionization attempt by the United Auto Workers at a Nissan plant, the union lost because workers were satisfied with the voice in decision making that Nissan's participatory style of management gave them. Likewise, when the United Grain Growers and Agricore Co-operative Ltd. merged in 2002, the employees of the Agricore United voted to reject union membership and become nonunion.[7]

Social and Status Concerns

Employees whose needs for status and recognition are being frustrated may join unions as a means of satisfying these needs. Through their union, they have an opportunity to fraternize with other employees who have similar desires, interests, and problems. Joining the union also enables them to put to use any leadership talents they may have. In the final analysis, the deciding factor is likely to be whether employees perceive that the benefits of joining a union outweigh the costs associated with membership.

HOW EMPLOYEES ORGANIZE

Once employees desire to unionize, a formal organizing campaign may be started either by a union organizer or by employees acting on their own behalf. Contrary to popular belief, most organizing campaigns are begun by employees rather than by union organizers. Large national unions like the Canadian Auto Workers, the United Brotherhood of Carpenters, the United Steelworkers, and the Teamsters, however, have formal organizing departments whose purpose is to identify organizing opportunities and launch organizing campaigns. It has been no secret that the labour movement has targeted certain types of employers. Larger unions have moved out of their traditional industries into other areas. This has been due to changes from a goods-producing society to a service-based society as well as a decline in union membership in industries such as mining and forestry.[8]

One of the more prominent campaigns has been to organize employees at McDonald's restaurants. However, to date, only one McDonald's is unionized—in the province of Quebec.[9] There had been a unionized McDonald's (organized by the Canadian Auto Workers) in British Columbia for a brief period of time, but the employees voted out the union after about two years. While it is difficult to determine exactly why McDonald's has not been unionized, some of the reasons appear to be the typical age of the workers (teenagers), the type of employment (part-time), and the difficulty unions have had in organizing the service sector. Even Starbucks, which has more than 250 outlets in Canada, has only had 11 of its outlets unionized.[10] Recently, Wal-Mart has been making headlines in relation to unionization attempts (discussed in more detail later in the chapter.)

Since organizing campaigns can be expensive, union leaders carefully evaluate their chances of success and the possible benefits to be gained from their efforts. Important in this evaluation is the employer's vulnerability to unionization. Union leaders also consider the effect that allowing an employer to remain nonunion may have on the strength of their union within the area. A nonunion employer can impair a union's efforts to standardize employment conditions within an industry or geographic area, as well as weaken the union's bargaining

Employees will frequently consider a union if there is dissatisfaction with how they are treated.

power with employers it has unionized. Unions will also assess whether there is a possibility that future employees may wish to decertify. Just as the costs of unionizing can be high, so can the challenges coming from employees wanting to cease having the union represent them.

Organizing Steps

Objective 4

The typical organizing campaign follows a series of progressive steps that can lead to employee representation. The organizing process normally includes the following steps:

1. Employee–union contact
2. Initial organizational meeting
3. Formation of in-house organizing committee
4. Application to labour relations board
5. Issuance of certificate by labour relations board
6. Election of bargaining committee and contract negotiations

Step 1   The first step begins when employees and union officials make contact to explore the possibility of unionization. During these discussions, employees will investigate the advantages of representation, and union officials will begin to gather information on employee needs, problems, and complaints. Union organizers will also seek specific information about the employer's financial health, supervisory styles, and organizational policies and practices. To win employee support, union organizers must build a case against the employer and for the union.

Supervisors and managers can become familiar with the questions unions ask employees during organizing drives and therefore better assess the effectiveness of their management practices. Manager's Toolkit 10.2 presents these questions.

Step 2   As an organizing campaign gathers momentum, the organizer will schedule an initial union meeting to attract more supporters. The organizer will use the information gathered in step 1 to address employee needs and explain how the union can secure these goals. Two additional purposes of organizational meetings are (1) to identify employees who can help the organizer direct the campaign, and (2) to establish communication chains that reach all employees.

Step 3   The third important step in the organizing drive is to form an in-house organizing committee composed of employees willing to provide leadership to the campaign. The committee's role is to interest other employees in joining the union and in supporting its campaign. An important task of the committee is to have employees sign a **membership card** (or authorization card) indicating their willingness to be represented by a labour union in collective bargaining with their employer. The number of signed membership cards demonstrates the potential strength of the labour union. Legislation across Canada states that unions must have a majority of employees as members in a bargaining unit before they can apply for certification election. However, most jurisdictions now interpret this to mean that at least 50% of those voting constitute a majority. In other words, those who do not cast ballots are not assumed to be voting against the certification of the union. The union membership card, once signed, is confidential, and only the labour relations board has access to the cards.

Membership card
A statement signed by an employee authorizing a union to act as a representative of the employee for purposes of collective bargaining

Step 4   Application is made to the appropriate labour relations board. In Canada, a majority of unions are certified without a vote if the labour relations board finds that the union has the support of the majority of the employees, based on the number of signed cards. However, in Ontario, if 40% or more of the employees sign membership cards, then a vote can be requested.

Manager's Toolkit **10.2** Manager's Toolkit 10.2

FREQUENTLY ASKED QUESTIONS

Many organizations find themselves unionized and are surprised that it has happened. There is also a mistaken belief that unions do not actively recruit new members. The following are the questions union organizers usually ask employees:

1. Do you think people get paid more in other organizations? (Unions will know how much people are paid in the industry and geographic area.)

2. Are decisions about how much employees are paid based on logic or favouritism? (Unions will have usually received information that supervisors make decisions in an arbitrary fashion.)

3. Are decisions about promotions based on merit or favouritism? (Unions usually have information about a particular individual that was promoted for reasons other than merit.)

4. If something happens that you feel is unfair, do you have recourse? Can you get your complaint heard? Who will hear it? Can they fix it?

(Many small companies do not have a way to handle employee complaints. Unions will talk about the formal grievance procedure and the protections that can be provided to employees who feel helpless in dealing with a problem.)

5. How are shift schedules determined? (Unions will say that shifts ought to be determined by seniority.)

6. How are performance problems handled? (Unions will convince potential members that a union can ensure that people are treated fairly if there are performance issues.)

7. Do you feel that your manager criticizes you unfairly? (Unions will describe the processes that can be used if employees feel that they have not been treated fairly.)

8. Does your boss treat you with respect? (Unions will indicate that the power of a collective group of people will make the employer treat everyone respectfully.)

Canadian Auto Workers
www.caw.ca

Step 5   The labour relations board reviews the application and initially informs both the employer and the employees about the application. This application is posted so that either employees or the employer have an opportunity to challenge.

Step 6   Once the labour relations board determines that the union is certified, a bargaining committee is put in place to start negotiating a collective agreement. If the union is a national union, such as the Canadian Auto Workers, usually a national representative works with the bargaining committee to negotiate the collective agreement with the company.

Employer Tactics

Employers must not interfere with the certification process. They are prohibited by law from dismissing, disciplining, or threatening employees for exercising their rights to form a union. Employers cannot promise better conditions, such as increased vacation days, if the employees vote for no union or choose one union over another. Nor can employers threaten to close the business as one company did as workers were voting.[11] They cannot unilaterally change wages and working conditions during certification proceedings or during collective bargaining. Like unions, they must bargain in good faith, meaning that they must demonstrate a commitment to bargain seriously and fairly. In addition, they cannot participate in the formation, selection, or support of unions representing employees.

None of these prohibitions prevents an employer from making the case that the employees have a right not to join a union or that they can deal directly with the employer on any issue. Employer resistance to unionization is the norm in Canada and opposition has been found to decrease the probability of successfully organizing.[12]

Attempts by employers to influence employees are scrutinized closely by officials of the organizing unions and the labour relations board. In one recent case, an employer in Ontario not only took the employees to the owner's home, but threatened to close the business if the union were voted in. The labour board determined that the employer had interfered by creating a mechanism by which the employees could not exercise their vote without being intimidated by the employer.[13]

Union Tactics

Unions also have a duty to act in accordance with labour legislation. Unions are prohibited from interfering with the operation of an employer's organization. They cannot intimidate or coerce employees to become or remain members of a union. Nor can they force employers to dismiss, discipline, or discriminate against nonunion employees. They must provide fair representation for all employees in the **bargaining unit**, whether in collective bargaining or in grievance procedure cases. Unions cannot engage in activities such as strikes before the expiration of the union contract.

Any of the prohibited activities discussed above for both employers and unions are considered **unfair labour practices**. Charges of unfair labour practices are made to the labour relations board, whose duty is to enforce the applicable labour laws and decide if an unfair labour practice occurred. An example of an unfair labour practice by an employer would be to threaten to fire people who wanted to join a union. Similarly, a union cannot threaten harm to employees if they don't join the union. Figure 10.2 provides a list of unfair labour practices on both the union and the management side.

Consequences of unfair labour practices can be quite costly. For example, in a recent decision by the Manitoba Labour Board, it ordered Buhler Versatile Inc. to pay its employees and its union (the Canadian Auto Workers Union) almost $6 million in costs and lost wages. In its decision, the board stated that the employer had overstepped the boundary of good behaviour in labour relations with its comments to the media and demands for certain concessions before bargaining could commence, and that prior to the strike employees were wrongly put on permanent layoff.[14]

Bargaining unit
Group of two or more employees who share common employment interests and conditions and may reasonably be grouped together for purposes of collective bargaining

Unfair labour practices
Specific employer and union illegal practices that operate to deny employees their rights and benefits under labour law

FIGURE 10.2 Unfair Labour Practices

Unfair labour practices by employers include the following.
- Helping to establish or administer a union.
- Altering the working conditions of the employees while a union is applying for certification without the union's consent.
- Using intimidation, coercion, threats, promises, or exercising undue influence while a union is being organized.
- Failing to recognize or bargain with the certified union.
- Hiring professional strike breakers.

Unfair labour practices by unions include the following.
- Contributing financial or other support to an employee's organization.
- Not representing fairly the employees in the bargaining unit.
- Bargaining or negotiating a collective agreement with an employer while another union represents the employees in the bargaining unit.
- Calling or authorizing an unlawful strike, or threatening to do so.

CERTIFICATION PROCEDURES

Certification
Acquisition of exclusive rights by
union to represent the employees

The procedures for union **certification** vary across Canadian jurisdictions. As mentioned earlier, if an applicant union can present documentation that it has sufficient support in the proposed bargaining unit, labour boards will grant certification to the union or grant a vote. The labour relations board must certify a union before it can act as a bargaining unit for a group of employees. The union normally provides evidence by submitting signed authorization cards and proof that initiation dues or fees have been paid.[15] Recognition of a union may be obtained through voluntary recognition, regular certification, or a prehearing vote.

However, there can be a situation whereby the legal framework of labour relations forces a person to join a particular union if the person wants to work. For example, the government of Quebec has legislation that forces all construction workers to belong to one of five unions. This also means that any construction company must hire only unionized workers. Even though this legislation was challenged, the Supreme Court of Canada ruled that the legislation does not violate the *Charter*.[16]

Voluntary Recognition

All employers, except those in the province of Quebec, may voluntarily recognize and accept a union. This rarely happens, except in the construction industry where there is a great reliance on union hiring halls.

Regular Certification

The regular certification process begins with the union submitting the required minimum membership evidence to the labour relations board. Generally, if an applicant union can demonstrate that it has sufficient support in the proposed bargaining unit, labour boards may grant certification on that basis. (However, with changes in

The CAW is Canada's
largest private-sector
union.

government, labour relations legislation is often reformed. Therefore, requirements for granting certification may change.) The labour relations board may order a representative vote if a sizable minority of workers have indicated either support for or opposition to the unionization.

Prehearing Votes

If there is evidence of irregularities, such as unfair labour practices taking place during the organizing drive, a prehearing vote may be taken. The purpose of this vote is to establish the level of support among the workers. Depending on the particular labour relations legislation, votes can be called if less than 50% of the employees indicate support for a union.

Once a union has been certified, employees are part of a collective and can no longer individually make special arrangements on pay, hours of work, and so on. Likewise, this means that the manager and supervisor can no longer treat individuals differently—that is, they can't make individual deals.

Contract Negotiations

Once a bargaining unit has been certified by the labour relations board, the employer and the union are legally obliged to bargain in good faith over the terms and conditions of a collective agreement. The collective agreement is for at least one year. As the contract expiry date approaches, either party must notify the other of its intention to bargain for a renewal collective agreement or contract negotiation.

Decertification

All legislation allows for decertification of unions under certain conditions. If the majority of employees indicate that they do not want to be represented by the union or that they want to be represented by another union, or if the union has failed to bargain, an application for decertification can be made to the labour relations board. If a collective agreement has been reached with the employer, this application can be made only at specified times, such as a few months before the agreement expires. The application for decertification can be initiated by either employees or the employer if the union fails to bargain.

Impact of Unionization on Managers

The unionization of employees can affect managers in many ways. Perhaps most significant is the effect it can have on the ability of managers to make decisions about employees. A union can assist employees if they believe they haven't been treated in accordance with the agreed-to employment conditions. As an example, if a company doesn't have a formal complaint mechanism, there is now a structured grievance procedure. And the decisions of a structured grievance procedure can be enforced through the courts (as will be discussed in Chapter 11). Unionization also restricts the freedom of management to formulate HR policy and practices unilaterally.

Challenges to Management Decisions

Unions typically attempt to achieve greater participation in management decisions that affect their members. Specifically, these decisions may often involve such issues as the subcontracting of work, productivity standards, and job content. Employers quite naturally seek to claim many of these decisions as their exclusive **management rights**. However, these rights are subject to challenge and erosion by the union. They may be challenged at the bargaining table, through the grievance procedure, and through strikes.

Management rights
Decisions regarding organizational operations over which management claims exclusive rights

Another way to challenge management decisions can also occur through the court system. In late 2004, the Supreme Court of Canada ruled against the United Steelworkers' in a claim that Stelco's bankruptcy protection should stop. The union argued that Stelco was not broke and that management had sought bankruptcy protection so that the company could cut jobs and reduce pensions. The court ruled in favour of Stelco, thus allowing it to continue with protection under bankruptcy laws.[17]

Loss of Supervisory Flexibility

At a recent labour–management conference a union official commented, "Contract terms covering wages, benefits, job security, and working hours are of major importance to our membership." However, for managers and supervisors, the focal point of the union's impact is at the operating level (the shop floor or office facility), where the terms of the collective agreement are implemented on a daily basis. For example, these terms can determine what corrective action is to be taken in directing and disciplining employees. When disciplining employees, supervisors must be certain they can demonstrate just cause (see Chapter 9) for their actions, because these actions can be challenged by the union and the supervisor can be called as defendant during a grievance hearing. If the challenge is upheld, the supervisor's effectiveness in coping with subsequent disciplinary problems may be impaired. Specific contract language can also reduce the supervisor's flexibility to manage in such areas as scheduling, training, performance evaluation, and promotions, to name a few.

Manager's Toolkit 10.3 Manager's Toolkit 10.3

CREATING A POSITIVE WORK ENVIRONMENT

1. If you have something to say to one of your employees, say it directly—and soon.
2. Praise employees publicly; criticize in private.
3. Remember: actions speak louder than words. Be sure your actions "say" what you want them to.
4. Be respectful of all your employees—even the poor performers.
5. Set up a file system for employee information where you can keep documentation on pay raises, performance reviews, and the like.

Allow employees access to their files and encourage them to review their files.
6. Create performance goals with each employee—goals that are challenging but attainable; monitor performance and provide feedback.
7. Share business information.
8. Seek input from employees when making changes that will affect them.
9. Ask employees for suggestions on how to improve business operations.

The list provided in Manager's Toolkit 10.3 offers guidelines to help managers and supervisors understand what they can do to create a work environment where there is no need to unionize.

HOW UNIONS OPERATE

Craft unions
Unions that represent skilled craft workers

Industrial unions
Unions that represent all workers— skilled, semiskilled, unskilled— employed along industry lines

Employee associations
Labour organizations that represent various groups of professional and white-collar employees in labour–management relations

International Brotherhood of Electrical Workers
www.ibew.org/

Brotherhood of Boilermakers
www.boilermakers.org/

Canadian Union of Postal Workers
www.cupw.ca

Ontario Secondary School Teachers' Federation
www.osstf.on.ca/

Canadian Labour Congress
www.clc-ctc.ca

Unions that represent skilled craft workers, such as carpenters or masons, are called **craft unions**, such as the International Brotherhood of Electrical Workers (IBEW) and the Brotherhood of Boilermakers. Unions that represent unskilled and semiskilled workers employed along industry lines are known as **industrial unions**, for example, the Canadian Union of Postal Workers and the Ontario Secondary School Teachers' Federation. While the distinction between craft and industrial unions still exists, technological changes and competition among unions for members have helped to reduce it. Today, skilled and unskilled workers, white-collar and blue-collar workers, and professional groups are being represented by both types of union.

Besides unions, there are also **employee associations** representing various groups of professional and white-collar employees. Examples of employee associations include the Federation of Quebec Nurses and the Alberta Teachers' Association. In competing with unions, these associations may function as unions and become just as aggressive as unions in representing members. These associations are nonunion; however, if the employee association met the necessary criteria under labour legislation, the association could become certified as a union.

Regardless of their type, labour organizations are diverse organizations, each with its own method of governance and objectives. And it is important to remember that unions are primarily political organizations. That is, they have elected leaders who can be voted out of office if the wishes of the members are not met.

Because of the political nature of unions, many unions have come together under an umbrella organization called the Canadian Labour Congress (CLC). Through this organization, the CLC attempts to influence government policy by commenting on economic conditions, such as the unemployment rate. Also, since most of the major unions in Canada are members of the CLC, it helps to referee between unions if they are seeking to organize the same group of workers. Because of its size and resources, the CLC is a very influential organization in Canada. For example, the CLC in late 2001 stated publicly that 200,000 more jobs could be created if less overtime were worked. The head (Ken Georgetti) of the CLC emphasized that even though many unionized employees relied on overtime to improve their quality of life, these same employees would gladly give this up if it meant creating more jobs.[18] On the other hand, Georgetti recently acknowledged that the free trade agreement with the United States was not the economic disaster organized labour feared—a major shift in union sentiment.[19] For further information on the CLC, go to its Web site at **www.clc-ctc.ca**.

Structure, Functions, and Leadership of International and National Unions

International unions tend to be affiliates of American unions, with headquarters in the United States. In Canada, there are 46 international unions (with membership of nearly 2 million workers) and 220 national unions (with membership of 2.7 million).[20] One of the more interesting cases involving a national Canadian union and a U.S.-based union was the 2004 merger of the Industrial, Wood & Allied Workers of Canada (IWA) with the United Steel Workers. The IWA leadership felt that it was no longer large or strong enough to deal with governmental policy makers and large companies.[21] The IWA had been a force in Canada for over 65 years but with the changing forestry sector, it had lost a significant number of its members. Even though there was not total support from the local unions for the merger, the national executive believed that such a merger would be better for the workers.[22]

Objective 5

Both international and national unions are made up of local unions. The objectives of these unions are to help organize local unions, to provide strike support, and to assist local unions with negotiations, grievance procedures, and the like. These unions also represent membership interest with internal and external constituents. By ensuring that all employers pay similar wages to their unionized workers, they serve the additional role of removing higher wages as a competitive disadvantage.[23]

Structure and Functions of Local Unions

Employees of any organization can form their own union, with no affiliation to a national or international union. In this case, the local is the union. However, most local unions are members of national or international unions or the Canadian Labour Congress, which make available to them financial resources and advice. There are an estimated 14,000 locals in Canada.

Canadian Auto Workers
www.caw.ca

Unionized employees pay union dues that finance the operation of the local union. The officers of a local union are usually responsible for negotiating the local collective agreement, for ensuring the agreement is adhered to, and for investigating and processing member grievances. At Work with HRM 10.1 describes how the Canadian Auto Workers union operates (see also **www.caw.ca**).

at work **with HRM 10.1**

THE CANADIAN AUTO WORKERS

Buzz Hargrove, president of the Canadian Auto Workers (CAW), oversees the operations of Canada's largest private-sector union. The CAW was established in 1985 after breaking away from its American affiliate, the United Auto Workers. Membership has since increased from 118,000 to 255,000 through mergers with other unions, including Mine Mill Workers, the Canadian Brotherhood of Railway Transportation, and General Workers.

In an interview, Hargrove explained the CAW structure:

> Our union is a centrally directed organization. The CAW council meets three times a year with our national workplace representatives to openly discuss issues and establish policies

that affect our members. The policy issues include social, collective-bargaining, economic, or international issues. Whatever could possibly affect our workers is discussed. This is referred to as an "accountability session." We are the only union that discusses matters with our local leadership on a national basis so frequently. Working collectively as a team brings the issues to the forefront of all our representatives' minds, and makes us a more solid force to better represent our members. The real strength in our union is this ability we have to bring local leadership together with the national leadership to collectively debate issues that affect our membership.

As part of the union's commitment to working collectively, its 2002 Bargaining Conference brought people together to discuss collective-bargaining issues. The outcome of the conference was to focus efforts on improved wages and benefits, shorter work time, greater job security, and renewed efforts by the CAW to minimize the effects of a changing Canadian economy on its members. This is a very different agenda from three years ago when the focus was on greater technological training to avoid job loss, wage increases that are comparable to those of managers, and involvement with the companies in redesigning jobs—not just for improved company performance but also for better employee satisfaction. It would appear that CAW is sounding like a traditional trade union.

Although the CAW has its roots in the auto industry, it has branched out into many other sectors of the Canadian economy. And because it started in the auto industry, most of the members originally were from Ontario. Today, one-third of the membership comes from outside Ontario. The union has achieved its growth by moving into other sectors and at the same time recognizing that young people need to be informed about the benefits of unions. It is having to do this because of declines in union membership in its traditional industries.

As Hargrove explains, the main issue confronting the CAW today is not only whether the union can survive, but also whether it can continue to play a crucial leadership role within Canadian labour and Canadian society:

> The future of the CAW is to increase the size of our union by signing on new members and more union mergers. There are a lot of smaller unions that do not have the resources to represent their membership appropriately; by pooling resources, they will be better represented. We also can't keep increasing our member dues. [Our members] have been faced with large tax increases and they just can't make any more financial sacrifices. The manufacturing sector will remain an important target, since we believe that it will continue to grow over the next few decades. The service sector will be another target. Key to these strategies will be the rebuilding of our political base in Canada and finding means to bring our members around to the concepts of equity and diversity.

CRITICAL THINKING QUESTIONS

1. What is your view of Buzz Hargrove's comments?
2. Do you think unions ought to be able to organize workers in any industry, like retail or fast food? Why?

Source: Adapted from *Bargaining in Tough Times*, www.caw.ca (retrieved May 17, 2002); Peter Brieger, "The CAW: Heading Down?" *Financial Post*, October 17, 2002, FP9.

Role of the Union (Shop) Steward

Union (shop) steward
Employee who, as a nonpaid union official, represents the interests of members in their relations with management

The **union (shop) steward** represents the interests of union members in their relations with their immediate supervisors and other members of management. Union stewards are employees of the company and are normally selected by union members within their department and serve without union pay.

A union steward can be viewed as a "person in the middle," caught between conflicting interests and groups. It cannot be assumed that stewards will always champion union members and routinely oppose managerial objectives. Union stewards are often

Buzz Hargrove, president of the Canadian Auto Workers, spends time at the union's annual convention with representatives of local unions.

insightful individuals working for the betterment of employees and the organization. Therefore supervisors and managers at all levels are encouraged to develop a positive working relationship with stewards and all union officials. This relationship can have an important bearing on union–management cooperation and demonstrate to the workers that labour and management can have common interests.[24]

Role of the Business Agent

Business agent
Normally a paid labour official responsible for negotiating and administering the collective agreement and working to resolve union members' problems

Negotiating and administering the collective agreement and working to resolve problems arising in connection with it are major responsibilities of the **business agent**. In performing these duties, business agents must be all things to all people within their unions. They frequently are required to assume the role of counsellor in helping union members with both personal and job-related problems. They are also expected to satisfactorily resolve grievances that cannot be settled by the union stewards. Administering the daily affairs of the local union is another significant part of the business agent's job.

Union Leadership Approaches and Philosophies

To evaluate the role of union leaders accurately, one must understand the nature of their backgrounds and ambitions and recognize the political nature of the offices they occupy. The leaders of many national unions have been able to develop political machines that enable them to defeat opposition and to perpetuate themselves in office. Tenure for the leaders of a local union, however, is less secure. If they are to remain in office, they must be able to convince a majority of the members that they are serving them effectively.

Although it is true that union leaders occupy positions of power within their organizations, rank-and-file members can and often do exercise a strong influence over these leaders, particularly with respect to the negotiation and administration of the collective agreement. It is important for managers to understand that union officials are elected to office and, like any political officials, must be responsive to the views of their constituency. The union leader who ignores the demands of union members may risk (1) being voted out of office, (2) having members vote the union out as their bargaining agent, (3) having members refuse to ratify the union agreement, or (4) having members engage in wildcat strikes or work stoppages.

To be effective leaders, union officials must also pay constant attention to the general goals and philosophies of the labour movement. Unions have historically been very politically active, backing such parties as the NDP. However, if the politicians are not sensitive enough to the goals of the labour movement, union leaders can be very vocal regarding their support of the politicians.[25] Currently, the general goals include increased pay and benefits, job security, and improved working conditions. However, there are times that a union will comment on government policy. For example, the Canadian Auto Workers is still taking issue with NAFTA (the free trade agreement) even though the CLC has recently indicated that the agreement hasn't been bad for Canada.[26] Finally, as part of Canada's adjustment to global competition, union leaders have been active in working with managers to make their respective industries more competitive.

LABOUR RELATIONS IN THE PUBLIC SECTOR

Canadian Union of Public Employees
www.cupe.ca

National Union of Public and General Employees
www.nupge.ca

Public Service Alliance of Canada
www.psac.com

Objective 6

Collective bargaining among federal, provincial, and municipal government employees, and among employees in parapublic agencies (private agencies or branches of the government acting as extensions of government programs), has increased dramatically since the 1960s. More than 75% of all public employees are now unionized.[27] The three largest unions in Canada represent public-sector employees. The Canadian Union of Public Employees (CUPE) is the largest union in Canada, representing 521,600 members. The second-largest union, with 325,000 members, is the National Union of Provincial Government Employees (NUPGE), which represents employees at the provincial level. The largest union representing employees at the federal level is the Public Service Alliance of Canada (PSAC), with 150,000 members.[28] Growth in these unions is threatened by increased cost-cutting efforts of governments at all levels, resulting in employee reductions. It should be noted that the federal government's desire to reform the public service is resulting in a threat to PSAC. Specifically, the government wants approximately 40,000 of its managers taken out of any union by allowing the managers to create an independent association. Part of the issue has to do with managers' image of themselves—where they are part of the decision-making processes in the government and their interests are more aligned with senior management.[29]

While public- and private-sector collective bargaining have many features in common, a number of factors differentiate the two sectors. This section will highlight several of the major differences between public- and private-sector industrial relations and discuss how these differences affect HRM. Three areas will be explored: (1) legislation governing collective bargaining in the public sector, (2) the political nature of the labour–management relationship, and (3) public-sector strikes.

Public-Sector Legislation

The Public Service Staff Relations Act (PSSRA) grants to federal civil servants bargaining rights, including the right to strike and the right to bargain for improvements in wages, hours, and working conditions. The PSSRA created the Public Service Staff Relations

Board, which, like the labour relations boards governing the private sector, has responsibility for certification of unions as bargaining agents and for conflict resolution.

At the provincial level, labour legislation applies to both the public and private sectors. For example, the Quebec Labour Code, the Saskatchewan Trade Union Act, and the British Columbia Labour Relations Code apply to both sectors. Other jurisdictions may operate under more than one piece of legislation; in Ontario, for example, seven different statutes are operative. Some statutes cover more than one sector; in New Brunswick, for instance, statutes cover hospitals, schools, and public utilities.

Political Nature of the Labour–Management Relationship

Government employees are not able to negotiate with their employers on the same basis as their counterparts in private organizations. It is doubtful that they will ever be able to do so because of inherent differences between the public and private sectors.

One of the significant differences is that labour relations in the private sector have an economic foundation, whereas in government their foundation tends to be political. Since private employers must stay in business in order to sell their goods or services, their employees are not likely to make demands that could bankrupt them. A strike in the private sector is a test of the employer's economic staying power, and usually the employer's customers have alternative sources of supply. Governments, on the other hand, must stay in business because alternative services are usually not available. For example, a strike between the Alberta government and the Alberta Teachers' Association was quite severe as there are very few alternatives to a public education. The government seriously considered ordering the teachers back to work to deal with the outcry from parents but in the end passed legislation forcing settlement of the dispute through binding arbitration.[30]

Strikes in the Public Sector

Strikes by government employees create a problem for lawmakers and for the general public. Because the services that government employees provide, such as police work and firefighting, are often considered essential to the well-being of the public, public policy is opposed to such strikes. However, various provincial legislatures have granted public employees the right to strike. Where striking is permitted, the right is limited to specific groups of employees—those performing nonessential services—and the strike cannot endanger the public's health, safety, or welfare. Public-sector unions contend, however, that denying them the same right to strike as employees in the private sector greatly reduces their power during collective bargaining.

One test of the unions' right to strike occurred when the federal government, under provisions in the Public Service Staff Relations Act, attempted to designate all air traffic controllers as essential, even though the parties had previously agreed that all commercial flights would be cancelled in the event of a strike by controllers. The dispute went all the way to the Supreme Court, which ruled in favour of the government and, furthermore, gave the government the authority to determine the necessary level of service. The federal government ultimately declared that 100% of the bargaining unit was essential employees.

Public employees who perform essential services do, in fact, strike. Teachers, sanitation employees, police, transit employees, firefighters, and postal employees have all engaged in strike action. To avoid a potentially critical situation, various arbitration methods are used for resolving collective-bargaining deadlocks in the public sector. One is **compulsory binding arbitration** for employees such as police officers, firefighters,

Compulsory binding arbitration
Binding method of resolving collective-bargaining deadlocks by a neutral third party

Public-sector workers picket to publicize their disputes and discourage people from entering the premises.

Final-offer arbitration
Method of resolving collective-bargaining deadlocks whereby the arbitrator has no power to compromise but must select one or another of the final offers submitted by the two parties

and others in jobs where strikes cannot be tolerated. Another method is **final-offer arbitration**, under which the arbitrator must select one or the other of the final offers submitted by the disputing parties. With this method, the arbitrator's award is more likely to go to the party whose final bargaining offer has moved the closest to a reasonable settlement. The government can also enact back-to-work legislation, an option being used with increasing frequency when there are concerns about public health or safety. For example, during the summer of 2002, the government of Ontario issued back-to-work legislation for the sanitation workers in Toronto. The government stated that there was a concern about the health risks of garbage piling up during very hot weather.[31]

CURRENT CHALLENGES FOR UNIONS

Objective **7**

Unions are no different than other organizations in terms of challenges that must be handled. These challenges are similar to those listed in Chapter 1 that included globalization and technology. In addition, unions are dealing with the changing nature of work, demographics, and innovative work practices.

Globalization

As mentioned in Chapter 1, Canadian organizations have had to respond to world-wide competition. Some of this has been as a result of trade agreements, such as NAFTA. Most unions have taken public stands against these types of trade agreements, such as the Canadian Auto Workers (CAW). CAW has continued to oppose free trade, citing that it leads to lost jobs in the manufacturing sector.[32]

Besides protesting free trade agreements, unions have taken issue with a recent federal government decision to allow foreign workers to be recruited into Canada. Specifically, trade unions in British Columbia challenged the decision to allow American workers into the province. The union stated that there were sufficient people in B.C. to fill jobs at a Surrey steel mill and that there was no need to allow non-Canadian workers to be hired.[33]

On the other hand, unions can be supportive of business approaches to enable the company to be more competitive. For example, when Hydro One (formerly Ontario Hydro) was considering privatization, its union, Power Workers Union, indicated support for this in a variety of ways, including a one-page ad in the *Financial Post*. Not only did the ad encourage the privatization and issuing of stock, but it suggested its members and general public buy shares as it represented an "investment and jobs."[34]

The issue of competition applies not just in Canada. Around the World with HRM 10.1 describes union concerns in China, the U.K., and Germany.

Technological Change

Improvements in computer technology and highly automated operating systems have lowered the demand for certain types of employees. Decline in membership in the auto, steel, rubber, and transportation unions illustrates this fact. Technological advances have also

---

around the world **with HRM 10.1** around the world

UNION CONCERNS IN OTHER COUNTRIES

In late 2004, Wal-Mart made headlines in China by allowing employees in Chinese stores to have trade unions. Wal-Mart has prided itself in being the largest nonunion store in the United States; therefore, this is quite a departure. The company indicated it is doing so to respect the wishes of employees and honour its obligations under Chinese law. However, some investors have expressed concern that if Chinese employees become unionized, it would reduce the company's ability to keep prices low. On the other hand, it is felt that the union drive is a last-ditch effort to penetrate the most dynamic sector of the Chinese economy and shore up a declining membership.[35]

Workers at Volkswagen's plant walked off the job in the fall of 2004 to protest potential job cuts. The company had warned that cost savings must happen and if collective bargaining can't achieve the necessary savings, then it would have to reduce its workforce. VW is looking to cut 30% from its costs by 2011. However, it did offer to guarantee the jobs of its more than 176,000 workers if they would agree to a wage freeze. Workers responded by striking.[36]

And in the U.K., Prime Minister Tony Blair refused to intervene in the London firefighters dispute—a strike by 50,000 firefighters. At the centre of the strike is the union demand for a 40% wage increase compared to an 11% (over two years) offer from the government. The government said it would not provide any change in its wage offer unless there were changes in working practices. Further, it would not do anything that would cause damage to the economy or be seen as unfair to other government workers, such as teachers, nurses, and police.[37]

In 2002, the United Auto Workers and the Canadian Auto Workers renewed their efforts to establish a presence in Mexico. The unions were concerned that Mexico's pro-government unions were helping the country attract investment and jobs from Canada and the United States. On one hand, these unions had an interest in keeping jobs where they were; on the other hand, there was an opportunity for the UAW and CAW to expand and create very powerful alliances to deal with the automakers.[38]

diminished the effectiveness of strikes because highly automated organizations are capable of maintaining satisfactory levels of operation with minimum staffing levels during work stoppages. At one point the CAW threatened to strike if Ford followed through on its plans to shut up to seven North American plants and reduce 35,000 jobs.[39]

Changes to the Nature of Work

The nature of work has and is changing. No longer are there as many large organizations with very stable workforces. Many organizations are small businesses with few employees. Also, more work is being done by contract, part-time employees.

In the past, white-collar employees tended to identify themselves with owners or managers as a group enjoying certain privileges (e.g., not having to punch a time clock) and socioeconomic status that blue-collar workers did not possess. Improvements in working conditions, for which union members had to make sacrifices, generally were extended to the white-collar group without any need for collective action on their part. The high turnover rate of employees in clerical jobs also increased the difficulty of organizing them. In recent years, however, growth in the size of private organizations has tended to depersonalize the work of white-collar groups and to isolate them from management. The lack of job security during economic downturns, together with growing difficulties in attempting to resolve complaints about working conditions, has helped to push white-collar workers toward unionization.

In response to these changes, unions are stepping up their efforts to organize white-collar workers. Some unions are targeting the financial sectors, including banking and insurance. Other unions are recruiting employees of small businesses and employees in the so-called pink-collar ghetto, a term describing low-paying clerical and sales positions traditionally held by women. For example, the CAW has unionized the following industries: food and beverage, hospitality and service, electrical and aerospace. Perhaps the most notable attempt to organize nonunion workers has been the drive by the United Food and Commercial Workers (UFCW) to unionize Wal-Mart. In 2004, a Wal-Mart store in Quebec was certified—the only one in North America.[40] The UFCW indicated it was concerned that the world's largest retailer could drive down wages in the food industry.[41] For a more complete understanding of the issues between Wal-Mart and the UFCW, read At Work with HRM 10.2.

CAW also has successfully organized the Casino Windsor, Fairmont Hotels, and some of the Delta Hotels. Issues with these employers have included ways and means to increase growth in tourism—especially important since September 11, 2001. Likewise, the Communications, Energy and Paperworkers (CEP) represents employees of the Web site torstar.com. These are just some of the examples of how unions have moved into the service sector.[42] To get a fuller appreciation of the range of different unions in different industries, review At Work with HRM 10.3.

Demographics

Union membership in Canada in 2001 constituted 31.3% of the workforce.[43] This percentage has declined steadily since the early 1990s. Despite the decrease in union membership, there has been a steep increase in the number of unionized female workers. As of 2003, 48% of union members were women, an increase from 12% in 1977. Part of the reason for this is the growing proportion of women in the paid workforce, the number of women in the public sector, and the drive to unionize the service sector— which is heavily dominated by women.[44]

at work **with HRM 10.2** at work with HRM 10.2

UNIONIZATION OF A WORLD GIANT

Union organizers at the United Food and Commercial Workers have targeted Wal-Mart to unionize its workers. But what are the issues and what is the success to date?

In mid-2004, the UFCW had been successful in organizing three retail outlets in Quebec. The union is concerned that Wal-Mart has been successful in keeping the wages of employees down. It is also fearful that as Wal-Mart continues to expand in Canada, wages in the food industry will be driven down. Wal-Mart, with over 230 stores in Canada, is planning to build "supercentres" which will sell groceries, household items, and clothing. This is a strategic direction to continue its growth and success.

However, it was within a few months of the first unionized store in Quebec that Wal-Mart Canada determined that the store was losing money. Wal-Mart indicated it had been a steady loser in sales since its opening in 2001 and that the workforce was too fractured to help with long-term success. For many people it wasn't a surprise when Wal-Mart announced in early 2005 that it would close that store. However, the UFCW immediately filed charges of bad-faith bargaining (a collective agreement had not as yet been concluded from the time it was unionized in 2004) and

unfair labour practices. It stated that this was a ploy to get rid of its unionized workers. Wal-Mart countered that the store was not meeting financial objectives. As of April 29, 2005, the store was closed and 200 employees were let go.

At the same time, the UFCW was attempting to organize workers in some Wal-Mart stores in northern British Columbia. But the Labour Relations Board determined that it had failed to sign up enough workers and the store in Terrace remains nonunion. The UCFW is continuing its drive to organize stores in other parts of British Columbia, Saskatchewan, and Ontario. In early March 2005, Wal-Mart employees at its Windsor, Ontario, store re-organized. It has been the first Wal-Mart to be certified (1997) and was decertified in 2002. However, the UCFW was able to have 40% of the staff sign union cards—the minimum amount required for a certification vote by the Ontario Labour Relations Board.

CRITICAL THINKING QUESTION

Do you think any union will be successful in unionizing many of Wal-Mart stores? Why or why not?

Sources: Adapted from "Board Rejects Wal-Mart Challenge to Unionization," *The Globe and Mail*, September 11, 2004, B6; Rachel Katz, "Wal-Mart Faces Opposition to 'Supercentres,'" *Financial Post*, October 6, 2004, FP3; Scott Simpson, "Unionizing Effort Fails at Terrace Wal-Mart," *The Vancouver Sun*, October7, 2004, D1; "Union Kept Out of North B.C. Wal-Mart," *Financial Post*, October 7, 2004, FP9; Sheila McGovern, "Wal-Mart Says Its Only Unionized Store Is Losing Money," *The Vancouver Sun*, October 14, 2004, D10; Derrick Penner, "Wal-Mart Faces New Union Fight," *The Vancouver Sun*, November 2, 2004, D1; and "Wal-Mart Union to File Charges," *National Post*, February 14, 2005, A7; Craig Pearson," "Certificate Vote at Windsor Wal-Mart," *The Vancouver Sun*, March 3, 2005, D6; Michael Forman, "No Wal-Mart Smile in Jonquière," UCFW, www.ufcw.ca/cgi-bin/full_story.cgi?story_id=1556&from_page=6 (retrieved May 30, 2005).

at work **with HRM 10.3** at work with HRM 10.3

DIFFERENT UNIONS IN DIFFERENT INDUSTRIES

Brewery, General and Professional Workers' Union (BG&PW)

- Bacardi-Martini Canada

- East Toronto Legal Services

- Glengarry Sports Palace

- Howard Johnson

- Olympia and York Properties

Canadian Auto Workers (CAW)

- AT&T Canada

- Pinkerton's

- University of Manitoba

- Holiday Inn

- Sheraton Hotels

Communication, Energy, and Paperworkers' Union of Canada (CEP)

- NOVA

- Patricia Gardens Nursery

- Calian Technology

- Mr. Furnace

- Secur Tech

CRITICAL THINKING QUESTION

Do you think unions can effectively represent the interests of its members in such diverse industries? Why or why not?

Sources: Information accessed on union Web sites: www.bgpwu.ca/; www.caw.ca; www.cep.ca (retrieved August 9, 2002).

With the shift away from the industrial sector, we are also seeing an increase in knowledge workers (see Chapter 1). People in these sectors are usually more educated and therefore tend to resist the idea of collective action. Knowledge workers are very individualistic and rely upon their own capabilities to succeed. Therefore, unions have a much more difficult time attempting to organize people who do not share the same concerns as the labour movement.[45]

Innovative Workplace Practices

Organizations have been using new and innovative work practices to increase organizational performance and employee satisfaction. As mentioned in Chapter 3, supervisors and managers are actively involving employees in making decisions in the workplace. By encouraging employees, and by being supportive of employees' desire to be involved, companies may change not just the performance of the company but also the labour–management relationship. For example, Bryan Baxter, a job trainer at Weyerhaeuser, encourages employees to think about global competition in the forest industry and to find ways of improving what they do. Although this isn't an unusual appeal, it is a new role for Baxter, a 24-year member of the Pulp, Paper and Woodworkers of Canada, the same militant union that conducted the longest strike (nine months) in the history of the Canadian pulp and paper industry.[46] By involving Baxter in a different way, Weyerhaeuser is helping to create a better relationship between the company and the union.

This type of work environment also changes the role of the supervisor to that of coach. Frequently in these new work arrangements, pay may be contingent on individual performance. Further, employees may also share in the success of the company with the possibility of profit sharing.

Lastly, there is some suggestion that as work practices change, there is a blending of various people practices in organizations and there is less need for the style of unionization that has existed for many years.[47]

SUMMARY

1. Explain the supervisor's role in labour relations.
   - Labour relations influences what a supervisor does and how an employee is treated.

2. Explain the federal and provincial legislation that provides the framework for labour relations.
   - Laws determine who can unionize.
   - Laws require that unions and employers bargain in good faith.
   - Laws provide for unions to strike and for employers to lock out.

3. Cite the reasons employees join unions.
   - Dissatisfaction with pay and benefits.
   - Dissatisfaction with managerial practices.
   - Desire for recognition and status.

4. Describe the process by which unions organize employees and gain recognition as their bargaining agent.
   - Employees make contact with a union representative.
   - Union schedules meeting with other employees.
   - Application is made to labour relations board.
   - Labour relations board grants bargaining rights.

5. Describe the functions labour unions perform at the national and local levels.
   - National unions help organize local unions.
   - National unions help train and educate local unions.
   - Local unions negotiate collective agreement and process member grievances.

6. Describe the differences between private-sector and public-sector labour relations.
   - There may be specialized legislation governing public-sector unions.
   - There is a political element in labour–management relations.
   - Strikes may be banned in the public sector.

7. List some of the current challenges for labour organizations.
   - Globalization.
   - Technological changes.
   - Changing nature of work, including more service workers, part-time workers, and contract workers.
   - Demographics.
   - Innovative workplace practices, resulting in increased employee satisfaction.

Need to Know

- Legislation in your province governing labour relations
- Steps employees go through to unionize
- Current challenges for unions

Need to Understand

- Relationship of supervisory actions and behaviours in employees unionizing
- Expected behaviours from employers and unions during organizing drive
- Impact of unionization on supervisory actions

Key Terms

bargaining unit 369

business agent 376

certification 370

closed shop 363

compulsory binding arbitration 378

craft unions 373

employee associations 373

final-offer arbitration 379

industrial unions 373

labour relations process 362

management rights 372

membership card 367

open shop 363

unfair labour practices 369

union (shop) steward 375

union shop 363

REVIEW QUESTIONS

1. Describe how labour relations are regulated at the federal and provincial levels.
2. Which unfair labour practices apply to (1) unions and (2) employers?
3. Describe the impact on supervisory actions after employees have become unionized.
4. What is the role of a business agent? A shop steward?
5. What are some of the challenges for unions today?

CRITICAL THINKING QUESTIONS

1. You have recently been appointed as a shop steward for your work unit. The supervisor of the unit tends to be fairly autocratic and directive in his approach to staff. However, you feel that the supervisor has always been fair in dealing with members of the bargaining unit. What type of relationship would you want to develop with the supervisor? Why?
2. Contrast the arguments concerning union membership that are likely to be presented by a union with those likely to be presented by an employer.
3. Provincial labour laws typically do not cover individuals who are self-employed. What arguments might you give for stating that the government ought to change its labour laws to protect self-employed individuals?

4. One of your friends is a supervisor in a fast-food restaurant. The restaurant has just become unionized and your friend is not sure how to treat his staff. What advice would you give?

DEVELOPING YOUR SKILLS

1. There has been a substantial increase (some estimate 40%) in the number of individuals who are self-employed. Some see this as a positive sign (i.e., of an increase in entrepreneurial activity); others see it as a response to the lack of permanent employment opportunities. The labour laws in each province effectively ignore independent workers. For many of them, wages (i.e., contract rates) are low, working conditions are difficult, and income security does not exist. Prepare to debate solutions to this issue, taking one of two sides: "Governments should change labour laws to recognize and protect self-employed workers," or "Unions should organize these independent contractors and fight for better treatment."

2. Get a copy of the labour code (or labour code guidelines) for your province. Explain each of the following provisions contained in the code:

   - organizing
   - certification and decertification
   - unfair labour practices
   - dispute resolution
   - strikes, lockouts
   - picketing

3. During a union organizing drive, labour and management will develop a plan to present their positions to employees. A goal of each side will be to collect information on the other that can be used to build a case for or against the union. Additionally, each side will seek to avoid committing unfair labour practices. Working in teams of union and management representatives, answer the following questions and be prepared to present your findings during a discussion period.

   a. What methods might the union use to contact employees?
   b. What information might the union collect on management in order to obtain employee support?
   c. What information might management want to collect on the union?
   d. What methods might unions and management use to tell their story to employees? What illegal actions will the union and management want to guard against?
   e. Access the following union Web sites:

      - **www.cupe.ca**
      - **www.caw.ca**
      - **www.iwa.ca**

   Review the profile of the union and the current issues it supports. Compare each union with regard to membership and issues. Bring your information to class and share it in groups of four to five. Identify at least one aspect of the Web site that surprised you and one thing that impressed you.

Canadian Union of Public Employees
www.cupe.ca

Canadian Auto Workers
www.caw.ca

Industrial, Wood, and Allied Workers of Canada
www.iwa.ca

Canadian Labour Congress

www.clc-ctc.ca

American Federation of Labor

www.aflcio.org

International Labour Organization

www.ilo.org/

f. Listed below are Web sites for umbrella labour organizations in Canada, the United States, and an international association. Check out each of the Web sites. Prepare a one- to two-page paper comparing and contrasting the key issues.

- **www.clc-ctc.ca**
- **www.aflcio.org**
- **www.ilo.org/**

Case Study **1**

Wal-Mart Stores in Canada

In 2003, Wal-Mart was operating more than 4,650 stores with 1.3 million employees around the world. In the early 1990s Wal-Mart Stores Inc. expanded into Canada, with the purchase of 122 stores from the failing Woolco chain. Wal-Mart had refused to purchase nine Woolco stores, which were unionized.

Wal-Mart tries to distinguish itself from other retailers by its culture. For example, it calls its workers "associates," not employees. Every day at 8:45 a.m., a compulsory meeting is held at each store during which company managers share financial information and performance targets and respond to questions. The meeting ends with the Wal-Mart cheer. The company operates an open-door policy, whereby any employee can talk to any member of management about issues, and receive answers, without being threatened with reprisal. The sundown rule ensures that management responds to the questions before sundown the same day.

The first Wal-Mart store ever to be unionized was in Windsor, Ontario, where the United Steelworkers (Retail and Wholesale Division) was certified by the Ontario Labour Relations Board. On April 14, 1997, the United Steelworkers began its organizing drive. On April 26, the store manager became aware that associates were being approached to sign unionization cards. The district manager was told of the organizing drive and the next morning attended the morning meeting. The district manager asked the associates why they would want to join a union and spent the day circulating through the store to discuss their problems or concerns. By April 27, 84 associates had signed cards. On April 29, an associate asked to speak at the morning meeting, and there expressed her opposition to the union, ending with the statement, "A union will only cause discontentment in our store, and I assure you as I am standing here, Wal-Mart will not put up with it." (Management did not ask, nor did the associate reveal, why she wanted to speak.) An inside organizer was prevented from responding because it was 9 a.m. and customers were waiting to enter the store.

Between May 4 and May 9, Wal-Mart managers—including managers from outside the store—responded to questions placed in a question-and-answer box, and to those raised while they wandered about the store. Most of the questions focused on compensation and hours of work. However, one associate testified that one manager said that things would change if the employees were unionized—for example, the profit-sharing plan would be revoked. During one meeting, the managers were asked if the store would close; they replied, "It would be inappropriate for your company to comment on what it will or will not do if the store is unionized." On May 9, the union lost the vote, with 151 employees voting against it, and 43 voting for it.

The Ontario Labour Relations Board nonetheless certified the union, because the employer violated the *Labour Relations Act* by not disassociating itself from the remarks made by the associate at the meeting; by not allowing the inside organizer to respond; by subtly threatening job security; and by allowing outside managers in the store from May 4 to 9. The OLRB stated that the union had 84 cards signed before the managers' visits, and a week later, this support had dropped. A second vote would not change the outcome, because the threat to job security could not be erased from employees' minds. The legislation that allows the OLRB to overturn a certification board has now been changed.

Despite numerous organizing drives, Wal-Mart has successfully prevented unionization, and most of their 213 Canadian stores remain union-free. The United Food and Commercial Workers Union (UFCW) charged Wal-Mart with unfair labour practices in thwarting a union organizing drive in British Columbia by discrediting the key organizer and by advising employees that if he turned up at their homes, they could call the police. The B.C. Labour Board said, "Wal-Mart has an anti-union history . . . and simply cannot resist the temptation to get involved in certification campaigns. While Wal-Mart has tended not to repeat its mistakes, there is no shortage of new ones that it finds ways to make."

Sources: Adapted from V. Galt, "Wal-Mart Must Give Union Access," *The Globe and Mail*, May 13, 2003: B5; J. Hobel, "Allegation of Union Vote Rigging Investigated at Wal-Mart," *Canadian HR Reporter*, September 20, 1999: 1, 19; "Employer Interference: The Wal-Mart Case," *Worklife Report* 11, no. 2: 1–4.

Questions

1. What were the rights of Wal-Mart, the employer, during these two organizing drives?
2. The certification of the first Wal-Mart was hailed by labour as a milestone event. Why?
3. In your opinion, can Wal-Mart remain union-free indefinitely? Why or why not?

Case Study **2**

Eastern Province Corporation: The Organizing Drive

Sally Sandhu, HR director for Eastern Province Corporation, had little experience with unions in general and no specific experience with union organizing campaigns. Unfortunately for Sandhu, the Brotherhood of Machine Engineers, Local 1463, began an organizing drive against Eastern Province on June 1. While the union's initial efforts were confined to passing out information notices about an organizational meeting, by June 10 it was obvious that employee support for the union had grown and union campaigning had greatly intensified. The question faced by Sandhu was no longer "Should Eastern Province do something?" but rather "What can Eastern Province do?" It was obvious to Sandhu that the union was committed to a full-fledged effort to unionize the company's employees. Supervisors reported to her that union supporters were passing out union membership cards in order to petition the labour relations board for a certification election.

Questions

1. Since the job of a labour organizer is to build a case for the union and against the company, what information about the organization do you think the union organizer would like to have?
2. What should Eastern Province do—both strategically and tactically—to defeat the organizing drive? Why would Eastern Province not want a union? Be specific in your answers.
3. List things that managers should *not* do for fear that they commit unfair labour practices.

NOTES AND REFERENCES

1. For a more complete understanding of the labour relations system, refer to J. T. Dunlop, *Industrial Relations Systems*, rev. ed. (Boston: Harvard Business School Press, 1993); and Alton W. J. Craig and Norma A. Solomon, *The System of Industrial Relations in Canada*, 5th ed. (Scarborough, Ont.: Prentice Hall Canada Inc., 1996).
2. Bruce E. Kaufman, "Reflections on Six Decades in Industrial Relations: An Interview with John Dunlop," *Industrial and Labor Relations Review* 55, no. 2 (January 2002): 324–48; C. Heron, *The Canadian Labour Movement: A Short History* (Toronto: James Lorimer & Company, 1989).
3. M. Gunderson, A. Ponak, and D. Gottlieb Taras, *Union Management Relations in Canada*, 4th ed. (Toronto: Addison Wesley Longman, 2001).
4. To read more about the labour relations process, consult John Pierce, *Canadian Industrial Relations*, 2nd ed. (Toronto: Pearson Education, 2003) and Gunderson, Ponak, and Taras, *Union–Management Relations in Canada*.
5. Robert R. Sinclair and Lois E. Tetrick, "Social Exchange and Union Commitment: A Comparison of Union Instrumentality and Union Support Perceptions," *Journal of Organizational Behavior* 16, no. 6 (November 1995): 669–79.
6. P. Kumar and G. Murray, "Union Bargaining Priorities in the New Economy: Results for the 2000 HRDC Survey on Innovation and Change in Labour Organizations in Canada," *Workplace Gazette*, Winter 2001, 43–45.
7. "Gricore Staff Reject Union, Company Says," *Financial Post*, March 19, 2002, FP4.
8. John Pierce, *Canadian Industrial Relations*, 2nd ed.: 125–34.
9. Conversation with the Vice-President, Human Resources, McDonald's Canada, March 2002.
10. John Greenwood, "CAW Calls for Job Action in Starbucks Talks," *Financial Post*, May 14, 2002, FP 9.
11. Lorna Harris, "Labour Board Punishes Employer for Heavy-Handed Efforts to Block Union," *Canadian HR Reporter* 15, no. 9 (May 6, 2002): 6.
12. K. J. Bentham, "Employer Resistance to Union Certification: A Study of Canadian Jurisdictions," *Relations Industrielles*, Winter 2002, 159–87.
13. Lorna Harris, "Labour Board Punishes Employer for Heavy-Handed Efforts to Block Union," 14.
14. Hugh Finnamore, "Imbalance on the Labour Scene Hurts Businesses," *The Vancouver Sun*, October 31, 2001, A23; www.caw.ca/news/videonews/recent/010720_1e.asp (retrieved August 7, 2002); and www.mfl.mb.ca/newsletter/archive/2001/newslet_mar2001.htm (retrieved August 7, 2002).
15. Canada Industrial Relations Board regulations and *Ontario Labour Relations Act*.
16. Kate Jaimet, "Supreme Court Upholds Quebec Law on Building Unions," *The Vancouver Sun*, October 20, 2001, A18.

17. Peter Breiger, "Union Loses Argument Stelco Not Insolvent," *Financial Post*, December 10, 2004, FP4.

18. Juliet O'Neill, "CLC Attacks Overtime, Says It Costs 200,000 Jobs," *The Vancouver Sun*, September 8, 2001, C3.

19. Bill Curry, "Labour Boss Georgetti Concedes Free Trade Good for Canada After All," *The Vancouver Sun*, September 22, 2004, A1.

20. Workplace Information Directorate, "Union Membership in Canada 2002."

21. Gordon Hamilton, "IWA Merger 'Done,'" *The Vancouver Sun*, August 28, 2004, F1.

22. Gordon Hamilton, "IWA Seeks Merger Partner," *The Vancouver Sun*, February 28, 2004, H1.

23. Godard, *Industrial Relations*, 228.

24. Katy Burnett, "Management and Labour Can Work Together," *Canadian HR Reporter*, October 11, 2004: 15–16.

25. Juliet O'Neill, "Hargrove Seeks Resignation of NDP Leader McDonough," *The Vancouver Sun*, November 23, 2001, A16.

26. Bill Curry, "CAW Still Wants to Scrap NAFTA," *The Vancouver Sun*, September 23, 2004, A3.

27. Visit these websites: www.cupe.ca; www.nupge.ca; www.psac.com; and www.clc-ctc.ca.

28. *Ibid.*

29. Kathryn May, "Middle Managers' Union Ties at Stake in Civil Service Row," *National Post*, January 7, 2002, A5.

30. Darren Yourk, "Alberta Teachers Win Reprieve," *The Globe and Mail*, February 19, 2002, www.globemandmail.com/ (retrieved February 20, 2002); News Release, Government of Alberta, March 7, 2002, "Government to Seek Arbitrated Settlement in Teachers' Dispute," http://WWW.GOV.AB.CA/acn/200203/12016.html (retrieved October 18, 2002).

31. Legislative Assembly, http://gateway.ontla.on.ca:80/hansard/house_debates/37_parl/Session3;L029.htm (retrieved August 7, 2002).

32. Bill Curry, "CAW Still Wants to Scrap NAFTA."

33. Adrienne Tanner, "Trade Unions Decry Decision to Import Labour," *Financial Post*, March 16, 2004, FP9.

34. Paul Vieira, "Power Union Backs Hydro One Bid for Privatization," *Financial Post*, April 23, 2002, F7–9.

35. "Wal-Mart Will Allow Unions in Chinese Stores," *The Vancouver Sun*, November 24, 2004, D11.

36. Matt Surman, "Workers Walk Out As VW Warns of Job Cuts," *The Vancouver Sun*, October 26, 2004, D12.

37. "Blair Won't Budget Despite Walkout by Firefighters," *National Post*, November 26, 2002, A17; "Soldiers Man U.K. Fire Hoses," *The Vancouver Sun*, November 15, 2002, A8.39.

38. Andrea Mandel-Campbell, "Mexican Standoff: Unions in Power Battle," *Financial Post*, May 14, 2002, FP1.

39. Doug Williamson, "Ford to Cut 35,000 Jobs."

40. Sheila McGovern, "Wal-Mart Says Its Only Unionized Store Is Losing Money," *The Vancouver Sun*, October 24, 2004, D10.

41. Frederic Tomesco, "Workers at Another Wal-Mart Seek Union," *Financial Post*, October 6, 2004, FP 3.

42. Information extracted from CAW and CEP Web sites, www.caw.ca and www.cep.ca, August 7, 2002.

43. Table 1, *Workplace Gazette*, Fall 2001, Vol. 4, No. 3, 36.

44. Bruce Little, "Women Play Increasing Role in Union Movement," *The Globe and Mail*, September 6, 2004.

45. Uyen Vu, "Are Knowledge Workers Beyond Unions' Reach?" *Canadian HR Reporter*, June 16, 2004, www.hrreporter.com/loginarea/members/viewing.asp?ArticleNo=3268&viewwhat=Print&subscriptionType=PRINT&callerpage=whoswho (retrieved February 19, 2005).

46. Jon Ferry, "The (New) Rules," *BC Business*, August 1999, 52–55.

47. Harry C. Katz and Owen Darbishire, "Converging Divergences: Worldwide Changes in Employment Systems," *Industrial and Labor Relations Review*, April 2001, 54, no. 3, 681–93.

CHAPTER 11

Collective Bargaining and Contract Administration

OBJECTIVES

After studying this chapter, you should be able to

1 Describe the bargaining process and the bargaining goals and strategies of a union and an employer.

2 Describe the forms of bargaining power that a union and an employer may utilize to enforce their bargaining demands.

3 Cite the principal methods by which bargaining deadlocks may be resolved.

4 Give examples of current collective bargaining trends.

5 Identify the major provisions of a collective agreement and describe the issue of management rights.

6 Describe a typical grievance procedure.

7 Explain the basis for arbitration awards.

OUTLINE

HRM
Close-Up

Aaron McKey, global prototype operations manager, Ford Motor Company

"If one trait characterizes labour relations at Essex, it's a mutual understanding about the business goals of the company."

Aaron McKey has spent most of his long career at the Ford Motor Company, where he started as an engineer and is currently global prototype operations manager. He spent several years at the Essex Engine Plant in Windsor, Ontario, where he oversaw 290 salaried employees (the supervisors and engineers who are *not* unionized), and 1,565 hourly workers (who are).

If improving quality and enhancing productivity are overriding goals, "developing a philosophy and sticking to it" remains McKey's managing mantra. His philosophy is simple: "Administer the contract fairly." Like all car companies, Ford of Canada has labour experts who negotiate new collective agreements every three years with the Canadian Auto Workers union. Although the industry remains highly structured, understanding the agreement—which "basically governs the responsibilities of the hourly workforce"—is not overly difficult, says McKey. Little substantial change occurs over time. As well as setting guidelines for what workers can and can't do, the agreement also outlines what management can and cannot *ask* them to do. A national contract is negotiated for all Ford plants, but each has its own bargaining committee so that local issues can be addressed.

Although plant managers have little to do with the process, McKey had some say in identifying the needs particular to the Essex Engine plant. For example, hourly employees in Canada cannot be made to work more than 48 hours a week. But Essex supplies both Canada and the United States—where overtime laws are less strict—so, McKey says, "there could be a need for a different operating pattern. So we would make a business case, put the requirement in front of the local committee, and ask for flexibility

to work around the needs of our customers: the assembly plants we ship to."

As the bargaining process can affect the working environment, negotiations take place off-site. "If we're making progress, it's invisible at the plant," McKey says. "But if talks break down, there can be some frustrating moments." Like most Ford managers, McKey has undergone training to understand what occurs during negotiating sessions and how to diffuse issues if they arise on the floor. However, both parties respect the process, says McKey, and understand that until a tentative deal is reached, "what's being negotiated stays behind closed doors." As for grievances, most occur when a worker doesn't understand the contractual rights and are easily settled. If an investigation does find a violation by management, "we put actions in place to prevent this from happening again," states McKey.

If one trait characterizes labour relations at the Essex Engine Plant, McKey says, "it's a mutual understanding about the business goals of the company." In today's automotive industry, people "don't really need to be managed." They do need to be given the right tools, the right training, and a clear understanding of the company's objectives. As McKey explains: "When you do that, I've found that 95% of the employees do a good job. And if management is fair in administering the agreement, issues won't surface that get in the way of producing the product."

INTRODUCTION

Once a union wins bargaining rights for employees, its two primary functions are to negotiate the collective agreement and resolve member complaints, usually through the grievance-arbitration process. Interestingly, according to labour law, once the union is certified to negotiate for bargaining-unit members, it must represent everyone in the unit equally, regardless of whether employees subsequently join the union or elect to remain nonmembers. The collective agreement that is ultimately negotiated establishes the wages, hours, employee benefits, job security, and other conditions under which represented employees agree to work.

In HRM Close-Up, Aaron McKey talks about the importance of understanding the collective agreement. This chapter is important to managers since it discusses the process by which an agreement is reached between labour and management. In addition, it describes the day-to-day administration of the agreement. It is concerned also with the changes that have occurred in the bargaining relationship as it has evolved from an adversarial relationship to a more cooperative one. Even under cooperative conditions, however, collective bargaining requires that negotiators possess special skills and knowledge if they are to represent their parties successfully. Union negotiators must be able to produce a collective agreement that members will find acceptable. An employer's negotiators, on the other hand, must come up with an agreement that will allow the employer to remain competitive. The agreement must be one that can be administered with a minimum of conflict and that facilitates other HR processes.

THE COLLECTIVE BARGAINING PROCESS

Objective **1**

Collective bargaining process
Process of negotiating a collective agreement, including the use of economic pressures by both parties

Those unfamiliar with contract negotiations often view the collective bargaining process as an emotional conflict between labour and management, complete with marathon sessions and fist pounding. In reality, negotiating a collective agreement entails long hours of extensive preparation combined with diplomatic manoeuvring and the development of bargaining strategies. Furthermore, negotiation is only one part of the **collective bargaining process**. Collective bargaining may also include the use of economic pressures in the form of strikes and boycotts by a union. Lockouts, plant closures, and the replacement of strikers are similar pressures used by an employer. In addition, either or both parties may seek support from the general public or from the courts as a means of pressuring the opposing side. To help you understand the collective bargaining process, review Figure 11.1.

Good-Faith Bargaining

Once a union has been recognized as the representative for employees, an employer is obligated to negotiate in good faith with the union's representatives over conditions of employment. Good faith requires the employer's negotiators to meet with their union counterparts at a reasonable time and place to discuss these conditions. In discussing the other party's proposals, each side will put forward their demands and attempt to justify their position.[1] Finally, at the conclusion of negotiations, a written document— the collective agreement—is produced, which governs the day-to-day employment

FIGURE 11.1   The Collective Bargaining Process

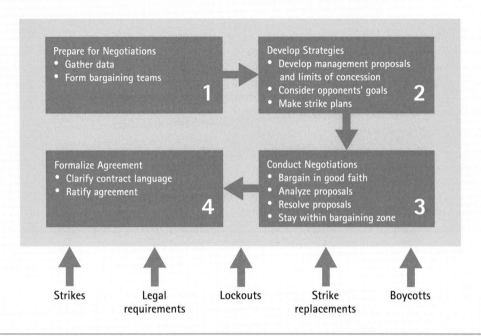

relationship.[2] Furthermore, an employer cannot override the bargaining process by making an offer directly to the employees. Figure 11.2 illustrates several common examples of bad-faith employer bargaining.

Preparing for Negotiations

Preparing for negotiations includes planning the strategy and assembling data to support bargaining proposals. This will permit collective bargaining to be conducted in an orderly fashion and on a factual and positive basis with a greater likelihood of achieving desired goals. Negotiators often develop a bargaining book that serves as a cross-reference file to determine which contract clauses would be affected by a demand. The bargaining book also contains a general history of contract terms and their relative importance to management.[3] Assuming that the collective agreement is not the first to be negotiated by the parties, preparation for negotiations ideally should start soon after the current agreement has been signed. This practice will allow negotiators to review and diagnose weaknesses and mistakes made during the previous negotiations while the experience is still current in their minds.

Gathering Bargaining Data

Internal data relating to grievances, disciplinary actions, transfers and promotions, layoffs, overtime, former arbitration awards, and wage payments are useful in formulating and supporting the employer's bargaining position. In addition, information can be obtained from other collective agreements negotiated in the company's industry. These agreements are usually available through the labour relations boards.

FIGURE 11.2   Examples of Bad-Faith Bargaining

Employer

- Using delaying tactics, such as frequent postponements of bargaining sessions
- Insisting that the union stop striking before resuming negotiations
- Unilaterally changing bargaining topics
- Negotiating with individual employees other than authorized union representatives
- Going through the motions of bargaining rather than conducting honest negotiations
- Refusing to meet with authorized union representatives

Union

- Using delaying tactics such as frequent postponements of bargaining sessions
- Withdrawing concessions previously granted
- Unilaterally changing bargaining topics
- Going through the motions of bargaining rather than conducting honest negotiations
- Refusing to meet with authorized employer representatives

The supervisors and managers who must live with and administer the collective agreement are the key sources of ideas and suggestions concerning changes that are needed in the next agreement. It is important that any concerns supervisors and managers might have with the collective agreement are thoroughly understood, considered, and incorporated as appropriate into the overall bargaining approach. Also, their contact with union members and representatives provides them with a firsthand knowledge of the changes that union negotiators are likely to propose. And since it is the supervisor who has to work with the collective agreement on a daily basis, it is important that the supervisors and managers be involved in the data collection process so that they understand and feel part of the bargaining process.

Today, most unions are professional and well-prepared. An example of such a union is the Saskatchewan Union of Nurses.

Data obtained from government sources, such as Statistics Canada bulletins and publications, and agencies, such as the Bureau of Labour Information, can help to support the employer's position during negotiations. These data sources can provide information on general economic conditions, cost-of-living trends, and geographical wage rates covering a wide range of occupations. Software is available to help analyze data. See **www.bargainingpower.com** for a sample.

Bargaining Power
www.bargainingpower.com

Bargaining Patterns

When negotiating contracts, union bargainers talk about "taking wages out of competition." This term refers to having similar contract provisions—particularly concerning wages and benefits—between different companies in order to prevent one employer from having a favourable labour cost advantage over another. **Pattern bargaining** is bargaining in which a settlement in one industry or employer sets the pattern for other settlements. This way unions can show their members that they are receiving similar provisions and employers will know what their costs are.[4] For example, the United Steelworkers of America negotiated a collective agreement for all of North America with Goodyear Tire & Rubber that also had implications for Ford, DaimlerChrysler, and General Motors.[5]

Pattern bargaining
Bargaining in which unions negotiate provisions covering wages and other benefits that are similar to those provided in other agreements existing within the industry or region

Developing Bargaining Strategies

It is critical that the organization develop a strategy for negotiations. Without adequately planning what it wants to achieve, a company could end up with an unwanted outcome. Negotiators for an employer should develop a written plan covering their bargaining strategy. The plan should consider the proposals that the union is likely to submit, based on the most recent agreements with other employers and the demands that remain unsatisfied from previous negotiations. The plan should also consider the goals the union is striving to achieve and the extent to which it may be willing to make concessions or to resort to strike action in order to achieve these goals. Likewise, it is essential that the company identify the point at which it is willing to let the employees strike or to lock out the employees. Not knowing the organization's limits can create difficulties at negotiations and perhaps incur job action that could have been avoided.

At a minimum, the employer's bargaining strategy must address these points:

- Identify the likely union objectives, including specific proposals and management responses to them.
- Develop a listing of organization objectives, including management demands, limits of concessions, and anticipated union responses.
- Identify the nature of the union–management relationship and the relationship the union has with its members.
- Determine if the company is prepared to lock out or take a strike.
- Develop a database to support management bargaining proposals and to counteract union demands.
- Determine whether the company will operate if employees strike and prepare a contingency operating plan.

Certain elements of strategy are common to both the employer and the union. Generally, the initial demands presented by each side are greater than those it actually may hope to achieve. This is done in order to provide room for compromise.

Moreover, each party will usually avoid giving up the maximum it is capable of conceding in order to allow for further compromise that may be needed to break a bargaining deadlock.

Conducting the Negotiations

Among the factors that tend to make each bargaining situation unique are the economic conditions under which negotiations take place, the experience and personalities of the negotiators on each side, the goals they are seeking to achieve, and the strength of the relative positions. Some collective agreements can be negotiated informally in a few hours, particularly if the contract is short and the terms are not overly complex. Other agreements, such as those negotiated with large organizations, such as Air Canada and Stelco, require months before settlements are reached. And sometimes agreements cannot be reached and other actions are taken, such as the cancellation of the NHL hockey season in 2005.

Bargaining Teams

The composition and size of bargaining teams are often a reflection of the desires and practices of the parties. Normally, each side will have four to six representatives at the negotiating table. The chief negotiator for management is usually the senior HR person; the chief negotiator for the union is usually the local union president or union business agent. Others making up management's team may include representatives from accounting or finance, operations, and other HR staff. The local union president is likely to be supported by the chief steward, various local union vice-presidents, and a representative from the national union. In some cases the representative from the national union will be the chief negotiator for the local union.

Labour negotiations have become increasingly complex and legalistic. Therefore, it is advisable that the parties have an experienced negotiator.

The initial meeting of the bargaining teams is a particularly important one because it establishes the climate that will prevail during the negotiations that follow. A cordial attitude, with perhaps the injection of a little humour, can contribute much to a relaxation of tensions and help the negotiations to begin smoothly.

Analyzing the Proposals

The negotiation of a collective agreement can have some of the characteristics of a poker game, with each side attempting to determine its opponent's position while not revealing its own. Each party will normally try to avoid disclosing the relative importance that it attaches to a proposal so that it will not be forced to pay a higher price than is necessary to have the proposal accepted. As with sellers who will try to get a higher price for their products if they think the prospective buyer strongly desires them, negotiators will try to get greater concessions in return for granting those their opponents want most.

As they develop their collective bargaining proposals, astute negotiators know that some demands are more important to their side than others—either for economic or for political reasons. Therefore the proposals that each side submits generally may be divided into those it feels it must achieve, those it would like to achieve, and those it is submitting primarily for trading purposes. As bargainers discuss the proposals from each side, they are constantly trying to determine the intensity with which each side is committed to its demands. The ability to accurately gauge "commitment" to various proposals can spell the difference between an agreement and a bargaining impasse.

Resolving the Proposals

For each bargaining issue to be resolved satisfactorily, the point at which agreement is reached must be within limits that the union and the employer are willing to accept.

Bargaining zone
Area within which the union and the employer are willing to concede when bargaining

For each bargaining issue to be resolved satisfactorily, the point at which agreement is reached must be within limits that the union and the employer are willing to accept. The area within these two limits is called the **bargaining zone**. In some bargaining situations, the solution desired by one party may exceed the limits of the other party. Thus that solution is outside the bargaining zone. If that party refuses to modify its demands sufficiently to bring them within the bargaining zone, or if the opposing party refuses to extend its limit to accommodate the demands of the other party, a bargaining deadlock will result.[6] For example, when bargaining a wage increase for employees, if the union's lowest limit is a 2% increase and management's top limit is 3%, an acceptable range—the bargaining zone—is available to both parties. If management's top limit is only 1%, however, a bargaining zone is not available to either side and a deadlock is likely to occur.

The Union's Power in Collective Bargaining

Objective **2**

During negotiations, it is necessary for each party to retreat sufficiently from its original position to permit an agreement to be achieved. If this does not occur, the negotiations will become deadlocked, and the union may resort to the use of economic power to achieve its demands. Otherwise its only alternative will be to have members continue working without a collective agreement once the old one has expired. The economic power of the union may be exercised by striking, picketing, or boycotting the employer's products and encouraging others to do likewise. As managers know well, the ability to engage or even threaten to engage in such activities also can serve as a form of pressure. And in some cases, employees do not actually strike, but slow down their work and create pressure on the company. Or the employees will "work to rule"—strictly following the terms of the collective agreement. This means that if the collective agreement specifies that employees will have a 45-minute lunch break, yet most employees take only 30 and work the other 15 minutes, in a work-to-rule, the employees would take the full 45 minutes.

Striking

Strike
A situation in which unionized workers refuse to perform their work during labour negotiations

A **strike** is the refusal of a group of employees to perform their jobs. This is only legal during negotiations after the collective agreement has expired. Employees cannot strike during the collective agreement as proscribed by labour legislation. Although strikes account for only a small portion of total workdays lost in industry each year, they are a costly and emotional event for all concerned. For example, in mid-2004, public-sector employees who had been on strike for 20 days shut down the Newfoundland legislature. The workers were frustrated with the lack of progress and wanted to put more pressure on the government.[7] Unions usually will seek strike authorization from their members to use as a bargaining ploy to gain concessions that will make a strike unnecessary. A strike vote by the members does not mean they actually want or expect to go out on strike. Rather, it is intended as a vote of confidence to strengthen the position of their leaders at the bargaining table. And the threat of a strike creates as much of a problem as an actual strike. This occurred with Stelco when the strike notice issued in late 2004 caused GM, a customer of Stelco, to find an alternative supply of steel.[8]

Since a strike can have serious effects on the union and its members, the prospects for its success must be analyzed carefully by the union. By late 2004, mine workers in two small Labrador communities had been on strike for over three months—far too long to keep the communities going. Local businesses had to lay off staff and, in some cases, went out of business as the strikers did not have the money to buy local items. But the strike has had provincial implications as these communities represent one-third of Labrador's population and the highest income per capita.[9] As recently as March 2005, gold mine operators in Prince George, B.C., were attempting to forestall a lengthy shutdown which would cause hardship in a fragile economy. However, the workers also knew at the time that gold prices were at an all-time high and therefore believed that the companies had the financial means to meet their demands.[10]

In the past, strikes have been crippling to many industries, but the number of strikes in Canada continues a 20-year decline.[11] Strikes can be disruptive and challenging to the organizations struck. Of critical importance is whether the employer will be able to continue operating using supervisory and nonstriking personnel and replacement workers. In organizations with high levels of technology and automation, and consequently fewer employees, continuing service with supervisors and managers is more likely. For example, among the highly automated telephone companies, supervisors can maintain most services during a strike. According to one authority, "Because of technological change, striking in many industries no longer has the effect of curtailing the employer's operations significantly."[12] The greater the ability of the employer to continue operating, the smaller the union's chances of achieving its demands through a strike. This is very well illustrated in the story of a company and its striking workers in At Work with HRM 11.1.

To understand more about the issues over which unions will strike, check out the Web sites of the International Association of Machinists and Aerospace Workers (**www.iamaw.ca**), Canadian Union of Public Employees (**www.cupe.ca**), and the IBEW International Brotherhood of Electrical Workers (**www.ibew.org**).

Picketing

When a union goes on strike, it will picket the employer by placing persons at business entrances to advertise the dispute and to discourage people from entering the premises. Even when the strikers represent only a small proportion of the employees within the organization, they can cause the shutdown of an entire organization if a sufficient number of the organization's remaining employees (i.e., sympathy strikers) refuse to cross their picket line. Also, because unions often refuse to cross another union's picket line, the pickets may serve to prevent trucks and railcars from entering the business to deliver and pick up goods.

If a strike fails to stop an employer's operations, the picket line may serve as more than a passive weapon. Employees who attempt to cross the line may be subjected to verbal insults and even physical violence. Mass picketing, in which large groups of pickets try to block the path of people attempting to enter an organization, may also be used. However, the use of picket lines to exert physical pressure and incite violence is illegal and may harm more than help the union cause.

International Association of Machinists and Aerospace Workers
www.iamaw.ca

Canadian Union of Public Employees
www.cupe.ca

International Brotherhood of Electrical Workers
www.ibew.org

at work **with HRM 11.1** at work with HRM 11.1

HOW LONG IS TOO LONG? A TRUE TESTAMENT OF PERSEVERANCE

None of the 15 men still striking would ever have thought that they would still be on the picket line over three years after walking off the job on January 24, 2002.

A small bumper refurbishing company, Modern Auto Plating in Vancouver, B.C., was a bustling company with plenty of business before job action began. The workers, members of United Steelworkers of America (USWA) Local 2952, had been together for a number of years, some for more than 15, so a strong bond was held among the employees. On January 24, 2002, 45 workers walked out and went on strike when the owner of the plant wouldn't negotiate a wage increase. When asked for reasons why they couldn't have a raise, the owner replied that he simply didn't have the money. At the time of the strike, as many as six delivery trucks would come and go on any given day. Each truck would carry as many as 30 bumpers per truck valued from $100 to $300 each. This was common knowledge to many of the employees; therefore, they felt that the company's lack of money wasn't the issue.

Although the wage increase was the major reason why the workers took job action, there was another minor issue: working conditions. One striking worker reported that one time while he was on shift, a WCB inspector dropped by for a surprise visit only to have the owner deny him access to the premises. The WCB official then returned with a court order and went through the site with "a fine-toothed comb" handing the owner approximately 25 to 30 infractions when finished.

Legal battles have gone back and forth over the years with the owner trying to overthrow the very union he himself had put in over 20 years ago. He once thought he had enough workers on the inside to have a decertification vote; thus, he took the union to court. The union won easily because

the owner failed to realize that the workers that had left for other jobs hadn't technically quit, and consequently were counted as striking workers.

Of the 45 workers who began the strike, 15 are still striking while the rest have moved to other jobs. Operations still continue to this day, but only at a fraction of the old business. Only one delivery truck leaves the plant on a daily basis with the occasional second truck. Compounding the decrease in volume of work is that the quality of workmanship may very well have suffered also.

The 15 men who are left cycle their shifts so that there are at least four of them outside the building during the working hours of the plant. They remain not only in good spirits but they also have a lot of support. Both the union president and the district manager of Canada have come to the line and supported their action with encouraging words and their motto, "One day longer." Additionally, many other unions come down and take part in the strike by standing on the picket line, including the bus drivers' union and firefighters' union. Quite recently the striking workers celebrated their third-year anniversary with several other unions joining in filling up the entire city block with over 300 supporters, horns, and banners.

For these 15 men, it's not a matter of money; it's a matter of principle. Some of the men who are working are still friends with some of the strikers. In fact, one of the men who went back to work with a wage cut is the brother of one of current strikers. The strikers just want to go back to work but the owner doesn't want to even go to the bargaining table. With both sides steadfast in their ways, there doesn't seem to be an end in sight. And in the words of one striker, "We'll be here as long as it takes to get resolved, but how long is too long?"

(Continued)

After negotiations had failed at the beginning of the strike, the owner took an interesting stance. He called off all negotiations, withdrew all previous offers, and stated that the striking workers would have to take a 20 to 30% wage decrease in order to come back to work. Some have done so while others still remain on strike.

CRITICAL THINKING QUESTION

If you were a striking worker, would you remain on strike for this long? Why or why not?

Source: Interview with striking workers, conducted by Ahren McIntee, February 2005.

Unions were recently given additional power to potentially expand the economic impact of picketing. The Supreme Court of Canada in January 2002 determined that striking workers had a constitutional right to picket secondary locations—i.e., locations of companies that were not directly involved in the dispute. This means that a union could picket a company's customers or directly contact customers to encourage them not to buy the product.[13]

Pickets are used during a strike to make customers and the general public aware of the dispute.

Boycotting

Boycott
Union tactic to encourage others
to refuse to patronize an employer

Another economic weapon of unions is the **boycott**, which is a refusal to patronize the employer. For, example, production employees on strike against a hand-tool manufacturer might picket a retail store that sells the tools made by the struck employer. Unions will also use handbills, radio announcements, and notices in newspapers to discourage purchase of the employer's product or service.

The Employer's Power in Collective Bargaining

The employer's power in collective bargaining largely rests in being able to shut down the organization or certain operations within it. The employer can transfer these operations to other locations or can subcontract them to other employers through outsourcing. General Motors outsources to foreign manufacturers many parts used in the assembly of North American cars. In exercising their economic freedom, however, employers must be careful that their actions are not interpreted by the provincial labour relations board to be an attempt to avoid bargaining with the union.

Operating During Strikes

When negotiations become deadlocked, typically it is the union that initiates action and the employer that reacts. In reacting, employers must balance the cost of taking a strike against the long- and short-term costs of agreeing to union demands. They must also consider how long operations might be suspended and the length of time that they and the unions will be able to endure a strike. An employer who chooses to accept a strike must then decide whether to continue operating if it is possible to do so.

Should employees strike the organization, employers in certain jurisdictions are limited in their ability to hire replacement workers. Quebec and British Columbia have passed "anti-scab" laws, forbidding the use of replacement workers during a strike. Employers have the right to dismiss workers who engage in sabotage or violence during a strike.

Workers are entitled to return to their jobs, but not necessarily their previous position, once a strike is settled. The right to return to work is often an issue to be negotiated. Although laws vary, in many cases employees must submit, in writing, their intention to return to their job once a strike is finalized.

Using the Lockout

Lockout
Strategy by which the employer
denies employees the opportunity to
work by closing its operations

Although not often used, a **lockout** occurs when an employer takes the initiative to close its operations. Besides being used in bargaining impasses, lockouts may be used by employers to combat union slowdowns, damage to their property, or violence within the organization that may occur in connection with a labour dispute.

Under Labour Relations Board provisions, an employer cannot enforce a lockout within a prescribed number of hours (48 to 72) of a strike vote. Lockouts affect non-striking workers. For example, when miners at Inco are locked out, administrative work ceases and office staff are locked out or laid off. Employers may be reluctant to resort to a lockout, however, because of their concern that denying work to regular employees might hurt the organization's image.

ethics **in HRM 11.1** ethics in HRM 11.1

WORKERS STAGE SIT-IN

What can happen when workers get frustrated with their employer during collective bargaining? Most people would think that the only thing workers might do is strike or picket. However, sometimes the usual methods don't appear to work and employees do something more dramatic.

In July 2002, the employees of Vidéotron, a cable-television company in Montreal, staged a sit-in at the offices of another company. The company, Caisse de dépôt et placement du Québec, owns a small portion of Vidéotron. Riot police were called to remove the employees since they were deemed to be trespassing. Caisse indicated that it has nothing to do with the employees and that the employees had to take the matter up with their employer, Vidéotron.

This latest incident was on top of alleged vandalism to the cable network to the 325,000 cable subscribers throughout Quebec. However, the company did not file any official complaints to the police about the vandalism.

Collective bargaining reached an impasse in May 2002 and Vidéotron locked out the employees and hired replacement workers.

Do you think what the employees did was right? Why or why not? Do you think what Vidéotron did was right? Why or why not?

Sources: Adapted from Frederick Tomesco, "Striking Videotron Workers Stage Sit-in," *Financial Post*, July 5, 2002, FP7, and "Videotron, Union Asks for Mediator in Lockout," *Financial Post*, July 9, 2002, FP2.

Selling the Business

Most companies will want to limit their power during collective bargaining to either operating or locking out employees. However, depending on the situation, a company may wish to actually sell an operation or business if the negotiations are not productive. The most visible example of this is Quebecor Inc., which in 2002 was unable to convince its union, CUPE Local 2815, that it needed to significantly reduce costs due to its high debt load. The union was unwilling to have its workers go from a 35-hour work week to a 40-hour work week for the same pay, as well as to have less paid vacation. Quebecor responded to this problem by selling the business unit to another company.[14] Whether this tactic would work in all situations depends on the actual labour legislation. In many provinces, when a business is sold, the collective agreement and the union go with the business.

Despite the power that both parties may have, the bargaining process can become very frustrating for the parties involved. Read Ethics in HRM 11.1 to better understand what people do when the frustration mounts.

Resolving Bargaining Deadlocks

Objective 3

When a strike or a lockout occurs, both parties are soon affected by it. The employer will suffer a loss of profits and customers, and possibly of public goodwill. The union members suffer a loss of income that is likely to be only partially offset by strike benefits or outside income. The union's leaders risk the possibility of losing members, of being voted out of office, of losing public support, or of having the members vote to decertify the union as their bargaining agent. As the losses to each side mount, the disputing parties usually feel more pressure to achieve a settlement.

Wal-Mart has made headlines by closing unionized stores in Quebec.

Mediation and Arbitration

When the disputing parties are unable to resolve a deadlock, a third party serving in the capacity of a conciliator, a mediator, or an arbitrator may be called on to provide assistance. In many jurisdictions, conciliation is compulsory before a legal strike or lockout. The conciliator, appointed by the provincial ministry of labour, helps the parties reconcile their differences in an attempt to reach a workable agreement. If the conciliation effort is unsuccessful, a report is filed with the ministry of labour, which in rare instances may appoint a conciliation board that accepts presentations from both parties and makes nonbinding formal recommendations. If a settlement cannot be reached at this stage, a strike is permitted, except in Manitoba, Alberta, Saskatchewan, and Quebec, where strikes are permissible during conciliation. This two-stage conciliation process is normally reserved for high-profile cases in which significant social and economic consequences would result from a strike.

Mediator
Third party in a labour dispute who meets with one party and then the other in order to suggest compromise solutions or to recommend concessions from each side that will lead to an agreement

Mediation is similar to conciliation except that it is voluntary (the two parties contract a neutral third party to help them), and the mediator assumes a more active role as a negotiator. A **mediator** serves primarily as a fact finder and someone to open up a channel of communication between the parties. Typically the mediator meets with one party and then the other in order to suggest compromise solutions or to recommend concessions from each side that will lead to an agreement without causing either to lose face. Mediators have no power or authority to force either side toward an agreement. They must have good interpersonal skills, such as active listening, a variety of assessment skills, and the ability to manage high-conflict situations.[15]

Facilitate.com inc.
www.facilitate.com

Mediate.com
www.mediate.com/odr/

ADR Resources
www.adrr.com

ADR Institute of Canada
www.adrcanada.ca

One of the newer forms of mediation is online mediation. Through using Internet-based help, ways can be found to use experts in helping solve the dispute without actually having the expert present. Check out some of these resources by visiting the following Web sites: Facilitate.com Inc. (**www.facilitate.com**), Mediate.com (**www.mediate.com/odr/**), ADR Resources (**www.adrr.com**), and ADR Institute of Canada (**www.adrcanada.ca**).

Arbitrator
Third-party neutral who resolves a labour dispute by issuing a final and binding decision in an agreement

Interest arbitration
A mechanism to renew or establish a new collective agreement for parties

Rights arbitration
A mechanism to resolve disputes about the interpretation and application of a collective agreement during the term of that collective agreement

Arbitration is the only third-party resolution form that results in binding decisions. An **arbitrator** assumes the role of a decision maker and determines what the settlement between the two parties will be. In other words, arbitrators write a final contract that the parties must accept. Compared with mediation, arbitration is not often used to settle private-sector bargaining disputes. In those essential-service areas within the public sector where strikes are prohibited, the use of **interest arbitration** is a common method to resolve bargaining deadlocks. Because one or both parties are generally reluctant to give a third party the power to make the settlement for them, a mediator typically is used to break a deadlock and assist the parties in reaching an agreement. Once an agreement is concluded, an arbitrator may be called on to resolve disputes arising in connection with the administration of the agreement. This type of arbitration is called grievance arbitration or **rights arbitration**.

TRENDS IN COLLECTIVE BARGAINING

Queen's University Industrial Relations Centre
www.qsilver.queensu.ca/irl

Centre for Industrial Relations
www.chass.utoronto.ca/cir/

Managers see the late 1990s and beyond as a period of great importance to labour–management relations. Advances in technology, innovative workplace practices, and continued competitive pressures will have their impact. These conditions will affect the attitudes and objectives of both employers and unions in collective bargaining. They will also influence the climate in which bargaining occurs and the bargaining power each side is able to exercise. Two centres in Canada track these trends by conducting research on union–management relations. Visit their Web sites: Queen's University Industrial Relations Centre (**www.qsilver.queensu.ca/irl**) and the Centre for Industrial Relations at the University of Toronto (**www.chass.utoronto.ca/cir/**).

Changes in Collective Bargaining Relationships

Traditionally, the collective bargaining relationship between an employer and a union has been an adversarial one. The union has held the position that, while the employer has the responsibility for managing the organization, the union has the right to challenge certain actions of management. Unions also have taken the position that the employer has an obligation to operate the organization in a manner that will provide adequate compensation to employees. Moreover, unions maintain that their members should not be expected to subsidize poor management by accepting less than their full entitlement.

With adversarial bargaining, negotiators start with defined positions and through deferral, persuasion, trade, or power, the parties work toward resolving individual bargaining demands. In traditional bargaining, with its give-and-take philosophy, the results may or may not be to the complete satisfaction of one or both parties. In fact, when one side feels it has received "the short end of the stick," bitter feelings may persist for the life of the agreement. As noted by one labour negotiator, "Adversarial bargaining does little to establish a long-term positive relationship based on open communications and trust. By its nature, it leads to suspicion and compromise."[16]

To overcome negative feelings, labour and management practitioners may follow a nonadversarial approach. **Interest-based bargaining (IBB)** is based on the identification and resolution of mutual interests rather than the resolve of specific bargaining

Interest-based bargaining
Problem-solving bargaining based on a win-win philosophy and the development of a positive long-term relationship

demands.[17] IBB is "a problem-solving process conducted in a principled way that creates effective solutions while improving the bargaining relationship."[18] The focus of this bargaining strategy is to discover mutual bargaining interests with the intent of formulating options and solutions for mutual gain.

Interest-based bargaining is novel in both its philosophy and process. Also distinct are the bargaining tools used to expedite a successful nonadversarial negotiating experience. Rather than using proposals and counterproposals to reach agreement (as with adversarial negotiations), participants use brainstorming, consensus decision making, active listening, process checking, and matrix building to settle issues. This style of negotiations was pioneered by Roger Fisher and William Ury, two professors at the Harvard Business School and published in their highly successful book *Getting to Yes*. They stressed the need to focus on the problem (not the positions of the parties), to separate the people from the problem, and to create options for mutual benefit. In this fashion, the parties strive to find solutions to problems and thus improve their overall relationship.[19] For a better understanding of IBB, read At Work with HRM 11.2, which describes how the *Ottawa Citizen* newspaper improved its relationship with its union.

at work **with HRM 11.2** at work with HRM 11.2

BUILDING TRUST THROUGH IBB

The *Ottawa Citizen*, a newspaper with a circulation of 145,000 newspapers, is the largest daily newspaper in Ottawa, and the eighth largest in Canada. Approximately 65% of its 595 full-time employees are unionized and belong to one of three unions: the Communication Energy & Paperworkers (CEP), the Graphic Communications Union (GCU), and the Newspaper Guild. These bargaining units are also called chapels (and the shop steward is called chapel chairman) in recognition of the time when it was illegal to hold union meetings so groups of employees wishing to meet collectively would say they were going to a "chapel [or church] meeting."

Debbie Bennett, vice-president of human resources and finance for the newspaper, describes the process: "In my opinion, IBB works when you have a good relationship that you want to improve upon, or when things are so bad that something has to change. I approached the [Newspaper] Guild, the largest union, with whom

we already had a good relationship, about IBB. At the time, it had about 325 members. I started by buying them some IBB books (*Getting to Yes* and *Getting Together*) to determine if there was interest. There was. Union and management advertised for, jointly selected, and paid for a facilitator, who took us through a three-day training and relationship-building session. The entire bargaining team from both parties took part in the workshop to make sure we all understood the differences between IBB and traditional bargaining.

"For example, one difference was the ways in which we communicated, both internally to build trust and externally to our stakeholders. In IBB, we brainstormed, with the rule that no repercussions would follow if an idea was presented that everyone liked but subsequently was not found workable. In traditional bargaining, if an idea is placed on the table and then removed, it could be seen as reneging or bargaining in bad

(Continued)

faith. The agreement to brainstorm led to very little caucus time, and a much faster bargaining pace, because the respective teams did not have to ask for a break to discuss new ideas in the hallway before presenting them to the other party.

"The tone of communications was also different. The objective at the table is to discuss issues in an open and honest manner. This objective would be hard to achieve if some of the more direct comments were quoted in public communiqués. Therefore, the parties agreed that communications to both management and union members were for the purpose of keeping everyone informed, not for the purpose of embarrassing the other party or belittling their position. The tone of communications was respectful.

"We started bargaining, with the facilitator at table, to ensure that we practised what we learned. After the third day, we no longer needed the facilitator. Usually our bargaining sessions took four to five months; this time, we finished in four to five days. Usually the changes to the collective agreement were mainly monetary; this time there were a lot of language changes. For example, like most organizations, when an employee is disciplined, a disciplinary letter is placed on file. The union wanted a sunset clause requiring automatic removal of the discipline letter after a period of time. The union's view was that a transgression should not be held against an employee forever. However, management felt a record of a serious infraction, like hitting another employee, should never be removed from the file nor should records of a repetitive problem. Through IBB, the teams came up with a clause, which said that a disciplinary letter will not automatically be removed, but will be taken to the VP who will decide on its removal based on clear criteria, such as the seriousness of the act and the repetitiveness of the behaviour.

"Overall, the effect of IBB on the labour relations climate, although always good, was to improve it."

CRITICAL THINKING QUESTIONS

1. Do you feel that IBB could work in all unionized environments? Why or why not?
2. What other factors in an organization are necessary to make IBB work?

Facilitating Labour–Management Cooperation

Improving labour–management relationships generally requires a restructuring of attitudes by both managers and union officials and members. John Calhoun Wells, director of the Federal Mediation and Conciliation Service, notes, "This cooperative model emphasizes trust, common ground, sharing of information, joint problem solving, risk taking, and innovation."[20] Joint labour–management committees are concerned not only with ensuring that regulatory standards are met but also with working together to bring about innovations in areas ranging from product development to customer service.[21]

Furthermore, the crisis of survival has forced unions, their members, and management to make concessions at the bargaining table and to collaborate in finding the solutions that will ensure survival. Recently, the Canadian Auto Workers and Canadian National Railway agreed to reduce overtime, thereby creating more jobs and minimizing layoffs.[22] If cooperation is to continue after the crisis has passed, however, it must rest on a solid foundation. For example, it has been noted that cooperation lasts only when both sides undertake the endeavour through a systems approach grounded in developmental activities.[23] Also, labour–management cooperation programs have a greater chance for success when both parties jointly establish goals and philosophies for mutual gain.

When building a cooperative environment, it is particularly important that union members believe that management is sincerely interested in their personal well-being.[24] Additionally, a review of meaningful labour–management cooperative endeavours indicates that success depends on an open and honest style of communication. Furthermore, both supervisors and employees must be trained in participative and problem-solving approaches to problem resolution.

Definition and Forms of Cooperation

While labour–management cooperation has become a positive trend in collective bargaining, there is no real consensus on how to define this cooperation or what it entails in practice. Two well-known labour writers, Neil Chamberlain and James Kuhn, define labour–management cooperation as any mode of bargaining or joint discussion in which the objective is to improve the well-being of both parties.[25] Though this is certainly a broad working definition, experimentation will continue on how cooperation can best be achieved.

Labour–management programs can be of many types. In fact, the purpose and structure of cooperative endeavours largely depend on the needs and desires of the parties. At Work with HRM 11.3 describes the necessary organizational components to achieve more cooperation.

at work **with HRM 11.3** at work with HRM 11.3

LABOUR–MANAGEMENT COOPERATION

Improved labour-management cooperation ought to be easy, but it isn't. Since labour and management have a "relationship," for cooperation to occur, the people involved in the relationship need to think and act differently. This means that the cultures of both the union and the employer need to change. But what is necessary in order to help the change happen? Here are some suggestions:

- Trust

- Willingness to change

- Willingness to work on the relationship

- Common goals

- Leadership

- Effective communication

For example, Irving Paper in New Brunswick had a bitter strike in very poor economic conditions. The company decided that there had to be better relations with its union if the company was to survive. It embarked upon a number of activities to first improve trust. The first step was to have a union–management committee visit other sites to see how things worked. From this the committee was asked to make recommendations. They did so and the company implemented them immediately. The results: better relations, more satisfied employees, and improved business.

CRITICAL THINKING QUESTION

How easy would it be to have a more cooperative relationship between union and management? Explain your reasoning.

Sources: Adapted from David A. Brown, "Can Unions and Management Learn to Co-Operate?" *Canadian HR Reporter*, November 6, 2001; "Collective Bargaining Highlights," Ontario Ministry of Labour, October 2001; and Pradeep Kumar and Gregor Murray, "Patterns of Innovation in Unions in Canada," *Workplace Gazette*, Fall 2001, Vol. 4, No. 3: 65–67.

Another recent development in cooperative labour–management relations has been the use of well-respected arbitrators who work with the union and management. Some arbitrators, such as Professor Joe Weiler, have developed long-term relationships with unions and employers through arbitral work. The parties have sought this individual because of both his knowledge and the respect held for his neutrality. Through this relationship, a new role of facilitator and interpreter has developed where the person is asked to help facilitate change outside of collective bargaining or grievances.[26]

As mentioned earlier in this section, it is important that union and management work together when examining how work gets done. Recent research into changes in the design of work at two different locations of a steel manufacturing company produced some very different results. The location that actively involved the union and the employees from the beginning, such as asking them for their ideas for job redesign, had higher levels of output along with reduced costs. However, the location that used a top-down approach met the cost reduction objectives but did not improve productivity levels or employee satisfaction levels.[27]

For more examples of collective bargaining trends, go to these Web sites: **www.ilo.org** and **www.cwrn-rcrmt.org**.

**International Labour
Organization**
www.ilo.org

**Canadian Workplace
Research Network**
www.cwrn-rcrmt.org

THE COLLECTIVE AGREEMENT

 Objective 5

At the conclusion of negotiations, a collective agreement is put in writing and ratified by the union membership. The union typically does this by asking that the members vote on the new terms. The representatives of both parties then sign the agreement. This is a legal, binding contract. The scope of the agreement (and the length of the written document) will vary with the size of the employer and the length of the bargaining relationship. Manager's Toolkit 11.1 shows some of the major articles in a collective agreement and also provides examples of some new and progressive contract clauses.

Two important items in any collective agreement pertain to the issue of management rights and the forms of security afforded the union.

The Issue of Management Rights

Management rights have to do with conditions of employment over which management is able to exercise exclusive jurisdiction. Since virtually every management right can and has been challenged successfully by unions, the ultimate determination of these rights will depend on the relative bargaining power of the two parties. Furthermore, to achieve union cooperation or concessions, employers have had to relinquish some of these time-honoured rights.

Residual Rights

Residual rights
Concept that management's authority is supreme in all matters except those it has expressly conceded to the union in the collective agreement

In the collective agreement, management rights may be treated as **residual rights** or as defined rights. The residual rights concept holds that

> management's authority is supreme in all matters except those it has expressly conceded in the collective agreement, or in those areas where its authority is restricted by law. Put another way, management does not look to the collective

Manager's Toolkit **11.1** Manager's Toolkit 11.1

TYPICAL ITEMS IN A COLLECTIVE AGREEMENT

Typical clauses will cover

- Wages
- Vacations
- Holidays
- Work schedules
- Management rights
- Union security
- Transfers
- Discipline

- Grievance procedures
- No strike/no lockout clause
- Overtime
- Safety procedures
- Severance pay
- Seniority
- Pensions and benefits

Progressive clauses will cover

- Employee access to records
- Limitations on use of performance evaluation
- Eldercare leave
- Flexible medical spending accounts
- Protection against hazards of technology (repetitive strain injuries or chemicals, such as PCBs)

- Limitations against electronic monitoring
- Procedures governing drug testing (or other substances)
- Bilingual stipends
- Domestic partnership benefits (same-sex benefits)

agreement to ascertain its rights; it looks to the agreement to find out which and how much of its rights and powers it has conceded outright or agreed to share with the union.[28]

Residual rights might include the right of management to determine the product to produce or to select production equipment and procedures. Employers who subscribe to the residual rights concept prefer not to mention management rights in the collective agreement on the grounds that they possess such rights already. To mention them might create an issue with the union.

Defined Rights

Defined rights
Concept that management's authority should be expressly defined and clarified in the collective agreement

The **defined rights** concept, on the other hand, is intended to reinforce and clarify which rights are exclusively those of management. This concept means that the employer only has those rights that are written into the collective agreement. It serves to reduce confusion and misunderstanding and to remind union officers, union stewards, and employees that management never relinquishes its right to operate the organization. For example, a defined right would include the right of management to take disciplinary action against problem employees. The great majority of collective agreements contain provisions covering management rights. The following is an example of a general statement defining management rights in one collective agreement:

> It is agreed that the company possesses all of the rights, powers, privileges, and authority it had prior to the execution of this agreement; and nothing in this agreement shall be construed to limit the company in any way in the exercise of the regular and customary functions of management and the operation of its business, except as it may be specifically relinquished or modified herein by an express provision of this agreement.[29]

Forms of Union Security

When a labour organization is certified by a labour relations board as the exclusive bargaining representative of all employees in a bargaining unit, it must, by law, represent all employees in the unit, nonunion and union members alike. In exchange for its obligation to represent all employees equally, union officials will seek to negotiate some form of compulsory membership as a condition of employment. Union officials argue that compulsory membership prevents the possibility that some employees will receive the benefits of unionization without paying their share of the costs. A standard union security provision is dues checkoff, which gives the employer the responsibility of withholding union dues from the paycheques of union members who agree to such a deduction.

The more common forms of union security found in collective agreements are the following:

1. The *closed shop* states that employers will hire only union members.
2. The *union shop* provides that any employee not a union member upon employment must join the union within 30 days or be terminated.
3. The *agency shop* states that union membership is voluntary yet all bargaining unit members must pay union dues and fees.
4. The *open shop* allows employees to join the union or not. Nonmembers do not pay union dues. This is the rarest form of union security.

Few issues in collective bargaining are more controversial than the negotiation of these agreements. Though rare, closed-shop clauses are perhaps the most adversarial because they require employers to recruit employees from a union hiring hall.

Working in conjunction with the union-shop clause are the various seniority provisions of the collective agreement. Unions prefer that many personnel decisions (promotions, job transfers, shift assignments, vacations) be based on seniority, a criterion that limits the discretion of managers to make such decisions on the basis of merit. However, depending on the words of the seniority clause, not all employees are totally protected. For example, the Hamilton Public Library was amalgamating a number of its facilities. In doing so, there were some jobs that it no longer needed. In laying off the necessary staff, a situation arose where two employees had exactly the same amount of seniority. In order to make the decision of which person would get the job, the collective agreement stated that a coin toss would break the tie.[30]

Administration of the Collective Agreement

Negotiation of the collective agreement, as mentioned earlier, is usually the most publicized and critical aspect of labour relations. Strike deadlines, press conferences, and employee picketing help create this image. Nevertheless, as managers in unionized organizations know, the bulk of labour relations activity comes from the day-to-day administration of the agreement. Once the collective agreement is signed, each party frequently will interpret clauses differently. These differences are traditionally resolved through the grievance procedure.

Manager's Toolkit 11.2 provides some examples of clauses from collective agreements.

Manager's Toolkit **11.2** Manager's Toolkit 11.2

CLAUSES FROM COLLECTIVE AGREEMENTS

1. Paid Education Leave

The Company agrees to pay into a special fund two cents (2¢) per hour per employee for all compensated hours for the purpose of providing paid education leave. Such leave shall be for upgrading the employee's skills in all aspects of trade union functions. Payments should be made on a quarterly basis into a trust fund established by the National Union, CAW, effective from date of ratification. Cheques shall be made payable to . . . .

The Company further agrees that members of the bargaining unit, selected by the Union to attend such courses, shall be granted a leave of absence without pay for twenty (20) days class time, plus travel time where necessary, said leave of absence to be intermittent over a twelve (12) month period from the first day of leave. Employees on said leave of absence shall continue to accrue seniority and benefits during such leave.

[Between The Eight (8) Rinks Hockey Complex and National Automobile, Aerospace, Transportation and General Workers Union (CAW-Canada) Local 3000].

2. Layoffs

   a. When there is a reduction in the workforce of the Employer, the most junior employee shall be laid off first.

   b. When an employee requests a layoff, for any reason, the said employee will not be allowed to bump a junior person upon return to work.

   c. Maternity Leave—Maternity leave shall be granted in accordance with Part 7 of the Employment Standards Act.

[Between Pacific Coast Traffic Control and Local Union 258 of the International Brotherhood Of Electrical Workers]

3. Pay for Overtime Worked

Overtime shall be compensated at the following rates:

   a. up to eight (8) hours in a regularly scheduled workday be paid at the regular rate of pay;

   b. time and one-half $(1\frac{1}{2})$ for the next three (3) hours of overtime on a regularly scheduled workday;

   c. double time for hours worked in excess of (b).

[Between Young Women's Christian Association of Vancouver (YWCA) and B.C. Government and Service Employees' Union (BCGEU)].

GRIEVANCE PROCEDURES

Grievance procedure
Formal procedure that provides for the union to represent members and nonmembers in processing a grievance

Objective 6

The **grievance procedure** typically provides for the union to represent the interests of its members (and nonmembers as well) in processing a complaint that something in the collective agreement has been violated. It is considered by some authorities to be the heart of the bargaining agreement—the safety valve that gives flexibility to the whole system of collective bargaining.[31] When negotiating a grievance procedure, one important concern for both sides is how effectively the system will serve the needs of employees and management. A well-written grievance procedure will allow grievances to be processed quickly and with as little red tape as possible. Furthermore, it should serve to foster cooperation, not conflict, between the employer and the union.

The operation of a grievance procedure is unique to each individual collective bargaining relationship but is required under Canadian labour relations codes. Grievance procedures are negotiated to address the organization's structure and labour–management philosophy and the specific desires of the parties. Although each procedure is unique, there are common elements among systems. For example, grievance procedures normally specify how the grievance procedure is to be initiated, the number and timing of steps that are to compose the procedure, and the identity of representatives from each side who are to be involved in the hearings at each step (see Figure 11.3). The purpose of this multi-step process is to allow higher levels of union and management representatives to look at the issue from different perspectives. When a grievance cannot be resolved at one of the specified steps, most agreements provide for the grievance to be submitted to a third party—usually an arbitrator—whose decision is final and binding. It is not the function of an arbitrator to help the two parties reach a compromise solution. Rather, it is the arbitrator's job to mandate how the grievance is to be resolved.

FIGURE 11.3   Grievance Procedure

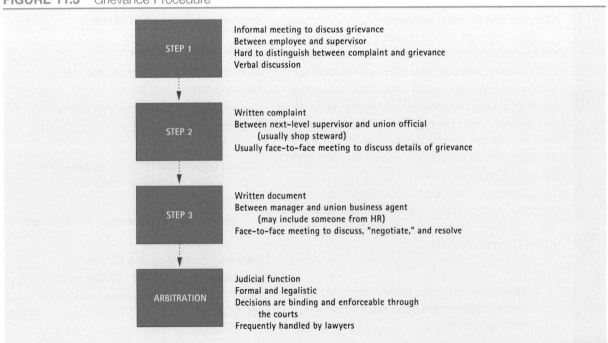

Initiating the Formal Grievance

In order for an employee's grievance to be considered formally, it must be expressed orally and/or in writing, ideally to the employee's immediate supervisor. If the employee feels unable to communicate effectively with the supervisor, the grievance may be taken to the union steward, who will discuss it with the supervisor. Since grievances are often the result of an oversight or a misunderstanding, many of them can be resolved at this point. Whether or not it is possible to resolve a grievance at the initial step will depend on the supervisor's ability and willingness to discuss the problem with the employee and the steward. Supervisors should be trained formally in resolving grievances. This training should include familiarization with the terms of the collective agreement and the development of counselling skills to facilitate a problem-solving approach.

In some instances, a satisfactory solution may not be possible at the first step because there are legitimate differences of opinion between the employee and the supervisor or because the supervisor does not have the authority to take the action required to satisfy the grievor. Personality conflicts, prejudices, emotionalism, stubbornness, or other factors may also be barriers to a satisfactory solution at this step.

Preparing the Grievance Statement

Most collective agreements require that grievances carried beyond the initial step be stated in writing, usually on a multicopy form similar to the one shown in Manager's Toolkit 11.3. It also forces employees to think more objectively about their grievances. When this is done, grievances that stem from trivial complaints or feelings of hostility are less likely to be pursued beyond the first step. Most grievances are specific to one employee, but a union could also initiate a policy grievance that would apply to all employees covered by the collective agreement.

Grievance Resolution

Grievance resolution
Process in which a neutral third party assists in the resolution of an employee grievance

Expedited arbitration
An agreement to bypass some steps in the grievance process

If a grievance is to be resolved successfully, representatives of both management and the union must be able to discuss the problem in a rational and objective manner. A grievance should not be viewed as something to be won or lost. Rather, both sides must view the situation as an attempt to solve a problem. Throughout the process, both parties will try to resolve the issue. And in many cases, people will use mediation skills, such as active listening, to help the process.[32] However, if the conflict cannot be resolved through discussion and compromise, all collective agreements in Canadian jurisdictions contain a provision for arbitration, or **grievance resolution**. An arbitrator (usually a lawyer or professional skilled in the arbitration process) or a board or panel (consisting of a union nominee, a management nominee, and a neutral chair) hears the case and submits a decision, including the rationale. The decision is final and the parties are legally bound to accept the decision unless there is a serious concern over the arbitrator's competence or integrity.

One criticism of the arbitration process is that it is slow (up to two years) and costly. One solution is **expedited arbitration**, which is an agreement to bypass some steps in the grievance process when the issue is particularly important or urgent, as in the case of employee dismissals. The United Steelworkers of America and the International Nickel Company of Canada Ltd. use expedited arbitration in their Sudbury and Port Colborne operations.

Manager's Toolkit **11.3** Manager's Toolkit 11.3

SAMPLE GRIEVANCE PROCEDURE RECORD

Level #1

Date Submitted to Union _____ Department _____
Grievor's Name _____ Nature of Grievance _____
_____

Articles Grieved _____
_____

Remedy Sought _____
_____

Grievor's Signature _____
Shop Steward's Signature _____
Department's Answer to Level #1
Date Answered _____
_____

❏ Accepted by Union   ❏ Not Accepted by the Union
Business Agent Signature _____
Grievor's Signature _____

Level #2

Date Submitted _____ Date Answered _____
Employer Response _____
_____
_____

❏ Accepted by the Union   ❏ Not Accepted by the Union
Business Agent Signature _____
Grievor's Signature _____
Date:

Level #3

Date Submitted _____ Date Answered _____
Company's Answer _____
_____
_____

❏ Accepted by the Union   ❏ Not Accepted by the Union
Business Agent Signature _____
Date: _____

Rights Arbitration

The function of rights (or grievance) arbitration is to provide the solution to a grievance that a union and an employer have been unable to resolve by themselves. As mentioned earlier, arbitration is performed by a neutral third party (an arbitrator or impartial umpire). This third party's decision dictates how the grievance is to be settled. Both parties are obligated to comply with the decision. Even if one of the parties believes the arbitrator's award is unfair, unwise, or inconsistent with the collective agreement, that party may have no alternative but to comply with the decision. And similar employment issues may be dealt with differently. Read HRM and the Law 11.1 for different decisions on theft in the workplace.

Sources of Arbitrators

An arbitrator must be acceptable to both disputing parties. An arbitrator who is retained on a permanent basis to resolve all grievances arising under an agreement has the advantage of being familiar with the agreement and the labour–management relationship. Arbitrators who are appointed on an ad hoc basis, however, resolve most grievances. If both parties are satisfied with an arbitrator's performance, that person may be called on to resolve subsequent grievances.[33]

Many collective agreements include a list of mutually acceptable arbitrators. In the absence of such a list, the provincial labour relations board can provide one. If both parties

---

HRM and **the law 11.1** HRM and the law 11.1

THEFT IN THE WORKPLACE

Not all cases involving theft in the workplace are decided the same way by arbitrators. Sometimes the situations are different and therefore arbitrators make decisions that will best solve the employment problem as they see it.

Case 1 involved a part-time worker who was accused of adding overtime hours onto the timesheet after the supervisor had signed the timesheet for just the regular hours. The person was fired. At the arbitration hearing, the supervisor testified that it was commonly known that the person was working extra hours. The employee verified that the time sheets had been filled in after the fact. The company stated that by doing this after the sheets were signed, the employee was stealing. The arbitrator disagreed, stated that the company knew the person was working overtime

and therefore had an obligation to pay, no matter how the payment was recorded, and ordered that the person be hired back.

Case 2 involved a bank teller who was fired for writing false cheques from the teller's personal account. The bank had expressly issued instructions to all employees that if any falsified transactions occurred in personal accounts, they could be fired. At the arbitration hearing, the employee testified that the bank did not go through proper procedures for being fired for theft but did not deny that the cheques had been written. The arbitrator decided that this was a serious offence at a bank and upheld the termination decision.

What do you think about these decisions? Should they both be the same? If so, what should the decision be? Why?

Sources: Adapted from "Former Bank Teller Justifiably Fired for Writing False Cheques," and "Fired Worker Reinstated with Full Back Pay," Library, Workplace Today, www.workplace.ca, retrieved August 9, 2002.

cannot agree on an arbitrator, the labour relations board may appoint one. Typically, arbitrators are professionals, such as professors, lawyers, or retired government labour arbitrators. Because of their professional backgrounds, they tend to be identified with neither labour nor management and are therefore able to occupy a position of neutrality.

The Decision to Arbitrate

If a grievance cannot be resolved through the grievance procedure, each disputing party must decide whether to use arbitration to resolve the case. The alternatives would be for the union to withdraw the grievance or for the employer to agree to union demands.

In deciding whether to use arbitration, each party must weigh the costs involved against the importance of the case and the prospects of gaining a favourable award. It would seem logical that neither party would allow a weak case to go to arbitration if there were little possibility of gaining a favourable award. But there may be other reasons for advancing a grievance. For example, it is not unusual for a union to take a weak case to arbitration in order to demonstrate to the members that the union is willing to exhaust every remedy in looking out for their interests. Union officers also are not likely to refuse to take to arbitration the grievances of members who are popular or politically powerful in the union, even though their cases are weak. Moreover, unions have a legal obligation to provide assistance to members who are pursuing grievances. Because members can bring suit against their unions for failing to process their grievances adequately, many union officers are reluctant to refuse taking even weak grievances to arbitration.

Management, on the other hand, may allow a weak case to go to arbitration to demonstrate to the union officers that management "cannot be pushed around." Also, managers at lower levels may be reluctant to risk the displeasure of top management by stating that a certain HR policy is unworkable or unsound. Stubbornness and mutual antagonism also may force many grievances into arbitration because neither party is willing to make concessions to reach an agreement, even when it may recognize that it is in the wrong.

The Arbitration Process

Submission to arbitrate
Statement that describes the issues to be resolved through arbitration

The issues to be resolved through arbitration may be described formally in a statement known as a **submission to arbitrate**. Each party makes a joint submission to the arbitrator indicating the rationale for the grievance. The submission to arbitrate must state the nature of the dispute with reference to the section of the collective agreement that has allegedly been breached. Such a statement might read: "Was the three-day suspension of Alex Hayden for just cause? If not, what is the appropriate remedy?" However, the two parties at the beginning of the hearing also present grievable issues orally to the arbitrator. The purpose of an arbitration hearing is to provide a full and fair hearing of the matter in dispute. If minutes and memoranda covering the meetings held at earlier stages of the grievance procedure have been prepared, these are sometimes submitted prior to the formal hearing to acquaint the arbitrator with the issues.

In arbitrating a dispute, it is the responsibility of the arbitrator to ensure that each side receives a fair hearing, during which it may present all the facts it considers pertinent to the case. In addition, any interested parties to an arbitration must be informed about the time and place of the hearing and be allowed to attend. This is particularly true if the grievance involves other union members, such as a promotional grievance. The procedures for conducting arbitration hearings and the restrictions governing the evidence that may be introduced during these hearings are more flexible than those permitted in a court of law. Hearsay evidence, for example, may be introduced, provided it is considered as such when evaluated with the other evidence presented. The primary purpose of the hearing is to assist the arbitrator in obtaining the facts necessary to resolve a human resources problem rather than a legal one. The arbitrator, therefore, has a right to question witnesses or to request additional facts from either party.

Depending on the importance of the case, the hearings may be conducted in an informal way or in a very formal manner not unlike that of a court trial. If desired by either or both parties, or by the arbitrator, a court reporter may be present during the hearing to prepare a transcript of the proceedings. If the proceedings have witnesses who will testify, the witnesses are sworn in. After conducting the hearing and receiving all written evidence, or any other submissions allowed, the arbitrator customarily has 30 days in which to consider the evidence and to prepare a decision. However, extensions beyond this period are not uncommon. In the majority of labour contracts, the parties share the costs of arbitration equally. In all grievance arbitrations except those involving any form of discipline, the "burden of proof" rests with the union. This means that the union must prove that the employer violated the written collective agreement.

The Arbitration Award

Arbitration award
Final and binding award issued by an arbitrator in a labour–management dispute

The **arbitration award** should include not only the arbitrator's decision but also the rationale for it. The reasoning behind the decision can help provide guidance concerning the interpretation of the collective agreement and the resolution of future disputes arising from its administration. In pointing out the merits of each party's position, the reasoning that underlies the award can help lessen the disappointment and protect the self-esteem of those representing the unsuccessful party. In short, tact and objective reasoning can help to reduce disappointment and hard feelings.

The foundation for an arbitrator's decision is the collective agreement and the rights it establishes for each party. In many instances, the decision may hinge on whether management's actions were justified under the terms of this agreement. Sometimes it may depend on the arbitrator's interpretation of the wording of a particular provision. Established HR policies and past practices can also provide the basis for determining the award. And it must be remembered that an arbitration decision, if need be, is enforceable through the courts.

In many grievances, such as those involving employee performance or behaviour on the job, the arbitrator must determine whether the evidence supports the employer's action against the grievor. The evidence must also indicate whether the employee was accorded the right of due process, which is the employee's right to be informed of unsatisfactory performance and to have an opportunity to respond to these charges. Under most collective agreements an employer is required to have just cause (i.e., a good reason) for the action it has taken, and such action should be confirmed by the evidence presented.

If the arbitration hearing indicates that an employee was accorded due process and the disciplinary action was for just cause, the severity of the penalty must then be assessed. Where the evidence supports the discipline imposed by the employer, the arbitrator will probably let the discipline stand intact. However, it is within the arbitrator's power, unless denied by the submission agreement, to reduce the penalty. It is not uncommon, for example, for an arbitrator to reduce a discharge to a suspension without pay for the period the grievor has been off the payroll.

Unlike decisions in a court of law, awards—at least in theory—are supposed to be reached on the basis of the facts of the case rather than on the basis of precedents established by previous cases. The reason for this is that no two cases are exactly alike. Each

Arbitration is a formal process to solve a grievance.

case should therefore be decided on its own merits. In practice, however, precedents do, at times, have some influence on the decision of an arbitrator, who may seek guidance from decisions of other arbitrators in somewhat similar cases. These decisions are compiled and published by the labour relations boards in each province.

How Arbitrators Decide Cases

Objective 7

Because of the importance and magnitude of arbitration in grievance resolution, the process by which arbitrators make decisions and the factors that influence those decisions are of continuing interest to managers. Typically, arbitrators use four factors when deciding cases:

1. The wording of the collective agreement.
2. The submission agreement as presented to the arbitrator.
3. Testimony and evidence offered during the hearing about how the collective agreement provisions have been interpreted.
4. Arbitration criteria or standards (i.e., similar to standards of common law) against which cases are judged.

When deciding the case of an employee discharged for absenteeism, for example, the arbitrator would consider these factors separately and/or jointly. Arbitrators are essentially constrained to decide cases on the basis of the wording of the collective agreement and the facts, testimony, and evidence presented at the hearing. For example, in a termination case, the employee was dismissed for unacceptable conduct. The employee grieved the action, stating that a disability had caused the conduct. The arbitration panel determined through the facts, testimony, and evidence presented that the person had been terminated with cause.[34]

Since discipline and dismissal issues generally constitute a majority of all grievance arbitration, it is informative to understand the reasons given by arbitrators when they overturn the decisions of managers in these cases. In one study, five reasons accounted for over 70% of all reversal cases:

1. The evidence did not support the charge of wrongdoing.
2. The evidence supported the charge, but there were mitigating circumstances.
3. Management committed procedural errors that prejudiced the grievor's rights.
4. The rule was fair, but punishment for its infraction was harsh.
5. Management was partly at fault in the incident.[35]

Arbitrators ask two basic questions regarding discipline during the arbitration process: (1) did the offence (misconduct) actually occur? and (2) if so, does the penalty imposed fit the misconduct? The answers to these and other related questions will help managers and supervisors when they prepare cases for arbitration. Other questions the supervisor needs to answer are the following:

1. Did the employee know about the rule or work standard?
2. Were the rules or standards applied consistently?
3. Did the employee know the consequences of the wrongdoing?
4. What was the employee's previous record? Was this an isolated incident?
5. How long has the person been employed?
6. Does the penalty create a special economic hardship on the employee?

The better prepared the supervisor is before taking disciplinary action, the more likely the discipline will be upheld if it is challenged by the union. Such preparation should include complete and accurate records and documentation of what happened, whether the employee knew the consequences of the action, whether the employee has a previous record of similar incidents, and whether the company has used discipline in the past for comparable situations.

In practice, arbitration decision making is not an exact science. In fact, the decisions of arbitrators can be rather subjective. Arbitrators can, and do, interpret contract language differently (e.g., What does "just-cause dismissal" actually mean?), they assign varying degrees of importance to testimony and evidence, they judge the truthfulness of witnesses differently, and they give arbitration standards greater or lesser weight as they apply to facts of the case. Each of these influences serves to introduce subjectivity into the decision-making process.

Problems with Rights Arbitration

Rights arbitration poses several critical problems today. Specifically, arbitration is criticized for taking too much time, being too expensive, and often creating frustration for the aggrieved employee and/or the supervisor in the dispute. The busy schedules of the arbitrator and the union and management officers, as well as a backlog of cases, frequently cause long delays in resolving relatively simple disputes.[36] "Creeping legalism" through the increased use of lawyers and legal procedures signals a movement away from the original purposes of labour arbitration. Therefore, in an effort to improve the overall labour–management relationship, supervisors and managers must understand the terms of the collective agreement and how to exercise their rights in a fair and reasonable way. By doing so, there is less risk that the supervisor or manager will violate the written contract.

SUMMARY

1. Describe the bargaining process and the bargaining goals and strategies of a union and an employer.
   - Each side will prepare a list of goals it wishes to achieve while additionally trying to anticipate the goals desired by the other side.
   - Both employer and union negotiators will be sensitive to current bargaining patterns within the industry, general cost-of-living trends, and geographical wage differentials.
   - The collective bargaining process includes not only the actual negotiations but also the power tactics used to support negotiating demands.

2. Describe the forms of bargaining power that a union and an employer may utilize to enforce their bargaining demands.
   - The union's power in collective bargaining comes from its ability to picket, strike, or boycott the employer.
   - The employer's power during negotiations comes from its ability to lock out employees or to operate during a strike by using managerial or replacement employees.

3. Cite the principal methods by which bargaining deadlocks may be resolved.
   - Mediation is the principal way of resolving negotiating deadlocks.
   - Interest arbitration is employed to finalize the collective agreement.
   - Interest arbitration is often used in the public sector, where unions are largely prohibited from striking.

4. Give examples of current collective-bargaining trends.
   - More cooperative labour–management endeavours.
   - Attitudes of less-adversarial collective bargaining.
   - A restructuring of attitudes by both managers and union officials and members.

5. Identify the major provisions of a collective agreement and describe the issue of management rights.
   - Typical collective agreements will contain numerous provisions governing the labour–management employment relationship.
   - Major areas of interest concern wages (rates of pay, overtime differentials, holiday pay), hours (shift times, days of work), and working conditions (safety issues, performance standards, retraining).
   - Management rights refers to the supremacy of management's authority in all issues except those shared with the union through the collective agreement.

6. Describe a typical grievance procedure.
   - The procedure will consist of three to five steps—each step having specific filing and reply times.
   - Higher-level managers and union officials will become involved in disputes at the higher steps of the grievance procedure.
   - The final step of the grievance procedure may be arbitration.
   - Arbitrators render a final decision for problems not resolved at lower grievance steps.

7. Explain the basis for arbitration awards.
   - The wording of the collective agreement.
   - Testimony and evidence offered during the hearing, including how the parties have interpreted the collective agreement.
   - Arbitration criteria against which cases are judged.
   - In discipline cases arbitrators will look at whether the offence actually occurred and whether the penalty imposed was appropriate.

Need to Know

- Definition of collective bargaining
- Definition of grievance
- Difference between mediation and arbitration
- Definition of defined rights and residual rights

Need to Understand

- Steps and importance of preparation for negotiations
- Steps in grievance process
- Types of negotiation approaches and impact on labour–management relationship
- Relationship of employer actions to arbitration outcomes

Key Terms

arbitration award 419

arbitrator 406

bargaining zone 399

boycott 403

collective bargaining process 394

defined rights 411

expedited arbitration 415

grievance procedure 414

grievance resolution 415

interest arbitration 406

interest-based bargaining (IBB) 406

lockout 403

mediator 405

pattern bargaining 397

residual rights 410

rights arbitration 406

strike 399

submission to arbitrate 418

REVIEW QUESTIONS

1. Describe the bargaining process.
2. List some examples of bad-faith bargaining
3. What information is necessary to prepare for collective bargaining?
4. What is a strike? A lockout?
5. What is the difference and similarities between mediation and arbitration?
6. What is interest-based bargaining?
7. What are some of the working conditions covered in a collective agreement?
8. What is a right (or grievance) arbitration?

CRITICAL THINKING QUESTIONS

1. At an election conducted among the 20 employees of the Exclusive Jewellery Store, all but two voted in favour of the Jewellery Workers Union, which subsequently was certified as their bargaining agent. In negotiating its first agreement, the union demanded that it be granted a union shop. The two employees who had voted against the union, however, informed the management that they would quit rather than join. Unfortunately for the store, the two employees were skilled gem cutters who were the most valuable of its employees and would be difficult to replace. What position should the store take with regard to the demand for a union shop?

2. You are on the bargaining team representing all the workers in a small manufacturing firm. Many of your fellow workers are in the age bracket 18 to 27. What are some items these workers might want in relation to hours of work and benefits?

3. The negotiations between Data Services International and its union have become deadlocked. What form of bargaining power does each side possess to enforce its bargaining demands? What are the advantages and disadvantages of each form of bargaining power for both the union and the employer?

4. A friend of yours was recently terminated due to poor work performance. The union business agent has grieved the action and a meeting has been scheduled between the union and the senior manager of the company. What type of evidence would you expect the company to put forward to prove that this termination was with cause?

5. Frequently, governments in Canada are encouraged by voters to ban public-sector employees from striking. Do you think laws should be passed to do this? Explain your reasons.

6. You have recently been elected shop steward at the hotel in which you work. Another employee approaches you asking that you launch a grievance about the manner in which shifts are assigned. What information would you want from the collective agreement? What information would you want from the employee? What information would you want from the employee's supervisor?

7. Indira Singh has decided to file a grievance with her union steward. The grievance alleges that she was by-passed by a junior employee for a promotion to a senior technician.

    a. Explain the steps her grievance will follow in a formal union–management grievance procedure.
    b. Should her grievance go to arbitration, explain the process of an arbitration hearing and identify the criteria used by the arbitrator to resolve her claim.

DEVELOPING YOUR SKILLS

1. A group of students wants a health food restaurant on their college campus. College administrators want a Burger King fast-food franchise. Resources allow for only one food outlet. Divide the class into bargaining teams, with one team representing the students, and the other team representing the college administrators. The objective is for each side to negotiate from that perspective and reach an agreement. (If there is another issue on your campus use the real and current issue instead.)

2. Using the information in Case Study 1, your instructor will conduct a mock arbitration. Students will be assigned roles and will be expected to prepare their case accordingly. The instructor will act as the arbitrator and make a final decision.

3. Using any search engine, conduct a search using the phrase "collective bargaining." Review at least 10 sites and determine if they would be useful for getting additional information about collective bargaining or collective agreements. Identify the sites you searched, pick one site, and prepare a one-page summary describing what the site is about and how you could use it if you were involved in collective bargaining.

4. Access the Canadian Industrial Relations Board Web site (**www.cirb-ccri.gc.ca/ publications/summaries/index_e.asp**) where summaries of cases can be found. Also, access the Web site of your provincial labour relations board (list of Web addresses can be found in Chapter 10, At Work with HRM 10.1) and access the link to decisions. Retrieve two or three decisions from each site. Prepare a two- to three-page report comparing the decisions.

Canadian Industrial Relations Board

www.cirb-ccri.gc.ca/
publications/summaries/
index_e.asp

Case Study **1**

The Arbitration Case of Jesse Stansky

At the arbitration hearing, both parties were adamant in their positions. Nancy Huang, HR manager of Phoenix Semiconductor, argued that the grievant, Jesse Stansky, was justly terminated for arguing and hitting a co-worker—a direct violation of company policy and the employee handbook. Stansky argued that he had been a good employee during his eight years of employment.

The submission agreement governing the case read, "It is the employer's position that just cause existed for the discharge of Mr. Jesse Stansky and the penalty was appropriate for the offence committed." Additionally, the employer introduced into evidence the labour agreement, which defined just cause termination as follows:

Just cause shall serve as the basis for disciplinary action and includes, but is not limited to: dishonesty, inefficiency, unprofessional conduct, failure to report absences, falsification of records, violation of company policy, destruction of property, or possession or being under the influence of alcohol or narcotics.

Stansky was hired as a systems technician on November 20, 1994, a position he held until his termination on October 25, 2002. According to the testimony of Huang, Phoenix Semiconductor strived to maintain a positive and cordial work environment among its employees. Fighting on the job was strictly prohibited. Stansky's performance evaluation showed him to be an average employee, although he had received several disciplinary warnings for poor attendance and one three-day suspension for a "systems control error." Stansky was generally liked by his co-workers, and several testified on his behalf at the arbitration hearing.

The termination of Stansky concerned an altercation between himself and Gary Lindekin, another systems technician. According to witnesses to the incident, both Stansky and Lindekin became visibly upset over the correct way to calibrate a sensitive piece of production equipment. The argument—one witness called it no more than a heated disagreement—lasted approximately three minutes and concluded when Stansky was seen forcefully placing his hand on Lindekin's shoulder. Lindekin took extreme exception to Stansky's behaviour and immediately reported the incident to management. After interviews with both Stansky and Lindekin, and those who observed the incident, Huang, Samantha Lowry, the employee's immediate supervisor, and Grant Ginn, department manager, decided that Stansky should be terminated for unprofessional conduct and violation of company policy.

Source: Adapted from an arbitration heard by George W. Bohlander. All names are fictitious.

Questions

1. Which arguments should be given more weight: those based on company policy, the employee handbook, and the collective agreement, or mitigating factors given by the grievant and his witnesses? Explain?
2. How might unprofessional conduct be defined? Explain.
3. If you were the arbitrator, how would you rule in this case? Explain fully the reasons for your decision.

Case Study 2

Tuned In or Turned Off?

For the past nine years, the use of personal radios while working has been an accepted practice at Vision-Trax Industries. Recently, however, Vision-Trax moved to a new location where an open-space facilities design permits close employee contact. Unfortunately, the new design also creates more noise, and, therefore, employees were told that all personal radios and cassettes, even those with earphones, were no longer permitted. On behalf of her employees, union steward Vera Freedman filed a grievance that resulted in arbitration.

At the hearing, the union argued these points:

- Employees' use of personal radios and cassette players is a right granted by the contract. The agreement specifically states that any right not mentioned in the contract, but in existence prior to the contract, is to remain in effect.
- Use of radios and cassette players equipped with earphones eliminates the noise concerns of managers and other employees.
- There has been no loss of productivity with the use of radios and cassette players.

During its presentation at the arbitration hearing, the company made these arguments:

- The rule prohibiting use of radios is consistent with management's right to run the organization in an efficient and effective manner.
- Employees had been warned that excessive noise could result in elimination of radios and cassette players. When noise levels were not reduced, the new rule was put in effect.
- Excessive radio noise can cause safety problems, including personal arguments between employees.
- The wearing of earphones presents an unprofessional appearance to visitors and customers.

Source: Adapted from "Tuned-in Employees," *Supervisory Management* 40, no. 4 (April 1995): 6.

Questions

1. Which arguments should receive more weight—those based on the contract or those alleging other concerns? Or should both types of argument be given equal weight? Explain.
2. How important is the company's argument that radios present an unprofessional appearance? Explain.
3. If you were the arbitrator, how would you rule in this case? Why?

NOTES AND REFERENCES

1. Larry Suffield, *Labour Relations* (Toronto: Pearson Education, 2005): 201–18.
2. Morley Gunderson, Allen Ponak, and Daphne G. Tars, *Union-Management Relations in Canada*, 5th ed. (Toronto: Pearson Education, 2005): 294–300.
3. John A. Fossum, *Labor Relations: Development, Structure, Process*, 6th ed. (Homewood, Ill.: BPI-Irwin, 1995): 278.
4. Gunderson, et al., *Union-Management Relations in Canada*, 264–65.
5. "Landmark Contract for Goodyear Workers," *Financial Post*, September 16, 2003, FP9.
6. Ross Stagner and Hjalmar Rosen, *Psychology of Union–Management Relations* (Belmont, Calif.: Wadsworth, 1965): 95–97. This is another classic in the field of labour–management relations.
7. Rob Antle, "Legislature Shut down in Newfoundland," *The Vancouver Sun*, April 20, 2004, A4.
8. Chris Sorensen and Peter Brieger, "Stelco in 11th-hour Talks with Labour to Save GM Steel Deal," *National Post*, November 19, 2004, FP9.
9. Becky Guthrie, "On the Line: Miners' Strikes Threaten the Survival of Two Small Labrador Communities," *Canadian Business*, September 27–October 10, 2004, 33.
10. Scott Simpson, "Gold Mine Faces Shutdown," *The Vancouver Sun*, February 23, 2005, D1; and Scott Simpson, "High Metal Prices Benefit Canadian Firms," *The Vancouver Sun*, February 23, 2005, D1.
11. D. Hynes, "New Climate of Collaboration in Labour Relations on the Horizon," *Canadian HR Reporter*, May 7, 2001, 9.
12. Eilene Zimmerman, "HR Lessons from a Strike," *Workforce* 79, no. 11 (November 2000): 36–42.
13. Brian Dartnell and J. Geoffrey Howard, "A Labour Relations Surprise," *PeopleTalk* 5, no. 3 (Spring 2002): 42; Janice Tibbetts, "Secondary Picketing Approved by Top Court," *The Vancouver Sun*, January 25, 2002, D1.
14. Sean Silcoff, "Quebecor and Union in Showdown Over Costs," *Financial Post*, February 26, 2002, FP3; "Quebecor Plays Hardball with Defiant Union," *Financial Post*, March 5, 2002, FP6.
15. Saskatchewan Department of Justice, www.saskjustice.gov.sk.ca/DisputeResolution/Careers/intro.shtml (retrieved March 3, 2005).
16. George W. Bohlander and Jim Naber, "Non-adversarial Negotiations: The FMCS Interest-Based Bargaining Program," *Journal of Collective Negotiations in the Public Sector* 28, no. 1, 1999.
17. Ira Lobel, "Is Interest Based Bargaining Really New?" *Dispute Resolution Journal* 55, no. 1 (January-February 2000): 8–17.
18. *Interest-Based Negotiations: Participants' Guidebook* (Washington, D.C.: Federal Mediation and Conciliation Service, 1998).
19. Roger Fisher and William Ury, *Getting to Yes* (Toronto: Penguin Books, 1991).
20. John Calhoun Wells, "Conflictive Partnership: A Strategy for Real World Labor–Management Cooperation," *Labor Law Journal* 47, no. 8 (August 1996): 484–92; Owen E. Herrnstadt, "Labor–Management Cooperation: Is Management Ready?" *Labor Law Journal* 46, no. 10 (October 1995): 636–38.
21. *Workplace Innovations Overview 1994*, Bureau of Labour Information, Human Resources Development Canada, 1994.
22. "CN and CAW Agree to Cushion Layoffs," *The Vancouver Sun*, February 17, 1999, D2c.
23. Jill Kriesky and Edwin Brown, "The Union Role in Labor–Management Cooperation: A Case Study at the Boise Cascade Company's Jackson Mill," *Labor Studies Journal* 18, no. 3 (Fall 1993): 17–32.
24. Tom Juravich, "Empirical Research on Employee Involvement: A Critical Review for Labor," *Labor*

Studies Journal 21, no. 2 (Summer 1996): 52–66; Douglas M. McCabe, "Labor–Management Cooperation: A Business Ethics and Business–Government Relations Perspective," *Labor Law Journal* 47, no. 8 (August 1996): 467–78.

25. Richard B. Peterson and Lane Tracy, "Lessons from Labor–Management Cooperation," *California Management Review* 31, no. 1 (Fall 1988): 41.

26. Talk given by Professor Joe Weiler on "New Role of Labour Relations Neutrals," Burnaby, B.C., February 28, 2002.

27. Ann C. Frost, "Labour-Management Collaboration over the Redesign of Work: The Impact of Alternative Approaches," Canadian Workplace Research Network, www.cwrn-rcrmt.org/eng/abs_01.cfm (retrieved August 10, 2002).

28. For an expanded discussion of management's residual rights, termed "reserved rights" in the United States, see Paul Prasow and Edward Peters, *Arbitration and Collective Bargaining*, 2nd ed. (New York: McGraw-Hill, 1983): 33–34. This book is considered an authority on management rights issues.

29. Labour agreement, Wabash Fibre Box Company and Paperworkers.

30. Mary Vallis, "Heads, She Keeps Library Job; Tails, She Loses," *National Post*, February 28, 2002, A10.

31. *Grievance Guide*, 9th ed. (Washington, D.C.: BNA Books, 1995). See also Frank Elkouri and Edna Asher Elkouri, *How Arbitration Works*, 4th ed. (Washington, D.C.: Bureau of National Affairs, 1985): 153. This book continues to be a leading reference on the topic of arbitration and the resolution of grievances.

32. Laurence Boulle and Kathleen J. Kelly, *Mediation: Principles, Process, Practice*, Canadian Edition (Toronto: Butterworths, 1998).

33. Some labour agreements call for the use of arbitration boards to resolve employee grievances. Arbitration boards, which may be either temporary or permanent, are composed of one or more members chosen by management and an equal number chosen by labour. A neutral member serves as chair. See Peter A. Veglahn, "Grievance Arbitration by Arbitration Boards: A Survey of the Parties," *Arbitration Journal* 42, no. 2 (July 1987): 47–53.

34. *Canada Post Corporation v. Nolan*, unreported, December 16, 1998, FCTD T 1373–97.

35. Donna Blancero and George W. Bohlander, "Minimizing Arbitrator Reversals in Discipline and Discharge Cases," *Labor Law Journal* 46, no. 10 (October 1995): 616–21. See also George W. Bohlander and Donna Blancero, "A Study of Reversal Determinants in Discipline and Discharge Arbitration Awards: The Impact of Just Cause Standards," *Labor Studies Journal* 21, no. 3 (Fall 1996): 3–18.

36. Allen Ponak, Wilfred Zerbe, Sarah Rose, and Corliss Olson, "Using Event History Analysis to Model Delay in Grievance Arbitration," *Industrial and Labor Relations Review* 50, no. 1 (October 1996): 105–21.

GLOSSARY

Achievement tests Measures of what a person knows or can do right now

Alternative dispute resolution (ADR) Term applied to different types of employee complaint or dispute-resolution procedures

Apprenticeship training System of training in which a worker entering the skilled trades is given thorough instruction and experience, both on and off the job, in the practical and theoretical aspects of the work

Aptitude tests Measures of a person's capacity to learn or acquire skills

Arbitration award Final and binding award issued by an arbitrator in a labour-management dispute

Arbitrator Third-party neutral who resolves a labour dispute by issuing a final decision in an agreement

Bargaining unit Group of two or more employees who share common employment interests and conditions and may reasonably be grouped together for purposes of collective bargaining

Bargaining zone Area within which the union and the employer are willing to concede when bargaining

Behavioural description interview (BDI) An interview in which applicants are asked questions about what they actually did in a given situation

Behaviourally anchored rating scale (BARS) A behavioural approach to performance review that consists of a series of vertical scales, one for each important dimension of job performance

Behaviour modification Technique that if behaviour is rewarded it will be exhibited more frequently in the future

Benchmarking Finding the best practices in other organizations that can be brought into a company to enhance performance

Bona fide occupational qualification (BFOQ) A justifiable reason for discrimination based on business reasons of safety or effectiveness

Boycott Union tactic to encourage others to refuse to patronize an employer

Business agent Normally a paid labour official responsible for negotiating and administering the collective agreement and working to resolve union members' problems

Certification Acquisition of exclusive rights by union to represent the employees

Closed shop Provision of the collective agreement that requires employers to hire only union members

Collective bargaining process Process of negotiating a collective agreement, including the use of economic pressures by both parties

Comparable value The concept that male and female jobs that are dissimilar, but equal in value or worth to the employer, should be paid the same

Competency-based pay Pay based on how many capabilities employees have or how many jobs they can perform

Compulsory binding arbitration Binding method of resolving collective-bargaining deadlocks by a neutral third party

Constructive dismissal Changing an employee's working conditions such that compensation, status, or prestige is reduced

Consumer price index (CPI) Measure of the average change in prices over time in a fixed "market basket" of goods and services

Contractual rights Rights that derive from contracts

Cooperative training Training program that combines practical on-the-job experience with formal education.

Core competencies Sets of integrated knowledge and capabilities in an organization that distinguish it from its competitors

Craft unions Unions that represent skilled craft workers

Cumulative trauma disorders Injuries involving tendons of the fingers, hands, and arms that become inflamed from repeated stresses and strains

Customer input Performance review that, like team review, is based on TQM concepts and seeks information from both external and internal customers

Defined rights Concept that management's authority should be expressly defined and clarified in the collective agreement

Designated groups Women, visible minorities, First Nations peoples, and persons with disabilities who have been disadvantaged in employment

Development The acquisition of skills, behaviours, and abilities to perform *future* work or to solve an organizational problem

Direct compensation Employee wages and salaries, incentives, bonuses, and commissions

Discipline (1) Treatment that punishes; (2) orderly behaviour in an organizational setting; or (3) training that moulds and strengthens desirable conduct—or corrects undesirable conduct—and develops self-control

Diversity management The optimization of an organization's multicultural workforce in order to reach business objectives

Downsizing The planned elimination of jobs

Due process Employee's right to a fair process in making a decision related to employment relationship

Eldercare Care provided to an elderly relative by an employee who remains actively at work

Employee assistance program (EAP) Program to provide short-term counselling and referrals to appropriate professionals

Employee associations Labour organizations that represent various groups of professional and white-collar employees in labour–management relations

Employee empowerment Granting employees power to initiate change, thereby encouraging them to take charge of what they do

Employee involvement groups (EIs) Groups of employees who meet to resolve problems or offer suggestions for organizational improvement

Employee rights Guarantees of fair treatment from employers

Employee teams An employee-contributions technique in which work functions are structured for groups rather than for individuals, and team members are given discretion in matters traditionally considered management prerogatives, such as process improvements, product or service development, and individual work assignments

Employment equity The employment of individuals in a fair and nonbiased manner

Equitable pay Compensation received is perceived to be equal to the value of the work performed

Ethics Set of standards of conduct and moral judgments that help to determine right and wrong behaviour

Expedited arbitration An agreement to bypass some steps in the grievance process

Final-offer arbitration Method of resolving collective-bargaining deadlocks whereby the arbitrator has no power to compromise but must select one or another of the final offers submitted by the two parties

Flexible benefit plans Plans that enable individual employees to choose the benefits that are best suited to their particular needs

Globalization Trend toward seeking out the most economical place in the world to do business

Graphic rating scales A trait approach to performance review whereby each employee is rated according to a scale of characteristics

Grievance procedure Formal procedure that provides for the union to represent members and nonmembers in processing a grievance

Grievance resolution Process in which a neutral third party assists in the resolution of an employee grievance

Hearing officer Person who holds a full-time position with an organization but assumes a neutral role when deciding cases between management and the aggrieved employees

Hourly work Work paid on an hourly basis

Human capital The individual's knowledge, skills, and abilities that have economic value to an organization

Human resource planning Process that the people required to run the company are being used as effectively as possible, where and when they are needed, in order to accomplish the organization's goals

Human resources information system (HRIS) Computerized system that provides current and accurate data for purposes of control and decision making

Human resources management (HRM) An integrated set of processes, programs, and systems in an organization that focuses on the effective deployment and development of its employees

Indirect compensation Benefits, such as dental plans and life insurance, supplied by employers

Industrial disease A disease resulting from exposure relating to a particular process, trade, or occupation in industry

Industrial unions Unions that represent all workers—skilled, semiskilled, unskilled—employed along industry lines

Instructional objectives Desired outcomes of a training program

Interest arbitration A mechanism to renew or establish a new collective agreement for parties

Interest-based bargaining (IBB) Problem-solving bargaining based on a win-win philosophy and the development of a positive long-term relationship

Internal job posting Method of communicating information about job openings

Internship programs Programs jointly sponsored by colleges, universities, and other organizations that offer students the opportunity to gain real-life experience while allowing them to find out how they will perform in work organizations

ISO 9000 World-wide quality standards program

Job A group of related activities and duties

Job analysis Process of obtaining information about jobs by determining the duties, tasks, or activities and the skills, knowledge, and abilities associated with those jobs

Job characteristics model An approach to job design that recognizes the link between motivational factors and components of the job to achieve improved work performance and job satisfaction

Job description A document that lists the tasks, duties, and responsibilities of a job to be performed along with the skills, knowledge and abilities, or competencies needed to successfully perform the work

Job design Process of defining and organizing tasks, roles, and other processes to achieve employee goals and organizational effectiveness

Job evaluation Systematic process of determining the relative worth of jobs in order to establish which jobs should be paid more than others within an organization

Job specifications Statement of the needed knowledge, skills, and abilities of the person who is to perform the position. The different duties and responsibilities performed by only one employee

Knowledge workers Workers whose responsibilities extend beyond the physical execution of work to include decision making, problem solving, and troubleshooting

Labour market Area from which applicants are recruited

Labour relations process Logical sequence of four events: (1) workers desire collective representation, (2) union begins its organizing campaign, (3) collective negotiations lead to a contract, and (4) the contract is administered

Lockout Strategy by which the employer denies employees the opportunity to work by closing its operations

Management by objectives (MBO) Philosophy of management that rates performance on the basis of employee achievement of goals

Management forecasts Opinions and judgments of supervisors or managers and others that are knowledgeable about the organization's future employment needs

Management rights Decisions regarding organizational operations over which management claims exclusive rights

Manager and/or supervisor review Performance review done by the employee's supervisor

Markov analysis Method for tracking the pattern of employee movements through various jobs

Material Safety Data Sheets (MSDS) Documents that contain vital information about hazardous substances

Mediation The use of an impartial third party to help facilitate a resolution to employment disputes

Mediator Third party in a labour dispute who meets with one party and then the other in order to suggest compromise solutions or to recommend concessions from each side that will lead to an agreement

Membership card A statement signed by an employee authorizing a union to act as a representative of the employee for purposes of collective bargaining

Mentors Executives who coach, advise, and encourage individuals of lesser rank

Negligence Failure to provide reasonable care where such failure results in injury to consumers or other employees

Occupational illness Abnormal condition or disorder resulting from exposure to environmental factors in the workplace

Occupational injury Any cut, fracture, sprain, or amputation resulting from a workplace accident

Ombudsperson Designated individual from whom employees may seek counsel for the resolution of their complaints

On-the-job training (OJT) Method by which employees are given hands-on experience with instructions from their supervisor or other trainer

Open-door policy Policy of settling grievances that identifies various levels of management above the immediate supervisor for employee contact

Open shop Provision of the collective agreement that allows employees to join or not join the union

Orientation Formal process of familiarizing new employees with the organization, their jobs, and their work unit and embedding organizational values, beliefs, and accepted behaviours

Outsourcing Contracting outside the organization for work that was formerly done by internal employees. The small-business owner saves money, time, and resources by outsourcing tasks such as accounting and payroll.

Panel interview An interview in which a board of interviewers questions and observes a single candidate

Pattern bargaining Bargaining in which unions negotiate provisions covering wages and other benefits that are similar to those provided in other agreements existing within the industry or region

Pay equity The practice of equal pay for work of equal value

Pay grades Groups of jobs within a particular class that are paid the same rate or rate range

Pay-for-performance standard Standard by which managers tie compensation to employee effort and performance

Peer review Performance reviews done by one's fellow employees, generally on forms that are compiled into a single profile for use in the performance interview conducted by the employee's manager

Performance management system A set of integrated management practices

Piecework Work paid according to the number of units produced

Position Specific duties and responsibilities performed by only one employee

Positive, or nonpunitive, discipline System of discipline that focuses on the early correction of employee misconduct, with the employee taking total responsibility for correcting the problem

Proactive response to change Change response initiated to take advantage of targeted opportunities

Progressive discipline Application of corrective measures by increasing degrees

Promotion Change of assignment to a job at a higher level in the organization

Reactive response to change Change response that occurs after external forces have already affected performance

Real wages Wage increases larger than rises in the consumer price index; that is, the real earning power of wages

Reasonable accommodation Attempt by employers to adjust the working conditions and employment practices of employees to prevent discrimination

Recruitment The process of locating and encouraging potential applicants to apply for jobs

Reliability The degree to which interviews, tests, and other selection procedures yield comparable data over time and alternative measures

Residual rights Concept that management's authority is supreme in all matters except those it has expressly conceded to the union in the collective agreement

Reverse discrimination Giving preference to members of certain groups, such that others feel they are the subjects of discrimination

Rights arbitration A mechanism to resolve disputes about the interpretation and application of a collective agreement during the term of that collective agreement

Selection The process of choosing individuals who have relevant qualifications and who will best perform on the job to fill existing or projected job openings

Self-review Performance review done by the employee being assessed, generally on a form completed by the employee prior to the performance interview

Sexual harassment Unwelcome advances, requests for sexual favours, and other verbal or physical conduct of a sexual nature in the working environment

Situational question Question in which an applicant is given a hypothetical incident and asked how he or she would respond to it

Six Sigma A process used to translate customer needs into a set of optimal tasks that are performed in concert with one another

Staffing table Graphic representations of organizational jobs along with the numbers of employees currently occupying those jobs and future employment needs

Standards of performance Set out the expected results of the job

Statutory rights Rights that derive from legislation

Step-review system System for reviewing employee complaints and disputes by successively higher levels of management

Strategic human resources management Identifying key HR processes and linking those to the overall business strategy

Stress Any adjustive demand caused by physical, mental, or emotional factors that requires coping behaviour

Strike A situation in which unionized workers refuse to perform their work during labour negotiations

Structured question Question which has an established set of answers

Submission to arbitrate Statement that describes the issues to be resolved through arbitration

Subordinate review Performance review of a superior by an employee, which is more appropriate for developmental than for administrative purposes

Systemic discrimination The exclusion of members of certain groups through the application of employment policies or practices based on criteria that are not job-related

Team review Performance review, based on TQM concepts, that recognizes team accomplishment rather than individual performance

Total quality management (TQM) A set of principles and practices whose core ideas include understanding customer needs, doing things right the first time, and striving for continuous improvement

Trainee readiness The consideration of a trainee's maturity and experience when assessing him or her

Training The acquisition of skills, behaviours, and abilities to perform *current* work

Transfer of training Effective application of principles learned to what is required on the job

Transfer Placement of an individual in another job for which the duties, responsibilities, status, and remuneration are approximately equal to those of the previous job

Trend analysis Quantitative approach to forecasting labour demand on an organizational index

Unfair labour practices Specific employer and union illegal practices that operate to deny employees their rights and benefits under labour law

Union (shop) steward Employee who, as a nonpaid union official, represents the interests of members in their relations with management

Union shop Provision of the collective agreement that requires employees to join the union as a condition of their employment

Validity How well a test or selection procedure measures a person's attributes

Wage and salary survey Survey of the wages paid to employees of other employers in the surveying organization's relevant labour market

Work Tasks or activities that need to be completed

Wrongful dismissal Terminating an employee's employment without just cause

NAME AND ORGANIZATION INDEX

SUBJECT INDEX

PHOTO CREDITS